*Ḥadīth* and Ethics through the Lens of Interdisciplinarity

الحديث والأخلاق: مقاربة متعددة التخصصات

# Studies in Islamic Ethics

*Editorial Board*

Mutaz al-Khatib (*Research Center for Islamic Legislation and Ethics,* HBKU)
Mohammed Ghaly (*Research Center for Islamic Legislation and Ethics,* HBKU)
Ray Jureidini (*Research Center for Islamic Legislation and Ethics,* HBKU)

*Managing Editor*

Abdurraouf Oueslati

VOLUME 5

The titles published in this series are listed at *brill.com/sie*

# *Ḥadīth* and Ethics through the Lens of Interdisciplinarity

# الحديث والأخلاق
# مقاربة متعددة التخصصات

*Edited by*

Mutaz al-Khatib

تحرير

معتز الخطيب

TUTA SUB AEGIDE PALLAS · 1683 ·

BRILL

LEIDEN | BOSTON

Cover illustration: Cover calligraphy by Nihad Nadam, 2022.

مركز دراسات التشريع الإسلامي والأخلاق
Research Center for Islamic Legislation and Ethics
عضو في جامعة حمد بن خليفة
Member of Hamad Bin Khalifa University

This publication is sponsored by the Research Center of Islamic Legislation and Ethics in Doha (Qatar), which is affiliated to the Faculty of Islamic Studies, Hamad Bin Khalifa University.

The Library of Congress Cataloging-in-Publication Data is available online at https://catalog.loc.gov
LC record available at https://lccn.loc.gov/2022050140

Typeface for the Latin, Greek, and Cyrillic scripts: "Brill". See and download: brill.com/brill-typeface.

ISSN 2589-3947
ISBN 978-90-04-52592-4 (hardback)
ISBN 978-90-04-52593-1 (e-book)



This book is printed on acid-free paper and produced in a sustainable manner.

*To my* shaykhs
*Nūr al-Dīn ʿItr and ʿAbd al-Fattāḥ Abū Ghudda*

*Also, to the future generation of* ḥadīth *scholars hoping that this work will inspire them to bridge the gap between* ḥadīth *and ethics*

## Contents


Notes on Style, Transliteration and Dates IX
Notes on Contributors X

Introduction: *Ḥadīth* and Ethics 1
*Mutaz al-Khatib*

1 *Ḥadīth*-Based Ethics
Ḥadīth *as a Scholarly Sub-discipline of Islamic Ethics* 8
*Mutaz al-Khatib*

2 *Ḥadīth* and the Concept of *Adab* as Moral Education 30
*Nuha Alshaar*

3 الأحاديث الكلية: من الأحكام التفصيلية إلى القواعد والمبادئ الأخلاقية 48
معتز الخطيب

4 الحافظ ابن أبي الدنيا والتأسيس لأخلاقيات المكارم 87
شفيق اكّريكّر

5 Narrations on Virtuous Acts in Epitomes of al-Ghazālī's *Iḥyā'*
*From Ibn al-Jawzī's* Minhāj al-Qāṣidīn *to Its Reception in Modernity* 120
*Pieter Coppens*

6 *Ḥadīth* and Sufism in Ethical Discourse
*Exploring ʿAbd al-Qādir al-Jīlānī's Conception of* Taḥbīb 147
*Salahudheen Kozhithodi and Khairil Husaini Bin Jamil*

7 Seclusion
*An Ethical Imperative Driven by the* Ḥadīth*?* 170
*M. Imran Khan*

8 The Ethical in the Transmission of Sunna
*Rethinking the* ʿUlamā'-Quṣṣāṣ *Conflict* 198
*Safwan Amir*

9 Abū Shuqqa's Approach to the *Ḥadīth*
*Towards an Egalitarian Islamic Gender Ethics* 221
*Faqihuddin Abdul Kodir*

10 Islamic Ethics and the *Ḥadīth* of Intention 248
*Ali Altaf Mian*

11 Consult Your Heart
*The Self as a Source of Moral Judgment* 268
*Mutaz al-Khatib*

12 مصنفات المحدثين في الأخلاق: كشاف أوليّ 306
معتز الخطيب

فهرس 337
Index 344

# Notes on Style, Transliteration and Dates

For referencing, this volume follows the *Chicago Manual of Style* author-date in-text citation system.

Arabic words and names are transliterated according to the system used in Brill's *Encyclopaedia of Islam Three*, which is also adopted in the *Journal of Islamic Ethics* (JIE):

Consonants: ʾ, b, t, th, j, ḥ, kh, d, dh, r, z, s, sh, ṣ, ḍ, ṭ, ẓ, ʿ, gh, f, q, k, l, m, n, h, w, y.
Short vowels: a, i, u.
Long vowels: ā, ī, ū.
Diphtongs: aw, ay.
*Tāʾ marbūṭa*: -a, -at (construct state).

While classical proper names are fully transliterated (e.g., al-Ghazālī), for modern names, i.e., since 1900, also the official or common spellings are adopted (e.g., Taha Abdurrahman). The "l" of the definite article "al-" is always retained, regardless of whether it is assimilated in pronunciation to the initial consonant of the word to which it is attached (*idghām*).

If not otherwise specified, the dates given are common era (CE) dates. If two dates are provided (e.g., 505/1111), the first one is the year according to the Islamic *hijrī* calendar (AH) and the second the CE date. For dates after 1900 only the CE date is provided.

# Notes on Contributors

*Faqihuddin Abdul Kodir* (فقيه الدين عبد القدير)
teaches *ḥadīth* and legal injunction at the faculty of Islamic Law at Institut Agama Islam Negeri (IAIN, State Institute for Islamic Studies) Syekh Nurjati Cirebon, Indonesia. Being one of the founders, he is also affiliated to the Institut Studi Islam Fahmina (ISIF, Fahmina Institute of Islamic Studies) in Cirebon, an Indonesian NGO working on gender, democracy and pluralism from an Islamic perspective. Abdul Kodir authored several books, including *Qirāʾah Mubādalah: Tafsir Progresif untuk Keadilan Gender dalam Islam* ("An Alternative Reading: Progressive Interpretation for Gender Justice in Islam" 2019), *Sunnah Monogami* ("Monogamous Sunna," 2017) and *Hadith and Gender Justice* (2007). He is also the founder of mubadalah.id, an Islamic portal about gender justice. At the Dar al-Tauhid in Cirebon he completed his Islamic boarding school education. Subsequently he moved to Syria to receive his undergraduate degree from Damascus University and Majmaʿ Abū l-Nūr al-Islāmī. He completed his MA degree at the International Islamic University Malaysia, and his PhD at the Universitas Gadjah Mada (UGM, Gadjah Mada University) in Yogyakarta, Indonesia. Currently he is involved with Muslim NGOs across Southeast Asia where he is trying to work out how gender justice can be culturally negotiated and adopted within Islamic perspectives.

*Nuha Alshaar* (نهى الشعار)
is Senior Research Associate at the Institute of Ismaili Studies in London and Associate Professor in Islamic Intellectual History and Thought at the American University of Sharjah. Alshaar obtained her PhD from the University of Cambridge (2009) and has taught at various academic institutions, including the School of Oriental and African Studies (SOAS) in London. Her research focuses on ethics and classical literary traditions (*adab*). Alshaar's publications include *Ethics in Islam: Friendship in the Political Thought of al-Tawḥīdī and his Contemporaries* (2015); *On God and the World: An Arabic Critical Edition and English Translation of Epistles 49–51* (co-authored with Wilfred Madelung, Cyril Uy and Carmela Baffioni, 2019); and *The Qur'an and Adab: The Shaping of Literary Traditions in Classical Islam* (editor, 2017).

*Safwan Amir* (صفوان أمير)
is Assistant Professor at the School of Arts and Sciences of Ahmedabad University, India. He was a Senior Research Associate with the World Humanities Report, India/South Asia (2019–2022) and a Fulbright Visiting Doctoral Fellow

at Columbia University in the City of New York (2017–2018). His research interests include the anthropology of religion, Islam and ethical possibilities of the margin. He is currently working on a book manuscript that draws on his PhD dissertation: "The Muslim Barbers of Malabar: Histories of Contempt and Ethics of Possibility."

*Khairil Husaini Bin Jamil* (خَيرئيل حسيني بن جميل)
is an Assistant Professor of Islamic Scriptural Sciences at the Department of Qur'an and Sunnah Studies, AHAS KIRKHS, International Islamic University Malaysia (IIUM). He obtained his BA and MA degrees from the Islamic University in Medina and received his PhD from the School of Oriental and African Studies (SOAS) in London. Bin Jamil is currently the Editor-in-Chief of *al-Burhān Journal of Qur'ān and Sunnah Studies*. The areas he focuses on in his research are Islamic scriptures, epistemology and theosophy. His publications include *Nasamāt al-ʿAwn: Terjemahan dan Syarahan 40 Hadis Bencana, Epidemik dan Taʿun* ("Breezes of Help: A Translation and Explanation of 40 *Ḥadīth*s on Disasters, Epidemics and Plagues," 2020) and *al-Gharā'ib al-Multaqaṭa min Musnad al-Firdaws al-Musammā "Zahr al-Firdaws" lil-Ḥāfiẓ Ibn Ḥajar al-ʿAsqalānī (t. 852H): Dirāsah wa Taḥqīq* ("Selected Rare Ḥadīths from *Musnad al-Firdaws* Named the 'The Flowers of Paradise' by al-Ḥāfiẓ Ibn Ḥajar al-ʿAsqalānī (d. 852 AH): A Critical Edition," 2018).

*Pieter Coppens* (پيتر كوپنس)
is Assistant Professor at the Faculty of Religion and Theology, Vrije Universiteit Amsterdam. He obtained his BA and MA degrees in Arabic Language and Culture from the Radboud University Nijmegen, and his PhD degree in Islamic Studies from Utrecht University. A reworked version of his dissertation was published under the title *Seeing God in Sufi Qur'an Commentaries: Crossings between This World and the Otherworld* (2018). Coppens has published on the history of Qur'ān commentaries (*tafsīr*), Islamic hermeneutics, and the history of Sufism. His current research project deals with the Qur'ān commentary of the Damascene Salafī scholar Jamāl al-Dīn al-Qāsimī (d. 1332/1914) and the influence of the rise of the printing press and modern book culture on the genre of *tafsīr*.

*Chafik Graiguer* (شفيق اݣريݣر)
is Senior Member of the Pedagogic Inspectorate Board at the Ministry of Education (Division of Philosophy) in Rabat, Morocco. He is currently working on a PhD project titled "The Ethical Autonomy in Classical Islam: A Controversy about Virtue" at Hassan II University, Casablanca, and has earned a Fulbright

scholarship grant at Vanderbilt University, Nashville, TN. His research interests include moral theology, Qur'ānic studies, philosophy of religion, the role of science and belief in society. Being an educational professional, he is particularly interested in the integration of critical thinking skills into school curricula. Graiguer is also running the website falsafa.info.

*Muhammad Imran Khan* (محمد عمران خان)
did his undergraduate degree in International Relations at the University of Leeds, obtained an MA in Islamic Theology at Leiden University and is now pursuing his PhD at the University of Cambridge. The title of his dissertation project is "Sociality and the Mystical Theology of ʿAbd al-Ghanī al-Nābulusī." He has spent several years studying at institutes in Syria, Pakistan, and Turkey, and worked at the al-Maktoum Institute of Higher Education, the University of St. Andrews, and the University of Cambridge. His main research interests are virtue ethics, Abrahamic wisdom literature, Sufism, *ḥadīth* exegeses and *tafsīr*, Islamic epistemology, philosophy of religion, Muslim charities and endowments, contextualising the pedagogy of seminaries, and Islam in South America. Currently, he is researching the Judaeo-Arabic Cairo Genizah corpus at the Trinity College, Dublin. His other affiliations include: the Woolf Institute, Centre for Forced Migration Studies, Gingko, Rosa Foundation and UCD Newman Centre for the Study of Religions.

*Mutaz al-Khatib* (معتز الخطيب)
is Associate Professor of Methodology and Ethics and coordinator of the MA programme in Applied Islamic Ethics at the College of Islamic Studies, Hamad Bin Khalifa University, Doha, Qatar. His research interests include ethics and moral philosophy, Islamic law (*fiqh*), *ḥadīth* criticism, the higher objectives of Sharīʿa (*maqāṣid al-Sharīʿa*) and Islamic intellectual history. Al-Khatib was visiting fellow at ZMO in Berlin (2006), and visiting scholar at the Forum Transregionale Studien, Berlin (2012–2013). Prior to that, al-Khatib served as Lecturer at the Islamic University of Beirut, Qatar University, and the American University in Beirut. Al-Khatib has given lectures at various universities such as the University of California-Berkeley, Princeton University, Cambridge University, Oxford University and the University of Tübingen. He authored and edited several books and over 30 academic articles. His publications include *Radd al-Ḥadīth min Jihat al-Matn: Dirāsa fī Manāhij al-Muḥaddithīn wa-l Uṣūliyyīn* ("*Matn* Criticism: A Study of the Methods of Traditionists and Muslim Jurists," 2011), *Maʾziq al-Dawla bayna al-Islāmiyyīn wa-l-ʿIlmāniyyīn* ("The Dilemma of the State between Islamists and Secularists," 2016), *al-ʿUnf al-Mustabāḥ: al-Sharīʿa fī Muwājahat al-Umma wa-l-Dawla* ("Violence Made

Permissible: 'Sharīʿa' versus the People and the State," 2017), *Qabūl al-Ḥadīth* ("The Reception of *Ḥadīth*," 2017) and *Islamic Ethics and the Trusteeship Paradigm* (co-editor, 2020).

*Salahudheen Kozhithodi* (صلاح الدين كوزهيتودي)
is Research Scholar at the Department of Quran and Sunnah Studies at the International Islamic University Malaysia (IIUM). His current research focuses on Sufi engagements with *ḥadīth*, with particular reference to ʿAbd al-Qādir al-Jīlānī's (d. 561/1166) works. After completing his first MA degree in Islamic Studies from Darul Huda Islamic University, Kerala, India (2010), and a second MA specifically in *ḥadīth* studies from IIUM (2013), he served as Assistant Professor at the Darul Huda till 2018 and part time Lecturer at the Department of Qur'an and Sunnah Studies in IIUM in 2019. He co-authored the work *Introduction to the Sciences of Qur'an* (forthcoming, International Institute of Islamic Thought).

*Ali Altaf Mian* (علي ألطاف ميان)
is Assistant Professor of Religion and the Izzat Hasan Sheikh Fellow in Islamic Studies at the University of Florida. He specialises in Islam in South Asia, Sufism, Islamic law and ethics, method and theory in the study of religion, gender and sexuality in contemporary Islam, and religion and colonialism. His published work has touched on the study of Islam and the affective turn, and has appeared in *Islamic Law and Society*, *History of Religions*, *Journal of Urdu Studies*, *Qui Parle*, *ReOrient* and *Religion Compass*. Mian is currently working on a book project titled *Surviving Genres: Muslim Ethics and Spiritual Sovereignty in Colonial India*.

# Introduction: *Ḥadīth* and Ethics

*Mutaz al-Khatib*

This edited volume addresses the link between *ḥadīth* (Prophetic reports) and ethics, or what can be termed as "*ḥadīth*-based ethics." Despite *ḥadīth* (or Sunna) historically being the second normative source in Islam after the Qurʾān, this topic has not received sufficient attention in the contemporary scholarship on Islamic ethics. Indeed, *ḥadīth* played a key role in the development of Islamic thought and in forming *ʿulūm al-sharīʿa* (Islamic sciences), as has been noted by some contemporary scholars.[1] This volume introduces *ḥadīth*-based ethics as a sub-discipline of Islamic ethics and fills the gap within the scholarship on Islamic ethics and *ḥadīth* studies since one of its key characteristics is applying an interdisciplinary approach to both *ḥadīth* and ethics.

Approaching *ḥadīth* as a reference for ethics reflects the intensity of the ethical content contained in the Prophetic traditions and practices. To do so, one can distinguish between two levels of analysis. At the first level, the Prophetic Sunna is approached as a revealed reference or an exemplary application of the revelation. At the second level, the Sunna is approached as a historical reference for the ethics that prevailed in the formative period of Islamic history.

The mainstream position in Islamic history has held that declaring things and actions as good (*taḥsīn*) or bad (*taqbīḥ*) should be premised on revelation, not on human intellect as claimed by the Muʿtazila (ʿAbd al-Jabbār 1960–1996, 6/1:7–8, 6/2:323; al-Taftāzānī 1998, 4:282–283; Hourani 1985, 57–66; Shihadeh 2016, 384–407). If this is the case, then it should have been the standard that the Qurʾān and *ḥadīth* are the sources of both legislation and ethics. Historical reality, however, shows such theorising in Islamic legal theory (*uṣūl al-fiqh*) and jurisprudence (*fiqh*) but not so much in the field of Islamic ethics, where the role of *ḥadīth* or Sunna, like the Qurʾān, has been marginalised in classical Islamic moral philosophy. Furthermore, Majid Fakhry (d. 2021), in his book *Ethical Theories in Islam*, and Muḥammad ʿĀbid al-Jābirī (d. 2010), in his book *al-ʿAql al-Akhlāqī l-ʿArabī* ("The Arabic Moral Reason"), introduced what were

1 For example, in *Athar al-Ḥadīth fī Khtilāf al-Fuqahāʾ* ("The Role of *Ḥadīth* in the Disagreement between Muslim Jurists"), Muḥammad ʿAwwāma quotes texts that reflect early arguments between *fuqahāʾ* and *muḥaddithūn* (traditionists) on the relationship between *fiqh* (jurisprudence) and *ḥadīth*. Likewise, John Burton discusses the impact of *ḥadīth* on the formation of Islamic knowledge historically. While he specifically underscores the political and theological dimensions, he neglects the ethical dimension (see ʿAwwāma 2007; Burton 1994).

claimed to be comprehensive overviews of Islamic literature on ethics in the Islamic tradition (Fakhry 1991; al-Jābirī 2001), but *ḥadīth* was, as clearly reflected in their works, absent in their overview of ethics in the Islamic tradition.

In contrast to the case of theoretical ethics, the practical and behavioural elements of the Prophetic *ḥadīth* have received extensive attention by *ḥadīth* scholars who have produced a vast genre, including the ethical aspects of Sunna. An extensive amount of *ḥadīth* literature has also been dedicated to *ādāb* (sing. *adab*, etiquettes and good manners) which have sometimes addressed professional ethics, such as the *ādāb* of the narrator of *ḥadīth* and the one who listens to him (*ādāb al-rāwī wa-l-sāmiʿ*), and the *ādāb* of the senior and junior jurists (*ādāb al-faqīh wa-l-mutafaqqih*). Additionally, some books have focused on outlining good and bad character (*maḥāsin al-akhlāq wa-masāwiʾuhā*), religious etiquettes (*al-ādāb al-sharʿiyya*), the etiquette of dealing with parents (*birr al-wālidayn*) and so forth. Other books are dedicated to the virtues and vices (*al-faḍāʾil wa-l-radhāʾil*); books enlisting incentives to do good (*targhīb*) and deterrents from doing evil (*tarhīb*); books concerned with the branches of faith (*shuʿab al-īmān*); books on virtues which vary according to persons, ages and times; and the Sufi literature on asceticism (*zuhd*), remembrance of God, supplication (*ādāb al-duʿāʾ*), spiritual diseases of the heart (*iʿtilāl al-qulūb*) and so on (al-Kattānī 1993, 50–60).

The six canonical collections of *ḥadīth* also had specific chapters dedicated to the *aḥādīth* on manners and ethics, whose total number reached more than 500 in the *Sunan* compiled by Abū Dāwūd (d. 275/888) and exceeded 600 in the *Ṣaḥīḥ* of Ibn Ḥibbān (d. 354/965) (al-Arnāʾūṭ and al-Qayyām 1999, 1:8). Moreover, the ethics of the Prophet (*akhlāq al-nabī*) were the subject of dedicated books, such as Abū l-Shaykh's work (1998), or occupied segments in books on the biography of the Prophet, meant to provide the exemplary model of ethics to be followed.

## This Book

Against this background, the majority of this volume's chapters originated from a seminar I convened on "*Ḥadīth* and Ethics: Concepts, Approaches and Theoretical Foundations," at the Research Center for Islamic Legislation and Ethics (CILE) between 30 April and 2 May 2019. This seminar complemented a previous initiative on "Qur'ān and Ethics" within CILE's broader vision, which seeks to canonise the field of Islamic ethics through two different methods:

teaching and producing reference works that help to fill the gaps and theorise the field.[2]

This volume consists of 12 chapters that address the interplay of *ḥadīth* and ethics and contribute to examining *ḥadīth*-based ethics, which will hopefully inspire future studies to cover further aspects of this emerging field.

Broadly speaking, the chapters included in this volume cover five main aspects related to *ḥadīth* and ethics:

1. a theoretical foundation for *ḥadīth*-based ethics as a scholarly sub-discipline of Islamic ethics (chapter 1);
2. virtue ethics: noble virtues (*makārim al-akhlāq*) and virtuous acts (*faḍāʾil al-aʿmāl*), covered by chapters 4 and 5;
3. moral concepts (*adab, taḥbīb, ʿuzla*), covered by chapters 2, 6 and 7;
4. *ḥadīth*-related sub-disciplines (*ḥadīth* transmission, gender ethics), covered by chapters 8 and 9; and
5. foundational *ḥadīths* on ethics (the *ḥadīth* of intention, consult your heart, and other key *ḥadīths*), which are covered by chapters 3, 10 and 11.

These five sections offer various approaches to studying ethics in *ḥadīth* works. Chapters 1 through 5 focus on the overarching framework to scriptural ethics. As is argued in chapter 2, *ḥadīth*-based ethics "initiated an epistemological shift in the understanding of *adab*; namely, that it had been informed solely by customary law and human knowledge but came to be seen as dictated by divine command and associated with religious sensitivity." In chapter 3, examining specific key traditions is employed as one approach to study ethics in *ḥadīth*. Chapter 4 on Ibn Abī l-Dunyā (d. 281/894) represents an attempt to establish a new field by Islamising common morality through *ḥadīth*. In chapter 5, which takes the case of al-Ghazālī (d. 505/1111) and his commentators, the author examines what "*ḥadīth*-based ethics" means: is it only its attribution to the Prophet as long as it is about common knowledge of morality, or should it strictly follow the technicalities of authenticity as outlined in the *ḥadīth* sciences?

Chapters 6–7 and 10–11 focus on discipline-based approaches where ethics is studied through (a) personal accounts: al-Jīlānī's (d. 561/1166) conception and practice of *taḥbīb*, and al-Nābulusī's (d. 1143/1731) conception and practice of seclusion, and (b) interdisciplinary approaches where individual *ḥadīth*s are

---

2 In January 2015, I dedicated one of the CILE international seminars to the theme of "Qurʾān and Ethics" and its proceedings were published as a thematic issue in the *Journal of Islamic Ethics* (al-Khatib 2017).

analysed through the lens of different disciplines, such as the *ḥadīth*s: "deeds are judged by intention" and "consult your heart." Chapters 8 and 9 especially focus on the role of interpretation in restoring the fundamental idea of *ḥadīh* as deeply intertwined with ethics. Chapter 8, in particular, utilises a Derridean trace to present the *quṣṣāṣ'* (storytellers/preachers) impact on the Sunna's transmission to the wider Muslim community. Meanwhile chapter 9 addresses "conflicting *ḥadīth*s" (*mukhtalif al-ḥadīth*) in searching for egalitarian gender ethics.

Chapter 12 can be considered as an appendix in which a classification of the key primary sources in the Islamic tradition that are relevant to the field of *ḥadīth* and ethics are presented in the form of an annotated bibliography.

After outlining the key ideas and approaches examined in this volume and the rationale of combining them together in one work, below, I provide a more elaborate overview of each chapter:

In chapter 1, "*Ḥadīth*-based Ethics: *Ḥadīth* as a Scholarly Sub-Discipline of Islamic Ethics," Mutaz al-Khatib lays out the foundations for *ḥadīth*-based ethics as a sub-discipline in Islamic ethics. This chapter provides the theoretical ground for the following chapters that tackle some of the issues in this emerging field. It reveals the value of *ḥadīth* as a corpus on ethics, conceptualises "*ḥadīth*-based ethics," classifies relevant works, and defines the key themes and issues in this emerging discipline.

In chapter 2, "*Ḥadīth* and the Concept of *Adab* as Moral Education," Nuha Alshaar treats the interaction between *ḥadīth* and the concept of "*adab*," historically a term with wide semantic meanings. *Adab* here is dealt with primarily as knowledge, an ethical call to action, and, especially, as a required form of training for those aspiring to maintain good manners, proper etiquette, and cleanse the soul.

In chapter 3, "al-Aḥādīth al-Kulliyya: Min al-Aḥkām al-Tafṣīliyya ilā al-Qawāʿid wa-l-Mabādiʾ al-Akhlāqiyya" ("Beyond *Aḥādīth al-Aḥkām*: From Detailed Rulings to Ethical Fundamentals and Principles"), Mutaz al-Khatib argues that the *ḥadīth* corpus comprises of key traditions that can serve as proper foundations for approaching *ḥadīth* literature as a repository of ethics, and where the focus will move: (a) from studying individual traditions to examining the overall governing system of *ḥadīth*; and (b) from the mono-disciplinary approach where *fiqh* is dominant, to an interdisciplinary approach where *fiqh* is one part of a much larger whole. The main part of this chapter analyses the key *ḥadīth*s categorised by *ḥadīth* scholars, including Abū Dāwūd (d. 275/888), Ibn al-Ṣalāḥ (d. 643/1245), al-Nawawī (d. 676/1277) and others, such as *jawāmiʿ al-kalim* or those upon which the edifice of the Islamic tradition is constructed (*al-aḥādīth allatī ʿalayhā madār al-islām*).

In chapter 4, "al-Ḥāfiẓ Ibn Abī l-Dunyā wa-l-Ta'sīs li-Akhlāqiyyāt al-Makārim" ("Ibn Abī l-Dunyā and the Formation of the Ethics of Noble Deeds"), Chafik Graiguer argues that Ibn Abī l-Dunyā's work can be seen as an attempt to establish a *ḥadīth*-based ethics where *makārim al-akhlāq* refers to: human dignity, *murūʾa* (which contains a set of values in Arab pre-Islamic morality) and rationality. Ibn Abī l-Dunyā's work also addresses *faḍāʾil*, hence the ethics in Ibn Abī l-Dunyā's work are scriptural, in terms of form, and rational, in terms of content and sources.

In chapter 5, "Narrations on Virtuous Acts in Epitomes of al-Ghazālī's *Iḥyāʾ*: From Ibn al-Jawzī's *Minhāj al-Qāṣidīn* to its Reception in Modernity," Pieter Coppens focuses on the reception of the *Iḥyāʾ* in the Ḥanbalī circles of Baghdad and Damascus, with the epitomes of Ibn al-Jawzī (d. 597/1201) and Ibn Qudāma (d. 689/1290) at its centre. He argues that their criticism of al-Ghazālī's use of unreliable *ḥadīth* in matters related to virtuous acts (*faḍāʾil al-aʿmāl*) was among their main motivations for composing their texts.

In chapter 6, "*Ḥadīth* and Sufism in Ethical Discourse: Exploring ʿAbd al-Qādir al-Jīlānī's Conception of *Taḥbīb*," Salahudheen Kozhithodi and Khairil Husaini Bin Jamil delve into the *ḥadīth al-taḥbīb* which reads: "I was made to love (*ḥubbiba ilay*) from your world; women and perfume, and I found the coolness of my eyes in the prayer." They argue for the intertwinement of *ḥadīth* and Sufism as a mechanism for ethical discourse where Sufi ethics claim a scriptural foundation, as evident in the scholarship of ʿAbd al-Qādir al-Jīlānī (d. 561/1166).

In chapter 7, "Seclusion: An Ethical Imperative Driven by the *Ḥadīth*," Mohammed Imran Khan explores ʿAbd al-Ghanī l-Nābulusī's (d. 1143/1730) seclusion (*ʿuzla*) in light of some of the moral and social dilemmas of associating with others. He argues that al-Nābulusī's concern for seclusion is justified by the *ḥadīth* traditions, and it is moral outrage which compels al-Nābulusī to write the tract as an ethical defence of his actions.

In chapter 8, "The Ethical in the Transmission of Sunna: Rethinking the *ʿUlamāʾ-Quṣṣāṣ* Conflict," Safwan Amir argues that the oft-neglected *quṣṣāṣ* (storyteller-preacher) played a vital role in directly conveying the Sunna to the larger public. He suggests that the *quṣṣāṣ* not only provide us with alternative histories to how knowledge was transmitted, taught, and realised in the Islamic tradition, but they also restore the fundamental idea of the *ḥadīth* as deeply intertwined with the ethical.

In chapter 9, "Abū Shuqqa's Approach to *Ḥadīth*: Towards an Egalitarian Islamic Gender Ethics," Faqihuddin Abdul Kodir tackles the question of how *ḥadīth*s have been reinterpreted to explain Islamic egalitarian gender ethics, through an analysis of ʿAbd al-Ḥalīm Muḥammad Abū Shuqqa's (d. 1995)

*Taḥrīr al-Mar'a fī 'Aṣr al-Risāla: Dirāsa 'an al-Mar'a Jāmi'a li-Nuṣūṣ al-Qur'ān wa-Ṣaḥīḥay al-Bukhārī wa-Muslim* ("The Liberation of Women at the Time of the Message: A Study on Women Composed of Qur'ānic Texts, and the *Ṣaḥīḥ*s of al-Bukhārī and Muslim").

In chapter 10, "Islamic Ethics and the *Ḥadīth* of Intention," Ali Altaf Mian contextualises "the *ḥadīth* of intention" in order to demonstrate, in part, the salience of *ḥadīth* texts as important sources for the study of Islamic ethics. He relates this *ḥadīth* to three broader themes in Islamic ethics. In doing so, he problematises the binary of the inner (*bāṭin*) and outer (*ẓāhir*) and highlights the social dimensions of intention through the illustration of migration, which signals the public – and not merely private – nature of intentions. The chapter also considers the multiple valences of intention in everyday Muslim religiosity.

In chapter 11, "Consult Your Heart: The Self as a Source of Moral Judgment," Mutaz al-Khatib explores the authority of the heart (*qalb*) as a potential locus of individual moral knowledge and normativity in Islamic ethics. To do so, he discusses two *ḥadīths* that ostensibly suggest that one's "self" is a potential source of the moral judgment. He argues that although the Islamic legal tradition, as a discipline, has focused on qualified external actions of individuals and the *ijtihād* (independent legal reasoning) of *mujtahid*s (jurists), it did not ignore the authority of the *bāṭin* over moral evaluation and the *ijtihād* of common individuals (*ijtihād al-mukallafīn*).

In chapter 12, "Muṣannafāt al-Muḥaddithīn fī l-Akhlāq: Kashshāf Awwalī" ("The Compendia of the Scholars of *Ḥadīth* on Ethics: A Preliminary Survey"), Mutaz al-Khatib presents a chronological bibliography of the key primary sources in the Islamic tradition with relevance to understanding the interplay of *ḥadīth* and ethics. The bibliography is preceded by an analytical introduction. This addition to the volume is meant to serve as a tool for future researchers to benefit from and build upon.

Although this volume is meant to provide theoretical foundations and insights about the study of *ḥadīth* as a crucial and rich source of Islamic ethics, there is a further thematic focus shared by various chapters, i.e., ethical subjectivity and relevant concepts such as intention, seclusion, noble virtues, *taḥbīb*, and consulting the heart.

The last editorial note I want to make here is that I have decided to pursue a systematic referencing to *ḥadīth* (*takhrīj*) and that is by referring to the book (*kitāb*) and the chapter (*bāb*). The purpose of that is not just for technical benefit and following the traditionists' method but also to highlight the thematic relevance and the moral argument behind each title if any.

Finally, I would like to thank the anonymous reviewers for their valuable comments. I am also grateful to the CILE research assistants Sara Abdelghany,

Rana Tahir and Yara Abdelbasset, as well as our MA students in Applied Islamic Ethics, Rasha Bader and Ibrahim Alledawi who helped me during the final step of this very long journey which started with a call-for-papers, followed by the submission of proposals of rough ideas about the seminar, revising the chapters several times, up until this publication. My gratitude also goes to all my colleagues working at CILE who helped and supported me through the ups and downs throughout the journey. Profound thanks and gratitude are due to my wife, Sawsan, whose dedicated support throughout the project was crucial. The last word is preserved for our newborn, Yaman, whose presence in our life, despite all the great noise he makes, was a great source of inspiration.

## Bibliography


ʿAbd al-Jabbār, Abū l-Ḥasan. 1960–1996. *Al-Mughnī fī Abwāb al-Tawḥīd wa-l-ʿAdl*, edited by Maḥmūd Muḥammad Qāsim, revised by Ibrāhīm Madkūr, and supervised by Ṭāhā Ḥusayn. Cairo: al-Dār al-Miṣriyya lil-Taʾlīf wa-l-Tarjama.

Abū l-Shaykh, ʿAbd Allāh. 1998. *Akhlāq al-Nabiyy wa-Ādābuh*, edited by Ṣāliḥ b. Muḥammad al-Waniyyān. Riyad: Dār al-Muslim.

al-Arnāʾūṭ, Shuʿayb and ʿUmar al-Qayyām Ibn Mufliḥ. 1999. "Muqaddimat al-Taḥqīq." In *Al-Ādāb al-Sharʿiyya*, by Ibn Mufliḥ. Beirut: Muʾassasat al-Risāla.

ʿAwwāma, Muḥammad. 2007. *Athar al-Ḥadīth al-Sharīf fī Khtilāf al-Aʾimma al-Fuqahāʾ*. Medina: Dār al-Yusr.

Burton, John. 1994. *An Introduction to the Hadith*. Edinburgh: Edinburgh University Press.

Fakhry, Majid. 1991. *Ethical Theories in Islam*. Leiden: Brill.

Hourani, George. 1985. *Reason and Tradition in Islamic Ethics*. Cambridge: Cambridge University Press.

al-Jābirī, Muḥammad ʿĀbid. 2001. *Al-ʿAql al-Akhlāqī l-ʿArabī*. Beirut: Markaz Dirāsāt al-Wiḥda al-ʿArabiyya.

al-Kattānī, Muḥammad b. Jaʿfar. 1993. *Al-Risāla al-Mustaṭrafa li-Bayān Mashhūr Kutub al-Sunna al-Musharrafa*. Beirut: Dār al-Bashāʾir al-Islāmiyya.

al-Khatib, Mutaz, ed. 2017. Thematic Issue: Qurʾan and Ethics. *Journal of Islamic Ethics* 1(1–2).

Shihadeh, Ayman. 2016. "Theories of Ethical Value in *Kalam*: A New Interpretation." In *The Oxford Handbook of Islamic Theology*, edited by Sabine Schmidtke, 384–407. Oxford: Oxford University Press.

al-Taftāzānī, Saʿd al-Dīn. 1998. *Sharḥ al-Maqāṣid*, edited by ʿAbd al-Raḥmān ʿUmayra. Beirut: ʿĀlam al-Kutub.

CHAPTER 1

# *Ḥadīth*-Based Ethics

## Ḥadīth *as a Scholarly Sub-discipline of Islamic Ethics*

*Mutaz al-Khatib*

The ethical content of *ḥadīth* has not received its due attention in contemporary scholarship on Islamic ethics: while some scholars completely disregarded it, others only briefly addressed it. So, this chapter will start with the section below to demonstrate this point.

## 1 *Ḥadīth* and Ethics in Contemporary Scholarship

Of the prominent scholars who disregarded the role of *ḥadīth* in Islamic ethics (*akhlāq*) is Bernard Carra de Vaux (d. 1953), who, in 1913, wrote the entry on "*Akhlāq*" in the first edition of *The Encyclopaedia of Islam*. In this entry, de Vaux adopted a limited understanding of Islamic ethics that was confined to the Greek philosophical tradition and argued that "the doctrine of the *akhlāq* is nothing but the ethics of the peripatetic philosophy" where "the science of moral philosophy … has an existence of its own; it is not an extract from different literary works, it is a science which is in fact connected with the tradition of Greek philosophy" (de Vaux 1987, 231). He thus concluded that "the Muslim authors who have written in a methodical manner about moral philosophy are comparatively few" (de Vaux 1987, 233).

Nine decades later, Muḥammad ʿĀbid al-Jābirī (d. 2010) also adopted a narrow conception of ethics in his *al-ʿAql al-Akhlāqī l-ʿArabī* ("The Arabic Moral Reason"), a large work in which he attempted to present a history of ethics in Islamic civilisation. However, al-Jābirī's work neglected specific contributions, most importantly Qurʾānic ethics, although he did reference the work of Muḥammad ʿAbd Allāh Drāz (d. 1958), *The Moral World of the Qurʾān*, but he undermined its value and contribution. Likewise, despite acknowledging that "the *ḥadīth* on ethics were countless," al-Jābirī downplayed the contribution of the *ḥadīth* corpus to ethics on grounds of differentiating between advocating and living (*ʿamal*) by the values of the Qurʾān and *ḥadīth*, on the one hand, and engaging in scholarly writing (*taʾlīf ʿilmī*) on Islamic values on the other. In other words, al-Jābirī restricted his historicisation to the theoretical works (*kalām*) on ethics and excluded the lived experience (*mumārasa*) of Muslim communities throughout history. In addition, he only included systematic works (*kitāba munaẓẓama*) which formulated a theoretical argument that follows scholarly methods (i.e., works that make use of typologies, analyses, and construction) (al-Jābirī 2001, 535, 537). Al-Jābirī also undermined the contribution of the *fuqahāʾ* to ethics, where he classified their work under *al-ādāb al-sharʿiyya*, by which he denotes "the best manner (*al-ṭarīqa al-fuḍlā*) to perform what is obligatory or recommended" and is thus "a formality (*shakliyya*) that is lacking in ethical content." To al-Jābirī, the work of the *fuqahāʾ* was enriched by the work of Sufis on *ādāb al-sulūk*, which address the etiquette of spiritual wayfaring, even though the Sufi contribution to *al-ādāb al-sharʿiyya* continued to be complementary to *fiqh*. These *ādāb sharʿiyya* entrenched "in the minds (*nufūs*) of the *fuqahāʾ*, *muḥaddithūn* (traditionists, sing. *muḥaddith*), and *mutakallimūn* the certainty that the sciences of religion (*ʿulūm al-dīn*) and *akhlāq* are one and the same" (al-Jābirī 2001, 536).

Accordingly, al-Jābirī was biased towards the philosophical ethics, despite his criticism of other scholars who confined themselves to the Greek tradition. In fact, al-Jābirī's conception of *akhlāq* is reductive: he presents a reductive conception of *adab* according to the *fuqahāʾ* under which he then classifies the works of the *muḥaddithūn*, while, in fact, the ethical content is present in both the rulings (*aḥkām*) and the *ādāb* (good manners and etiquette). For example, to the *fuqahāʾ adab* is used to denote (1) good character traits (*khiṣāl ḥamīda*), (2) the recommended (to the exclusion of the obligatory),[1] (3) all that is commanded, be it obligatory or recommended, or (4) inflicting discretionary punishment (*al-zajr wa-l-taʿzīr*).

As for the *muḥddithūn*, they were among the first to write on topics such as *zuhd* (asceticism), starting in the middle of the second *hijrī* century. If *zuhd* is to be included within al-Jābirī's conception of *adab*, then it cannot be considered a formality since *zuhd* served as the impetus for the development of Sufism as a discipline rich in ethics. Additionally, the *muḥddithūn*'s works span different genres of *adab*, as in *al-Adab al-Mufrad* of Abū ʿAbd Allah al-Bukhārī (d. 256/870),[2] *al-Mujālasa wa-Jawāhir al-ʿIlm* of Abū Bakr al-Dīnawarī

1 *Fuqahāʾ* used several definitions such as: *nafl* (supererogatory), *mustaḥab* (recommended/desirable), and *taṭawwuʿ* (volunteerism), as well as the better action to be carried out (*mā fiʿluhu khayrun min tarkihi*), what the person who is accountable is praised for doing but would not be criticised for disregarding (*mā yumdaḥu bihi al-mukallaf wa-lā yudhammu*), and what is required to be done but would not cause criticism if not done (*al-maṭlūb fiʿluhu sharʿan min ghayri dhammin ʿalā tarkihi*) (see Wizārat al-Awqāf 1983, 2:345–346).

2 Al-Bukhārī entitled this work *al-Adab al-Mufrad* to distinguish it from the chapter (*kitāb*) on *adab* under the *Ṣaḥīḥ* of al-Bukhārī. The book *al-Adab al-Mufrad* contains *ḥadīths* that

(d. 333/944), *Adab al-Nufūs* by Abū Bakr al-Ājurrī (d. 360/971), *Adab al-Ṣuḥba* by Abū 'Abd al-Raḥmān al-Sulamī (d. 412/1021), *al-Jāmiʿ li-Akhlāq al-Rāwī wa-Ādāb al-Sāmiʿ* by Abū Bakr al-Khaṭīb al-Baghdādī (d. 463/1071), and *Adab al-Imlāʾ wa-l-Istimlāʾ* by Abū Saʿd al-Samʿānī (d. 562/1167). These works reflect a conception of *adab* that is broader than what al-Jābirī labels as *al-mawrūth al-ʿarabī* (Arab heritage) which is limited to individual manners (*adab al-nafs*) and etiquettes of speech (*adab al-lisān*). In fact, from an ethical perspective the works of the *muḥaddithūn* are so rich and they demonstrate the Islamic ethical heritage, a heritage that al-Jābirī searched for. The *muḥaddithūn*'s works further demonstrate some of the scholarly criteria that al-Jābirī set as conditions for inclusion, namely the use of typology, analysis, and construction, through which the *muḥaddithūn* classified their collections thematically under chapters (*kutub*, sing. *kitāb*) and sections (*abwāb*, sing. *bāb*). This idea will be further elaborated under the third section of this introductory chapter.

As in the works of de Vaux and al-Jābirī, a bibliography on Islamic ethics commissioned by Oxford University Press and written by Andrew March also disregarded the contribution of *ḥadīth*, despite adopting a broad conception for ethics that included various Islamic disciplines. The bibliography moves from Qurʾānic ethics to theological ethics, and other disciplines, without examining the discipline of *ḥadīth* (March 2009).

Conversely, there were studies that addressed the ethical aspects in *ḥadīth*, but while some simply mentioned *ḥadīth* as a source on ethics, others dedicated a chapter or a few pages to the topic. The following paragraphs chronologically present a critical review of these studies and their key ideas.

Dwight M. Donaldson (d. 1976) was probably the only scholar who dedicated a whole chapter in his book *Studies in Muslim Ethics* to *ḥadīth*, titled "The Ethics of the Traditions." In this chapter, Donaldson noted the significance of the practical dimension of *īmān* (faith) in Islam; that is, emulating the Prophet's guidance as depicted in his words, actions, and approvals. In other words, the Prophet serves as a role model and exemplar to be followed, thus offering the *ḥadīth* their "utmost importance". In his discussion, Donaldson differentiated between three concepts: Sunna, *sīra*, and *adab*. Sunna serves as a source for determining "ceremonial duties, legal practices, necessary beliefs, etc." *Sīra* recounts the Prophet's biography, his life events, and the circumstances in which he lived and taught others. *Adab* addresses "the requisites for good manners, education, and general culture" (Donaldson 1953, 60–61). Accordingly, Donaldson built his

---

are not part of the *Ṣaḥīḥ* of al-Bukhārī in addition to some that are *mawqūf* (whose chain of transmission stops at the Prophet's Companions). This book, according to Muḥammad b. Jaʿfar al-Kattānī (d. 1345/1926) is of significant value and benefit (al-Kattānī 1993, 53).

chapter around these three concepts to stress the historical and ethical value of *ḥadīth*, as "it represents the Prophet's ethical as well as religious consciousness". Indeed, as Donaldson explained "though it is said that there were thousands of instances in which traditions were falsely attributed to the Prophet, still these very traditions may have evidential value for the religious and moral syncretism that took place in the development of the Muslim community after the all-absorbing period of rapid expansion" (Donaldson 1953, 61).

In the first volume of *The Encyclopaedia of Islam*'s second edition, published in 1960, Richard Walzer (d. 1975) and Hamilton Gibb (d. 1971) highlighted the role of the *muḥaddithūn* in supplementing "the religious ethics of the Ḳur'ān" (Walzer and Gibb 1960, 326). They argued that "the importance of the *ḥadīth* in forming and maintaining the common ethical ideas of the Muslim Community in all ages and all regions has been incalculable; but in addition it was largely responsible for the ethical framework of the developing Islamic Law, and for laying the foundations which made possible the process of integration" of different and sometimes conflicting kinds of morality. As they correctly explain, "… the whole corpus of *ḥadīth* constitutes a handbook of Islamic ethics" (Walzer and Gibb 1960, 326).

Later in 1975, George Hourani (d. 1984) listed *ḥadīth*, alongside the Qur'ān, as sources for "rules of law and morality for man", or what he termed "normative religious ethics" (Hourani 1975, 128–135; Hourani 1985, 15). Hourani concluded that the texts of the *ḥadīth*, just like those of the Qur'ān, "contain […] suggestions for answers to some more general questions of ethics" and serve as content of analytical ethics, but "all these kinds of normative religious books provided materials for analytical ethics, without themselves analysing ethical terms," since they are neither philosophical nor theological (*kalām*) texts (Hourani 1985, 15–16).

In 1991, Majid Fakhry (d. 2021) briefly addressed the ethical dimensions in the Qur'ān and *ḥadīth* under what he referred to as "scriptural morality" (Fakhry 1991, 10). Yet, given his focus on theoretical ethics, he set three parameters to his search for ethics in the Qur'ān and *ḥadīth*: (a) the nature of right and wrong, (b) divine justice and power, and (c) moral freedom and responsibility. Through his reading of a few *ḥadīth* which are of definite ethical relevance, Fakhry concluded that the *ḥadīth* is not as explicit as the Qur'ān, that it provides "an even dimmer view of the intricate correlations between the three ethical concepts," and that it only casually touches upon ethics. While Fakhry seems aware that this cursory review of his may appear "sketchy" (Fakhry 1991, 28), he proceeded to conclude that the *ḥadīth* does not articulate a substantive and systematic theory of justice and moral responsibility. This is clear through three observations (Fakhry 1991, 28):

1. With the exception of the problem of free will and predestination (*qadar*), not much systematic material can be produced from *ḥadīth*. Even this little material is of questionable historical value, since it appears to reflect the theological partisanship of the major theological and legal controversies that followed the Prophet's death. In fact, the theological trends that prevailed at those times "are of far greater significance" than *ḥadīth* to understanding "the standpoint of ethical development" of moral theology in Islam.
2. It cannot be assumed "that a substantive and systematic theory of justice and moral responsibility is articulately laid out in the canonical [*ḥadīth*] collections."
3. Given the circumstantial nature of utterances and legal pronouncements, and the personal or communal opinions embedded in the reports, it would be a mistake to premise profound and far-reaching moral constructions on these *ḥadīth*.

Fakhry's analysis seems methodologically flawed since he admits to a cursory reading but still draws general conclusions about the value of the *ḥadīth* corpus to ethics. Moreover, his methodology is biased since he focuses on philosophical and theological meta-ethics, while excluding other branches of ethics. Finally, in his search for the three parameters that he set for his analysis, he restricts himself to a few *ḥadīth* that appear in the *kutub* on *īmān* (faith) and *qadar* (predestination) in the *Ṣaḥīḥ* of al-Bukhārī and the *Ṣaḥīḥ* of Muslim (d. 261/875), to the exclusion of the other *kutub* in these collections and to the exclusion of other canonical collections. This confirms the cursory nature of his reading, since he concludes that these two collections do not include content on divine justice, or justice in general, while in fact the texts of the Qur'ān and *ḥadīth* served as rich content for the discipline of *kalām*. Fakhry also seems to have missed that *ḥadīth* on justice do not necessarily need to appear under a chapter on justice, since the classification of *ḥadīth* under chapters and sections is a function of authorial discretion, rather than a function of the value of the *ḥadīth* as a proof. In fact, other *ḥadīth* collections across time did feature sections on justice.[3]

3 For example, Abū Muḥammad al-Dārimī (d. 255/869) has a chapter on "justice among the people" in his *Musnad* (2015, 3:70), Nūr al-Dīn al-Haythamī (d. 807/1404) dedicated a section to "justice and transgression/wrongdoing/injustice" (1994, 5:196), and Abū l-ʿAbbās al-Būṣīrī (d. 840/1436) dedicated a section to "justice in ruling between the people on the day of judgement" (1999, 8:169). Shihāb al-Dīn Ibn Ḥajar al-Haytamī (d. 973/1566) also compiled 40 *ḥadīths* on justice in a treatise (2012). Issues concerning justice have been addressed in several *ḥadīths* under other *kutub* in *Ṣaḥīḥ* al-Bukhārī including those on *īmān, maẓālim*

Contrastingly, Scott C. Lucas acknowledged, in his 2008 work, the important influence of *ḥadīth* on Muslims and that such an influence persisted for over a millennium. Yet, Lucas pointed out that the content of *ḥadīth* remained largely inaccessible to non-Arabs, partly due to the "Western scholars' preoccupation with its authenticity rather than the function of *ḥadīth* in Islamic thought" (Lucas 2008, 226). In his journal article, Lucas provided an overview of the content of the key Sunnī canonical *ḥadīth* collections, presenting a sample of the *ḥadīth* with ethical content from the *Sunan* of Abū Dāwūd (d. 275/888). He also presented a comparison between the *Ṣaḥīḥ* of Muslim and the *Sunan* of Abū Dāwūd, where he listed 26 chapter titles common to both compilations. In doing so, he stressed that although "most of these topics relate to Islamic law and address the three broad legal categories of acts of worship (*ʿibādāt*), transactions (*muʿāmalāt*), and punishments (*ʿuqūbāt*)," ethical topics were *still* observable in a *kitāb* in Abū Dāwūd's *Sunan*, which includes 502 *ḥadīth*, while in Muslim's *Ṣaḥīḥ* ethical topics are more observable and an almost equivalent number of the *ḥadīth* are scattered across several *kutub*. He then listed 22 "ethical *ḥadīth*" from the *Sunan* of Abū Dāwūd, and indicated that *al-Arbaʿūn al-Nawawiyya* ("al-Nawawī's Collection of 40 *Ḥadīths*") is primarily about ethical teachings. Lucas also argued that the hierarchy – Islam (submission), *īmān* (faith), and *iḥsān* (beautiful conduct) – favoured by Sufis is of an ethical nature, and that a comparative thematic analysis of the major *ḥadīth* collections "ha[s] the potential to shed light on the role of *ḥadīth* in Islamic law, ethics, and theology" (Lucas 2008, 226–239).

In her 2010 book, Mariam al-Attar dedicated a few pages to what she termed "ethical presuppositions of *ḥadīth*" (al-Attar 2010, 21–25). She first listed a few *ḥadīths* that discourage documenting *ḥadīth*, confirm the Prophet's humanity, underscore the distinctness of *ḥalāl* (permissible) from *ḥarām* (impermissible), and highlight the centrality of the *qalb* (heart). She then deduced that "such reports are rare, and one cannot conclude that the *ḥadīth* reports support objective ethics, especially when considering [that there are] many reports that tend to emphasise predestination, and others in which goodness is given a political dimension advocating conformity to the will of the community and its leader, while evil is said to consist simply in following any heretical group" (al-Attar 2010, 21–22). Al-Attar also echoed Fakhry's philosophical ethical concepts, but rearranged them under four headings, while similarly limiting her examination to the *Ṣaḥīḥ* of al-Bukhārī and the *Ṣaḥīḥ* of Muslim. She thus concluded that "from Bukhārī and Muslim one cannot produce much

(complaints against authority, oppression), *qadar, aḥkām* (rulings) and *tawḥīd* (asserting Allāh's Oneness).

systematic material pertaining to the problem of the nature and knowledge of ethical values and divine justice," and that "the terms *qaḍā'* and *qadar* are used to refer to God's predetermination of everything, including ethical values, human moral choices, and the destiny of every individual," thus, those *ḥadīths* that align with orthodoxy, especially that of the Ashʿarī theology, are dubious and, in fact, fabricated (al-Attar 2010, 24). As was the case with Fakhry, al-Attar's research is selective and restricted to a few *ḥadīths* of al-Bukhārī and Muslim without presenting a justification for this selectivity or outlining the methodology used for her analysis. Further, she seems to overlook *ḥadīth* commentaries, which tips the balance towards a Muʿtazilī view at the expense of highlighting the historical and ethical value of *ḥadīth*.

Finally, it is also worth highlighting a critical bibliography produced by some Iranian researchers in 2012, which brought together what they term as "the ethical schools in the Islamic thought" (*al-madāris al-akhlāqiyya fī l-fikr al-islāmī*) (Islāmī et al. 2012). The bibliography lists some works, both from the Sunnī and the Shīʿī literature, and provide a description for each. In it, the scholars dedicated a section to what they called *madrasat al-akhlāq al-athariyya* (the narration-based ethical school) (Islāmī et al. 2012, 75–80). To them, this school encompasses the works that included and classified the reports on ethics which depict a narrative style, which makes these works more of examples of compilations than ones on ethics (*kutub riwāya*) (Islāmī et al. 2012, 77–78). Specifically, these works include repetitions and contradictions with no attempt at reconciling these *ḥadīths*, nor do they depict an acceptable methodical classification, rather they depict some conflation of Islamic ethics and *ādāb* (Islāmī et al. 2012, 77, 79–80). The researchers thus build their bibliography on the presumption that *al-akhlāq al-athariyya* is premised in revelation as the only, or most important, source of ethics – which, in their view, seems to align with the Ashʿarī position on *sharʿ* being the source of normativity (*al-taḥsīn wa-l-taqbīḥ*) – although the authors admit to having no proof for this presumption and acknowledge that some *muḥaddithūn* produced their works based on specialization, where the main concern is to narrate and compile reports (Islāmī et al. 2012, 30–31, 75–76).

Despite the diversity depicted in the Iranian bibliography, which includes works from the four different schools of philosophical (*falsafiyya*), Sufi (*ʿirfāniyya*), narration-based (*athariyya*), and reconciliatory (*tawfīqiyya*) ethics, it fails to offer a clear conception for *akhlāq*. In the introduction to the bibliography, *akhlāq* seems limited to *afʿāl al-bāṭin* (inner actions) and *tahdhīb al-nafs* (disciplining the self). Yet, under the section on *al-akhlāq al-athariyya*, the authors talk about the *akhlāq* of the individual, the family, the community, and of serving God (Islāmī et al. 2012, 17, 30, 80). However, while in the introduction the authors conclude that the Islamic tradition's content in terms of theoretical works on Islamic ethics does not match those on *fiqh, tafsīr* (exegesis), *kalām*, or even philosophy, they still conclude, under the section on *al-akhlāq al-athariyya*, that the literature of this school on *akhlāq* is richer than the literature of other schools of ethics (Islāmī et al. 2012, 19, 79).

While we could have deduced from the Iranian bibliography that the researchers differentiated theoretical ethics from applied ethics, since *al-akhlāq al-athariyya* is classified as applied ethics, the authors still criticise the works on *al-akhlāq al-athariyya* for conflating *akhlāq* and *ādāb*, without providing a definition for these two concepts. The authors also do not clearly differentiate theoretical ethics from applied ethics, nor do they clarify whether they consider all works on *al-akhlāq al-athariyya* as devoid of theory. Further, the authors do not provide proof for how they classified the sources on *al-akhlāq al-athariyya* as aligned with the Ashʿarī position, nor do they provide an opinion on whether applied ethics can stand without an explicit or implicit theoretical base. On top of that, the authors do not provide any discussion on how the works on *al-akhlāq al-athariyya*, which they consider as purely narrative works (*kutub riwāya*), can be classified as a school on their own, and whether an underlying classification is sufficient to establish this group of works as a school or approach in ethics. In short, it seems that the authors of this bibliography were more preoccupied with describing these sources at the expense of critically analysing their contents, so they adopted a limited conception of *akhlāq*. In fact, had the authors adopted an interdisciplinary approach to *akhlāq*, they may have succeeded in touching on the intersections between *akhlāq* and the other Islamic disciplines including *fiqh, kalām*, and philosophy, which may have enabled them to broaden their conception of *riwāyāt akhlāqiyya* (ethical narrative) beyond *aḥwāl al-bāṭin* (states of the heart) and *ādāb*.

## 2 *Ḥadīth* as a Corpus on Ethics

*Ḥadīth*, specifically that which is characterised as *marfūʿ* – meaning that the chain of transmission is traced to the Prophet – includes all that is attributed to the Prophet, in: words, actions, tacit approval (*taqrīr*), physical traits (*ṣifa khalqiyya*), or character traits (*ṣifa khuluqiyya*). In the terminology of *muḥaddithūn*, the scope of *ḥadīth* extends beyond that of Sunna, where the latter is restricted to the actions and behaviours of the Prophet (see al-Shumunnī 2004, 92; al-Kattānī 1993, 3, 32). To some *muḥaddithūn*, the word "*ḥadīth*" also extends to encompass the *mawqūf*, for which the chain of transmission ends at a Companion (*ṣaḥābī*), and the *maqṭūʿ*, for which the chain of transmission ends at a Successor (*tābiʿī*); although, they still acknowledge the inferiority of these two *ḥadīth* forms to the *marfūʿ*, in serving as a source of law (al-Zarkashī 1998, 1:420–421).

There are thus two levels to studying *ḥadīth*. The first is specifically concerned with its sources and depicts various approaches to compilation, such as arranging content according to the Companion transmitting the *ḥadīth* (*musnad*, pl. *masānīd*), the scholar through which the compiler received the *ḥadīth* (*muʿjam*, pl. *maʿājim*), or according to an existing arrangement by another *muḥaddith*, but using the compiler's relevant chain of transmission instead (*mustakhraj*, pl. *mustakhrajāt*). The second level, which has been largely disregarded in Western academia,[4] is concerned with the texts (*mutūn*, sing. *matn*) reporting the Prophet's words, actions, or approvals, which, in totality, form the corpus of *ḥadīth*. This second approach gained traction in different forms during the classical period, including *ḥadīth* commentaries and collecting as much of these texts, in a single book, as possible. Examples of this form of *ḥadīth* collection include, *Jamʿ al-Jawāmiʿ* by Jalāl al-Dīn al-Suyūṭī (d. 911/1505) and *Kanz al-ʿUmmāl fī Sunan al-Aqwāl wa-l-Afʿāl* by ʿAlāʾ al-Dīn al-Muttaqī l-Hindī (d. 975 /1567) in the Mamluk era (al-Suyūṭī 2005; al-Muttaqī l-Hindī 1981).

In studying these texts, Muslim scholars were largely concerned with their value to generating *fiqhī* (juristic) rulings, or to serving as proofs, and were, accordingly, preoccupied with collecting and commenting on *ahādīth al-aḥkām* (traditions on *fiqhī* rulings). Yet, in fact, the *ḥadīth* corpus extends beyond rulings to encompass *sunan* (exemplary behaviour), stories, *ādāb* (manners) and *mawāʿiẓ* (moral exhortations), historical narratives with moral content (*ʿiẓa*), and creed. Accordingly, the examination of the *ḥadīth* corpus should extend beyond a discipline-based approach to, instead, adopt an interdisciplinary one.

With this expanded conception, *ḥadīth* serves as a corpus on ethics, in the broad conception of ethics, as is demonstrated through both the historical context and the actual content in *ḥadīth* sources. With respect to the historical context, the *ḥadīth* corpus documents, in detail, issues, concerns, and questions of the early Muslim community, who were in need of normative judgement relevant to all aspects of life at the communal, family, and individual levels. It was this level of detail that allowed *ḥadīth* to serve as a normative authority

4 Textual reporting has recently started to gain traction in Western scholarship in different forms, including *ḥadīth* commentary (Blecher 2018), the narrative elements in the *ḥadīth* literature (Calamawy 1983; Günther 1998; Sperl 2007), the Prophet's example as a husband (Ali 2004; Chaudhry 2011), Prophetic authority (Brown 1999, 60–80; Musa 2008), the use of *ḥadīth* in theology (Holtzman 2010), and studies on single *ḥadīth*s or *muḥaddith*s (Leirvik 2010; Bellamy 1963).

among the *fuqahāʾ* (Muslim jurists) who examined *ḥadīth* both theoretically, under Islamic legal theory (*uṣūl al-fiqh*), and practically, under *fiqh*. Compared to the Qurʾān, which lays out general principles and which, in the eyes of the *fuqahāʾ*, includes a limited number of verses on rulings (*āyāt al-aḥkām*), it was *ḥadīth* that played the more significant role in *fiqh* (jurisprudence). In fact, even when some *ḥadīth*s are not necessarily sound (*ṣaḥīḥ*), they still carry a normative value where, at the minimum, they reflect the norms of their times. In addition, the *ḥadīth* corpus carries significance for narrative ethics as it provides insight into the complexity of specific incidents, the drivers of normativity, and the character traits of subjects, albeit many texts were transmitted devoid of such details (al-Shāfiʿī 1938, 213, 216).

As for the *ḥadīth* corpus' content, it may be classified into three categories: words, actions, and character traits, where these categories correspond to the contemporary dichotomy of ethics of action versus virtue ethics. While the sources on *ḥadīth* are generally concerned with words and actions, character traits, at times referred to as *akhlāq*, were the concern of other genres, such as those on *sīra* (Prophetic biography), on *shamāʾil* (Prophetic perfections), and of other distinct works entitled *ṣifāt al-nabīʾ* and *akhlāq al-nabī* such as the works of Muḥammad b. Hārūn (d. 353/964), Abū l-Shaykh al-Aṣbahānī (d. 369/979), Abū Ḥayyān al-Aṣfahānī (d. 429/1038), Ḍiyāʾ al-Dīn al-Maqdisī (d. 643/1245), and others.

It is through these three categories that Sunna established its normative authority as the second source of Islamic law, after the Qurʾān. Additionally, these three categories positioned the Prophet as the role model and exemplar whose words, actions, and character traits are to be emulated, consequently establishing his rights over Muslims, starting with the duty to love him,[5] extending to other duties which are compiled in books such as that of al-Qāḍī ʿIyāḍ (d. 544/1149) entitled *al-Shifāʾ bi-Taʿrīf Ḥuqūq al-Muṣṭafā* (2013). The Prophet's position as an exemplary role model is central to the *ḥadīth* corpus and is premised in the Qurʾānic exhortation "The Messenger of God is an excellent model for those of you who put your hope in God and the Last Day and remember Him often" (Q 33:21, tr. Abdel Haleem). This exemplary role is also cemented through the use of the term "Sunna," which indicates that which is set to be followed, making Sunna the second source of Islamic law. Finally, this exemplary role is also cemented through exclusion, specifically, the emergence of a genre on "Prophetic characteristics" (*khaṣāʾiṣ nabawiyya*) that seeks to delineate what is specific to the Prophet and is not to be emulated, as in the

5 See, for example, al-Bukhārī (2001, 2:125): *Kitāb al-Īmān* ("Book of Faith"), *Bāb Ḥubb al-Rasūl min al-Īmān* ("Chapter on Loving the Prophet is Part of Faith").

works of Abū l-Khaṭṭāb Ibn Diḥya al-Kalbī (d. 633/1236), ʿIzz al-Dīn Ibn ʿAbd al-Salām (d. 660/1262), Sirāj al-Dīn Ibn al-Mulaqqin (d. 804/1401), and others.

By excluding that in which the Prophet is unique, these works indirectly confirm that, apart from these exclusions, perfection and happiness are attainable by following the Prophet as a role model. In other words, Sunna defines what a Muslim should be to achieve the ultimate ends of perfection and happiness in both lives: the here and the hereafter.

In addition, *ḥadīth* as a corpus on ethics is not limited to the outer actions (*afʿāl al-jawāriḥ* or *al-ẓāhir*) but extends to include the inner actions (*afʿāl al-bāṭin*) to which specific works were dedicated such as those by Ibn Abī l-Dunyā (d. 281/894), Abū Muḥammad al-Ḥasan b. Ismāʿīl al-Ḍarrāb (d. 392/1002), and others. Others dedicated *kutub* (chapters) in their canonical books on *ḥadīth* to the inner actions, such as the *kitāb al-riqāq* (softening the heart) in the *Ṣaḥīḥ* of al-Bukhārī and in the *Ṣaḥīḥ* of Ibn Ḥibbān (d. 354/965) (as ordered by Ibn Balabān [d. 739/1338]), and the *kitāb al-birr wa-l-ṣila wa-l-ādāb* (virtue, caring for kin, and manners) in the *Ṣaḥīḥ* of Muslim. Finally, *ḥadīth* as a corpus on ethics encompasses both texts that address casuistries, as well as texts that establish general principles such as those of *al-Arbaʿūn al-Nawawiyya* ("The Forty *Ḥadīth*s of al-Nawawī [d. 676/1277]") (al-Nawawī 2009).

Considering ethics in its broad conception, the content on ethics in the *ḥadīth* collections can be found dispersed in several *kutub*, as in those on rulings (*aḥkām*), grievances and usurpation (*maẓālim wa-ghaṣb*), coercion (*ikrāh*), tricks (*ḥiyal*), destiny (*qadar*), and others in the *Ṣaḥīḥ* of al-Bukhārī, for example. However, if we consider ethics in its most restricted conception, the texts that serve as a corpus on ethics can be found under two types of sources. The first are those works dedicated to a specific topic such as *dhamm al-riyāʾ* (blameworthiness of insincerity) or to a group of virtues. These works will be further classified later in this introductory chapter. The second type of sources are the key collections where the texts on *akhlāq* (ethics) are listed under specific *kutub*, as in the *kitāb al-adab* in *Sunan Abī Dāwūd* which includes more than 500 reports (Abū Dāwūd 2009, 7:153–545), and the *kitāb al-birr wa-l-iḥsān* (virtue and good deeds) and *kitāb al-raqāʾiq* (softening the heart) in the *Ṣaḥīḥ* of Ibn Ḥibbān (as ordered by Ibn Balabān) with more than 767 reports (Ibn Ḥibbān 1988, 1:506, 3:310). A survey of the six canonical collections highlights specific *kutub* as pertinent to ethics in its most restricted conception, namely *kitāb al-manāqib* (merits) which highlights certain virtues, and *kitāb al-adab*, *kitāb al-riqāq*, *kitāb al-birr wa-l-ṣila*, and *kitāb al-zuhd* (asceticism). Specific to the *Ṣaḥīḥ* of Muslim, the texts with ethical content are spread across *kitāb al-salām* (greeting), *kitāb alfāẓ min al-adab* (the use of correct words), *kitāb al-birr wa-l-ṣila*, *kitāb al-ādāb*, *kitāb al-faḍāʾil* (virtues), *kitāb al-tawba* (repentance), *kitāb al-dhikr wa-l-duʿāʾ* (remembrance and supplication), *kitāb ṣifāt al-munāfiqīn* (characteristics of the hypocrites), and *kitāb al-zuhd*. It is clear here that *ādāb* is distinguished from *adab* in the *Ṣaḥīḥ* of Muslim, to which he dedicates separate chapters, as did al-Tirmidhī.

However, the *ḥadīth*'s contribution to ethics is not limited to that of the texts included in the collections, it also extends to the contribution of *uṣūl al-ḥadīth*, or the sciences of *ḥadīth*, which serve a theoretical purpose, parallel to that which *uṣūl al-fiqh* serves in the discipline of *fiqh*. These sciences address the *ādāb* (manners) of the *muḥaddith*, the knowledge seeker (*ṭālib al-ḥadīth*), documenting *ḥadīth* (*kitābat al-ḥadīth*), travelling in pursuit of collecting *ḥadīth* (*al-riḥla fī ṭalab al-ḥadīth*), and of dictating and transcribing *ḥadīth* (*al-imlāʾ wa-l-istimlāʾ*). While these sciences were originally addressed in distinct books, they were later brought together under the genre of *anwāʿ ʿulūm al-ḥadīth* (types of *ḥadīth* sciences), starting with the work of Abū ʿAmr Ibn al-Ṣalāḥ (d. 643/1245). For example, in discussing *ādāb al-muḥaddith*, Ibn al-Ṣalāḥ underscores the fit of a virtuous character free from vices for this noble science (i.e., *ḥadīth* sciences) (Ibn al-Ṣalāḥ 1986, 236), while al-Nawawī, in discussing the *ādāb* of dictating *ḥadīth* (*imlāʾ al-ḥadīth*), encourages *muḥaddith* to conclude dictation by including texts on asceticism and virtues (al-Nawawī 1985, 81; al-Suyūṭī 1994, 2:581).

*Ḥadīth* sciences also include that of *rijāl* (transmitters), or *al-jarḥ wa-l-taʿdīl* (disparaging and declaring trustworthiness), by which the trustworthiness and reliability of the transmitters themselves were examined, which is of relevance to ethics. As noted by Muṣṭafā Ṣādiq al-Rāfiʿī (d. 1937) early on, this science is closely linked to ethics. Specifically, to al-Rāfiʿī this science may be considered the "historical science of ethics" (*ʿilm al-akhlāq al-tārīkhī*) where transmitters were assessed based on their accuracy, trustworthiness, their endeavour in fulfilling their religious obligations, their character traits, and their *akhlāq* (al-Rāfiʿī 1911, 1:297). In that sense, the sources on *al-jarḥ wa-l-taʿdīl* present transmitters as exemplars and offer some rich content on virtues and vices. In addition, these sources can serve the study of *murūʾa* (chivalry) which played a critical role in determining the trustworthiness of transmitters, and is yet to receive significant attention in contemporary scholarship.

## 3 *Ḥadīth*-Based Ethics: Its Nature, Classification, and Scope

Thus, *ḥadīth* is rich in ethical content as evident in the conception of *ḥadīth* and Sunna, in the content of the *ḥadīth* corpus, itself, and through the *ḥadīth* sciences. We can now speak of *ḥadīth*-based ethics. Yet, it is imperative to also delve into examining the nature of such ethics since the works of the *muḥaddithūn* on *akhlāq* are usually perceived as *ḥadīth* collections, devoid of any theoretical framework or introduction, where the *muḥaddith* is simply reporting texts and chains of transmission rather than contributing their own ideas.

It is true that the collections of the *muḥaddithūn* on *akhlāq* do not follow the theoretical approach common to works on ethics, since their methodology holds knowledge to be in the narrative form rather than in the scholar's opinion or analysis. Yet, despite their faithfulness to this methodology, a theoretical component is evident in the sciences of *ḥadīth*, as well as in the collections themselves. Since the latter may need some clarification, al-Bukhārī's collection, for example, demonstrates the *fiqh* of the *muḥaddithūn*, whereby he embeds a theoretical framework in the narrative that he offers. Accordingly, those engaging in commentary on his work highlighted that while al-Bukhārī does not provide a theoretical introduction to his work, his contribution to *fiqh* is in his classification and categorisation of texts, and in the titles that he uses for chapters and sections (*fiqh al-Bukhārī fī tarājimih*). Indeed, Ibn Ḥajar al-ʿAsqalānī (d. 852/1448) concluded through induction (*istiqrāʾ*) that al-Bukhārī relies on implicit rather than explicit means to present his argument (Ibn Ḥajar n.d. a, 1: 8). As for al-Nawawī, he stressed that al-Bukhārī sought to make an argument and used the texts as proofs for that argument, rather than simply offering a collection or compilation of *ḥadīth*s, which explains his tendency to drop the chains of transmission at times (Ibn Ḥajar n.d.(b), 8). In other words, the theoretical dimension in the work of al-Bukhārī is implicit and is to be extracted, a task for which many commentators dedicated their works, including Ibn al-Munayyir (d. 683/1284), Walī Allāh al-Dihlawī (d. 1176/1762), Muḥammad Zakariyyā al-Kāndihlawī (d. 1402/1632) and others (Ibn al-Munayyir 1987; al-Dihlawī 2018; al-Kāndihlawī 2012).

One can further appreciate the theoretical dimension found in the collections of *ḥadīth* by recognising that classifying and compiling reports under chapters or titles is a form of presenting an argument: an undertaking that extends beyond *masānīd*, *maʿājim*, or according to reasons for rejection of the *ḥadīth* (*ʿilal al-ḥadīth*). Nonetheless, some *muḥaddithūn* attempted to combine both methodologies, such as al-Nasāʾī (d. 303/915) who offered a thematic classification, comparable to commenting on reasons for rejection where relevant. In fact, it was in the second *hijrī* century that the *muḥaddithūn* started to offer a thematic classification (*al-taṣnīf ʿalā l-abwāb*) of *ḥadīth*, as in the work of ʿAbd Allah Ibn al-Mubārak (d. 181/797) – an approach that was initially criticised given its departure from the established methods (Abū Nuʿaym 1974, 8:165). Yet, thematic classification continued to gain traction until it was recognised as an approved methodology under *ḥadīth* sciences (al-Ḥākim 2001, 43; Ibn al-Ṣalāḥ 1986, 253; Ibn Ḥajar 2000, 147), and later it was considered as an independent branch of *ḥadīth* sciences by Abū ʿAbd Allāh Muḥammad b. ʿUmar b. Rashīd (d. 721/1321) (al-Suyūṭī 2003, 1:22).

In fact, the theoretical dimension that underlies thematic classification was recognised by al-Ḥākim al-Naysābūrī (d. 405/1014) and Ibn al-Ṣalāḥ who believed that a *muḥaddith* who classifies *ḥadīth* by themes or titles is, in actuality, generating a ruling and considering the texts listed under a specific title fit to serve as proofs for it (al-Ḥākim 2001, 43; Ibn al-Ṣalāḥ 1986, 38). Likewise, Ibn Ḥajar came to recognise that, in general, whoever classifies *ḥadīth* thematically is arguing for the ruling presented as the theme or title under which texts are listed, a method that is very different from classifying according to the transmitting Companion (*al-taṣnīf ʿalā l-masānīd*) where no conclusion about the fitness of the texts to serve as proofs can be made. At any rate, Ibn Ḥajar was aware of irregularities, since some *muḥaddithūn* who adopted a thematic classification still included texts that were unfit to serve as proofs (Ibn Ḥajar 1984, 1:446–447, 449). Accordingly, some *ḥadīth* scholars were keen to emphasise that whoever adopts a thematic classification should avoid including week or unsound *ḥadīth* (*ḥadīth al-ḍuʿafāʾ*) unless they serve specific purposes, such as identifying reasons for rejection (*iʿtibār*) or confirming the essence of a text in question (*shāhid*) (al-Isʿardī 1989, 36; al-Zarkashī 1998, 1:270; al-Suyūṭī 1994, 1:141).

In conclusion, an implicit theoretical framework does underlie thematic *ḥadīth* classification, including the chapters or sections on ethics. Yet, this framework is different from those employed by both the philosophers and the *fuqahāʾ*. This framework also overrides the dichotomy of normative (or narrative) ethics versus analytical ethics adopted by George Hourani and Mohammed Arkoun (Hourani 1985, 15; Arkoun 1990, 89), since *ḥadīth*-based ethics combines the narrative and the analytical, as will be demonstrated in this book's chapter on Ibn Abī l-Dunyā, and as evident in the works of al-Ḥakīm al-Tirmidhī (d. *c.*320/932), Abū Bakr al-Kalābādhī (d. 380/990), al-ʿIzz Ibn ʿAbd al-Salām, and others. Thus, there is a need to invest in unearthing and examining the framework that underlies thematic classification of *ḥadīth*.

In examining the Islamic literature to identify works on ethics, Muḥammad ʿAbd Allāh Drāz (d. 1958) (1998, 4), and others, were limited by their search for works that demonstrated the methods of the philosophers. In doing so, they overlooked the books compiled by the *muḥaddithūn* on ethical themes, which makes coming up with a classification of works on *ḥadīth*-based ethics a challenging undertaking. Yet, our attempt will exclude the *kutub* (chapters) listed earlier under the canonical works, as well as the chapters on *ḥadīth* on rulings that extend to encompass some texts with a restricted conception of ethics. Therefore, when focusing on books that were specifically dedicated to *ḥadīth*-based ethics, I propose the following classification:

- *Adab* genre: which discusses manners and etiquette as relevant to the different disciplines, including those applicable to: the narrator and the listener, the *faqīh* and the student of *fiqh*, to the one who dictates and the one who transcribes, and others. This genre also includes works on individual manners (*adab al-nufūs*), treating the parents, and other works that follow the *muḥaddithūn*'s method in narrating reports with their chain of transmitters (*al-aḥādīth al-musnada*).
- Works on noble virtues (*makārim al-akhlāq*), or on good and bad character traits (*maḥāsin wa-masāwiʾ al-akhlāq*), which came to be treated as a standalone genre.
- Works on *al-targhīb wa-l-tarhīb* (persuasion and intimidation) that address praiseworthy and blameworthy actions, and that cover both religious and ethical aspects.
- Works on *shuʿab al-īmān* (branches of faith) that seek to survey what falls under these branches, building on the well-known *ḥadīth* that offer a foundation for these branches. These works bring together *kalām, fiqh*, and ethics, as well as both belief and action.
- Works on *manāqib* (merits) and excellences (*faḍāʾil*), depicting a diversity of literature according to specific individuals and times.
- Works on asceticism, which emerged starting in the second *hijrī* century and which pioneered thematic classification.
- Works that present Prophetic guidance (*hady al-nabī*), his character traits (*akhlāq*), and his perfections (*shamāʾil*) as a role model and exemplar. These came to stand as a distinct genre after being included as part of the *Sīra* works.
- Works dedicated to a specific topic, such as the blameworthiness of the attachment to this life (*dhamm al-dunyā*), the blameworthiness of insincerity (*dhamm al-riyāʾ*), diseases of the heart (*iʿtilāl al-qulūb*), and others.

Some of the most notable authors with works classified under these genres are Ibn al-Mubārak, Aḥmad Ibn Ḥanbal (d. 241/855), al-Bukhārī, al-Tirmidhī (d. 279/892), Ibn Abī l-Dunyā, al-Ḥakīm al-Tirmidhī, al-Kharāʾiṭī (d. 327/939), al-Ṭabarānī (d. 360/971), Abū l-Shaykh b. Ḥayyān (d. 369/979), al-Ḥalīmī (d. 403/1012), al-Bayhaqī (d. 458/1066), and others.

## 4 Concluding Remarks: Suggested Research Topics

The above listed writings on ethics show the richness of the *ḥadīth* literature and its great potential for the field of Islamic ethics. It can be also of added value to the field of *ḥadīth*. Although practical and behavioural ethics can be clearly observed in this literature, it should not be perceived only as narrative-based ethics or merely as a collection of reports on advice and good manners (*adab*). It is true that *ḥadīth* collections are devoid of any philosophical framework since philosophical theorisation does not fit within the traditionists' (*muḥaddithūn*) mindset, which perceives knowledge through the lens of transmitted knowledge (*naql*) rather than intellectual reasoning (*ʿaql*). But this doesn't mean that they are free of any indirect theoretical foundations or implicit frameworks (including concepts, analysis, classification, structure, and implicit argument). This is why this literature ended up producing what I called "*ḥadīth*-based ethics" which, being diverse and variable, needs to be studied and analysed from an interdisciplinary approach. My hope is that this edited volume comes as the first step in this direction.

With this in mind, theorising ethics in the works on *ḥadīth* can be conceptualised through the following six broad themes:

1. Terminology and Ethical Concepts in *Ḥadīth* Collections
   - *A ḥadīth-based* dictionary of ethics: noble virtues (*makārim al-akhlāq*), immoral qualities (*masāwiʾ al-akhlāq*), etiquette and good manners (*adab*), virtuous acts (*faḍāʾil al-aʿmāl*), branches of faith (*shuʿab al-īmān*), the ethics of the Prophet, and *shamāʾil*.
   - Tackling the problem of distinguishing between juristic rulings (*aḥkām*), on the one hand, and *faḍāʾil al-aʿmāl*, on the other.
   - Examining the concept of Sharīʿa as outlined in the works on rulings and those which study good manners (*ādāb*), compared to the writings on the "branches of faith" which incorporate ethics. This may result in the adoption of an interdisciplinary approach that combines the disciplines of Islamic theology, jurisprudence, and ethics.
   - Analysing the diverse and rich typologies of morals from the various disciplines that invoke ethics, and observing their impact on both ethical form and content. This also involves studying the implications of specialist works on ethics and how they relate to the other collections of *ḥadīth*.
2. *Ḥadīth*-based Ethics: History, Development, and Approaches
   - Examining the history and evolution of writings dedicated to *ḥadīth*-based ethics by introducing a historical-epistemological reading that analyses the evolution of this genre in light of the developments of the three other genres, namely: (1) philosophical ethics, such as the writings of Abū Yūsuf al-Kindī (d. 256/870), Abū Bakr al-Rāzī (d. 311/923), Abū ʿAlī Miskawayh (d. 421/1030) and others; (2) *adab*-based ethics, such as the writings of Ibn al-Muqaffaʿ (d. 142/759) and others; and (3) juristic rulings, such as the early works on *fiqh* written by Abū Yūsuf (d. 182/798), Muḥammad b. al-Ḥasan (d. 189/805), al-Shāfiʿī (d. 204/819) and others.

- Studying the *ḥadīth* in al-Ghazālī's *Iḥyāʾ ʿUlūm al-Dīn* ("Revival of the Religious Sciences") – without imposing the standards of *ḥadīth* scholars to verify the authenticity of these traditions – in search of the ethical model that was possibly served by the *ḥadīth* that was widely circulating in the Sufi discourse. To what extent did these traditions serve as foundation for a certain vision, or were they simply quoted to support an already existing vision?
- Examining the question of ethics in the collections of *ḥadīth* commentaries – its scope, dimensions, and theoretical issues.
- Recognising the theoretical potential that can be captured from the prolific ethical compilations provided by scholars like al-Ḥārith al-Muḥāsibī (d. 243/857), Ibn Abī l-Dunyā and others.
- Studying the ethical visions provided by some early *ḥadīth* collections, such as the *Muṣannaf* of ʿAbd al-Razzāq al-Ṣanʿānī (d. 211/826), to understand the ethical vision of the formative period of Islamic history as reflected in the miscellaneous *ḥadīth* narrated by ʿAbd al-Razzāq, irrespective of the authenticity of these *ḥadīth*.
- Conducting an ethical analysis of the biography of the Prophet and the *shamāʾil* genre, to identify the practical side of the "exemplar model" (*uswa*) and the traits that should be followed by believers.

3. The Nature of *Ḥadīth*-based Ethics

- Can *ḥadīth*-based ethics be classified as religious ethics, or does it fit under one of the key Western moral theories (deontology and utilitarianism), or is it not restricted to the current theories, thus producing a third category?
- Examining the concept of *targhīb/tarhīb*, its applicability and the problems it raises in moral philosophy. For example, this concept may support the idea of religious-based ethics, with praise and blame being in the hereafter, whereas Draz (2008, 285–290) and others argue that Islamic ethics are not exclusively religious in nature.
- Exploring the possible reasons that prompted jurists (*fuqahāʾ*) and traditionists to be lenient with regards to the traditions that talk about virtuous acts (*faḍāʾil al-aʿmāl*), while strictly scrutinising those traditions that imply rulings (*aḥādīth al-aḥkām*). How does this differentiation relate to disagreements regarding the epistemological sources that justify judging actions as "good" or "bad"? In the same vein, to what extent would the low probability of attributing the weak *ḥadīth* on *faḍāʾil al-aʿmāl* to the Prophet, provide a sufficient basis to make it a religious virtue although it will not be enough in the case of a ruling produced by the human intellect, which the Muʿtazilīs considered one of God's messengers.

– Further exploring the relationship between ethics and religion, and the nature of the ethics provided by *ḥadīth* collections in terms of authority, relationships, and sources. Do they produce religious-based ethics?

4. Sunna as a Source: Towards the Fundamentals of Ethics

– Studying the theoretical aspects of ethics as elaborated by Muslim legal theorists (*uṣūliyyūn*) in the chapter dedicated to Sunna (*mabāḥith al-sunna*) in the books of Islamic legal theory (*uṣūl al-fiqh*). How far can these theoretical elements be integrated into the study of meta-ethics or normative ethics?

– Studying ethical concepts in the Prophetic *ḥadīth*, but based on a theoretical foundation. In studying these concepts, it is also possible to search for key values in *ḥadīth* corpus (*birr, taqwā, ḥayāʾ, amāna*, etc.).

– Reviewing major ethical propositions in Sunna using a thematic approach; that is conducting theme-based studies (*ḥadīth mawḍūʿī*) premised in a theoretical foundation before proceeding to the applied examples.

– Extracting the key and governing ethical principles in *ḥadīth* corpus and developing potential methodologies for such identification and extraction.

– Developing a theoretical basis for the Prophetic traditions on ethics (*aḥādīth al-akhlāq*), similar to what was done with the genre of traditions on rulings (*aḥādīth al-aḥkām*) which has received considerable attention from both traditionists and jurists.

5. *Ḥadīth*-based Ethics: Comparative Studies

– Comparing *ḥadīth*-based ethics to other ethical traditions, such as pre-Islamic Arab values, Christianity and Judaism. Enabling comparative critical studies demonstrating what was adopted, added or subjected to amendment or correction.

– Comparing the all-comprehensive words (*jawāmiʿ al-kalim*) in the *ḥadīth* corpus to similar genres of other cultures that were known to Muslims in early Islamic history.

6. Applied Studies on Ethical Values in *Ḥadīth* Corpus

– Advancing applied studies on select ethical values that are mentioned in *ḥadīth* collections and discussed in Islamic theology, such as the creation of deeds (*khalq al-afʿāl*), compulsion and freedom, or determining the good (*taḥsīn*) and the bad (*taqbīḥ*).

– Initiating applied studies that address some of the *ḥadīth*-based values in fields such as politics (obeying the ruler, commanding right and forbidding wrong, the rights of common people, freedom, justice, etc.), and economics (social justice, distribution of wealth, equal opportunities, etc.), as well as in other fields.

## Bibliography

Abdel Haleem, Muhammad. 2005. *The Qur'an: A New Translation*. Oxford: Oxford University Press.

Abū Dāwūd, Sulaymān b. al-Ashʿath. 2009. *Sunan Abī Dāwūd*. Beirut: Dār al-Risāla al-ʿĀlamiyya.

Ali, Kecia. 2004. "A Beautiful Example: The Prophet Muḥammad as a Model for Muslim Husbands." *Islamic Studies* 43(2): 273–291.

Arkoun, Muḥammad. 1990. *Al-Islām wa-l-Akhlāq wa-l-Siyāsa*, translated by Hāshim Ṣāliḥ. Paris: UNESCO, Beirut: Markaz al-Inmāʾ al-Qawmī.

Al-Attar, Mariam. 2010. *Islamic Ethics: Divine Command Theory in Arabo-Islamic Thought*. London: Routledge.

al-Aṣbahānī, Abū Nuʿaym Aḥmad. 1974. *Ḥilyat al-Awliyāʾ wa-Ṭabāqāt al-Aṣfiyāʾ*. Cairo: Dār al-Saʿāda.

Bellamy, James A. 1963. "The *Makārim al-Akhlāq* by Ibn Abīʾl-Dunyā (A Preliminary Study)." *Muslim World* 53: 106–119.

Blecher, Joel. 2018. *Said the Prophet of God: Hadith Commentary across a Millennium*. University of California Press.

Brown, Daniel W. 1999. *Rethinking Tradition in Modern Islamic Thought*. Cambridge: Cambridge University Press.

al-Bukhārī, Muḥammad b. Ismāʿīl. 1422 [2001]. *Ṣaḥīḥ al-Bukhārī*, edited by Muḥammad Zuhayr b. Nāṣir al-Nāṣir. Beirut: Dār Ṭawq al-Najāt.

al-Būṣīrī, Shihāb al-Dīn Abū l-ʿAbbās. 1999. *Itḥāf al-Khiyara al-Mahara bi-Zawāʾid al-Masānīd al-ʿAshara*, edited by Dār al-Mishkāt lil-Baḥth al-ʿIlmī. Riyad: Dār al-Waṭan.

Chaudhry, Ayesha S. 2011. "'I WANTED ONE THING AND GOD WANTED ANOTHER …': The Dilemma of the Prophetic Example and the Qurʾanic Injunction on Wife-Beating." *Journal of Religious Ethics* 39(3): 416–439.

al-Dārimī, ʿAbd Allāh b. ʿAbd al-Raḥmān. 2015. *Al-Musnad*, edited by Markaz al-Buḥūth bi-Dār al-Taʾṣīl. Cairo: Dār al-Taʾṣīl.

de Vaux, Bernard Carra. 1987. "Akhlāḳ (Ethics)." In *The Encyclopaedia of Islam, First Edition (1913–1936)*, edited by M. TH. Houtsma, T.W. Arnold, R. Basset and Hartmann. Leiden: Brill. DOI: 10.1163/2214-871X_ei1_SIM_0520.

Donaldson, Dwight M. 1953. *Studies in Muslim Ethics*. London: S.P.C.K.

Draz, M.A. 2008. *The Moral World of the Quran*, translated by Daniel Robinson and Rebecca Masterton. London, New York: I.B.Tauris.

Drāz, Muḥammad ʿAbd Allāh. 1998. *Dustūr al-Akhlāq fī l-Qurʾān*, translated by ʿAbd al-Ṣabūr Shāhīn. Beirut: Muʾassasat al-Risāla.

al-Dihlawī, Walī Allāh. 2018. *Sharḥ Tarājim Abwāb Ṣaḥīḥ al-Bukhārī*, edited by Fāyiz Aṣṭīla. Damascus: Dār al-Taqwā lil-Ṭibāʿa wa-l-Nashr.

El Calamawy, Sahair. 1983. "Narrative Elements in the Ḥadīth Literature." In *Arabic Literature to the End of the Umayyad Period*, edited by A.F.L. Beeston, T.M. Johnstone, R.B. Serjeant, and G.R. Smith, 308–316. Cambridge: Cambridge University Press.

Fakhry, Majid. 1994. *Ethical Theories in Islam*. Leiden: Brill.

Günther, Sebastian. 1998. "Fictional Narration and Imagination within an Authoritative Framework: Towards a New Understanding of Ḥadīth." In *Story-telling in the Framework of Non-fictional Arabic Literature*, edited by Stefan Leder, 433–471. Harrassowitz: Wiesbaden.

al-Ḥākim, Abū ʿAbd Allāh. 2001. *Al-Madkhal ilā Maʿrifat Kitāb al-Iklīl*, edited by Muʿtazz al-Khaṭīb. Damascus: Dār al-Fayḥāʾ.

al-Haytamī, Ibn Ḥajar Shihāb al-Dīn. 2012. *Arbaʿūna Ḥadīthan fī l-ʿAdl*. edited by Samīr al-Kattānī, Riyad: Manshūrāt al-Jamal.

al-Haythamī, Abū al-Ḥasan Nūr al-Dīn. 1994. *Majmaʿ al-Zawāʾid wa-Manbaʿ al-Fawāʾid*, edited by Ḥusām al-Dīn al-Qudsī. Cairo: Maktabat al-Qudsī.

Holtzman, Livnat. 2010. "Human Choice, Divine Guidance and the *Fiṭra* Tradition: The Use of Hadith in Theological Treatises by Ibn Taymiyya and Ibn Qayyim al-Jawziyya." In *Ibn Taymiyya and his Times*, edited by Yossef Rapoport and Shahab Ahmad, 163–88. Oxford: Oxford University Press.

Hourani, George F. 1975. "Ethics in Medieval Islam: A Conspectus." In *Essays on Islamic Philosophy and Science*, 128–135. Albany: State University of New York Press.

Hourani, George F. 1985. *Reason and Tradition in Islamic Ethics*. Cambridge: Cambridge University Press.

Ibn al-Munayyir, Abū l-ʿAbbās Aḥmad. 1987. *Al-Mutawārī ʿalā Tarājim Abwāb al-Bukhārī*, edited by Ṣalāḥ al-Dīn Maqbūl Aḥmad. Beirut: Maktabat al-Muʿallā.

Ibn al-Ṣalāḥ, Abū ʿAmr ʿUthmān. 1986. *ʿUlūm al-Ḥadīth*, edited by Nūr al-Dīn ʿItr. Damascus: Dār al-Fikr.

Ibn Ḥajar al-ʿAsqalānī, Aḥmad b. ʿAlī. 1984. *Al-Nukat ʿalā Kitāb Ibn al-Ṣalāḥ*, edited by Rabīʿ b. Hādī ʿUmayr al-Madkhalī. Medina: ʿImādat al-Baḥth al-ʿIlmī bi-l-Jāmiʿa al-Islāmiyya.

Ibn Ḥajar al-ʿAsqalānī, Aḥmad b. ʿAlī. 2000. *Nuzhat al-Naẓar fī Tawḍīḥ Nukhbat al-Fikar fī Musṭalaḥ Ahl al-Athar*, edited by Nūr al-Dīn ʿItr. Damascus: Dār al-Ṣabāḥ.

Ibn Ḥajar al-ʿAsqalānī, Aḥmad b. ʿAlī. n.d.(a). *Fatḥ al-Bārī Sharḥ Ṣaḥīḥ al-Bukhārī*, edited by Muḥibb al-Dīn al-Khaṭīb. Cairo: al-Dār al-Salafiyya.

Ibn Ḥajar al-ʿAsqalānī, Aḥmad b. ʿAlī. n.d.(b). *Hady al-Sārī Muqaddimat Fatḥ al-Bārī*, edited by Muḥibb al-Dīn al-Khaṭīb. Cairo: al-Dār al-Salafiyya.

Ibn Ḥibbān, Muḥammad b. Ḥibbān. 1988. *Al-Iḥsān fī Taqrīb Ṣaḥīḥ Ibn Ḥibbān*, edited by Shuʿayb al-Arnāʾūṭ. Beirut: Muʾassasat al-Risāla.

al-Isʿardī, Taqī l-Dīn ʿUbayd Allāh. 1989. *Faḍāʾil al-Jāmiʿ li-Abī ʿĪsā l-Tirmidhī*, edited by al-Sayyid Ṣubḥī al-Sāmarrāʾī. Beirut: ʿĀlam al-Kutub, Maktabat al-Nahḍa al-ʿArabiyya.

Islāmī et al. 2012. *Al-Madāris al-Akhlāqiyya fī l-Fikr al-Islāmī*, translated by ʿAbd al-Ḥasan Bahbahānī Būr. Beirut: Markaz al-Ḥaḍāra li-Tanmiyat al-Fikr al-Islāmī.

ʿIyāḍ, Abū l-Faḍl ʿIyāḍ b. Mūsā. 2013. *Al-Shifā bi-Taʿrīf Ḥuqūq al-Muṣṭafā*, edited by ʿAbduh ʿAlī Kūshak. Dubai: Ḥukūmat Dubayy.

al-Jābirī, Muḥammad ʿĀbid. 2001. *Al-ʿAql al-Akhlāqī l-ʿArabī: Dirāsa Taḥlīliyya Naqdiyya li-Nuẓum al-Qiyam fī l-Thaqāfa al-ʿArabiyya*. Beirut: Markaz Dirāsāt al-Wiḥda al-ʿArabiyya.

al-Kāndihlawī, Muḥammad Zakariyyā. 2012. *Al-Abwāb wa-l-Tarājim li-Ṣaḥīḥ al-Bukhārī*, edited by Walī l-Dīn al-Nadwī. Beirut: Dār al-Bashā'ir al-Islāmiyya.

al-Kattānī, Muḥammad b. Jaʿfar. 1993. *Al-Risāla al-Mustaṭrafa li-Bayān Mashhūr Kutub al-Sunna al-Musharrafa*. Beirut: Dār al-Bashā'ir al-Islāmiyya.

Leirvik, Oddbjørn. 2010. "Aw Qāla: 'Li-Jārihi': Some Observations on Brotherhood and Neighborly Love in Islamic Tradition." *Islam and Christian–Muslim Relations* 21(4): 357–372.

Lucas, Scott C. 2008. "Major Topics of the Hadith." *Religion Compass* 2(2): 226–239.

March, Andrew. 2009. *Ethics: Oxford Bibliographies Online Research Guide*. Oxford: Oxford University Press. DOI: 10.1093/OBO/9780195390155-0021.

Musa, Aisha Y. 2008. *Hadith as Scripture: Discussions on the Authority of Prophetic Traditions in Islam*. New York: Palgrave and Macmillan.

al-Muttaqī l-Hindī, ʿAlā' al-Dīn. 1981. *Kanz al-ʿUmmāl fī Sunan al-Aqwāl wa-l-Afʿāl*, edited by Bakrī Ḥayyānī and Ṣafwa al-Saqqā. Beirut: Mu'assasat al-Risāla.

al-Nawawī, Muḥyī l-Dīn Abū Zakariyyā. 1985. *Al-Taqrīb wa-l-Taysīr li-Maʿrifat Sunan al-Bashīr al-Nadhīr fī Uṣūl al-Ḥadīth*, edited by Muḥammad ʿUthmān al-Khusht. Beirut: Dār al-Kitāb al-ʿArabī.

al-Nawawī, Muḥyī l-Dīn Abū Zakariyyā. 2009. *Al-Arbaʿūn al-Nawawiyya*, edited by Quṣayy Muḥammad Nawras al-Ḥallāq and Anwar b. Abī Bakr al-Shaykhī. Beirut: Dār al-Minhāj.

al-Rāfiʿī, Muṣṭafā Ṣādiq. 1911. *Tārīkh Ādāb al-ʿArab*. Beirut: Dār al-Kitāb al-ʿArabī.

al-Shāfiʿī, Muḥammad b. Idrīs. 1938. *Al-Risāla*, edited by Aḥmad Muḥammad Shākir. Cairo: Maṭbaʿat Muṣṭafā al-Bābī l-Ḥalabī.

al-Shumunnī, Aḥmad. 2004. *Al-ʿĀlī l-Rutba fī Sharḥ Naẓm al-Nukhba*, edited by Muʿtazz al-Khaṭīb. Damascus: Mu'assasat al-Risāla.

Sperl, Stefan. 2007. "Man's 'Hollow Core': Ethics and Aesthetics in Ḥadīth Literature and Classical Arabic Adab." *Bulletin of the School of Oriental and African Studies* 70 (3): 459–486.

al-Suyūṭī, Jalāl al-Dīn ʿAbd al-Raḥmān. 1415 [1994]. *Tadrīb al-Rāwī fī Sharḥ Taqrīb al-Nawāwī*, edited by Abū Qutayba Naẓar Muḥammad al-Fāryābī. Riyad: Dār al-Kawthar.

al-Suyūṭī, Jalāl al-Dīn ʿAbd al-Raḥmān. 1424 [2003]. *Qūt al-Mughtadhī ʿalā Jāmiʿ al-Tirmidhī*, edited by Nāṣir b. Muḥammad b. Ḥāmid al-Gharībī. Mecca: Umm al-Qurā University.

al-Suyūṭī, Jalāl al-Dīn ʿAbd al-Raḥmān. 2005. *Jamʿ al-Jawāmiʿ (al-Jāmiʿ al-Kabīr)*, edited by Mukhtār Ibrahīm al-Hāʾij, ʿAbd al-Ḥamīd Muḥammad Nadā, and Ḥasan ʿĪsā ʿAbd al-Ẓāhir. Egypt: al-Azhar al-Sharīf.

Walzer, R. and H.A.R. Gibb. 1960. "Akhlāḳ (Ethics)." In *The Encyclopaedia of Islam, Second Edition*, vol. 1, 325–327. Leiden: Brill. DOI: 10.1163/1573-3912_islam_COM_0035.

Wizārat al-Awqāf wa-l-Shuʾūn al-Islāmiyya. 1983. *Al-Mawsūʿa al-Fiqhiyya*. Kuwait: Ṭibāʿat Dhāt al-Salāsil.

al-Zarkashī, Badr al-Dīn Muḥammad. 1998. *Al-Nukat ʿalā Kitāb Ibn al-Ṣalāḥ*, edited by Zayn al-ʿĀbidīn b. Muḥammad Balāfrīj. Riyad: Dār Aḍwāʾ al-Salaf.

CHAPTER 2

# *Ḥadīth* and the Concept of *Adab* as Moral Education

*Nuha Alshaar*

## 1 Introduction

This chapter discusses the interaction between *ḥadīth* and the concept of *adab* as sources for moral education and training. The term "*adab*" has wide semantic implications and nuances that have evolved over time due to religious, cultural and social development in Muslim societies (Sperl 2007, 459; Alshaar 2017, 1–48). However, for the purpose of this chapter, the term *adab* will be treated from the point of view of its ethical dimension and will be considered here, as rightly suggested by Stefan Sperl, as "practical ethics" (Sperl 2007, 459). In other words, knowledge that is a call to action and a required form of training for those aspiring to good manners, proper etiquette and cleansing of their souls.

*Ḥadīth*s originated in an oral society, which was, with the introduction of writing and the documentation of the Qur'ān, slowly changing into a new community by adopting the religious authority of the divine scripture and the Prophetic paradigm (Neuwirth 2014, 72). The Prophet was endowed with the authority to teach and interpret the divine scripture and he had the opportunity to put his teaching into practice. This Prophetic model of dictating the Muslim community's moral norms underlined the intersections of the private and public domains, as well as the role of interpretive narrative in forming patterns of moral behaviour and standards for different situations.

Building on existing literature, including Sperl's seminal work on the ethics and aesthetics of *ḥadīth* literature and classical Arabic *adab* compilations of the third/ninth century (Sperl 2007), this chapter will explore the interaction between Prophetic traditions and the term *adab* in two ways: at an epistemological level, and at an authoritative level. The epistemological level underlines how the circulation of certain *ḥadīth* materials shaped the conceptualisation of *adab* and its moral paradigm, which was a shift from viewing *adab* as solely informed by customary law and human knowledge to viewing it as dictated by divine commands and aligned to religious sensitivity. The authoritative level demonstrates the role of the Prophet as an *uswa* (*qudwa*, role-model) who has provided Muslims with a living example of how to behave in different situations. It also explains the role of *ḥadīth* narratives as explanatory and interpretive vehicles that erect ethical discourses and invoke moral and religious authority, as well as a linguistic authority. This linguistic authority emerges from the famous maxim that the Prophet had been endowed with "*jawāmiʿ al-kalim*," a phrase that came to be interpreted as the ability to express oneself with brevity, wit and fluency.

## 2 *Ḥadīth* as a Moral Source and its Influence on the Conceptualisation of *Adab*

Recorded in oral memory and through means of writing, *ḥadīth* rapidly became an authoritative repository of the community's early religious and historical experiences (Khalidi 1994, 17). After the Prophet's death, the early Muslim community collected the speeches and reports about him and disseminated them for exemplary use and guidance under the term "*ḥadīth*." This term is found together with others such as *khabar* (report), *nabaʾ* (news) and *ʿilm* (knowledge), and is used in the Qurʾān to refer to reports and the representations of the past. The basic meaning of the word is also a story or narration, parable, or report, which, as suggested by Tarif Khalidi, could indicate a shift in the function of *ḥadīth* from a private to a more public role of guidance (Khalidi 1994, 17–18).

The connection of the term *ḥadīth* with those for report, news and parable reflect a moral content, while the connection with the word *ʿilm* implies knowledge and wisdom derived from sacred scripture. In the sense of unveiling the past, the term *ḥadīth* covered various content, including narrative emanating from the Prophet Muḥammad and his Companions. This material varied in importance and religious seriousness, ranging from legal injunctions, rituals, the virtues of individuals or tribes, eschatology, ethical conduct, biographical fragments, the Prophet's expeditions, correct manners, admonitions and homilies.

## 3 The Prophet as *Uswa* (*Qudwa*, Ethical Role-Model)

*Ḥadīth* materials included interpretive narratives, which not only complemented the teaching of the Qurʾān but also provided an authoritative body of knowledge on "how to act" and "what is right and what is wrong" in different themes and aspects of life. This allowed *ḥadīth* to compete with other forms of knowledge. It also established the authority of the Prophet as an ethical role-model whose behaviour in different situations guided his Companions and followers. They imitated his example and in turn contributed examples for other situations, for later Muslims. The Prophet acted as the main educator (*mu'addib*) of his community and provided materials for other educators (*mu'addibūn*) or the practitioners of *adab*, thus shifting the notion of moral and educational endeavour. Before analysing the circulation of specific *ḥadīth* that influenced the conceptualisation of *adab* and established the authority of the Prophet as an educator and ethical role-model, it is useful to look at some of the pre-Islamic uses of *adab*.

The term *adab* had several pre-Islamic uses, according to early and medieval lexicologists. For example, al-Khalīl b. Aḥmad al-Farāhīdī (d. 175/791) links the "*adīb*" and "*adab*" to the concept of *ta'dīb*, a form of offering education or training for those aspiring to acquire good manners and to learn proper etiquette. Al-Farāhīdī says that the *adīb* "is the educator who educates others" (*mu'addib yu'addibu ghayrah*), or "is educated by others" (*yata'addabu bi-ghayrih*). Al-Farāhīdī also associates the term *adab* with "correction" and "punishment" (al-Farāhīdī 1980–1985, 8:85); this definition was used among the nomads to indicate the domestication of animals (Bonebakker 1984, 405–410).

This pre-Islamic understanding of *adab* as educating someone about correct manners and appropriate behaviour was a recurrent theme discussed in poetry, proverbs and anecdotes. In these cultural and literary records, *adab* was described in relation to the concept of *muruwwa* or *murū'a*; a pre-Islamic moral term that combines the notion of manliness with virtuous conduct that was informed by tribal law and customs (Montgomery 1986, 7). *Muruwwa* also represented a moral code by which to judge the moral and social standing of individuals and their relations and obligations towards their communities. Thus, the discussion on *muruwwa* and *adab* not only bridged the gap between the community and the person, but also encompassed the substantive moral issues of the time, including people's aspirations, their struggle for survival and their attempt to create coherent communities.

Pre-Islamic Arabs also linked *adab* to forms of sociability and social interactions, such as offering food and sharing a meal, which were indicators of social status and part of portraying friendship (Alshaar 2020). In this culture, banquets were recurrent themes in the literature, celebrating moral and social values, such as generosity, through which individuals reached moral refinement and commonly accepted etiquettes. Al-Farāhīdī links *adab* and the root *'-d-b* to the meaning "invitation to a banquet" and the *adīb* to a "*ṣāḥib al-ma'duba*," where *ma'duba* or *ma'daba* is a banquet, and the *adīb* is the host who invites and entertains the guests (al-Farāhīdī 1980–1985, 8:85).

Although *adab*, as a form of practical moral guide, was informed by inherited customary norms, it also developed over time, incorporating religious elements (see Alshaar 2017, 7; 2020, 182–183). With the coming of Islam, and the circulation of *ḥadīths* that communicated ethics inspired by the revelation, *adab* gained a new point of reference, leading to a shift in its nature and sources. While the *ḥadīth* functioned as an interpretive and subordinate source to the Qurʾān, it was a central reference point for different religious endeavours and for moral values. The ethical underpinning of *ḥadīth* narratives produced not only moral knowledge that determines norms or accepted standards, but also guidance for practical reasoning and problem-solving, focusing on situations or circumstances where the Prophet himself, as an exemplary model, approved or disapproved. In one *ḥadīth*, the Prophet Muḥammad is reported as saying,

> My Lord has educated me, and so He excelled in educating me and I was brought up among the tribe of Saʿd (*addabanī rabbī fa-aḥsana taʾdībī wa rubbītu fī banī Saʿd*).[1]

Another *ḥadīth*, related by al-Ḥākim al-Naysābūrī (d. 405/1014) and attributed to Ibn Shihāb al-Zuhrī (d. 124/742) says,

> Verily this knowledge [referring to *ʿilm al-ḥadīth*] is "God's *adab*," through which He has educated his Prophet, and through which the Prophet has educated his community.
>
> AL-ḤĀKIM AL-NAYSĀBŪRĪ 2003, 247–248

In both cases, *adab* constitutes the sum of divine knowledge that protects one from errors in speech, acts and character, and dictates the best form of behaviour.

In many Prophetic reports, the Prophet is depicted with a disposition naturally in line with the moral teaching of the Qurʾān. He also encouraged his followers to cultivate the best moral character. For example, in a report narrated by al-Bayhaqī (d. 458/1065), the Prophet declares that the essence of his message is to guide people to perfect their moral character: "Indeed I was sent [by God] to perfect good moral character."[2] He also equates the notion of *birr*

---

1 This *ḥadīth* is related by al-Samʿānī (d. 562/1166) (al-Samʿānī 1981, 1) and considered by some late *ḥadīth* scholars as a weak tradition that bears a true meaning (see Ibn al-Athīr 1963–1965, 1:4; al-Sakhāwī 1985, 73–74).

2 Al-Bukhārī 1955, 78: *Bāb Ḥusn al-Khuluq* ("Chapter on the Excellence of Character").

(righteous virtue), which is a central theme in the Qur'ān, with "having the best moral character" (*al-birr ḥusn al-khuluq*).[3] Acting morally is equal to sincerity in performing the five prescribed pillars, and a person whose actions are guided by the best moral character is equal in rank to the believer who performs much supererogatory fasting and praying, "indeed, a believer with good character attains the same degree of the one who fasts and prays throughout the night."[4] As the moral guide for Muslims, the Prophet asked his followers to acquire unwavering moral character and said this is the way to receive his love: "Those of you who have the best moral character will be the closest to me on the Day of Judgement."[5] In another *ḥadīth*, the Prophet says "nothing is weightier on the scale [on the Day of Judgement] than good (*ḥusn*) character."[6] In this *ḥadīth*, the need to cultivate good character is seen as an aesthetic quality (*ḥusn*), the origin of which is divine knowledge. In another famous report, ʿĀ'isha (d. 58/678) described her husband, the Prophet, as having a disposition and a character that mirrors the Qur'ān and as embodying the essence of its values and moral virtues.[7] In this statement, the Qur'ān constitutes the ideal source that informs the disciplining of the soul, which results in proper behaviour.

Thus, the imitation of Prophet Muḥammad and fulfilling the reciprocal rights and duties that he established becomes an important part of Muslim moral and ethical teaching and practices, a position that the Qur'ān asserts: "Indeed you have been endowed with a noble character" (*khuluq ʿaẓīm*) (Q 68:4). This exact point provides grounds for the Muslim community's acceptance of the Prophet's words as authoritative and of a different register of speech than other forms of human language. This is because they not only erect moral discourses that embody the essence of God's divine wisdom, but also manifest the ability to express their intended meanings with brevity and fluency, as expressed in the famous maxim about the Prophet that he was endowed with "*jawāmiʿ al-kalim.*" The Prophet is considered as proof of God's divine generosity, a medium of metaphysical force and the eloquent

3 Muslim 1991, 255: *Kitāb al-Birr wa-l-Ṣila wa-l-Ādāb* ("Book on Virtue, Maintaining the Ties of Kinship and Manners"), *Bāb Tafsīr al-Birr wa-l-Ithm* ("Chapter on the Interpretation of Virtue and Sin").

4 Abū Dāwūd 2009: *Kitāb al-Adab* ("Book of Manners").

5 Al-Nawawī 2001: *Kitāb al-Umūr al-Manhī ʿAnhā* ("Book on Prohibited Actions").

6 Al-Bukhārī 1955, 78: *Bāb Ḥusn al-Khuluq* ("Chapter on Good Moral Character").

7 Muslim 1991, 1:513: *Kitāb Ṣalāt al-Musāfirīn wa-Qaṣruhā* ("Book on the Travellers' Prayers and its Shortening"), *Bāb Jāmiʿ Ṣalāt al-Layl wa-man Nāma ʿAnhu aw-Mariḍ* ("Chapter on the One Who Performs the Night Prayers Together, Sleeps through Them or Falls Ill Without Performing Them").

communicator of divine knowledge to people, which educates them and helps them refine their characters (Q 2:129).

On this basis, a strong link between *ḥadīth*s and divine *ʿilm* provides *ḥadīth* with legitimacy as an edifying source of knowledge. This source transcends the personal realm, that is, the life and actions of the Prophet to communal practice through emulation. Thus, *ḥadīth* can be described as intermediary communication, conveying divine teaching and values to humans through verbal interpretation, and as a linguistic moral source based on the Prophet's mastery of pure Arabic. The Prophet asserted, as mentioned in the *ḥadīth* cited above, that he spoke the Arabic of the Bedouins (Banū Saʿd) and he received the revealed scripture, which contains the best meanings expressed in the most eloquent words. Such *ḥadīth*s draw attention to the rhetorical and aesthetical features of *ḥadīth* and could explain why a *muʾaddib* who is interested in the moral education of others finds *ḥadīth* an important and necessary source.

Hence, the correct use of language, including certain words and expressions, is seen as a religious and moral act, which is a topic covered in *ḥadīth* literature. For example, in the chapter on *adab* in al-Bukhārī's collection of *ḥadīth*s, the edifying power of speech is a metanarrative manifested in the intrinsic relationship between word and deed, and speech and action. As outlined by Sperl, worthy action as induced by eloquent and laudable speech seems to form common ground between several *ḥadīth* compilations and premodern literary compilations (Sperl 2007, 466–467). This link between word and action leads to an important shift, embodied in *ḥadīth* literature, in which the Qurʾān as the divine and eloquent words of God induced good actions in people.

## 4 *Ḥadīth* and the Shift in the Pre-Islamic Notion of *Adab*

A number of *ḥadīth*s introduced a new twist to the pre-Islamic notion of an *adīb* as someone who invites others to a "banquet" in order to promote Islamic moral and literary sensibilities. For example, ʿAbd Allāh Ibn Masʿūd (d. 32/652–653) narrates a *ḥadīth* comparing the Qurʾān to a divine banquet sent by God:

> Indeed, the Qurʾān is the banquet of God [on earth], so you should learn from its banquet whatever you can (*inna hadhā l-Qurʾān maʾdubat Allāh fa-taʿallamū min maʾdubatih mā staṭaʿtum*).

This *ḥadīth* is reported on the authority of Ibn Masʿūd in different wordings; in some sources it is reported as Ibn Masʿūd's own statement (*mawqūf*), while in others it is elevated to the Prophet (*marfūʿ*).[8] In this *ḥadīth*, the banquet is the divine knowledge that educates people and helps them to refine their behaviour (Alshaar 2017, 11).

From the third/ninth century onwards, scholars continued to use this first/seventh-century allegory of the Qurʾān as a divine banquet providing the "nourishment" of knowledge, goodness and guidance and might have influenced the conceptualisation of *adab* and the role of the *adīb*. In the chapter on *daʿawāt* (invitations) in his *Kitāb al-Alfāẓ* ("The Book of Words"), the grammarian Ibn al-Sikkīt (d. 244/858) defines *maʾduba* and *maʾdaba* as a banquet that is prepared by someone who invites his brothers. Next, he explains the verb form *adaba* and the subject noun *ādib*. He then quotes the *ḥadīth* on the authority of Ibn Masʿūd, discussing how God compares the Qurʾān to a banquet, as something He makes for people's welfare and benefit. Following this analogy, he states that the practitioner of *adab* (the *adīb*) is the one who invites people to religion (Ibn al-Sikkīt 1998, 456). In *Maqāyīs al-Lugha* ("Analogical Templates of Language"), Aḥmad b. Fāris al-Qazwīnī (d. 395/1004) mentions the root *ʾ-d-b*, listing two main derived meanings: *adb*, which is the act of gathering people to a banquet, and *adab* which is something that there is collective agreement for its praise (*mujmiʿūn ʿalā istiḥsānih*). He also quotes the *ḥadīth* on the authority of Ibn Masʿūd, adding that from the same metaphor of the Qurʾān as God's banquet, one could make the analogy that the *adīb* is one who gathers people to guide them to achieve inner excellence (*istiḥsān*) (Ibn Fāris al-Qazwīnī 1946–1952, 1:74–75). Thus, there are two shifts: One is related to the scope and the nature of knowledge that leads to *adab*, and another is linked to the social function of *adab*, which became more religiously oriented in search of inner goodness, based on satisfying a divine standard.

This conceptual shift continued into later literature. In his *al-Jāmiʿ li-Aḥkām al-Qurʾān* ("Compilation of the Rulings of the Qurʾān"), Muḥammad b. Aḥmad al-Qurṭubī (d. 671/1272) quotes two *ḥadīth*s describing the Qurʾān as a divine banquet. He begins by citing:

---

8 For the *mawqūf ḥadīth*, see al-Ṣanʿānī 1983, 3:368, 375: *Kitāb Faḍāʾil al-Qurʾān* ("Book on the Virtues of the Qurʾān"), *Bāb Taʿlīm al-Qurʾān wa-Faḍlih* ("Chapter on Teaching the Qurʾān and Its Virtue"); Ibn Abī Shayba 2006, 15:464: *Kitāb Faḍāʾil al-Qurʾān* ("Book on the Virtues of the Qurʾan"), *Bāb fī l-Tamassuk bi-l-Qurʾān* ("Chapter on Holding Fast to [the Teachings of] the Qurʾān"); al-Dārimī 2000, 2:2083–2093: *Kitāb wa-min Faḍāʾil al-Qurʾān* ("Book on What Belongs to the Virtues of the Qurʾān"), *Bāb Faḍl Man Qaraʾa l-Qurʾān* ("Chapter on the Benefits of the One Who Reads the Qurʾān"). For the *marfūʿ ḥadīth*, see Ibn Abī Shayba 1997, 1:251; 2006, 15:462–463: *Kitāb Faḍāʾil al-Qurʾān* ("Book on the Virtues of the Qurʾān"), *Bāb fī l-Tamassuk bi-l-Qurʾān* ("Chapter on Holding Fast to [the Teachings of] the Qurʾān"); al-Naysābūrī 1997, 1:753: *Kitāb Faḍāʾil al-Qurʾān* ("Book on the Virtues of the Qurʾān"), *Bāb fī Faḍāʾil al-Qurʾān Jumlatan* ("Chapter a Sentence on the Virtues of the Qurʾān").

> The Qur'ān is the banquet of God on earth, and the one who seeks refuge in it is safe, so you should learn from its banquet (*al-Qur'ān ma'dubat Allāh fī l-arḍ fa-man dakhala fīh fa-huwa āmin*).
>
> AL-QURṬUBĪ 2006, 1:12

Al-Qurṭubī explains this *ḥadīth* by citing Abū ʿUbayda Maʿmar b. al-Muthannā (d. 210/825), who says in his *Gharīb al-Ḥadīth* ("Strange Traditions") that this is a proverb in which the Prophet compares the Qur'ān to something that God has made for people, in which lies their welfare and benefit. Al-Qurṭubī adds, still drawing on Abū ʿUbayda:

> It [the word *ma'duba*] can be pronounced *ma'duba* and *ma'daba*. The one who reads it as *ma'duba* refers to the making that is made by God (*al-ṣanīʿ ṣanaʿahu Allāh*), while the one who reads it as *ma'daba* refers to *adab*, so he takes it as the derivative form *mafʿala* from the word *adab*.

Abū ʿUbayda supports this opinion by quoting another similar *ḥadīth*: "Indeed this Qur'ān is the banquet of God on earth, so you should learn from His banquet (*ma'daba*)." Abū ʿUbayda then associates the allegory of the Qur'ān as *ma'daba* with *adab*, underlining its benefit as a proof of God's divine generosity (al-Qurṭubī 2006, 1:12–13).

The shift in the meaning of *adab* and its religious, moral and social function is further elaborated in later philological works. The association of *adab* with *duʿā'* (supplication in prayer) is a prominent example in the literature, for example in *Lisān al-ʿArab* ("The Tongue of the Arabs") by Abū al-Faḍl Jamāl al-Dīn Muḥammad Ibn Manẓūr (d. 711/1311). Furthermore, in order to emphasise the moral and religious orientation of *adab*, Ibn Manẓūr identified the *adīb* as someone who educates people, calls for praiseworthy actions and forbids blameable ones (*summiya adaban li-annahu yu'addibu al-nās ilā l-maḥāmid wa-yanhāhum ʿan al-maqābiḥ*). Ibn Manẓūr cites Abū Isḥāq al-Zajjāj (d. 310/922), who said that the best form of *adab* is that which God used to educate His Prophet (Ibn Manẓūr 1955–1956, 1:200).

Jalāl al-Dīn al-Suyūṭī (d. 911/1505), in *al-Tawshīḥ ʿalā al-Jāmiʿ al-Ṣaḥīḥ* ("The Strophic Work on the Authentic Collection") in the chapter on *adab*, explains *adab* as "the use of that which is praiseworthy in speech and deed" (*istiʿmāl mā yuḥmadu qawlan wa-fiʿlan*); he also says it means "applying one's moral character." Al-Suyūṭī adds that *adab* is derived from *ma'duba* (banquet), and that this banquet is the call for morality (al-Suyūṭī 2000, 5:37). He further cites several *ḥadīth*s concerning the ethics of action and companionship in which the Prophet states that the best deeds that lead to reward and satisfaction of

God are performing prayers on time and being kind and caring towards parents (al-Suyūṭī 2000, 5:37–38). This point illustrates how *adab* was influenced by religion as conveyed in the teachings of *ḥadīth*, echoing the Qur'ānic spirit.

Thus, the religiously informed moral dimension of *adab* as every type of praiseworthy training, which leads a person to reach one of the many virtues and excellence, and a tool for acquiring the discipline of the soul and the best of character is maintained in various Prophetic *ḥadīth*s. This underlines the educational function of this form of *adab* as imparting exemplary instruction and rules in the social domain as taught by the Prophet and the early Muslim community.

## 5 *Adab* Chapters in *Ḥadīth* Collections, Their Edifying Function and Reception

*Ḥadīth*s were initially collected as recorded, heard or remembered. However, as they began to be compiled in authoritative collections, *ḥadīth*s were classified by subject-matter and there was an awareness of their educational and moral value. Sperl explains that this specific function manifested in the development of canonical *ḥadīth* compendia in the late third/ninth century, which he compares with literary compilations of the same period, showing a common interest in chapters under the heading of *adab* (Sperl 2007, 459–486). He identifies the spread of derivatives, such as *ta'addub and ta'dīb* ("to acquire education" and "to educate" respectively), and a common interest for good conduct in these compilations. Sperl notes the brevity of a *ḥadīth* from Thābit (d. 123/741 or 127/745) on the authority of Anas (d. 93/712) that the Prophet said:

> When God created Adam in Paradise, He left him as He wished to leave him, and Satan began to walk around him to see what he was. When he realised that he was hollow he knew that he had been created unable to control himself (Muslim 1991, 4:2016: *Kitāb al-Birr wa-l-Ṣila wa-l-Ādāb* ("Book on Virtue, Maintaining the Ties of Kinship and Manners"), *Bāb Khalq al-Insān Khalqan lā Yatamālak* ("Chapter on the Creation of Humankind in a Way that He Would Not Control Himself").[9]

According to Sperl, this *ḥadīth* evokes a metanarrative underlying the phenomenon of *ḥadīth* in general, concerning the inability of the human being to control himself or herself, hence suceptible to the danger of Satan and

9 In Sperl's article it is "Thābit b. Anas," but in the *Ṣaḥīḥ* of Muslim it is "Thābit *'an* Anas."

temptation, and in need for help and divine guidance. This divine guidance is provided "by a succession of divine messengers despatched to earth as a sign of God's mercy," a message that resonates with Qur'ānic teachings (Sperl 2007, 461–462).

Thus, as explained in the above discussion about the Prophet as an ethical role-model, *ḥadīths* from Muḥammad, the last Prophet responsible for teaching and interpreting divine guidance, offer a metanarrative that surpasses other forms of human language in their emotional, spiritual and didactic impact on religiously oriented audiences. On this basis, *ḥadīth* presents authorised codes of practice and ethical conduct in order to promote a coherent community. Thus, the importance of *ḥadīth* is manifested by how many Muslims see the Prophet not only as someone who preached an alternative and continually relevant way of living, but who also implemented his religious and moral teachings in all facets of life, whether personal in relation to God, his family, or at social and political levels. Therefore, his practice "was not mere private conduct, but a detailed interpretation and application of his teachings" (Hamidullah 1992, 23). Tarif Khalidi has also showed that for centuries the Islamic community has continued to centre its attention on the Prophet Muḥammad even more than the Qur'ān itself. He showed how the persona, sayings and deeds of the Prophet Muḥammad have been conceived in various ways by Muslims in different places, to reflect their aspirations and the demands of living (Khalidi 2009).

The traditions of the Prophet proved important for *adab* (as practical ethics) and for devoted Muslims in their search for a moral agent who could influence their practices and perspective on life. *Ḥadīth* narratives offered an authoritative guide for most aspects of Muslim daily life and thus form the basis of what could be termed as "ordinary ethics," a form of ethics which has been described by Michael Lambek as intrinsic to action (Lambek 2010, 39–63). Here, this can be seen in two ways: narratives specific to acts in terms of performance (what the Prophet said or did) and narratives specific to actions in terms of passing judgements or establishing a practice (what the Prophet approved or did not approve). Hence, *adab*'s basic function in *ḥadīth,* as pointed out by Sperl, is to define the basic behavioural standards of the Muslim community and to outline the moral ground for the interpersonal relationship of different groups (Sperl 2007, 472).

The five canonical collections of *ḥadīth,* namely, those of al-Bukhārī (d. 256/870), Muslim (d. 261/875), Abū Dāwūd (d. 275/889), al-Tirmidhī (d. 279/892) and Ibn Māja (d. 273/887), all contain chapters devoted to *adab.* Each compiler maintained his own method and approach of including or excluding certain *ḥadīths*. However, the *ḥadīths* they included in these chapters share a common interest in creating a set of moral behavioural codes, an awareness of the self in relation to others and self-control. For example, in the *Ṣaḥīḥ* of Muslim in *Kitāb al-Birr wa-l-Ṣila wa-l-Ādāb* ("Book on Virtue, Maintaining the Ties of Kinship and Manners") and in the *Ṣaḥīḥ* of al-Bukhārī in *Kitāb al-Adab* ("Book of Manners"), *ḥadīth*s are arranged to provide practical advice on forms of relationships and how a person could lead a pious life. *ḥadīth*s have covered many aspects starting with one's responsibilities towards others, including care and love for parents, observing bonds of kinship and extending righteousness, mercy and forgiveness towards neighbours and fellow humans. These are followed by additional *ḥadīth*s that act as parables for how a person may gain control over his or her emotions, including anger, avoidance of conflict, commanding right and forbidding wrong, as well as *ḥadīth*s that show the importance of cultivating virtues such as honesty and telling the truth, cheerfulness and joviality, humility and compassion.

Abū Dāwūd starts his chapter on *adab* with reports on the moral qualities of the Prophet. He seems to give more importance to certain aspects, including the need for self-control (*ḥilm*), anger management, decency and detesting praising a person in their presence. There are also *ḥadīth*s relating to the rules of behaviours in specific situations.

Another example is Ibn Abī l-Dunyā (d. 281/894), an ascetic at the ʿAbbāsid court, whose main pre-occupation as an educator and tutor of several ʿAbbāsid caliphs and princes (Dietrich 1968) influence greatly his selection criteria of *ḥadīths*. Being interested in providing an authoritative basis for proper conduct and moderate morality, Ibn Abī l-Dunyā included *ḥadīth*s and *āthār* (reports generally concerning the Companions of the Prophet) that served a moral purpose, including piety, *tazkiyat al-nafs* (purification of the soul), *zuhd* (asceticism) and *adab* (moral rectitude) and self-control. For example, in his work *Makārim al-Akhlāq* ("The Noblest Moral Character") (see Ibn Abī l-Dunyā 1989). Ibn Abī l-Dunyā introduced *ḥadīth* (especially *qudsī* [divine]) that dealt with noble qualities of character and personal piety, which were addressed to religiously oriented audiences. These *ḥadīth*s are not consulted in the work of jurists, but they function as metanarratives offering overarching accounts, or interpretations of particular events, or a set of circumstances concerning the Prophet and his early companions to provide patterns for correct behaviour and a set of values and beliefs that give meaning to people's experiences.

The link between *ḥadīth* and *adab* is also clear in al-Nawawī's (d. 676/1277) *ḥadīth* collection, *Riyāḍ al-Ṣāliḥīn* ("Gardens of the Righteous"). In his authorial remarks of *Riyāḍ al-Ṣāliḥīn*, al-Nawawī stated that human beings were created to worship God and to refrain from anything that distracts from this. He added that the best way to achieve this moral rectitude and refinement of character is through the authentic reports about the Prophet (*al-taʾaddub bi-mā ṣaḥḥa ʿan Nabiyyinā*) (al-Nawawī 2001, 18). Likewise, for al-Suyūṭī (d. 911/1505) anyone who is ignorant of *ḥadīth* is deprived of great goodness, but the one who knows it obtains great goodness. Therefore, the one who has this form of knowledge should rectify his intention and purify his heart from worldly desires. Indeed, al-Suyūṭī underlines the moral value of Imām al-Nawawī's compilation. He mentions that the *ḥadīth*s which are combined and explained by Imām al-Nawawī are the link to the Prophet and provide a source for the person interested in rectifying his speech and actions (al-Suyūṭī n.d., 6). Thus, the relationship of *ḥadīth* to ethics is manifested in pre-modern collections by the sheer number of *ḥadīth*s that cover various topics on morality and by the ways in which these moral ideas are presented as intrinsically related to actions and practises in most aspects of Muslim daily life.

However, in the third/ninth and the fourth/tenth centuries, which were a period of cultural, polemical and intellectual tension, the reception and status of *ḥadīth* as a source of moral knowledge was often debated in various circles. In the field of *adab* (literary traditions) and with the introduction of elements coming from other cultures, several practitioners of *adab*, especially those driven by anti-Arab sentiment (*shuʿūbiyya*) and professional pride rejected the use of *ḥadīth* and devalued the reports about the Prophet and his Companions (Ibn Qutayba 1982, 7). Ibn Qutayba (d. 276/889) and Abū ʿUthmān ʿAmr b. Baḥr al-Jāḥiẓ (d. 255/868), however, emphasised the moral dimension of the art of writing, arguing for the unique place of the Qurʾān, Prophetic traditions and science of the Arabic language to achieve moral rectitude and a model of piety (see Ibn Qutayba 1982, 7; Van Gelder 1998, 1:361; Sperl 2007, 462; Alshaar 2017, 15; Khalidi 1996, 104–108; Montgomery 2013). Studying and memorising the Qurʾān and *ḥadīth* in learning sessions (*majālis al-taʿlīm*) continued to be part of the education and training that many *udabāʾ* received, and some engaged in the transmission and teaching of *ḥadīth*, such as Ibn Qutayba and Abū ʿAlī al-Tanūkhī (d. 384/994). Thus, acquiring knowledge of the Qurʾān and Prophetic traditions was seen as the basis for three-dimensional moral education, which focuses on inner personal development, that is, spiritual progress that comes about through the internalisation of collective Islamic values and its implementation at the social level. This use of Prophetic traditions manifests a strong connection between rhetoric and the manifestation of moral values in action and practices.

Ibn Qutayba, in his *Adab al-Kātib* ("Manners of the Scribe"), acknowledges the inherent elements in *ḥadīth* as a source for wisdom and mentions that a chancery writer, or an *adīb*, should particularly memorise *ḥadīth* that concern *fiqh* (jurisprudence) and its rulings (Ibn Qutayba 1982, 9). This point was also suggested by al-Qalqashandī (d. 821/1418), who drew attention to memorising *ḥadīth* on various subjects and added that a writer needs also to memorise more general *ḥadīth* (as *khabar*) concerning wisdom, *siyar* (biographies) or historical events, which people often cite in their speech or texts (al-Qalqashandī 1987, 202–203).

*Ḥadīth* narratives as examples of wisdom derive their legitimacy from the Prophet's statement, "I have been given the ability to combine many meanings in a few words and to arrive at new ones," (*uʿṭītu jawāmiʿ al-kalim*). Therefore, his utterances are considered above ordinary human wisdom and above other forms of Arabic style and rhetoric. For this reason, *ḥadīth* and Qurʾānic citations (*iqtibās*) are commonly accepted as authoritative (Sanni 1998). Many authors used *ḥadīth* alongside Qurʾānic citations to support their views and to advance their goals by providing a persuasive voice in the religious and political disputes of the time. Therefore, authors were advised to comprehend *al-Muwaṭṭaʾ* ("The Well-Trodden Path") of Mālik b. Anas (d. 179/796), the *Ṣaḥīḥ*s of al-Bukhārī and Muslim, the *Sunan* of al-Tirmidhī, Abū Dāwūd, al-Nasāʾī and other *ḥadīth* collections. This inclusive approach to *ḥadīth* is adopted in *al-Kāmil fī l-Lugha wa-l-Adab* ("The Comprehensive Work on Language and Manners") by al-Mubarrid (d. 286/898), whose motive to compose a work that combines forms of *adab*, or materials that provide training in virtue as well as eloquence, led him to cite many sayings of the Prophet alongside eloquent prose from the early Companions, well-composed poetry, popular proverbs, wisdom and oratory (al-Mubarrid 1937, 3–4.).

Often, *ḥadīth* was positioned after Qurʾānic verses, creating a hierarchy of knowledge that reinforces the understanding of *ḥadīth* as explanatory and subordinate to the Qurʾān. This position of *ḥadīth* is maintained by many pre-modern authors. For example, the Prophet's customs (Sunna) are second within the hierarchy of sources for Abū Ḥayyān al-Tawḥīdī (d. 414/1023), whose moral vision was influenced by his spiritual commitment to the example of the Prophet and his early Companions. In his epistle *Risāla fī l-ʿUlūm* ("Epistle on the Classification of Knowledge"), the Prophetic Sunna is subordinate to the Qurʾān and elucidates its principles and terms. He argues that part of the Prophetic Sunna gives rise to knowledge, while another part necessitates action and demands rules of behaviour, which is the highest degree of moral knowledge (al-Tawḥīdī 1968, 107; Alshaar 2015, 70). This knowledge seems the highest degree and it includes elements that qualify it as wisdom (*ḥikma*) with religious reference ascribed to the Prophet's sayings and practices. This position is similar to that of al-Shāfiʿī (d. 204/820), who also links *ḥikma* to the Sunna of the Prophet within the framework of divine revelation. The Prophet's Sunna and the divine revelation are the best sources to determine right and wrong (al-Tawḥīdī 1984, 1:515).

As subordinate and explanatory to God's Qur'ānic commands, the Prophetic Sunna provides the foundation for moral education in Islam, disseminating knowledge of what people should do (*ḥalāl*, permitted) and should not do (*ḥarām*, forbidden), and motivating them to act in accordance with the examples provided in the *ḥadīth* narratives and with God's commands. This knowledge can be divided into three main types: a) relating to *akhlāq*, moral traits concerning religious duties and responsibilities as set out by Qur'ānic commands; b) relating to people's dealings with each other and manners associated with good behaviour (*adab*) and judgments about them; c) the qualities of personal character emulating the ideal example of the Prophet.

Thus, *ḥadīth* contains elements considered worthy of preserving by the Muslim community and provides a strong basis for the interface between religion, morality and rhetoric, by delivering outstanding moral claims on the basis of being secondary to the Qur'ān. *ḥadīth* narratives provide a form of timeless morality based on timeless religious principles. Thus, Sunna became part of the law that enforces this form of religious collective morality rather than an autonomous one.

Modern scholarship has recently come to appreciate the value of *ḥadīth* as "*khabar*" or narrative that presents a situation or an understanding of a situation (Günther 1998, 433–471; El Calamawy 1983, 308–316). Sahair El Calamawy particularly addresses the narrative elements of *ḥadīth*, especially their "aspects of storytelling" due to their oral popular transmission, and how the details of certain narratives woven around the persona of the Prophet functioned to arouse emotion (El Calamawy 1983, 308–316). Daniel Beaumont also discusses the act of narrating in *ḥadīth* and argues that while the *isnād* provides a sense of needed legitimacy, the *matn* provides elements for comparison and drawing similarities (Beaumont 2010, 4:1–28), which help to form moral judgements. These elements help readers to compare their situations with knowledge about the life of the Prophet, who is seen by devoted Muslims as the exemplar of the ideal man. This aspect of storytelling in the domain of *ḥadīth* highlights the links between stories, reports and storytelling and that of ethics and morality. Thus, moral values form an integral part of *ḥadīth* reports, since the narratives deal explicitly with questions, as mentioned above, related to behaviour or action and to judgements about different situations.

## 6 Conclusion

In conclusion, the reception of *ḥadīth* narratives was closely linked to questions of *adab* and morality in Islamic culture along with their use in legal discussions. *Ḥadīth* has continued for centuries to provide models of piety and morality, based on the ideals of the Prophet and his companions, for the Muslim community seeking to define its place and identity, while interacting with Qur'ānic scripture.

Islamic scholarship in numerous fields manifested a great interest in using reports on the Prophet and his early companions as normative sources for moral knowledge. This practice not only shows the role of stories, narrative and their interpretations in shaping ethical discourses in Islamic culture, but also a conscious attempt to limit sources and thus possibilities for moral knowledge, putting forward a religio-Arab moral source of knowledge in a culture of competing ethical claims.

The fact that many contemporary Muslim communities still look to the Prophet as an ideal model emphasises the continued role of *ḥadīth* in forming ideas about morality. Religious language based on *ḥadīth* plays an important role in raising the emotions of members of the community and adding a human psychological example to their understanding of ethics and morality. Therefore, Prophetic traditions have become an integral part of Muslim social imaginary and cultural memory, in which the morality of the Prophet, through his deeds and sayings, have been received and appropriated in various contexts.

## Bibliography

### *Sources*

Abū Dāwūd. 2009. *Sunan Abī Dāwūd*, edited by Shuʿayb al-Arnāʾūṭ et al., 6 vols. Beirut: Dār al-Risāla al-ʿĀlamiyya.

al-Bukhārī. 1955. *Al-Adab al-Mufrad*, edited by Muḥammad Fūʾād ʿAbd al-Bāqī. Cairo: al-Maṭbaʿa al-Salafiyya.

al-Dārimī. 2000. *Musnad al-Dārimī*, edited by Ḥusayn Salīm Asad al-Dārānī, 4 vols. Riyad: Dār al-Mughnī.

al-Farāhīdī, al-Khalīl b. Aḥmad. 1980–1985. *Kitāb al-ʿAyn*, edited by Mahdī al-Makhzūmī and Ibrāhīm al-Sāmarrāʾī, 8 vols. Baghdad: Wizārat al-Thaqāfa wa-l-Iʿlām.

al-Ḥākim al-Naysābūrī. 1997. *Al-Mustadrak ʿalā al-Ṣaḥīḥayn*, edited by Muqbil b. Hādī l-Wādiʿī, 5 vols. Cairo: Dār al-Ḥaramayn.

al-Ḥākim al-Naysābūrī. 2003. *Maʿrifat ʿUlūm al-Ḥadīth wa-Kammiyyat Ajnāsih*, edited by Aḥmad b. Fāris al-Sallūm. Beirut: Dār Ibn Ḥazm.

Ibn al-Athīr, Majd al-Dīn. 1963–1965. *Al-Nihāya fī Gharīb al-Ḥadīth wa-l-Athar*, edited by Maḥmūd Muḥammad Ṭanāhī and al-Ṭāhir Aḥmad al-Zāwī, 5 vols. Cairo: ʿĪsā l-Bābī al-Ḥalabī.

Ibn Abī l-Dunyā, ʿAbd Allāh b. Muḥammad. 1989. *Makārim al-Akhlāq*, edited by Muḥammad ʿAbd al-Qādir ʿAṭā. Beirut: Dār al-Kutub al-ʿIlmiyya.

Ibn Abī Shayba, Abū Bakr. 1997. *Musnad Ibn Abī Shayba*, edited by ʿĀdil al-ʿIzzāwī and Aḥmad al-Mazīdī, 2 vols. Riyad: Dār al-Waṭan.

Ibn Abī Shayba, Abū Bakr. 2006. *Al-Muṣannaf*, edited by Muḥammad ʿAwwāma, 26 vols. Jedda: Dār al-Qibla and Beirut: Muʾassasat ʿUlūm al-Qurʾān.

Ibn Fāris al-Qazwīnī. 1946–1952. *Maqāyīs al-Lugha*, edited by ʿAbd al-Salām Muḥammad Hārūn, 6 vols. Cairo: ʿĪsā al-Bābī l-Ḥalabī.

Ibn Manẓūr, Muḥammad b. Mukarram. 1955–1956. *Lisān al-ʿArab*, 20 vols. Beirut: Dār Ṣādir.

Ibn Qutayba, ʿAbd Allāh b. Muslim. 1963. *ʿUyūn al-Akhbār*, edited by Aḥmad Zakī al-ʿAdawī, 4 vols. Cairo: al-Muʾassasa al-Miṣriyya al-ʿĀmma.

Ibn Qutayba, ʿAbd Allāh b. Muslim. 1982. *Adab al-Kātib*, edited by Muḥammad al-Dālī. Beirut: Muʾassasat al-Risāla.

Ibn Qutayba, ʿAbd Allāh b. Muslim. 1999. *Kitāb Taʾwīl Mukhtalif al-Ḥadīth*, edited by Muḥamad Muḥyī l-Dīn al-Aṣfar. Cairo: Dār al-Ishrāq.

Ibn al-Sikkīt, Yaʿqūb b. Isḥāq. 1998. *Kitāb al-Alfāẓ*, edited by Fakhr al-Dīn Qabāwa. Beirut: Maktabat Lubnān.

al-Jāḥiẓ, Abū ʿUthmān ʿAmr b. Baḥr. 1948–1950. *Kitāb al-Bayān wa-l-Tabyīn*, edited by ʿAbd al-Salām Muḥammad Hārūn, 4 vols. Cairo: Maṭbaʿat Lajnat al-Taʾlīf wa-l-Tarjama wa-l-Nashr.

al-Mubarrid, Abū l-ʿAbbās. 1937. *Al-Kāmil fī l-Lugha wa-l-Adab*, edited by Zakī Mubārak and Aḥmad Shākir, 3 vols. Cairo: Maṭbaʿat Muṣṭafā l-Bābī al-Ḥalabī.

Muslim b. al-Ḥajjāj. 1991. *Ṣaḥīḥ Muslim*, edited by Muḥammad Fuʾād ʿAbd al-Bāqī, 5 vols. Cairo: Dār Iḥyāʾ al-Kutub al-ʿArabiyya, ʿĪsā al-Bābī l-Ḥalabī wa-Shurakāʾuh.

al-Nawawī, Yaḥyā b. Sharaf. 2001. *Riyāḍ al-Ṣāliḥīn min Kalām Sayyid al-Mursalīn*. Cairo: Maktabat al-Muṣṭafā.

al-Qalqashandī, Aḥmad b. ʿAlī. 1987. *Ṣubḥ al-Aʿshā fī Ṣināʿat al-Inshāʾ*, edited by Muḥammad Ḥusayn Shams al-Dīn, vol. 1. Beirut: Dār al-Kutub al-ʿIlmiyya.

al-Qurṭubī, Muḥammad b. Aḥmad. 2006. *Al-Jāmiʿ li-Aḥkām al-Qurʾān wa-l-Mubayyin li-mā Taḍammanahu min al-Sunna wa-Āy al-Furqān*, edited by ʿAbd Allāh b. ʿAbd al-Muḥsin al-Turkī, 24 vols. Beirut: Muʾassasat al-Risāla.

al-Sakhāwī, ʿAbd al-Raḥmān. 1985. *Al-Maqāṣid al-Ḥasana fī Bayān Kathīr min al-Aḥādīth al-Mushtahara ʿalā al-Alsina*, edited by Muḥammad ʿUthmān al-Khusht. Beirut: Dār al-Kitāb al-ʿArabī.

al-Samʿānī, Abū Saʿd ʿAbd al-Karīm. 1981. *Adab al-Imlāʾ wa-l-Istimlāʾ*. Beirut: Dār al-Kutub al-ʿIlmiyya.

al-Ṣanʿānī, ʿAbd al-Razzāq. 1983. *Al-Muṣannaf*, edited by Ḥabīb al-Raḥmān al-Aʿẓamī, 11 vols. Beirut: al-Maktab al-Islāmī.

al-Sharīf al-Raḍī. 1937. *Al-Majāzāt al-Nabawiyya*, edited by Ṭāha Muḥammad al-Zaynī. Cairo: Mu'asasat al-Ḥalabī.

al-Suyūṭī, Jalāl al-Dīn. 2000. *Al-Tawshīḥ ʿalā al-Jāmiʿ al-Ṣaḥīḥ*, edited by ʿAlāʾ Ibrāhīm al-Azharī, 5 vols. Beirut: Dār al-Kutub al-ʿIlmiyya.

al-Suyūṭī, Jalāl al-Dīn. n.d. *Sharḥ ʿUqūd al-Jumān*, edited by Muḥammad ʿUthmān. Beirut: Dār al-Fikr.

al-Tawḥīdī, Abū Ḥayyān. 1953. *Al-Imtāʿ wa-l-Muʾānasa*, edited by Aḥmad Amīn and Aḥmad al-Zayn, 2 vols. Beirut: al-Maktaba al-ʿAṣriyya.

al-Tawḥīdī, Abū Ḥayyān. 1968. *Rasāʾil Abī Ḥayyān al-Tawḥīdī*, edited by Ibrāhīm Kīlānī. Damascus: Manshūrāt Dār Majallat al-Thaqāfa.

al-Tawḥīdī, Abū Ḥayyān. 1984. *Al-Baṣāʾir wa-l-Dhakhāʾir*, edited by Wadād al-Qāḍī, 10 vols. Beirut: Dār Ṣādir.

### *Studies*

Alshaar, Nuha. 2015. *Ethics in Islam: Friendship in the Political Thought of al-Tawḥīdī and His Contemporaries*. London: Routledge.

Alshaar, Nuha. 2017. "Introduction. The Relation of Adab to the Qurʾan: Conceptual and Historical Framework." In *The Qurʾan and Adab: The Shaping of Literary Traditions in Classical Islam*, edited by Nuha Alshaar, 1–61. Oxford: Oxford University Press in association with the Institute of Ismaili Studies.

Alshaar, Nuha. 2020. "Meal Custom, VIII, Islam." In *Encyclopaedia of the Bible and its Reception*, vol. 18, coll. 238–240. Berlin: De Gruyter.

Beaumont, Daniel. 2010. "Hard-Boiled: Narrative Discourse in Early Muslim Traditions." In *The Ḥadīth: Critical Concepts in Islamic Studies*, edited by Mustafa Shah, 1–28. London: Routledge.

Bonebakker, Seeger A. 1984. "Early Arabic Literature and the Term *Adab*." *Jerusalem Studies in Arabic and Islam* 5: 389–421.

Dietrich, A. 1968. "Ibn Abi l-Dunyā." In *Encyclopaedia of Islam, Second Edition*, vol. 3, 684. Leiden: Brill. DOI: 10.1163/1573-3912_islam_SIM_3046.

El Calamawy, Sahair. 1983. "Narrative Elements in the Ḥadīth Literature." In *Arabic Literature to the End of the Umayyad Period*, edited by A.F.L. Beeston, T.M. Johnstone, R.B. Serjeant and G.R. Smith, 308–316. Cambridge: Cambridge University Press.

Günther, Sebastian. 1998. "Fictional Narration and Imagination within an Authoritative Framework: Towards a New Understanding of Ḥadīth." In *Story-telling in the Framework of Non-fictional Arabic Literature*, edited by Stefan Leder, 433–471. Harrassowitz: Wiesbaden.

Hamidullah, Muhammad. 1992. *Introduction to Islam*. Delhi: Kitab Bhavan.

Khalidi, Tarif. 1994. *Arabic Historical Thought in the Classical Period*. Cambridge: Cambridge University Press.

Khalidi, Tarif. 2009. *Images of Muhammad: Narratives of the Prophet in Islam across the Centuries*. New York: Doubleday Religion.

Lambek, Michael. 2010. "Toward an Ethics of the Act." In *Ordinary Ethics: Anthropology, Language, and Action*, edited by Michael Lambek, 39–63. New York: Fordham University Press.

Librande, Leonarde. 2005. "Ibn Abī al-Dunyā: Certainty and Morality." *Studia Islamica* 100/101: 5–42.

Montgomery, James. 1986. "Dichotomy in Jāhilī Poetry." *Journal of Arabic Literature* 17(7): 1–20.

Montgomery, James. 2006. "Al-Jāḥiẓ's Kitāb al-Bayān wa al-Tabyīn." In *Writing and Representations in Medieval Islam: Muslim Horizons*, edited by Julia Bray, 91–153. London: Routledge.

Montgomery, James. 2013. *Al-Jāḥiẓ: In Praise of Books*. Edinburgh: Edinburgh University Press.

Neuwirth, Angelika. 2014. *Scripture, Poetry and the Making of a Community: Reading the Qur'an as a Literary Text*. Oxford: Oxford University Press in association with the Institute of Ismaili Studies.

Sanni, Amidu. 1998. *The Arabic Theory of Prosification and Versification: On Ḥall and Naẓm in Arabic Theoretical Discourse*. Stuttgart: Steiner.

Sperl, Stefan. 2007. "Man's 'Hollow Core': Ethics and Aesthetics in *Ḥadīth* Literature and Classical Arabic *Adab*." *Bulletin of the School of Oriental and African Studies* 70(3): 459–486.

Thomas, David. 2012. "Images of Muhammad: Narratives of the Prophet in Islam across the Centuries." *Islam and Christian–Muslim Relations* 23(1): 105–106.

Van Gelder, Geert Jan. 1998. "Ibn Qutayba." *Encyclopaedia of Arabic Literature*, vol. 1, 361.

Wiener, Alfred. 1913. "Die Farağ ba'd aš-Šidda-Literatur." *Der Islam* 4: 270–298.

Zubaidi, A.M. 1983. "The Impact of the Qur'ān and Ḥadīth on Medieval Arabic Literature." In *The Cambridge History of Arabic Literature: Arabic Literature to the End of the Umayyad Period*, edited by Alfred F.L. Beeston et al., 322–343. Cambridge: Cambridge University Press.

الفصل 3

# الأحاديث الكلية: من الأحكام التفصيلية إلى القواعد والمبادئ الأخلاقية

معتز الخطيب

## 1 مقدمة

يرجع تعبير «الأحاديث الكلية» إلى الإمام أبي عمرو بن الصلاح (ت. 1245/643) الذي كان أول من أملى - في مجلسٍ حديثي - مجموعة من الأحاديث سماها «الأحاديث الكلية»، وقد شكلت أحاديثه فاتحةً للاشتغال بنوعٍ يجمع أحاديث مخصوصة شرطُها أن تؤسس لقاعدة من قواعد الدين أو مبدأ من مبادئه. لم يُعن ابن الصلاح بالرقم أربعين، وكان قد بنى عمله على أقوال سابقة لعدد من المحدثين المتقدمين ممن عُنوا ببيان «أصول الأحاديث» التي يمكن ردّ مجموع الحديث إليها على وجه كلّي. ولكن الإمام محيي الدين النووي (ت. 1277/676) الذي عُني بالأحاديث الكلية، أدخلها في نوع الأربعينات فجمع في أحاديثه بين خصيصتي الكلّي والأربعين متجاوزًا لتقليد سابق كان يجمع أربعين حديثًا في باب أو معنى جزئي.

وقد اعتنى المحدثون بطرائق التصنيف في الحديث ونوّعوها، واعتنوا ببيان أهمية التمييز بين بعضها وبعض بحسب الموضوع؛ حتى قال علي بن المديني (ت. 849/234) مثلًا: "إذا رأيت الحَدَث أول ما يكتب الحديث يجمع حديث الغُسل وحديث من كذب فاكتب على قفاه: لا يُفلح" (الخطيب 1983، 301/2)، كما أن حديث النية - وهو من الأحاديث الكلية - حظي باهتمام بالغ؛ حتى إن أئمة الحديث كعبد الرحمن بن مهدي (ت. 814/198) ومحمد بن إسماعيل البخاري (ت. 870/256) قالوا: إنه يجب أن يُبدأ به، وأن يكون فاتحة كل تصنيف أو رأس كل باب من أبواب العلم (الخطيب 1983، 300/2). وقد استقر أن ثمة طريقتين يُصنَّف الحديثُ عليهما ويمكن ردّ عموم مدوناته إليهما، وهما: التصنيف على الأبواب أو الموضوعات، والتصنيف على المسند بضمّ أحاديث كل صحابي بعضها إلى بعض (الحاكم 2001، 43؛ الخطيب 1983، 284/2؛ ابن الصلاح 1986، 253؛ ابن حجر العسقلاني 2000، 147)، وقد قابل يحيى بن سعيد القطان (ت. 813/198) بين الطريقتين؛ حين قال: "كان شعبة [بن الحجاج (ت. 777/160)]

© معتز الخطيب, 2023 | DOI:10.1163/9789004525931_005

أعلمَ بالرجال: فلان عن فلان كذا وكذا، وكان سفيان [الثوري (ت. 778/161)] صاحب أبواب" (الخطيب 1983، 286/2)؛ رغم أن من المحدثين من جمع بين الطريقتين.

ولكن أين تقع الأحاديث الكلية من هاتين الطريقتين؟ تنوعت المصنفات على الأبواب؛ فبعضها اقتصر على باب واحد أفرده عن الكتب الطوال، وبعضها جمع أبوابًا مختلفة سُميت جوامع وسننًا وغير ذلك، وقد انشغل كثيرون بتصنيف السنن وتخريجها على الأحكام وطريقة الفقه، وكان الخطيب البغدادي (ت. 1071/363) قد أفرد بابًا بعنوان: "الأحاديث التي تدور أبواب الفقه عليها،" ساق فيه روايتين عن أبي داود (ت. 888/275) في أن "الفقه يدور على أربعة أحاديث" أو "على خمسة أحاديث" وهي من الأحاديث الكلية التي ستأتي لاحقًا، وخصص أيضًا بابًا آخر لـ"معرفة الشيوخ الذين تُروى عنهم الأحاديث الحُكْمية والمسائل الفقهية" (الخطيب 1983، 288/2–290)، وقد آل تصنيف السنن على الأحكام - لدى المتأخرين - إلى ما سمي «أحاديث الأحكام» التي يَجمع فيها كل مصنِّف أدلة الفقه على مذهب معين محذوفةَ الأسانيد، وهي نظير آيات الأحكام.

ولكن الفقه - وإن غلبَ - لم يستوعب طريقةَ التصنيف على الأبواب؛ التي شملت أيضًا أبوابًا أخرى غير الفقه، كالزهد والرِّقاق (أو الرقائق) والأخلاق والآداب وشعب الإيمان وجوامع الكلم والحكم والمواعظ والترغيب والترهيب والفضائل وغيرها.

فالأحاديث الكلية تبدو خارج طريقتي التصنيف السابقتين ومتجاوزة لفكرة الأبواب؛ في انتقال من الجزئي إلى الكلي، ومن الفروع إلى الأصول، ومع ذلك يمكن أن تُدرج الأحاديث الكلية ضمن الأخلاق الحديثية أو المصنفات الحديثية المتصلة بحقل الأخلاق؛ من جهة مضامينها -كما سيتضح لاحقًا - ومن جهة كونها تعبر عن قواعد ومبادئ كلية متجاوزة للنزعة التفصيلية لأحاديث الأحكام التي تجمع بين الجوانب الأخلاقية والقانونية والتعبدية. وإذا كان بعض متقدمي المحدثين قد اعتبر التصنيف على الأبواب يدخل في طلب الآخرة (الخطيب 1983، 285/2)؛ فإن الانشغال بالأحاديث الكلية يدخل في أمرين: الأول: طلب طريق الآخرة؛ فقد قال النووي في مقدمة أربعينه: "وينبغي لكل راغب في الآخرة أن يعرف هذه الأحاديث؛ لما اشتملت عليه من المهمات، واحتوت عليه من التنبيه على جميع الطاعات" (النووي 2009، 45)، والثاني: تحصيل الأخلاق؛ لما اشتملت عليه هذه الأحاديث من المبادئ والمفاهيم الكلية الناظمة لسلوك الفرد في علاقته بنفسه وبالله تعالى وبالآخرين.

يناقش هذا الفصل الأحاديث الكلية من خلال ثلاثة محاور بالإضافة إلى مقدمة وخاتمة. في المحور الأول يحرر مفهوم الأحاديث الكلية وعلاقته بمفهوم جوامع الكلم، وفي المحور الثاني يؤرخ لفكرة الأحاديث الكلية وتطوراتها، وفي المحور الثالث يحلل المضامين الأخلاقية للأحاديث الكلية.

## 2 مفهوم الأحاديث الكلية وصلتها بجوامع الكلم

اختلفت عبارات علماء الحديث وشراحه في وصف الأحاديث المجموعة في هذا الباب، ولكن ثمة تعبيرات مفتاحية وهي: جوامع الكلم، والأحاديث التي عليها مدار الإسلام، وقواعد الدين أو أصول الإسلام، والأحاديث الكلية. ولم أجد للعلماء كلامًا صريحًا حول ما إذا كانت هذه التعبيرات مترادفة أم متباينة المدلول، ولذلك سأتناول استعمالات العلماء لهذه التعبيرات أولًا، ثم أحرر القول في مفهوم «جوامع الكلم» ثانيًا؛ لأن ذلك سيعين على تحرير المفاهيم ومن ثم تنزيل عبارات العلماء عليها.

### 2.1 جوامع الكلم والأحاديث الكلية في نصوص العلماء

تجنب ابن الصلاح ومحيي الدين النووي تعبير «جوامع الكلم» في وصفهما للأحاديث التي جمعاها؛ ما يشير إلى أنهما ربما يميزان بين المفهومين. فقد استعمل ابن الصلاح تعبير «الأحاديث الكلية»، في حين اقتصر النووي – في مقدمته للأربعين – على وصف النبي صلى الله عليه وسلم بأنه "المخصوص بجوامع الكلم،" ولكن حين وصف الأحاديث التي جمعها لم يستعمل تعبير «جوامع الكلم»، واكتفى بإيضاح شرطه فيها فقال: "من العلماء من جمع الأربعين في أصول الدين، وبعضهم في الفروع، وبعضهم في الجهاد، وبعضهم في الزهد، وبعضهم في الآداب، وبعضهم في الخطب، وكلها مقاصد صالحة رضي الله تعالى عن قاصديها. وقد رأيت جمع أربعين أهم من هذا كله، وهي أربعون حديثًا مشتملة على جميع ذلك. وكل حديث منها قاعدة عظيمة من قواعد الدين، قد وصفه العلماء بأن مدار الإسلام عليه، أو هو نصف الإسلام أو ثلثه أو نحو ذلك ..." (النووي 2009، 43–44)، ثم قال في خاتمة الأربعين: "هذا آخر ما قصدته من بيان الأحاديث التي جمعت قواعد الإسلام، وتضمنت ما لا يُحصى من أنواع العلوم في الأصول والفروع والآداب وسائر وجوه الأحكام" (النووي 2009، 116).

ويظهر مِن تتبع كلام النووي في أعماله المختلفة أنه تجنب – عمدًا – استخدام تعبير "جوامع الكلم" في هذا السياق؛ ففي خاتمة كتاب الأذكار قال: "وقد رأيتُ أن أضمَّ إليه أحاديث تتمُّ محاسن الكتاب بها إن شاء الله تعالى، وهي الأحاديث التي عليها مدارُ الإسلام، وقد اختلفَ العلماءُ فيها اختلافًا منتشرًا، وقد اجتمع مِن تداخل أقوالهم – مع ما ضممتُه إليها – ثلاثون حديثًا" (النووي 1994، 405)، وفي شرحه على صحيح مسلم قال في حديث «إن الله طيب لا يقبل إلا طيبًا»:[1]

---

1 سأتجنب – في هذا الفصل – تخريج الأحاديث الواردة في الأربعين النووية لعدة أسباب: أولها: أن النووي اشترط فيها الصحة وفق حكمه على الأحاديث، فقال: "ألتزم في هذه الأربعين أن تكون صحيحة، ومعظمها في صحيحي البخاري ومسلم" (النووي 2009، 44)، وثانيها: أنها طُبعت بتحقيقات

"وهذا الحديث أحد الأحاديث التي هي قواعد الإسلام ومباني الأحكام، وقد جمعت منها أربعين حديثًا في جزء" (النووي 1929، 7/100)، ومن ثم جعل عنوان أربعينه هكذا: «**الأربعين (أو الأربعون) في مباني الإسلام وقواعد الأحكام**»،[2] أي أنه تجنب - أيضًا - استخدام «جوامع الكلم» في العنوان على خلاف ابن رجب الحنبلي (ت. 795/1393)، وملا علي القاري (ت. 1014/1606) مثلًا. وفي كتابه «**بستان العارفين**» قال: "ومما ينبغي الاعتناء به بيان الأحاديث التي قيل: إنها أصول الإسلام، وأصول الدين، أو عليها مدار الإسلام، أو مدار الفقه والعلم، ... ولأنها مهمة فينبغي أن تُقَدَّم. وقد اختلف العلماء في عددها اختلافا كثيرا، وقد اجتهد في جمعها وتبيينها الشيخ الإمام الحافظ أبو عمرو عثمان بن عبد الرحمن المعروف بابن الصلاح - رحمه الله تعالى - ولا مزيد على تحقيقه وإتقانه، فأنا أنقل ما ذكره - رحمه الله - مختصرًا، وأضم إليه ما تيسر مما لم يذكره" (النووي 2006، 47)، وفي «**تهذيب الأسماء واللغات**» قال: "قد قيل: مدار الإسلام على حديث: الدين النصيحة، وقيل: غير ذلك، وقد جمعت كل ذلك فى كتاب الأربعين" (النووي د.ت.(أ)، 2/226).

ويؤكد فكرة التمييز بين جوامع الكلم والأحاديث الكلية، ما ذهب إليه نجم الدين الطوفي (ت. 716/1316) في مقدمة شرحه على الأربعين النووية؛ إذ قال: "ثم أضاف النَّاس إلى هذه الأحاديث ما هو من جنسها من الأحاديث الكلية ممَّا ذكر المصنف. وسنبين وجه كون كل حديث منها قاعدةً كليةً من قواعد الإسلام إن شاء الله تعالى،" ثم قال: "وخاصية هذه الأحاديث كونها مشتملة على قواعد الدين وكلياته" (الطوفي 1998، 23). ولكن قد يُشكل على فكرة التمييز بين جوامع الكلم والأحاديث الكلية (أو مدار الإسلام أو قواعد الدين) أمور ثلاثة اتضحت لي بالتتبع والمقارنة، وهي:

الأمر الأول: أن ثمة أحاديث وصفها شراح الحديث بأنها من جوامع الكلم، وهي في الأربعين التي بناها النووي على «الأحاديث الكلية» لابن الصلاح. من ذلك أن النووي نفسه حين جاء إلى

---

عدة مع العناية بتخريجها، كما أنه طُبعت شروح عديدة لها، من أشهرها شرح ابن رجب الحنبلي الذي اعتنى بتخريج هذه الأحاديث، وثالثها: تحاشياً للتطويل في هذا الفصل من دون داعٍ؛ فمن السهل العودة إلى الأربعين النووية نفسها لمعرفة تخريج حديث منها.

2 كما ثبت في عدد من النسخ الخطية وفي عدد من النسخ المطبوعة. انظر مثلًا طبعة نظام اليعقوبي (المغرب: دار الحديث الكتّانية، 2012)، ومحمد بن يوسف الحوراني (عمان: دار الذخائر، 2019)، ورياض حسين الطائي (الكويت: ركائز للنشر 2022)، وأحمد حاج محمد عثمان (الرياض: دار الفردوس للبحث والنشر ودار الصميعي، 2015)، وقاسم بن محمد ضاهر البقاعي (بيروت: دار اللؤلؤة، 2022).

حديث جبريل عن الإسلام والإيمان والإحسان (النووي 1929، 157/1)، وحديث «إذا أمرتكم بشيء فأتوا منه ما استطعتم» (النووي 1929، 102/9) قال: إن كل واحد منهما من جوامع الكلم، وكذلك فعل ابن دقيق العيد (ت. 1302/702) في حديث «قل آمنت بالله ثم استقم» وغيره (ابن دقيق 2003، 80). بل نُقل عن أبي الزناد: عبد الله بن ذكوان (ت. 748/130) في حديث "لا يؤمن أحدكم حتى أكون أحب إليه من والده وولده والناس أجمعين" قوله: "هذا من جوامع الكلم، لأنه قد جمعت هذه الألفاظ اليسيرة معانيَ كثيرة" (ابن دقيق 2003، 136)، وقال بدر الدين العيني (ت. 1451/855) في حديث «فإن لم تكن تراه، فإنه يراك»: هذا من جوامع الكلم (العيني د.ت.، 289/1)، ومثل هذه الأقوال قد يُفيد الترادف أو التداخل.

الأمر الثاني: أن تعبيري جوامع الكلم وقواعد الدين قد يجتمعان في عبارة واحدة لوصف أحاديث في الأربعين النووية، مما قد يوحي بالترادف أيضًا، كقول النووي نفسه في حديث «فإذا أمرتكم بشيء فأتوا منه ما استطعتم»: "هذا من قواعد الإسلام المهمة، ومن جوامع الكلم" (النووي 1929، 102/9)، وكقول ابن دقيق العيد في حديث «من أحدث في أمرنا هذا ما ليس منه فهو ردٌّ»: "هذا الحديث قاعدة عظيمة من قواعد الدين، وهو من جوامع الكلم" (ابن دقيق 2003، 41، وانظر 57)، وكقول ابن رجب الحنبلي في حديث « كل بدعة ضلالة»: "من جوامع الكلم لا يخرج عنه شيء، وهو أصل عظيم من أصول الدين" (ابن رجب 2001، 128/2)، وقول ابن حجر العسقلاني (ت. 1449/852) في حديث «من كان يؤمن بالله واليوم الآخر فليقل خيراً أو ليصمت»: "هذا من جوامع الكلم، لأن القول كله إما خير وإما شر، وإما آيل إلى أحدهما" (ابن حجر العسقلاني د.ت.، 446/10)، وقول بدر الديني العيني في حديث «من كان يؤمن بالله واليوم الآخر فلا يؤْذ جاره، ومن كان يؤمن بالله واليوم الآخر فَلْيُكْرِمْ ضيفه، ومن كان يؤمن بالله واليوم الآخر فَلْيَقُلْ خيرًا أو ليصمت»: "هذا الكلام من جوامع الكلم، لأنها هي الأصول، إذ الثالث منها إشارة إلى القولية، والأولان إلى الفعلية ..." (العيني د.ت.، 110/22–111). بل إن ابن رجب رأى أن "الأحاديث الكلية" التي جمعها ابن الصلاح "جمع فيها الأحاديث الجوامع التي يقال: إن مدار الدين عليها، وما كان في معناها من الكلمات الجامعة الوجيزة"، ثم سمى ابن رجب كتابه هكذا: "جامع العلوم والحكم في شرح خمسين حديثًا من جوامع الكلم" (ابن رجب 2001، 56/1)، ورأى في مقدمته أن يَضم إلى أحاديث النووي "أحاديث أخر من جوامع الكلم الجامعة لأنواع العلوم والحكم" (ابن رجب 2001، 128/2). فهذه قرائنُ قد تدل على الترادف بين الأحاديث الكلية وجوامع الكلم.

الأمر الثالث: أن ثمة أحاديث وُصفت بأنها من جوامع الكلم ولم تُدرج ضمن الأحاديث الكلية أو التي عليها مدار الإسلام. من ذلك الأمثلة التي ضربها أبو سليمان الخطابي (ت. 998/388)

لجوامع الكلم وجعلها دالة على ما وراءها من نظائرها وأخواتها، وهي: حديث «المؤمنون تكافأُ دماؤهم ويسعى بذمتهم أدناهم، وهم يدٌ على مَن سواهم»،[3] وحديث «المِنْحة مردودة، والعاريّة مؤداة، والدَّين مَقضي، والزعيم غارم»،[4] وحديث «سلوا الله اليقين والعافية»[5] (الخطابي 1982، 64/1–65)، وكذلك بعض الأمثلة التي ساقها ابن حجر العسقلاني لجوامع الكلم مما هو خارج الأربعين، بل ليس في زيادات ابن رجب أيضًا، كحديثي: «كل شرط ليس في كتاب الله فهو باطل»،[6] و«ما ملأ ابن آدم وعاء شرًّا من بطنه»،[7] ثم قال ابن حجر: "إلى غير ذلك مما يكثر بالتتبع" (ابن حجر العسقلاني د.ت.، 250/13)، ومن ذلك أيضًا قول أبي بكر بن العربي (ت. 543/1148) في حديث «لا تَسأل المرأة طلاق أختها لتستفرغ صَحْفَتَها ولتنكح، فإنما لها ما قُدِّر لها»:[8] "هذا الحديث من أصول الدين في السلوك على مجاري القدر" (العراقي د.ت.، 39/7)، ووصف بدر الدين العيني حديث «يَسِّروا ولا تُعسِّروا وبَشِّروا ولا تُنفِّروا»[9] بأنه "من جوامع

---

3 رواه أبو داود (2009، 587/6)، كتاب الديات، باب: أيُقاد المسلم بالكافر؟، وأحمد (2001، 268/2)، وغيرهما.

4 رواه أبو داود (2009، 417/5)، أول كتاب البيوع، باب: في تضمين العارية، والترمذي (1996، 556/2)، كتاب أبواب البيوع، باب: ما جاء في أن العارية مؤداة، وابن ماجه (2009، 477/3)، أبواب الصدقات، باب: العارية.

5 رواه ابن المبارك (د.ت.، 196)، باب: التوكل والتواضع، وابن أبي شيبة (2006، 96/15)، كتاب الدعاء، باب الدعاء بالعافية، والبزار (1988، 90/1)، وأبو يعلى (1984، 123/1).

6 رواه ابن ماجه (2009، 563/3)، كتاب أبواب العتق، باب: المُكاتَب، وأحمد (2001، 42، 321، 516)، والبزار (1988، 30/11).

7 رواه الترمذي (1996، 168/4)، أبواب الزهد، باب: ما جاء في كراهية كثرة الأكل، وابن ماجه (2009، 448/4)، أبواب الأطعمة، باب: الاقتصاد في الأكل وكراهية الشبع، وأحمد (2001، 422/28)، وغيرهم.

8 رواه البخاري (1312 [1894]، 69/3، 191، 21/7، 123/8)، كتاب البيوع، باب: لا يبيع على بيع أخيه، ولا يسوم على سَوم أخيه، حتى يأذن له أو يترك، وكتاب الشروط، باب: ما لا يجوز من الشروط في النكاح، وباب: الشروط في الطلاق، وكتاب النكاح، باب: لا تُنكح المرأة على عمتها، وكتاب القدر، باب: ﴿وَكَانَ أَمْرُ اللَّهِ قَدَرًا مَقْدُورًا﴾ [الأحزاب: 38]، ومسلم (1991، 1029/2)، كتاب النكاح، باب: تحريم الجمع بين المرأة وعمتها أو خالتها في النكاح.

9 رواه البخاري (1312 [1894]، 25/1)، كتاب العلم، باب: ما كان النبي صلى الله عليه وسلم يتخولهم بالموعظة والعلم كي لا ينفروا، وكتاب الأدب، باب: قول النبي صلى الله عليه وسلم: "يسروا ولا تعسروا"، ومسلم (1991، 1359/3)، كتاب الجهاد والسير، باب: في الأمر بالتيسير وترك التنفير.

الكلم، لاشتماله على خيري الدنيا والآخرة" (العيني د.ت.، 47/2)، وقال كذلك في حديث «فمن وُلِيَ شيئًا من أمة محمد صلى الله عليه وسلم فاستطاع أن يُضِرَّ فيه أحدا أو يَنْفَعَ فيه أحدا فلْيَقبلْ من محْسِنِهِم ويتَجاوَزْ عن مسيئهم»:[10] "من جوامع الكلم، لأن الحال منحصر في الضَر أو النَّفع، والشخص في المحسن والمسيء" (العيني د.ت.، 228/6)، ووصف غيرُ واحد حديث «كل شراب أسكر فهو حرام»[11] بأنه من جوامع الكلم (العيني د.ت.، 171/21؛ البِرماوي 2012، 352/2، 186/14؛ العلوي الهرَري 2009، 83/21)؛ فهذه قرائن دالة على التمييز بين جوامع الكلم والأحاديث الكلية، وإن وقع التداخل بينهما في الجملة.

## 2.2 مفهوم «جوامع الكلم»

ولتحرير القول في ما سبق، لا بد أن نناقش مفهوم «جوامع الكلم» نفسه، لأنه سيساعد على تحديد مفهوم الأحاديث الكلية وصلته بها من جهة، وعلى فهم عبارات العلماء السابقين من جهة أخرى.

جاء في الأحاديث النبوية أن النبي صلى الله عليه وسلم بُعث بجوامع الكلم (أو أُعطي جوامع الكلم) كما في الصحيحين وغيرهما،[12] وفي رواية "أوتيت فواتح الكلم وخواتمه وجوامعه،" وفي أخرى "أوتيت جوامع الكلم وخواتمه، واختُصر لي الحديث اختصارًا،" وفي رواية "أعطيت فواتح الكلم وخواتمه وجوامعه،" والألفاظ متقاربة في المعنى.[13] ولعل أقدم تفسير لجوامع الكلم هو قول محمد بن شهاب الزهري (ت. 742/125): "بلغني أن جوامع الكلم أن الله عز وجل يجمع له الأمور الكثيرة التي كانت تُكتب في الكتب قبله في الأمر الواحد والأمرين، أو نحو ذلك" (أبو نعيم الحداد 2010، 42/4؛ ابن الملقن 2008، 107/18؛ ابن رجب 2001، 53/1؛ ابن الأثير 1969، 530/8). وقد جرى كثير من العلماء على هذا المعنى في تحديد جوامع الكلم، وهو أنها جَمع المعاني

10 رواه البخاري (1312 [1894]، 11/2، 204/4، 35/5)، كتاب الجمعة، باب: من قال في الخطبة بعد الثناء: أما بعد، وكتاب المناقب، باب: علامات النبوة في الإسلام، وباب قول النبي صلى الله عليه وسلم: "اقبلوا من محسنهم وتجاوزوا عن مسيئهم".

11 رواه البخاري (1312، 58/1، 105/7)، كتاب الوضوء، باب: لا يجوز الوضوء بالنبيذ، ولا المسكر، وكتاب الأشربة، باب: الخمر من العسل وهو البِتْع، ومسلم (1991، 1585/3)، كتاب الأشربة، باب: بيان أن كل مسكر خمر وأن كل خمر حرام.

12 رواه البخاري (1312 [1894]، 36/9)، كتاب التعبير، باب: المفاتيح في اليد، وكتاب الاعتصام بالكتاب والسنة، باب: الاقتداء بسنن رسول الله صلى الله عليه وسلم؛ مسلم (1991، 371/1)، كتاب المساجد ومواضع الصلاة، باب: جُعلت لي الأرض مسجدا وطهورا.

13 استقصى ابن رجب الحنبلي الروايات في هذا (ابن رجب 2001، 53–54).

الكثيرة في الألفاظ اليسيرة (النووي 1929، 170/13؛ ابن الأثير د.ت.، 80/1؛ ابن الملقن 2012، 195؛ العيني د.ت.، 235/14)، وقد جعل الجاحظ (ت. 868/255) «جوامع الكلم» أحد فنون كلام النبي – صلّى الله عليه وسلّم – "وهو الكلام الذي قلّ عدد حروفه وكثر عدد معانيه، وجلّ عن الصنعة، ونَزِه عن التكلف" (الجاحظ 1988، 17/2)، ثم جاء أبو سليمان الخطابي فعرّفها بأنها "إيجاز الكلام في إشباعٍ للمعاني؛ يقول الكلمة القليلة الحروف فتنتظم الكثير من المعنى، وتتضمن أنواعًا من الأحكام" (الخطابي 1988، 1422/2). وتتفق هذه التحديدات على معنى عامّ هو صفة للكلام، وشكل من أساليب البيان.

ولكن هذا المفهوم العام لجوامع الكلم يشمل القرآن أيضًا، ولاسيما أنه قد خُصّ به النبي صلى الله عليه وسلم، بل ربما كان هو الأقرب إلى الفهم، ولهذا فسّر أبو عبيد الهروي (ت. 1011/401) جوامع الكلم بأنها القرآن، قال: "جمع الله – بلطفه – في الألفاظ اليسيرة منه معاني كثيرة" (الهروي 1999، 365/1)، وهو ما مال إليه – فيما يبدو – الحافظ أبو عبد الله الحميدي (ت. 1095/488)، وتبعه ابن الأثير الجزري (ت. 1233/630) (الحميدي 1995، 285؛ ابن الأثير 1979، 295/1). ولكن جرى القول بعد ذلك على أن جوامع الكلم صفة لكلام النبي صلى الله عليه وسلم، ثم صار العلماء إلى حكاية هذا الاختلاف في مدلول جوامع الكلم: إما القرآن وإما حديث النبي (العراقي د.ت.، 111/2)، إلى أن جمع ابن التين (ت. 1214/611) وابن رجب وغيرهما بين القولين فجعلوا جوامع الكلم على نوعين: الأول ما هو في القرآن كقوله عز وجل: ﴿إِنَّ ٱللَّهَ يَأْمُرُ بِٱلْعَدْلِ وَٱلْإِحْسَـٰنِ وَإِيتَآئِ ذِى ٱلْقُرْبَىٰ وَيَنْهَىٰ عَنِ ٱلْفَحْشَآءِ وَٱلْمُنكَرِ وَٱلْبَغْيِ﴾ [النحل: 90]، والثاني ما هو في كلامه صلى الله عليه وسلم، "وهو منتشر موجود في السنن المأثورة عنه" (ابن رجب 2001، 55/1–56؛ العيني د.ت.، 235/14). بل إن النووي بعد أن ذكر كلام الهروي أضاف: "وكلامه – صلى الله عليه وسلم – كان بالجوامع؛ قليل اللفظ كثير المعاني" (النووي 1929، 5/5)، ما يدل على أنه جمع بين المعنيين (القرآن والحديث)؛ جريًا على المدلول العام لجوامع الكلم، ولهذا حين جاء إلى حديث «أُعطي جوامع الكلم بخواتمه»[14] قال: "قوله: «بخواتمه» أي كأنه يختم على المعاني الكثيرة التي تضمنها اللفظ اليسير؛ فلا يخرج منها شيء عن طالبه ومستنبطه؛ لعذوبة لفظه وجزالته" (النووي 1929، 170/13). ثم نقل في كتاب آخر عن العلماء أن الاستقامة – وهي لزوم طاعة الله تعالى – "من جوامع الكلم" (النووي 1998، 62).

ولكن هل كل كلامه صلى الله عليه وسلم جوامع أم بعضه فقط؟ وكيف نحدده أو نتتبعه؟

ظاهر عبارة النووي "وكلامه – صلى الله عليه وسلم – كان بالجوامع" أن عامة كلامه كذلك، وقرر ضياء الدين بن الأثير (ت. 1239/637) أن "جُلّ كلام النبي – صلى الله عليه وسلم – جارٍ

14 رواه مسلم (1991، 1586/3)، كتاب الأشربة، باب: بيان أن كل مسكر خمر وأن كل خمر حرام.

هذا المجرى،" أي في إيجاز اللفظ وسعة المعنى (ابن الأثير د.ت.، 80/1)، وقال ابن حجر: إن جوامع الكلم في كلامه – صلى الله عليه وسلم – "مما يكثر بالتتبع" (ابن حجر العسقلاني د.ت، 250/13). وهذا لأن خَصيصة الإيجاز في اللفظ مع سعة المعنى سمةٌ غالبة على الحديث النبوي؛ بالرغم من وجود بعض المطولات في كلامه، ولكنها تبقى استثناءً لأغراض تختص بها، ولهذا فلا حاجة إلى تكلف التمييز بين قولين هنا: قول يرى أن كل كلام النبي جوامع، وقول آخر يرى أن بعض كلامه فقط جوامع، كما فعل بعض المعاصرين (اللوغاني 2018، 10–12)؛ لأن مدونة الحديث تنطوي على أحاديث طويلة، وأحاديث تفصيلية تتناول مسائل ووقائع جزئية أو خاصة، ولكن الجوامع صفة لأسلوب البيان، وهو الإيجاز والإقلال من الكلام، وقد كان هذا السمةَ العامة للحديث النبوي، وهي أيضًا سمة فصاحة، ومن ثم جعل الخطابي جوامع الكلم "من ألوان فصاحة النبي وحسن بيانه" التي تعددت أشكالها، كتكَلُّمه بألفاظ اقتضبها لم تُسمع من العرب قبله (الخطابي 1982، 64/1–67)، وقد أدرج ملا علي القاري هذه الألفاظَ المقتضبة تحت جوامع الكلم (القاري 2013). وقد مثَّل الخطابي لنوعين من جوامع الكلم هما: القضايا والأحكام، والوصايا (الخطابي 1982، 64/1–65)، ويمكن أن نضيف إليهما أيضًا الأمثال والحكم والأدعية النبوية وغيرها.

فجوامع الكلم – إذن – أوسع من الأحاديث الكلية؛ فكل حديث كلي هو من جوامع الكلم من دون عكس، وقد تَنبه إلى هذا الفرق – فيما أفهم – بعضُ العلماء، فعبد الله النبراوي (ت. 1275/1859) – مثلًا – وصف **«الأربعين النووية»** بأنها "من جوامع كلمه – صلى الله عليه وسلم – مشتملةً على أبلغ المعاني وأحكم المباني" (النبراوي د.ت.، 2)، وأدرج نور الدين عتر (ت. 2020) تحت ألوان جوامع الكلم: "الأحاديث التي قيل: إنها تجمع أمور الإسلام، وعليها قام أساس الجمع للأربعين حديثا التي استتمها الإمام النووي" (عتر 2013، 389–394)، وجمع صالح الشامي الأحاديث التي عليها مدار الدين أو أصول الإسلام أو الأحكام فبلغت – عنده – عشرة أحاديث، ثم قال: "وهذه الأحاديث هي من جوامع الكلم التي خُص بها النبي صلى الله عليه وسلم" (الشامي 2014، 7)، ونوّع عبد الرحمن بن ناصر السعدي (ت. 1376/1957) الجوامع إلى "جوامع في جنس أو نوع أو باب من أبواب العلم" (السعدي 2011، 7). فالجوامع – في رأيي – معنى عامٌّ لسمتي الإيجاز في اللفظ والسعة في المعنى، وهذا سمة عامة في كلامه صلى الله عليه وسلم، ويشمل أقسامًا؛ ما يعني أن المطول من حديثه يختل فيه شرط الإيجاز في اللفظ، والخاص من حديثه يختل فيه شرط سعة المعاني، وفي حديثه الرواية بالمعنى أيضًا فيختل شرط اللفظ النبوي، ولهذا قال ابن حجر: "وانما يَسلم ذلك فيما لم تتصرف الرواة في ألفاظه. والطريق إلى معرفة ذلك أن تَقِل مخارج الحديث، وتتفق ألفاظه، وإلا فإن مخارج الحديث إذا كثرت قلّ

أن تتفق ألفاظه، لتوارد أكثر الرواة على الاقتصار على الرواية بالمعنى بحسب ما يظهر لأحدهم أنه واف به" (ابن حجر العسقلاني د.ت.، 250/13).

### 2.3 مفهوم «الأحاديث الكلية»

فالأحاديث الكليّة من جوامع الكلم وليست هي جوامع الكلم، وهو المعنى الذي قصده ابن الصلاح ثم توسع فيه النووي، إذ شرط الكليّ أنه يتناول قاعدة من قواعد الإسلام ومباني الأحكام أو عليه مدار الإسلام، وهو ما عبر عنه النووي حين قال في مقدمة أربعينه: "وكل حديث منها قاعدة عظيمة من قواعد الدين، قد وصفه العلماء بأن مدار الإسلام عليه، أو هو نصف الإسلام أو ثلثه أو نحو ذلك" (النووي 2009، 44)، واعتبره الطوفي "خاصية هذه الأحاديث" (الطوفي 1998، 23). وقد تنوعت أوصاف العلماء المتقدمين لـ«الأحاديث الكلية»، ومنها وصفهم للحديث بأنه ثلث العلم أو ربعه، ووصفهم للأحاديث بأن عليها مدار الدين، وأنها «أصول الإسلام» أو «أصول الأحاديث» (وهو يختلف عن «الأحاديث الأصول»)، و«أصول السنن». وقد استخدم شراح الحديث تعبير قواعد الإسلام، وأصول الشريعة، واستخدم ابن الصلاح تعبير «مِلاك أمر الدين والدنيا». ووجود الكلي في الحديث مهم لجهة وفاء نصوص الشريعة بالوقائع المستمرة، ولهذا قال ابن تيمية (ت. 1328/728) في الجواب على من قال: إن النصوص لا تفي بعُشر معشار الشريعة: "إن الله بعث محمدًا – صلى الله عليه وسلم – بجوامع الكلم فيتكلم بالكلمة الجامعة العامة التي هي قضية كلية وقاعدة عامة تتناول أنواعا كثيرة، وتلك الأنواع تتناول أعيانا لا تُحصى، فبهذا الوجه تكون النصوص محيطة بأحكام أفعال العباد" (ابن تيمية 2004، 280/19).

وبناء على هذا التحديد المفهومي للكلي، يمكن لنا أن نقوّم الزيادات على «**الأربعين النووية**»، كزيادات ابن رجب التي منها: «ألحقوا الفرائض بأهلها»،[15] و«يَحْرُم من الرضاع ما يحرم من

15 رواه البخاري (1312 [1894]، 8/150–153)، كتاب الفرائض، باب: ميراث الولد من أبيه وأمه، وباب: ميراث ابن الابن إذا لم يكن ابن، وباب: ميراث الجد مع الأب والإخوة، وباب ابني عم: أحدهما أخ للأم والآخر زوج، ومسلم (1991، 3/1233)، كتاب الفرائض، باب: ألحقوا الفرائض بأهلها، فما بقي فلأولى رجل ذكر.

النسب»،[16] و«إن الله إذا حرم شيئا حرم ثمنه»،[17] و«كل مسكر حرام»،[18] و«ما ملأ آدمي وعاء شرًّا من بطنه» (ابن رجب 2001، 57/1)؛ فهذه أحاديث لا تتوفر على شرط الكلي الذي بحثه ابن الصلاح والنووي؛ ولكن ابن رجب لحظ - كما هو عنوان كتابه - مفهوم «جوامع الكلم» أكثر مما لحظ مفهوم «الكلي».

وقد جرى بعض المعاصرين على تقسيم الأحاديث الكلية إلى قسمين: كلي في أكثر من باب، وكلي في باب واحد (السعدي 2011، 7؛ اللوغاني 2018، 12؛ المقبل 2017، 73)، ولكن ما سُمي كليًّا في باب ليس كليًّا بالمعنى الذي أراده ابن الصلاح والنووي والذي شرطه أن يكون من قواعد الدين أو كلياته، ويبدو لي أن التمييز بين جوامع الكلم والأحاديث الكلية يُغني عن تكَلف هذا التمييز بين أنواع من الكلي، سواءٌ بناء على تناوله لباب أو أبواب أم على تناوله مجالًا أو أكثر، كالكلي في الفقه والكلي في العقيدة، وهكذا. فما سمي كلي الباب يُعبَّر عنه بالأصل، فنجد في كلام النووي - مثلًا - وصف أحاديث عدة بأنها "أصل عظيم،" ولكن عند التدقيق نجدها تنقسم إلى نوعين: نوع أدرجه النووي في الأربعين، وهو أصل كلي، ونوعٌ هو جزئي، ولذلك لم يُدرجه ضمن الأربعين بالرغم من كونه أصلًا؛ فالحديث الأصل قد يكون كليًّا وقد يكون أصلًا في باب معين من أبواب العلم. فحديث «بُني الإسلام على خمس» - مثلًا - قال فيه النووي: هو "أصل عظيم في معرفة الدين، وعليه اعتماده، وقد جَمَع أركانه" (النووي 1929، 176/1) وهو أحد الأربعين، في حين أن هناك أحاديثَ أصولًا مقيدة بباب فقط، كباب الطهارة أو باب الوضوء أو باب الحج أو باب البيوع أو باب الولاية وهكذا، وقد أشار النووي في أعماله إلى حديثٍ أصلٍ في كل باب من هذه الأبواب.

16 رواه البخاري (1312 [1894]، 170/3)، كتاب الشهادات، باب: الشهادة على الأنساب والرضاع المستفيض والموت القديم؛ ومسلم (1991، 1070/2)، كتاب الرضاع، باب: تحريم الرضاعة من ماء الفحل.

17 رواه أحمد (2001، 416/4)؛ وابن الجعد (1996، 479)؛ وابن حبان (1988، 313/11)، كتاب البيوع، باب: البيع المنهي عنه، وغيرهم.

18 رواه البخاري (1312 [1894]، 161/5، 30/8، 70/9)، كتاب المغازي، باب: بعث أبي موسى ومعاذ إلى اليمن قبل حجة الوداع، وكتاب الأدب، باب: قول النبي صلى الله عليه وسلم: "يسروا ولا تعسروا،" وكتاب الأحكام، باب: أمر الوالي إذا وَجه أميرين إلى موضع: أن يتطاوعا ولا يتعاصيا؛ ومسلم (1991، 1586/3)، كتاب الأشربة، باب: بيان أن كل مسكر خمر وأن كل خمر حرام.

ففي حديث عثمان أنه «دعا بوَضوء فتوضأ فغسل كفيه ثلاث مرات ...»،[19] قال النووي: "هذا الحديث أصل عظيم في صفة الوضوء" (النووي 1929، 106/3)، وفي أبواب الطهارة ذكر النووي عدة أحاديث، كحديث «إن ماء الرجل غليظ أبيض، وماء المرأة رقيق أصفر»[20] ثم قال فيه: "هذا أصلٌ عظيم في بيان صفة المنيّ" (النووي 1929، 222/3)، وكحديث «إن المؤمن لا يَنجس»[21] الذي قال فيه: "هذا الحديث أصل عظيم في طهارة المسلم حيًّا وميتاً" (النووي 1929، 66/4)، وكحديث «هو الطَّهور ماؤه الحِلّ مَيْتته»[22] قال: هو "أصل عظيم من أصول الطهارة. ذكر [الماوردي (ت. 1058/450)] صاحب الحاوي عن الحُميدي (ت. 834/219) شيخ البخاري وصاحب الشافعي قال: قال الشافعي (ت. 820/204): "هذا الحديث نصف علم الطهارة" (النووي د.ت.(ب)، 84/1؛ الماوردي 1994، 37/1)؛ فكونه نصف علم الطهارة لا نصف العلم أخرجه عن أن يكون أصلًا كليًّا. وكحديث «لتأخذوا عني مناسككم»[23] قال: "وهذا الحديث أصل عظيم في مناسك الحج، وهو نحو قوله صلى الله عليه وسلم في الصلاة: صلوا كما رأيتموني أصلي"[24] (النووي 1929، 45/9)، وكحديث النهي عن بيع الغَرَر[25] قال: "هو أصل عظيم من أصول كتاب البيوع، ولهذا قدمه مسلم، ويدخل فيه مسائل كثيرة غير منحصرة" (النووي 1929، 156/10)، وكحديث «لا تَأَمَّرَنَّ على اثنين ولا تولَّيَنَّ مال يتيم»[26] قال فيه: "هذا الحديث أصل عظيم في اجتناب الولايات ولاسيما لمن كان فيه ضعف عن القيام بوظائف تلك الولاية"

19 رواه البخاري (1312 [1894]، 44/1)، كتاب الوضوء، باب: المضمضة في الوضوء؛ ومسلم (1991، 204/1)، كتاب الطهارة، باب: صفة الوضوء وكماله.

20 رواه مسلم (1991، 250/1)، كتاب الحيض، باب: وجوب الغسل على المرأة بخروج المني منها.

21 رواه البخاري (1312 [1894]، 65/1، 73/2)، كتاب الغسل، باب: الجُنب يخرج ويمشي في السوق وغيره، وقال عطاء: "يحتجم الجنب ويقلم أظفاره، ويحلق رأسه وإن لم يتوضأ"، وكتاب الجنائز، باب غسل الميت ووضوئه بالماء والسدر؛ ومسلم (1991، 282/1)، كتاب الحيض، باب: الدليل على أن المسلم لا ينجس.

22 رواه أبو داود (2009، 62/1)، كتاب الطهارة، باب: الوضوء بماء البحر؛ وابن ماجه (2009، 250/1)، أبواب الطهارة وسننها، باب: الوضوء بماء البحر؛ ومالك (2004، 29/2)، وُقوت الصلاة، الطَّهُور للوَضوء، وغيرهم.

23 رواه مسلم (1991، 943/2)، كتاب الحج، باب: استحباب رمي جمرة العقبة يوم النحر راكبا وبيان قوله صلى الله عليه وسلم: "لتأخذوا مناسككم".

24 رواه البخاري (1312 [1894]، 128/1)، كتاب الأذان، باب: الأذان للمسافر إذا كانوا جماعة والإقامة، وكذلك بعرفة وجَمْع، وقول المؤذن: الصلاة في الرحال في الليلة الباردة أو المطيرة.

25 رواه مسلم (1991، 1153/3)، كتاب البيوع، باب: بطلان بيع الحصاة، والبيع الذي فيه غرر.

26 رواه مسلم (1991، 1457/3)، كتاب الإمارة، باب: كراهة الإمارة بغير ضرورة.

(النووي 1929، 210/12). فالأصل في باب لا يسمى كليًّا على هذا الاصطلاح، وإن دخل في جوامع الكلم، من جهة اشتماله على شرطي الإيجاز في اللفظ وكثرة المعنى.

## 3 من الجزئي إلى الكلي: محاولة لتأريخ «الأحاديث الكلية»

في تعليقه على قول النووي: إن كل حديث من الأربعين يشكل "قاعدة عظيمة من قواعد الدين"، قال الطوفي: "قلت: أول من علمناه قال نحو هذا أبو داود" (الطوفي 1998، 22–23)، ولكن يظهر - بالتتبع - أن فكرة الأحاديث الكلية ظهرت في القرن الثاني الهجري ثم شاعت في القرنين الثالث والرابع الهجريين حتى إن الحافظ حمزة بن محمد الكناني (ت. 968/357) قال: "سمعت أهل العلم يقولون: هذه الثلاثة أحاديث هي الإسلام،"[27] ما يفيد أن الفكرة صارت شائعة بين أهل العلم. ويَظهر من جمع أقوالهم وجود اختلاف في تحديد الأحاديث الكلية وعددها، الأمر الذي سيدفع بعض متأخري المحدثين - كابن الصلاح - إلى جمع الأحاديث التي وردت في أقوال الأئمة المتقدمين فبلغت معه 26 حديثًا، ثم جاء النووي فاستتمها وزاد عليها بالتدريج حتى بلغت أربعين حديثًا، ثم زاد على الأربعين حديثين على سبيل الخاتمة كما فهم غير واحد، ثم جاء مَن زاد على النووي زيادات أخرى كابن رجب الحنبلي وغيره، في حين نحا آخرون إلى جمع وإحصاء الأقوال، كما فعل ابن الملقن (ت. 1401/804) فبلغ بها عشرة أقوال، ثم زاد عليها واحدًا فبلغت أحد عشر قولًا، وكان قد نقل بعض هذه الأقوال عن كتاب "الأقسام والخصال" لأبي بكر الخفّاف (أحد قدماء فقهاء الشافعية ومن علماء القرن الرابع الهجري/العاشر الميلادي) ثم قال: "ولم أر لغيره تَعرضًا لذلك فاستفده" (ابن الملقن 2004، 663/1). وسأجعل تأريخ الفكرة على قسمين: ظهور الفكرة لدى المتقدمين، ثم تطوراتها اللاحقة لدى المتأخرين.

### 3.1 الأحاديث الكلية عند الأئمة المتقدمين

برزت فكرة الأحاديث الكلية في القرن الثاني الهجري، وساهم في صياغتها عدد من الأئمة ممن جمع بين الفقه والحديث في الغالب، وهم: عبد الرحمن بن مهدي، ومحمد بن إدريس الشافعي (ت. 820/204)، وأبو عبيد القاسم بن سلام (ت. 838/224)، وعلي بن المديني، وإسحاق بن راهويه (ت. 851/238)، وأحمد بن حنبل (ت. 855/241)، وأبو داود السِّجستاني، وعثمان بن سعيد الدارِمي (ت. 893/280)، وحمزة بن محمد الكِنَاني، وأبو الحسن الدارَقُطْني (ت. 995/385)، وابن أبي زيد القيرواني (ت. 996/386). ويشكل أبو داود محطة بارزة في صياغة الفكرة، فقد

27 سيأتي لاحقًا ذكر هذه الأحاديث.

نُقل عنه خمسُ روايات مختلفة في تحديد الأحاديث الكلية وكثر ناقلوها، ولهذا ظن نجم الدين الطوفي أنه أول من قال بذلك. سأقدم فيما يأتي تأريخًا للفكرة من خلال حصر الأقوال وتوثيقها أولًا، ثم تحليلها عبر التدقيق في العبارات المستعملة ودلالاتها ثانيًا، وتحرير الاختلاف في عدد الأحاديث الكلية وفي تعيينها ثالثًا، ثم النظر في المتفق والمفترق بين الأقوال رابعًا، وهذا التأريخ يتجاوز مجرد سرد الأقوال المختلفة في الأحاديث الكلية، كما فعل ابن الملقن مثلًا.

1. عبد الرحمن بن مهدي:

نقل أبو بكر الخَفاف عنه قوله: مدار الإسلام على أربعة أحاديث هي: «الأعمال بالنيات»، و«لا يَحل دم امرئ مسلم إلَّا بإحدى ثلاث»، و«بني الإسلام على خمس»، و«البينة على المدعي واليمين على من أنكر» (ابن الملقن 1997، 155/1؛ ابن الملقن 2004، 662/1).

2. الشافعي:

نقل أبو بكر الخفاف عنه أنه قال: "مدار الإسلام على أربعمئة حديث". قال ابن الملقن: "كذا رأيته أربعمئة، ثم رأيت في أصول الفقه لابن سُراقة العامري (ت. نحو 410/1019) من أصحابنا يذكر أربعة أحاديث، وكأنه أصوب" (ابن الملقن 2004، 662/1؛ ابن الملقن 1997، 154/1).

3. أبو عبيد القاسم بن سلام[28]:

قال: "جمع النبي صلى الله عليه وسلم جميع أمر الآخرة في كلمة: «من أحدث في أمرنا ما ليس منه فهو رد»، وجمع أمر الدنيا في كلمة: «إنما الأعمال بالنيات»؛ يدخلان في كل باب" (الهروي 1998، 26/1؛ البغوي 1983، 218/1؛ الطيبي 1997، 603/2؛ ابن رجب 2001، 62/1).[29]

4. علي بن المديني:

نُقل عنه قولان: أولهما من رواية ابنه محمد بن علي بن المديني قال: سمعت أبي يقول: "إنما يدور حديث رسول الله صلى الله عليه وسلم على أربعة أحاديث: حديث عمر بن الخطاب (ت. 23/644) عن رسول الله صلى الله عليه وسلم في «الأعمال بالنيات»، وحديث زيد بن وَهْب (ت. 83/702) عن ابن مسعود (ت. 32/650): حدثنا رسول الله صلى الله عليه وسلم - وهو الصادق المصدوق - «إنّ خَلقَ أحدِكُم يُجمَعُ في بَطنِ أُمّه أربعين يومًا»، وحديث عثمان بن عفان (ت. 35/656) أن النبي صلى الله عليه وسلم قال: «لا يَحل دم

28 حكت مصادر عدة عن أبي عبيد ولم تسمه، وأغلب الظن أنه أبو عبيد القاسم بن سلام الذي وُلد قبل المئتين بقليل وتوفي سنة 224/838 (الذهبي 1983، 490/10).

29 عند الهروي وابن رجب: عثمان بن سعيد قال سمعت أبا عبيد. وعند البغوي والطيبي: عن يحيى بن سعيد قال: سمعت أبا عبيد.

مسلم إلا بإحدى ثلاث»، وحديث النبي صلى الله عليه وسلم «أُمرت أن أقاتل الناس حتى يقولوا لا إله إلا الله»" (الخليلي 1989، 538/2).

أما القول الثاني عنه – وهو مثل قول عبد الرحمن بن مهدي السابق – فنقله عنه أبو بكر الخفاف وهو أن مدار الإسلام على أربعة أحاديث هي: «الأعمال بالنيات»، و«لا يحل دم امرئ مسلم إلَّا بإحدى ثلاث»، و«بني الإسلام على خمس»، و«البينة على المدعي واليمين على من أنكر» (ابن الملقن 1997، 155/1؛ ابن الملقن 2004، 662/1).

5. إسحاق بن راهويه:

نقل عنه قولان، الأول: أن "أربعة أحاديث هي من أصول الدين" وهي: حديث عمر «إنما الأعمال بالنيات»، وحديث «الحلال بين والحرام بين»، وحديث «إن خلق أحدكم يجمع في بطن أمه أربعين يوما»، وحديث «من صنع في أمرنا شيئا ما ليس منه فهو رَد» (ابن رجب 2001، 62/1). أما القول الثاني فنقله عنه أبو بكر الخفاف، وهو أن "مداره على ثلاثة" لا أربعة، وهي: «إنما الأعمال بالنيات»، وحديث عائشة: «من أدخل في أمرنا ما ليس منه فهو رد»، وحديث النعمان: «الحلال بين» (ابن الملقن 2004، 622/1؛ ابن الملقن 1997، 155/1). وقد نُقل مثل هذا القول الأخير عن الإمام أحمد كما سيأتي.

6. أحمد بن حنبل:

رُوي عنه روايتان: الأولى: أنه قال: "أصول الإسلام على ثلاثة أحاديث" وهي: حديث عمر: «إنما الأعمال بالنيات»، وحديث عائشة (ت. 678/58): «من أحدث في أمرنا هذا ما ليس منه فهو رد»، وحديث النعمان بن بشير (ت. 685/65): «الحلال بين والحرام بين» (ابن أبي يعلى د.ت.، 47/1؛ ابن الجوزي 1997أ، 85/1؛ ابن الجوزي 1997ب، 298؛ ابن رجب 2001، 61/1؛ العراقي د.ت.، 5/2؛ ابن مفلح 1990، 109/1؛ ابن الملقن 1997، 155/1).

أما الرواية الثانية فقال الحاكم النيسابوري (ت. 1014/405): "حدثونا عن عبد الله بن أحمد عن أبيه أنه ذكر قوله عليه الصلاة والسلام: «الأعمال بالنيات»، وقوله: «إن خلق أحدكم يجمع في بطن أمه أربعين يوما»، وقوله: «من أحدث في ديننا ما ليس منه فهو رد». فقال: ينبغي أن يُبدأ بهذه الأحاديث في كل تصنيف، فإنها أصول الأحاديث" (ابن رجب 2001، 61/1).

7. أبو داود:

كثرت أقوال أبي داود في هذا الباب، فقد أحصيت خمس روايات مختلفة عنه، وهي كالآتي:

الأولى: رواية أحمد بن محمد بن الأعرابي (ت. 952/341) وجاء فيها: "حدثنا أبو داود سليمان بن الأشعث قال: "أقمت بطَرَسوس عشرين سنة كتبت المسند، فكتبت أربعة

آلاف حديث، ثم نظرت فإذا مدار أربعة آلاف على أربعة أحاديث لمن وفقه الله جل ثناؤه، فأولها حديث النعمان بن بشير: «الحلال بين والحرام بين»، وثانيها حديث عمر: «الأعمال بالنيات»، وثالثها حديث أبي هريرة (ت. 679/59): «إن الله طيب لا يقبل إلّا الطيب»، ورابعها حديث أبي هريرة أيضًا: «من حسن إسلام المرء تركه ما لا يعنيه»" (الخطابي 1932، 366/4؛ النووي د.ت.(أ)، 226/2؛ العلائي 2008، 44؛ العراقي د.ت.، 6/2).[30] وقد جمع نصر بن إبراهيم المقدسي (ت. 1097/490) شيخ الشافعية بالشام جزءًا مفردًا أسند فيه هذه الأحاديث الأربعة إلى أبي داود، ونقل عنه في حديث «الحلال بين ...» قوله: "هذا ربع العلم" (المقدسي 2012، 23)، ثم نقل عنه في حديث «الأعمال بالنيات» قوله: "هذا نصف العلم" (المقدسي 2012، 24)، ثم نقل عنه في حديث «إن الله طيب» قوله: "فهذا ثلاثة أرباع العلم" (المقدسي 2012، 25)، ثم ختم بعد الحديث الرابع بقول أبي داود: "فهذه الأربعة الأحاديث - لمن وفقه الله تعالى - تجزئ الأربعة آلاف" (المقدسي 2012، 27).[31]

الثانية: رواية عبد الله بن أبي داود (ت. 928/316) عن أبيه أبي داود قال: "الفقه يدور على أربعة أحاديث: «الحلال بين والحرام بين»، و«الأعمال بالنيات»، و«ما نهيتكم عنه فاجتنبوه وما أمرتكم به فأتوا منه ما استطعتم»، و«لا ضرر ولا ضرار»". (ابن مسلمة 2002، 46، 182؛ الخطيب 1983، 289/2، وبوّب عليه: الأحاديث التي تدور أبواب الفقه عليها؛ الطائي الهمذاني 1999، 41).

الثالثة: رواية محمد بن بكر بن داسة (ت. 957/346)، وجاء فيها أن أبا داود قال: "كتبت عن رسول الله صلى الله عليه وسلم خمسمئة ألف حديث. انتخبت منها ما ضمّنته هذا الكتاب - يعني كتاب السنن - جمعت فيه أربعة آلاف وثمانمئة حديث. ذكرت الصحيح وما يشبهه ويقاربه، ويكفي الإنسانَ لدينه من ذلك أربعةُ أحاديث: أحدها: قول النبي - صلى الله عليه وسلم -: «الأعمال بالنيات». الثاني قوله: «من حسن إسلام المرء تركه ما لا يعنيه». الثالث قوله: «لا يكون المؤمن مؤمنًا حتى يرضى لأخيه ما يرضى لنفسه». الرابع قوله صلى الله عليه وسلم: «الحلال بين والحرام بين»" (الخطيب 2001،

---

30 جاء عند العراقي بلفظ: "اجتهدت في الحديث المسند ..." وجاء عند النووي هكذا: "وقال محمد بن صالح الهاشمي: قال لنا أبو داود: أقمت بطرسوس ..."

31 كان أولى بمحقق جزء المقدسي أن يورد اختلاف الروايات عن أبي داود، وأن يحرر القول فيها وفي الاختلاف بين بعضها وبعض، ولماذا اختار المقدسي هذه الرواية دون غيرها، ولكنه اكتفى بالإشارة المجملة إلى وجود اختلاف فيها (المقدسي 2012، 3).

10/78–79؛ ابن بلبان 2004، 35؛ الخطابي 1932، 365/4؛ ابن أبي يعلى د.ت.، 161/1؛ ابن الجوزي 1997أ، 86/1؛ ابن دقيق العيد 2009، 43/1؛ ابن الصلاح 1992، 185/1؛ التجيبي 1981، 98؛ الكرماني 1981، 203/1؛ ابن رجب 2001، 62/1–63؛ العراقي د.ت.، 6/2). وقد خرّج أبو عمرو الداني المقرئ هذه الأحاديث الأربعة في جزء (التجيبي 1981، 98).

الرابعة: رواية عبد الله بن أبي داود أيضًا عن أبيه أنه قال: "الفقه يدور على خمسة أحاديث: «الحلال بين والحرام بين»، وقوله صلى الله عليه وسلم: «لا ضرر ولا ضرار»، وقوله: «الأعمال بالنيات»، وقوله: «الدين النصيحة»، وقوله: «ما نهيتكم عنه فاجتنبوه، وما أمرتكم به فأتوا منه ما استطعتم»" (الخطيب 1983، 290/2؛ أبو طاهر السلفي 2003، 53–55؛ أبو طاهر السلفي 2008، 42؛ ابن الجوزي 1997أ، 85/1؛ ابن الصلاح 1984، 219؛ ابن رجب 2001، 63/1؛ العراقي د.ت.، 6/2).

الخامسة: أن أبا داود قال: "أصول السنن في كل فن أربعة أحاديث: حديث عمر: «الأعمال بالنيات»، وحديث: «الحلال بين والحرام بين»، وحديث: «من حسن إسلام المرء تركه ما لا يعنيه»، وحديث: «ازهد في الدنيا يحبك الله وازهد فيما في أيدي الناس يحبك الناس»" (ابن عبد البر 1981، 201/9؛ ابن رجب 2001، 6/1؛ ابن الملقن 2012، 195).

من الواضح أن الروايات الخمس اتفقت على حديثين هما: حديث النية وحديث «الحلال بيّن»، واختلفت في الباقي. وقد قال ابن حجر: "والمعروف عن أبي داود عَدُّ «ما نهيتكم عنه فاجتنبوه ...» الحديث، بدل «ازهد فيما في أيدي الناس»" (ابن حجر العسقلاني د.ت.، 129/1).

8. عثمان بن سعيد الدارمي:

نقل عنه ابن الملقن أنه قال: "أمهات الحديث أربعة، وحديث النية أحدها" ولكن ابن الملقن لم يذكر البقية (ابن الملقن 2004، 663/1؛ ابن الملقن 1997، 154/1).

9. حمزة بن محمد الكناني:

ذكر حديث النية، وحديث «من حسن إسلام المرء تركه ما لا يعنيه»، وحديث «الحلال بين والحرام بين»، ثم قال: "سمعت أهل العلم يقولون: هذه الثلاثة أحاديث هي الإسلام، وكل حديث منها ثلث الإسلام" (ابن الملقن 2004، 662/1؛ ابن الملقن 1997، 154/1).

10. الدارقطني:

نقل عنه أنه قال: "أصول الأحاديث أربعة: «الأعمال بالنيات»، و«من حسن إسلام المرء تركه ما لا يعنيه»، و«الحلال بين»، و«ازهد في الدنيا يحبك الله»" (ابن الملقن 2004، 662/1؛ ابن الملقن 1997، 154/1؛ السيوطي 1983، 9؛ المناوي 1988، 144/1).

11. ابن أبي زيد القيرواني:
قال في رسالته المشهورة: "وجماع آداب الخير وأَزِمّته تتفرع عن أربعة أحاديث: قول النبي عليه السلام: «من كان يؤمن بالله واليوم الآخر فليقل خيرا أو ليصمت». وقوله عليه السلام: «من حسن إسلام المرء تركه ما لا يعنيه»، وقوله للذي اختصر له في الوصية: «لا تغضب»، وقوله: «المؤمن يحب لأخيه المؤمن ما يحبه لنفسه»" (ابن أبي زيد 1986، 268؛ وزروق 2006، 1028/2؛ ابن ناجي التنوخي 2007، 444/2؛ وأسنده السلفي إلى ابن أبي زيد: أبو طاهر السلفي 1994، 196–198؛ وانظر: ابن الصلاح 1984، 203؛ ابن الملقن 2012، 214؛ النفراوي 1995، 297/2).

تدور هذه الأقوال – بمجموعها – على تحديد الأحاديث التي عليها مدار الإسلام أو هي الإسلام أو أصول الإسلام، أو من أصول الدين، أو التي تجمع أمري الدنيا والآخرة، أو التي عليها مدار الحديث أو هي أصول الأحاديث أو أمهات الحديث، أو عليها مدار السنن أو خلاصة كتابِ السنن لأبي داود، أو عليها مدار الفقه، أو ما يكفي الإنسانَ لدينه، أو هي جِماع آداب الخير وأَزِمَّته. ويبدو أن النووي قد أجمل هذه العبارات حين جعل شرط الأربعين أن "كل حديث منها قاعدة عظيمة من قواعد الدين قد وصفه العلماء بأن مدار الإسلام عليه، أو هو نصف الإسلام أو ثلثه أو نحو ذلك" (النووي 2009، 44)، ولعل هذا يفيد أنه رأى هذه التعبيرات المختلفة واردة على معنى واحد، وربما يؤكد ترادفَها أيضًا اختلافُ العبارات الواردة عن الشخص الواحد مع وجود اختلاف جزئي في تعيين تلك الأحاديث بحسب كل رواية، كما وجدنا مع أبي داود مثلًا، ولكن تعبيرات مثل أصول الإسلام أو مدار الإسلام أو أصول الدين ربما تحمل دلالة أشمل من تعبير أصول الأحاديث، أو دلالة كلامية في مقابل تعبير مدار الفقه أو السنن مثلًا، ولكن بما أن المسألة أغلبية ففي التعبير سعة، ولذلك حملها النووي – فيما يبدو – على معنى واحد. وإذا تأملنا تلك العبارات بالمقارنة مع مضمون الأحاديث التي تحتها وجدنا أن الأحاديث التي عليها مدار الإسلام تنطوي على حديث أركان الإسلام: «بُني الإسلام على خمس»، وهو غير مدرج ضمن المجموعات الأخرى التي حملت عناوين مختلفة. وكذلك نجد حديث الابتداع في الدين: «من أحدث في أمرنا ما ليس منه»، وحديث الخلق والقدر: «إن خلق أحدكم ليجمع في بطن أمه ...» مُدرَجَين تحت عنوان «أصول الدين»، ولكنهما يَردان – أيضًا – تحت عناوين أخرى؛ فحديث «إن خلق أحدكم» جاء – أيضًا – تحت «مدار الحديث» و«أصول الأحاديث». وحديث «من أحدث في أمرنا» يرد تحت عنوان مثل «أمر الآخرة»، و«مدار الإسلام»، و«أصول الإسلام»، و«أصول الأحاديث». ومن اللافت – كذلك – أن الأحاديث الكلية الواردة في أقوال أبي داود المختلفة، هي ذات طابع عملي يتصل بالأحكام؛ ما يجعل من العبارات المختلفة الواردة عن أبي داود – وهي: «مدار السنن» أو «أصول السنن» أو «مدار الفقه» أو «ما يكفي

الإنسان لدينه» – معبِّرة بدقة عن محتوى تلك الأحاديث، ولاسيما أن أبا داود نفسه قد قال: "وإنما لم أصنف في كتاب السنن إلا الأحكام، ولم أصنف كتب الزهد وفضائل الأعمال وغيرها؛ فهذه الأربعة آلاف والثمانمئة كلها في الأحكام. فأما أحاديث كثيرة في الزهد والفضائل وغيرها من غير هذا فلم أخرجه" (أبو داود 1984، 33–34؛ التجيبي 1981، 98)، وقد شرح الخطابي هذا فقال: "وقد جمع أبو داود في كتابه هذا من الحديث في أصول العلم وأمهات السنن وأحكام الفقه ما لا نعلم متقدمًا سبقه إليه ولا متأخرًا لحقه فيه" (الخطابي 1932، 8/1). أما تعبير «جِماع آداب الخير»، فإن الأحاديث التي تحته تتناول أخلاق النفس المتمثلة في أربعة هي: حفظ اللسان عن اللغو، وعدم التدخل فيما لا يعني، وعدم الغضب، وأن يحب المرء لأخيه ما يحب لنفسه.

تؤكد هذه التعبيرات المختلفة مفهوم الكليّ الذي سبقت مناقشته، وأنه معنى أدق من مطلق جوامع الكلم، وهو السمة الأساسية التي تميز هذه التعبيرات رغم اختلافها؛ فجميعها يؤكد الخروج من فكرة الباب أو المجال إلى الأبواب أو عموم الإسلام أو الدين أو عموم مدونة الحديث التي هي مصدر رئيس للإسلام، وهو معنى سأزيده بيانًا فيما بعد.

أما من جهة تقدير العدد، فالأقوال الواردة تدور على اثنين وثلاثة وأربعة وخمسة، ولكن ابن الملقن حكى قولًا مبهمًا يرى أنها ترجع إلى واحد فقط هو حديث «الحلال بين»، ولكنه لم يبين قائله (ابن الملقن 2008، 196/2؛ ابن الملقن 1997، 154/1).[32]

وأما من جهة تعيين الأحاديث الكلية والاختلاف الواقع فيه، فمن الواضح أن ثمة اتفاقًا على مركزية حديث النية باستثناء ما ورد عن ابن أبي زيد؛ فإن أحاديثه أخص من أحاديث الباقين، ولذلك عبر عنها بـ«آداب الخير». وهذا الاتفاق يؤكد ما قاله الحافظ ابن حجر: "وقد تواتر النقل عن الأئمة في تعظيم قدر هذا الحديث. قال أبو عبيد:[33] ليس في أخبار النبي صلى الله عليه وسلم شيء أجمع وأغنى وأكثر فائدة من هذا الحديث" (ابن حجر العسقلاني د.ت.، 11/1).

وإذا أردنا أن نختبر دقة ما نسبه حمزة الكناني إلى «أهل العلم» من اتفاقهم على الأحاديث الثلاثة: حديث النية و«من حسن إسلام المرء» وحديث «الحلال بين»، سنجد أن الاتفاق وقع على حديث النية فقط، أما حديث «من حسن إسلام المرء»، فإنه ورد في ثلاث روايات عن

32 من اللافت أن ابن الملقن ذكر هذا القول – ضمن أربعة أقوال اقتصر عليها – في شرحه على صحيح البخاري، وعيّن هذا الحديث الفرد، ولكنه حين ذكر هذا القول في "الإعلام بفوائد عمدة الأحكام" لم يذكر الحديث، بالرغم من أنه أحال في شرح البخاري إلى الإعلام؛ فمن الواضح أنه كتبه بعد «الإعلام».

33 اضطربت المصادر في تعيين هذا الاسم؛ ففي بعضها أبو عبد الله، وفي بعضها أبو عبيدة. والواضح أنه أبو عبيد صاحب أحد الأقوال المذكورة سابقًا.

أبي داود، كما ورد عن الدارقطني وابن أبي زيد فقط. أما حديث «الحلال بين»، فإنه جاء عن إسحاق في الروايتين عنه، وعن أحمد في رواية، وعن أبي داود الذي اتفقت الروايات الخمس عنه على عدّه من الأحاديث الكلية، كما جاء عن الدارقطني أيضًا.

وقد اجتمع من مجموع هذه الأقوال الأحد عشر برواياتها المختلفة 17 حديثًا هي: «الأعمال بالنيات»، و«لا يحل دم امرئ مسلم إلّا بإحدى ثلاث»، و«بني الإسلام على خمس»، و«البينة على المدعي واليمين على من أنكر»، و«من أحدث في أمرنا ما ليس منه فهو رد»، و«إنّ خَلقَ أحدِكُمُ يُجمَعُ في بطنِ أُمّه أربعين يومًا»، و«أمرت أن أقاتل الناس حتى يقولوا لا إله إلا الله»، و«الحلال بين والحرام بين»، و«إن الله طيب لا يقبل إلّا الطيب»، و«من حسن إسلام المرء تركه ما لا يعنيه»، و«ما نهيتكم عنه فاجتنبوه وما أمرتكم به فأتوا منه ما استطعتم»، و«لا ضرر ولا ضرار»، و«لا يكون المؤمن مؤمنًا حتى يرضى لأخيه ما يرضى لنفسه»، و«الدين النصيحة»، و«ازهد في الدنيا يحبك الله»، و«من كان يؤمن بالله واليوم الآخر فليقل خيرا أو ليصمت»، و«لا تغضب».[34]

وتُظهر أقوال الأئمة المتقدمين الانتقال من الجزئي إلى الكلي، ومن الأحاديث المفردة إلى أصول الأحاديث، فبعد جمع مدونات الحديث جرى البحث في كلياته أو أصوله، وهو نظير حصر الأحكام ثم البحث – لاحقًا – عن قواعد كلية ترجع إليها، فقد نقل البويطي (ت. 846/231) أن الشافعي سئل: كم أصول الأحكام؟ فقال: خمسمئة. قيل له: كم أصول السنن؟ قال: خمسمئة. قيل له: كم منها عند مالك (ت. 795/179)؟ قال: كلها إلا خمسة وثلاثين حديثا. قيل له: كم عند ابن عيينة (ت. 814/198)؟ قال: كلها إلا خمسة (البيهقي 1970، 519/1؛ الذهبي 1983، 54/10؛ الذهبي 2003، 146/5؛ ابن كثير 2004، 47/1)، وهو ما مهد لظهور القواعد

34 جمع صالح الشامي (الشامي 2014، 7، 11) «الكلمات التي صدرت عن الرعيل الأول» تحت عنوان «الأحاديث النبوية الكلية» فبلغت – بحسبه – 10 أحاديث، في حين أن الحاصل من مجموع أقوالهم هو 17 حديثًا لا عشرة. وقد قال الشامي: إنما جمعها من أقوال المتقدمين؛ لأنها "أكثر دقة في الدلالة على ما ذهبوا إليه من اختيار الأحاديث التي هي أصول الأحكام بل وأصول الإسلام، وما أضيف إليها بعد ذلك فهو في معظمه شروح وتطبيقات لتلك الأصول المختارة،" ولكنه وقع في إشكالين: الأول: أنه حذف منها حديثين؛ بزعم أنهما لم يبلغا مبلغ الصحة، وهما «من حسن إسلام المرء»، و«لا ضرر ولا ضرار»؛ لأنه لا يُعقل – وفق قوله – أن يكون الحديث من الأصول ولم يرتق إلى الصحة، ثم أضاف حديثين آخرين فبلغت الأحاديث عشرة. فبما أن أقوال المتقدمين أكثر دقة، كان عليه أن يعتبر ذلك تصحيحا لها؛ فعَدُّها من الأصول مُشعِرٌ بتصحيحها لا العكس، ثم بما أن أقوال المتقدمين – بحسبه – أكثر دقة كان عليه ألا يزيد عليها، وإلا لزمه قبول الزيادات التي وقعت من المتأخرين!

الفقهية في القرن الرابع الهجري، والتي آلت – فيما بعد – إلى القواعد الخمس الكبرى التي تُرد إليها الأحكام. وثمة صلة بين القواعد الفقهية والأحاديث الكلية، فقد فُهِم من قول أحمد: حديث النية ثلث العلم، أنه يُرُد جميع الأحكام إلى قواعد ثلاث (ابن حجر العسقلاني د.ت.، 11/1؛ السيوطي 1983، 9)، بل إن قاعدتين من القواعد الفقهية الخمس الكبرى بُنيتا على حديثين من الأحاديث الكلية وهما: «حديث النية» و«حديث لا ضرر ولا ضرار»، فضلًا عن أن بعض الأحاديث الكلية الأخرى بُني عليها قواعد فقهية صغرى، كحديث «البينة على المدعي» الذي تحول إلى قاعدة فقهية، وكحديث «الحلال بين» الذي بُني عليه قاعدة «الحريم له حكم ما هو حريم له» (السيوطي 1983، 126)، وكحديث «فأتوا منه ما استطعتم»، فقد بني عليه قواعد فقهية منها: «الميسور لا يسقط بالمعسور» (السبكي 1991، 155/1؛ ابن الملقن 2010، 174/1)، و«درء المفاسد أولى من جلب المصالح» (السيوطي 1983، 87؛ ابن نجيم 1999، 78).

ويبدو أن فكرة الكليات كانت مطروحة أيضًا قبل ذلك، فقد أورد عمران الزَّناتي (ت. 1314/714) حكاية لها دلالة هنا، وهي أن أحدهم كتب إلى ابن عمر رضي الله عنهما (ت. 693/73) أن اكتب لي بالعلم كله. فكتب إليه: العلم كثير، ولكن إن استطعت أن تلقى الله تعالى خميص البطن من أموال الناس، خفيف الظهر من دنياهم، كافّ اللسان عن أعراضهم، ملازمًا لجماعاتهم، فافعل. قال: "فكانوا يقولون: جمع العلم في أربع كلمات" (ابن الملقن 1997، 157/1).

### 3.2 الأحاديث الكلية عند المتأخرين

أول من عرفناه من المتأخرين اهتم بـ«الأحاديث الكلية» ابن الصلاح الذي انتقلت معه الفكرة إلى مسار آخر من خلال المجلس الحديثي الذي أملاه تحت هذا العنوان، فشكل فاتحة للزيادة والاستدراك والعناية بهذا الباب من أبواب الحديث الذي ركز عليه النووي (2006، 47). وكان ابن الصلاح قد قصد إلى استقصاء خلاف المتقدمين في تعيين تلك الأحاديث التي عليها مدار الإسلام أو أصول الدين أو ما شابه، فبلغت – بمجموعها – 26 حديثًا كما سبق. وهذه الرسالة – وإن لم نقف عليها – فقد وصفها غير واحد، من أبرزهم النووي الذي أوضح – في غير موضع – أن ابن الصلاح حكى فيها "أقوال الأئمة في تعيين الأحاديث التي عليها مدار الإسلام واختلافهم في أعيانها وعددها"، وأنه "قد اجتهد في جمعها وتبيينها" (النووي 2006، 47، 49؛ الطوفي 1998، 23)، وتابعه تاج الدين الفاكِهاني (ت. 1331/731) فقال: "وذكر أبو عمرو ابن الصلاح أقوال الأئمة في تعيين الأحاديث التي عليها مدار الإسلام واختلافهم في أعيانها" (الفاكهاني 2007، 36).

وقد أوضح ابن الصلاح – في بعض أعماله – محل بحثه فقال: "وكنت قد قلت: إن مِلاك أمر الدين والدنيا في أربعة أحاديث،" ومَظِنة ذلك هو رسالته في «الأحاديث الكلية» التي جمع فيها الأقوال المختلفة، ويبدو أنه مال إلى قول مفرد فيها، والأربعة التي يعنيها هنا هي حديث معاذ بن جبل (ت، 639/18): «قلت يا رسول الله أوصني. قال: اتق الله حيثما كنت. قلت: زدني. قال: أتبع السيئة الحسنة تَمحها. قلت: زدني. قال: خالق الناس بخلق حسن»، وحديث معاذ أيضًا: «يا رسول الله أخبرني بعمل يُدخلني الجنة ويباعدني من النار. قال: لقد سألتَ عن عظيم ...» قال ابن الصلاح: "اشتمل على مباني الإسلام وأبواب الخير من الصوم والصدقة وصلاة الليل، وعلى الجهاد وحفظ اللسان". وحديث العِرباض بن سارية (ت، 694/75) أن رسول الله صلى الله عليه وسلم قال: «أوصيكم بتقوى الله والسمع والطاعة وإن تَأَمَّر عليكم عبدٌ ...» قال ابن الصلاح: "وفيه الحث على اتباع سنته وسنة الخلفاء الراشدين وعلى مجانبة البدع." وحديث ابن عباس (ت، 687/68) أن رسول الله صلى الله عليه وسلم قال: «احفظ الله يحفظك. احفظ الله تجده تُجاهك. وإذا سألتَ فلتسأل الله وإذا استعنت فاستعن بالله ...» (ابن الصلاح 2017، 207–212).

ولكن الأحاديث التي أملاها ابن الصلاح بلغت 26 حديثًا كما ساقها النووي، في حين أن مجموع الأحاديث الواردة في الأقوال الأحد عشر السابقة هو 17 حديثًا، فقد يكون ابن الصلاح قد اطلع على أقوال أخرى لم نطلع عليها، أو أنه زاد عليها تسعة أحاديث رأى هو – باجتهاده – أنها داخلة في معناها؛ خصوصًا أن الأربعة التي اعتبرها "ملاك أمر الدين والدنيا" هي – جميعا – من الأحاديث الزائدة على الـ17 والتي أُدرجت ضمن الأربعين النووية. أما الخمسة الباقية من عدة الـ26 حديثًا فهي: «دع ما يَريبك إلى ما لا يريبك»، و«استفت قلبك» وتممه بحديث آخر هو: «البر حسن الخلق»،[35] و«إن الله كتب الإحسان على كل شيء ...»، و«إن الله فرض فرائض فلا تضيعوها ...»، وحديث جبريل في الإيمان والإسلام والإحسان والساعة.

ثم جاء النووي فوسع الفكرة لجمع كل الأحاديث التي تحقق فيها الشرط الموضح سابقًا، وزاد عليها ما وجده من زيادات بشكل متتابع حتى بلغت 40 حديثًا كما سبق. وقد وقع له ذلك على ثلاث مراحل: في المرحلة الأولى زاد على أحاديث ابن الصلاح ثلاثة أحاديث افتتحها بقوله: "ومما في معناها" (النووي 2006، 119–131)، وفي المرحلة الثانية زاد عليها حديثًا واحدًا وقال: "وقد اجتمع من تداخل أقوالهم – مع ما ضممته إليها – ثلاثون حديثا" (النووي 1994، 405)، وفي المرحلة الثالثة أوصلها إلى أربعين، ثم زاد حديثين، "كأنه رأى الختم بهما على الأربعين؛

35 وتبعه النووي على ذلك لاحقًا فأعطى الحديثين رقمًا واحدًا، ولكنه قدم حديث النوّاس: البر حسن الخلق؛ فقد رواه مسلم، وأخّر حديث وابصة: استفت قلبك؛ فإنه ليس في الكتب الستة ولكن النووي حسّنه.

لكون أحدهما من باب الوعظ لمخالفة الهوى ومتابعة الشرع، وثانيهما: من باب الرجاء والدعاء والاستغفار والإطماع في الرحمة" كما قال الطوفي وتبعه ابن الملقن (الطوفي 1998، 336؛ ابن الملقن 2012، 31–32). وبهذا بلغ مجموع ما زاده النووي 16 حديثًا.

وقد جاء في زيادته الأولى الأحاديث الآتية: «قل آمنت بالله ثم استقم»، و«إذا لم تستح فاصنع ما شئت»، وأن رجلًا سأل النبي: «أرأيتَ إذا صليتُ المكتوبات وصمت رمضان وأَحْللتُ الحلال وحرمتُ الحرام ولم أزد على ذلك شيئا أأدخل الجنة؟ قال: نعم». وفي زيادته الثانية زاد حديثًا في خاتمة كتاب **الأذكار** وهو: «يا عبادي إني حرمتُ الظلم على نفسي وجعلته بينكم محرمًا فلا تَظالموا ...»، ثم زاد الأحاديث الآتية في أربعينه: «الطُّهور شطر الإيمان والحمد لله تملأ الميزان ...»، و«أوليس قد جعل الله لكم ما تَصَّدَّقون؟...»، و«كل سُلامى من الناس عليه صدقة ...»، و«من رأى منكم منكرا فليغيره بيده ...»، و«المسلم أخو المسلم لا يظلمه ولا يخذله ولا يكذبه ...»، و«من نفَّس عن مؤمن كُربة من كرب الدنيا ...»، و«إن الله تعالى كتب الحسنات والسيئات ثم بين ذلك ...»، و«من عادى لي وليًّا فقد آذنته بالحرب...»، و«إن الله تجاوز لي عن أمتي الخطأ والنسيان وما استُكرهوا عليه»، و«كن في الدنيا كأنك غريب أو عابر سبيل»، ثم ختم بالحديثين الآتيين: «لا يؤمن أحدكم حتى يكون هواه تبعا لما جئت به»، و«يا ابن آدم إنك ما دعوتني ورجوتني غفرت لك على ما كان منك ولا أبالي...».

ثم صنف عمر بن المظفر (ت. 632/1234) كتاب الأربعين المسمى بـ«دار السلام في مدار الإسلام» (كحالة د.ت.، 8/3)، وقال القاسم بن يوسف التجيبي (ت. 730/1329) – بعد ذكره كلام أبي داود في الأحاديث الكلية – "وقد ذكرت في كتاب **مستفاد الرحلة والاغتراب**، في ترجمة أبي العباس البطرني المقري (ت. 793/1390) الأحاديث التي قيل فيها: إنها أصول الإسلام أو أصول الدين أو عليها مدار الإسلام أو مدار الفقه أو العلم، وبلغ جميع ما ذكرته هناك منها ستة وعشرين حديثًا" (التجيبي 1981، 98)، وهو العدد نفسه الذي انتهى إليه ابن الصلاح.

ثم جاء ابن رجب الحنبلي فزاد عليها ثمانية أحاديث وأبلغها خمسين حديثًا، وكان قد عزا إلى بعض شراح الأربعين النووية أنهم تعقبوها بزيادات تلخصت في الأحاديث الآتية: حديث «ألحقوا الفرائض بأهلها، فما أبقت الفرائض، فلأولى رجل ذكر»، بحجة أنه "جامعٌ لقواعد الفرائض التي هي نصف العلم، فكان ينبغي ذكره في هذه الأحاديث الجامعة،"[36] وحديث «البينة

36 هذا الحديث مما استدركه الطوفي على النووي حيث قال: "فات الشيخَ أن يُلحق بالأربعين حديثَ: ألحقوا الفرائض بأهلها، فما أبقت الفروض فلأولى رجل ذكر؛ فإنه من الجوامع في علم الفرائض، وهو نصف العلم" (الطوفي 1998، 338)، وكونه جامعًا في باب دون آخر يُخرجه من الكلي على ما سبق.

على المدعي، واليمين على من أنكر»[37]، لأنه "جمع أحكام القضاء،" ثم سرد زياداته التي تمثلت في الأحاديث الآتية: «ألحقوا الفرائض بأهلها»، و«يحرم من الرضاع ما يحرم من النسب»، و«إن الله إذا حرم شيئا حرم ثمنه»، و« كل مسكر حرام»، و«ما ملأ آدمي وعاء شرا من بطن»، و«أربع من كن فيه كان منافقا»،[38] و«لو أنكم تَوَكَّلون على الله حق توكله، لرزقكم كما يرزق الطير»،[39] و«لا يزال لسانك رطباً من ذكر الله عز وجل».[40]

انشغل المتقدمون برد مجموع الحديث النبوي إلى أصول كبرى معدودة تراوح عددها بين ثلاثة وخمسة، وساهم في تحديدها أئمة كبار أحاطوا بديوان الحديث رواية ودراية، ولكن طرأ لدى المتأخرين تحولان:

الأول: الانتقال من فكرة «الأحاديث الكلية» إلى فكرة جمع كل ما عُدّ من الأحاديث الكلية مع ابن الصلاح، وما يدخل في جنسه مع النووي الذي وسعها على ثلاث مراحل.

والثاني: الانتقال من «الأحاديث الكلية» إلى «الأحاديث الجوامع» من خلال الزيادة على ابن الصلاح والنووي، والعناية بالأحاديث الجوامع توجهٌ كان قد بدأ مع أبي بكر القفال الشاشي الكبير (ت. 976/365) في كتابه «**جوامع الكلم وبدائع الحكم**» (مخطوط)، وأبي نُعيم الأصبهاني (ت. 1038/430) في كتابه «**الإيجاز وجوامع الكلم**»،[41] وأبي عبد الله القُضاعي (ت. 1062/454) في كتابه «**الشهاب في الحكم والآداب**» (القضاعي 1985)، وشيرويه بن شهردار الديلمي (ت. 1115/509) في كتابه «**الفِردوس بمأثور الخطاب**» (الديلمي 1986) ومن بعدهم.

---

37 سبق أن هذا الحديث مما عده عبد الرحمن بن مهدي وعلي بن المديني - في رواية - في الأحاديث الكلية.

38 رواه البخاري (1312 [1894]، 16/1، 127/3)، **كتاب الإيمان، باب: علامة المنافق، وكتاب المظالم والغصب، باب: إذا خاصم فجر**؛ ومسلم (1991، 78/1)، **كتاب الإيمان، باب: بيان خصال المنافق**.

39 رواه الترمذي (1996، 151/4)، **أبواب الزهد، باب: في التوكل على الله**؛ وابن ماجه (2009، 266/5)، **أبواب الزهد، باب التوكل واليقين**، وغيرهما.

40 رواه الترمذي (1996، 318/5)، **أبواب الدعوات، باب: ما جاء في فضل الذكر**؛ وابن ماجه (2009، 708/4)، **أبواب الأدب، باب: فضل الذكر**، وغيرهما.

41 عزاه ابن رجب الحنبلي (2001، 56/1) لأبي بكر بن السُّني (ت. 974/364)، ولكن عزاه إلى أبي نعيم كلٌّ من: السمعاني 1996، 582/1؛ السمعاني 1975، 180/1؛ الذهبي 1983، 306/19؛ الذهبي 2003، 232/11؛ وخرّج منه العراقي بعض الأحاديث وعزاه لأبي نعيم أيضًا (العراقي 2005، 254/1، 595/2). ومن العجيب أن المقبل (2017، 42) عزاه لأبي علي الحداد (ت. 1122/515)، ظنًّا منه أنه له في حين أن الذي في المصادر التي عزا إليها هو أن أبا عليّ سمعه من مصنِّفه أبي نعيم الأصبهاني.

وقد مثّل ابن رجب محطة مهمة هنا؛ إذ إنه فهم من عمل ابن الصلاح أنه "جمع فيه الأحاديث الجوامع التي يقال: إن مدار الدين عليها، وما كان في معناها من الكلمات الجامعة الوجيزة" (ابن رجب 2001، 56/1)، أي أنه رادف بين مفهومي «الأحاديث الكلية» و«جوامع الكلم» التي هي عبارة عن «الكلمات الجامعة الوجيزة»، وهي عبارة فيها توسع لم يُرده ابن الصلاح ولا النووي، ومن ثم وقع الالتباس بين المفهومين، ومن زاد عليهما لم يحقق شرطهما، ومن ثم وقع الخروج عن مسار الأئمة المتقدمين الذين انشغلوا بالأحاديث الكلية قليلة العدد. ونحو ذلك نجده عند شمس الدين الذهبي (ت. 1348/748)؛ فإنه حين جاء إلى قول أبي داود: إنه "يكفي الإنسان لدينه أربعة أحاديث،" علق قائلًا: هذا "ممنوع؛ بل يحتاج المسلم إلى عدد كثير من السنن الصحيحة مع القرآن" (الذهبي 1983، 210/13). لا يبدو أن الذهبي حرر مفهوم الأحاديث الكلية ومقصود أبي داود وغيره هنا. وقد استمر هذا الخلط مع بعض المعاصرين كعبد الله بن الصديق الغماري (ت. 1993)؛ فإنه قال – في تعليقه على رسالة ابن الصلاح "**وصل البلاغات الأربعة في الموطأ**": "وفاتهما [أي ابن الصلاح والنووي] كثير من الأحاديث الوجيزة الجامعة للمعاني الكثيرة،" ثم راح يسوق بعض المؤلفات في "الكلم الجوامع من أحاديث النبي صلى الله عليه وسلم" (ابن الصلاح 2017، 210). فمن لم يميز بين الأحاديث الكلية والأحاديث الجوامع خلط بين مصنفات كلٍّ منهما؛ فجعل الجميع شيئًا واحدًا، ولا بد من التمييز هنا.

## 4 الأحاديث الكلية وسؤال الأخلاق

ثم أبين وجه صلتها بعلم الأخلاق بفروعه الثلاثة: أخلاقيات الفعل وأخلاقيات الفاعل وما بعد الأخلاق، ثم أختم ببيان وجه كونها أحاديث كلية على التفصيل.

### 4.1 الموضوعات المفتاحية للأحاديث الكلية

تدور الأحاديث السبعة عشر المشار إليها سابقًا على قضايا هي: النية، وعصمة دم المسلم (وفيها حديثان)، وأركان الإسلام (وفيها حديثان)، واتباع السنة وعدم الابتداع في الدين، ومراحل خلق الإنسان والقدر والعمل، والحلال والحرام وترك الشبهات وصلاح القلب، وأن قبول الأعمال مشروط بالطيب، وترك المسلم ما لا يعنيه، واجتناب المنهيات كلية والإتيان بالأوامر على قدر الاستطاعة، ولا ضرر ولا ضرار، وحب الخير للناس، والنصيحة، والزهد في الدنيا، والاقتصار على قول الخير وإكرامُ الجار والضيف، وترك الغضب، والبينة واليمين.

وتدور زيادات ابن الصلاح والنووي على قضايا هي: ترك ما يَريب، والإيمان والإحسان والساعة (الجزاء)، وأن الإحسان كُتب على كل شيء، والتقوى وحسن الخلق، والإخلاص

لله والإيمان بالقدر، والحياء، والاستقامة، وأن فعل المأمورات واجتناب المنهيات كاف لدخول الجنة، وجوامع الخير التي تشمل الذكر والصلاة والصدقة والصبر، وتحريم الظلم وسعة إنعام الله وأن الجزاء مرتبط بالعمل، وسعة مفهوم الصدقة، وتنوع أفعال الخير التي تشمل الذكر والأمر بالمعروف والنهي عن المنكر والمعاشرة الزوجية وإعانة الناس والكلمة الطيبة وإماطة الأذى عن الطريق وحفظ اللسان وغيرها (وفي هذا حديثان)، والبر والإثم واستفتاء القلب، وتقوى الله والسمع والطاعة والالتزام بالسنة، والأوامر والنواهي وحدود الله، والزهد، وتغيير المنكر ومراتبه، والأخوة وحقوق المسلم، وقضاء حوائج المسلمين، والحسنات والسيئات، والسلوك إلى الله عز وجل والوصول إلى معرفته ومحبته، والعفو عن الخطأ والنسيان والإكراه، وتهذيب النفس ليكون الهوى تبعًا لشريعة النبي.

ويمكن أن نلحظ من خلال هذه الموضوعات أمرين:

الأول: أنها ذات مضمون أخلاقيٍ واضحٍ، والأخلاق هنا مفهومٍ موسّع يتناول تقويم الأفعال وصفات الفاعل وفضائله، وهي حقلٌ متعدد التخصصات، وعبارةُ النووي قد تدل لهذا المعنى؛ فقد ختم أربعينه بقوله: "هذا آخر ما قصدته من بيان الأحاديث التي جمعت قواعد الإسلام، وتضمنت ما لا يُحصى من أنواع العلوم في الأصول والفروع والآداب، وسائر وجوه الأحكام" (النووي 2009، 116)؛ فالأخلاق بهذا المعنى تشمل الأصول والفروع والآداب وغيرها، وقد أدخل النووي كل هذا في جنس الأحكام (التقويمات)؛ التي تبدو - لديه - جنسًا يشمل أنواعًا.

والثاني: أن بعض الزيادات التي في الأربعين جاءت مؤكِّدة لمعانٍ وردت في الأحاديث الكلية السبعة عشر، مثل الزهد (كما في حديث «كن في الدنيا كأنك غريب»)، والإخلاص لله (كما في حديث النية وحديث «إن الله طيب لا يقبل إلا طيبًا»)، والورع (كما في حديث «دع ما يَريبك»)، وتحليل الحلال وتحريم الحرام (كما في حديث «أرأيت إذا صليت المكتوبات»، وحديث «إن الله فرض فرائض»)، وسببية الأعمال للجزاء (كما في حديث «إني حرمت الظلم على نفسي» وكحديث «إن أحدكم يُجمع خلقه»). ولكن تمت إضافة كليات أخرى تتصل بالتقوى، والإحسان، والحياء، والاستقامة، وسعة أبواب الخير (فيه ثلاثة أحاديث)، وسعة مفهوم الصدقة التي تشمل الأفعال أيضًا وليس الأموال فقط، والبر والإثم واستفتاء القلب، والسمع والطاعة، والأخوة وحقوق المسلم، والعفو عن الخطأ والنسيان والإكراه، والحسنات وسعة فضل الله في الجزاء عليها. نستنتج من هذا عدم دقة ما فهمه صالح الشامي حين اعتبر أن ما زاده المتأخرون "معظمه شروح وتطبيقات لتلك الأصول المختارة" من قبل الرعيل الأول (الشامي 2014، 7، 11).

### 4.2 الأحاديث الكلية وحقل الأخلاق

تتصل مضامين الأحاديث الكلية بالمحاور الثلاثة لعلم الأخلاق وهي: أخلاق الفعل، وأخلاق الفاعل، وما بعد الأخلاق.

ففيما يخص أخلاق الفعل، ينقسم الفعل الإنساني إلى نوعين: اختياري وغير اختياري، والأخلاق إنما تتناول الأفعال الاختيارية، وهنا يأتي حديث «إن الله تجاوز لأمتي...» الذي يُخرج الخطأ والنسيان والإكراه من دائرة المحاسبة إلى دائرة العفو؛ لفقدان حرية الاختيار. ثم إن الأفعال الاختيارية يمكن أن تنقسم أحكامها إلى تقسيمات عدة، فهي:

- إما حلال وحرام ومشتبه، وهنا يأتي حديث «الحلال بين»، وحديث «دع ما يَريبك»، وحديث «استفت قلبك»، وحديث «البر حسن الخلق». ثم إن الريبة وصفٌ شامل لأفعال متنوعة؛ فقد تقع في أفعال العبادات والمعاملات والمناكحات وسائر الأبواب.
- أو أنها تنقسم إلى ما يُستحى منه وما لا يُستحى منه، وهذه قسمة يفيدها حديث «إذا لم تستح فاصنع ما شئت».
- أو أنها تنقسم إلى معروف يجب الأمر به، ومنكر يجب النهي عنه، وهذه قسمة يفيدها حديث «من رأى منكم منكرا».

والحلال والحرام، وما يُستحى منه وما لا يُستحى منه، والمعروف والمنكر: تقسيماتٌ يمكن أن ترجع إلى الأحكام الخمسة التي تستوعب أفعال المكلفين التي لا تنحصر، ومن ثم فهي تقويمات أخلاقية. ومدار التكليف على منظومة حقوق ثلاثية تتناول حقوق الله وحقوق المكلف وحقوق العباد، وهذا مستفادٌ من حديث «اتق الله حيثما كنت»، وحديث «قل آمنت بالله ثم استقم»؛ فالتقوى تعبر عن حقوق الله، وفعل الحسنات لتكفير السيئات يعبر عن حقوق المكلف، ومخالقة الناس بخُلق حسن تعبر عن حقوق العباد. وعلى هذا فإن التكليف يتناول جميع أفعال العباد الظاهرة والباطنة (أعمال القلب وأعمال البدن) المتعلقة بأنواع الحقوق الثلاثة.

وقد جاءت تفصيلات هذه الحقوق في أحاديث أخرى؛ فحديث «يا غلام إني أعلمك كلمات» يتناول رعاية حقوق الله، وحديث «من عادى لي وليًّا» هو أصل في السلوك إلى الله وبيان طريقة أداء المفروضات، أي في رعاية حقوق الله. أما حديث «من حسن إسلام المرء تركه ما لا يعنيه» فيتناول حقوق العباد؛ فالترك والفعل إنما يتناولان الأعمال الظاهرة، وهي هنا عدم التدخل في شؤون الآخرين، وحديث «لا يؤمن أحدكم حتى يحب لأخيه» يتناول الأعمال الباطنة التي تأتي بعد تهذيب النفس لتصل إلى ترك حب الأثرة ومساواة الغير بالنفس. ومما يتصل أيضًا بحقوق العباد: أحاديث عصمة دم المسلم، والأحاديث التي توضح تنوع أبواب الخير واتساعها – ومنها حديث «من نفَّس عن مؤمن كربة» – ؛ فأبواب الخير تتناول التيسير على المعسر، وستر عورة المسلم، وعون الأخ على أموره، وإكرام الجار، وإكرام الضيف، والنهي عن

التحاسد والتباغض والتناجش والتدابر وبيع بعض على بعض. ثم إن الأحاديث التي توضح سعة مفهوم الصدقة (صدقة الأموال وصدقة الأفعال التي تتلخص في عبادة الله ونفع العباد) تتصل ببيان منظومة الحقوق - على اختلاف أنواعها وتفاوت درجاتها - ومنها حديث «أوليس قد جعل الله لكم ما تَصَّدقون»، وحديث «كل سلامى من الناس عليه صدقة». أما حقوق المكلف فترد في أحاديث أخرى؛ كحديث «لا تغضب» الذي يتصل بحق النفس وتهذيبها؛ لأن الغضب والشهوة مصدرا الشرور، بالإضافة إلى ما سبق من أن المكلف إذا فعل سيئة عليه أن يُتبعها حسنة تمحوها وتدفع عنه وزرها. بل إن منظومة الحقوق تتسع لتشمل حتى الحيوان؛ فالإحسان بوصفه مفهومًا شاملًا لكل شيء، تشمل جزئياته التخفيف عن الحيوان في الذبح والقتل كما في حديث «إن الله كتب الإحسان على كل شيء». وبناء على هذا جاء التأكيد في الأحاديث - كحديث «أرأيت إذا صليت المكتوبات» - على أن تحليل الحلال وتحريم الحرام كلامٌ جامع لأصول الدين وفروعه، وأن الأعمال سببٌ للجزاء إن خيرًا فخير وإن شرًّا فشر، كما في حديث «إن أحدكم يُجمع خلقه»، وحديث «يا عبادي إني حرمت الظلم».

ومما يدخل في أخلاق الفضيلة جملةٌ من الفضائل التي انطوت عليها الأحاديث الكلية، منها: التقوى؛ فحديث «اتق الله حيثما كنت» أصل فيها، والورع؛ فحديث «الحلال بين» وحديث «دع ما يريبك» أصلان فيه، والإخلاص؛ فحديث النية التي هي من أعمال القلوب، وحديث «إن الله طيب» أصلان فيه، والعدل (ونقيضه الظلم)؛ فحديث «إني حرمت الظلم على نفسي» أصل فيه، والأخوة؛ فحديث «لا تحاسدوا ولا تناجشوا» أصل فيها، وترك الأثرة ومحبة الخير للغير؛ فحديث «لا يؤمن أحدكم حتى يحب لأخيه» أصل فيهما، وفضائل إكرام الجار وإكرام الضيف؛ فحديث «من كان يؤمن بالله واليوم الآخر» أصل فيه، وهذه الفضائل تقود - جميعًا - إلى فضيلة أعلى وهي الأخوة وائتلاف القلوب (الألفة والمحبة بين الناس). ومن الفضائل التي انطوت عليها الأحاديث الكلية أيضًا، فضائل اللسان المتعلقة بالاقتصار على قول الخير والصمت عن غيره، والحِلم وترك الغضب، وتهذيب أهواء النفس لتكون تبعًا للشريعة، كما في حديث «لا يؤمن أحدكم حتى يكون هواه تبعًا لما جئت به»، والإحسان الذي كُتب على كل شيء، والحياء كما في حديث «إذا لم تستحِ»، والزهد كما في حديث «ازهد في الدنيا» وحديث «كن في الدنيا كأنك غريب»، والصلاح المستفاد من رعاية المصالح ونفي المفاسد جملة، والاستقامة كما في حديث «قل آمنت بالله ثم استقم»، وقد عُد حديث جبريل في الإيمان والإسلام والإحسان أصلًا في مقامات السالكين من التوكل والزهد والإخلاص والمراقبة والتوبة واليقظة ونحوها.

وقد اشتملت الأحاديث الكلية كذلك على مباحث تتصل بما بعد الأخلاق (meta-ethics) التي تبحث في اللغة الأخلاقية ومصادر التقويم الأخلاقي؛ فقد تضمنت قاموسًا أخلاقيًّا ثريًّا

يشمل الحسنات والسيئات، والحلال والحرام والمشتبه، والبر والإثم، والخطأ والإكراه، والمعروف والمنكر. ويمكن البحث في الفروق المحتملة بين الحلال والمعروف وما لا يُستحى منه من جهة، والحرام والمنكر وما يُستحى منه من جهة أخرى؛ والاشتباه والريبة وما يتصل بهما من مفاهيم فقهية كخلاف الأولى والأحوط مثلًا من جهة ثالثة. فالمعروف والحياء مفهومان أخلاقيّان يفيدان معنى زائدًا على مجرد الحل والحرمة، كما أنهما قد يُحيلان إلى مصادر أخرى غير الوحي، كالعرف الاجتماعي مثلًا، بينما الحل والحرمة يتحددان بالوحي؛ إذ ليس للإنسان سلطة التحليل والتحريم، وحديث «من أحدث في أمرنا هذا» صريح في هذا المعنى. ومما يدخل في مصادر التقويم الأخلاقي حديث «استفت قلبك» الذي هو أصل في إثبات الضمير الأخلاقي بوصفه مصدرا لتقويم الأفعال. ثم إن التكليف الشرعي أو الإلزام الخلقي ثابت على عباد الله (كل مسلم بالغ عاقل مختار)، ولكن الحكم الشرعي قد يكون متكلَّمًا به (صراحة أو استنباطًا) أو مسكوتًا عنه، وهذا مستفاد من حديث «إن الله فرض فرائض». وقانون التكليف العام أن المنهي عنه يجب تركه بالكلية، وأن المأمور به مقيّد بالاستطاعة وهذا كله مستفاد من حديث «ما نهيتكم عنه فاجتنبوه، وما أمرتكم به فأتوا منه ما استطعتم ...»، وقد بُني على هذا ثلاث قواعد أخلاقية: أولها: نظرية الحد الأدنى والحد الأعلى التي تَسِم النظر الأخلاقي، وهو ما سماه محمد عبد الله دراز «الجهد المبدع» (دراز 1998، 613)، وثانيها: أن الميسور لا يسقط بالمعسور، وثالثها: أن درء المفاسد مقدم على جلب المصالح.

### 4.3 بيان وجه الكلي في الأحاديث الكلية

وممن اعتنى – من الشراح – ببيان وجه كون الأحاديث الأربعين قواعد كليةً، الإمام نجم الدين الطوفي؛ إذ قال: "وسنبين وجه كون كلّ حديث منها قاعدةً كليةً من قواعد الإسلام إن شاء الله تعالى" (الطوفي 1998، 23)، ولكنه لم يطّرد في ذلك؛ فثمة أحاديث عدة لم يبين وجه كونها قاعدة كلية، كحديث «أُمرت أن أقاتل الناس»، وحديث «لا يَحل دم امرئ» وحديث «الطُّهور شطر الإيمان»، وحديث «البر حسن الخلق»، وحديث «أوليس قد جعل الله لكم ما تَصدقون؟»، وحديث «ازهد في الدنيا»، وحديث «لا تَحاسدوا»، وغيرها. ولكن يدور بيانه لوجه كون الأحاديث الأربعين كليةً على أربعة أوجه:

الأول: أنه وصف بعض الأحاديث بأنها تعبر عن الشريعة بكليتها، كحديث جبريل في الإسلام والإيمان والإحسان بقوله: هو "وافٍ بأحكام الشريعة، لاشتماله على جُملها مطابَقَة، وعلى تفصيلها تَضَمنًا، وجَمْعه بين الطاعات المتعلقة بالقلب والبدن: أصولًا وفروعًا" (الطوفي 1998، 76–77)، وقوله في حديث «إن الله كتب الإحسان على كل شيء»: هو "قاعدة الدين العامة، فهو متضمن لجميعه؛ لأن الإحسان في الفعل هو إيقاعه على مقتضى الشرع أو العقل،" ثم جعل

الأفعال التي تصدر عن الشخص على قسمين: ما يتعلق بمعاشه وما يتعلق بمعاده، فـ"المتعلق بمعاشه إما سياسة نفسه وبدنه، أو سياسة أهله وإخوانه ومِلكه، أو سياسة باقي الناس." أما "المتعلق بمعاده: فإما الإيمان وهو عمل القلب، أو الإسلام وهو عمل البدن كما مر في حديث جبريل،" ثم خلص الطوفي إلى القول: "فإذا أحسن الإنسان في هذا كله وأتى به على مقتضى الشرع، فقد حصّل على خير، وسَلِم من كل شر، ووفّى بجميع عهد الشرع" (الطوفي 1998، 148). وقال في حديث «أرأيت إذا صليت المكتوبات»: "تحليل الحلال وتحريم الحرام كلام جامع لأصول الدين وفروعه، لأن أحكام الشرع إما قلبية أو بدنية" (الطوفي 1998، 173).

الثاني: أنه وصف أحاديث أخرى بأنها نصف العلم أو نصف الشريعة أو نصف أدلة الشرع، كحديث «من أحدث في أمرنا»، فقد قال فيه: "وهذا الحديث يصلح أن يسمى نصف أدلة الشرع" (الطوفي 1998، 93–94)، وقال في حديث «من رأى منكم منكرا»: "يصلح أن يكون نصف الشريعة، لأن أعمال الشريعة: إما معروف يجب الأمر به، أو منكر يجب النهي عنه" (الطوفي 1998، 292)، وقال في حديث «إن الله تجاوز لي عن أمتي»: إنه "عام النفع عظيم الوقع، وهو يصلح أن يسمى نصف الشريعة، لأن فعل الإنسان: إما أن يصدر عن قصد واختيار وهو العمد مع الذكر اختيارًا، أو لا عن قصد واختيار وهو الخطأ والنسيان والإكراه، وهذا القسم معفوٌّ عنه والأول مؤاخَذٌ به" (الطوفي 1998، 322).

الثالث: أنه أدار جملة أحاديث على ثنائية الأمر والنهي أو أعمال القلب وأعمال البدن، وربطها بالأحكام الخمسة كأحاديث «الحلال بين» (الطوفي 1998، 98)، و«إذا لم تستح» (الطوفي 1998، 168)، و«قل آمنت بالله ثم استقم» (الطوفي 1998، 170)، و«إن الله فرض فرائض» (الطوفي 1998، 227)، و«ما أمرتكم به فأتوا منه ما استطعتم» (الطوفي 1998، 111).

الرابع: أنه وصف أحاديث بأنها أصل من الأصول في موضوع معين ولكن هذا الأصل سارٍ في جملة أبواب، لتناوله لأفعال المكلفين جملةً، كحديث «يا غلام إني أعلمك كلمات» قال فيه: "هذا الحديث أصل في رعاية حقوق الله تعالى" (الطوفي 1998، 166)، وكحديث «لا ضرر ولا ضرار» الذي استفاض فيه واعتبره أصلًا في رعاية المصالح ودرء المفاسد بل قدّمه على باقي أصول الشريعة (الطوفي 1998، 237–278)، وكحديث «من عادى لي وليًّا»، فقد قال فيه: "هذا الحديث أصل في السلوك إلى الله عز وجل والوصول إلى معرفته ومحبته، وطريقة أداء المفروضات" (الطوفي 1998، 321)، وكحديث «كن في الدنيا كأنك غريب» الذي قال: إنه "أصل في الفراغ عن الدنيا والزهد فيها" (الطوفي 1998، 329)، وكحديثي «دع ما يريبك» و«الحلال بين» اللذين وصف كل واحد منهما بأنه "أصل في الورع" (الطوفي 1998، 120، 103)، وحديث النية الذي وصفه بأنه "أصلٌ في الإخلاص" (الطوفي 1998، 41).

ويمكن توضيح وجه كون هذه الأحاديث كليةً من خلال أمرين:

الأول: كونها متجاوزة للأبواب، وهو المعنى الذي عُبر عنه بتعبيرات مختلفة كالقول بأن علوم الشريعة راجعة إليه، أو هو ثلث أو ربع الإسلام، أو نصف العلم، أو يمكن أن تُرد جميع الأحكام إليه، أو يَجمع أحكام الدين كلها، أو استوفى أقسام الفضل وأوفى حقوق الدين، أو لا يخرج عنه عمل أصلاً، أو تناول جميع الطاعات، أو غير ذلك مما يفيد معنى الكلي مما ورد في كتب شراح الحديث، وخاصة شراح الأربعين النووية. فقد قيل في حديث جبريل: إنه يشتمل على شرح الدين كله، وقال القاضي عياض (ت. 1149/544): "علوم الشريعة كلها راجعة إليه ومتشعبة منه" (القرطبي 1996، 152/1؛ العيني د.ت.، 289/1)، وقال ابن رجب: "جميع العلوم والمعارف ترجع إليه وتدخل تحته" (ابن رجب 2001، 134/1)، وقال ابن العربي في حديث «الحلال بين»: "يمكن أن يُنتزع منه – وحده – جميع الأحكام" (ابن حجر العسقلاني د.ت.، 129/1).

وأبرز مثال هنا هو حديث النية؛ فقد قال فيه عبد الرحمن بن مهدي: "ينبغي أن يُجعل رأسَ كل باب" (ابن حجر العسقلاني د.ت.، 11/1)؛ فهو أصل في الإخلاص الذي يدخل في عموم الأفعال، أي أنه متجاوز للأبواب، ولهذا قال ابن مهدي أيضًا: إنه "يدخل في ثلاثين بابًا من الفقه،" وقال الشافعي: إنه يدخل "في سبعين بابًا من الفقه،"[42] وراح الشراح يَعدون هذه الأبواب جميعًا؛ وذكروا أن مراد الشافعي الأبواب الكلية كالطهارة بأنواعها، والصلاة بأقسامها، والزكاة، والصيام، والاعتكاف، وهكذا (ابن الملقن 1997، 160/1–162؛ ابن الملقن 2008، 197/2)، وقال ابن حجر الهيتمي (ت. 1566/974): إن الشافعي لم يُرد المبالغة؛ فالنية "تدخل في ربع العبادات بكماله، وكنايات العقود، والحلول، والإقرار، والأيمان، والظهار، والقذف، والأمان، والردة، وفي الهدايا، والضحايا، والنذور، والكفارات، والجهاد، وسائر القُرَب؛ كنشر العلم، وكل ما يتعاطاه الحُكَّام، بل وسائر المباحات؛ إذا قَصد بها التقوي على الطاعة، أو التوصل إليها؛ ... وتدخل في غير ذلك ممَّا لا يخفى عليك استحضاره بعدما تقرر؛ فعُلم أنه إنما أراد التحديد بالسبعين بالنسبة إلى جملة الأبواب، وأما بالنسبة إلى جزئيات المسائل فذلك لا ينحصر" (ابن حجر الهيتمي 2008، 127–128).

وقال ابن حجر العسقلاني: "اتفق عبد الرحمن بن مهدي والشافعي – فيما نقله البويطي عنه – وأحمد بن حنبل وعلي بن المديني وأبو داود والترمذي (ت. 892/279) والدارقطني وحمزة الكناني على أنه ثلث الإسلام، ومنهم من قال: ربعه، واختلفوا في تعيين الباقي" (ابن حجر

42 نقل هذا عنهما عامة شراح الحديث وشراح الأربعين النووية. وروى قولَ الشافعي: الربيع بن سليمان، وأسنده الخطيب (1983، 290/2).

العسقلاني د.ت.، 11/1). ووجّه أبو بكر البيهقي الشافعي (ت. 1066/458) كونه ثلث العلم بأن "كسب العبد إنما يكون بقلبه ولسانه وبنانه، والنية واحدةٌ من ثلاثة أقسامٍ اكتسابه. ثم لقسم النية ترجيحٌ على القسمين الآخرين، فإن النية تكون عبادةً بانفرادها، والقولُ العاري عن النية، والعملُ الخالي عن العقيدة: لا يكونان عبادة بأنفسهما"، فالنية لا يدخلها الرياء على خلاف العمل (البيهقي 1989، 8/1).

الأمر الثاني: أن بعض الأحاديث الكلية يتناول الفضائل والمفاهيم الكلية التي لا تنحصر تعيناتها، كالتقوى والحياء والبر والإثم، والحسنات والسيئات، والصدقة، والإحسان، وغير ذلك مما سبق ذكره. وإن اعتبرنا «البينة» مفهومًا مجردًا غير خاص بالقضاء فقط، فإن وجه كون الحديث الوارد فيها كليًّا واضحٌ، وإن قصرنا البينة على باب القضاء فقط خرج الحديث عن كونه كليًّا، ولكن البينات تُشترط في كل دعوى سواءٌ كانت قضائية أم غير قضائية، سواءٌ في الخصومات الحقوقية أم في الجدل والحِجاج.

ويمكن أن نُجمل موارد الكليّ – في هذه الأحاديث – في اشتمال الحديث على القولي والفعلي، أو تناوله لأفعال الظاهر والباطن أو أعمال القلب وأعمال البدن، أو تناوله لكسب العبد بأنواعه الثلاثة المشار إليها سابقًا، أو تناوله للأحكام الخمسة، أو اشتماله على التخلية عن الرذائل والتحلية بالفضائل، أو استيعابه لأحكام الله: الفرائض والمحارم والحدود والمسكوت عنه، أو استيعابه للأصول والفروع، أو تناوله لرعاية المصالح ودرء المفاسد، أو اشتماله على مفهوم من المفاهيم الكلية كما سبق، وغير ذلك.

## 5 خاتمة

تبدو «الأحاديث الكلية» – إذن – انتقالًا من الجزئي إلى الكلي، ومن الفروع إلى الأصول؛ فهي تتجاوز طريقتي التصنيف في الحديث اللتين سادتا في الأزمنة الأولى. فالأحاديث الكلية تنشغل بالقواعد والمبادئ العامة التي يرجع إليها الدين أو يدور عليها الإسلام، أو هي أصول الأحاديث التي تختزن المعاني الكلية لمدونة الحديث، ومن ثم شكلت مادة خصبة للأخلاق؛ بوصفها حقلًا متعدد التخصصات، ويشمل الفعل والفاعل ومصادر التقويم الأخلاقي المختلفة، كما يشمل دوائر النشاط الإنساني المتعددة في علاقته بنفسه (أخلاق العناية بالذات) وبالآخرين (الأخلاق الاجتماعية) وبالله تعالى (الأخلاق الدينية). فمن جهة أخلاقيات الأفعال تتناول نوعي الأفعال: الاختياري وغير الاختياري (الخطأ والنسيان والإكراه)، وفيما يخص الأفعال الاختيارية التي هي ميدان التقويم الأخلاقي تزودنا بتقويمات عديدة للأفعال أمكن الحديث فيها عن تقسيمات عدة لأحكام

الأفعال تتصل بالحلال والحرام والمشتبه من جهة، وبالحياء والمعروف والمنكر من جهة أخرى، ثم هي تفصل في منظومة الحقوق الثلاثية: حقوق المكلف وحقوق العباد وحقوق الله تعالى، بل وتتناول بعض حقوق الحيوان أيضًا. وفيما يخص أخلاقيات الفاعل تنطوي الأحاديث على العديد من الفضائل مثل التقوى، والورع، والإخلاص، والعدل (ونقيضه الظلم)، والأخوة، وترك الأثرة ومحبة الخير للغير، وفضائل إكرام الجار وإكرام الضيف، وفضائل اللسان، والحِلم وترك الغضب، وتهذيب أهواء النفس، والإحسان، والحياء، والزهد، والاستقامة، وغيرها. ثم إنها تضمنت كذلك مفاهيم أخلاقية كلية عديدة شملت الحسنات والسيئات، والحلال والحرام والمشتبه، والبر والإثم، والخطأ والإكراه، والمعروف والمنكر، كما تطرقت إلى مصادر التقويم الأخلاقي التي تتمثل في الوحي، والعرف، والقلب أو الضمير.

## قائمة المصادر


ابن أبي زيد، أبو محمد عبد الله. 1986. **الرسالة الفقهية**، إعداد وتحقيق الهادي حمّو ومحمد أبو الأجفان. بيروت: دار الغرب الإسلامي.

ابن أبي شيبة، أبو بكر عبد الله. 2006. **المُصَنَّف**، تحقيق محمد عوامة. الرياض: دار القبلة.

ابن أبي يعلى، أبو الحسين. د.ت. **طبقات الحنابلة**، تحقيق محمد حامد الفقي. القاهرة: مطبعة السنة المحمدية.

ابن الأثير، ضياء الدين نصر الله. د.ت. **المثل السائر في أدب الكاتب والشاعر**، تحقيق أحمد الحوفي، وبدوي طبانة. القاهرة: دار نهضة مصر للطباعة والنشر والتوزيع.

ابن الأثير، مجد الدين أبو السعادات. 1969. **جامع الأصول في أحاديث الرسول**، تحقيق عبد القادر الأرنؤوط، دمشق: مكتبة الحلواني، مطبعة الملاح، مكتبة دار البيان.

ابن الأثير، مجد الدين أبو السعادات. 1979. **النهاية في غريب الحديث والأثر**، تحقيق طاهر أحمد الزاوى ومحمود محمد الطناحي. بيروت: المكتبة العلمية.

ابن الجعد، علي. 1996. **مسند ابن الجعد**، تحقيق عامر أحمد حيدر. بيروت: مؤسسة نادر.

ابن الجوزي، جمال الدين أبو الفرج. 1997أ. **تلقيح فهوم أهل الأثر في عيون التاريخ والسير**. بيروت: شركة دار الأرقم بن أبي الأرقم.

ابن الجوزي، جمال الدين أبو الفرج. 1997ب. **كشف المشكل من حديث الصحيحين**، تحقيق علي حسين البواب. الرياض: دار الوطن.

ابن الصلاح، أبو عمرو. 1984. **صيانة صحيح مسلم من الإخلال والغلط وحمايته من الإسقاط والسقط**، تحقيق موفق عبد الله عبد القادر. بيروت: دار الغرب الإسلامي.

ابن الصلاح، أبو عمرو. 1986. **علوم الحديث**. تحقيق نور الدين عتر. دمشق: دار الفكر.

ابن الصلاح، أبو عمرو. 1992. **طبقات الفقهاء الشافعية**، تحقيق محيي الدين علي نجيب. بيروت: دار البشائر الإسلامية.

ابن الصلاح، أبو عمرو. 2017. **وصل بلاغات الموطأ** (مطبوع ضمن «**خمس رسائل في علوم الحديث**»)، تحقيق عبد الفتاح أبو غدة. القاهرة: دار السلام.

ابن المبارك، عبد الله. د.ت. **الزهد والرقائق**، تحقيق حبيب الرحمن الأعظمي، بيروت: مؤسسة الرسالة.

ابن الملقن، سراج الدين أبو حفص. 1997. **الإعلام بفوائد عمدة الأحكام**، تحقيق عبد العزيز بن أحمد المشيقح. الرياض: دار العاصمة للنشر والتوزيع.

ابن الملقن، سراج الدين أبو حفص. 2004. **البدر المنير في تخريج الأحاديث والأثار الواقعة في الشرح الكبير**، تحقيق مصطفى أبو الغيط وعبد الله بن سليمان وياسر بن كمال. الرياض: دار الهجرة للنشر والتوزيع.

ابن الملقن، سراج الدين أبو حفص. 2008. **التوضيح لشرح الجامع الصحيح**، تحقيق دار الفلاح للبحث العلمي وتحقيق التراث. دمشق: دار النوادر.

ابن الملقن، سراج الدين أبو حفص. 2010. **قواعد ابن الملقن أو الأشباه والنظائر في قواعد الفقه**. تحقيق مصطفى محمود الأزهري. الرياض: دار ابن القيم، القاهرة: دار ابن عفان.

ابن الملقن، سراج الدين أبو حفص. 2012. **المعين على تفهم الأربعين**، تحقيق دغش بن شبيب العجمي. الكويت: مكتبة أهل الأثر للنشر والتوزيع.

ابن بلبان، علي أبو الحسن. 2004. **جزء فيه خمسة أحاديث عن الأئمة الخمسة**، تحقيق: رياض حسين الطائي. الرياض: دار المغني.

ابن تيمية، تقي الدين أبو العباس أحمد. 2004. **مجموع الفتاوى**، تحقيق عبد الرحمن بن محمد بن قاسم. المدينة: مجمع الملك فهد لطباعة المصحف الشريف.

ابن حبان، أبو حاتم محمد. 1988. **الإحسان في تقريب صحيح ابن حبان**. ترتيب الأمير علاء الدين علي بن بلبان الفارسي، تحقيق شعيب الأرناؤوط. بيروت: مؤسسة الرسالة.

ابن حجر الهيتمي، أحمد بن محمد. 2008. **الفتح المبين بشرح الأربعين**، تحقيق أحمد جاسم محمد المحمد وقصي محمد نورس الحلاق وأبو حمزة أنور بن أبي بكر الشيخي الدّاغستاني، جدة: دار المنهاج.

ابن حجرالعسقلاني، أحمد بن علي. د.ت. **فتح الباري شرح صحيح البخاري**، رقم كتبه وأبوابه وأحاديثه محمد فؤاد عبد الباقي. قام بإخراجه وصححه وأشرف على طبعه محب الدين الخطيب، عليه تعليقات عبد العزيز بن عبد الله بن باز. القاهرة: المكتبة السلفية.

ابن حجر العسقلاني، أبو الفضل أحمد بن علي. 2000. **نزهة النظر في توضيح نخبة الفكر في مصطلح أهل الأثر**، تحقيق نور الدين عتر. دمشق: مطبعة الصباح.

ابن دقيق العيد، تقي الدين أبو الفتح. 2003. **شرح الأربعين النووية في الأحاديث الصحيحة النبوية**. بيروت: مؤسسة الريان.

ابن دقيق العيد، تقي الدين أبو الفتح. 2009. **شرح الإلمام بأحاديث الأحكام**، حققه وعلق عليه وخرج أحاديثه: محمد خلوف العبد الله. سوريا: دار النوادر.

ابن رجب، زين الدين. 2001. **جامع العلوم والحكم في شرح خمسين حديثا من جوامع الكلم**، تحقيق شعيب الأرناؤوط، وإبراهيم باجس. بيروت: مؤسسة الرسالة.

ابن عبد البر، أبو عمر. 1981. **التمهيد لما في الموطأ من المعاني والأسانيد**، تحقيق مصطفى بن أحمد العلوي، ومحمد عبد الكبير البكري. المغرب: وزارة عموم الأوقاف والشؤون الإسلامية.

ابن كثير، أبو الفداء إسماعيل. **طبقات الفقهاء الشافعيين**، تحقيق أنور الباز. المنصورة: دار الوفاء.

ابن ماجه، محمد بن يزيد. 2009. **سنن ابن ماجه**، تحقيق شعيب الأرناؤوط وعادل مرشد ومحَّد كامل قره بللي وعَبد اللّطيف حرز الله. بيروت: دار الرسالة العالمية.

ابن مسلمة، رشيد الدين. 2002. **المشيخة البغدادية**، تخريج زكي الدين محمد بن يوسف البِرزالي، حققه وعلق عليه كامران سعد الله الدَّلَوي، أشرف عليه وراجعه بشار عواد معروف. بيروت: دار الغرب الإسلامي.

ابن مفلح، أبو إسحاق. 1990. **المقصد الأرشد في ذكر أصحاب الإمام أحمد**، تحقيق عبد الرحمن بن سليمان العثيمين. الرياض: مكتبة الرشد.

ابن ناجي التنوخي، قاسم بن عيسى. 2007. **شرح ابن ناجي التنوخي على متن الرسالة لابن أبي زيد القيرواني**، اعتنى به أحمد فريد المزيدي. بيروت: دار الكتب العلمية.

ابن نجيم، زين الدين. 1999. **الأشباه والنظائر على مذهب أبي حنيفة النعمان**، وضع حواشيه وخرج أحاديثه زكريا عميرات. بيروت: دار الكتب العلمية.

أبو داود، سليمان بن الأشعث. 1984. **رسالة أبي داود إلى أهل مكة وغيرهم في وصف سننه**، تحقيق محمد الصباغ. بيروت: المكتب الإسلامي.

أبو داود، سليمان بن الأشعث. 2009. **سنن أبي داود**، تحقيق شعَيب الأرناؤوط ومحمد كامِل قره بللي. بيروت: دار الرسالة العالمية.

أبو طاهر السلفي، صدر الدين. 1994. **مشيخة الشيخ الأجل أبي عبد الله محمد بن أحمد بن إبراهيم الرازي**، قرأه وعلق عليه الشريف حاتم بن عارف العوني. الرياض: دار الهجرة.

أبو طاهر السِلَفي، صدر الدين أحمد. 2003. **منتقى من السفينة البغدادية**، تحقيق أبي عبد الباري رضا بوشامة الجزائري. الرياض: دار ابن حزم.

أبو طاهر السِلَفي، صدر الدين. 2008. **شرط القراءة على الشيوخ** (مطبوع مع "فوائد حسان")، قرأهما وعلق عليهما وخرج أحاديثهما أبو عبيدة محمد بن فريد زريوح. الرياض: دار التوحيد للنشر.

أبو نعيم الحداد، عبيد الله بن الحسن. 2010. **جامع الصحيحين بحذف المعاد والطرق**، تحقيق لجنة من المحققين بإشراف نور الدين طالب. دمشق، بيروت: دار النوادر.

أبو يعلى، أحمد بن علي. 1984. **مسند أبي يعلى**، تحقيق حسين سليم أسد. دمشق: دار المأمون للتراث.

أحمد، بن حنبل. 2001. **مسند الإمام أحمد بن حنبل**، تحقيق شعيب الأرنؤوط وعادل مرشد وآخرين. بيروت: مؤسسة الرسالة.

البخاري، محمد بن إسماعيل. 1312 [1894]. **الجامع المسند الصحيح المختصر من أمور رسول الله صلى الله عليه وسلم وسننه وأيامه**، ضبط محمد زهير بن ناصر الناصر. بيروت: دار طوق النجاة (مصورة عن السلطانية بإضافة ترقيم ترقيم محمد فؤاد عبد الباقي).

البِرْماوي، شمس الدين. 2012. **اللامع الصبيح بشرح الجامع الصحيح**، تحقيق لجنة من المحققين بإشراف نور الدين طالب. دمشق: دار النوادر.

البزار، أبو بكر أحمد. 1988. **مسند البزار المنشور باسم البحر الزخار**، تحقيق محفوظ الرحمن زين الله وعادل بن سعد وصبري عبد الخالق الشافعي. المدينة: مكتبة العلوم والحكم.

البغوي، أبو محمد الحسين. 1983. **شرح السنة**، تحقيق شعيب الأرناؤوط، ومحمد زهير الشاويش. بيروت، دمشق: المكتب الإسلامي.

البيهقي، أبو بكر أحمد بن الحسين. 1970. **مناقب الشافعي**، تحقيق السيد أحمد صقر. القاهرة: مكتبة دار التراث.

البيهقي، أحمد بن الحسين. 1989. **السنن الصغير**، تحقيق عبد المعطي أمين قلعجي، كراتشي: جامعة الدراسات الإسلامية.

التجيبي، القاسم بن يوسف. 1981. **برنامج التجيبي**، تحقيق عبد الحفيظ منصور. طرابلس، تونس: الدار العربية للكتّاب.

الترمذي، محمد بن عيسى. 1996. **الجامع الكبير**، تحقيق بشار عواد معروف. بيروت: دار الغرب الإسلامي.

الجاحظ، أبو عثمان عمرو بن بحر. 1988. **البيان والتبيين**، تحقيق وشرح عبد السلام هارون. القاهرة: مكتبة الخانجي.

الحاكم، أبو عبد الله. 2001. **المدخل إلى معرفة كتاب الإكليل**. تحقيق معتز الخطيب. دمشق: دار الفيحاء.

الحميدي، محمد بن فتوح. 1995. **تفسير غريب ما في الصحيحين البخاري ومسلم**، تحقيق زبيدة محمد سعيد عبد العزيز. القاهرة: مكتبة السنة.

الخطابي، أبو سليمان حمْد. 1932. **معالم السنن (وهو شرح سنن الإمام أبي داود)**، طبعه وصححه محمد راغب الطباخ. حلب: المطبعة العلمية.

الخطابي، أبو سليمان حمد. 1982. **غريب الحديث**، تحقيق عبد الكريم إبراهيم الغرباوي، خرج أحاديثه عبد القيوم عبد رب النبي. دمشق: دار الفكر.

الخطابي، أبو سليمان حمد. 1988. **أعلام الحديث في شرح صحيح البخاري**، تحقيق محمد بن سعد بن عبد الرحمن آل سعود. مكة: جامعة أم القرى: مركز البحوث العلمية وإحياء التراث الإسلامي.

الخطيب، أبو بكر أحمد بن علي. 1983. **الجامع لأخلاق الراوي وآداب السامع**، تحقيق محمود الطحان. الرياض: مكتبة المعارف.

الخطيب، أبو بكر أحمد بن علي. 2001. **تاريخ بغداد**، تحقيق بشار عواد معروف. بيروت: دار الغرب الإسلامي.

دراز، محمد بن عبد الله. 1998. **دستور الأخلاق في القرآن**، ترجمة عبد الصبور شاهين. بيروت: مؤسسة الرسالة.

الديلمي، شيرويه بن شهردار. 1986. **الفردوس بمأثور الخطاب**، تحقيق السعيد بن بسيوني زغلول. بيروت: دار الكتب العلمية.

الذهبي، شمس الدين أبو عبد الله. 1983. **سير أعلام النبلاء**، تحقيق مجموعة من المحققين بإشراف الشيخ شعيب الأرناؤوط. بيروت: مؤسسة الرسالة.

الذهبي، شمس الدين أبو عبد الله. 2003. **تاريخ الإسلام وَوَفيات المشاهير وَالأعلام**، تحقيق بشار عوّاد معروف. بيروت: دار الغرب الإسلامي.

زروق، شهاب الدين أبو العباس. 2006. **شرح زروق على متن الرسالة لابن أبي زيد القيرواني**، اعتنى به أحمد فريد المزيدي. بيروت: دار الكتب العلمية.

السبكي، تاج الدين. 1991. **الأشباه والنظائر**، تحقيق عادل أحمد عبد الموجود، وعلي محمد معوض. بيروت: دار الكتب العلمية.

السعدي، عبد الرحمن بن ناصر. 2011. **بهجة قلوب الأبرار وقرة عيون الأخبار في شرح جوامع الأخبار**، تحقيق هشام برغش. الرياض: دار الوطن للنشر.

السمعاني، عبد الكريم أبو سعد. 1975. **التحبير في المعجم الكبير**، تحقيق منيرة ناجي سالم، بغداد: رئاسة ديوان الأوقاف.

السمعاني، عبد الكريم أبو سعد. 1996. **المنتخب من معجم شيوخ السمعاني**، تحقيق موفق بن عبد الله بن عبد القادر. الرياض: دار عالم الكتب.

السيوطي، جلال الدين. 1983. **الأشباه والنظائر**. بيروت: دار الكتب العلمية.

السيوطي، جلال الدين. د.ت. **البحر الذي زخر في شرح ألفية الأثر**، تحقيق أبي أنس أنيس بن أحمد بن طاهر الأندونوسي. الرياض: مكتبة الغرباء الأثرية.

الشامي، صالح. 2014. **الأحاديث النبوية الكلية التي عليها مدار أحكام الإسلام، ويليه أحاديث الأربعين النووية**. دمشق: دار القلم.

الطائي الهمذاني، أبو الفتوح محمد بن محمد. 1999. **كتاب الأربعين في إرشاد السائرين إلى منازل المتقين (الأربعين الطائية)**، تحقيق عبد الستار أبو غدة. بيروت: دار البشائر الإسلامية.

الطوفي، نجم الدين سليمان. 1998. **التعيين في شرح الأربعين**، تحقيق أحمد حَاج محمّد عثمان. بيروت: مؤسسة الريان، ومكة: المكتبة المكيّة.

الطيبي، شرف الدين الحسين بن عبد الله. 1997. **شرح الطيبي على مشكاة المصابيح (المسمى الكاشف عن حقائق السنن)**، تحقيق عبد الحميد هنداوي. مكة المكرمة، الرياض: مكتبة نزار مصطفى الباز.

عتر، نور الدين. 2013. **في ظلال الحديث النبوي ومعالم البيان النبوي**. القاهرة: دار السلام للطباعة والنشر والتوزيع والترجمة.

العراقي، أبو الفضل زين الدين عبد الرحيم. د.ت. **طرح التثريب في شرح التقريب**، أكمله ابنه أحمد بن عبد الرحيم. بيروت: تصوير دار إحياء التراث العربي.

العراقي، أبو الفضل زين الدين عبد الرحيم. 2005. **المغني عن حمل الأسفار في الأسفار في تخريج ما في الإحياء من الأخبار** (مطبوع بهامش إحياء علوم الدين). بيروت: دار ابن حزم.

العلائي، خليل بن كيكلدي. 2008. **كتاب الأربعين المغنية بعيون فنونها عن المعين**، تحقيق أبو عبيدة مشهور بن حسن آل سلمان. عمّان: الدار الأثرية.

العَلَوي الهَرَري، محمد الأمين بن عبد الله. 2009. **شرح صحيح مسلم المسمَّى الكوكب الوهَّاج والرَّوض البهَّاج في شرح صحيح مسلم بن الحجاج**، مراجعة لجنة من العلماء برئاسة هاشم محمد علي مهدي. الرياض: دار المنهاج، بيروت: دار طوق النجاة.

العيني، أبو محمد محمود بن أحمد. د.ت. **عمدة القاري شرح صحيح البخاري**. القاهرة: إدارة الطباعة المنيرية.

الفاكهاني، أبو حفص تاج الدين. 2007. **الفتح المبين في شرح الأربعين**، حققه وخرج أحاديثه شوكت بن رفقي بن شوكت. الرياض: دار الصميعي.

القاري، ملا علي. 2013. **أربعون حديثا من جوامع الكلم**، تحقيق السيد حسن الحسيني. بيروت: دار البشائر الإسلامية.

القرطبي، أبو العباس. 1996. **المفهم لما أشكل من تلخيص كتاب مسلم**، تحقيق محيي الدين ديب مستو وأحمد محمد السيد ويوسف علي بديوي ومحمود إبراهيم بزال. دمشق-بيروت: دار ابن كثير، دار الكلم الطيب.

القزويني، أبو يعلى الخليلي. 1989. **الإرشاد في معرفة علماء الحديث**، تحقيق محمد سعيد عمر إدريس. الرياض: مكتبة الرشد.

القضاعي، أبو عبد الله. 1985. **مسند الشهاب**، تحقيق حمدي بن عبد المجيد السلفي. بيروت: مؤسسة الرسالة.

كحالة، عمر رضا. د.ت. **معجم المؤلفين**. بيروت: دار إحياء التراث العربي، ومكتبة المثنى.

الكرماني، شمس الدين. 1981. **الكواكب الدراري في شرح صحيح البخاري**. بيروت: دار إحياء التراث العربي.

اللوغاني، ناصر بن خليفة. 2018. **الأربعون الكلية في التذييل على الأربعين النووية**. بيروت، إسطنبول: دار الغوثاني للدراسات القرآنية.

مالك، ابن أنس. 2004. **الموطأ**، تحقيق محمد مصطفى الأعظمي. أبو ظبي: مؤسسة زايد بن سلطان آل نهيان للأعمال الخيرية والإنسانية.

الماوردي، أبو الحسن. 1994. **الحاوي الكبير في فقه مذهب الإمام الشافعي رضي الله عنه وهو شرح مختصر المزني**، تحقيق علي محمد معوض وعادل أحمد عبد الموجود. بيروت: دار الكتب العلمية.

مسلم ابن الحجاج، أبو الحسن. 1991. **المسند الصحيح المختصر بنقل العدل عن العدل إلى رسول الله صلى الله عليه وسلم**، تحقيق محمد فؤاد عبد الباقي. القاهرة: دار إحياء الكتب العربية.

مسلم ابن الحجاج. **المسند الصحيح المختصر بنقل العدل عن العدل إلى رسول الله صلى الله عليه وسلم**، تحقيق محمد فؤاد عبد الباقي. بيروت: دار إحياء التراث العربي.

المقبل، عمر بن عبد الله. 2017. **جوامع الكلم النبوي**. الخبر: تكوين للدراسات والأبحاث.

المقدسي، نصر بن إبراهيم. 2012. **جزء فيه أربعة أحاديث مروية عن النبي صلى الله عليه وسلم**، تحقيق محمد زياد بن عمر التكلة. بيروت: دار البشائر الإسلامية.

المناوي، زين الدين عبد الرؤوف. 1972. **فيض القدير شرح الجامع الصغير**. بيروت: دار المعرفة.

المناوي، زين الدين عبد الرؤوف. 1988. **التيسير بشرح الجامع الصغير**. الرياض: مكتبة الإمام الشافعي.

النبراوي، عبد الله. د.ت. **حاشية النبراوي على الأربعين النووية في الأحاديث القدسية والنبوية**. د.ن.

النفراوي، أحمد بن غنيم. 1995. **الفواكه الدواني على رسالة ابن أبي زيد القيرواني**. بيروت: دار الفكر.

النووي، أبو زكريا محيي الدين. 1929. **صحيح مسلم بشرح النووي**. القاهرة: المطبعة المصرية بالأزهر.

النووي، أبو زكريا محيي الدين. 1990. **الأذكار النووية أو حلية الأبرار وشعار الأخيار في تلخيص الدعوات والأذكار المستحبة في الليل والنهار**، تحقيق محيي الدين مستو. دمشق، بيروت: دار ابن كثير.

النووي، أبو زكريا محيي الدين. 1998. **رياض الصالحين**، تحقيق شعيب الأرناؤوط. بيروت: مؤسسة الرسالة.

النووي، أبو زكريا محيي الدين. 2006. **بستان العارفين**، تحقيق محمد الحجار. بيروت: دار البشائر الإسلامية.

النووي، أبو زكريا محيي الدين. 2009. **الأربعون النووية**، عُنِيَ بِهِ قصي محمد نورس الحلاق، وأنور بن أبي بكر الشيخي. بيروت: دار المنهاج للنشر والتوزيع.

النووي، أبو زكريا محيي الدين. د.ت.(أ). **المجموع شرح المهذب (مع تكملة السبكي والمطيعي)**. القاهرة: إدارة الطباعة المنيرية.

النووي، أبو زكريا محيي الدين. د.ت.(ب). **تهذيب الأسماء واللغات**، عنيت بنشره وتصحيحه والتعليق عليه ومقابلة أصوله شركة العلماء بمساعدة إدارة الطباعة المنيرية. بيروت: دار الكتب العلمية.

الهروي، أبو إسماعيل عبد الله. 1998. **ذم الكلام وأهله**، تحقيق عبد الرحمن عبد العزيز الشبل. المدينة المنورة: مكتبة العلوم والحكم.

الهروي، أبو عبيد أحمد بن محمد. 1999. **كتاب الغريبين في القرآن والحديث**، تحقيق أحمد فريد المزيدي، قدم له وراجعه: فتحي حجازي. الرياض: مكتبة نزار مصطفى الباز.

الفصل 4

# الحافظ ابن أبي الدنيا والتأسيس لأخلاقيات المكارم

شفيق اكّريكّر

## 1 مقدمة*

يسعى هذا الفصل إلى استنباط المعاني الخلقية الكامنة في عمل ابن أبي الدنيا (ت. 281/894)، واستكشاف النظرية الأخلاقية الثاوية خلفها، من خلال قراءة تحليلية لرسالتيه: «**العقل وفضله**» و«**مكارم الأخلاق**».[1] وسيتضح من خلال هذه القراءة أن «أخلاقيات المكارم» – عند ابن أبي الدنيا – تستعمل الحديث لتبرهن على قضيتين متواشجتين: أولوية العقل بوصفه مصدرًا رئيسًا للهدى الأخلاقي، ومركزية مفهوم «مكارم الأخلاق». أما المثل الأعلى الذي ينشده الجهد الأخلاقي للإنسان – عنده – فهو التحقق بالمروءة، أي بما به يكون الإنسان إنسانًا على التحقيق.

عند الحديث عن مكارم الأخلاق، ينصرف الذهن مباشرة إلى الراغب الأصفهاني (ت. القرن الرابع/العاشر على الأرجح) الذي رفع «**مكارم الأخلاق**» مكانًا عليًا من خلال «**الذريعة إلى مكارم الشريعة**»، المصنف الذي قَرَن فيه مكارم الأخلاق بخلافة الإنسان لله تعالى، جاعلًا خلافة الله تعالى سِدرة منتهى منازل الوجود الإنساني بعد منزلتيْ عمارة الأرض وعبادة الله، وبهذا صارت الغايات التي وُجد لأجلها الإنسان ثلاثًا (الراغب الأصفهاني 2007، 59–60). ولكن ابن أبي الدنيا كان أسبقَ إلى العناية بمكارم الأخلاق والتنبيه عليها باعتبارها جماع الفضائل والمثل الأخلاقية التي ينبغي للمرء الاجتهاد في تحصيلها. وقد أمكن للراغب أن يطلع على الترجمات اليونانية في عصره وأن يقتبس منها بعض الأفكار والتصورات، فيُكيّفها مع التصور الإسلامي ضمن بنيان نظري رصّ لبناته بعناية. أما ابن أبي الدنيا فقد سلك مسلكًا أثريًّا محضًا اقتصر فيه على الرواية المسندة جمعًا وتبويبًا، من غير تدخل مباشر منه بالشرح أو التعليق. ولا

* لا يفوتني هنا أن أتقدم بالشكر الجزيل إلى كل من المحكَّمَين اللذين تفضلا بإبداء ملاحظاتهما، وإلى محرر الكتّاب الذي راجع هذا العمل، المرة تلو الأخرى، وتفضل بإبداء ملاحظات واقتراح تصويبات وإضافات. وقد أغنى ذلك كله البحث، ومكّنه من الاستواء على عوده.

[1] نُشرت الرسالتان ضمن مجموع رسائل ابن أبي الدنيا (ابن أبي الدنيا 2000، 252–432)، ونشرتا أيضًا مستقلتين (ابن أبي الدنيا 1365؛ وابن أبي الدنيا 1990أ). وقد كان لجيمس بيلمي فضل السبق في نشر رسالة «**مكارم الأخلاق**» سنة 1973 في فيسبادن بألمانيا، وأعيد نشرها في القاهرة (ابن أبي الدنيا 1990ب).

تستحق أخلاقيات ابن أبي الدنيا الدرس والتحليل بسبب هذه الأسبقية التاريخية فحسب؛ فقد انطوت – أيضًا – على معان أخلاقية لطيفة تجعلها معاصرةً لمسلمي اليوم، وملهمةً في تَدَبُّر المأزق الأخلاقي المعاصر، وهو مأزقٌ يسائل المسلمين الذين يعتقدون في أنفسهم أنهم خير أمة، وأنهم جزء من الإنسانية المعاصرة التي عليهم أن يصلوا معها إلى كلمة سواء.

أما ابن أبي الدنيا فهو عبد الله بن محمد، ولد في بغداد وكان قليل الرحلة، ولكنه أخذ العلم عن خلق كثير حتى إن الحافظ جمال الدين المزي (ت. 742/1342) جمع أسماء شيوخه على حروف المعجم. وقد اشتُهر ابن أبي الدنيا بالفصاحة والبلاغة، وكان واعظًا ومؤدِّبًا؛ فقد أدّب غير واحد من أولاد الخلفاء. قال عنه الحافظ شمس الدين الذهبي (ت. 748/1348): "تصانيفه كثيرة جدًّا، فيها مُخَبآت وعجائب" (الذهبي 1985، 13/399)، وقال المؤرخ ابن تغري بردي (ت. 874/1470): "الناس بعده عيالٌ عليه في الفنون التي جمعها" (ابن تغري بردي د.ت.، 3/86). وقد ساق له الذهبيّ أكثر من 160 رسالةً ورتبها على حروف المعجم، ولكن الناظر فيها يلحظ بوضوح مركزية الأخلاق فيها؛ رغم أنه صنف في فنون أخرى تتصل بالأخبار والتاريخ وغيرها. وقد جمع بعض المعاصرين رسائله في الأخلاق والرقائق وهي كثيرة. وهذا التصنيف المتنوع والغزير في مجال الأخلاق يدل على انشغاله به. وتدل هذه الغزارة على أنه من أوائل الذين فطنوا للأفق الأخلاقي للمدونة الحديثية، بل لعله لم ير فيها إلا هذا الجانب بالذات (ethical appeal)، حتى إن "معظم مؤلفاته لا تكاد تخرج عن المضمون الأخلاقي والرسالة التربوية" (إبراهيم 1990، 10).

وبالتأمل في جملة رسائله، نجد أنها تنقسم إلى قسمين: (1) قسم أداره على فضائل دينية[2] مثل التوكل والشكر والزهد والدعاء والولاية والبكاء، ويدخل في ذلك أيضًا الرسائل التي جمعها عبد الله سعداوي[3] تحت الكتب الآتية: «**كتاب التوحيد والتوكل**»، و«**كتاب أخبار الصالحين**»، و«**كتاب المذمومات**». (2) وقسم وَقَفَه على فضائل أخلاقية صرفة، ويشمل الرسائل المجموعة تحت عنوان «**كتاب العقل ومكارم الأخلاق**» الذي ينطوي على رسالتين: العقل وفضله ومكارم الأخلاق، بالإضافة إلى بقية الرسائل التي يتقاطع مضمونها مع رسالة «**مكارم الأخلاق**»، وتتناول: الحِلم، والقناعة والتعفف، وقضاء الحوائج، والأمر بالمعروف والنهي عن المنكر، وقِرى الضيف، واصطناع المعروف. وقد أحسن سعداوي عندما افتتح الكتاب برسالة «**العقل وفضله**»، ثم أتبعها برسالة «**مكارم الأخلاق**»، لأن العقل عند ابن أبي الدنيا هو المقدمة والذريعة

2 يشبه ذلك تمييز التقليد المسيحي بين فضائل لاهوتية هي الإيمان والمحبة والرجاء، وأخرى فلسفية هي الفطنة والاعتدال والشجاعة والعدالة (انظر مثلًا الهيبي 2010، 113).

3 ناشر الطبعة التي أحيل إليها في هذا الفصل.

إلى مكارم الأخلاق، كما سأبيّن، ولذا أفردت رسالتيْ «**العقل وفضله**» و«**مكارم الأخلاق**» بالاهتمام دون سائر الرسائل.

## 2 ابن أبي الدنيا والأخلاق الأثرية

نعني بالأخلاق الأثرية هنا "مجموعة التصانيف التي تُعنى بالتأكيد على الروايات الأخلاقية جمعًا وتبويبًا" (تقي إسلامي وآخرون 2012، 75). ولئن وقع الخلاف في مفهوم «الأثر»، فإنه – على المعنى الشائع – يشمل الأحاديث المرفوعة والموقوفة والمقطوعة (أقوال النبي والصحابة والتابعين)، وعلى هذا المعنى تجري مصنفات الأخلاق الأثرية، بل إن بعض مصنفات الأخلاق الأثرية قد يضيف إلى تلك الآثار أقوال المفسرين ونكت الحكماء والبلغاء، وإن كان ثمة هيمنة واضحة للحديث النبوي فيها. ولذلك وُفّق بعض الدارسين (تقي إسلامي وآخرون 2012) عندما سمّوها بهذا الاسم، وعدّوها مدرسة قائمة بذاتها إزاء ثلاث مدارس أخلاقية أخرى هي: الأخلاق العرفانية، والأخلاق الفلسفية، والأخلاق التوفيقية.

عُني دارسو الفكر الأخلاقي الإسلامي بتحليل المنظورات الأخلاقية التي استوت على عودها ولم ينشغلوا باستنباط ما كان مضمراً منها، فلم تستوقفهم مصنفات الأخلاق الأثرية بما فيها مصنفات ابن أبي الدنيا. ويعتقد هؤلاء الدارسون أن هذه المصنفات تقوم أصالة على سرد المرويات وتبويبها تحت تراجم معينة، وقلّما يكون للمحدّث، في حدود هذه المهمة «الروائية»، مقالة أو خطاب نظري خاص به. وفي أحسن الأحوال تختفي شجرة المحدثين خلف غابة الفقهاء كما هو الحال عند محمد عابد الجابري الذي رأى أن المحدّثين عملوا في صلة وثيقة بالفقهاء، الأمر الذي ترك أثره على رؤية المحدثين للآداب. فالفقه يعتبر "مكارم الأخلاق هي نفسها الآداب الشرعية التي تحدد كيفية أداء الفروض بمكملاتها والسنن بمتمماتها" (الجابري 2001، 536، 618). وظل هذا المنظور الفقهي – في نظر الجابري – شكليًّا فقيرًا في مضمونه الأخلاقي، ولم يغْتنِ إلا عند انتشار «آداب السلوك» عند المتصوفة. بيد أن لهذا التعميم استثناءات كما سنرى مع ابن أبي الدنيا الذي تخفّف نسبيًا من الخطاطة الفقهية وألّف في مكارم الأخلاق. وعلى خلاف الجابري، يفرد ماجد فخري في صُنافته (typology) الرباعية، بابا خاصا للأخلاق النصية (scriptural ethics)، التي مردها إلى النص قرآنًا وحديثا (Fakhry 1994, xi). وعند استكشافه لمتون الحديث، راح فخري يلتمس هذه الأخلاق النصية في الصحيحين فقط مهملا بذلك محدثين أقل شهرة، لكنهم جمعوا أحاديث تحت عناوين أخلاقية صريحة، وعلى رأسهم ابن أبي الدنيا. صحيح أن فخري أدرج اسم ابن أبي الدنيا مع الحسن البصري (ت. 110/728) ضمن

ما سماه النزعة النقلية في الأخلاق (ethical traditionalism)، إلا أنه قد خصص معظم كلامه - تقريبا - للحسن البصري (Fakhry 1994, 151–157).

حظيت أخلاقيات ابن أبي الدنيا بعناية أفضل في مقالة ليونارد لبراند (Librande 2005) الذي حلل «**كتاب اليقين**» لابن أبي الدنيا، وخلص إلى أن اليقين عنده هو الفضيلة الأولى للحياة الأخلاقية، وهي فضيلة أدرك ابن أبي الدنيا أن الإسلام يقترحها علاجًا للمخاوف والشكوك وضروب القلق التي تساور كل سالك لطريق التخلق (Librande 2005, 42). أما العنوانان العريضان اللذان يضع الكاتب أخلاقيات ابن أبي الدنيا تحتهما فهما الزهد والرقائق (Librande 2005, 8). ولا شك أن هذه الخلاصة صحيحة إلى حد بعيد، ولكن هل يسع هذان العنوانان رسالتيْ "فضل العقل" و"مكارم الأخلاق"؟ لا أعتقد ذلك، إذ ثمة عناوين أخلاقية أخرى، يمكن أن نضع تحتها جزءًا من التأليف الأخلاقي لهذا المحدِّث. وما من شك أن الذي منع الدارسين من استكشاف هذه العناوين الأخرى هو تلك الفكرة العامة التي كوّنوها عن الأخلاق عند المحدثين، من ذلك مثلًا أن مؤلفي كتاب «**المدارس الأخلاقية في الفكر الإسلامي**» (تقي إسلامي وآخرون 2012) استبعدوا إطلاق اسم «مدرسة» على أعمال بعض المحدثين وإن أفردوا أبوابًا خاصة للموضوعات الأخلاقية؛ فالمحدّثون، في نظرهم، كانوا بصدد تأليف كتبٍ في الحديث لا كتب في الأخلاق؛ ومن ثم لم يتوان المحدثون - في رأيهم - عن تدوين مرويات مكررة وأخرى متعارضة، من دون منهجية أو ترتيب مقبول، ثم إنهم خلطوا - بحسبهم - بين الأخلاق الإسلامية والآداب الإسلامية، واستبطنوا فكرة الأشاعرة التي تجعل الحسن والقبح مطابقًا لما جاء به النقل (أو الوحي) وتابعًا له (تقي إسلامي وآخرون 2012، 76–80). صحيح أن بعض هذه السمات ينطبق على ابن أبي الدنيا؛ ولكن ذلك لا يكفي للقول: إن عمله يندرج - فقط - تحت الآداب الإسلامية؛ إذ قدم أخلاقًا إسلامية، والتزم - في عرض مروياته - تبويبًا معقولًا، فلم يكن يصدر عن نظرة أشعرية للحسن والقبح (رغم أنه سابق على أبي الحسن الأشعري ت. 935/324)، بل عن نظرة أقرب إلى الاعتزال إذا ما حكمنا عليه انطلاقًا من حجم المرويات التي ساقها في مدح العقل والإشادة بمنزلته وأولويته الأخلاقية بل والأنطولوجية.

وفي هذا الإطار، امتازت دراسة جيمس بيلمي (Bellamy 1963, 106–119) عن الدراسات المذكورة أعلاه، بأنها كانت رائدة في إنصاف الفكر الأخلاقي الثاوي في مرويات ابن أبي الدنيا. وبما أن رسالة «**مكارم الأخلاق**» كانت لا تزال مخطوطة حينئذ، خصّص بيلمي نصف مقالته لترجمة مقتطفات منها (Bellamy 1963, 111–117)، وانصرف في بقيتها إلى التنبيه على أهمية هذه الرسالة وريادتها في مجال النثر العربي المخصص لمكارم الأخلاق (Bellamy 1963, 106–108)، كما وصف مضمون الرسالة، سواء لجهة بنيتها الكلية من حيث انطواؤها على مقدمة وأبواب

بعدد المكارم الواردة في حديث للسيدة عائشة، أم لجهة بنية كل باب منها من حيث ابتداؤه أولًا بالحديث النبوي ثم آثار التابعين مرتبة زمنيًّا، ثم الاقتباسات الشعرية، ثم الاستشهادات القرآنية. أما بالنسبة لفكر ابن أبي الدنيا، فقد لاحظ بيلمي - بحق - أن رسائله تدور على التقوى الشخصية التي لا يُعنى بها الفقهاء عادة (Bellamy 1963, 108, 118)، ولكن فاته أن يلحظ محورية مفهوم «مكارم الأخلاق» في الرسالة نفسها وصلته برسالته الأخرى في فضل العقل، وكان محمد زاهد الكوثري (ت. 1952م) قد نشر هذه الرسالة الأخيرة قبل نحو عقدين من ذلك (ابن أبي الدنيا 1365). ولئن كان بيلمي قد فطن لكون أخلاقيات ابن أبي الدنيا تضع الإسلام على خط الاستمرارية مع نمط الحياة العربية (Bellamy 1963, 118)، فإن هذه الأخلاقيات لا تُفهم، في نظره، إلا بما هي رد فعل على ضعف الدولة العباسية آنذاك، وبما هي تعبير عن ميول أموية وحنين إلى العصر الذهبي للسيادة العربية (Bellamy 1963, 119). ومن ثم فاته أن يرى فيها أمشاج مدرسة أثرية في الأخلاق تتقاطع مع الكثير من المؤلفات التي أدخلها الجابري تحت عنوان الموروث العربي الدائر على قيمة المروءة.

وهكذا نرى أن أخلاقيات ابن أبي الدنيا لم تنل ما تستحقه من عناية، فبقيت تعاني مما عانت منه الأخلاق الأثرية عامة من إهمال في الدراسات المسحية (studies survey)، فضلًا عن عدم ربطها بباقي الرسائل التي تركها هذا المصنِّف. والحال أن الربط بين رسالة «**مكارم الأخلاق**» ورسالة «**فضل العقل**» كاف لإبراز البعد النسقي لفكر ابن أبي الدنيا الأخلاقي وتفاصيل نظريته الثاوية خلف مروياته، والمتمحورة حول مفهوم «مكارم الأخلاق» بما هي فضائل عالية، وهو ما سأوضحه فيما يأتي.

## 3 أخلاقيات المكارم عند ابن أبي الدنيا

في هذا القسم سأقوم بتحليل مضامين رسالتي ابن أبي الدنيا، وسأخصص قسمًا لكل رسالة على حدة، بادئًا برسالة «**العقل وفضله**»، ثم أثني برسالة «**مكارم الأخلاق**» وكيف أسسها ابن أبي الدنيا على مركزية العقل.

### 3.1 العقل وفضله على الأخلاق

رسالة «**العقل وفضله**» هي رسالة في إثبات شرعية العقل حيث يلتمس ابن أبي الدنيا لهذه الشرعية أدلة من داخل النص القرآني والحديث والأثر. ولكن ابن أبي الدنيا وإن كان يختفي وراء الروايات المسندة والأخبار التي ينقلها، فإن قارئه يمكن أن يستنبط من هذه المرويات خصائص ومائية العقل وموقعه المركزي بوصفه أول الموجودات وقوام الدين لدى ابن أبي الدنيا.

تبدأ رسالة «**العقل وفضله**» بحديث ابن عباس (ابن أبي الدنيا 2000، 255، ح1)[4] قال: "قال رسول الله صلى الله عليه وسلم: أنا الشاهد على الله لا يعثر عاقل إلا رفعه الله، ثم لا يعثر إلا رفعه، حتى يجعل مصيره إلى الجنة."[5] أي أن العاقل لا يزال مشمولًا بالمدد والتسديد الإلهيين حتى يدخل الجنة. وفي موضع آخر (ابن أبي الدنيا 2000، 256، ح4) يروي ما يفيد أن العقل والمروءة شيءٌ واحد: "كرم المرء دينه، ومروءته عقله، وحسبه خلقه."[6] ويرد المعنى نفسه عن عمر بن الخطاب (ت. 644/23) من قوله، ولفظه: "حسَب المرء دينه، وأصله عقله، ومروءته خلقه" (ابن أبي الدنيا 2000، 256، ح5). ويبدو أن ابن حبان البستي (ت. 965/354) قد تابعه على هذا المعنى؛ إذ أسند في باب «ذكر الحث على إقامة المروءات» حديث «ومروءته عقله»، وأوضح المعنى بقوله: "صرح النبي صلى الله عليه وسلم في هذا الحديث بأن المروءة هي العقل" (ابن حبان 1977، 229). وهي جميعها أخبارٌ تلح على ثلاثة أمور هي: الدين، والعقل، والمروءة. والمروءة تارة عقلٌ، وأخرى خُلقٌ.

ومما يؤكد فضل العقل - عند ابن أبي الدنيا - تلك الإحالات القرآنية له، وهي قد تأتي صريحة وقد تأتي مؤوَّلة. وفي الحالة الثانية يستعين ابن أبي الدنيا بأقوال بعض المفسرين لإثبات أن المراد بها العقل. فمن الألفاظ الصريحة ما جاء في تفسير ﴿هَلْ فِي ذَٰلِكَ قَسَمٌ لِّذِي حِجْرٍ﴾ (الفجر: 5)، إذ يروي ابن أبي الدنيا عن ابن عباس أن «الحِجر» هو النُّهى والعقل (ابن أبي الدنيا 2000، 260، ح27)، ومن الألفاظ المؤولة التي تحيل إلى العقل ما رواه عن التابعي مجاهد بن جَبْر (ت. 722/104) في تفسير ﴿أُوْلِي ٱلْأَيْدِي وَٱلْأَبْصَٰرِ﴾ (ص: 45) من أن "الأيدي هي القوة، والأبصار هي العقل" (ابن أبي الدنيا 2000، 256، ح7)، وما نقله في تفسير ﴿أَطِيعُوا اللَّهَ

4 من الآن فصاعدًا سأذكر رقم الصفحة متبوعا برقم الحديث الذي أرمز له بحرف الحاء، نظرًا لأنني سأحيل إلى أحاديث بعينها على مدار الفصل لصلة ذلك بالمضمون الذي سأقوم بتحليله.

5 الطبراني (1995، 160/6)، وقال الحافظ نور الدين الهيثمي (1994، 282/6): "رواه الطبراني في الصغير والأوسط وإسناده حسن،" وضعفه ناصر الدين الألباني (1408، 188).

6 روى الحديث محدثون تقدموا ابن أبي الدنيا وآخرون جاؤوا بعده. رواه مثلًا: ابن الجعد (1990، 435)، وأحمد بن حنبل (2001، 381/14)؛ والطبراني (1989، 28): باب فضل الرفق والحلم والأناة؛ والقضاعي (1986، 143/1)؛ والحاكم النيسابوري (1990، 212/1): **كتاب العلم، فصل في توقير العالم**، ولكن بلفظ: "كرم المؤمن" بدل "كرم المرء"؛ وابن حبان (1988، 233/2): باب حسن الخلق، **ذكر البيان بأن من أحب العباد إلى الله وأقربهم من النبي صلى الله عليه وسلم في القيامة من كان أحسن خلقًا**؛ والبيهقي (2003، 365/6). وقد قال الحاكم: "صحيح على شرط مسلم ولم يخرجاه وله شاهد،" فعقب عليه الذهبي بأن مسلمًا بن خالد الزنجي - أحد رواة الحديث - ضعيف، وما خرج له مسلم بن الحجاج، ولكن قال: "له شاهد."

وَأَطِيعُوا الرَّسُولَ وَأُولِي الْأَمْرِ مِنكُمْ﴾ (النساء: 59) من أن «أولي الأمر» هم أولو العقل والفقه في دين الله (ابن أبي الدنيا 2000، 270، ح78)، وما نقله عن سعيد بن المسيَّب (ت. حوالي 712/93) في تفسير ﴿وَأَشْهِدُواْ ذَوَىْ عَدْلٍ مِّنكُمْ﴾ (الطلاق: 2) من أن «العدل» يعني العقل، وما نقله عن الضحاك بن مزاحم (ت. 102–720/106–724) في تفسير ﴿لِيُنذِرَ مَنْ كَانَ حَيًّا﴾ (يس: 7) من أن «الحي» هو العاقل (ابن أبي الدنيا 2000، 262، ح33).

فإذا كان «الحِجر» أو النُّهى أو العقل بمعنى واحد أو متقارب، فإن في تأويل أولي الأبصار والأمرِ والعدلِ والحياة بأصحاب العقل حرصا واضحا على إنزال العقل منزلة الأساس لكل شيء، وبهذا يصير العقل مبدأً ميتافيزيقيًّا للموجودات العقلية منها والمحسوسة. ثم يُسند ابن أبي الدنيا إلى الحسن البصري قوله في ﴿فَاتَّقُوا اللَّهَ يَا أُولِي الْأَلْبَابِ﴾ (الطلاق: 10): "إنما عاتبهم لأنه يحبهم" (ابن أبي الدنيا 2000، 269، ح68)، فكأنه يريد بذلك الإيحاء بأن العقل الذي هو مناط التسديد الإلهي هو أيضًا مناط المحبة الإلهية والعتاب.

وفيما يخص مائية العقل، فإن ابن أبي الدنيا يختلف عن الحارث المحاسبي (ت. 857/243) الذي استهل كتاب «**مائية العقل ومعناه**» بتعريفات صريحة له (المحاسبي 1971، 201)، في حين أننا لا نقف عند ابن أبي الدنيا على تعريفٍ محدد للعقل، وإن كان يمكن استنباط عناصره من جملة المرويات التي يسندها، وهي عناصر لها صلة بالفلسفة تستحق أن تُفرَد ببحث مستقل. من ذلك هذا التعريف الجنيني الذي ساقه على لسان أحد الحكماء الذي قال: "العقل أمران: أحدهما: صحة الفكر في الذكاء والفِطنة، والآخر: حسن التمييز وكثرة الإصابة" (ابن أبي الدنيا 2000، 272، ح91)، وهو تعريف يذكرنا بقول ديكارت: "إن قوة الإصابة في الحكم، وتمييز الحق من الباطل – وهي التي تسمى في الحقيقة بالعقل أو النطق – تتساوى بين كل الناس بالفطرة" (ديكارت 1968، 110). ويعزو ابن أبي الدنيا إلى معاوية بن أبي سفيان (ت. 680/60) التمييز بين العقل الفطري والعقل المكتسب في قوله: "العقل عقلان: عقل تجارب وعقل نحيزة" أي فطرة (ابن أبي الدنيا 2000، 263، ح37)، ويثنّيه مباشرة بخبر عن عبيد الله بن سعد بن إبراهيم القرشي (ت. 873/260) قال سمعت أبي يحدث عن أبيه قال: سئل بعض العرب عن العقل فقال: "لبٌّ أعنتَه بتجريب." وثمة مرويات أخرى عن العقل لا تخفى إيحاءاتها السقراطية، إما لجهة امتداح السؤال كما نجد فيما نقله عن محمد بن سيرين (ت. 729/110) من قوله: "كانوا يرْون حسن السؤال يزيد في عقل الرجل" (ابن أبي الدنيا 2000، 269، ح70)؛ أو لجهة الجهل الواعي (*docta ignorantia*) كما نجد في ما يرويه عن مولى لبني هاشم عن بعض الحكماء أنه قال: "من ظن أنه عاقل والناس حمقى، كمُل جهله،" أو قوله: "قيل لبعض الحكماء: من الأديب العاقل؟ قال: الفطِن المتغافل" (ابن أبي الدنيا 2000، 269، ح74)، ومثله ما نقله عن الخليل

بن أحمد (ت. 786/170) بشأن الأصناف الأربعة من الناس، وأن أسوأهم من لا يَعرف ولا يَعرف أنه لا يعرف (ابن أبي الدنيا 2000، 271، ح83).

يمكن لنا أيضًا أن نستنبط من مرويات ابن أبي الدنيا تصورًا معيّنًا لعلاقة العقل بباقي ملكات الإنسان من قلب وجسد وكلام، فالعقل يبدو كما لو كان المبدأ الفعال المنتج المجدد لما يحويه القلب، وذلك من خلال ما يرويه عن عليّ بن عبيدة:[7] "القلوب أوعية والعقول معادن، فما في الوعاء يَنفد إذا لم تُمده المعادن" (ابن أبي الدنيا 2000، 269، ح72). ويعضده ما نقله من قول علي بن أبي طالب (ت. 661/40): "إن هذه القلوب تملّ كما تملّ الأبدان، فالتمسوا لها الحكمة طرفًا" (ابن أبي الدنيا 2000، 273، ح98)،[8] وأن "طول النظر في الحكمة تلقيح للعقل" (ابن أبي الدنيا 2000، 265، ح46). ثم نقل عن عبد الله بن خَبيق الأنطاكي (ت. ق. 624/3) – وكان أحد الزهاد في الكوفة – أنه كان يقال: "العقل سراج ما بطن، وملاك ما عَلن، وسائس الجسد، وزينة كل أحد، فلا تصلح الحياة إلا به، ولا تدور الأمور إلا عليه" (ابن أبي الدنيا 2000، 269، ح73)، ويكاد هذا يشبه المعنى الأفلاطوني للنفس العاقلة السائسة. أما ميزان العلاقة بين النطقيْن، أي العقل والكلام، فيوضحه الخليفة الأموي سليمان بن عبد الملك (ت. 717/99)؛ إذ أُعجب بكلام رجل، فلما اختبره ألفاهُ مضعوف العقل، فقال: "زيادة منطق على عقل خدعة، وزيادة عقل على منطق هُجنة، ولكن أحسن ذلك ما زَين بعضُه بعضًا" (ابن أبي الدنيا 2000، 268، ح62).

وللعقل عند ابن أبي الدنيا مضمون أخلاقي واضح، أي أنه عقل عملي أو موجه نحو العمل، ولهذا نجد لديه تلك الثنائية التي هيمنت على الفكر الأخلاقي في الإسلام بتأثير من الفلسفة اليونانية، وهي ثنائية العقل والهوى؛ فقد نقل عن أحد الحكماء: "ليس من أحد إلا ومعه قاضيان باطنان: أحدهما ناصح والآخر غاشّ. فأما الناصح فالعقل، وأما الغاش فالهوى، وهما ضدان فأيّهما مِلت معه وَهِيَ الآخرُ" (ابن أبي الدنيا 2000، 272، ح93).[9] ويتضح المضمون الأخلاقي في

---

7 قال ياقوت الحموي: "علي بن عبيدة الريحاني: أحد البلغاء الفصحاء. من الناس من يفضله على الجاحظ في البلاغة وحسن التصنيف ... وكان له اختصاص بالمأمون (ت. 833/218) ويسلك في تأليفاته وتصنيفاته طريقة الحكمة وكان يرمى بالزندقة" (الحموي 1993، 1814/4)، ولم أجد ذكرًا لتاريخ وفاته في كتب التراجم.

8 استشهد الماوردي بهذا الأثر ليسوغ اشتمال كتابه على أمثال الحكماء وآداب البلغاء وأقوال الشعراء إلى جانب آي القرآن وأحاديث السنة (الماوردي 1985، 5–6).

9 لا يُستبعد أن يكون صاحب هذا القول فيلسوفًا لم يشأ ابن أبي الدنيا أن يدعوه بهذه الصفة، وذلك لأن ثنائية العقل الناصح الأمين والهوى الناصح الغشاش من الموضوعات المفضلة عند الفلاسفة المسلمين

ما ينقله عن عبد الملك بن جريج (ت. 768/150) في أقسام العقل الثلاثة وهي: "حسن المعرفة بالله، وحسن الطاعة، وحسن الصبر على أمره" (87: 272)، ومثله أيضًا رد العقل إلى القيمة العربية العريقة وهي الحِلم، وذلك عندما ينقل كلامًا لورد بن محمد نَصْرَوَيه (ت. ؟) يفيد بأن العقل هو غلبة الحلم على الجهل والهوى (ابن أبي الدنيا 2000، 263، ح39)، ويعضده لاحقًا كلام منسوب إلى أكثم بن صيفي (ت. 631/9)، رمز الحكمة العربية، وهو قوله: "دعامة العقل الحِلم" (ابن أبي الدنيا 2000، 266، ح51).

ونقل ابن أبي الدنيا عن وهب بن مُنَبِّه (ت. 732/114) كلامًا يكاد يتحول معه المؤمن إلى حكيم رواقي طرح عن نفسه الأهواء والانفعالات فاستعاد السكينة والحرية الداخلية؛ أو إلى فيلسوف أفلوطيني يتأمل الحقائق الخالدة والموجودات الأزلية. يقول وهب: "المؤمن مفكر مذكّر، فمن ذَكَر تَفكر فَعَلَتْه السكينة وقنع فلم يهتم، ورفض الشهوات فصار حرًا، وألقى الحسد فظهرت له المحبة، وزهد في كل فانٍ فاستكمل العقل، ورغب في كل شيء باق فَعَقل المعرفة" (ابن أبي الدنيا 2000، 273–274، ح101). ولا يبدو أن هذا يختلف في شيء عما نجده عند الفيلسوف أبي يوسف الكندي (ت. 870/256) والفيلسوف والطبيب ابن زكريا الرازي (ت. 925/313) عن استعمال العقل لطرد الهم والجزع وجلب السكينة، والزهد فيما يصيبه، والانصراف إلى تعقل ما هو خالد من الموجودات والحقائق.

ويكاد العاقل عند ابن أبي الدنيا يصير ذلك المؤمن العابر لحدود المِلل والعصور؛ فهو ينقل عن وهب بن منبه أنه قرأ في حكمة آل داود أن للعاقل أربع ساعات: مناجاة ربه، ومحاسبة نفسه، وخلوة إلى صديق يبصّره بعيوب نفسه،[10] وساعة لنفسه في لذة الحلال (ابن أبي الدنيا 2000، 261–262، ح31). وبهذا يكون العقل هنا هو الباعث على كل مناشط الإنسان، سواء تعلقت بربه أم بنفسه أو بصديقه أو بجسمه؛ بل ينقل عن قَتادة بن دِعامة السَّدوسي (ت. 736/118) كلامًا للقمان الحكيم ناصحًا ابنه بما يفيد أن "العقل غاية السؤدد والشرف في الدنيا والآخرة" (ابن أبي الدنيا 2000، 262، ح35). وعن أيوب بن القِرِّيَّة (ت. 703/84) أحد الفصحاء والبلغاء في الدولة الأموية، أن الرجال ثلاثة أصناف: "عاقل وأحمق وفاجر" (ابن أبي الدنيا 2000، 262، ح32). وبموجب هذه القسمة يغدو العاقل مرادفًا للمؤمن الكامل، متحلّيًا بالعقل الذي ينقص الأحمق، وبالتقوى التي تُعوز الفاجر. لا عجب والحالة هذه إن كان من علامات فساد الزمان

(انظر الرازي 1939، 89؛ والراغب الأصفهاني 2007، 93)، ويبدو أن الراغب هنا ينقل عن الرازي دون أن يسميه.

10 "الصديق المبصّر بالعيوب" من الموضوعات الفلسفية المشهورة التي بدأها أرسطو، وصادفت هوى في نفوس الفلاسفة المسلمين (انظر مثلا الرازي 1939، 32–35).

(أو أشراط الساعة إن جاز القول) رفع العقل وفشو التحامق (ابن أبي الدنيا 2000، 266، ح52–56).

والعقل أيضًا هو الفاروق الذي يُعرض عليه دين المرء، فإن صح من المتدين العقلُ صحت منه العبادات، وإلا فهي مردودة عليه. هذا ما يُستنتج من خمسة آثار (ابن أبي الدنيا 2000، 257، ح8–12) تجعل إسلام المرء ونواله الزلفى من الله، وإتيانه الخير وما يحصّله من الثواب على أعمال العبادة والورع والقراءة: متوقفًا على رجحان عقله. وينقل عن وكيع بن الجراح (ت. 196–811/197–812) أن "العاقل من عقل عن الله أمره،" ومفهوم «العقل عن الله» هو الذي أدار عليه الحارث المحاسبي أخلاقياته،[11] وعند وكيع أن الحمق أفدح من الفجور (ابن أبي الدنيا 2000، 266، ح50). ونقل ابن أبي الدنيا عن الضحاك بن مُزاحم أن تمام صلاح الرجل الصالح متوقف على ثلاثة شروط: أولها العقل ثم نعمة الإسلام ثم وجه تحصيله لمعاشه (ابن أبي الدنيا 2000، 264، ح44). وفي رسالة «**مكارم الأخلاق**» – وسيأتي الكلام عليها – يحرص ابن أبي الدنيا على رواية صيغة أخرى لحديث "الحياء شعبة من شعب الإيمان" تتضمن طرفًا في مدح العقل وهي: "الحياء شعبة من شعب الإيمان، ولا إيمان لمن لا حياء له، وإنما يُدرَك الخير كله بالعقل، ولا دين لمن لا عقل له" (ابن أبي الدنيا 2000، 304، ح111)[12] بل ينقل عن ابن جريج ما يفيد أكثر من ذلك، إذ يغدو العقل قوام الإنسان والدين معا: "قوام المرء عقله، ولا دين لمن لا عقل له" (ابن أبي الدنيا 2000، 272، ح89).

إن العقل عند ابن أبي الدنيا ليس مجرد ملكة أو فعل قائم في ذات إنسانية، بل هو مخلوق من مخلوقات الله ومخاطَب بالأمر الإلهي، وفي هذا المعنى، يروي حديثًا مرفوعًا نصه: "لما خلق الله تعالى العقل، قال له: قم، فقام، ثم قال له: أدبر، فأدبر، ثم قال له: أقبل، فأقبل، ثم قال له: اقعد، فقعد، فقال: ما خلقت خلقًا خيرًا منك ولا أكرم منك ولا أفضل منك ولا أحسن

---

11 حول مواضع ورود هذه العبارة في كتب المحاسبي ومعانيها، انظر مقدمة القوتلي (1971، 66، 144–146).

12 والصيغة المشهورة للحديث: "الْإِيمَانُ بِضْعٌ وَسِتُّونَ شُعْبَةً، وَالْحَيَاءُ شُعْبَةٌ مِنَ الْإِيمَانِ،" رواها البخاري (2002، 1/13–14): **كتاب الإيمان، باب أمور الإيمان**؛ وبنحوه رواه مسلم (1952، 1/63): **كتاب الإيمان، باب شعب الإيمان**. والجزء المتعلق بالعقل جاء في حديث مستقل مرفوع بلفظ: "قوام المرء عقله ولا دين لمن لا عقل له." رواه الحارث – وهو معاصر لابن أبي الدنيا – (الهيثمي 1992، 2/803)؛ والبيهقي (2003، 6/355)، ومن اللافت أن ابن أبي الدنيا نفسه روى هذا اللفظ الأخير من قول عبد الملك بن جريج.

منك. بك آخذ وبك أعطي وبك أعزّ، وإياك أعاتب. بك الثواب وعليك العقاب" (ابن أبي الدنيا 2000، 258، ح15).[13]

من المهم أن نلاحظ هنا ذلك التطابق التام بين العقل والإرادة الإلهية (قم فقام ...)، بما يجعل العاقل مطيعًا لله بحكم طبيعة العقل وخلْقه، وأن العقل اشتمل على منتهى الخير والكرم والفضل والحسن بين المخلوقات، وأنه أخيرًا أساس الثواب والعقاب، وهي الفكرة التي شغلت المتكلمين بصدد مصدر التحسين والتقبيح ومبدأ استحقاق الثواب أو العقاب. وتتضح هذه الفكرة في حديثين آخرين (ابن أبي الدنيا 2000، 261، ح28–29) يحضر فيهما العقل متزامنًا هذه المرة مع خلق الإنسان لا مع خلق الأكوان، ويظهر منهما أن آدم قد خُيّر في مبتدأ حياته الأرضية بين العقل والدين وحسن الخلق (أو العلم كما في الحديث الثاني) فاختار العقل. ولكنه في النهاية يحصل على الجميع؛ لأن الدين وحسن الخلق لا ينفكّان عن العقل، ويكونان معه حيث يكون. ومن الطريف أن يكون آدم متمتعًا بحرية الاختيار وقادرًا على التمييز قبل الحصول على أداة الاختيار وآلة التمييز وهي العقل!

هكذا تتضح أولوية العقل – عند ابن أبي الدنيا – من الناحية المعرفية والأخلاقية والوجودية، بل إنه – وهو المحدِّث – لا يتردد في أن يروي عن الحَسن البصري ما يجعل الدراية فوق الرواية: "من لم يكن له عقل يسوسه لم ينتفع بكثرة روايات الرجال" (ابن أبي الدنيا 2000، 270، ح76). ومن المرجح أن إمعان ابن أبي الدنيا في مدح العقل وفي الاحتجاج لفضله بالمرويات كان على قدر إمعان بعض معاصريه في معاداة العقل، أو على الأقل ازدرائه والزراية بمادحيه. هذا على الأقل ما يُستشف من هذه الرواية الطريفة عن منصور بن المعتمر (ت. 132/750) الذي كان يختم مجالسه بالدعاء بالتقوى والجنة، وهذا مما يدعو به كل مسلم؛ ولكنه كان يضيف: "وخُلقًا نعيش به بين الناس، وعقلًا تنفعنا به،" فإذا قال هذا، كان محمد بن أبي إسماعيل (ت. 142/759)[14] إذا ذكر العقل يأخذه منه الضحك، فسأله منصور: "لأي شيء تضحك؟ إن الرجل يكون عنده ويكون عنده، ولا يكون عنده عقل فلا يكون له شيء" (ابن أبي الدنيا 2000، 271، ح84).

13 والحديث رواه الطبراني (1995، 190/7)؛ والبيهقي (2003، 349/6) وحكاه الحكيم الترمذي (2010، 442/4) بصيغة التمريض من دون إسناد فقال: "روي في الخبر عن رسول الله صلى الله عليه وسلم." وقال الهيثمي (1994، 28/8): "رواه الطبراني في الكبير والأوسط وفيه عمر بن أبي صالح. قال الذهبي: لا يُعرف."

14 في المطبوع من رسالة «العقل»: "حسين الجعفي عن زائدة عن أبي إسماعيل مؤذن البراجم،" ولكن في «شعب الإيمان» للبيهقي (2003، 170/4): "حسين الجعفي عن محمد بن أبي إسماعيل."

على هذا النحو، تبدو رسالة «**العقل وفضله**» بيانًا من أجل العقل عامة ومن أجل إمامته في الأخلاق خاصة. لم يدّخر له ابن أبي الدنيا حجةً مما بلغه من مرويات وآثار، ويفعل ذلك بحماس وإخلاص إلى درجة يصح معها اعتبار الرسالة بمثابة النسخة الحديثية الباكرة من أدبيات مدح العقل التي سنجدها لاحقًا ضمن فصول مكرسة لـ "فضل العقل وذم الهوى" في مُفتَتح كتب ألّفها محدّثون وفقهاء مثل ابن حبان (1977، 16–25)، أو متفلسفة مثل ابن زكريا الرازي (1939، 17–19) أو أصحاب فنون مثل الماوردي (ت. 450/1058) (1985، 6–33) والراغب الأصفهاني (2007، 133–134) وابن الجوزي (ت. 597/1201) (1986، 7–10).

## 3.2 مكارم الأخلاق

بحسب ترتيب ناشر الطبعة التي اعتمدتها هنا، تأتي رسالة «**مكارم الأخلاق**» بعد رسالة «**العقل وفضله**»، وهي كذلك فعلًا في النظام العام لفكر ابن أبي الدنيا الأخلاقي. وتتكون الرسالة من 486 مادة بين حديث وأثر وخبر وحكمة وشعر. وهي تأليف فريد، لا لجهة مضمونها الذي سنعرضه بعد قليل، بل لجهة الترتيب المنطقي لهذا المضمون. ويمكن تقسيم الرسالة إلى مقدمة ومحورين يقطع اتصالهما استطراد ذو علاقة بالمقدمة. وتنتظم المواد وفق الترتيب الآتي:

- **مقدمة في المكارم**، وتشمل المرويات (1–36)، في التقوى والمكارم والحِلم وبقاء الذكر الحسن.
- **واسطة عقد الرسالة**، وهي عبارة عن ثلاث روايات (34–36)، عن السيدة عائشة بنت أبي بكر الصديق (ت. 58/678) تعدد فيها عشر مكارم.
- **واستطراد** ويشمل المرويات (37–72).
- ثم **تفصيل القول في مكارم** الأخلاق العشرة المستقاة من حديث السيدة عائشة، وهي المرويات (73–486).

وسأناقش هذه المحاور على هذا الترتيب فيما يأتي.

### 3.2.1 مقدمة في الكرم والمكارم

تدور الفكرة المركزية للمقدمة (والاستطراد كذلك) على الوصل بين المكارم والكرم، ويشكلان معًا عند ابن أبي الدنيا الفضيلة المطلقة الجامعة لكل خير؛ فالمكارم كالكرم ليست أفعالًا معزولة، بل هيئة راسخة في النفس. وإذا كانت هذه المعاني تبدو ألصق بالموروث العربي، فإن الكرم يستمد أيضًا صفة الفضيلة العالية من كونه صفة إلهية وعمود الدين أيضًا. وبذلك تخضع مكارم الأخلاق – عند ابن أبي الدنيا – لعملية تأويل معقدة يمتزج فيها الأخلاقي بالديني.

يبدأ ابن أبي الدنيا رسالة «**المكارم**» بنفس ما بدأ به رسالة «**العقل**»؛ أي بالحديث المرفوع المذكور سابقًا وهو "كرم المرء دينه، ومروءته عقله، وحسبه خلقه" (ابن أبي الدنيا 2000، 277،

ح1)، ويثنّي بحديث مرفوع في التقوى (ابن أبي الدنيا 2000، 272، ح2) ونصه: "قيل يا رسول الله من أكرم الناس؟ قال: أتقاهم."[15] ويَعقبه حديثان (ابن أبي الدنيا 2000، 278، ح4–5) يطابقان أيضًا بين التقوى والكرم. ويتصل مفهوم «الكرم» – عند ابن أبي الدنيا – بمفهوم «المكارم» لفظًا ومعنىً، فالكرم من معانيه الجود، ولكنه عند ابن أبي الدنيا يعني أيضًا الفضيلة المطلقة التي تسمو بجِبِلّة الإنسان فتقلبها إلى جوهر كريم شريف كالأحجار الكريمة، وتُظل بظلها كل الفضائل الجزئية أو الأفعال المخصوصة. وهذه السعة الدلالية لمفهوم «الكرم» (أو المكارم) – عند ابن أبي الدنيا – يعبر عنها الراغب الأصفهاني بقوله: "وأما الكرم فاسم لجميع الأخلاق والأفعال المحمودة إن ظهرت بالفعل" (الأصفهاني 2007، 117)، ويوضحها ابن منظور (ت. 1311/711) فيما بعد حين يُفيد أن الكريم "الجامع لأنواع الخير والشرف والفضائل،" وأنه "اسم جامع لكل ما يُحمَد،" والكرم – وإن كان أصله صفة للناس – فإنه يُستعمل "في الخيل والإبل والشجر وغيرها من الجواهر إذا عَنَوا العتق." قال ابن الأعرابي (ت. 846/231): "كَرَم الفرَس: أن يَرِقّ جلده ويلين شعره وتطيب رائحته." قال يحي بن زياد الفراء (ت. 822/207): "العرب تجعل الكريم تابعًا لكل شيء نفت عنه فعلًا تنوي به الذم" (الفراء 1972، 127/3).

تحقق في مفهوم «الكرم» – إذن – صفة «الجامعية»، فهو اسم جامع لكل ما يُحمَد، مانع من كل ما يُذم في البشر والحيوان والجماد، والتكرمُ تنزيه النفس عما يشين. يروي ابن أبي الدنيا ما يفيد هذا المفهوم الواسع للكرم فيُسند إلى مالك بن دينار (ت. 127–745/130–748): "المؤمن كريم في كل حالة. لا يحب أن يؤذي جاره، ولا يفتقرَ أحد من أقربائه. قال: ثم يبكي مالك ويقول: وهو والله مع ذلك غني القلب لا يملك من الدنيا شيئًا. إن أزلته عن دينه لم يزُل، وإن خدعته عن ماله انخدع. لا يرى الدنيا من الآخرة عِوَضًا، ولا يرى البخل من الجود. تراه منكسر القلب. ذو هموم قد تفرد بها، مكتئب محزون ليس له في فرح الدنيا نصيب. إن أتاه منها شيء فرّقه، وإن زُوي عنه كل شيء فيها لم يطلبه. قال: ثم يبكي ويقول: هذا والله الكرم! هذا والله الكرم!" (ابن أبي الدنيا 2000، 292، ح63). ومن المؤكد أن ابن أبي الدنيا (على لسان مالك بن دينار) يتوسع في معنى «الكريم» ويحمّله فوق ما هو معهود من اللفظ؛ لأن من يتأمل هذا الكلام لا يملك إلا أن يرى فيه مثالًا من مُثل الأخلاق الرواقية التي امتدحها الكندي والرازي، كالثبات والجَلَد ونبذ الجزع وترك التعلق بالأشياء، مُضافًا إليها فضائل عربية إسلامية كأخلاق العناية (بالجار

15 رواه البخاري (2002، 864/6)، كتاب المناقب، باب قول الله تعالى: ﴿يَٰٓأَيُّهَا ٱلنَّاسُ إِنَّا خَلَقۡنَٰكُم مِّن ذَكَرٖ وَأُنثَىٰ﴾، وفي مواضع أخرى؛ ورواه مسلم (1952، 1846/4)، كتاب الفضائل، باب من فضائل يوسف عليه السلام.

والقريب)، وفضائل الجود والثبات على الدين وانكسار القلب، ومن اللافت أن هذه المعاني لا تسمى هنا زهدًا بل كرمًا.

ويبدو أن توظيف مفهوم «الكرم» قد أتاح لابن أبي الدنيا الوصول إلى أنه لما كان الكرم هيئة راسخة في النفس، كانت طاعة الله إكرامًا للنفس قبل أن تكون امتثالًا، ومعصيته إهانةً للنفس قبل أن تكون عصيانًا وجحودًا، وسيعبر لاحقًا عن هذا المعنى عند حديثه عن الحياء. ولتأكيد هذا المعنى، يُسند إلى يحيى بن أبي كثير (ت. 746/129) قوله: "كان يقال: ما أكرم العباد أنفسهم بمثل طاعة الله، ولا أهان العباد أنفسهم بمثل معصية الله" (ابن أبي الدنيا 2000، 292، ح64)، وأسند إلى زيد بن أسلم (ت. 753/136) قوله: "خلّتان من أخبرك أن الكرم إلا فيهما[16] فكذّبه: إكرامك نفسك بطاعة الله، وإكرامك نفسك عن معاصي الله" (ابن أبي الدنيا 2000، 292، ح65). وهذا من المعاني اللطيفة التي لم تتم العناية بها أو تطويرها في الفكر الإسلامي، باستثناء ما نجده عند المعتزلة – وخاصة القاضي عبد الجبار (ت. 1024/415) – في تعريف الحسن والقبح تعريفًا يصلهما بالقيمة الاعتبارية لذات الفاعل؛ فالحسن عنده ما يستوجب فاعله المدح، والقبح ما يستوجب فاعله الذم (القاضي عبد الجبار 1965، 6/26، 31).

ولئن كان الإسلام قد جعل للصالحات جزاءً أخرويًا، فلا ينبغي أن ننسى أن المكارم لم تكن تنفصل – قبل الإسلام – عن شيء من الثواب **الدنيوي** يناله صاحبها. وأعلى الثواب ذيوع سيرته بين الناس وثناؤهم عليه، وبقاء ذكره بينهم، ومن ثم اتقاء العار الذي يلحقه إذا تنكب عن هذه المكارم. ولا يهتم الرجل لأمر الثناء والعار مدة حياته فحسب، بل بعد مماته أيضًا؛ لأنه يلحق ذويه كذلك في مجتمع عربي احتفى بشدة بالأنساب، وذلك ما يفسّر الآثار المتعددة التي أوردها ابن أبي الدنيا (ابن أبي الدنيا 2000، 280–281، ح14–18) في بقاء الذِكر الحسن، نافيًا أن يكون السعي إليه محبطًا للعمل. من ذلك أنه قيل لزيد بن أسلم: "الرجل يعمل بشيء من الخير فيسمع الذاكر له فيُسر، هل يُحبط ذلك شيئًا من عمله؟ قال: ومن ذا الذي يحب أن يكون له لسان سوء؟!" بعدها يسوق ابن أبي الدنيا آيات قرآنية مؤيدة لذلك المعنى، ومنها: ﴿وَاجْعَل لِّي لِسَانَ صِدْقٍ فِي الْآخِرِينَ﴾ (الشعراء: 84)، ﴿وَتَرَكْنَا عَلَيْهِ فِي الْآخِرِينَ﴾ (الصافات: 78)، ﴿وَآتَيْنَاهُ أَجْرَهُ فِي الدُّنْيَا﴾ (العنكبوت: 27)، ويروي من التفاسير ما يوضح أن المقصود منها هو بقاء الذكر الحسن. ويدخل في هذا المعنى ما نقله عن سفيان (ولم يحدد أيّ السفيانين) من قوله: "لو أن

16 "إلا فيهما" هكذا هي في المطبوع من أعمال ابن أبي الدنيا ككتابي «التوبة» و«**مكارم الأخلاق**»، وهي كذلك في «**تاريخ دمشق**» لابن عساكر (1995، 19/289)، ولكنها وردت في النسخة المطبوعة من كتاب «**مختصر تاريخ دمشق**» لابن منظور (1984، 9/113) "أن الكرم فيهما." وفي نسخة من «**شعب الإيمان**» للبيهقي جاءت بصيغة "أن الكرامة إلا فيهما" (انظر مثلًا 2000، 5/450)، وفي نسخة أخرى (2003، 9/393) جاءت "ليست فيهما."

الرجل عمل عمره كله ليقع عليه اسم من هذه الأسماء أن يقال: حليم أو يقال: كريم" (ابن أبي الدنيا 2000، 286، ح33). ثم يعود إلى الذكر الحسن، مستشهدًا بنصيحة وزير إلى ملك قائلا: "إنما الدنيا حديث، فإن استطعت أن تكون منها حديثًا حسنًا فافعل" (ابن أبي الدنيا 2000، 287، ح39)، ويتكرر المعنى نفسه في بعض المرويات (ابن أبي الدنيا 2000، 288، ح40-41).[17] ولا ينبغي أن نستغرب مرويات "بقاء الذكر الحسن"، لأن الأخلاق - عند ابن أبي الدنيا - هي أخلاق حثّ، فهي تستحث الفاعل على تكريم نفسه وصون مروءته، أكثر منها أخلاقيات أمر تطالبه بالامتثال. وكرم الذات يزكو في عين الفاعل الأخلاقي عندما يتصور بقاء ذكره الحسن في الناس بعده.

بيد أنه إن كانت المكارم، من الناحية الموضوعية، تضرب بسبب إلى الأخلاقيات العربية الدنيوية، فإن ابن أبي الدنيا حريص بالقدر نفسه على تدينها. وفي هذا الصدد يروي جملة أحاديث تفيد أن المكارم يحبها الله الموصوف بالكرم، ويدعو بها النبي الذي ما بُعث إلا لإتمامها. ففيما يتصل بمفهوم «الكريم» الذي هو الله تعالى، تأتي تلك المرويات التي يسوقها ابن أبي الدنيا وتتحدث عن أخلاق الله الكريم، كالأحاديث المرفوعة (ابن أبي الدنيا 2000، 278-280، ح6-13) ومنها أيضا: "إن لله مئة وسبعة عشر خلقًا" (ابن أبي الدنيا 2000، 284، ح27)،[18] و"إن الله كريم يحب الكرم، جواد يحب الجود ومعالي الأخلاق ويُبغض سَفسافها" (ابن أبي الدنيا 2000، 279، ح8)،[19] و"إن لله عز وجل لوحًا من زُمُرُّدة خضراء جعله تحت العرش وكتب فيه: إني أنا الله لا إله إلا أنا أرحم وأُتَرَحم، خلقت بضعة عشر وثلاثمئة خُلُق، من جاء بخلق منها مع شهادة أن لا إله إلا الله دخل الجنة" (ابن أبي الدنيا 2000، 284، ح28)،[20] وأن الخير "أربعون

17 نقع أيضًا على أهمية الثناء والحمد بالنسبة إلى الرجل الفاضل في تعريف المروءة الوارد عند أبي حيان التوحيدي الذي يقول: "هي القيام بخواص ما للإنسان مما يكون عليه محمودا وبه ممدوحا" (التوحيدي 1986، 256).

18 والحكيم الترمذي (2010، 293/2)، وفي موضع آخر من دون إسناد، ولكنه أسنده في (167/6، 168).

19 وكرر ابن أبي الدنيا الحديث بصيغتين مختلفتين قليلا (ابن أبي الدنيا 2000، 278، ح6؛ 279، ح10) والحديث وجد في بعض مدونات الحديث المبكرة كجامع معمر بن راشد (الصنعاني 1983، 143/11) ورواه عبد الرزاق (2015، 38/9)؛ والحاكم النيسابوري (1990، 111/1)، كتاب الإيمان، والبيهقي (2003، 372/10).

20 والطبراني (1990، 20/2)، والبيهقي (2003، 64/11). قال الهيثمي (1994، 36/1): "رواه الطبراني في الأوسط، وفي إسناده أبو ظلال القَسْمَلِيّ وثقه ابن حبان والأكثر على تضعيفه." وجاء عند الطبراني "زَبَرجَد خَضِرًا،" وعند البيهقي والهيثمي "زَبَرجدة خضراء" بدل "زمردة".

خصلة، أعلاها مِنحة العَنْز. لا يعمل عبدٌ بخصلة منها رجاء ثوابها وتصديق موعودها إلا أدخله الله عز وجل بها الجنة" (ابن أبي الدنيا 2000، 285، ح30).[21] ورغم التباين في العدد، فإن هذه الأخلاق في النهاية -كما ينقل ابن أبي الدنيا عن بعض السلف - "منائح يمنحها الله من يشاء من عباده" (ابن أبي الدنيا 2000، 286، ح32؛ 288، ح43)، ومن جاء بأحدها دخل الجنة، وإذا أراد الله بعبد خيرًا جعل فيه واحدة منها. هذا عن الكرم بما هو صفة إلهية، أما المكارم بما هي تاج الدعوة المحمدية، فترِد في أحاديث مرفوعة مثل "اللهم اهدني لأحسن الأخلاق، فإنه لا يهدي لأحسنها إلا أنت، واصرف عني سيئها، لا يصرف عني سيئها إلا أنت" (ابن أبي الدنيا 2000، 279، ح9)،[22] و"إن مكارم الأخلاق من أعمال أهل الجنة" (ابن أبي الدنيا 2000، 280، ح12)،[23] و"بعثت لأتم صالح الأخلاق" (ابن أبي الدنيا 2000، 280، ح13)[24] و"إنما بعثت على تمام محاسن الأخلاق" (ابن أبي الدنيا 2000، 280–281، ح14).[25]

ومن **القيم الأخلاقية-الدينية التي** تنطوي عليها المكارم: قيمة الحِلم التي يخصص لها ابن أبي الدنيا بعض المرويات (ابن أبي الدنيا 2000، 281–284، ح19–26)، ولعلها تستحوذ على النصيب الأوفر من معنى المكارم. وللحلم معان يتصل فيها بالعقل والرشد ويضاد بها السفه، وهذه

---

21 ورواه البخاري (2001، 638/2): **كتاب الهبة، باب المنيحة**، كما رواه غيرُ واحدٍ. وفي لفظ البخاري: "قال حسان [بن عطية أحد رواة الحديث]: "فعددنا ما دون منيحة العنز من رد السلام وتشميت العاطس وإماطة الأذى عن الطريق ونحوه، فما استطعنا أن نبلغ خمس عشرة خصلة." و"مَنحة العنز" - كما هي عند ابن أبي الدنيا وغيره - و"مَنِيحة العنز" - كما هي عند البخاري وغيره - هي أنثى العنز تعطى ليُنْتَفع بلبنها ثم تُرد.

22 رواه مسلم (1952، 534/1)، **كتاب صلاة المسافرين وقصرها، باب الدعاء في صلاة الليل وقيامه**، ورواه غير واحد، منهم أبو داود والترمذي والنسائي، وغيرهم ممن التزم رواية الصحيح كابن خزيمة وابن حبان، وغيرهما.

23 الطبراني (1995، 313/6)، والقضاعي (1986، 108/2) قال الهيثمي (1994، 177/8):"رواه الطبراني في الأوسط وإسناده جيد،" وقال ابن أبي حاتم (2006، 96/5): "قال أبي: هذا حديث باطل، وطَلْق [بن السمح أحد رواة الحديث] مجهول."

24 رواه أحمد بن حنبل (2001، 513/14).

25 ورواه الطبراني (1983، 65/20)، والبيهقي (2003، 353/10). قال الهيثمي (1994، 23/8): "رواه الطبراني والبزار إلا أنه قال: إنما بعثت بمحاسن الأخلاق. وفيه عبد الرحمن بن أبي بكر الجُدْعاني وهو ضعيف." ولكن للحديث شواهد أخرى من حديث جابر بن عبد الله وأبي هريرة (انظر أحمد 2001، 513/14؛ القضاعي 1986، 192/2؛ والبغوي 1983، 202/13). وقال الهيثمي (1994، 188/8) في حديث أبي هريرة: "رواه أحمد ورجاله رجال الصحيح."

المعاني كامنة في استعمال ابن أبي الدينا لهذا المفهوم وإن كان لا يصرّح بها. وفي المرويات المذكورة، يتحدد الحِلم إجمالًا بوصفه نوعًا من العفو الذي يدفع السيئة بالحسنة: صلة من قطع، والعفو عمن ظلم، وإعطاء من منع. ولا يكتفي ابن أبي الدنيا بهذه المعاني الأخلاقية الصرفة للحِلم، بل يقرنها كالعادة بالمعنى الديني، فيجعل العفو شرطًا لبلوغ صريح الإيمان (ابن أبي الدنيا 2000، 282، ح22)، ووسيلة إلى مقام الرفعة عند الله (ابن أبي الدنيا 2000، 283، ح23). وعلى عادته، يأتي ابن أبي الدنيا في ختام هذه السلسلة (ابن أبي الدنيا 2000، 283، ح25) بآية قرآنية هي ﴿خُذِ الْعَفْوَ وَأْمُرْ بِالْعُرْفِ وَأَعْرِضْ عَنِ الْجَاهِلِينَ﴾ (الأعراف: 119)، مع تفسيرها في ضوء ما سبق من خصال الحِلم.[26]

هكذا نرى كيف تجري، مع توالي المرويات، عملية تأويل وصهر معقدة للمكارم يمتزج فيها الأخلاقي بالديني، بحيث تغدو أخلاق المكارم ملازمة للدين أو مؤطرة له. ويبدو ابن أبي الدنيا مقتنعا بأن الأخلاق الكريمة هي أحد أعمدة الدين، وأن الإيمان هو عبارة عن فضائل كالصبر والسماحة وأن أفضل مراتبه الخلق الحسن، وأن دناءة الأخلاق تناظر الحرام، وكلاهما مطلوب الاجتناب في الدين. يُسند إلى عبد الله بن عمر (ت. 693/73) حديثًا مرفوعًا (ابن أبي الدنيا 2000، 289، ح50) يماهي بين أخلاق العرب ودين الإسلام، ونصه: "خصلتان من أخلاق العرب - وهما من **عمود الدين** - توشكون أن تَدَعوهما: الحياء والأخلاق الكريمة." ويروي أحاديث أخرى (ابن أبي الدنيا 2000، 291، ح59–61) تفيد بأن الإيمان صبر وسماحة، وأن أفضلَ الإيمان الخلقُ الحسن. وينقل عن أحدهم قوله: "فليتق الرجل دناءة الأخلاق كما يتقي الحرام، فإن الكرم من الدين" (ابن أبي الدنيا 2000، 290، ح55)، وهذا يفيد أن الحظر الشرعي (أو الحرام) يماثل الحظر الأخلاقي (أو الدناءة).

### 3.2.2 حديث المكارم العشر أو واسطة العقد

بعد تلك المقدمة، تأتي ثلاث روايات سميتها واسطة العقد في رسالة «**المكارم**»، لأنها تتضمن المبدأ الذي تنتظم وفقه لائحة المرويات التي يوردها ابن أبي الدنيا تحت خانة المكارم. ووضع هذه الروايات الثلاث هذا الموضع يمنح التأليف (والتفكر) الأخلاقي عند ابن أبي الدنيا فرادة لا تتأتى فقط من مضمونه الذي عرضناه؛ بل أيضًا من شكله ونظام عرضه، أي نسقيته؛ وإلى نفس هذه الحكم خلص زيليو غراندي (Zilio-Grandi 2015, 89). فلم يعمد مصنِّفنا إلى سرد المرويات الأخلاقية كيفما اتفق، أو تحت أبواب أعفى نفسه من مشقة تسويغها والدفاع عنها؛ بل اتخذ من كلامٍ للسيدة عائشة إطارًا مفهوميًا مرجعيًا ومُسوّغًا لتنظيم مادة المرويات، فجاء تنظيم الكتاب

26 خصص ابن أبي الدنيا للحِلم رسالة مستقلة، درسها زيليو-غراندي (Zilio-Grandi 2015, 88–95).

معقولًا ومحكمًا وإن لم يخل من الاستطراد الذي وسم طريقة القدماء في التصنيف. ولم يجانب بيلمي الصواب حين اعتبر كتاب «**مكارم الأخلاق**» بمنزلة كتاب الكتب، أي الجامع لما تفرق في الرسائل أو الكتب الأخرى من خصال (Bellamy 1963, 111). تقول السيدة عائشة – بحسب ما رواه ابن أبي الدنيا (ابن أبي الدنيا 2000، 286–287، ح36): "إن المكارم عشرة: صدق الحديث، وصدق البأس في طاعة الله، وإعطاء السائل، ومكافأة الصنيع، وصلة الرحم، وأداء الأمانة، والتذمم للجار، والتذمم للصاحب، وقِرى الضيف، ورأسهن الحياء".[27] ولقد بلغ من عناية ابن أبي الدنيا بالترتيب المنطقي لمرويات مصنَّفه، أن بدأ – كما سنرى – عرض الخصال بالحياء؛ لأنه رأسهن، رغم ذكره آخِرًا في كلام السيدة عائشة.

ويتوسط هذا الحديثُ المرجعي حديثين آخرين للسيدة عائشة أيضًا من قولها؛ بحيث يشكل الثلاثة واسطة العقد. أول هذين الحديثين قولها: "لقد جاء الإسلام وفي العرب بضع وستون خصلة، كلها زادها الإسلام شدة، منها قِرى الضيف وحسن الجوار والوفاء بالعهد" (ابن أبي الدنيا 2000، 286، ح35). ويعزز هذا الحديث الفكرة الراسخة عند ابن أبي الدنيا بأن الإسلام ما أحدث قطيعة مع محصول التجربة الإنسانية التي كانت للعرب في الجاهلية، وخاصة في جانبها الأخلاقي. أما ثاني الحديثين فتقول فيه السيدة عائشة: "مكارم الأخلاق عشرة: تكون في الرجل ولا تكون في ابنه، وتكون في ابنه ولا تكون فيه، وتكون في السيد ولا تكون في عبده، وتكون في العبد ولا تكون في سيده" (ابن أبي الدنيا 2000، 287، ح37). وهذا الحديث يُدخل التعددية إلى الأشكال التي تتحقق بها المكارم؛ إذ ليس معيار الفضيلة واحدًا يقاس به الأداء الأخلاقي لكل الناس من غير تمييز، بل كل إنسان يأتي من المكارم بما يناسب خصائصه النفسية أو وظائفه أو مقامه الاجتماعي.[28]

---

27 روي هذا الحديث في بعض المصنفات المبكرة المتقدمة على ابن أبي الدنيا، كالجامع لعبد الله بن وهب (ت. 197/813) (ابن وهب 1995، 595) من قول عائشة، ورواه البيهقي أيضًا (2003، 162/10) عن عائشة من قولها، ورواه الحكيم الترمذي (2010، 341/4)، والبيهقي (2003، 161/10) عن عائشة مرفوعًا. وقد حكم المحدثون بعدم صحته مرفوعًا؛ قال ابن حبان: "وهذا ما لا أصل له من كلام رسول الله" (ابن حبان 1398، 91/3)، وقال ابن الجوزي (1981، 242/2): "هذا حديث لا يصح عن رسول الله صلى الله عليه وسلم، ولعله من كلام بعض السلف."

28 يقرّ الرازي أيضًا تنوع معايير الأداء الأخلاقي بين المتنعم والفقير (الرازي 1939، 106–107)، كما يقرها الراغب الأصفهاني بخصوص المرأة والرجل (الراغب الأصفهاني 2007، 116). وليس هذا بمستغرب؛ فالعصور ما قبل الحديثة لم تكن تنظر إلى الأفراد نظرة الحداثة؛ أي من زاوية المساواة المبدئية الصورية التي تجعل من كل شخص ذاتية (subjectivity) متعالية، لا تتطابق ولا تختزل بالضرورة إلى الدور الاجتماعي الذي تلعبه، والذي يظل عرضيا لا يمس جوهر الشخص

بعد هذه الأحاديث الثلاثة، يتحدث ابن أبي الدنيا بلسانه – ونادرًا ما يفعل ذلك – فيشرح لنا خطته فيما تبقى من رسالته قائلا: "ونحن ذاكرون في كتابنا هذا في كل خصلة من الخصال التي ذكرت أم المؤمنين – رضوان الله عليها – بعض ما انتهى إلينا عن النبي وعن أصحابه رضوان الله عليهم ومن بعدهم من التابعين لهم بإحسان وأهل الفضل والذكر من العلماء؛ ليزداد ذو البصر في بصيرته، وينتبه المقصر عن ذلك من طول غفلته؛ فيرغب في الأخلاق الكريمة، وينافس في الأفعال الجميلة التي جعلها الله حِلْية لدينه، وزينة لأوليائه. وقد كان يقال: ليس من خلق كريم ولا فعل جميل إلا وقد وصله الله بالدين" (ابن أبي الدنيا 2000، 287، ح38).

تدلنا هذه الفقرة المفتاحية على منطق العرض الذي ستخضع له المرويات اللاحقة، ومن ثم لا يتعلق الأمر بجمع وحفظ مرويات كيفما اتفق؛ بل ثمة هيكل يسند البنيان وقصد يوجّه التصنيف. بيد أن أهم ما في كلام ابن أبي الدنيا هو العبارةُ الأخيرة التي تعلن عن «الفلسفة» التي تقف وراء تأليفه رسالته، وربما باقي رسائله الأخلاقية، وهي إثبات الصلة التي أقامها الله بين الدين وكل خلق جميل، أو بالأحرى تجسير الهوة بين الدين والأخلاق، والتي كانت قد بدأت تتسع في زمن ابن أبي الدنيا لصالح تدين شكلي ليس فيه من روح الدين (الأخلاقية) شيء.

### 3.2.3 تفصيل القول في المكارم

في ضوء الحديث المرجعي للسيدة عائشة، يشرع ابن أبي الدنيا في عرض المرويات المتعلقة بالمكارم العشر التي يتضح بعد التأمل أنها جملة الفضائل العالية.[29] وبما أنها أنواع تحت جنس المكارم، فإن ماهية الكرم تعمها؛ منها ما هو إكرام للنفس، ومنها ما هو إكرام للغير من ذوي القربى، ومنها أخيرا ما هو إكرام لعموم الناس. وفضلا عن ذلك، فإنها ترث من «المكارم» طابعها الرسوخي؛ أي كونها خُلقًا على التحقيق، والخلق – كما عرّفه المؤلفون المسلمون – هيئة راسخة في النفس تصدر عنها الأفعال بيسر متى تحققت في النفس (الجرجاني د.ت.، 89). وسأذكر الآن هذه المكارم العشر بإيجاز، وأتوقف عند الحياء بشيء من التفصيل.

يبدأ ابن أبي الدنيا بمرويات عن المكارم يمكن اعتبارها متعلقة بإكرام النفس، وهي الحياء والصدق وصدق البأس. وكما سبق يبدأ ابن أبي الدنيا بالحياء مبررًا ذلك بالقول: "بدأنا بذكر الحياء وما جاء في فضله لقول أم المؤمنين رضي الله عنها: رأس مكارم الأخلاق الحياء" (ابن أبي الدنيا

---

بما هو ذات أخلاقية. فلم تكن كينونة الشخص في العصور ما قبل الحديثة تنفصل عن مقامه الاجتماعي، فهو جوهريا واحد سواء كان من العامة أم من الخاصة، سيدًا أم عبدًا، رجلًا أم امرأة. يُنظر (Di Vito 1999, 223, 231).

29 وعليه، أتفق مع بِشر فارس عندما آثر ترجمة «مكارم الأخلاق» إلى الفرنسية بعبارة «الفضائل الرفيعة vertus éminentes» (فارس 1939، 37، حاشية 30).

2000، 294). وتدور جل مرويات باب الحياء على فكرة أن الدين والإيمان هما الحياء أو هما حياء. فلما قيل لعمر بن عبد العزيز (ت. 720/101): "الحياء من الدين،" أجاب: "بل هو الدين كله" (ابن أبي الدنيا 2000، 298، ح87). ومثله الحديث المرفوع: "إن لأهل كل دين خُلُقًا، وإن خلق الإسلام الحياء" (ابن أبي الدنيا 2000، 301، ح98).[30] وبناء على مركزية الحياء بالنسبة إلى الإيمان، فإن من كان فيه الحياء رفعه الله ولم تمسسه النار (ابن أبي الدنيا 2000، 304، ح108–109)، وحتى المنافق يرجى له الخير إن كان فيه حياء بحسب الحديث المرفوع (ابن أبي الدنيا 2000، 303، ح104) المروي عن معاوية بن قرة (ت. 731/113)، ويبينه حديث "من لم يكن ذا حياء فلا دين له، ومن لم يكن ذا حياء في الدنيا لا يدخل الجنة" (ابن أبي الدنيا 2000، 302، ح100). بل إن "قلة الحياء كفر" بحسب سعيد بن المسيب (ابن أبي الدنيا 2000، 297، ح84)، والمعنى نفسه يرد من حديث عمر بن عبد العزيز مرفوعًا حيث يجعل عديم الحياء كافرًا (ابن أبي الدنيا 2000، 303، ح106). ليس الحياء هو الدين كله فحسب، بل هو الخير كله. إنه خير محض إن صح القول، فلا يكون منه أو معه شر مطلقًا (ابن أبي الدنيا 2000، 295–296، ح76–79)، وكأن بين الحياء والشر تناقضًا منطقيًا، إذا ثبت أحدهما ارتفع الآخر.

ولما كان ابن أبي الدنيا لا يتدخل بوضع تعريفات وحدود للمفاهيم والقيم التي يمتدحها، مراهنًا - فيما يبدو - على وضوح معناها وبداهة مدلولها في ذهن القارئ الذي كان يكتب له، لا يبقى أمامنا سوى استنباط تعريفات ضمنية للمفاهيم من الاستعمال والسياق. هكذا، نستشف من وصف أحوال الرسول صلى الله عليه وسلم في حيائه، أن الحياء: تَرْكُ مصارحة الناس بما يكرهون سماعه، بما في ذلك ترك تنبيههم على ما ينجم عن سلوكهم من أذى للمستحيي (ابن أبي الدنيا 2000، 296–297، ح80–82)؛ بل هو عند سعيد بن جبير (ت. 714/95): استثقال نهي رجل عن فعل ما يُكرَه (ابن أبي الدنيا 2000، 304، ح110)، وترك الفحش (ابن أبي الدنيا 2000، 298، ح86). ويكشف لنا كلامٌ لأبي بكر الصديق (ت. 634/13) عن بعد آخر للحياء هو ستر العورة ولو في خلاءٍ، تهيّبًا من الله (ابن أبي الدنيا 2000، 300، ح92). وبالجملة، إنه غاية التأدب، أو غاية التفضل أو الكرم مع الله والناس.

وربما كان كلام أبي بكر الصديق مرشدًا إلى الحقيقة العميقة للحياء بما هو خجل المرء من عوراته، الجسماني منها والمعنوي، وهو معنى يتأكد بمصادر مختلفة تشتمل على الحديث (ابن

30 ورواه مالك (1985، 905/2)، كتاب الجامع، باب ما جاء في الحياء، وابن الجعد (1990، 421)، وابن ماجه (1952، 399/2)، أبواب الزهد، باب الحياء، والطبراني (1983، 389/10)، والبيهقي (2003، 155/10). وقال العقيلي (1984، 201/2): «والصحيح عن النبي صلى الله عليه وسلم أنه قال: "الحياء من الإيمان، والحياء خير كله" وأسانيدها جياد».

أبي الدنيا 2000، 302، ح102)، والأثر كقول لوهب بن منبه (ابن أبي الدنيا 2000، 301، ح97)، والشعر المتنوع كشعر الأعرابية (ابن أبي الدنيا 2000، 301، ح95) وآخر محكي عن بعض العرب (ابن أبي الدنيا 2000، 304، ح107). وهي مصادر تؤكد - جميعًا - أن الحياء لباس الإيمان كاللحاء للعود، ييبَس ويموت إذا نُزع عنه، بل هو لباس للتقوى نفسها (ابن أبي الدنيا 2000، 305، ح114). ولهذا السبب أنشدت تلك المرأة التي سمعها عمر بن الخطاب قائلة:

دَعَتْنِي النَّفْسُ بَعْدَ خُروجِ عَمْرٍو إِلَى اللَّذَّاتِ تطَّلع اطلاعا
فَقُلْتُ لَهَا: عَجِلْتِ فَلَنْ تُطَاعِي وَلَوْ طَالَتْ إِقَامَتُهُ رِبَاعا
أُحَاذِرُ – إِنْ أُطِيعُكِ – سَبَّ نَفْسِي وَمَخْزَاةً تُجَلِّلُنِي قِنَاعَا

ولما سألها عمر عما منعها أجابت: "الحياء وإكرام عرضي،" فعقّب عمر محللًا كلامها ومفسرًا سلوكها: "إن الحياء ليدل على هَناتٍ ذات ألوان. من استحيا استخفى، ومن استخفى اتقى، ومن اتقى وُقي" (ابن أبي الدنيا 2000، 301، ح94). وإن جواب المرأة ليخرج عن المعهود الإسلامي؛ إذ المعهود استدعاء مقولة "خوف الله وخشيته" في المواقف التي يتعرض فيها المرء للغواية وهو مستخف آمن من الفضيحة أو من تقريع الناس. نستنتج من هذا أن الحياء واعظ ذاتي ومحاسب مدقِّق، وأنه يحمل على اتقاء الخزي الذي قد يلحق المرء من نفسه عند فشله في الالتزام بالواجب الأخلاقي. إنه انحصار النفس خوف إتيان القبائح.

هذا عن الحياء وهو أهم المكارم في الحقيقة؛ لأنه رأسها كما ورد في كلام السيدة عائشة. ويأتي بعده ضربان من الصدق يصبان في إكرام النفس:

**أولهما:** الصدق (ابن أبي الدنيا 2000، 306–313، ح115–153)، ويورد فيه ابن أبي الدنيا مرويات تشدد على الصلة بين الصدق والإيمان، وأخبارًا تتحدث عن صدق الصالحين من السلف والملوك، وقد سبق أن ثمة صلة بين الإيمان والحياء، ثم يختم الباب بهذا الكلام البالغ الدلالة لمحمد بن كعب (ت. 108/726): "إنما يكذب الكاذب من مهانة نفسه عليه" (ابن أبي الدنيا 2000، 316، ح153)، وهو قول يُظهر أن الكذب نقص في الحياء، أو بالأحرى نقص في احترام المرء لنفسه وتفريط في إكرامها.

**وثانيهما:** صدق البأس (ابن أبي الدنيا 2000، 317–334، ح154–202). وليس هو عنده سوى ما يسميه غيره من المؤلفين المتأثرين بالفلسفة "فضيلة الشجاعة"، ولكنه يؤثر لها هذا الاسم، كما يؤثر لها الشواهد من التاريخ الإسلامي بدءًا بشجاعة النبي صلى الله عليه وسلم ثم علي بن أبي

طالب والزبير بن العوام (ت. 656/36) وطلحة بن عبيد (ت. 656/36) وخالد بن الوليد (ت. 642/21) رضي الله عنهم أجمعين وآخرين.

وفي مقابل إكرام النفس، يأتي – من المكارم – إكرام الغير من ذوي القربى، ويجمع ذلك مكرمة صلة الرحم (ابن أبي الدنيا 2000، 335–352، ح203–263) والبر بالوالدين وخاصة الأم، فابن أبي الدنيا يورد أخبارًا كثيرة عن سِير الصالحين في مبالغتهم في بِرّ أمهاتهم.

أما القسم الأخير من المكارم فقد جمع فيه ابن أبي الدنيا، ما يتعلق بإكرام مطلق الناس، ويشمل الآتي:

- **أداء الأمانة** (ابن أبي الدنيا 2000، 353–356، ح264–279) حيث يورد أحاديث وآثارًا في الحث على أداء الأمانات، ويستهل ابن أبي الدنيا هذا الباب بحديث مرفوع يقرن قرانًا دالًا بين الأمانة والحياء وهو" :أول ما يُرفع عن هذه الأمة **الحياء والأمانة**، فسلوهما الله تعالى" (ابن أبي الدنيا2000، 353 ، ح264).[31]
- **التذمم للصاحب** (ابن أبي الدنيا 2000، 357–364، ح280–318) وإكرام الأصحاب والسؤال عنهم وقضاء حوائجهم وديونهم، ورعاية أهليهم.
- **التذمم للجار** (ابن أبي الدنيا 2000، 365–372، ح319–354) وهو باب يدور على التحذير من إيذاء الجار والحث على الإحسان إليه، وذكر مآثر الصالحين في ذلك.
- **المكافأة بالصنائع** (ابن أبي الدنيا 2000، 373–377، ح355–375)، حيث يتحدث فيها عن رد الجميل، ورد الهدية بمثلها.
- **الجود وإعطاء السائل** (ابن أبي الدنيا 2000، 378–434، ح376–486)، وهو أكبر الأبواب، ويكثر فيه من الأحاديث عن جود النبي صلى الله عليه وسلم، والراشدين والصحابة وخلفاء بني أمية، مع شواهد شعرية كثيرة.

تلك هي جملة المكارم. والملاحظ أنه لم يخصص بابًا لقِرى الضيف، فجاءت الخصال تِسعًا لا عشرًا. ولعل مردّ ذلك إلى أن إكرام الضيف داخل في الأبواب الأخرى مثل إعطاء السائل والتذمم للجار أو الصاحب،[32] فضلا عن كونه واقعا تحت ماصَدَق الكرم بمعناه الشاسع. وهذه المكارم مرتبة ترتيبًا لا يخفى منطقه: مكارم إكرام النفس وهي لاحقة بالحياء (الصدق،

31 أبو يعلى (1984، 511/11)، والقضاعي (1986، 155/1)، والبيهقي (2003، 216/7)، **باب الأمانات وما يجب من أدائها إلى أهلها.**

32 ربما لهذا السبب عنون ناشر آخر لرسائل ابن أبي الدنيا باب إعطاء السائل بـ«الجود وإعطاء السائل» (انظر ابن أبي الدنيا 1990أ، 113).

الشجاعة)، ومكارم إكرام الغير من ذوي القربى (صلة الرحم)، ومكارم إكرام مطلق الناس (الأمانة، والتذمم للجار، والتذمم للصاحب، ورد الجميل، وإعطاء السائل).

## 4 حدود أخلاقيات ابن أبي الدنيا ضمن تقاليد المحدثين

بتشديده على قيمة العقل، وبإدارته الفضائل والدين على الكرم والمكارم، وبحرصه على تسويغ الترتيب الذي اختاره عند عرض مرويات المكارم، يكون ابن أبي الدنيا قد فارق السمة الغالبة على الأخلاق الأثرية؛ ولكنه مع ذلك بقي أمينًا لصنعة أهل الأثر، وما تفرضه من قيود على أسلوب التأليف. وأبرزها التمسك بقانون الرواية والاستشهاد؛ ولهذا لا يتكلم بلسان نفسه، أي أنه – كما قال بيلمي – "ضيّق على نفسه بشدة في ما يخص الموارد التي اعتمدها" (Bellamy 1963, 109). وقد أوقعه ذلك حتما في طلب شديد على الرواية أدت به إلى التماس المرويات بأي ثمن، فروى أحاديث ضعّفها بعض نقاد الحديث فيما بعد. وبالرغم من هذا، فهو يكتسب -في نظري – مكانته في تاريخ الأخلاق الإسلامية بقدرته على تحقيق أمرين: **الأول** اجتراح طريق ثالث بين فريقين متنابذين (المستغنون بالموروث الإسلامي عما عداه في مقابل المقبلين – بانبهار – على الموروثات الأجنبية)؛ **الثاني** تصوره للأخلاق باعتبارها صونا لإنسانية الإنسان، أو لمروءته وكرم نفسه، وكان الأمر الثاني شرطًا لتحقق الأمر الأول.

وفي الواقع، ينطوي المسعى الذي انتهجه ابن أبي الدنيا على نوع من التحدي؛ فقيم المكارم والمروءة والاهتداء بالعقل ليست قيمًا نصية فقط؛ إذ يمكن تبريرها تبريرًا عقليًا خالصًا أيضًا، ودليل ذلك أنها كانت من أمهات المثل الأخلاقية لدى العرب قبل الإسلام. فكأنه اجتهد في التأسيس لأخلاقيات عقلية اعتمادا على أدوات نقلية. وقد تقصّى في سبيل ذلك عددًا كبيرًا ومتنوعًا من المرويات التي جاءت ملائمة جدًا لمنظوره الأخلاقي، لكننا – بالمقابل – لا نقع في كتب الحديث الصحيح، وخاصة صحيحي البخاري (ت. 870/256) ومسلم (ت. 875/261)، على الكثير من تلك الأحاديث، وخاصة الأحاديث المفاتيح التي بنى عليها تصوره الأخلاقي، بل على العكس انتقد بعض المحدّثين اللاحقين بعض أحاديثه، كما سبق في حديث "أنا الشاهد على الله، لا يعثر عاقل إلا رفعه الله،" وحديث السيدة عائشة الذي هو بمنزلة قطب الرحى في تصوره الأخلاقي، ينطبق الحال نفسه على حديثين مفتاحييْن هما: حديث "كرم المرء دينه ومروءته عقله وحسبه خلقه،" وحديث "أول ما خلق الله العقل." فالحديث الأول ضعفه شمس الدين الذهبي (ت. 1348/748) وغيره، وصححه ابن حبان والحاكم النيسابوري (ت. 1014/405). والحديث الثاني اشتد نقد المحدثين اللاحقين له؛ بل إن ابن تيمية (ت. 1328/728) قال فيه: "وهؤلاء

[الفلاسفة] يدعون أن العقول قديمة أزلية، وأن العقل الفعال هو رب ما تحت فلك القمر ... والملاحدة الذين دخلوا معهم ... كملاحدة المتصوفة، يحتجون لمثل ذلك بالحديث الموضوع: أول ما خلق الله العقل ... فيأخذ هؤلاء العبارات الإسلامية ويودعونها معاني هؤلاء" (ابن تيمية 2004، 17/332–333). وإلى مثل هذا الرأي ذهب غولدتسيهر معتبرًا أن الحديث يحمل آثار الأفلاطونية المحدثة التي تقول بأن العقل الكوني هو أول شيء صدر مباشرة عن الذات الإلهية، ومن ثم عَدّه من جملة الأحاديث التي وُضعت بتأثير الإسماعيلية (غولدتسيهر 1980، 219).

وعلى العموم، فللعقل في مدونات الحديث قصة غريبة بعض الشيء كما قال حسين القوتلي في مقدمته الوافية لكتاب «**العقل وفهم القرآن**» للمحاسبي الذي يعتقد أن علماء الجرح والتعديل ورجال الفقه من أهل السنة – بوجه خاص – قد بالغوا في حملتهم على أحاديث العقل، خوفًا من أن ينساق المسلمون وراء العقل وحده، فيجعلوه إمامهم المكتفي بنفسه بحيث يعقل عن ذاته لا عن الله.[33]

وبغض النظر عن موقف المحدثين، فقد حمل ابن أبي الدنيا لواء المعتقدين بصحة "أحاديث العقل" عن الرسول صلى الله عليه وسلم. ومهما قيل في أسانيدها، فيبدو أنه كان مقتنعًا بصحة متنها على الأقل، وربما كان مقتنعًا بأولية العقل في سلم الوجود والخلَق وأنها فرضية ضرورية من وجهة نظر أخلاقية على الأقل، ما دام المتجمّلون بالمكارم والمادحون لها قد وُجدوا قبل ورود شريعة الإسلام، وما دام حث المرء على العيش وفق مطالب المروءة لا يحتاج منا أن نناشد فيه غير طبيعته العاقلة وكرامته. ولئن كان نقد الإسناد مركزيًّا في علم الحديث، فهو أقل أهمية في علم الأخلاق؛ لأن الحديث – سواء ثبت أم لم يثبت – إنما يشهد على رغبة في شرعنة تأسيس الأخلاق على العقل باستعمال طريقة الأثريين في الحجج النقلية. ومن ثم فلا يخلو أن يكون ابن أبي الدنيا أحدَ رَجلينْ، فهو إما منافس لأطراف في الجبهة الخارجية، أي لغير المحدّثين ممن رفعوا من شأن العقل في ميدان الأخلاق معتمدين على مصادر غير نصية وعلى رأس هؤلاء الفلاسفة والمتأدبون، أو مقاوم على الجبهة الداخلية، أي لأترابه من المحدّثين ممن جمدوا على الرواية وحصروا الفضيلة في هدي السمع وبخسوا العقل قدره.

وبعيدًا عن نقد المرويات، فقد سلك ابن أبي الدنيا نهجًا امتاز به عن فئتين: اكتفت الأولى بالمدونة الأخلاقية الإسلامية، بينما اختارت الأخرى الاقتباس عن الموروث الأجنبي. أراد ابن أبي الدنيا أن يؤسس الأخلاق على الحديث وآثار السلف والحكمة السائرة في زمنه، وما يُروى عن الأنبياء السابقين، فطفق يقيم منها جسرًا يربط بين الخلق الكريم والفعل الجميل من جهة، والدين من جهة أخرى. وههنا كان رائدًا لغيره ممن تصدوا لهذه المهمة **التوفيقية**، سواءٌ من أهل

33 القوتلي (1971، 124، و21 وما بعدها) حيث أورد جملة من أحاديث ابن أبي الدنيا وناقشها.

الحديث – كابن حِبان البُستي في «**روضة العقلاء ونزهة الفضلاء**» – ممن اكتفى بجمع الأحاديث والآثار ذات الصلة بالزهد أو الرقائق أو السنن أو الآداب، وقدمها هَدْيًا دينيًا أو تعبديًّا، أم من أهل الفلسفة ممن بنى على الموروثين الفارسي واليوناني محاولًا أسلمته بالاحتجاج له بما يؤيده من النقل، كما فعل الراغب الأصفهاني. فمفاهيم ابن أبي الدنيا إسلامية خالصة أو هذا ما حرص على إظهاره على الأقل، ومضامينه عربيّة خالصة، ومن ثم فهو أقرب إلى التوجه الإنساني الأخلاقي الذي يدور على قيم المروءة والمكارم والكرم والحِلم، وما في معناها من القيم.

وإذا ما قارنا عمل ابن أبي الدنيا بعمل المُكتفين بالمدونة الأخلاقية الإسلامية، نجد أن ابن أبي الدنيا امتاز عن أترابه من المحدثين بمصنفاته التي استقلت بأغراض خاصة، ولم تكن خادمة للفقه الذي إن عني بالأخلاق مال إلى «فضائل الأعمال» أكثر من «فضائل الخصال». ولم يجانب جيمس بيلمي الصواب عندما رأى أن ابن أبي الدنيا تأثر بمعاصريه من علماء اللغة والكتّاب. وهو، وإن كان محدّثا، إلا أن مؤلفاته ليست من النوع الذي يمكن للفقهاء توظيفه؛ لأنها منصرفة إلى التقوى الشخصية والزهد بالمعنى الواسع (Bellamy 1963, 106). وكما قال جورج حوراني: إن "كتب المكارم واحدة من الأجناس المنضوية تحت الأدب الأخلاقي ذي المنحى الديني، ولا تُعنى بالتفصيلات الفقهية بل بالفضائل الدينية" (Hourani 1985, 16)، ولهذا السبب فَقَد التصور الأخلاقي لابن أبي الدنيا تأثيره عند منتصف القرن الثالث لصالح كل من التصوف والفهم التشريعي للإسلام (legalistic) (Bellamy 1963, 106).

وفي تأسيسه لمكارم الأخلاق، لم يتوسل ابن أبي الدنيا بشيء من خارج الموروث العربي الإسلامي، فعلى خلاف ابن قتيبة (ت. 276/889)، لا نجد عنده ذكرًا لحكمة الهنود أو فلسفة اليونان أو إرث الساسانيين أو حكماء الفرس، بل لا نجد لديه ذكرًا لابن المقفع (ت. 142/760) نفسه (Bellamy 1963, 109). وينبغي ألا يفاجئنا زهده في تراث الآخرين؛ فالمكارم موضوع عربي خالص مبنى ومعنى، ولا يمكن للشواهد الأجنبية إلا أن توهن قوة ندائها الأخلاقي. وها هو أبو الحسن العامري (ت. 381/992) المتشرب للفلسفة، يبخس كتاب ابن المقفع قيمته؛ رغم ما فيه من الحث على مكارم الأخلاق قائلا: "ولعمري إن للمجوس كتابًا يُعرف بـ«**أبستا**» وهو يأمر بـ«مكارم الأخلاق» ويوصي بها، وقد أتى بمجامعها عبد الله بن المقفع في كتابه المعروف بـ«**الأدب الكبير**»، إلا أنه مع تقدمه في ذلك غير لائق شيئًا منه بالقرآن" (العامري 1988، 159–160). ولربما كان العامري "مُحقًّا" في الجملة الأخيرة؛ لأن «**مكارم الأخلاق**» أوضح وأيسر استخراجًا من السيرة والأحاديث والآثار منها في القرآن.

ولا تباين في موقف ابن أبي الدنيا من مكونات الموروث الأجنبي المختلفة؛ إذ لا يقل تحاشيه للموروث اليوناني عن تفاديه للموروث الفارسي. وعلى خلاف المتفلسفة المسلمين، لم يتخذ من

العدالة فضيلة الفضائل التي تحف بالفضائل الثلاث «العفة»، و«الشجاعة»، و«الحكمة»، والراجح أن مفهوم «مكارم الأخلاق» كان مفهومًا جامعًا أغناه عنها، كما أننا لا نجد لديه أثرًا لمفهوم الوسط الذي قبِله الكثير من مفكري الإسلام بوصفه معيار الفضيلة، وهو بذلك من الذين يصح القول فيهم: إنهم "اعتبروا أن النفس بتعاليها تحصّل الفضائل، وبتسافلها تحصل الرذائل، وأنه لا حد وسط بين الأمرين عند النفس" (جرادي 2010، 98). والأخلاق عنده ليست أخلاق الحكيم اليوناني أو الرواقي السعيد – أبدًا – بذاته، بل أخلاق عناية ومواساة، أو أخلاق محبة. هي أخلاق تحصل فيها السعادة بإسعاد الآخرين والتخفيف من شقائهم: التذمم للجار، وإعطاء المحتاج، والعفو عن المسيء، وقِرى الضيف.

ولئن كانت الأخلاق في الموروث الإسلامي الخالص تتردد بين أخلاقيات أمرٍ مرجعها القرآن، وأخلاقيات قدوة موردها السُّنة (Goodman 1999, 119)، فإن الأخلاق عند مصنّفنا أقرب إلى الثانية منها إلى الأولى، بل إن القدوة عنده لا تقتصر على صاحب الشريعة؛ بل تشمل كل الصالحين من صحابة وتابعين، وكل ذي عقل وحكمة ومروءة وكرم من دون تمييز.[34] وبهذا المعنى، فالأخلاق – عنده – نداء صادر من قدوة تحثنا على الاقتداء أكثر مما هي **أمر** يطالب بالطاعة والامتثال.

وإذا كان الفرنسي دو بوفون (de Buffon) قد قال في القرن 18: إن "الأسلوب هو الرجل نفسه" (Dürrenmatt 2010, 66) فلا نبالغ إن قلنا: إن ابن أبي الدنيا يعُدّ المكارم هي الرجل نفسه. يشهد لذلك ما يرويه ابن أبي الدنيا من كلام عمر بن الخطاب: "لا تَغرنّكم طنطنة الرجل بالليل – يعني صلاته –، **فإن الرجل كل الرجل** من أدى الأمانة إلى من ائتمنه، ومن سلم المسلمون من يده ولسانه" (ابن أبي الدنيا 2000، 354، ح268). يتعلق الأمر بما يحقق الرجلَ في كلّيته، لا في بعضه دون بعض. فإذا أبدلنا «الرجل» بـ«المرء» صحّ اعتبار المكارم تحقيقًا للمروءة أي للإنسانية (سليم 1986، 9). وهذا ما فطن له جيمس بيلمي عندما قال: إن كلمة «vir-tues» (فضائل) تترجِم جيّدًا في بعض المواضع العبارةَ العربية «مكارم الأخلاق» (Bellamy 1963, 107). والأمر نفسه ذهب إليه محمد أركون حينما لاحظ أن المترجمين العرب القدماء وضعوا «الفضيلة» مقابلًا للفظ اليوناني «آريتي» (arete). والحال أن المعنى المستخدم به عند هوميروس ذو إيحاءات أرستقراطية، فيكون مقابله هو «المروءة»، مثلما أن «aidos» المرافق لها هو نفسه الحِلم الملازم للمروءة (Arkoun 1982, 298).

---

34 في «رسالة الإخلاص والنية» – مثلا – لا يورد ابن أبي الدنيا (2000، 67-77) غير بضعة أحاديث نبوية وسط عدد هائل من أقوال السلف والمرويات عن الأنبياء السابقين.

من هذه الناحية، تلتقي أخلاقيات ابن أبي الدنيا مع الأخلاق الأرسطية من حيث إنهما أخلاقيات فضيلة لا أخلاقيات واجب (deontological ethics). يبدأ أرسطو بتحديد غائية الوجود الإنساني انطلاقًا من الطبيعة المميزة للإنسان، فتغدو غايةُ الإتيقا هي ينّعانُ (flourishing) الشخص الإنساني وتحقيق الكمالات التي له بالقوة (Broadie 2006, 342–345). وبالمثل، إذا أعدنا بناء مرويات ابن أبي الدنيا مُسبغين عليها نسقية لا تتوفر عليها مقارنة بمصنفات أرسطو، سنراه يبدأ بدوره مما للإنسان من إنسانية، أي من عقل ومروءة وكرم، فيستحثه من خلال المرويات والنماذج الإنسانية الفاضلة على تحقيق مروءته/إنسانيته أو بالأحرى صونها.[35] والانحدار الأخلاقي للإنسان هنا ليس معصية لأوامر خارجية، بقدر ما هو فشلٌ في الاستجابة لنداء داخلي، ومن ثم إهانةٌ لهذه المروءة والكرامة. وإذا جاز لنا تشبيه ساحة الأخلاق بحلبة رهان، فإن ما يراهن به المرء ويخاطر به ليس شيئًا آخر غير مروءته، فله أن يصونها أو يخسرها.

بهذا نفهم تربُّع الحياء على عرش الخصال العشر المكونة للمكارم،[36] فما الحياء إلا تهيُّب المرء وتصاغره عند الإقدام أو التفكير في الإقدام على ما ينتقص من مروءته أو كرم نفسه، كما بيّنّا أعلاه. والأمر نفسه يصح على الصدق وحفظ الأمانة والشجاعة، بل إن كُلًّا من العطاء والتذمم للجار والتذمم للصاحب إنما تبتغي صون هذه المروءة والكرامة عند الآخرين، على أساس أنه حيثما أهدرت كرامة واحد من الناس فكأنما أهدرت كرامة الناس جميعا. ومن باب حفظ المروءة ألّف مصنِّفنا بابًا في "ذم المسألة والزجر عنها" ضمن رسالة «**القناعة والتعفف**»، وأسند فيه إلى سعيد بن العاص (ت. 679/59) من قوله: "أخزى الله المعروف إذا لم يكن ابتداءً من غير مسألة. أما إذا أتاك [السائل] تكاد ترى دمه من وجهه ومخاطرًا لا يدري أتعطيه أم تمنعه، فوالله لو خرجت له من جميع مالك ما كافأته" (ابن أبي الدنيا 2000، 481، ح45). فـالأخلاق عنده إنما هي صون المرء لمروءته أي لإنسانيته. ولأن الأمر يتعلق بإنسانية الإنسان، فقد أتاح له ذلك استعادة المُثل الأخلاقية للعرب في حقبة ما قبل الإسلام من دون حرج، بعيدًا عن موقف الإدانة الأخلاقية الذي طالما طال تلك الفترة.

35 ذاك ما فطن له الراغب الأصفهاني، فبعد أن ذكر الفضائل النفسية الأربع (العقل، والشجاعة، والعفة، والعدالة) وفروعها، اضطر لأن يضيف: "والإنسانية والكرم يجمعان هذه الفضائل" (الراغب الأصفهاني 2007، 142).

36 وهو كذلك عند المعاصرين، انظر الفصل السادس («الحياء أساسًا للأخلاق») في: عبد الرحمن (2017، 1/181–207).

## 5 خاتمة

بهذا تتبين محورية مكارم الأخلاق لدى ابن أبي الدنيا، وكيف أنها عنوان لتوجه أخلاقي قائم بذاته داخل الأخلاق الأثرية، بل داخل اتجاهات الفكر الأخلاقي في الإسلام عامة. ويتبين هذا من ظاهرتين ثقافيتين: **أولاهما** فُشوّ هذا المصطلح في عناوين الكثير من المصنفات التي ظهرت جميعها في وقت لاحق على ابن أبي الدنيا،[37] حتى إن بيلمي يرى أن "كل دراسة لجنس أو أدبيات المكارم في النثر العربي تبدأ حتمًا مع ابن أبي الدنيا" (Bellamy 1963, 108). أما **ثانيهما** – وهي الأهم – فهي تلك "الحياة المديدة المجيدة" التي قُيِّضت لعبارة «مكارم الأخلاق» ضمن حديث "إنما بعثت لأتمم مكارم الأخلاق،" بالرغم من أن الحديث لا يرد بهذا اللفظ في أيّ من مدونات الحديث الرئيسة (الكتب الستة).[38]

لا يحصر علو مكانة تصانيف ابن أبي الدنيا – بين المصنفات الأثرية ذات المنحى الأخلاقي – في المضمون والمنظور فحسب، بل يتعداه إلى الشكل أيضًا؛ إذ يخضع سرد المرويات عنده لترتيب موضوعي (thematic) ومنطقي بفضل الإطار النظري الموجِّه الذي اشتقّه من كلام السيدة عائشة. وقد حافظ مصنّفنا على هذا النسق؛ رغم العدد الهائل من المرويات التي تميل بالمؤلف عادة إلى الاستطراد وتَنَكُّب سبيل الوحدة الموضوعية. ولهذا قيل عن مصنفاته على العموم: إنها تتصف "بالوحدة الموضوعية، وجودة الترتيب" (ابن حميد وابن ملوح 1998، 72/1). لكن تصانيف ابن أبي الدنيا تظل مقيدة بما تفرضه صنعته الحديثية؛ كغياب المؤلف وتواريه خلف سيل المرويات والآثار التي يُسندها. ولقد رأينا أنه لم يفتح غير كُوّة واحدة صغيرة – في الجدار الطويل المتصل من المرويات – كي يتحدث بلسانه مفصحًا عن خطة الكتاب، ومُعربًا عن رأيه في العلاقة بين الأخلاق والدين. وحتى في هذه اللحظة النادرة من لحظات انكشاف الذاتية، وجد ابن أبي الدنيا نفسه مضطراً إلى نسبة الرأي إلى غيره في صيغة المبني للمجهول، فقال: "وقد قيل: ليس من خلق كريم ولا فعل جميل إلا وقد وصله الله بالدين" (ابن أبي الدنيا 2000، 287، ح38).

بهذا نكون قد بيّنا أن أخلاقيات ابن أبي الدنيا هي أخلاقيات أثرية المادة عقلية الصورة، وهي بذلك تُشَكّل جيب مقاومة فريدًا داخل الاتجاه السائد – لدى أترابه – الذي يقرر أن مصدر التحسين والتقبيح شرعي لا عقلي. وضمن مناخ التنوع الأممي (cosmopolitical)

---

37 أحصى بِشر فارس (1939، 32–34، الحواشي 2–11) عناوين 15 كتابا يرد فيها لفظ «المكارم»، ولكن لم يصلنا منها إلا القليل.

38 من أجل عرض وافٍ لمختلف الصيغ اللغوية التي ورد بها الحديث (انظر فارس 1939، 38–44).

للدولة الإسلامية في النصف الثاني من القرن الثالث الهجري، كانت أخلاقياته – بحسب الظاهر – تخاطب المسلمين، لكنها كانت – في العمق – دعوةً للناس إلى كلمة أخلاقية سواء، شعاره في ذلك أن الفضيلة (مكارم الأخلاق) ضالة المؤمن أنّى وجدها فهو أحق بها، أن المؤمن امرؤ قبل أن يأتيه الدين.

## قائمة المصادر


إبراهيم، مجدي السيد. 1990. «مقدمة». ضمن: **مكارم الأخلاق**، لأبو بكر بن أبي الدنيا. القاهرة: مكتبة القرآن.

ابن أبي الدنيا، أبو بكر. 1365هـ [1946]. **العقل وفضله**، عرَّف الكتاب وترجم للمؤلف وصحَّحه محمد بن زاهد الكوثري. القاهرة: مكتبة نشر الثقافة الإسلامية.

ابن أبي الدنيا، أبو بكر. 1988. **الإخوان**، تحقيق وتعليق محمد عبد الرحمن طوالبة، إشراف ومراجعة نجم عبد الرحمن خلف. القاهرة: دار الاعتصام.

ابن أبي الدنيا، أبو بكر. 1990أ. **مكارم الأخلاق**، تحقيق وتعليق مجدي السيد إبراهيم. القاهرة: مكتبة القرآن.

ابن أبي الدنيا، أبو بكر. 1990ب. **مكارم الأخلاق**، حققه وشرحه وقدم له جميز بيلمي. القاهرة: مكتبة ابن تيمية.

ابن أبي الدنيا، أبو بكر. 2000. «كتاب العقل ومكارم الأخلاق». ضمن: **رسائل ابن أبي الدنيا في الزهد والرقائق والورع**، لابن أبي الدنيا، الجزء الأول، جمع وضبط وتعليق أبي بكر بن عبد الله سعداوي. الشارقة: المنتدى الإسلامي.

ابن أبي حاتم، أبو محمد. 2006. **العلل**، تحقيق فريق من الباحثين بإشراف سعد بن عبد الله الحميد وخالد بن عبد الرحمن الجريسي. الرياض: مطابع الحميضي.

ابن تغري بردي، أبو المحاسن. د.ت. **النجوم الزاهرة في ملوك مصر والقاهرة**. القاهرة: وزارة الثقافة والإرشاد القومي، دار الكتب.

ابن تيمية، أحمد بن عبد الحليم. 2004. **مجموع الفتاوى**، جمع وترتيب عبد الرحمن بن محمد بن قاسم. الرياض: مجمع الملك فهد لطباعة المصحف الشريف.

ابن الجعد، علي. 1990. **مسند ابن الجعد**، تحقيق عامر أحمد حيدر. بيروت: مؤسسة نادر.

ابن الجوزي، أبو الفرج. 1986. **الطب الروحاني**، تحقيق محمد السعيد زغلول. القاهرة: مكتبة الثقافة الدينية.

ابن الجوزي، أبو الفرج. 1981. **العلل المتناهية في الأحاديث الواهية**، تحقيق إرشاد الحق الأثري. إسلام أباد: إدارة العلوم الأثرية.

ابن حبان البستي. 1396هـ. **المجروحين من المحدثين والضعفاء والمتروكين**، تحقيق محمود إبراهيم زايد. حلب: دار الوعي.

ابن حبان البستي. 1977. **روضة العقلاء ونزهة الفضلاء**، تحقيق محمد محي الدين عبد الحميد. بيروت: دار الكتب العلمية.

ابن حبان البستي. 1988. **الإحسان في تقريب صحيح ابن حبان**، ترتيب علاء الدين بن بلبان، حققه وخرج أحاديثه وعلق عليه شعيب الأرناؤوط. بيروت: مؤسسة الرسالة.

ابن حميد، صالح وعبد الرحمن ابن ملوح، إشراف. 1998. **موسوعة نضرة النعيم في أخلاق الرسول الكريم**، 12 ج. جدة: دار الوسيلة للنشر والتوزيع.

ابن عساكر، أبو القاسم. 1995. **تاريخ دمشق**، تحقيق عمرو بن غرامة العمروي. بيروت: دار الفكر للطباعة والنشر والتوزيع.

ابن ماجه، أبو عبد الله. 1952. **سنن ابن ماجة**، تحقيق محمد فؤاد عبد الباقي. القاهرة: دار إحياء الكتب العربية، البابي الحلبي.

ابن منظور. 1414 هـ. **لسان العرب**، ط3. بيروت: دار صادر.

ابن منظور. 1984. **مختصر تاريخ دمشق لابن عساكر**، تحقيق روحية النحاس ورياض عبد الحميد مراد ومحمد مطيع الحافظ. دمشق: دار الفكر للطباعة والتوزيع والنشر.

ابن وهب، أبو محمد. 1995. **الجامع في الحديث لابن وهب**، تحقيق مصطفى حسن. الرياض: دار ابن الجوزي.

أبو يعلى، أحمد بن علي. 1984. **مسند أبي يعلى**، تحقيق حسين سليم أسد. دمشق: دار المأمون للتراث.

أحمد بن حنبل. 2001. **مسند الإمام أحمد**، تحقيق شعيب الأرناؤوط وآخرون. بيروت: مؤسسة الرسالة.

الألباني، محمد ناصر الدين. 1408هـ. **ضعيف الجامع الصغير وزيادته**، ط٢، أشرف على طبعه زهير الشاويش. بيروت: المكتب الإسلامي.

الألباني، محمد ناصر الدين. 1992. **سلسلة الأحاديث الضعيفة والموضوعة وأثرها السيء في الأمة**. الرياض: دار المعارف.

البخاري، محمد بن إسماعيل. 2002. **صحيح البخاري**، طبعة جديدة مضبوطة ومصححة ومفهرسة. دمشق، بيروت: دار ابن كثير.

البغوي، أبو محمد. 1983. **شرح السنة**، تحقيق: شعيب الأرناؤوط ومحمد زهير الشاويش. بيروت: المكتب الإسلامي.

البيهقي، أحمد بن الحسين. 2000. **شعب الإيمان**، تحقيق محمد السعيد زغلول. بيروت: دار الكتب العلمية.

البيهقي، أحمد بن الحسين. 2003. **شعب الإيمان**، حققه وراجع نصوصه وخرج أحاديثه عبد العلي عبد الحميد حامد، أشرف على تحقيقه وتخريج أحاديثه مختار أحمد الندوي، صاحب الدار السلفية ببومباي – الهند. الرياض: مكتبة الرشد.

الترمذي، أبو عيسى محمد بن عيسى. 1996. **سنن الترمذي (الجامع الكبير)**، تحقيق بشار عواد معروف. بيروت: دار الغرب الإسلامي.

تقي إسلامي، محمد وآخرون. 2012. **المدارس الأخلاقية في الفكر الإسلامي دراسة منهجية في المصادر والاتجاهات**، ترجمة عبد الحسن بهبهاني بور. بيروت: مركز الحضارة لتنمية الفكر الإسلامي.

التوحيدي، أبو حيان. 1986. **المقابسات**، تحقيق علي شلق. بيروت: دار المدى للطباعة والنشر.

الجابري، محمد عابد. 2001. **العقل الأخلاقي العربي: دراسة لمنظومة القيم في الثقافة العربية**. القاهرة: مركز دراسات الوحدة العربية.

جرادي، شفيق. 2010. «المرتكز الأساسي في نظام القيم الإسلامي». ضمن: **الدين في التصورات الإسلامية والمسيحية**، لمجموعة من الباحثين. بيروت: دار المعارف الحكمية.

الجرجاني، محمد السيد الشريف. د.ت. **معجم التعريفات**، تحقيق ودراسة محمد صديق المنشاوي. القاهرة: دار الفضيلة.

الحاكم النيسابوري، أبو عبد الله. 1990. **المستدرك على الصحيحين**، تحقيق مصطفى عبد القادر عطا. بيروت: دار الكتب العلمية.

الحكيم الترمذي، أبو عبد الله. 2010. **نوادر الأصول في معرفة أحاديث الرسول صلى الله عليه وسلم**، تحقيق توفيق محمد تكلة. بيروت: دار النوادر.

الحموي، ياقوت. 1993. **معجم الأدباء (إرشاد الأريب إلى معرفة الأديب)**، تحقيق إحسان عباس، ط1. بيروت: دار الغرب الإسلامي.

ديكارت، رونيه. 1968. **مقال في المنهج**، ترجمة محمود محمد الخضيري، ط2. بيروت: دار الفكر.

الديلمي، أبو شجاع. 1986. **الفردوس بمأثور الخطاب**، تحقيق السعيد بن بسيوني زغلول. بيروت: دار الكتب العلمية.

الذهبي، شمس الدين. 1985. **سير أعلام النبلاء**، ط٣، تحقيق مجموعة من المحققين بإشراف شعيب الأرناؤوط. القاهرة: مؤسسة الرسالة.

الرازي، أبو بكر محمد بن زكريا. 1939. **رسائل فلسفية**، جمعه وصححه بول كراوس. القاهرة: مطبعة بول باربي.

الراغب الأصفهاني. 2007. **الذريعة إلى مكارم الشريعة**، تحقيق ودراسة أبو اليزيد أو زيد العجمي. القاهرة: دار السلام.

سليم، محمد إبراهيم. 1986. **المروءة الغائبة**. القاهرة: مكتبة القرآن.

الصنعاني، عبد الرزاق. 2015. **المصنف**، تحقيق مركز البحوث بدار التأصيل. القاهرة: دار التأصيل.

الطبراني، أبو القاسم. 1983. **المعجم الكبير**، تحقيق حمدي بن عبد المجيد السلفي. القاهرة: مكتبة ابن تيمية.

الطبراني، أبو القاسم. 1989. **مكارم الأخلاق** (مطبوع مع مكارم الأخلاق لابن أبي الدنيا)، كتب هوامشه أحمد شمس الدين. بيروت: دار الكتب العلمية.

الطبراني، أبو القاسم. 1995. **المعجم الأوسط**، تحقيق طارق بن عوض وعبد المحسن الحسيني. القاهرة: دار الحرمين.

العامري، أبو الحسن. 1988. **الإعلام بمناقب الإسلام**، تحقيق ودراسة أحمد عبد الحميد غراب. الرياض: دار الأصالة.

عبد الجبار، القاضي أبو الحسن. 1965. **المغني: التعديل والتجوير**، تحقيق محمود محمد قاسم. القاهرة: وزارة الثقافة والإرشاد القومي.

عبد الرحمن، طه. 2017. **دين الحياء: من الفقه الائتماري إلى الفقه الائتماني**. بيروت: المؤسسة العربية للفكر والإبداع.

العقيلي، أبو جعفر. 1984. **الضعفاء الكبير**، تحقيق عبد المعطي أمين قلعجي. بيروت: دار الكتب العلمية.

غولدتسهير، إغناتس. 1980.«العناصر الأفلاطونية المحدثة والغنوصية في الحديث». ضمن: **التراث اليوناني في الحضارة الإسلامية**، بتحرير من عبد الرحمن بدوي، ط4 بيروت: دار القلم.

فارس، بِشر. 1939. **مباحث عربية في المكارم والمروءة والفرد والقبيلة**. القاهرة: مطبعة المعارف ومكتبتها.

فخري، ماجد. 1978. **الفكر الأخلاقي العربي، نصوص اختارها وقدم لها الدكتور ماجد فخري**. الجزء 1: الفقهاء والمتكلمون. بيروت: الأهلية للنشر.

الفراء، يحيى بن زياد. 1972. **معاني القرآن**، تحقيق أحمد يوسف النجاتي ومحمد علي النجار وعبد الفتاح إسماعيل الشلبي. القاهرة: الدار المصرية للتأليف والترجمة.

القضاعي، أبو عبد الله. 1986. **مسند الشهاب**، تحقيق حمدي بن عبد المجيد السلفي. بيروت: مؤسسة الرسالة.

القوتلي، حسين. 1971. «مقدمة». ضمن: **العقل وفهم القرآن**، للحارث المحاسبي، قدم له وحقق نصوصه حسين القوتلي، 192–195. بيروت: دار الفكر.

اللخمي، صالح بن جناح. 1992. **الأدب والمروءة**، تحقيق قسم التحقيق بالدار. طنطا: دار الصحابة للتراث.

مالك بن أنس. 1985. **الموطأ**، صححه ورقمه وخرج أحاديثه وعلق عليه محمد فؤاد عبد الباقي. بيروت: دار إحياء التراث العربي.

الماوردي، أبو الحسن. 1985. **أدب الدنيا والدين**، شرح وتعليق محمد كريم راجح، ط4. بيروت: دار اقرأ.

المحاسبي، الحارث بن أسد. 1971. **العقل وفهم القرآن**، قدم له وحقق نصوصه حسين القوتلي. بيروت: دار الفكر.

مسكويه، أبو علي أحمد بن محمد بن يعقوب. 2011. **تهذيب الأخلاق**، دراسة وتحقيق عماد الهلالي. بيروت، بغداد: منشورات الجمل.

معمر، بن أبي عمرو. 1983. **الجامع** (منشور في آخر مصنف عبد الرزاق)، تحقيق حبيب الرحمن الأعظمي. إسلام أباد: المجلس العلمي بباكستان.

الهيبي، الأب إدغار. 2010. «الدين ونظام القيم». ضمن: **الدين في التصورات الإسلامية والمسيحية**، بتحرير من مجموعة من الباحثين. بيروت: دار المعارف الحكمية.

الهيثمي، نور الدين. 1992. **بغية الباحث عن زوائد مسند الحارث**، تحقيق حسين أحمد صالح الباكري. المدينة المنورة: مركز خدمة السنة والسيرة النبوية.

الهيثمي، نور الدين. 1994. **مجمع الزوائد ومنبع الفوائد**، تحقيق حسام الدين القدسي. القاهرة: مكتبة القدسي.

Arkoun, Mohammed. 1982. *L'humanisme arabe au IV$^{e}$/X$^{e}$ siècle: Miskawayh, philosophe et historien.* Paris: Vrin.

Bellamy, James A. 1963. "The Makārim al-Akhlāq by Ibn Abī'l-Dunyā (A Preliminary Study)." *Muslim World* 53: 106–119. DOI: 10.1111/j.1478-1913.1963.tb01144.x.

Broadie, Sarah. 2006. "Aristotle and Contemporary Ethics." In *The Blackwell Guide to Aristotle's Nicomachean Ethics*, edited by Richard Kraut. Oxford: Blackwell.

Di Vito, Robert A. 1999. "Old Testament Anthropology and the Construction of Personal Identity." *The Catholic Biblical Quarterly* 61(2): 217–238.

Dürrenmatt, Jacques. 2010. "Le style est l'homme même: destin d'une buffonnerie à l'époque romantique." *Romantisme* 148(2): 63–76.

Fakhry, Majid. 1994. *Ethical Theories in Islam*, 2nd ed. Leiden: Brill.

Goodman, Lenn. 1999. *Jewish and Islamic Philosophy: Crosspollinations in the Classic Age*. New Jersey: Rutgers University Press.

Hourani, George. 1985. *Reason and Tradition in Islamic Ethics.* Cambridge: Cambridge University Press.

Librande, Leonard. 2005. "Ibn Abī al-Dunyā: Certainty and Morality." *Studia Islamica* 100/101: 5–42.

Zilio-Grandi, Ida. 2015. "*Ḥilm* or Judiciousness: A Contribution to the Study of Islamic Ethics." *Studia Islamica* 110: 88–95.

CHAPTER 5

# Narrations on Virtuous Acts in Epitomes of al-Ghazālī's *Iḥyāʾ*

***From Ibn al-Jawzī's* Minhāj al-Qāṣidīn *to Its Reception in Modernity***

*Pieter Coppens*

## 1 Introduction

The genre of narrative virtue ethics in the Islamic tradition arguably finds its clearest expression in the field of *ḥadīth* literature, more particularly in the category of virtuous acts (*faḍāʾil al-aʿmāl*), as well as in sayings attributed to the earliest generations (*al-salaf al-ṣāliḥ*), and in the sayings and stories of prominent early Sufi figures. Abū Ḥāmid al-Ghazālī's (d. 505/1111) *Iḥyāʾ ʿUlūm al-Dīn* ("Revival of the Religious Sciences") is a rich source for such narrative virtue ethics, which he copied from works from the earlier tradition, mainly Abū Ṭālib al-Makkī's (d. 386/996) *Qūt al-Qulūb* ("Nourishment of the Hearts"). His seemingly uncritical incorporation of Prophetic narrations on virtuous acts, that were often classified as weak (*ḍaʿīf*) or forged (*mawḍūʿ*), has not been without dispute in the later tradition. Whether unreliable *ḥadīth* material on virtuous acts can be transmitted uncritically and acted upon plays a prominent role in modern critiques on the reliability of the *Iḥyāʾ*.

Historically, the role of this specific point of criticism on the *Iḥyāʾ* was more marginal, although always present. The eventual relative absence of *ḥadīth* criticism in early polemics against the *Iḥyāʾ* may have to do with the topics for which al-Ghazālī used Prophetic narrations. The *Iḥyāʾ* hardly deals with matters of *fiqh*, for which scholars historically have always demanded the highest standards of reliability for Prophetic narrations. Most narrations that al-Ghazālī employs are parenetic, stressing certain supererogatory acts of worship, addressing the ethical topics of good manners and virtuous character (*adab* and *akhlāq*), as well as "softeners" (*raqāʾiq*) and "exhortation and dissuasion" (*al-targhīb wa-l-tarhīb*), to all of which scholars historically applied different standards of reliability than to creed- and *fiqh*-related topics.

The idea that this type of *ḥadīth* material may be held to lower standards of reliability than legal material has a long history in Islamic scholarship. According to many scholars, the positive and ethically desired effects of such narrations legitimised sharing them, despite them being weak or forged. The dominant position in the premodern period was that unreliable *aḥādīth* could be accepted in the realm of non-legal virtue ethics to encourage believers to act virtuously (Fudge 2006, 120; Brown 2011, 4; Brown 2014, 224–254; Lange 2015, 82, 84f). This was not an exclusive position of Sufis. The only exception to this permissive viewpoint was a small group of Ḥanbalīs from Baghdad and Damascus, among them ʿAbd al-Raḥmān b. ʿAlī Ibn al-Jawzī (d. 597/1201), some of the Damascene Maqdisī-family, and a score of scholars influenced by them.

It is to the reception of the *Iḥyāʾ* by these pivotal Ḥanbalī figures that we will have a closer look in this chapter, through an investigation of the appropriation of the *Iḥyāʾ* by two prominent Ḥanbalī scholars from the sixth/twelfth and seventh/thirteenth centuries: Ibn al-Jawzī's *Minhāj al-Qāṣidīn wa-Mufīd al-Ṣādiqīn* ("The Way of the Strivers and the Benefit of the Truthful"), and Aḥmad b. ʿAbd al-Raḥmān Ibn Qudāma al-Maqdisī's (d. 689/1290) epitome of that work, *Mukhtaṣar Minhāj al-Qāṣidīn* ("Summary of the Way of the Strivers"), as well as their reception in both reformist and puritan Salafī circles of the twentieth century.[1] My purpose is twofold. First, I shed light on their

1 Ibn al-Jawzī needs no further introduction here as a well-known scholar. The most important academic source for his biography is the work of Merlin Swartz (2002). There is an unresolved discussion about the identity of the more obscure author of *Mukhtaṣar Minhāj al-Qāṣidīn*, who should by any means not be confused with Muwaffaq al-Dīn Ibn Qudāma (d. 620/1223), the famous author of the *Mughnī*. According to the *ṭabaqāt*-works of Ḥanbalī scholars, his full name was Najm al-Dīn Abū l-ʿAbbās Aḥmad b. ʿAbd al-Raḥmān b. Muḥammad b. Aḥmad b. Muḥammad Ibn Qudāma al-Maqdisī (Ibn Rajab 2005, 4:231–232). The introduction to the *Mukhtaṣar* also names him as Najm al-Dīn Abū l-ʿAbbās Aḥmad, but then names him as the son of ʿIzz al-Dīn Abū ʿAbd Allāh Muḥammad, mentions his grandfather as Shams al-Dīn Abū Muḥammad ʿAbd al-Raḥmān, and his great-grandfather as Abū ʿUmar Muḥammad b. Aḥmad b. Muḥammad Ibn Qudāma al-Maqdisī al-Ḥanbalī. So, there is an extra chain in the lineage (ʿIzz al-Dīn) that the *ṭabaqāt* do not mention (Ibn Qudāma 1991, 9). All names in this lineage belong to a family of prominent scholars from the Ḥanbalī school that came to Damascus from Nablus as refugees from the Crusaders. They put their mark on the city, from the sixth/twelfth to the seventh/fourteenth centuries, with a unique combination of thorough knowledge of scriptural sources and religious charisma as popular preachers. The settlement of al-Ṣāliḥiyya, on the mount of Qāsiyūn, in his age was the gathering place of scholars and followers of the Ḥanbalī school, often with roots in Jerusalem (hence the prevalent *kunyā* al-Maqdisī among scholars from this part of the city). It was known for its vivid tradition of religious education and preaching, and brought forth many prominent scholars of the Ḥanbalī school (Leder 1997). The *ṭabaqāt*-works do not mention much details about his life. As may be expected from hagiographical literature, he is described as someone of noble character, who memorised texts with great ease and had great insight. He was appointed as a judge before his thirtieth, worked as a teacher at the famous Dār al-Ḥadīth al-Ashrafiyya in al-Ṣāliḥiyya, and was instructor of the Ḥanbalī study circle in the Grand Umayyad Mosque of Damascus. The *ṭabaqāt* sources also report that he regularly bravely participated as a sworded horseman in *jihād* expeditions. He is said to have fought in the recapture of Tripoli on the Crusaders in 688/1289, under the auspices of the Mamluk sultan al-Malik al-Manṣūr

reception of the *Iḥyā'* specifically on the aspect of narrative virtue ethics, to see what the consequences of their strong opinions have been for the way they dealt with the abundant *aḥādīth* and sayings of early pious figures (*āthār*) used by al-Ghazālī in his magnum opus. Second, I explain how and why their works and approach rose to prominence in the twentieth century after being relatively marginal in the preceding centuries.

I contend that the work of al-Ghazālī was appreciated by both of these medieval Ḥanbalīs, and their appropriators in the twentieth century, exactly because of the virtue ethics propagated in it. They raised the bar of *ḥadīth* criticism on this specific aspect to be able to convincingly convey this central purpose of the *Iḥyā'*, that had their sympathy, to their intended audiences without compromising their specific Ḥanbalī values of *ḥadīth* criticism and rejection of certain mystical aspects of the Sufi tradition. Although they at times also censored and replaced certain narrations to steer the virtue ethics content proposed by al-Ghazālī in a slightly different direction, this was not the main purpose of their *ḥadīth* criticism: their main stake was raising the religious credibility of these propagated virtues. While the intended audience in medieval times mainly consisted of students of religion and fellow scholars, from the twentieth century onwards these epitomes received a more general audience as part of the project of "moral refinement" (*tahdhīb al-akhlāq*) in reformist movements. This put the bars of textual criticism even higher: where fellow scholars and students in medieval times had the scholarly tools to distinguish between strong and weak narrations, the general audience should only be presented with the strongest narrations to avoid confusion.

Al-Ghazālī's *Iḥyā' 'Ulūm al-Dīn* is widely celebrated as a classic of Islamic literature and has, as has its author, received generous scholarly attention (Ormsby 2007; Griffel 2009; Garden 2013). The work's author, structure, and content thus do not need further introduction here. An encompassing reception history of the work, and the story of how it has become a widely spread classic, both praised and criticised, still largely remains unwritten, however. As noted by Michael Cook, "The wide diffusion of the work [..] is documented by a mass of evidence that remains largely unstudied" (Cook 2001, 450–451). This still holds true today. Part of this reception history should entail an investigation of the critiques the work received on its use and propagation of narrative virtue ethics in different Islamic intellectual and sectarian environments. This chapter is a first modest step towards such a wider reception history. Through this endeavour I intend to contribute to discussions on the relation between

---

Qalāwūn (d. 689/1290). He passed away at the age of 38 (Ibn Qudāma 1991, 7–8; Ibn Rajab 2005, 4:231–232).

Sufism and Ḥanbalī-traditionalism, a field in which more and more key texts are covered by academic research (Makdisi 1979; Anjum 2010; Picken 2011; Post 2016; 2020), as well as their revival and reception in modern and contemporary Salafī circles. In this endeavour I pay particular attention to the field of narrative virtue ethics, as reflected in these works. I intend to uncover how the stress on reliable *ḥadīth* – especially when pertaining to virtue ethics – in these circles influenced the way the *Iḥyāʾ* was received and restructured from the twentieth century onwards.

## 2 The Virtue Ethics of Knowledge in the *Iḥyāʾ* and the Knowledge Discipline of *Ḥadīth*

It has been suggested that al-Ghazālī simply did not know much about *ḥadīth* and its discipline of knowledge, because of the school of al-Juwaynī (d. 478/1085) in which he was formally trained. This school allegedly did not pay great attention to the discipline of *ḥadīth* because of its emphasis on rational knowledge disciplines and disputation (al-Shāmī 1993a, 166–169; al-Qaraḍāwī 1994, 150; Siddiqui 2019, 135–162). In medieval biographical literature, several biographers suggested that al-Ghazālī only delved into the two *Ṣaḥīḥ*s of al-Bukhārī (d. 256/870) and Muslim (d. 261/875) at the end of his life. This is most probably a trope to accentuate the importance of the *Ṣaḥīḥayn*, by showing how even speculative theologians, philosophers and Sufis ultimately returned to the authority of these works (al-Qaraḍāwī 1994, 154–155; Griffel 2009, 56–57). Does al-Ghazālī himself have anything to say about the knowledge discipline of *ḥadīth* and its practitioners in his *Iḥyāʾ* that may prove this perception of him either right or wrong?

The first book of the *Iḥyāʾ*, *Kitāb al-ʿIlm* ("The Book of Knowledge"), contains ample reflection on the Islamic knowledge disciplines and the abominable inner state of its practitioners according to al-Ghazālī. One might even argue, as has Garden (2013), that this first Book contains the entire intention of the *Iḥyāʾ*. The "Revival" that al-Ghazālī proposes may be considered a call to return to virtue ethics for the scholarly class of his age. Al-Ghazālī laments the dry technical state that the Islamic knowledge disciplines have turned into, and how Islamic scholarship has rather become a career path than a path to a good outcome in the Hereafter. Al-Ghazālī envisions a return of the Islamic knowledge disciplines to "knowledge of the path to the Hereafter" (*ʿilm ṭarīq al-ākhira*), where these knowledge disciplines are only studied for the sake of God and the Hereafter, and not for positions, power, and prestige. He therefore favours knowledge disciplines that deal with the inner state of people, their hearts and souls, which he considers to be the true knowledge disciplines of the Hereafter, over theology and law, which he ultimately considers this-worldly knowledge disciplines (Garden 2005, 218–219; al-Ghazālī 2011, 1:66–67).

Where does this leave the study of *ḥadīth* in his project of reviving the Islamic knowledge disciplines in their perceived original goal of attaining the Hereafter? In a passage on individual obligation (*farḍ ʿayn*) in knowledge, al-Ghazālī criticises every group of scholars for considering their own branch of knowledge as an individual obligation. Scholars of *ḥadīth* also have this illusion according to him: "Each group considers his own branch of knowledge as obligatory. (…) The exegetes of the Qur'ān and the *ḥadīth* scholars say: 'It is knowledge of the Qur'ān and the Sunna, because, through these, one reaches all disciplines of knowledge'" (al-Ghazālī 2011, 1:54–55). Al-Ghazālī himself classifies *ḥadīth* as part of the knowledge disciplines that are a communal obligation (*farḍ kifāya*) (al-Ghazālī 2011, 1:65–66). He considers them praiseworthy as long as they are studied as an instrumental knowledge discipline, in service of the higher goals of the inward knowledge disciplines and the "knowledge of the path to the Hereafter." In a commentary on a supplication of al-Sarī al-Saqaṭī (d. between 251/865 and 258/871) for his student al-Junayd (d. 298/910), "May God make you a companion of *ḥadīth* that is a Sufi, not a Sufi that is a companion of *ḥadīth*," al-Ghazālī explains that to be a successful Sufi, one first needs to master the knowledge discipline of *ḥadīth* and religious knowledge in general as a prerequisite (al-Ghazālī 2011, 1:83). *ḥadīth* should only be studied to a limited extent, not as a hyper-specialisation. Ironically, he considers the study of the works of al-Bukhārī and Muslim as the absolute minimal, and the works that contain sound (*ṣaḥīḥ*) narrations as the maximum extent (al-Ghazālī 2011, 1:146–149). The fact that he mentions this as such, makes it more plausible that the reason why he included so many unsound narrations in the *Iḥyā'* is perhaps indeed because of his uncritical copying of passages from earlier works like the *Qūt al-Qulūb*, trusting in the reliability of their selection, as claimed by Ibn al-Jawzī and Rashīd Riḍā (d. 1354/1935), which we will see later.

## 3 Premodern *Ḥadīth* Criticism on the *Iḥyā'*: *Minhāj al-Qāṣidīn* and Its *Mukhtaṣar*

The *Iḥyā'* received a lot of criticism during the lifetime of the author himself (Cook 2001, 455–456; Garden 2005). This criticism has persisted throughout the centuries and has increased even further in the course of the twentieth century, mostly due to a general revival of *ḥadīth* studies, the rise in popularity of Salafī-inclined Islamic scholarship, as well as movements of Islamic reform and modernism. These reform movements criticised the work for its use of weak Prophetic narrations, and increasingly problematised (certain aspects of) Sufism and speculative theology (*kalām*) as a legitimate part of the Islamic heritage (ʿAbd al-Ḥamīd 1988; al-Shāmī 1993a, 157–182; al-Qaraḍāwī 1994, 117–127, 158–159; al-Ṭanṭāwī 2001, 2:253). Many of these modern and contemporary critiques on the *Iḥyāʾ* echo premodern critiques. The three perpetual points of criticism are: al-Ghazālī's use of problematic Prophetic narratives, his embrace of perceived excesses of the Sufi tradition, and his use of illegitimate philosophical ideas.

In his own age, the *Iḥyāʾ* already caused controversy in Nishapur, where al-Ghazālī returned to teach after the wanderings that followed his much-discussed crisis. In the Islamic West (the *Maghrib*), where Sufism was not yet as strongly rooted within Islamic tradition as it was in the Islamic East (the *Mashriq*), several fierce treatises were written against the work (Garden 2005, 141–184). The controversy reached such heights that al-Ghazālī even felt compelled to write a defence of the work himself, as well as his own epitome in Persian (al-Ghazālī 2011, 10:213–354; Hillenbrand 2013). The main accusations in his own age were propagation of too extreme Sufi ideas, inappropriate philosophical ideas in matters of creed, errors in Arabic grammar, and poor Persian (Garden 2005, 76–78). His use of problematic Prophetic narrations was still only a minor part of the criticism in his own age, not so much aimed at his use of weak (*ḍaʿīf*) and forged (*mawḍūʿ*) material, but rather at his laxity in naming sources, and did not play any role in his own rebuttal of the criticisms. These accusations had a social and political angle as well: al-Ghazālī had made enemies because of his critical stance towards the career-minded scholars and governors of the region, a criticism that is at the heart of the *Iḥyāʾ* (Garden 2005, 118–140).

This perpetual criticism on the *Iḥyāʾ*, which rose simultaneously with its popularity, also caused another more constructive trend among Islamic scholars. Many scholars from different Islamic intellectual and sectarian traditions sought a middle way between completely renouncing the work and uncritically accepting it. To that purpose they wrote commentaries on the work, or works, classifying the *aḥādīth* used by al-Ghazālī, in which they articulated their mild criticism, but also showed their praise. Another strategy of finding a balance between criticism and praise was through composition of positive-critical epitomes of the work, in which the composer conserved what he agreed with, and scrapped what he deemed problematic (Ḥaddād 1987; al-Shāmī 1993b; Cook 2001, 453–456; Reichmuth 2009, 269–275).

The works of Ibn al-Jawzī and Ibn Qudāma belong to that second category of positive-critical epitomes. As scholars of the Ḥanbalī school, and part of the very vivid Ḥanbalī culture of learning in their age in Baghdad and al-Ṣāliḥiyya, a suburb of Damascus, they summarised the *Iḥyāʾ* in such a way that it would become suitable to teach and consume within their own circles, conforming with their specific religious views. It is likely that these authors very well realised that the popularity and influence of this work had become so pervasive that it was inevitable that scholars and students in their own circles would come into contact with it. Composing a purified version of the work was, possibly, a way to take advantage of the immense popularity of the work to propagate ideas they agreed with.

In his *al-Muntaẓam fī Tārīkh al-Mulūk wa-l-Umam* ("Compilation on the History of Kings and Nations"), Ibn al-Jawzī mentions having composed a treatise more emphatically against the *Iḥyāʾ*, with the title *Iʿlām al-Aḥyāʾ bi-Aghlāṭ al-Iḥyāʾ* ("Informing the Living about the Mistakes in the Revival"). Yet, there is no manuscript left of the treatise. Some of the criticism in this treatise can be found in his entry on al-Ghazālī in *al-Muntaẓam* however (Ibn al-Jawzī 1992, 17:124–127; Brown 2007, 354). In this encyclopaedic work, Ibn al-Jawzī criticises al-Ghazālī for having neglected the knowledge discipline of *fiqh* completely and only focusing on Sufism in an unbalanced and irresponsible way. Ibn al-Jawzī accuses al-Ghazālī of being much too attracted to the works of the early Sufis, like Abū Ṭālib al-Makkī's *Qūt al-Qulūb* – indeed one of the main sources for the *Iḥyāʾ* – which distracted him from remaining within the boundaries of *fiqh*. He, for example, blames al-Ghazālī for including a story on a man who wanted to rid himself of his good reputation (*jāh*) and therefore stole a cloak from the bathing house only to intentionally be discovered as a thief. Following the same logic as in his criticism of forged narrations for the sake of *al-targhīb wa-l-tarhīb*, Ibn al-Jawzī considers these kinds of stories on virtue ethics to have damaging social consequences. It is therefore immoral (*qabīḥ*) to share them with novices, even if the goal is learning. According to Ibn al-Jawzī too much was at stake if such material would be accepted and spread: the whole concept of a noble lie would undermine the integrity and authority of *ḥadīth* as a source of guidance. The extreme behaviour these false narrations often endorsed would lead to undesirable social consequences. These ideas of Ibn al-Jawzī on *ḥadīth* criticism were an exception in his own age and subsequent centuries, and only became more influential in the late nineteenth century. His contemporaries and later *ḥadīth* theorists generally considered Ibn al-Jawzī too strict, and criticised him for not upholding his own standards (Brown 2011, 20–21; al-Khaṭīb 2011, 103–106).

Ibn al-Jawzī gives similar examples of what he considers crucial mistakes of al-Ghazālī, among which is his use of *ḥadīth* in the *Iḥyāʾ*. He rebukes him for narrating a *ḥadīth* attributed to ʿĀʾisha (d. 58/678) in which she says "You are the one who pretends to be the messenger of God," which according to him has no basis of reliability and simply cannot be true considering its meaning. Ibn al-Jawzī emphatically considers al-Ghazālī weak in the knowledge discipline of *ḥadīth*, which is the reason why, according to him, the majority of narrations in the *Iḥyāʾ* belong to the category of forged narrations (*aḥādīth mawḍūʿa*). He suggests it would be better if al-Ghazālī had his work checked on this aspect by a specialist, because now his transmission is worthless. He does mention that al-Ghazālī spent the last moments of his life memorising the Qurʾān and occupying himself with the two *Ṣaḥīḥ*s, which may be interpreted as a way to further underline his lack of knowledge of *ḥadīth*. Ibn al-Jawzī also mentions his own epitome in this entry on al-Ghazālī in *al-Muntaẓam*: "Someone craved for the *Iḥyāʾ* so I pointed out its flaws to him. Then I (re)wrote it for him and left out what was suitable to be left out, and added what was [suitable to be] added" (Ibn al-Jawzī 1992, 17:124–127).

Brockelmann (d. 1956) specifically mentioned Ibn al-Jawzī's epitome in the context of his zeal for purifying the Sunna from false transmissions, which he considered an exaggerated and extreme application of the Sunna-fanaticism of the Ḥanbalī school (Brockelmann 1909, 177). The entry on *Minhāj al-Qāṣidīn* in Ḥājjī Khalīfa's (d. 1067/1657) *Kashf al-Ẓunūn* ("Removal of Uncertainties") also mentions his obliteration of incorrect Prophetic narrations and Sufi ideas: "It follows the method of the *Iḥyāʾ*, but he has removed tenuous Prophetic narrations and ways of the Sufis that have no foundation" (Ḥājjī Khalīfa n.d., 2:1878). Both Brockelmann and Ḥājjī Khalīfa do not mention Ibn Qudāma's epitome. This is probably due to the popularity and fame of Ibn al-Jawzī, especially compared to the relative obscurity of Ibn Qudāma.

The introduction of Ibn al-Jawzī's epitome confirms this motive of purification (Ibn al-Jawzī 2010, 5–9). Ibn al-Jawzī directs his words, as is a common style form in spiritual treatises, to one of his pupils who intends to seclude himself in silence with the *Iḥyāʾ*.[2] Ibn al-Jawzī first praises the student for choosing the *Iḥyāʾ*, which he calls a unique work in its kind. However, he warns his pupil that the work of his choice contains many things that will lead to actions unacceptable in the religion. His first criticism concerns, as can be expected, al-Ghazālī's use of *ḥadīth* material. According to Ibn al-Jawzī the work contains many weak and fabricated narrations, upon which one cannot build one's acts of worship. He blames al-Ghazālī for narrating "halted" (*mawqūf*) narrations of the Companions as if they are "elevated" (*marfūʿ*) to the Prophet, and for uncritically copying them from his earlier Sufi sources.

2 See al-Ghazālī's *Ayyuhā l-Walad* ("Dear Pupil") as a comparison to al-Jawzī's use of this introductory writing style.

He also names the example of supererogatory prayers that al-Ghazālī falsely attributes to the Prophet. In Ibn al-Jawzī's view, it would be useless to act upon such baseless narrations, since religious acts should always be based on sound knowledge to be valid.

His second criticism concerns the way the work deals with Sufism. Ibn al-Jawzī considers many things that al-Ghazālī mentions in this regard to be excessive and unnecessarily harsh. As examples, he mentions discourses about annihilation and subsistence (*al-fanāʾ wa-l-baqāʾ*), commanding deliberate excessive hunger, and religious dwellings (*siyāḥa*). For this, he refers to his arguably most famous work *Talbīs Iblīs* ("The Deception of the Devil"), in which he repeats his criticism of al-Ghazālī's laxity in blindly copying unreliable *aḥādīth*, grave transgressions in creedal matters and *fiqh*, and repeatedly gives examples of al-Ghazālī's mistakes in the realm of Sufism (Ibn al-Jawzī 1983, 160).

When his student exclaims his disappointment that Ibn al-Jawzī has made him detest this book after having loved it so much, he promises his student that he will write a version purified from all mistakes and wrong ideas, only narrating the most sound and well-known narrations and well-established meanings:

> You said to me: "You have made me uneasy with this book, after my intimacy [with it]." I said: "I wish for you what I wish for myself, so I will write it in a book that does not abandon its merits, and rids it from its bad elements. I will use the most sound and well-known narrations in it, and the most well-established and excellent meanings. I will leave out what is suitable to leave out, and will add to it what is suitable to add. I will not be unnecessarily lengthy".
>
> IBN AL-JAWZĪ 2010, 1:7

He stresses that he will leave out many narrations, not out of forgetfulness, but because he believes them not to be sound. He promises not to repeat his criticism on the *Iḥyāʾ*, noted down in his other treatise, in this work to keep the reader focused on its positive message.

Ibn Qudāma's introduction, of his summary of Ibn al-Jawzī's work, largely consists of a literal repetition of Ibn al-Jawzī's words (Ibn Qudāma 1991, 9–12). The only thing he adds is praise for Ibn al-Jawzī's book, adding that it is still too large and that he wished to shorten it further, by leaving out discussions pertaining to details of jurisprudence. He considers these well known in the works of *fiqh* and does not deem it necessary to repeat them. Both works stick to the same organisation of the *Iḥyāʾ*, a total of forty books (chapters) divided equally over four quarters. Ibn Qudāma's work merges several books for practical reasons of length. He omits the *Qawāʿid al-ʿAqāʾid* ("The Foundations of Religious Convictions") completely, a book that Ibn al-Jawzī also drastically shortens because of his aversion of the knowledge discipline of *kalām*. The content of the *Kitāb al-Samāʿ wa-l-Wajd* ("Book on Audition and Ecstasy"), in which al-Ghazālī praises both religious sessions of audition (*samāʿ*) and the ecstasy they provoke, is also drastically replaced with a complete rejection of the matter. Ibn Qudāma even files it under the *Kitāb al-Amr bi-l-Maʿrūf wa-l-Nahy ʿan al-Munkar* ("Book of Commanding the Right and Forbidding the Wrong") (Black MacDonald 1902; Ibn Qudāma 1991, 143–144; Ibn al-Jawzī 2010, 1:499–502; al-Ghazālī 2011, 4:409–533).

## 4 A Sample: Narrative Virtue Ethics on Earning and Livelihood (*al-Kasb wa-l-Maʿāsh*)

Let us first have a closer look at *al-Kasb wa-l-Maʿāsh* ("Earning and Livelihood"), to see how this scrutiny of *ḥadīth* material affects the treatment of this chapter on the virtue ethics of acquiring one's livelihood. This is a good example of narrative virtue ethics in a Sufi context. The issue of whether a wayfarer should earn one's own livelihood through one's own acquisition of God's decree (*kasb*), or should completely rely on God's decree without acquiring it oneself, is an old theme in Sufism, closely related to the themes of reliance on God (*tawakkul*), renunciation (*zuhd*), and poverty (*faqr*), as pious ideals (Reinert 1968, 141–156; Gramlich 1995a, 1:158–160; Ritter 2013, 217–226; Melchert 2020, 147–151). Al-Ghazālī was clearly relating to this discussion in this book of the *Iḥyāʾ*, taking the position that although God is the absolute and only provider of sustenance, one should still work for it oneself and actively acquire one's livelihood.

This third book of the *Rubʿ al-ʿĀdāt* ("Quarter of Habits") is divided into five chapters. The first chapter is most relevant for the topic of *ḥadīth* on virtue ethics. It deals with the merits of working for one's earnings and starts – as is typical for most books of the *Iḥyāʾ* – with a summary of relevant Qurʾānic verses on the topic, followed by sayings attributed to the Prophet, and, after that, sayings of Companions, Successors, and wise men from earlier generations (*āthār*) related to the topic. A comparison with the chapter with the same name from Abū Ṭālib al-Makkī's *Qūt al-Qulūb* shows that most of this material is directly copied from the *Qūt* (Gramlich 1995b, 3:610–612; al-Ghazālī 2011, 3:239–246). This rules out any deliberate organisation of *ḥadīth* material by al-Ghazālī to make some kind of sophisticated ethical point through his composition, to be discovered by us as readers, and shows that Ibn al-Jawzī and Riḍā were right in their observation that he uncritically copied passages from earlier works.

In this first subchapter, al-Ghazālī mentions fourteen narrations attributed to the Prophet, only one of which can be related back to the six canonical collections, al-Tirmidhī's (d. 279/892). As is also typical for the *Iḥyāʾ*, and as was already the criticism from his early adversaries in the Islamic West, al-Ghazālī himself does not include any chains of transmission or sources for these narrations, he only attributes them directly to the Prophet. Thematically, these narrations all support the idea that earning one's own livelihood and trade are acts of high religious merit and virtue, and much better than just profiting from others or waiting for one's livelihood to fall from the sky, such as "There is a category of sins that are only expiated by concern with seeking livelihood;" "The trustworthy trader is resurrected on the day of resurrection with the upright and the martyrs;" "The most permissible food that a man can eat is from what he has earned, and from every blessed sale" (al-Ghazālī 2011, 3:239–242).

The main difference between the *Iḥyāʾ* and the epitome of Ibn al-Jawzī in this chapter is in the choice of narrations: Ibn al-Jawzī selects only five narrations, of which only one, a narration that can be traced back to Aḥmad b. Ḥanbal's (d. 241/855) *Musnad*, corresponds with the selection of al-Ghazālī. The other fourteen do not survive his critical redaction of weak material, an exceptionally high number. The second difference lies in that Ibn al-Jawzī does mention the source of each *ḥadīth* that he includes. For two narrations, he even lists the full chains of transmission from himself back to the Prophet, transmitting through his direct teachers ʿAbd al-Wahhāb b. al-Ḥāfiẓ (fl. 6th/12th century) and ʿAbd al-Awwal b. ʿĪsā (d. 553/1159). Ibn al-Jawzī does, thus, not only refer these transmissions back to the compilations in which they can be found, but really shows in his work that he is part of the living tradition of narrating these Prophetic narrations with a full chain of transmission, attaining the highest level of scrutiny of the chains of transmission as possible. From the other three narrations two go back to the collections of al-Bukhārī and Muslim, already firmly canonised as the most reliable compilations, by the time of Ibn al-Jawzī (Brown 2007, 169).

Despite the completely different set of narrations that Ibn al-Jawzī offers, thematically there is no large difference in the *ḥadīth* material selected. For Ibn al-Jawzī, the main goal in his selection is to show the merit of earning one's livelihood by the work of one's own hands or by trade, and a rejection of passivity in awaiting God's provision. He, for example, mentions a narration that compares earning one's livelihood to *jihād*, another that mentions the food that one brought forth by one's own hands as the best type of food, and a narration that describes the professions of Prophets as farmers, carpenters, tailors and shepherds (Ibn al-Jawzī 2010, 1:362–363). While Ibn Qudāma has no major deviations from Ibn al-Jawzī, he only reduced the number of cited narrations to four (Ibn Qudāma 1991, 82–84).

When we look at the *āthār*, we see a similar dynamic of reducing the number of narrations and sometimes replacing them with other more reliable narrations. Here also, al-Ghazālī mentions fifteen sayings attributed to a mixture of former Prophets, Companions of Muhammad, and illustrious Sufi figures, such as Luqmān the Wise, ʿUmar b. al-Khaṭṭāb (d. 24/644), Zayd b. Thābit (d. 45/665), ʿAbd Allāh b. Masʿūd (d. 32/650), Ibrāhīm b. Adham (d. 161/777–778), the Prophet Job, Aḥmad b. Ḥanbal and Abū Sulaymān al-Dārānī (d. 215/830) (al-Ghazālī 2011, 3:243–246). The thematic content of these *āthār* is similar to the Prophetic narrations: working is lauded as *jihād* and an elevated form of worship, and as a way to become independent from other people. All sayings somehow suggest that begging and preferring worship over working is ethically frowned upon. Of these fifteen *āthār*, Ibn al-Jawzī preserves only six in his redaction: those by Luqmān, ʿUmar, Job, Ibrāhīm b. Adham, Aḥmad b. Ḥanbal and Abū Sulaymān al-Dārānī; Ibn Qudāma only leaves Luqmān, Aḥmad and Abū Sulaymān (Ibn Qudāma 1991, 82–83; Ibn al-Jawzī 2010, 1:363). Here, it is harder to say which criteria Ibn al-Jawzī used to narrow these options down, whether it was a critique on their reliability, or a critique on their contents, or perhaps both.

Saliant is that Ibn al-Jawzī censures or changes the sayings attributed to Companions (ʿUmar, Ibn Masʿūd, Zayd) while he leaves the sayings of Sufi figures like Ibn Adham and al-Dārānī intact. A reason for this might be that he demands a higher level of authenticity for the former, since the Companions have a higher status as a source of religious guidance. From attributions to ʿUmar for example, al-Ghazālī included two sayings directly from *Qūt al-Qulūb*: "Let none of you sit down from seeking livelihood and say, 'O God, provide me with livelihood.' You know that the heaven does not let gold and silver rain down;" and "No place is more beloved to me to have death come to me than a place in which I am trading for my family, buying and selling." Ibn al-Jawzī replaces these with only one saying attributed to ʿUmar. He thus leaves the authority cited intact as a sign of respect to the original composition, and replaces it with a saying with a similar meaning: "To die between two work-related travels in which I seek livelihood is more beloved to me than to die warring on the path of God" (Ibn al-Jawzī 2010, 1:363). We can state that, in this particular case, Ibn al-Jawzī's critical redaction did not lead to a shift in the intended parenetic meaning of al-Ghazālī's selection of sayings on virtue ethics. Rather he shows that, both in the case of *ḥadīth* and *āthār*, more reliable alternatives can be used without losing the scope of the book out of sight.

## 5 A Related Sample: Divine Unity and Reliance (*al-Tawḥīd wa-l-Tawakkul*)

As stated earlier, the themes of poverty and renunciation (*al-faqr wa-l-zuhd*), as well as trust in divine providence (*tawakkul*), are closely related to the theme of earning one's livelihood, and may be considered typical Sufi themes (Reinert 1968), as well as its preceding movement of renunciants (*zuhhād*) (Melchert 2020). In the following section, I will therefore analyse the theme of *tawakkul* as well, to see whether the same approach to narrative virtue ethics can be found here.

To understand al-Ghazālī's coupling of *tawḥīd* with *tawakkul*, one should turn to the first book, *Kitāb al-ʿIlm*, where al-Ghazālī redefines the knowledge discipline of *tawḥīd* as

> that one sees everything coming from God, with a vision that stops one from turning to causes and means, and only sees good and evil as coming from Him. This is an honourable station, the fruit of which is trust in divine providence.
>
> AL-GHAZĀLĪ 2011, 1:125

Al-Ghazālī complains how it has now become an expression for the art of theological dispute, which was reprehensible among the *salaf*. He wishes to replace it with a practical theology of virtue, in which an experiential understanding of the unity of God leads to complete reliance upon him: God is the only agent in the universe, and thus the only one upon which one should rely. This is a way for al-Ghazālī to reclaim the definition of *tawḥīd* as part of the inward knowledge discipline of the heart, related to Sufism, rather than as a knowledge discipline of dialectical disputation and speculative theology as practiced by the *mutakallimūn*.[3] This definition remains in the epitomes of Ibn al-Jawzī and Ibn Qudāma, likely because it fit their disapproval of *kalām* very well, as well as their sober understanding of Sufism (Ibn Qudāma 1991, 19; Ibn al-Jawzī 2010, 1:41). To convey this inward vision on *tawḥīd* as *tawakkul* in the book of the *Iḥyāʾ* dedicated to that specific subject, al-Ghazālī takes his resort to *ḥadīth* literature and pious examples of earlier Sufi figures quite prominently in this book. I shall now analyse what of that material remains in the epitomes of Ibn al-Jawzī and Ibn Qudāma.

3 This speculative theology is also followed in a mild form in *Kitāb Qawāʿid al-ʿAqāʾid* ("The Foundations of Religious Convictions") in the *Iḥyāʾ*, but profoundly changed in the epitome of Ibn al-Jawzī, and completely censored in the recension of Ibn Qudāma.

As we are used to in the *Iḥyā'*, al-Ghazālī also starts this book with a series of quotes from the Qur'ān on the topic, and then moves on to Prophetic narrations and sayings from pious early figures (*āthār*). He quotes a total of six Prophetic narrations, two sayings attributed to earlier Prophets (Ibrāhīm and Dāwūd), and eight sayings from early pious figures. The material he quotes can be categorised in the following themes: (1) those who trust in God alone are guaranteed Paradise without reckoning; (2) those with full trust in God's providence are fully provided for by Him; (3) recourse to anything other than God, like sorcery and superstitions, is detrimental to one's trust in God. None of these themes seem to be something that Ibn al-Jawzī would take offence at from his particular view on matters of creed and Sufism. The *āthār* largely revolve around the same themes, but here a fourth theme is added that is absent from the *ḥadīth* material: sustenance comes to the believer without actively striving for it: this is the greatest proof that God is the Sustainer.

In the recension of Ibn al-Jawzī, the same three basic themes indeed recur in the *ḥadīth* material, and he also quotes six Prophetic narrations in total. However, as we earlier saw in the *al-Kasb wa-l-Maʿāsh*, Ibn al-Jawzī, in some cases, replaces the *aḥādīth* with thematically similar material that he deems more trustworthy. Al-Ghazālī for example cites a *ḥadīth* attributed to ʿAbd Allāh b. Masʿūd, about gathering on the day of ʿArafāt during the Ḥajj season, in which the Prophet states that among those present of his community there will be 70,000 people who will enter Paradise without reckoning, because they fully trust on God and do not engage in sorcery or trickery. This narration in these exact wordings can only be found in the *Musnad* of Abū Dāwūd al-Ṭayālisī (d. 204/819) (al-Ghazālī 2011, 8:196–197).[4] Ibn al-Jawzī replaces this with a *ḥadīth* supported by a full chain of transmission instead, from himself to Ibn ʿAbbās (d. *c.*68/687), through Aḥmad b. Ḥanbal, that deals with the same event and the same saying of the Prophet, but with different details in the narrative (Ibn al-Jawzī 2010, 3:1228–1229). Contrary to the narration that al-Ghazālī relates, the narrative attributed to Ibn ʿAbbās can be found in the the two *Ṣaḥīḥ*s.[5] It likely had higher status in the eyes of Ibn al-Jawzī, especially because he himself had his own unique chain of transmission of the narration through Aḥmad as well, underlining his identity as a Ḥanbalī. Ibn al-Jawzī

4 Abū Dāwūd 1999, 1:320–322: *Mā Asnada ʿAbd Allāh b. Masʿūd* ("What ʿAbd Allāh b. Masʿūd Compiled").

5 al-Bukhārī 1422/2001, 8:113: *Kitāb al-Riqāq* ("Book on Heart Softeners"), *Bāb Yadkhul al-Janna Sabʿūn Alfan bi-Ghayr Ḥisāb* ("Chapter on 70,000 Who Enter Paradise without Reckoning"); Muslim n.d., 1:98: *Kitāb al-Īmān* ("Book of Faith"), *Bāb al-Dalīl ʿalā Dukhūl Ṭawāʾif min al-Muslimīn al-Janna bi-Ghayr Ḥisāb wa-lā ʿAdhāb* ("Chapter on the Evidence that Groups of Muslims Enter Paradise without Reckoning and Punishment").

keeps the famous *ḥadīth* that compares the believer with full trust in God with birds in his recension, but also with his own chain of transmission included to underline its reliability (Ibn al-Jawzī 2010, 3:1229). The other four *aḥādīth* that al-Ghazālī quotes, Ibn al-Jawzī leaves out, replacing them with four supplications attributed to the Prophet, that he derived from Abū Bakr b. Abī l-Dunyā's (d. 281/894) *Kitāb al-Tawakkul* ("Book on Providence"), who had an equal reputation of very cautious scrutiny of *ḥadīth* material, citing them without full chains of transmission (Ibn al-Jawzī 2010, 3:1229–1230; Ibn Abī l-Dunyā 1987). As in the Book analysed above, here Ibn al-Jawzī radically chooses to replace all sayings that he does not consider reliable enough with narrations that conform to his high standards. He is very consistent in this. He does decide to leave the topics addressed intact however: his objection and censorship, in this particular case, is not related to the content of the narrations, as was the case in *Kitāb al-Samāʿ*, but only with their reliability.

Let us now see what happens to the category of *āthār* in his epitome, as well as the sayings of early Sufi figures. From the *āthār* that al-Ghazālī quotes, half of them from unnamed authorities, Ibn al-Jawzī edits none. He replaces them completely with other sayings, all with the authorities named, of which only one authority is overlapping and includes a different saying. Reliability of the chain of transmission was not the issue here however, nor was the supposed creedal integrity of the figures quoted. Here is clearly a case of criticism of the content. The main theme of the sayings quoted by al-Ghazālī can be interpreted as a type of quietism in understanding reliance on God: it comes to the true believer without actively seeking it oneself, indeed a fatalist conception of *tawakkul*. There is a strange conflict here with what al-Ghazālī propagated earlier in *Kitāb al-Kasb*, as well as what he propagates in the remainder of *Kitāb al-Tawḥīd wa-l-Tawakkul* ("Divine Unity and Reliance"): he himself is obviously not in favour of such a fatalist conception, and rather agitates against that himself. Al-Ghazālī himself did not seem troubled by this inconsistency however, which further confirms the idea that he was uncritical in copying such sayings from earlier sources. Al-Ghazālī's selection of sayings seems more motivated by what was accidentally available to him at that moment than by a well-crafted and meticulous selection that fitted what he himself propagated. This was an unacceptable idea for Ibn al-Jawzī. As we have already learned from his introduction discussed above, passively waiting for one's sustenance was something he considered to belong to the category of unacceptable and excessive forms of Sufism. He thus replaces the narrative virtue ethics that al-Ghazālī offers with a narrative virtue ethics that stresses a sober lifestyle (*zuhd*), remembrance of death (*dhikr al-mawt*), and the fundamental link of *tawakkul* to one's belief.

In the second part of *Kitāb al-Tawḥīd wa-l-Tawakkul*, al-Ghazālī relates several stories on *tawakkul* from earlier pious Sufi figures (al-Ghazālī 2011, 8:262–265). According to David Burrell, the goal of al-Ghazālī with his presentation of these narratives is "to offer one object lesson after another of a way to take esoteric Sufi lore and allow it to inspire one's practice" (Burrell 2001, xxi). This is completely omitted by Ibn al-Jawzī, who clearly did not agree with the approach of these early Sufis. Here the conflict is clearer and harsher, which leads to a more drastic censure than in the case of earlier discussed *ḥadīth* material.

## 6 The Reception of the *Iḥyā'* in Modernity and the Problematisation of *Ḥadīth* on Virtue Ethics

Given the perpetual popularity of and praise for the *Iḥyā'* in later centuries, the criticism of Ibn al-Jawzī did not directly lead to a paradigm shift in the tradition after him (al-Shāmī 1993a, 157–161; Cook 2001, 450–456). The very scarce remaining manuscript evidence (only three) of Ibn al-Jawzī's work, which both the editor and the publisher give as a reason for its late edition, also suggests that it was not a highly popular book in the premodern age, certainly not as popular as the *Iḥyā'* itself (Ibn al-Jawzī 2010, 1:5, 14–15). The same can be said of Ibn Qudāma's epitome, the first printed edition of which was also based only on three manuscripts (Ibn Qudāma 1928). Both thus remained relatively marginal within the boundaries of their own school, with the *Iḥyā'* itself triumphant. Apparently, their fundamental criticism was not shared widely enough to also be adopted outside their own local branch of the Ḥanbalī school.

This only changed in the course of the twentieth century, with the rise of printing. This made many forgotten manuscripts see the light of day as printed texts, often with an agenda of "purification" of the Islamic tradition according to Taymiyyan standards. Both early reformist and later puritan Salafīs were keen to make use of printing to advance their causes (Khan 2016, 54–55; El Shamsy 2020, 182–191; Bosanquet 2021). Islamic reform movements in the late nineteenth and early twentieth century cared deeply about promoting virtues (*faḍā'il*), morality (*akhlāq*), and refinement (*tahdhīb*), as part of their "civilisation" (*tamaddun*) programs (Kateman 2019, 96–115). To promote religious virtues and morality in society, the *Iḥyā'* remained the most suitable text in their view, but it needed some revisions to fit their broader agenda of textual criticism and critique of Sufi excesses considered to be irrational and too miraculous. Their renewed criticism of weak and forged *ḥadīth* and perceived irrationalities of Sufism thus had repercussions for the reception of al-Ghazālī's *Iḥyāʾ*. The Salafī-reformist scholar Rashīd Riḍā, for example, famously discussed the status of problematic *ḥadīth* material in the *Iḥyāʾ* as a response to a reader's question in the widespread and influential journal *al-Manār* ("The Lighthouse"), an article which is claimed to have been the major impetus for Nāṣir al-Dīn al-Albānī's (d. 1420/1999) career in *ḥadīth* studies (Riḍā 1909; Brown 2011, 34–35). Riḍā admits al-Ghazālī had weaknesses in his knowledge of the classification of *ḥadīth*, but acquits him from intentionally including weak and forged transmissions in his work. Most of them, claims Riḍā, come from *Qūt al-qulūb*, which al-Ghazālī, according to Riḍā, copied in blind trust of the original author. As we have seen, this indeed was an important source text for the *Iḥyāʾ*.

Both *Qūt al-Qulūb* and the *Iḥyāʾ* were epitomised by the Syrian Salafī-reformist and *ḥadīth*-specialist Jamāl al-Dīn al-Qāsimī (d. 1332/1914), who maintained good contacts with Muḥammad ʿAbduh (d. 1323/1905) and his student Riḍā. Al-Qāsimī even summarised the *Iḥyāʾ* on personal advice from ʿAbduh, "on condition they be edited to omit weak oral reports and spurious stories" (Commins 1990, 62; al-Qāsimī 2009, 33). Also, his published collection of Friday sermons is largely based on the structure and content of the *Iḥyāʾ*, which further confirms the desire of these reformists to bring the virtues propagated in the work to the masses (al-Qāsimī 1907).[6] Al-Qāsimī gave an impetus to the revival of the knowledge disciplines of *muṣṭalaḥ al-ḥadīth* (*ḥadīth* classification) and *al-jarḥ wa-l-taʿdīl* (impugning and approving) in his circles, mainly through his *Qawāʿid al-Taḥdīth* ("The Foundations of Narrating Prophetic Traditions"), which contains large portions of the works of Ibn al-Jawzī (al-Qāsimī 1925; al-Sarmīnī 2010). In his introduction to his epitome of Abū Ṭālib al-Makkī's work, *al-Waʿẓ al-Maṭlūb min Qūt al-Qulūb* ("The Required Exhortation from The Nourishment of the Hearts"), al-Qāsimī mentions purification from problematic Prophetic reports as a main motive:

> This book of his has nevertheless never been criticised in this time, on the objectionable reports and narrations among the people of knowledge that it contains. Removing these from it is one of the greatest priorities and the best things to do, because it increases its benefit and use.
>
> AL-QĀSIMĪ 2010, 28

In the introduction to his *Iḥyāʾ*-epitome *Mawʿiẓat al-Muʾminīn min Iḥyāʾ ʿUlūm al-Dīn* ("Exhortation of the Believers from the *Iḥyāʾ*") he explains that he

6 I owe this insight to my conversations with Melle Lyklema (Utrecht University), who is preparing a dissertation on the subject of literature on preaching in the Islamic world.

wished to make a version of the *Iḥyāʾ* which would be more accessible to the lay people, who had difficulty understanding the literal readings of the work in public teaching sessions by scholars. He does not make specific reference to the problem of unreliable *aḥādīth*, but does mention how ʿAbduh suggested that it would be the best work for the purpose of instructing Islamic virtues to lay people "after purifying it" (*baʿda tajrīdihi*) (al-Qāsimī 2009, 41). A glance at the content of the book, however, immediately reveals that he omitted a lot of *ḥadīth* material and mainly focused on summarising its other contents in his own wordings. In his summary of the earlier discussed *al-Kasb wa-l-Maʿāsh* for example, he only preserves four narrations from the fifteen in the original redaction of al-Ghazālī, one of which can be traced back to the two *Ṣaḥīḥ*s, two to Aḥmad's *Musnad*, and one to al-Ṭabarānī. Only the last of these is ranked as weak (*ḍaʿīf*) by the editor, the son of the Damascene Salafī scholar Muḥammad Bahjat al-Bīṭār (1893–1976), a close friend of al-Qāsimī and Riḍā (al-Qāsimī 2009, 176–177; Weismann and Adawi 2021). Al-Qāsimī formally held a more lenient position than Ibn al-Jawzī on using weak *ḥadīth*, agreeing with the mainstream position that it is allowed outside the realm of legal opinions, but in his redaction, he remained strict (al-Qāsimī 1925, 94–95; Brown 2011, 31–32).

This renewed interest in the *Iḥyāʾ*, making it suitable for a larger audience than only the learned class, as part of the reformist mission of stimulating moral refinement (*tahdhīb al-akhlāq*) among all layers of society, also led to a renewed interest in and printed publication of its medieval Ḥanbalī epitomes. In the preceding discussion, most attention has gone to Ibn al-Jawzī's epitome, with Ibn Qudāma's epitome proving to be nothing more than a further curtailment for practical reasons without a deeper ideological agenda. Why then still include Ibn Qudāma in this discussion? This has to do with the modern reception of these works, in which Ibn Qudāma's work was dominant. Ibn Qudāma's epitome has seen several editions in the twentieth century, most of them from Syria, where it has been part of Islamic secondary and higher education since the 1930s. The relatively small size of the work, its emphasis on pedagogy (*tarbiya*) and good manners (*adab*), as well as its broad acceptability for different strands of Islamic thought, from traditionalist to modernist, from Sufi to Salafī, made it very suitable for that.

Given their renewed stress on reliable *ḥadīth* material and the irrational excesses of Sufism, it is no coincidence that named epitomes by Ibn al-Jawzī and most notably Ibn Qudāma became specifically popular with the advent of the Salafī movement in the twentieth century. Although the text became popular in a much wider circle and was certainly not limited to this group, their engagement with editions of this work seem relatively larger than other groups. The modern appropriation of the *Mukhtaṣar* starts in 1346/1927–1928, when the Islamic scholar and historian Muḥammad Aḥmad Dahmān (d. 1988), belonging to the emerging Salafī trend in Damascus, sees the manuscript and edits it for publication for the first time (Ibn Qudāma 1928). According to his own testimony, his purpose was to use it as education material in the religious institutions of higher education (*al-kulliyyāt al-sharʿiyya*) of Syria, which according to him indeed adopted the work in all major cities (Ibn Qudāma 1978, 5–6).

The most current popular edition seems to be the edition of Shuʿayb al-Arnāʾūṭ (d. 1438/2016) and ʿAbd al-Qādir al-Arnāʾūṭ (d. 1415/2004), which has the endorsement of Dahmān and is based on his earlier edition (Ibn Qudāma, 1991). Both Shuʿayb and ʿAbd al-Qādir al-Arnāʾūṭ are not coincidentally modern major figures in the knowledge discipline of *ḥadīth* from Damascus, with the latter subscribing to more or less the same Salafī method as al-Albānī, and with a large following (Pierret 2013, 106, 108, 111). Al-Maktab al-Islāmī, an important puritan Salafī publishing house, also has issued its own edition edited by its founder, the Damascene Salafī scholar Zuhayr al-Shāwīsh (d. 1434/2013). In the introduction, when the editor discusses other existing epitomes, he mentions al-Qāsimī as "the *shaykh* of our *shaykhs*." He explains that in his methodology of classifying its *aḥādīth* he consulted the works and followed the methodology of "my teacher" Nāṣir al-Dīn al-Albānī, with whom he indeed stood in close contact (Pierret 2013, 20). Ibn al-Jawzī's epitome was only critically edited and published for the first time in history in 2010. This critical edition was made by Kāmil Muḥammad al-Kharrāṭ, with a preface by Naʿīm al-ʿIrqsūsī (b. 1951), currently one of the most important *ḥadīth* scholars from Damascus (Ibn al-Jawzī 2010; Blecher 2018, 11–13).

These modern editions show the ongoing engagement of *ḥadīth* scholars with criticism on this particular aspect of the *Iḥyāʾ* and the relatively royal embrace of Salafī scholars and publishing houses of this specific text. The involvement of scholars like Shuʿayb al-Arnāʾūṭ and Naʿīm al-ʿIrqsūsī not belonging to the Salafī trend, however, shows that it was also part of a broader trend of renewed interest in *ḥadīth* criticism in twentieth-century Damascus (ʿĪdū 2017; Snober 2020). As we will see, this broader revival of interest in *ḥadīth* criticism also had its influence on other epitomes in the twentieth century from Syria.

This tradition of epitomes apparently left most of its traces in Syria. This is likely because of the influence of al-Qāsimī on the emerging Syrian (and global) Salafī trend and the edition of Ibn Qudāma's epitome on the religious educational curriculum. Not only the Salafī scholars of Syria engaged themselves with epitomes of the *Iḥyāʾ*, the practice also gained ground in Syrian Sufi-oriented circles, with the same criticism of al-Ghazālī's use of *ḥadīth*. The scholar and activist Saʿīd Ḥawwā (d. 1989) from Hama, a former leading figure in Syria's Muslim Brotherhood and committed Naqshbandī, also compiled an epitome of the *Iḥyāʾ* in the 1970s. In his vision, Islamic political movements, also in their more militant forms, could not be successful without proper spiritual training for their activists (Weismann 1993; 1997). Therefore, books like the *Iḥyāʾ* were direly needed in a more simplified form according to Ḥawwā, since many challenges from al-Ghazālī's times were similar to theirs (Ḥawwā 2004, 5–10). In his introduction, Ḥawwā also explicitly mentions the question of *ḥadīth*, like most authors addressing the issue of weak and forged narrations in the *Iḥyāʾ*. He says he has removed weak narrations from his epitome, as well as the thoughts constructed on these narrations, but stresses that they are not equal to forged narrations, since there is still a chance that the weak narrations are really the words of the Prophet. Wherever he has left the problematic narrations from al-Ghazālī intact, he explains, he has added the commentary of al-Ḥāfiẓ Zayn al-Dīn ʿAbd al-Raḥīm al-ʿIrāqī (d. 806/1403) to them, as well as the classification of the strength of the narrations and their sources, but only when they are sound in their meaning. Narrations from Prophets other than Muḥammad he has also excluded, since their reliability cannot be confirmed (Ḥawwā 2004, 5–6). Ḥawwā thus adopted an academic rigour in *ḥadīth* criticism typical of the twentieth century in his approach to the *ḥadīth* material in the *Iḥyāʾ*, stricter than the standards that one would thus far expect in the scholarly circles that he emerged from.

Ṣāliḥ al-Shāmī (b. 1934), the author of a book on al-Ghazālī that reads as an apology for his legacy, produced an epitome as well, in which he is relatively mild towards the problematic narrations al-Ghazālī included (al-Shāmī 1993a; 1993b). In his apology, al-Shāmī recognises that al-Ghazālī did indeed use a lot of problematic narrations, as is the consensus among his critics, and states that "every reader of the *Iḥyāʾ* wished he had not done so" (al-Shāmī 1993a, 166). In his defence he adds that the knowledge discipline of *ḥadīth* was not part of al-Ghazālī's formal training, while he was highly cultured in almost every other discipline of knowledge. He also defends al-Ghazālī's use of *ḥadīth* on the ground, that this was very common in his age for this type of topic. He quotes Abū l-Fidāʾ Ismāʿīl b. ʿUmar Ibn Kathīr's (d. 774/1373) defence of al-Ghazālī in this matter, and criticises Ibn al-Jawzī for himself not living up to the high standards on which he judges al-Ghazālī in his own parenetic works, like *Dhamm al-Hawā* ("Disparagement of Passion"). Even *Minhāj al-Qāṣidīn* and Ibn Qudāma's *Mukhtaṣar* contain weak narrations after all, he states, and also scholars like Ibn al-Qayyim (d. 751/1350), known for his rigour in the knowledge discipline of *ḥadīth*, still includes weak material (al-Shāmī 1993a, 166–168). He thus concludes that "therefore the reasonable among the scholars held that the weak narrations in the *Iḥyāʾ* have influence on its value, but do not completely make it lose its status; especially after God made the classification of its narrations easy upon al-Ḥāfiẓ al-ʿIrāqī" (al-Shāmī 1993a, 168). In the introduction to his epitome, he accentuates that he did not make yet another summary of the *Iḥyāʾ*, but rather a refinement (*tahdhīb*), which in its essence still includes everything the *Iḥyāʾ* contains. He does not delve deeply into its critics on the topic of *ḥadīth*, mentioning Murtaḍā al-Zabīdī's (d. 1205/1791) and Tāj al-Dīn al-Subkī's (d. 771/1370) defenses of the work in this matter as sufficient (al-Shāmī 1993b, 10–11, 15; Reichmuth 2009, 269–334). He does consider offering a version of the texts without weak and forged narrations as a goal, as suggested by al-Qaraḍāwī (d. 2022) in his work on al-Ghazālī, which he explicitly names as an inspiration to compose this refinement (al-Shāmī 1993b, 27). His summary of the *al-Kasb wa-l-Maʿāsh* shows that he perhaps was the strictest of all in this matter, leaving only three narrations intact, mentioning their classification as either sound (*ṣaḥīḥ*) or good (*ḥasan*). Thus, we also see here that the importance of *ḥadīth* criticism in the twentieth century has become so strong that it is adopted by scholars from trends that historically would not see a problem in citing weak material related to *faḍāʾil al-aʿmāl*. This was increasingly considered important to keep the credibility of the *Iḥyāʾ* intact, not only among scholars, as was already the case in premodern times, but even more when aiming at a lay audience who did not have the scholarly tools to classify the quality of narrations.

The method of Ḥawwā and al-Shāmī is fundamentally different from Ibn al-Jawzī however: where Ibn al-Jawzī chose to radically replace the material cited by al-Ghazālī for material that he favoured, often with his own *isnād*s attached, these two modern authors, rather, adopted the milder criticism of al-Ḥāfiẓ al-ʿIrāqī, and kept al-Ghazālī's own selection as the basis in their works. It is not so much the rigorous method of Ibn al-Jawzī that they adopted, but rather the mindset of *ḥadīth* criticism that had become popular for a much wider audience than only scholars, in the twentieth century, and the new audience created by the rise of the printing press that they likely kept in mind. These epitomes were no longer intended for colleague scholars or religious students only, who would be well aware of the pitfalls of the *Iḥyāʾ*, but would also be read by lay people without any religious training, who would not be able to distinguish reliable from unreliable material themselves. This may have made a rigorous selection of material more necessary in their eyes.

## 7 Conclusion

This chapter has only scratched a very small surface of the reception of the *Iḥyāʾ* through the ages, only focusing on the aspect of *ḥadīth* on virtue ethics in epitomes from Ḥanbalī and Salafī circles. First, I have shed light on the aspect of narrative virtue ethics in the Ḥanbalī epitomes of the *Iḥyāʾ* from Ibn al-Jawzī and Ibn Qudāma, to see what the consequences of their refusal of using unreliable *ḥadīth* on virtuous acts (*faḍāʾil al-aʿmāl*) has been for the way they dealt with the abundant *aḥādīth* and *āthār* used by al-Ghazālī in his magnum opus. It appears that in the case of virtue ethics on earning and livelihood (*al-kasb wa-l-maʿāsh*) thematically Ibn al-Jawzī remained true to the selection of al-Ghazālī, but he replaced all narrations that he considered unreliable with *ḥadīth* material that he considered reliable, often with complete chains of narration (*isnād*) through his own teachers. In the case of reliance on God (*tawakkul*) he changed the themes of the narrations as well, however, because he did not agree with al-Ghazālī's excessive Sufi opinions on *tawakkul*, for which al-Ghazālī used unreliable *ḥadīth* material as support. Ibn al-Jawzī thus intended to offer his readers and students a summarised version of the *Iḥyāʾ* as an alternative to the original work, which had become too popular among a large audience to debunk or neglect completely. By conforming the work to his high standards of *ḥadīth* criticism he hoped that it would no longer undermine the elevated position of *ḥadīth* in Islamic culture, as was his fear that would happen by the widespread practice of accepting lesser standards in the case of virtuous acts.

Second, I have reconstructed how and why these Ḥanbalī works with their exceptionally strict approach to *ḥadīth* on virtue ethics rose to prominence in the twentieth century after being relatively marginal in the preceding centuries. The rigour of Ibn al-Jawzī on this particular aspect of the *Iḥyāʾ* was an exception in his own age and was only further popularised in the twentieth century, mainly through the impact of Ibn Qudāma's summary in reformist circles after its rediscovery and first print in 1928 by the Damascene Salafī scholar Muḥammad Aḥmad Dahmān. *ḥadīth* criticism on the aspect of virtue ethics of the *Iḥyāʾ* had always been present historically but was not the main point of criticism on the work: it was commonly accepted to use unreliable *ḥadīth* on virtuous acts (*faḍāʾil al-aʿmāl*). When reformist movements in the late nineteenth and early twentieth century revived the ideas of Ibn al-Jawzī on *ḥadīth* criticism and consequently no longer accepted unreliable *ḥadīth* on virtuous acts, this gradually changed. This point of criticism on the *Iḥyāʾ* became so paradigmatic in modernity, that even authorities such as al-Shāmī and Ḥawwā, who defended al-Ghazālī on this point in their introductions and were more inclined towards Sufism than Salafism, became extra rigorous on this particular aspect of *ḥadīth* than one would expect from them based on their scholarly persuasions.

Given the small sample presented here of the large reservoir of both premodern and modern epitomes of and commentaries on the *Iḥyāʾ*, we should not be too hasty in attaching grand conclusions to this revival of *ḥadīth* criticism on the *Iḥyāʾ*. It would go too far for example to state that the rise of Salafism was so paradigmatic in the twentieth century that it completely changed the approach to *ḥadīth* on virtue ethics in non-Salafī circles. For that criticism on aspects of al-Ghazālī's use of *ḥadīth* has been too persistent in earlier times as well. It may be plausible, however, that non-Salafī authors became extra wary of this criticism to keep their works acceptable for a larger audience than only their own circle, and thus further implicated the scholarly criticism of the likes of al-Ḥāfiẓ al-ʿIrāqī, now that their works were intended for a larger popular audience than only specialist scholars.

These premodern Ḥanbalī epitomes still need further academic study to properly appreciate the reception of al-Ghazālī's creedal and Sufi ideas in the circles of the Ḥanbalīs of Baghdad and Damascus, and in modern and contemporary Salafism, where these premodern Ḥanbalī scholars found a unique reception history, their works entering completely different dynamics than originally intended. This will not only potentially shed new light on the relation between historical Ḥanbalism, Sufism, and speculative theology, it may also lead to new insight on the historical continuity between premodern Ḥanbalism and modern/contemporary Salafism, a relation that is not yet properly and systematically investigated.

Classics of Islamic literature like al-Ghazālī's *Iḥyāʾ* deserve a proper reception history to come to a deeper understanding of how this author and work have become such icons of Islamic thought. Epitomes keep appearing all over the Islamic world to this day, in very diverse settings (Garden 2016). I hope to have shown that the tradition of summaries on iconic works may prove rewarding to understand the reception history of these works. The study of commentary traditions has by now become a well-established trend in Islamic intellectual history. Perhaps it is time to place epitome traditions firmly on the map as well.

## Acknowledgment

This work is part of the research program "The origins, growth and dissemination of Salafī Qurʾān interpretation: the role of al-Qāsimī (d. 1914) in the shift from premodern to modern modes of interpretation," with project number 016.Veni.195.105, financed by the Dutch Research Council (NWO).

## Bibliography

ʿAbd al-Ḥamīd, ʿAlī b. Ḥasan. 1988. *Kitāb Iḥyāʾ ʿUlūm al-Dīn fī Mīzān al-ʿUlamāʾ wa-l-Muʾarrakhīn*. Hofuf: Maktabat Ibn al-Jawzī.

Abū Dāwūd al-Ṭayālisī. 1999. *Musnad*, edited by Muḥammad b. ʿAbd al-Muḥsin al-Turkī, 4 vols. Cairo: Dār Hajr.

Anjum, Ovamir. 2010. "Sufism without Mysticism? Ibn Qayyim al-Ǧawziyyah's Objectives in Madāriǧ al-Sālikīn." *Oriente Moderno* 90: 153–80.

Black MacDonald, Duncan. 1902. "Emotional Religion in Islam as Affected by Music and Singing. Being a Translation of a Book of the Iḥyāʾ ʿUlūm al-Dīn of al-Ghazzālī with Analysis, Annotation and Appendices." *Journal of the Royal Asiatic Society of Great Britain and Ireland* 3: 195–252.

Blecher, Joel. 2018. *Said the Prophet of God: Hadith Commentary across a Millennium*. Oakland, CA: University of California Press.

Bosanquet, Antonia. 2021. "One Manuscript, Many Books: the Manuscript and Editing History of Aḥkām Ahl al-Dhimma." *Die Welt des Islams* 61(2): 153–80.

Brockelmann, Carl. 1909. *Geschichte der arabischen Litteratur*. Leipzig: C.F. Amelangs Verlag.

Brown, Jonathan A.C. 2007. *The Canonization of al-Bukhārī and Muslim: The Formation and Function of the Sunnī Ḥadīth Canon*. Leiden: Brill.

Brown, Jonathan A.C. 2011. "Even if It's Not True It's True: Using Unreliable Ḥadīths in Sunni Islam." *Islamic Law and Society* 18: 1–52.

Brown, Jonathan A.C. 2014. *Misquoting Muhammad: The Challenge and Choices of Interpreting the Prophet's Legacy*. London: Oneworld Publications.

al-Bukhārī, Muḥammad b. Ismāʿīl. 1422/2001. *Al-Jāmiʿ al-Ṣaḥīḥ al-Mukhtaṣar min Umūr Rasūl Allāh*, edited by Muḥammad Zuhayr b. Nāṣir al-Nāṣir, 9 vols. Beirut: Dār Ṭawq al-Najāt.

Burrell, David. 2001. *Al-Ghazali: Faith in Divine Unity and Trust in Divine Providence* (*Kitab al-Tawhid wa l-Tawakkul*). Louisville, KY: Fons Vitae.

Commins, David. 1990. *Islamic Reform: Politics and Social Change in Late Ottoman Syria*. Oxford: Oxford University Press.

Cook, Michael. 2001. *Commanding Right and Forbidding Wrong in Islamic Thought*. Cambridge: Cambridge University Press.

El Shamsy, Ahmed, 2020. *Rediscovering the Islamic Classics: How Editors and Print Culture Transformed an Intellectual Tradition*. Princeton: Princeton University Press.

Fudge, Bruce. 2006. "Qurʾānic Exegesis in Medieval Islam and Modern Orientalism." *Die Welt des Islams* 46(2): 115–147.

Garden, Kenneth. 2005. "Al-Ghazālī's Contested Revival: *Iḥyāʾ ʿUlūm al-Dīn* and its critics in Khorasan and the Maghrib." PhD diss., Chicago University.

Garden, Kenneth. 2013. *The First Islamic Reviver: Abu Hamid al-Ghazali and his Revival of the Religious Sciences*. Oxford: Oxford University Press.

Garden, Kenneth. 2016. "The Revival of the Religious Sciences in the Twenty-First Century: Suʿād al-Ḥakīm's Adaptation of al-Ghazālī's Revival." In *Islam and Rationality: The Impact of al-Ghazālī; Papers Collected on His 900th Anniversary*, edited by Frank Griffel, vol. 2, 310–331. Leiden: Brill.

al-Ghazālī, Abū Ḥāmid. 2011. *Iḥyāʾ ʿUlūm al-Dīn*, 10 vols. Jedda: Dār al-Minhāj lil-Nashr wa-l-Tawzīʿ.

Gramlich, Richard. 1995a. *Alte Vorbilder des Sufitums*, 2 vols. Wiesbaden: Harrasowitz Verlag.

Gramlich, Richard. 1995b. *Die Nahrung der Herzen: Abū Ṭālib al-Makkī's Qūt al-qulūb eingeleitet, übersetzt und kommentiert*, 4 vols. Stuttgart: Franz Steiner Verlag.

Griffel, Frank. 2009. *Al-Ghazali's Philosophical Theology*. Oxford: Oxford University Press.

Ḥaddād, Abū ʿAbd Allāh Maḥmūd b. Muḥammad. 1987. *Takhrīj Aḥādīth Iḥyāʾ ʿUlūm al-Dīn lil-ʿIrāqī (725–806) wa-Ibn al-Subkī (727–771) wa-l-Zabīdī (1145–1205)*, 7 vols. Riyad: Dār al-ʿĀṣima.

Ḥawwā, Saʿīd. 2004. *Al-Mustakhlaṣ fī Tazkiyat al-Anfus*. Cairo: Dār al-Salām.

Hillenbrand, Carole. 2013. "The *Kimiya-yi Saʿadat* (The Alchemy of Happiness) of al-Ghazali: A Misunderstood Work?" In *Ferdowsi, the Mongols and the History of Iran: Art, Literature and Culture from Early Islam to Qajar Persia*, edited by Robert Hillenbrand, A.C.S. Peacock and Firuza Abdullaeva, 59–69. London: I.B. Tauris.

Ibn Abī l-Dunyā, Abū Bakr. 1987. *Kitāb al-Tawakkul ʿalā Llāh*. Beirut: Dār al-Bashāʾir al-Islāmiyya.

Ibn al-Jawzī, ʿAbd al-Raḥmān b. ʿAlī. 1983. *Talbīs Iblīs*. Beirut: Dār al-Qalam.

Ibn al-Jawzī, ʿAbd al-Raḥmān b. ʿAlī. 1992. *Al-Muntaẓam fī Taʾrīkh al-Mulūk wa-l-Umam*, edited by Muḥammad ʿAbd al-Qādir ʿAṭā and Muṣṭafā ʿAbd al-Qādir ʿAṭā, 19 vols. Beirut: Dār al-Kutub al-ʿIlmiyya.

Ibn al-Jawzī, ʿAbd al-Raḥmān b. ʿAlī. 2010. *Minhāj al-Qāṣidīn wa-Mufīd al-Ṣādiqīn*, edited by Kāmil Muḥammad Kharrāṭ, 3 vols. Damascus: Dār al-Tawfīq lil-Ṭibāʿa wa-l-Nashr wa-l-Tawzīʿ.

Ibn Qudāma al-Maqdisī, Aḥmad b. ʿAbd al-Raḥmān. 1928. *Mukhtaṣar Minhāj al-Qāṣidīn*, edited by Muḥammad Aḥmad Dahmān. Damascus: Maṭbaʿat Ibn Zaydūn.

Ibn Qudāma al-Maqdisī, Aḥmad b. ʿAbd al-Raḥmān. 1978. *Mukhtaṣar Minhāj al-Qāṣidīn*, edited by Shuʿayb al-Arnāʾūṭ and ʿAbd al-Qādir al-Arnāʾūṭ, first edition. Damascus: Maktabat Dār al-Bayān.

Ibn Qudāma al-Maqdisī, Aḥmad b. ʿAbd al-Raḥmān. 1991. *Mukhtaṣar Minhāj al-Qāṣidīn*, edited by Shuʿayb al-Arnāʾūṭ and ʿAbd al-Qādir al-Arnāʾūṭ, fourth edition. Damascus: Maktabat Dār al-Bayān.

Ibn Qudāma al-Maqdisī, Aḥmad b. ʿAbd al-Raḥmān. 2000. *Mukhtaṣar Minhāj al-Qāṣidīn*, edited by Zuhayr al-Shāwīsh, ninth edition. Damascus: al-Maktab al-Islāmī.

Ibn Rajab al-Ḥanbalī, ʿAbd al-Raḥmān b. Aḥmad. 2005. *Al-Dhayl ʿalā Ṭabaqāt al-Ḥanābila*, edited by ʿAbd al-Raḥmān b. Sulaymān al-ʿUthaymīn, 5 vols. Riyad: Maktabat al-ʿUbaykān.

ʿĪdū, ʿIṣām. 2017. "Ṣiyāgha Musta'nafa li-ʿIlm al-Ḥadīth." In *al-Dars al-Ḥadīthī al-Muʿāṣir*, edited by Aḥmad al-Jābirī, 385–390. Beirut: Markaz Namā' lil-Buḥūth wa-l-Dirāsāt.

Kateman, Ammeke. 2019. *Muḥammad ʿAbduh and His Interlocutors: Conceptualizing Religion in a Globalizing World*. Leiden: Brill.

Khalīfa, Ḥājjī. n.d. *Kashf al-Ẓunūn*. Beirut: Dār Iḥyā' al-Turāth al-ʿArabī.

Khan, Ahmad. 2016. "Islamic Tradition in an Age of Print: Editing, Printing, and Publishing the Classical Heritage." In *Reclaiming Islamic Tradition: Modern Interpretations of the Classical Heritage*, edited by Elisabeth Kendall and Ahmad Khan, 52–100. Edinburgh: Edinburgh University Press.

al-Khaṭīb, Muʿtazz. 2011. *Radd al-Ḥadīth min Jihat al-Matn: Dirāsa fī Manāhij al-Muḥaddithīn wa-l-Uṣūliyyīn*. Beirut: al-Shabaka al-ʿArabiyya lil-Abḥāth wa-l-Nashr.

Lange, Christian. 2015. *Paradise and Hell in Islamic Traditions*. Cambridge: Cambridge University Press.

Leder, Stefan. 1997. "Charismatic Scripturalism: The Ḥanbalī Maqdisīs of Damascus." *Der Islam* 74(2): 297–304.

Makdisi, George. 1979. "The Hanbali School and Sufism." *Boletín de la Associación Espanola de Orientalistas* 15: 115–126.

Melchert, Christopher. 2020. *Before Sufism: Early Islamic Renunciant Piety*. Berlin: De Gruyter.

Ormsby, Eric. 2007. *Ghazali*. Oxford: Oneworld Publications.

Picken, Gavin N. 2011. "The Quest for Orthodoxy and Tradition in Islam: Ḥanbalī Responses to Sufism." *Fundamentalism in the Modern World* 2: 237–263.

Pierret, Thomas. 2013. *Religion and State in Syria: The Sunni Ulama from Coup to Revolution*. Cambridge: Cambridge University Press.

Post, Arjan. 2016. "A Glimpse of Sufism from the Circle of Ibn Taymiyya: An Edition and Translation of al-Baʿlabakkī's (d. 734/1333) Epistle on the Spiritual Way (Risālat al-Sulūk)." *Journal of Sufi Studies* 5: 156–87.

Post, Arjan. 2020. *The Journeys of a Taymiyyan Sufi: Sufism through the Eyes of ʿImād al-Dīn Aḥmad al-Wāsiṭī (d. 711/1311)*. Leiden: Brill.

al-Qaraḍāwī, Yūsuf. 1994. *Al-Imām al-Ghazālī bayna Mādiḥīhi wa-Nāqidīh*. Beirut: Mu'assasat al-Risāla.

al-Qāsimī, Jamāl al-Dīn. 1907. *Majmūʿat Khuṭab*. Damascus: al-Maktaba al-Hāshimiyya.

al-Qāsimī, Jamāl al-Dīn. 1925. *Qawāʿid al-Taḥdīth min Funūn Muṣṭalaḥ al-Ḥadīth*, edited by Muḥammad Bahjat al-Bīṭār. Damascus: Maktab al-Nashr al-ʿArabī.

al-Qāsimī, Jamāl al-Dīn. 2009. *Maw'iẓat al-Mu'minīn min Iḥyā' 'Ulūm al-Dīn*, edited by 'Āṣim Bahjat al-Bīṭār. Beirut: Dār al-Nafā'is.

al-Qāsimī, Jamāl al-Dīn. 2010. *Al-Wa'ẓ al-Maṭlūb min Qūt al-Qulūb*, edited by Muḥammad b. Nāṣir al-'Ajmī. Beirut: Dār al-Bashā'ir al-Islāmiyya.

al-Qushayrī, Muslim b. al-Ḥajjāj. n.d. *Al-Musnad al-Ṣaḥīḥ al-Mukhtaṣar bi-Naql al-'Adl 'an al-'Adl ilā Rasūl Allāh*, edited by Muḥammad Fu'ād 'Abd al-Bāqī, 5 vols. Beirut: Dār Iḥyā' al-Turāth al-'Arabī.

Reichmuth, Stefan. 2009. *The World of Murtaḍā al-Zabīdī (1732–91): Life, Networks and Writings*. Cambridge: Gibb Memorial Trust.

Reinert, Benedikt. 1968. *Die Lehre vom tawakkul in der klassischen Sufik*. Berlin: De Gruyter.

Riḍā, Rashīd. 1909. "Al-Aḥādīth al-Mawḍū'a fī *Kitāb al-Iḥyā'* wa-Riwāyatuhā." *Al-Manār* 12: 911–912.

Ritter, Hellmut. 2013. *The Ocean of the Soul: Men, the World and God in the Stories of Farīd al-Dīn 'Aṭṭār*, translated by John O'Kane. Leiden: Brill.

al-Sarmīnī, Muḥammad Anas. 2010. *Al-Shaykh Muḥammad Jamāl al-Dīn al-Qāsimī wa-Juhūduh al-Ḥadīthiyya*. Beirut: Dār al-Bashā'ir al-Islāmiyya.

al-Shāmī, Ṣāliḥ Aḥmad. 1993a. *Al-Imām al-Ghazālī: Ḥujjat al-Islām wa-Mujaddid al-Mi'a al-Khāmisa*. Damascus: Dār al-Qalam.

al-Shāmī, Ṣāliḥ Aḥmad. 1993b. *Al-Muhadhdhab min Iḥyā' 'Ulūm al-Dīn*, 2 vols. Damascus: Dār al-Qalam.

Siddiqui, Sohaira Z.M. 2019. *Law and Politics under the Abbasids: An Intellectual Portrait of al-Juwayni*. Cambridge: Cambridge University Press.

Snober, Ahmed. 2020. "Hadith Criticism in the Levant in the Twentieth Century: From *Ẓāhir al-Isnād* to *'Ilal al-Ḥadīth*." In *Modern Ḥadīth Studies: Continued Debates and New Approaches*, edited by Belal Abu-Alabbas, Michael Dann and Christopher Melchert, 151–170. Edinburgh: Edinburgh University Press.

Swartz, Merlin. 2002. *A Medieval Critique of Anthropomorphism: Ibn al-Jawzī's Kitāb Akhbār al-Ṣifāt*. Leiden: Brill.

al-Ṭanṭāwī, 'Alī. 2001. *Fatāwā 'Alī al-Ṭanṭāwī: al-Juz' al-Thānī*, edited by Mujāhid Dayrāniyya. Jedda: Dār al-Manāra.

Weismann, Itzchak. 1993. "Sa'id Hawwa: The Making of a Radical Muslim Thinker in Modern Syria." *Middle Eastern Studies* 29(4): 601–623.

Weismann, Itzchak. 1997. "Sa'id Hawwa and Islamic Revivalism in Ba'thist Syria." *Studia Islamica* 85: 131–154.

Weismann, Itzchak and Rokaya Adawi. 2021. "Muḥammad Bahjat al-Bīṭār and the Decline of Modernist Salafism in Twentieth-Century Syria." *Journal of Islamic Studies* 22(2): 237–256.

CHAPTER 6

# *Ḥadīth* and Sufism in Ethical Discourse

## *Exploring ʿAbd al-Qādir al-Jīlānī's Conception of* Taḥbīb

*Salahudheen Kozhithodi and Khairil Husaini Bin Jamil*

## 1 Introduction

The Ḥanbalī Sufi scholar ʿAbd al-Qādir al-Jīlānī (d. 561/1166) argues in his works, *Futūḥ al-Ghayb* ("Revelations of the Unseen") and *al-Fatḥ al-Rabbānī* ("The Sublime Revelation"), that a Sufi may enjoy certain worldly pleasures after struggling through various stages of asceticism (*zuhd*). This chapter discusses the scriptural foundation of this idea and how al-Jīlānī avoided the contradiction between the enjoyment of worldly pleasures and Sufi ethics, which is based on "self-purification." We will analyse *ḥadīth al-taḥbīb* that translates as "I was made to love (*ḥubbiba ilayya*) from your world women and perfume, and I found the coolness of my eyes (*qurratu ʿaynī*) in performing the prayer," and compare al-Jīlānī's interpretation with that of other scholars in pre and post Jīlānī era.

Some ascetics and Sufis believed that marriage and family life are hindrances to achieving excellence in the path of Allāh, as evident from different quotations recorded in Sufi and *zuhd* literature. However, the majority refuted this idea pointing to the life of the Prophet and his encouragement for marital life. At the same time, the former opinion highlights the Prophet's foresight of later generations becoming worse overtime, and in such a time, it will be better for a person to live isolated from people.[1] Likewise, some scholars found two key terms in the *ḥadīth*, "*ḥubbiba*" and "*dunyā*" problematic, hence necessitating explanation. How could the Prophet say that he loves things from this world (*dunyā*), whilst he has described it as a damned place elsewhere. Abstaining from the *dunyā* has often been regarded as the fundamental principle of asceticism and Sufism. These contradictions have triggered various interpretations and have sometimes placed the Sufis in a defensive mode.

1 The *ḥadīth* has been recorded in various corpuses including the *Ṣaḥīḥ* of al-Bukhārī (see al-Bukhārī 1987, 1:15: *Kitāb al-Īmān* ("Book of Faith"), *Bāb min al-Dīn al-Firār min al-Fitan* ("Chapter on Avoiding/Escaping Temptation belongs to Religion")). Scholars have used this *ḥadīth* to justify celibacy (see Ibn al-ʿArabī 2003, 3:144).

Furthermore, some have criticised Sufis for enjoying worldly pleasures, and even al-Jīlānī himself had faced such criticism.[2] By intertwining *ḥadīth* with Sufi perspectives, al-Jilānī responded to this criticism and apparent contradictions. At the same time, he tried to establish that the Sufi concepts of *fanāʾ* and *baqāʾ*, which refer to the developed form of asceticism, are not contradictory to the Qurʾān and Sunna as some may have claimed. Indeed, the *ḥadīth* mentioned above is a piece of excellent scriptural evidence to substantiate his stance.

## 2 *Takhrīj* and the Form of the *Ḥadīth*

The *ḥadīth* was recorded on the authority of Anas b. Mālik (d. 93/712) from the beginning of the third/ninth century in different sources, including those which were arranged according to themes and narrators such as *Sunan*s and *Musnad*s. Yet, among the six canonical ones, only al-Nasāʾī (d. 303/915) recorded it in his compendium.[3] Al-Ḥākim al-Naysābūrī (d. 405/1014) recorded it in his *Mustadrak* and evaluated it as authentic by the standard of Muslim, though the latter did not record it in his work. Nevertheless, the great *ḥadīth* scholar and verifier, Ibn Ḥajar al-ʿAsqalānī (d. 852/1448), treated it as a considerable one (*ḥasan*) (Ibn Ḥajar al-ʿAsqalānī 1995, 3:249).

In the primary thematic sources of *ḥadīth*, the *ḥadīth* of *taḥbīb* has been cited to highlight various issues including the status of *ṣalāt* (prayer) in Islam as found in Muḥammad b. Naṣr al-Marwazī's (d. 294/906) *Taʿẓīm Qadr al-Ṣalāt* ("The Aggrandisement of the Status of Prayer") (al-Marwazī 1986, 1:331). Al-Marwazī stated that *ṣalāt* is the most significant act of worship in the eyes of Allāh; thus, He made it dearer to His dearest servant. It is also recorded as an encouragement towards marriage in the book of *Nikāḥ* ("Marriage"), in Abū ʿAwāna's (d. 316/928) *Mustakhraj* ("The Extracted") and al-Bayḥaqī's (d. 458/1066) *al-Sunan al-Kubrā* ("The Great Sunnas").[4] Unlike the latter, the former gave quite a long title for his chapter to project the *ḥadīth* as an instruction by the Prophet to all Muslims to marry more than one wife whenever possible, to bring forth

2 See the questions he encountered pertaining to his marriage below.

3 Al-Nasāʾī 1986, 7:61: *Kitāb ʿIshrat al-Nisāʾ* ("Book on Living with Women"), *Bāb Ḥubb al-Nisāʾ* ("Chapter on the Love for Women").

4 Al-Isfarāyīnī 1998, 3:12: *Kitāb al-Nikāḥ* ("Book of Marriage"), *Bāb Dhikr Ḥaḍḍ al-Nabī ʿalā Tazwīj al-Abkār al-Wadūd al-Walūd wa-ʿalā Ibtighāʾ al-Nasl fa-Yukāthir bihinna l-Umam* ("Chapter on the Prophet's Encouragement of the Marriage of Amiable and Fertile Virgin Women and on Pursuing Offspring to Increase the Population"); al-Bayhaqī 2003, 7:124: *Kitāb al-Nikāḥ* ("Book of Marriage"), *Bāb al-Raghba fī l-Nikāḥ* ("Chapter on Desiring Marriage").

more good people into their community. For al-Nasāʾī, the *ḥadīth* instructs men to observe fair treatment of women. Therefore, he included it in the chapter of *Kitāb ʿIshrat al-Nisāʾ* ("Kind Treatment of Women") under the subheading of *Bāb Ḥubb al-Nisāʾ* ("Loving Women/Wives").

On the other hand, the part of the *ḥadīth* regarding fragrance has been the concern of other *ḥadīth* compilers such as ʿAbd al-Razzāq (d. 211/827) and Abū l-Shaykh (d. 369/979) (al-Aṣbahānī 1998, 2:58). The former presented it in a chapter titled *Bāb al-Marʾa Tuṣallī wa-Laysa fī Raqabatihā Qilāda wa-Taṭayyub al-Rijāl* ("A Woman Prays without a Necklace on Her Neck and Perfume of Men") in his *Muṣannaf* ("The Topically Arranged"), whereas the latter employed it in a chapter titled *Bāb Dhikr Maḥabbatihi lil-Ṭībi wa-Taṭayyubihi bihi* ("The Mention of the Prophet's Love for Perfumes"). Quite intriguingly, Ibn Abī ʿĀṣim (d.287/900) in his collection on asceticism alluded to the fact that wives and perfumes could not be considered as something against asceticism. His chapter is titled *Bāb Ḥubbiba ilayya min Dunyākum al-Nisāʾ wa-l-Ṭīb* ("Wives and Perfumes are Made Dearer to Me [the Prophet]") (Ibn Abī ʿĀṣim 1988, 1:119). The *ḥadīth* was also recorded in the *Musnad* ("The Supported") of Aḥmad b. Ḥanbal (d. 241/855) and *al-Muʿjam al-Awsaṭ* ("The Middle Sized *Muʿjam*") of al-Ṭabarānī (d. 360/971) on the authority of Anas b. Mālik (Aḥmad b. Ḥanbal 2001, 19:305; al-Ṭabarānī 1995, 5:241).

Though the scholars have no serious disagreement on the authenticity of the *ḥadīth*, they have different opinions regarding its textual form. The most significant amongst such debates is the one concerning the number "three" (*thalāth*) found in some versions of the *ḥadīth*, i.e., "three things from your *dunyā* are made dear to me." While scholars like Ibn Fūrak (d. 406/1015), al-Kalābādhī (d. 380/990) and al-Ghazālī (d. 505/1111) have tried to justify it, others like Ibn Qayyim al-Jawziyya (d. 751/1350) have argued that it is not part of the original *ḥadīth*; instead, it was later added into the text.[5] According to Ibn Ḥajar al-ʿAsqalānī and others, the addition "three" was not found in any primary sources of the *ḥadīth*. It was only found in some non-*ḥadīth* experts' works such as *Iḥyāʾ ʿUlūm al-Dīn* ("The Revival of Religious Sciences") of al-Ghazālī and *al-Kashshāf* ("The Revealer") of al-Zamakhsharī (al-Sakhāwī 1985, 1:292).

Finally, another genre that could be said to have also pursued the debate on the literal form of the *ḥadīth* is the genre of *al-aḥādīth al-mushtahira* (viral *ḥadīth*). Some of the works of this genre include *al-Maqāṣid al-Ḥasana* ("The Good Purposes") of al-Sakhāwī (al-Sakhāwī 1985, 1:292) and *Kashf al-Khafāʾ* ("Uncovering the Hidden") of al-ʿAjlūnī (d. 1162/1749) (al-ʿAjlūnī 2000,

5 See their interpretations below. For Ibn Fūrak's and Ibn al-Qayyim's justifications, see Ibn Fūrak 2015; Ibn Qayyim al-Jawziyya 1997, 238.

1:391–393). The authors validated the *ḥadīth* by referring to various narrations and additions found in different reports. However, both affirmed that the addition of the words "three things" was not found in any narrations recorded in the primary sources. For them, this addition affects the meaning of the *ḥadīth* because prayer should not be qualified as one of the worldly matters. Nevertheless, al-ʿAjlūnī, a later contributor to this genre, did not object to the views of those who report and interpret the "three things." He attempted to justify that the third of the three things could have been omitted from the narration. It could be retrieved from a version reported by Aḥmad b. Ḥanbal on the authority of ʿĀʾisha (d. 58/678), which reads, "He likes three things from this world: women, perfumes, and food. He gained two but not the third. He got women and perfumes but not the food" (al-ʿAjlūnī 2000, 1:391–393).

## 3 *Ḥadīth* of *Taḥbīb*: Interpretations in *Ḥadīth* Commentaries

In the pre-Jīlānī era, Sufis and people of *zuhd* were the individuals most interested in this *ḥadīth*. After al-Jīlānī, the *ḥadīth* of *taḥbīb* can be said to have gained wider attention. The main reason could be the increasing scholarly engagements with the *Sunan* of al-Nasāʾī. Another secondary source of the *ḥadīth*, which has also attracted numerous great exegetes to advance worthful discussions about its meaning, is *al-Shifā* ("The Healing") of al-Qāḍī ʿIyāḍ (d. 544/1149). The *ḥadīth* was considered as a part of the *shamāʾil* (qualities and attributes) of the Prophet, particularly concerning his marital life. Continuous discussion on the *ḥadīth* within this genre could be appreciated from *al-Mawāhib al-Ladunniyya* ("The Divine Providences") of al-Qasṭallānī (d. 686/1287). On the other hand, scholars of jurisprudence deduced rulings on fragrance from the *ḥadīth*. Due to the multidimensional nature of its interpretation, debates surrounding the *ḥadīth* will be tackled in several sections as follows.

## 4 *Zuhd* and Marriage: Conflict or Harmony?

The most critical point with regards to this debate is that, as far as the available sources are concerned, no scholar has connected this *ḥadīth* with the concepts of *fanāʾ* and *baqāʾ* prior to al-Jīlānī. A contemporary scholar of al-Jīlānī, al-Qāḍī ʿIyāḍ, did discuss this *ḥadīth*, however with an attempt to suit the *ḥadīth* to the notion of *zuhd* (al-Qāḍī ʿIyāḍ 1987, 1:19–46). He averred that married life does not contradict with the practice of *zuhd* by citing the examples of married

Prophets. Although there were unmarried Prophets, according to him, the ones who got married and fulfilled their family duties are deemed higher in status. Al-Qāḍī ʿIyāḍ perceived the *ḥadīth* as a general promotion for marriage whereas al-Jīlānī undoubtedly proclaimed that *nikāḥ* is prohibited for a *murīd*, and in terms of *murād*, he has no choice but to follow what has been determined by God.

Al-Qāḍī ʿIyāḍ's appropriation of this *ḥadīth* to *zuhd* was a response to those who thought that marriage is a hindrance on the path towards Allāh. In *Qūṭ al-Qulūb* ("The Nourishment of the Hearts") of Abū Ṭālib al-Makkī (d. 386/996) and *Iḥyā ʿUlūm al-Dīn* of al-Ghazālī, *imām* Aḥmad was quoted as saying that he had debated a group of scholars regarding Ḥasan al-Baṣrī's (d. 110/728) claim that "if Allāh wishes *khayr* (goodness) for a person He will not occupy him with family and wealth" (al-Makkī 2005, 2, 413). The well-known Sufi contemporary to Aḥmad, Bishr al-Ḥāfī (d. 227/841) was not married, and when he was asked about it, he replied that he preferred to be engaged with obligatory deeds to the supererogatory ones (al-Ghazālī n.d., 2:23). The great Sufi literature, such as the two mentioned above, discusses both views that encourage or discourage marriage in detail and provide many traditions in support of both arguments.

As mentioned earlier, Ibn Abī ʿĀṣim argues that wives and perfumes could not be considered as something against asceticism. Yet, other works on asceticism included a section on *Bāb man Kariha al-Māla wa-l-Walad* ("Disinterest in Offspring and Wealth") in which some ascetics were reported to ask Allāh to be free from offspring and wealth. Astonishingly, when those ascetics wish to pray against anyone, they will pray that Allāh increase the person's wealth and children, so that he will be burdened with them (Ibn al-Jarrāḥ 1984, 415–417).

On another note, the Mālikī scholar Ibn al-ʿArabī (d. 543/1148) attempted reconciliation by exploiting the change of condition across generations. Marriage was not a hindrance in the path of Allāh for the early generation. However, in later times, some scholars and ascetics found that the world had become more challenging, and people became compelled to commit prohibited acts to earn their livelihood and provide for their families. Therefore, the scholars and ascetics rejected family life and preferred seclusion (*ʿuzla*). Ibn al-ʿArabī viewed this stance as a strong position since the Messenger of Allāh had said: "The best possession of a Muslim will be a herd of sheep with which he retires to the top of a mountain or places where rain is expected to fall (pastures), in order to safeguard his faith from tribulation."[6] However, he made it clear that there is no monasticism in Islam as found in Christianity, and one is

6 Al-Bukhārī 1987, 1:15: *Kitāb al-Īmān* ("Book of Faith"), *Bāb min al-Dīn al-Firār min al-Fitan* ("Chapter on Avoiding/Escaping Temptation belongs to Religion").

not supposed to immerse in worship and avoid all worldly matters, including the family. The scholars who seem to favour a life similar to monasticism were actually referring to extraordinary circumstances due to the widespread of crisis (Ibn al-ʿArabī 2003, 3:144).

The tenth/seventeenth century scholar al-Ghazzī (d. 1061/1651) also quoted this *ḥadīth* to change the perception of people who manipulated the sayings of early scholars to discourage marriage, and to depict it as an act contradictory to asceticism. He treated all these statements as conditional; when a marriage diverts a person's attention from obeying Allāh and from abiding by His rules, then it is a hindrance in the path of worshipping Allāh. Any comforts with wives and fragrance in this world could not be treated generally as blameworthy. However, he did not provide explanation on how they deviate man from the straight path and how a person can overcome them (al-Ghazzī 2011, 1:184).

A pro-Salafī contemporary interpreter, ʿAbd al-Raḥmān Nāṣir al-Barrāk (b. 1933–1934) used this *ḥadīth* to criticise Ibn Rajab al-Ḥanbalī's (d. 795/1392) position on *Kalimat al-Ikhlāṣ* ("The Word of Devotion"). Ibn Rajab stated that "the *ʿārifūn* have no engagements other than what they have with their Lord and no concerns about something other than Him …" According al-Barrāk, it is nothing but an utterance of some extreme ascetics who transcended the limits with a wrong *ijtihād* due to their ignorance. Al-Barrāk criticised this position on the ground that it contradicts the *ḥadīth* of *taḥbīb*. He finds no issue in engaging with family, children, and other lawful comforts. However, unlike his predecessors, he resorts to criticising Ibn Rajab instead of offering a reconciling interpretation (al-Barrāk 2014, 110).

## 5 Material World: Love or Curse?

In his commentary, al-Qāḍī ʿIyāḍ had given attention to the apparent contradiction between this *ḥadīth* and the Islamic concept of cursing the material world (*dunyā*), since this *ḥadīth* treats three things among worldly matters and depicts the *dunyā* as the loved one. Therefore, he noted that the Prophet did not see women and perfume as *his* worldly matters, but he used the words "*your* worldly matters." This was concluded from the addition found in some versions, i.e., the phrase *ḥubbiba ilayya min dunyākum*, which means some of your worldly matters that have been made dear to me.[7] According to al-Qāḍī

7 The *ḥadīth* has been recorded without the possessive pronoun "*kum*" (see al-Maqdisī 2000, 5:122; Abū Yaʿlā l-Mawṣilī 1984, 6:237; Aḥmad b. Ḥanbal 2001, 21:433). So, the meaning would be "I was made to love from the world …"

ʿIyāḍ, the Prophet perceived these matters as his *ākhira* (the Hereafter) affairs since a Muslim can convert any worldly matter to that of the Hereafter by having the right *niyya* (insight). Nevertheless, a question remains due to this interpretation – it leaves no specific reason to the mention of only these two things since all worldly matters share the same potential of convertibility.

Other interpretations offered to solve this contradiction are those by al-Kalābādhī and al-Ghazālī. Al-Kalābādhī opines that the article "*min*" in the *ḥadīth* could be given the meaning of "*fī*" which then indicates that women, fragrance, and prayer are the three things made dear to the Prophet during his life *in* this world (*ḥubbiba ilayya wa-anā fī l-dunyā*), but they are not part of this world. Unlike later *ḥadīth* scholars, he treated the word *three* as a part of the *ḥadīth* and tried to answer two questions simultaneously: firstly, how can the Prophet love something that is a part of this world? and secondly, how can prayers be attributed as a part of this material world? Hence, these non-worldly affairs are made dear *in* this world while he was here. He further elaborated that this *ḥadīth* indicates a very high stage of *ʿubūdiyya* (worship) achieved by the Prophet. Prayer is the most elegant form of glorification (*taʿẓīm*) of Allāh, and this *ḥadīth* implies that the Prophet had attained it. The other two matters, women and fragrance, represent excellent interaction with the creations of Allāh, which should be done by fulfilling their due rights as well as being kind and generous towards them. He further added that fragrance is amongst the rights of the angels, and the Prophet was applying it to fulfil their rights. Indeed, the Prophet himself is the most beautiful fragrance in this world and he does not need any fragrance (al-Kalābādhī 1999, 25). In short, al-Kalābādhī attempted to establish that the love mentioned in this *ḥadīth* was not a mere love of comforts in the material world, rather it was part of achieving the finest form of *ʿubūdiyya* and excellent dealing with others.

Al-Ghazālī also viewed this *ḥadīth* as apparently contradicting with the basic principles of asceticism and Sufism, discussing it in the book of *Dhamm al-Dunyā* ("Condemnation of the Worldly"). He argued that the things found in the *dunyā* are of mainly three categories, the first of which are the things that will go to the next world, such as one's knowledge and actions. By knowledge he means the recognition of God, His attributes, His actions and His sovereignty over heaven and earth, and by actions, the actions done for the sake of God. To him, though it is part of the *dunyā*, it is not blameworthy but praiseworthy. To substantiate his position, he cited the *ḥadīth* of *taḥbīb*. Even though prayer is classified with the *dunyā*, it is an action done in the *dunyā* for the *ākhira*. Consequently, actions related to marriage and using fragrance, although mentioned as part of the *dunyā*, do not fall into the category of a blameworthy *dunyā* (al-Ghazālī n.d., 23).

## 6 Jurisprudential Perspective

In dealing with the *ḥadīth* of *taḥbīb*, most of the scholars of jurisprudence focused on the subject of fragrance. The Mālikī Ibn al-ʿArabī referenced this *ḥadīth* in his interpretation of *al-Muwaṭṭaʾ* ("The Well-Trodden Path"), titled *Kitāb al-Qabas* ("The Book of Allusion"), to explain away other *ḥadīth* that claimed the Prophet applied perfumes during *ḥajj* whilst it is considered a prohibition to do so during such ritual. Ibn al-ʿArabī grouped different opinions of scholars into four, the first of which is that applying perfumes while performing *ḥajj* and *ʿumra* is an exclusive right (*khuṣūṣiyya*) of the Prophet. It is allowed exclusively to him because it was specifically made dear to him by Allāh. Ibn al-ʿArabī further observed that the Prophet was given some privileges regarding whatever was made dear to him. In terms of prayer, it was obligatory for him to pray at night whilst it was only supererogatory for others. Likewise, he was allowed to marry more than four wives, as well as conduct his marriages without the presence of guardians and witnesses. Therefore, according to Ibn al-ʿArabī, it is not strange to have a special privilege for the Prophet in applying perfume during pilgrimage (Ibn al-ʿArabī 1992, 1:553). Ibn al-ʿArabī also discussed this *ḥadīth* in his commentary on *Jāmiʿ al-Tirmidhī* ("The Compilation of al-Tirmidhī") explaining that the Prophet never rejected perfume when it was offered to him because he needed it and at the same time, it was made dear to him, combining need and love here. It is possible in his case to reject things other than perfume if there is any reason to do so (Ibn al-ʿArabī n.d., 10:236). Obviously, the Prophet does not need fragrance since he himself is fragrant, therefore, by "need," Ibn al-ʿArabī might have intended his need to fulfill the rights of angels as mentioned above.

## 7 *Taḥbīb* as a Sublime Quality of the Prophet

As seen above, some jurists and Sufis have considered this *ḥadīth* as addressing a specific privilege of the Prophet. While al-Kalābādhī treated it as an indication of the most excellent form of human being reserved for the Prophet, Ibn al-ʿArabī treated it as a reason for a concession to marrying more than four wives and applying perfumes during pilgrimage. Likewise, this *ḥadīth* has been much discussed as part of the Prophet's *shamāʾil* (sublime qualities of the Prophet). Al-Suyūṭī (d. 911/1505), in his commentary on *Sunan al-Nasāʾī* ("The Traditions of al-Nasāʾī"), investigates the wisdom behind the *taḥbīb* from two different angles. On the one hand, it is a *balāʾ* (hardship from God) because world matters have been made dear to a person whereas he needs to dedicate his love solely to God. Therefore, life has become the most challenging task for him. On the other hand, when the enemy of the Prophet accused him as being a *sāḥir* (sorcerer), or a poet who was oblivious to ordinary life, he became concerned with worldly matters to refute their claims. In that sense, it is not a hardship, but rather a mercy from God (al-Suyūṭī 1986, 61–63).

Al-Sindī (d. 170/787) added that the divine wisdom behind the Prophet's love towards women was educational. His wives could convey many lessons from his private affairs to the coming generations. As for the perfume, it was the dearest thing to the angels and as a prophet who dealt with angels, he was using it to please them. Al-Sindī infers that his *ḥubb* was not a mere love of worldly matters, but by doing so, he was fulfilling some noble objectives. However, the coolness of the eyes is located in the Prophet's conversation with God during his prayers. It conveys the idea that if a worldly pleasure hinders the love towards God, it is not a praiseworthy thing. It is only laudable when it enhances the love towards God (al-Sindī 1986, 61–62).

On another part, most of the interpreters of *Mishkāt al-Maṣābīḥ* ("The Niche of Lamps") such ʿAbd al-Ḥaqq al-Dihlawī (d. 1052/1642) and ʿAlī l-Qārī (d. 1014/1606) also elaborated on the meaning of the *ḥadīth*. They have given some attention to the word "*ḥubbiba*" as it denotes that the love did not originate from the Prophet's nature or self, but that Allāh compelled him to be so as a mercy for mankind (al-Dihlawī 2014, 8:480; ʿAlī l-Qārī 2002, 8:3294). Though both of them were seen as coming from Sufi backgrounds, they did not relate *taḥbīb* with the Sufi concepts of *baqāʾ* and *fanāʾ* as found with al-Jīlānī.

In *Nuzhat al-Majālis wa-Muntakhab al-Nafāʾis* ("Unwinding Councils and Precious Selections"), al-Ṣaffūrī (d. 894/1489) narrated a background story, without any *isnād*, to offer context for the *ḥadīth*. It says that when the Prophet mentioned this *ḥadīth*, Abū Bakr (d. 13/634), ʿUmar (d. 23/644), ʿUthmān (d. 35/656) and ʿAlī (d. 40/661) responded one after another by citing the things that were made dear to them. Abū Bakr said that he was made to love three things from this world – to sit in front of the Prophet, to recite *ṣalawāt* (prayers) upon him and to spend his wealth for him. Thereupon ʿUmar said: "I was made to love three things from this world; commanding good, forbidding evil, and establishing the *ḥudūd* (the prescribed punishments)." Then ʿUthmān responded that he was made to love feeding the hungry, spreading *salām* (peace greeting), and praying at night while people are sleeping. Finally, ʿAlī said: "I was made to love three things from this world; fighting with the sword, fasting in summer and serving guests." Then the angel Gabriel informed the Prophet about things that he was made to love, saying: "I was made to love descending upon Prophets, carrying the message to Messengers, and praising Allāh the Lord of the Worlds." Then Allāh informed the Prophet about the three things that He likes most: a tongue that always recites *dhikr*, a thankful heart and a body that is patient during hardship (al-Ṣaffūrī 1867, 1:52–53). Al-Ṣaffūrī commented that when this *ḥadīth* reached the four eponymous founders of the legal *madhāhib* (legal schools), Abū Ḥanīfa (d. 150/767) was reported to say: "I was made to love acquiring knowledge throughout the nights, avoiding self-praise and arrogance, and having a heart that avoids the love of *dunyā*." Mālik (d. 179/796) also related the three things that were made dear to him: being a neighbour to the Prophet's grave, attachment with his soil, and paying respect to his relatives (*ahl al-bayt*). Al-Shāfiʿī (d. 204/820) said that he was made to love dealing with people with compassion, avoiding things that lead to pretentiousness, and following the way of *taṣawwuf*. Aḥmad responded that he was made to love following the Prophet in his sayings, seeking God's blessings with his lights, and embarking on the path of his examples (al-Ṣaffūrī 1867, 1:52–53). Indeed, al-Ṣaffūrī's extended story includes many of the major early Islamic figures, truly providing a lesson of "three" important loveable actions for later generations.

This long narration was repeated with some variations in al-Qasṭallānī's *al-Mawāhib al-Laduniyya* and al-ʿAjlūnī's *Kashf al-Khafāʾ*. Though the authenticity is questionable, this provides another unique understanding of the *ḥadīth*. It indicates that the things made dearer to people could be of anything apart from women and perfume. In a sense, it is congruent with al-Jīlānī's concept of *taḥbīb* where certain worldly pleasures are made dearer to specific individuals (al-ʿAjlūnī 2000, 1:391–393; al-Qasṭallānī n.d., 2:221).

## 8 Theosophical Perspective

It is not surprising to find that the one who treated this *ḥadīth* from a theosophical perspective was the renowned Sufi luminary Muḥyī l-Dīn Ibn al-ʿArabī. He interpreted this *ḥadīth* in *Fuṣūṣ al-Ḥikam* ("Bezels of Wisdom") appropriating it to a theosophical system called by others as "the unity of being" (*waḥdat al-wujūd*). Starting with Adam, each of the 27 chapters of *Fuṣūṣ* is dedicated to a Prophet mentioned in the Qurʾān. The chapters are based on a specific Qurʾānic verse or Prophetic *ḥadīth* that describes the characteristics of the respective Prophet. The final chapter is dedicated to the last Prophet Muḥammad, and its entire discussion is based on the *ḥadīth* of *taḥbīb*.

According to Ibn al-ʿArabī, all things are reflections of a unique and unified Absolute Reality, God. Some things are a greater manifestation compared to others, such as the Prophets amongst other creatures and Prophet Muḥammad amongst other Prophets – he is the highest manifestation. He also believed that a woman is the one who completes a man's recognition of the divine, and a man's witnessing of God in a woman is the most excellent witnessing. After quoting the first part of the *ḥadīth*, "three things from your *dunyā* are made dear to me," Ibn al-ʿArabī said that among the three, Allāh started with women even before prayer due to this state (Bālī Zādah 2002, 312–313). Unlike other interpreters, he gave much attention to the order stated in the *ḥadīth*. To him, knowing a woman is part of knowing one's self since she is an excellent manifestation of the oneness of being. Only those who achieve that knowledge can reach the core of prayer, which is a part of knowing God. Whoever knows himself knows his Lord. According to him:

> When man witnesses Allāh in women, his witnessing is in the passive; when he witnesses Him in himself, regarding the appearance of woman from Him, he witnesses Him in the active. When he witnesses Him from himself without the presence of any from him, his witnessing is in the passive directly from Allāh without any intermediary. So, his witnessing of Allāh in the woman is the most complete and perfect because he witnesses Allāh inasmuch as He is both active and passive. For this reason, the Prophet, may Allāh bless him and grant him peace, loved women.
>
> IBN ʿARABĪ 2014, 128

According to his interpretation, the love of women is not a matter of worldly pleasure; instead, it is a medium for acquiring the ultimate knowledge about God, which is called *maʿrifa* (gnosis). He further argued that every subject yearns for its origin. Man yearns for his Lord[8] because He created man in His image by blowing His *rūḥ* (spirit). God loves him, who is in His image. Likewise, He makes loveable to man the woman whom He extracted for him from him and who appeared in His image. When a man loves a woman, he desires their union, and the best way to achieve it is through marriage. Ibn al-ʿArabī states:

> When a man loves a woman, he seeks union with her, that is to say the most complete union possible in love, and there is in the elemental sphere no greater union than that between the sexes. It is [precisely] because such desire pervades all his parts that man is commanded to perform

8 This is based on the Qurʾānic verse 32:9, which reads: "Then He proportioned him and breathed into him from His [created] spirit and made for you hearing and vision and hearts; little are you grateful," and the *ḥadīth* "The Prophet, peace and blessings be upon him said, 'Allāh created Adam in His image …'" (al-Bukhārī 1987, 5:2299: *Kitāb al-Istiʾdhān* ("Book of Asking Permission"), *Bāb Badʾ al-Salām* ("Chapter on Commencing with the Peace Greeting")).

> the major ablution. Thus, the purification is total, just as his annihilation in her was total at the moment of consummation. God is jealous of his servant that he should find pleasure in any but Him, so He purifies him by the ablution, so that he might once again behold Him in the one in whom he was annihilated, since it is none other than He Whom he sees in her.
>
> IBN ʿARABĪ 2014, 128

In terms of the fragrance (*ṭīb*), the Prophet mentioned it after women because women are the best perfume. They have fragrance in their form (*takwīn*) itself, and the best perfume is the embracement of the well-beloved (Ibn ʿArabī 2014, 128).

Ultimately, within the domain of *ḥadīth* literature, the association of *taḥbīb* with the concepts of *fanāʾ* and *baqāʾ* was only found in the writings of ʿAbd al-Raʾūf al-Munāwī (d. 1031/1622), an Ottoman scholar from Cairo. He was known for his works on the early history of Islam and the history of Sufism in Egypt, and he was also a disciple of al-Shaʿrānī (d. 973/1565). In his seminal work, *Fayḍ al-Qadīr* ("Revelation of the Omnipotent"), al-Munāwī mentions that some scholars have related *taḥbīb* with *fanāʾ* and *baqāʾ* and, to them, the *ḥadīth* refers to a state after *fanāʾ*. When an aspirant annihilates in God without having any personal intention and desire, God places some worldly matters in his mind. Yet, al-Munāwī did not mention al-Jīlānī by name. Nevertheless, it is after al-Munāwī that this concept found extensive elaboration in *ḥadīth* interpretive discourse (al-Munāwī 1937, 3:371).

## 9 *Ḥadīth al-Taḥbīb* in al-Jīlānī's Works

The *ḥadīth* of *taḥbīb* was mentioned two times in *al-Fatḥ al-Rabbānī* and once in *Futūḥ al-Ghayb*.[9] In *al-Fatḥ*, the *ḥadīth* has been quoted as: "I was made to love from your world women and perfume, and the delight of my eyes has always been in the prayer." In some latest editions of *al-Fatḥ*, there is an addition of the words "three things," i.e., "I was made to love three things from your world;" however, they were absent in the earliest one. The addition was also found in the early editions of *Futūḥ al-Ghayb*. This addition has caught the

9 This *ḥadīth* has been mentioned in *al-Fatḥ* in the seventh discourse on patience, and in the 25th discourse on ascetic detachment in the world (*al-zuhd fī l-dunyā*) (al-Jīlānī 1988, 44, 114). It has also been mentioned in *Futūḥ* in the sixth discourse on *al-fanāʾ ʿan al-khalq* (al-Jīlānī 1973, 14).

attention of many *ḥadīth* scholars since it raises some questions as explained above.

The apparent meaning that an ordinary reader gets from the *ḥadīth* is that the Prophet likes perfumes and women, yet he still found real happiness whilst performing prayers. *Qurrat al-ʿayn* (literally, the coolness of the eyes) is an Arabic metaphor for enjoyment as the tears become cold when a person becomes extremely happy (Ibn Manẓūr 1993, 12:582).

In the seventh discourse on "patience" in *al-Fatḥ al-Rabbānī*, a lecture that al-Jīlānī delivered in his *ribāṭ* (Sufi lodge) on 17 Shawwāl 545 (13 February 1151), he elaborated on the *ḥadīth* of *taḥbīb* uttering the following:

> Hate all things and love the creator of all things. Then if He makes you love one of the things you have hated, you may do so in safety, because He is the one giving rise to the love, not you. This is why the Prophet, Allāh bless him and give him peace, said: "I have been made to love three things: perfume, women, and the coolness of my eyes (chief comfort) is in the prayer." He was made to love them after disliking, forsaking, renouncing, and shunning them. You must now rid your heart of everything aside from Him until He makes you love whatever part thereof, He will.
>
> ʿABD AL-QĀDIR AL-JĪLĀNĪ 1992, trans. HOLLAND, 61

Again, in his speech on "renouncing worldly affairs" on 19 Dhū l-Ḥijja 545 (15 April 1151), he quoted the same *ḥadīth* saying:

> When a person is sincere (*ṣādiq*) in his asceticism, his allotted shares (of worldly things) come to him. He receives them and uses them to clothe himself outwardly, while his heart is filled with abstemiousness toward them and other such things. This is why our Prophet Muḥammad, Allāh bless him and give him peace, was more ascetic than Jesus, blessings and peace be upon him, and the other Prophets, blessings and peace be upon them, although he did say: "I have been made to love three things belonging to this world of yours: perfume, women and my chief comfort is given in prayer."
>
> He loved all these, despite his abstemiousness towards them and other things, because they were part of his allotted share, of which his Lord, almighty and Glorious is He, had foreknowledge. So, he accepted them in fulfilment of the (Lord's) commandment. Carrying out that commandment is obedience, so whoever receives his allotted shares in this manner is in a state of obedience, even if he is fully involved in this world.
>
> ʿABD AL-QĀDIR AL-JĪLĀNĪ 1992, trans. HOLLAND, 178

In the two quotes above, al-Jīlānī did not connect the *ḥadīth* to the concepts of *fanāʾ* and *baqāʾ*, two well-known concepts in Sufism. However, in *Futūḥ al-Ghayb*, the *ḥadīth* was discussed in the sixth discourse on *al-fanāʾ ʿan al-khalq* (vanishing from the creature). Apart from this, two other stages of *fanāʾ* were explained here: vanishing from desires, and vanishing from one's own will, together with the signs of each stage. For the first, a person should completely avoid all social contact with people to free his mind from desiring what they possess (al-Jīlānī 1973, 14). For the second, it is a sign to discard all efforts for, and contact, with worldly means in acquiring any benefits and avoiding any harms. Al-Jīlānī explained it as:

> to not move oneself in one's own interest and to not rely on oneself in matters concerning oneself and to not protect oneself nor help oneself, instead, leave the entire things to God; because He had the charge of it in the beginning, so will have it till the end, just as the charge rested on Him, when you were hidden in the womb (of your mother) as also when you were being suckled as a baby in the cradle.
>
> AL-JĪLĀNĪ 1973, 14

The sign of vanishing from one's will is to maintain the passivity of the organs of his body and the calmness of his heart at the time of the manifestation of the will and act of God, without entertaining any resolve or having any desire. This passivity is not unique to *taḥbīb*, rather it is discussed with the highest level of almost all other Sufi concepts, for example, *riḍā* (satisfaction) (Khalil 2014, 378). At this moment, one will not have any feeling of internal need nor any purpose, God will be his only objective (al-Jīlānī n.d., trans. Ahmad, 31–32).

Passing these three stages, an aspirant will reach into a phase called *baqāʾ* (subsistence). Al-Jīlānī explains the ultimate stage, *baqāʾ*, an aspirant reaches by passing through the above-mentioned three different levels:

> After this experience, you will never remain broken down. Neither any sensual desire nor any will remain in you like a broken vessel that retains neither any water nor any dreg. And you will be devoid of all human actions so that your inner self will accept nothing but the will of God. At this stage, miracles and supernatural things will be ascribed to you. These things will be seen as if proceeding from you when in fact they will be acts of God and His will.
>
> Thus, you will be admitted to the company of those whose hearts have been smashed and their animal passions have vanished. Hence, they have been inspired by the Divine will and new desires of daily existence.

> It is about this stage that the Holy Prophet PBUH, says: "Three things have been made dearer to me …"
>
> AL-JĪLĀNĪ n.d., trans AHMAD, 31–32

In his work, *al-Ghunya li-Ṭālibī Ṭarīq al-Ḥaqq* ("Richness for the Seeker of the Truth"), al-Jīlānī does not reference the *ḥadīth* neither to encourage marital life nor to promote the use of perfumes as many early and later scholars had done. Unlike his two works mentioned above, *al-Ghunya* focuses on human faith and actions in day-to-day affairs, including the etiquette of marriage. While readers would expect to find the *ḥadīth* in the work, with the scholar exploiting its popular sense of promoting marital life and perfuming, this was not the case. Al-Jīlānī's neglect of the *ḥadīth* in *al-Ghunya* while having given detailed discussion in the other two works supports the perception that he did not give any attention to its apparent and popular meaning.

## 10 Al-Jīlānī's Interpretation of the *Ḥadīth* and *Taḥbīb*

In his interpretation of the *ḥadīth*, al-Jīlānī focuses on the word "*ḥubbiba*" which means made to love. Given this passive form, a reader would become curious about the actor who influences the Prophet. Who made those things dearer to him? There are four possible answers; he is either controlled by his own passion, by his *hawā* (desire), by Satan, or by God. For Muslims, the first three are impossible in the case of the Prophet, for a prophet could not be a person who is driven by his desire, passion, or Satan. The basics of Islamic teachings emphasise disobeying satanic inspirations; therefore, it could not be expected from a prophet. The only remaining possibility is God, the Almighty. If that is the case, further clarification is much needed.

Although some scholars have tried to elaborate on the word *ḥubbiba*, they confine this *ḥadīth* to the life of the Prophet, as can be learned from the aforementioned discussions of the pre- and post-Jīlānī interpretations. However, al-Jīlānī generalised *taḥbīb* by describing it as a stage in a Sufi's life, which contributes a significant addition in the *ḥadīth* interpretive discourse and Sufi tradition. He says: "… Thus you will be admitted to the company of those whose hearts have been smashed and their animal passions have vanished." Hence, they have been inspired by the Divine will and new desires of daily existence. It is about this stage that the Holy Prophet, peace and blessings of Allāh be upon him, says "Three things have been made dearer to me …" (al-Jīlānī n.d., trans. Ahmad, 31–32). That means a Sufi may be made to enjoy certain worldly pleasures after struggling through various stages of asceticism (*zuhd*) to eventually end up in the ultimate goal, *fanāʾ*. At this stage, God will make him long for some worldly comforts according to His will – and this can be concluded as an act of *taḥbīb*.

Al-Jīlānī applies this concept even to marriage, which is generally perceived as an act of Sunna by the majority of scholars. It indicates that if an act is not an obligatory one, it would be subjected to this theory as well. That is very clear from the application of this concept in his own life. Nevertheless, in his commentary on al-Jīlānī's *Futūḥ al-Ghayb*, Ibn Taymiyya (d. 728/1328) attempted to reconcile this theory, and the concept of *fanāʾ* in general, with the principles of Sharīʿa by reducing them to worldly affairs usually treated as merely permissible (*mubāḥ*) and not as praiseworthy in Islam. For Ibn Taymiyya, something which is praiseworthy should not be forbidden, even according to the path of Sufism. However, this could be regarded as a bend of al-Jīlānī's thought, as it does not bode well with what al-Jīlānī himself had proposed and explained, or how he applied it in his own life (Ibn Taymiyya n.d., 31).

## 11 The Exemplification of the Concept in al-Jīlānī's Personal Life

Al-Jīlānī seems to have believed that he had reached the prime stage of Sufism, *fanāʾ*, wherein a Sufi will experience *taḥbīb* in his life. A perfect example for this is his own marriage life. Although Islam encourages marriage, as in various Qurʾānic verses and Prophetic *ḥadīth*s, a Sufi's understanding of marriage is quite different from that of the layman. When al-Jīlānī was asked about marriage, he answered – after giving a brief remark on its jurisprudential aspect – that, from a Sufi perspective, marriage is prohibited for a *murīd*, a person who strives in the path of God and has not achieved his goal. In terms of a *murād*, a person who has reached the prime stage of Sufism, Allāh will engage him either with marriage or with something else, and he need not bother about it (al-Jīlānī 1988, 345).

The above two Sufi terminologies (*fanāʾ* and *taḥbīb*), indicate two different stages in Sufism. However, once a Sufi reaches the paramount, he has no choice to wish something for himself. Instead, Allāh will wish for him something and make him love it, and he will wholeheartedly accept it. After getting married in his forties, al-Jīlānī was addressed with several questions concerning his marriage. He then answered: "I waited for consent from the Prophet until he suggested [to] me to do so [the Prophet appeared to him in a dream]. Then I married four wives. Therefore, they never became a hindrance in my spiritual path" (al-Suhrawardī 1971, 1:343). The marriage, thus, was instructed. One could also notice from al-Jīlānī's response that he considered the Prophet's instruction through dreams as one of the signs of *taḥbīb*.

Another exemplification of *taḥbīb* theory in his life were his own lectures in which he says:

> Allāh's destiny made me sit here although I did not wish to do it. O pupils, I have spoken out, but you are running away and not practising! My name in other countries is *akhras* (dumb, mute). I used to pretend to be crazy, dumb, or unable to speak Arabic, but it was not correct for me. Destiny brought me out here to you. I was in the underground storage bins when it pulled me out and made me sit on the lecture seat.
>
> AL-JĪLĀNĪ 1992, trans. HOLLAND, 398; AL-JĪLĀNĪ 1988, 235

Similar expressions about him being exposed can be found in many places in his two major works, *al-Fatḥ* and *Futūḥ*. This association with people has been justified as *wujūd* (existence) after *fanāʾ* (annihilation). It is also represented by other terminologies such as *basṭ* (expansion) after *qabḍ* (contraction), and *jamʿ* (gathering) after *tafriqa* (separation), and *ṣaḥw* (sobriety) after *sukr* (intoxication) (al-Jīlānī 1988, 213, 173, 364).

How does Allāh make a person who reached that stage love worldly affairs and how do we know whether God or others caused that inclination? These are questions that arise from the points mentioned above. As previously mentioned, sometimes the Prophet comes in a dream and gives direction to symbolise *taḥbīb*. A similar experience was reported to occur to the early Sufi, Abū l-Qāsim al-Junayd (d. 297/910) (al-Jīlānī 1988, 356). Interestingly, al-Jīlānī himself was confronted with these questions as related in the sixty-first discourse in *al-Fatḥ al-Rabbānī*. Al-Jīlānī's reply was:

> How to explain to you what notions are? Your notions come from the devil (*shayṭān*), natural impulses (*ṭabʿ*), the passion (*hawā*) and this world. Your interest (*hamm*) and concern are whatever is more important to you (*ahammaka*). Your notions correspond in kind to your interest while it is active. A notion (*khāṭir*) inspired by the Lord of Truth (Almighty and Glorious is He) comes only to the heart, free from anything apart from Him. He said: Allāh forbid that we should seize anyone except him with whom we found our property (Q 12:79). If Allāh and His remembrance (*dhikr*) are present with you, your heart will certainly be filled with His nearness, and the notions suggested by the devil, the passions and this world will all avoid your company. There is a kind of notion belonging

> to this world and a notion belonging to the Hereafter. There is a notion belonging to the angels, and a notion belonging to the lower self (*nafs*), and a notion belonging to the heart. There is also a notion belonging to the Lord of Truth (Almighty and glorious is He). If you reject the notion of the lower self, the notion of the passions, the devil's notion and the notion of the world, the notion of the Hereafter will come to you. Then you will receive the angel's notion, then finally the notion of the Lord of Turth (Almighty and Glorious is He). This is the ultimate stage.
>
> AL-JĪLĀNĪ 1992, trans. HOLLAND, 417

He further says:

> When your heart is sound, it will pause to ask each notion as it arises: What kind of notion are you? From what source do you come? So, they will tell him in return: "I am the notion of such and such. I am a true notion from the Truth (*khāṭir ḥaqq min al-ḥaqq*). I am a loving counsellor; the Lord of Truth (Almighty and Glorious is He) loves you so love you too. I am ambassador (*safīr*). I am the portion of the spiritual state (*ḥāl*) of the prophethood (*nubuwwa*)."
>
> O young man! You must devote your attention to real knowledge (*maʿrifa*) of Allāh (Almighty and glorious is He), for it is the root of all that is good. If you are constant in obedience to Him, He will grant you real knowledge of Himself.
>
> AL-JĪLĀNĪ 1992, trans. HOLLAND, 418

From his lengthy explanation, it can be understood that, at a particular stage, a person will be able to differentiate between notions, whether they come from God or others. However, it is difficult to explain the form of each notion to someone who has not attained such a status. For those who have attained it, the forms are not at all relevant to them, since they can identify the notions without prior knowledge of the forms.

## 12 *Taḥbīb* and the Concepts of *Fanāʾ* and *Baqāʾ*

The state of *taḥbīb* is a stage after *fanāʾ*, and it can be perceived as a stage associated with *baqāʾ*, the ultimate goal of an aspirant. *Fanāʾ* indicates the notion of "dying metaphorically before the real death," which represents a breaking down of the individual ego and a recognition of the fundamental unity of God, creation, and the individual self. Individuals who have entered this enlightened state obtain awareness of the intrinsic unity (*tawḥīd*) between Allāh and all that exists, including the individual's mind. It is coupled conceptually with *baqāʾ*, subsistence, the state of pure consciousness and abidance in God (see *fanāʾ* and *baqāʾ* in Murata 2018).

In *Futūḥ al-Ghayb*, al-Jīlānī related *taḥbīb* with the concept of *fanāʾ*, whereas, in two other places in *al-Fatḥ al-Rabbānī*, he connected it with two different ideas. In one of them it is related to asceticism, as explained in the first part of this chapter. According to al-Jīlānī, *zuhd* is the way to achieve *fanāʾ*, and that is also apprehended when the statements in *Futūḥ* and *Fath* are considered together. While he talks about *zuhd* in *Futūḥ*, al-Jīlānī uses the term *fanāʾ*; he says "*ifna ʿan al-khalq*," that means to abstain from the creatures. The state represents the beginning of the ultimate *fanāʾ*. *Zuhd* is *fanāʾ ʿan* (abstain from), but the real *fanāʾ* is *fanāʾ fī*, annihilation or dissolution in God. After *fanāʾ* from people, an aspirant should go forward to *fanāʾ* from desires, then, *fanāʾ* from his own will. Eventually, he will acquire *fanāʾ* in God.

The other context wherein this *ḥadīth* was quoted in *Fatḥ* is where it was related to *ṣabr* (patience) or being content with *qaḍāʾ* (divine decree) and *qadar* (fate). In this regard, al-Jīlānī says: "Hate all things and love the Creator of all things. Then, if He makes you love one of the things you have hated …" To hate things calls for *zuhd*, and only by going through different stages of *zuhd*, one can reach *fanāʾ* in Allāh and subsequently the stage of *taḥbīb*.

To denote the stages of *fanāʾ*, the central theme of the two books, al-Jīlānī sometimes uses different words, such as *inkisār* (to be broken), and called the heart of such a person "broken hearted." He says:

> This world belongs to one set of people, the hereafter belongs to another set of people, and the Lord of Truth (Almighty and Glorious is He) belongs to yet another set of people, namely the truly convinced believers … who are grief-stricken and broken-hearted for His sake.
>
> AL-JĪLĀNĪ 1992, trans. HOLLAND, 53; AL-JĪLĀNĪ 1988, 37

Broken-hearted here indicates that no self-interest or intention has remained in the heart; it is broken and keeps nothing. Likewise, al-Jīlānī's statement of "*al-akhdh* (possess) after *al-tark* (renounce)," indicates that a *zāhid* fears to take from this world because he fears to lose his beloved, the Almighty (al-Jīlānī 1988, 362). But the one who achieved the ultimate *zuhd* takes from it without any fear, while gnosis emanates from Him. That appears as the meaning of his statement "*al-tark zuhd wa-l-akhdh maʿrifa*" (to renounce is ascetism and to possess is gnosis) (al-Jīlānī 1988, 362). Whoever reaches this stage attains real happiness in this world (al-Jīlānī 1988, 62).

## 13 Conclusion

ʿAbd al-Qādir al-Jīlānī, a Ḥanbalī Sufi scholar, can be regarded as first interpreter of the *taḥbīb ḥadīth* who blended it with two essential Sufi concepts; *fanāʾ* and *baqāʾ*. However, his interpretation does not attract much attention from the exegetes of *ḥadīth*, and this was the case for five centuries, until al-Munāwī accentuated this discussion in his seminal work *Fayḍ al-Qadīr*. Al-Jīlānī's exposition differs from the popular understanding of the *ḥadīth*. According to him, it could not be treated as an unconditional encouragement for marriage and perfuming, it could have pointed otherwise. Moreover, there is no point, according to him, to restrict the love mentioned in the *ḥadīth* to only the two subjects. Instead, the *ḥadīth* refers to a stage associated with *baqāʾ* (subsistence) that an aspirant has achieved after passing through the different states of *fanāʾ* (annihilation) by being persistent in asceticism. Once he achieves it, Allāh will make him love some worldly comforts. Yet, in the case of the Prophet, women and perfumes were the things that were made dearer to him. The concept of *fanāʾ* and *baqāʾ* was not something new to medieval Sufism. Instead, they were already embraced by al-Jīlānī's great predecessors such as al-Kharrāz (d. 286/899) and al-Junayd. In this regard, al-Jīlānī's approach could be treated as a defensive response to those who depicted Sufis as the adversaries of the Qurʾān and Sunna. This exploration of al-Jīlānī's idea could be appreciated as an invitation to study his attempt to substantiate other Sufi concepts with the scriptural basis, particularly the *ḥadīth*. This study covered almost all interpretations by the exegetes of *ḥadīth* in the pre- and post-Jīlānī era. However, the influence of al-Jīlānī's new understanding of the *ḥadīth* on Sufis themselves requires further analysis. Ultimately, the intertwinement of *ḥadīth* and Sufism can be appreciated as a mechanism for ethical discourse as evident in the scholarship of ʿAbd al-Qādir al-Jīlānī.

## Bibliography

Aḥmad b. Ḥanbal. 2001. *Musnad al-Imām Aḥmad*, edited by Shuʿayb al-Arnāʾūṭ. Beirut: Muʾassasat al-Risāla.

al-ʿAjlūnī, ʿIsmāʿīl b. Muḥammad b. ʿAbd al-Hādī. 2000. *Kashf al-Khafāʾ wa-Muzīl al-Ilbās,* edited by ʿAbd al-Ḥāmid b. Aḥmad b. Yūsuf al-Hindāwī. Beirut: al-Maktaba al-ʿAṣriyya.

ʿAlī al-Qārī. 2002. *Mirqāt al-Mafātīḥ Sharḥ Mishkāt al-Maṣābīḥ.* Beirut: Dār al-Fikr.

al-Aṣbahānī, Abū Muḥammad ʿAbd Allāh b. Muḥammad b. Jaʿfar b. Ḥayyān Abū l-Shaykh. 1998. *Akhlāq al-Nabī wa-Ādābuh,* edited by Ṣāliḥ b. Muḥammad al-Wanīyān. Riyad: Dār al-Muslim.

Bālī Zādah, Muṣṭafā b. Sulaymān. 2002. *Sharḥ Fuṣūṣ al-Ḥikam l-Ibn ʿArabī.* Beirut: Dār al-Kutub al-ʿIlmiyya.

al-Barrāk, ʿAbd al-Raḥmān b. Nāṣir. 2014. *Sharḥ Kalimat al-Ikhlāṣ,* edited by Yāsir b. Badr al-ʿAskar. Khobar: Dār Ibn al-Jawzī.

al-Bukhārī. 1987. *Ṣaḥīḥ al-Bukhārī,* edited by Muṣṭafā Dīb al-Bughā. Beirut: Dār Ibn Kathīr.

al-Bayhaqī, Abū Bakr Aḥmad b. Ḥusayn. 2003. *Al-Sunan al-Kubrā,* edited by Muḥammad ʿAbd al-Qādir ʿAṭā. Beirut: Dār al-Kutub al-ʿIlmiyya.

al-Dihlawī, ʿAbd al-Ḥaqq b. Sayf al-Dīn b. Saʿd Allāh. 2014. *Lamaʿāt al-Tanqīḥ fī Sharḥ Mishkāt al-Maṣābīḥ,* edited by Taqī al-Dīn al-Nadwī. Damascus: Dār al-Nawādir.

al-Ghazalī, Abū Ḥāmid. n.d. *Iḥyāʾ ʿUlūm al-Dīn.* Beirut: Dār al-Maʿrifa.

al-Ghazzī, Najm al-Dīn. 2011. *Ḥusn al-Tanabbuh li-mā Warada fī l-Tashabbuh.* Syria: Dār al-Nūr.

Ibn Abī ʿĀṣim, Abū Bakr. 1988. *Al-Zuhd,* edited by ʿAbd al-ʿAlī ʿAbd al-Ḥamīd. Cairo: Dār al-Rayyān lil-Turāth.

Ibn al-ʿArabī, Abū Bakr. 1992. *Al-Qabas fī Sharḥ Muwaṭṭaʾ Mālik b. Anas,* edited by Muḥammad ʿAbd Allāh Walad Karīm. Beirut: Dār al-Gharb al-Islāmī.

Ibn al-ʿArabī, Abū Bakr. n.d. *ʿĀriḍat al-Aḥwadhī.* Beirut: Dār al-Kutub al-ʿIlmiyya.

Ibn al-ʿArabī, Abū Bakr. 2003. *Aḥkām al-Qurʾān,* edited by Muḥammad ʿAbd al-Qādir ʿAṭā. Beirut: Dār al-Kutub al-ʿIlmiyya.

Ibn ʿArabī, Muḥyī l-Dīn. 2014. *Fuṣūṣ al-Ḥikam,* translated by Aisha Bewley. Berkeley: Ibn ʿArabī Society.

Ibn Ḥajar al-ʿAsqalānī. 1995. *Talkhīṣ al-Ḥabīr fī Takhrīj Aḥādīth al-Rāfiʿī al-Kabīr,* edited by Ḥasan b. ʿAbbas. Cairo: Muʾassasat Qurṭuba.

Ibn Fūrak, Abū Bakr Muḥammad al-Aṣbahānī. 2015. *Juzʾ fīh Sharḥ Ḥadīth Ḥubbiba Ilayya min Dunyākum, Muḥammad ʿAlwān.* Tangier: Dār al-Ḥadīth al-Kattāniyya.

Ibn al-Jarrāḥ, Abū Sufyān Wakīʿ. 1984. *Kitāb al-Zuhd,* edited by ʿAbd al-Raḥmān ʿAbd al-Jabbār al-Furaywāʾī. Medina: Maktabat al-Dār.

Ibn Manẓūr, Abū al-Faḍl Muḥammad b. Mukarram Jamāl al-Dīn. 1993. *Lisan al-ʿArab.* Beirut: Dār Ṣādir.

Ibn al-Qayyim al-Jawziyya. 1997. *Al-Jawāb al-Kāfī li-man Saʾala ʿan al-Dawāʾ al-Shāfī.* Casablanca: Dār al-Maʿrifa.

Ibn Taymiyya. n.d. *Sharḥ Futūḥ al-Ghayb*. Lahore: Mu'assasat al-Sharaf.

al-Isfarāyīnī, Abū ʿAwāna Yaʿqūb b. Isḥāq. 1998. *Al-Mustakhraj alā Ṣaḥīḥ Muslim*, edited by Ayman b. ʿĀrif. Beirut: Dār al-Maʿrifa.

al-Jīlānī, ʿAbd al-Qādir. 1973. *Futūḥ al-Ghayb*. Cairo: Muṣṭafā l-Bābī l-Ḥalabī.

al-Jīlānī, ʿAbd al-Qādir. 1988. *Al-Fatḥ al-Rabbānī wa-l-Fayḍ al-Raḥmānī*. Cairo: Dār al-Rayyān lil-Turāth.

al-Jīlānī, ʿAbd al-Qādir. 1992. *The Sublime Revelation* (*al-Fatḥ ar-Rabbānī*), translated by Muhtar Holland. Houston: al-Baz Publishing.

al-Jīlānī, ʿAbd al-Qādir. n.d. *Futuh al-Ghaib* [*The Revelations of the Unseen*], translated by Aftab-ud-Din Ahmad. Lahore: SH. Muhammad Ashraf.

al-Kalābādhī, Abū Bakr Muḥammad b. Abī Isḥāq. 1999. *Baḥr al-Fawā'id*, edited by Muḥammad Ḥasan Ismāʿīl and Aḥmad Farīd al-Mazīdī. Beirut: Dār al-Kutub al-ʿIlmiyya.

Khalil, Atif. 2014. "Contentment, Satisfaction and Good-Pleasure: Rida in Early Sufi Moral Psychology." *Studies in Religion/Sciences Religieuses* 43(3): 371–389.

al-Makkī, Abū Ṭālib. 2005. *Qūt al-Qulūb fī Muʿāmalat al-Maḥbūb wa-Waṣf Ṭarīq al-Murīd ilā Maqām al-Tawḥīd*, edited by ʿĀṣim Ibrāhīm al-Kayālī. Beirut: Dār al-Kutub al-ʿIlmiyya.

al-Maqdisī, Abū ʿAbd Allāh Ḍiyā' al-Dīn. 2000. *Al-Aḥādīth al-Mukhtāra*, edited by ʿAbd al-Malik. Beirut: Dār Khiḍr.

al-Marwazī, Abū ʿAbd Allāh Muḥammad b. Naṣr. 1986. *Taʿẓīm Qadr al-Ṣalāt*, edited by ʿAbd al-Raḥmān ʿAbd al-Jabbār al-Furaywā'ī. Medina: Maktabat al-Dār.

al-Mawṣilī, Abū Yaʿlā Aḥmad b. ʿAlī. 1984. *Musnad Abī Yaʿlā*, edited by Ḥusayn Salīm Asad. Damascus: Dār al-Ma'mūn lil-Turāth.

al-Munāwī, ʿAbd al-Ra'ūf b. Tāj al-Dīn. 1937. *Fayḍ al-Qadīr: Sharḥ al-Jāmiʿ al-Ṣaghīr*. Cairo: al-Maktaba al-Tijāriyya al-Kubrā.

Murata, Kazyo. 2018. "Fana and Baqa." In: *Oxford Bibliographies*. www.oxfordbibliographies.com/view/document/obo-9780195390155/obo-9780195390155-0256.xml.

al-Nasā'ī. 1986. *Sunan al-Nasā'ī*, edited by ʿAbd al-Fattāḥ Abū Ghudda. Beirut: Maktabat al-Maṭbūʿāt al-Islāmiyya.

al-Qāḍī ʿIyāḍ. 1987. *Al-Shifā' bi-Taʿrīf Ḥuqūq al-Muṣṭafā*. Muscat: Dār al-Fayḥā'.

al-Qasṭallānī, Abū l-ʿAbbās. n.d. *Al-Mawāhib al-Ladunniyya bi-l-Minaḥ al-Muḥammadiyya*. Cairo: al-Maktaba al-Tawfīqiyya.

al-Ṣaffūrī, ʿAbd al-Raḥmān b. ʿAbd al-Salām. 1867. *Nuzhat al-Majālis wa-Muntakhab al-Nafā'is*. Cairo: al-Maṭbaʿa al-Kāstaliyya.

al-Sakhāwī, Shams al-Dīn Abū l-Khayr Muḥammad b. ʿAbd al-Raḥmān. 1985. *Al-Maqāsid al-Ḥasana fī Bayān Kathīr min al-Aḥādīth al-Mushtahira ʿalā Alsinat al-Nās*, edited by Muḥammad ʿUthman al-Khisht. Beirut: Dār al-Kitāb al-ʿArabī.

al-Sindī, Muḥammad b. ʿAbd al-Hādī Nūr al-Dīn. 1986. *Ḥāshiyat al-Sindī ʿalā Sunan al-Nasā'ī*. Aleppo: Maktabat al-Maṭbūʿāt al-Islāmiyya.

al-Suhrawardī, Shihāb al-Dīn Abū Ḥafṣ ʿUmar. 1971. *ʿAwārif al-Maʿārif*, edited by ʿAbd al-Ḥalīm Maḥmūd and Muḥammad b. al-Sharīf. Cairo: Maṭbaʿat al-Saʿāda.

al-Suyūṭī, Jalāl al-Dīn. 1986. *Ḥāshiyat al-Suyūṭī ʿalā Sunan al-Nasāʾī*. Aleppo: Maktabat al-Maṭbūʿāt al-Islāmiyya.

al-Ṭabarānī, Abū l-Qāsim Sulaymān b. Aḥmad. 1995. *Al-Muʿjam al-Awsaṭ*, edited by Abū l-Muʿādh Ṭāriq b. ʿIwaḍ Allāh and Abū l-Faḍl ʿAbd al-Muḥsin. Cairo: Dār al-Ḥaramayn.

CHAPTER 7

# Seclusion

## *An Ethical Imperative Driven by the* Ḥadīth?

*M. Imran Khan*

## 1 Introduction

This chapter focuses on seclusion (*ʿuzla*),[1] which is a contentious theme that has barely been analysed, not least from an ethical perspective, as opposed to a mystical one. It behoves us to delve into this topic from the perspective of earlier works and other figures who wrote or compiled traditions on seclusion. I will begin therefore with a brief historiography of *ʿuzla* in Islam so that we may understand various ideas and works on this subject to better realise ʿAbd al-Ghanī l-Nābulusī's (d. 1143/1731) contributions. This will follow with some historical context, followed by a selection of traditions which seem to capture al-Nābulusī's motives, while a subsequent section will consider whether withdrawing benefit from society presents a problem, despite corruption within society. Finally, the virtue of humility will be evaluated to consider whether it may be congruent with secluding oneself from society.

Notions of "sociality" or interaction are inevitably bound by judgments of morality and relate to ethics, which means the nature and tensions of these relations may provide valuable insights, but the converse is also true, as argued by John Barbour, who believes that there is an urgent need for an ethics of seclusion (Barbour 2004, 4). This begs the question how seclusion relates to ethics and how this understanding may be achieved. If sociality, synonymous in Arabic with *ṣuḥba* (companionship) and *mukhālaṭa* (social interaction) among Muslims, has been understudied, seclusion has had almost no

1 "Seclusion" has a number of synonyms besides *ʿuzla* in Arabic which all connote voluntary seclusion, self-imposed isolation or retreat and these constitute a fundamental principle of asceticism (*zuhd*): *khalwa, waḥda, infirād, inqitāʿ* (see Knysh 1999, 314–316). A further word introduced by Ibn Bājja (d. 533/1139) is *tawaḥḥud* for the isolation undertaken by a philosopher, such philosophers are referred to as *ghurabāʾ* by the Sufis. He does this because he does not live in a virtuous city where people base their actions on rationality and the use of the intellect (see Ibn Bājja 1978, 18–19).

 | DOI:10.1163/9789004525931_009

attention.[2] Yet, we are given the impression by al-Nābulusī, in his main work on the topic: *Takmīl al-Nuʿūt fī Luzūm al-Buyūt* ("Perfecting Praiseworthy Qualities by Imposing Home-Seclusion"),[3] that his seclusion was motivated by the *ḥadīth* traditions which urge this practice, primarily in times of severe trials due to moral decline. The ensuing practice is meant to act as a protective buffer from society. Yet, it is undeniable that al-Nābulusī felt little appreciated by society too, and this caused him considerable consternation. In fact, he turned his attention to seclusion partly for having failed to attain a prominent teaching position (Schlegell 1997). As an eminent scholar in an antagonistic society, he felt the need to justify his rationale via the application of the Islamic tradition to his social reality, which thereby granted him the prerogative to seek separation from society on theological grounds. Such an assessment appears in line with the task of moral knowledge, determining the right action in a particular situation, as Hans Gadamer argued, and the requirement for seclusion certainly demanded an appropriate response for a scholar of al-Nābulusī's stature (Gadamer 1989, 313–317). We may furthermore extend what Gadamer said about law, to the sources al-Nābulusī uses and his approach towards them, that is that they do not exist solely "in order to be understood historically, but to be concretised in [their] legal validity by being interpreted" such that the interpretations may function in contexts (Gadamer 1989, 309). The *Takmīl*'s and *Ghāyat al-Maṭlūb fī Maḥabbat al-Maḥbūb*'s ("The Peak of the Goal in Loving the Beloved") self-referential and part-ethnographical appraisals represent al-Nābulusī's style of argument and showcase his deft use of the *aḥadīth*. Whereas moral texts written by preceding Muslim authors (such as many of those mentioned below) are usually written timelessly and, therefore, offer

2 One of the most extensive works on ethical social conduct with others is Abū Ḥāmid al-Ghazālī's (d. 505/1111) *Kitāb Ādāb al-Ulfa wa-l-Ukhuwwa wa-l-Ṣuḥba wa-l-Muʿāshara* ("The Book of Etiquettes of Affection, Brotherhood, Companionship and Social Interaction") in *Iḥyāʾ ʿUlūm al-Dīn* ("Revival of the Religious Sciences") (al-Ghazālī 2002, 213–299). According to Hellmut Ritter the fervour behind al-Ghazālī's penning of this section "arises from the spirit of Islamic mysticism" established by Sufis (Ritter 2003, 324–325). Ritter says that Ignaz Goldziher (1888–1890, 1–39) has dealt with the concept of brotherly solidarity in the Islamic social ethic but his concern is chiefly with the early period of Islam: "*Muruwwa und Dīn*."

3 For the manuscript of this work, see al-Nābulusī n.d., fols. 356b–376a. There is also an edited version published under *al-Muslimūn fī Zaman al-Fitan Kamā Akhbara al-Rasūl* ("Muslims in the Time of Strife as Told by the Messenger"), and edited by Majdī b. Manṣūr b. Sayyid al-Shūra (al-Nābulusī 1998), referred to in-text by the author's original designation: *Takmīl al-Nuʿūt fī Luzūm al-Buyūt*. A non-academic translation of this text exists in English with a lengthy introduction praising the work and lauding its importance, based on the former work, entitled: *The Virtues of Seclusion in Times of Confusion* (al-Nābulusī 2017). Excerpts from passages in the *Takmīl*, which are translated here, are my own translations.

little or no insight into how the authors' practical lives, relations and experiences may have shaped their opinions or determined their intellectual trajectories and lived experiences.[4]

In Islam interpersonal social links are meant to strengthen people's disposition to act in the correct way, while seclusion is typically discouraged (Leaman 1999, 125). Although al-Nābulusī presents the Prophet as a moral exemplar, he does not make explicit comparisons between his own sequestering and the Prophet's retreats, nor that he is undertaking it as part of his affiliation to the Sufi Naqshabandī path. The main motivation for the Sufis to withdraw from society is *imitatio prophetae* – for our purposes here – the custom of the Prophet Muḥammad to isolate himself in a cave on Mount Ḥirā' prior to Islam (Knysh 1999, 316). Maḥmūd b. ʿAlī al-Kāshānī (d. 735/1334) in the *Misbāḥ al-Hidāya* ("Lantern of Guidance") goes as far as to proclaim *khalwa* (seclusion) an innovation of the Sufis – the Sunna was, in fact, "social engagement" (*ṣuḥba*) and its "excellence excelleth other excellences" – since the Prophet's retreats preceded the sending of the Sunna. Al-Kāshānī does however soften his objection noting that for the seekers of God *khalwa* might be *wājib*, just as Moses required it to achieve propinquity to God so that he could converse with him (Suhrawardī 1891, 41–42). Additionally, when one's faith is at peril we find the requirement to disassociate rather emphatic in the traditions around which al-Nābulusī's arguments and conduct revolve.

Regarding emulation, "true Islam," according to ʿAlī Sharīʿatī (d. 1977), must be discovered "not in scripture but in the activity of exemplary Muslims" something our figure is keen to emphasise (Lee 2018, 122).[5] Indeed, one of the ways in which moral judgements are evaluated, modified and corrected is by "consulting the behaviours of moral exemplars, who are widely acknowledged as deserving emulation," or, at least, looked to for inspiration (Cuneo 2014, 17). Not only did al-Nābulusī achieve such prominent acceptance among his contemporaries, his legacy was also spoken fondly of, even in the mid-twentieth century, although it had faded somewhat in the interim period after a few

4 In arguing for the importance of moral considerations today, Osvaldo Rossi argues that self-perception has now incorporated a new self-subjectivity, a broadly focussed one that centres on relationships: "as a 'self' in front of the others, [which] referred to the world, to meaning, to God and so on" which has led to a more balanced equilibrium between knowing and acting (Rossi 1990, 107–110).

5 According to Sharīʿatī, the knowledge of this authentic version of the religion depends on: the history of Islam, especially in its early days; study of the contemporary world and its needs; familiarity with Islamic scripture, and receptivity to the most mystical elements of religion (Lee 2018, 121).

decades since his death. The preeminent Levantine scholar, Yūsuf al-Nabhānī (d. 1350/1932), for instance, regarded him to be the "greatest gnostic sage" of the past three hundred years (al-Nabhānī 1983, 194).

Nevertheless, there had to be a higher ethical perspective that ennobled the action and attracted the respect of others even if this may not have initially featured as a motivation for al-Nābulusī. Indeed, duty, obligation and rightness are but one part of ethics or morality, "there is the whole other area of the values of personal and interpersonal relations and activities" (Stocker 1976, 455). Such values belong to the throbbing centre of the human moral constitution, and, as Mark Sainsbury reminds us, "the throbbing centres of our lives appear to be describable only in vague terms" (Sainsbury 1996, 251). For the purposes of this study then, considering al-Nābulusī's arguments in a phenomenological frame will be vital to aver a distinctive epistemological enterprise, and whether his attitude was influenced at all by personal relations. Even though his stated aim is to gather *aḥadīth* for instance, both the introduction as well as digressions further in the *Takmīl* expressing moral outrage reveal his discontent and loathing of society. These factors appear so dominant that even his mystical proclivities surprisingly pale beside them. The purpose of this chapter will be to evaluate the ethical stance of al-Nābulusī regarding seclusion by assessing his use of *ḥadīth* through a critical analysis of his works which deal with this topic, mainly the *Takmīl al-Nuʿūt fī Luzūm al-Buyūt, Ghāyat al-Maṭlūb fī Maḥabbat al-Maḥbūb* and briefly the *Wasāʾil al-Taḥqīq wa Rasāʾil al-Tawfīq* ("The Means of Truth-Seeking and the Letters of Providential Guidance").

## 2 Historiography

Writings on seclusion in the very early period of Islam (around the second/eighth and third/ninth centuries) are mainly compilations of *ḥadīth* traditions subsumed in various works of *ḥadīth* literature, usually as chapters with varying lengths of traditions. The genre lodges itself embryonically into the broader works on *zuhd* (asceticism), which overlap chronologically with the earlier works on *ḥadīth* (sometimes even preceding them) and often taking the form of mere compilations of traditions. We begin to see some philosophical observations with more original theological contributions on the topic in the fourth century by Abū Sulaymān Ḥamd b. Muḥammad al-Khaṭṭābī (d. 386/996 or 388/998) which reaches its apogee in Abū Ḥāmid al-Ghazālī (d. 505/1111), whose disquisition is the most thorough of all works reviewed on this topic. Al-Nābulusī's work blends this latter trend with a concerted delivery of two chapters of traditions with virtually no commentary, while in other areas of his work, he veers into a sociocultural critique interspersed with invectives aimed mostly at fellow scholars.

ʿAbd Allāh b. al-Mubārak's (d. 181/797) *al-Zuhd wa-l-Raqāʾiq* ("The Renunciation and Heart-Softening Reports") has 1627 traditions and according to Fuat Sezgin (d. 2018) it is the oldest book to have reached us from this period on the topic of *zuhd* (renunciation). According to Yunus Yaldiz's study on Ibn al-Mubārak, seclusion was generally practiced by ascetics and renunciants (Yaldiz 2016, 46, 145). *Zuhd* is also connected to the idea of *ṣamt* (silence) and *dhikr* (the recollection of God), as these are related acts of obedience which acquire greater significance during seclusion, as exemplified in the lives of personalities such as the Companion Abū Ḥudhayfa b. al-Yamān (d. 36/656) and Rabīʿ b. Khuthaym (d. 62/682). In fact, *ṣamt* and *dhikr* were sometimes used as metonyms for *khalwa* and *ʿuzla* (Yaldiz 2016, 164–165). Although the latter work is not about "seclusion" per se it contains abundant traditions that refer to it.[6]

Abū Bakr b. Abī l-Dunyā al-Baghdādī (d. 281/894) compiled a work, *al-ʿUzla wa-l-Infirād* ("Seclusion and Isolation"), which continues in the vain of the early *muḥaddithīn* by including a *sanad* (chain of transmission) for each report, many of which are statements by the *salaf* who gave importance to seclusion. In one such report a man comes to Shuʿayb b. Ḥarb (d. 196/811 or 197/812) and says he has come to socialise with him, whereupon he tells him that he has taken to isolation for forty-years. Ibn Abī l-Dunyā thereupon beseeches: "O God: I seek refuge in propinquity to one whose closeness distances me from you" (Ibn Abī l-Dunyā 1997, 94). Ibn Abī l-Dunyā does not directly share his own thoughts on the topic although it seems quite likely that discussion of the subject arises from a favourable sentiment towards seclusion.

The earliest systematic monograph dedicated to the topic of seclusion appears to be *Kitāb al-ʿUzla* ("The Book of Seclusion") by al-Khaṭṭābī who was a Shāfiʿī jurist and litterateur. Al-Khaṭṭābī was not promulgating isolation by

6 This work is representative of a genre of works which include *al-Zuhd* by Hannād b. al-Sariyy (d. 243/857) and a work of the same title by Abū Bakr b. Abī ʿĀṣim (d. 287/900); *al-Tafarrud wa-l-ʿUzla* (The Tract on Aloofness and Isolation) by Abū Bakr Muḥammad b. al-Ḥusayn al-Ājurrī (d. 360/970); *al-Risāla al-Mughniya fī l-Sukūt wa-Luzūm al-Buyūt* ("The Comprehensive Epistle on Silence and Connubial Confinement") by Abū ʿAlī al-Ḥasan b. Aḥmad b. ʿAbd Allāh al-Baghdādī (d. 471/1078); *ʿIzz al-ʿUzla* ("The Honour of Isolation") by Abū Saʿīd ʿAbd al-Karīm b. Muḥammad al-Samʿānī (d. 562/1166); *al-ʿUzla* ("The Tract on Seclusion") by Abū l-Faraj ʿAbd al-Raḥmān b. ʿAlī al-Jawzī (d. 597/1201); *Uns al-Munqaṭiʿīn ilā ʿIbādat Rabb al-ʿĀlamīn* ("The Congeniality of those Sparing themselves for the Worship of the Lord of the Worlds") by al-Muʿāfā b. Ismāʿīl al-Shaybānī (d. 623/1233); *al-ʿIbādat wa-l-Khalwa* ("The Tract on Worship and Seclusion") by Muḥammad b. Shākir al-Dārānī b. Shākir al-Kutbī (d. 764/1363).

any means, rather, he was arguing for avoiding the company of bad associates even if that meant quarantining oneself. He argued: "an excess in all things is reprehensive. The best of affairs is in moderation; virtue is flanked by evil" (al-Khaṭṭābī 1990, 236). Moreover, isolation, does not entail leaving the Friday or quotidian congregational prayers nor avoiding greeting others or abandoning various noble customary practices – although the latter may be "conditional exceptions" (*fa-innahā mustathnātun bi-sharāʾiṭihā*). Al-Khaṭṭābī pragmatically explores beyond textual precepts to advise people (by which he means scholars), who are uniquely fit to undertake this practice to consider whether they have the independence to distance themselves, and, if it is the case, then, the choice is theirs to make individually. But this should never extend to shunning members of one's household and neighbours. Excessive socialising is the main target of his reprobation (al-Khaṭṭābī 1990, 58–59). In a commentary of several Qurʾānic verses and a tradition by an early Muslim scholar on the theme of animals, al-Khaṭṭābī demonstrates his expository skill by linking them to represent the variation in dominant human character traits and then uses, among others, the metaphor of a dog's barking as being zoomorphic for an irascible person's pugnacity. He then attempts to provide some psychological relief for those that must endure such incivility by stating that they are to regard such individuals as their animal counterpart and not pity them since their physicality is not like that of an animal, for which they supposedly have sufficient a respite (al-Khaṭṭābī 1990, 159–163). This nuance by the author highlights the rich variation in the way in which seclusion has been retreated.

References to isolation were made in works even prior to al-Khaṭṭābī, albeit these were typically brief, including a single page in *al-Waṣāyā* ("The Commandments") of al-Ḥārith al-Muḥāsibī (d. 243/857).[7] The latter argues that one ought not to part with their religion when the devils from *jinn* and humans inspire one another (towards heedlessness) with adorned speech. Two types of people's company should be kept: one type is those who inspire you to virtue and reverence of God, the other type is those that assist one in their temporal affairs. If both needs may be fulfilled by one person, then others besides that individual should be avoided. Only the helper to virtue is not harmful to one's religion, which is why the most meritorious act and safest precaution is keeping aloof from people, it is greater than that which is feared. He advises his companions not to mix with people, yet acknowledges that few

---

7 Avoiding people was a common trope that was frequently mentioned in works of exhortation. Gibril Fouad Haddad gives several references to the practice of "silence" (*ṣamt*) which al-Muḥāsibī mentions, namely, that nine tenths of worship is in avoiding people (see Haddad 2017, 101).

people can accept this advice because enduring patience in this regard is difficult to bear (*al-ṣabr ʿalā l-waḥda shadīd*). He then delimits sociality by saying "shun people from the heart, afford them connection [only] through greetings and by means necessitated as per their rights as Muslims" (al-Muḥāsibī 1986, 104). There is also a book attributed to al-Muḥāsibī entitled *Kitāb al-Khalwa wa-l-Tanaqqul fī l-ʿIbāda wa-Darajāt al-ʿĀbidīn* ("The Book of Seclusion and Movement in Worship, and the Levels of Worshippers"), which according to Gavin Picken, extolls the virtues of spiritual retreat (*khalwa*) from worldly life and particularly when it is simultaneous with frequent recitation and reflection upon the Qurʾān. The one pursuing seclusion is advised to adopt silence and to view necessary speech "as a disaster that has struck" (Picken 2010, 83).

Scholars have also discussed seclusion's relationship to travel, and how the two can further one's relationship with God. Al-Ḥakīm al-Tirmidhī (d. 298/910) stated, for example:

> I came to love withdrawing in seclusion (*khalwa*) at home, as well as going forth into the [deserted] countryside. And I would wander about in the ruins and amongst the tombs situated near the city. This was my constant practice. And I sought sincere companions who might be of assistance to me in this matter, but I did not succeed and I withdrew into those ruins and places of retirement.
>
> RADTKE and O'KANE 1996, 17

These words seem to have been expressed after al-Ḥakīm al-Tirmidhī's return from pilgrimage in Mecca, where he underwent a spiritual experience that led him to resolve to live a life devoted to God. However, he was unsuccessful in finding kindred spirits on his sojourn, nor effective spiritual tutelage. It is especially important to consider al-Ḥakīm al-Tirmidhī as his popularity ascended greatly due to the theosophist-mystic Muḥyī l-Dīn Ibn al-ʿArabī's (d. 638/1240) writing on him; who, of course, greatly influenced al-Nābulusī (Radtke and O'Kane 1996, 17). Indeed, Ibn ʿArabī whom al-Nābulusī considered *al-shaykh al-akbar* (his greatest master) deemed *ṣamt* and *ʿuzla* as some of the prerequisites that the traveller ought to strive to acquire on his journey toward union with God (Ateş 1968).

Not only did seclusion play an important role in the thought of Muslim scholars, but also a central one in the rituals of many Sufi orders. Aḥmad b. Ḥusayn al-Bayhaqī's (d. 458/1066) *al-Zuhd al-Kabīr* ("The Major Epistle on Asceticism") has one section of six on the theme of "seclusion and obscurity" (*al-ʿuzla wa-l-khumūl*). While Shihāb al-Dīn al-Suhrawardī (d. 632/1191) dedicates three chapters of his *ʿAwārif al-Maʿārif* ("The Esoteric Insights of the Gnostics") describing the rules of *khalwa* (retreating). *Khalwa* played an important role in the rites of Sufi orders, including the Kubrāwiyya,[8] the Qādiriyya,[9] the Shādhiliyya,[10] and the Khalwatiyya,[11] which derives its name from it (Knysh 1999, 314–316). Both in earlier examples of *zuhd* among Sufis and their later counterparts, including al-Nābulusī, the focus is usually a lifestyle preoccupied with interior conscionable concerns and scrupulous behaviour (Yaldiz 2016, 165).

The most extensive and systematic work on the topic is al-Ghazālī's *Iḥyāʾ ʿUlūm al-Dīn*'s ("Revival of the Religious Sciences") sixth book from the quarter designated for "worship," which lists the preconditions of undertaking *ʿuzla*; he also covers the topic broadly in his *Minhāj al-ʿĀbidīn* ("The Curriculum of the Worshippers") and his *Minhāj al-ʿĀrifīn* ("The Curriculum of the Gnostics"). The arguments for both sides are presented in the *Iḥyāʾ* and al-Ghazālī sets out to explain these meticulously. He proffers seven benefits of socialising with people (which receives virtually no treatment in al-Nābulusī's main work on the subject), and offers a partial retreat as an alternative. He stresses that seclusion might even be undertaken for selfish ends, such as gaining a reputation as a mystic, or other such sanctimonious purposes (al-Zabīdī 2012, 380–416). Murtaḍā al-Zabīdī's (d. 1205/1790) commentary on the *Iḥyāʾ* entitled *Itḥāf al-Sāda al-Muttaqīn* ("The Benefactions of the Cultivated-Faithful") expands on the seminal work by adding useful explanations and inputs. For example, al-Zabīdī says that certain early Muslim scholars believed every believer had the power of intercession and that this ought to be a motivating factor in forging abundant relations with other "believers" – rather than secluding oneself – since you may ultimately benefit from a specific believer whom you had befriended (al-Zabīdī 2012, 314–317). Al-Nābulusī does not address the conundrum of scholars withdrawing in times of corruption, and unwittingly further perpetuating corruption through their absence from the role of publicly guiding people, although he may have appealed to his dedication to publishing works and teaching some students in his defence (al-Nābulusī 2010, 138). Again, al-Ghazālī is far more exacting and nuanced in his treatise on this point as on so many others on the subject.

---

8 A Sufi order founded by Najm al-Dīn Kubrā (d. 618/1221) which is based on *al-mawt al-irādī* (death by volition).

9 A Sufi order founded by ʿAbd al-Qādir al-Jīlānī (d. 561/1166) rooted in service to humanity and submission to the will of God.

10 A Sufi order founded by Abū l-Ḥasan al-Shādhilī (d. 656/1258) that is known for lifelong learning and gratitude to God, for which it is sometimes known as the *ṭarīqa* of gratitude.

11 This order was founded by ʿUmar al-Khalwatī (d. 800/1397) which was fundamentally about withdrawing from the world for mystical purposes.

More recently scholars have examined the *Takmīl* and discussed the spiritual seclusion practiced by Muslim scholars. Gibril Fouad Haddad critiqued the *Takmīl* of al-Nābulusī in a journal article that also mentioned accounts of various Muslim renunciants (Haddad 2017, 91). The nature of isolated retreats by prominent Muslim figures are worth considering in light of Hermann Landolt's point in his entry on *khalwa* for the *Encyclopaedia of Islam*: "spiritual isolation from the world was considered higher than material seclusion and it is clear that periodic retreats rather than permanent seclusion were practiced in reality" (Landolt 1977). Even prolonged durations away from interaction with people tended to be punctuated by occasional visits to others or receiving guests as al-Nābulusī's case reveals.

## 3 Historical Context around the Time of al-Nābulusī's Seclusion

The first half of the eighteenth century was argued by Ottoman specialists, such as Andre Raymond, to be a period of urban development and commercial expansion, rejecting the theory of decline (Aladdin 1985, 23). Lejla Demiri and Samuela Pagani agree that "decline" is no longer an acceptable "descriptive term to characterise the Ottoman period in the Arab-speaking territories" while cautioning that concepts differ across civilisations (Demiri and Pagani 2019, 6).

Intriguingly and perhaps in contradistinction to "urban development and commercial expansion" salving the decline narrative, al-Nābulusī's primary disquiet with the sociocultural atmosphere of late eleventh/seventeenth century Damascus was, in fact, its "decline," albeit in morality. "Moral degeneration" was posited as the primary justification for his retreat from public life (al-Nābulusī 1998, 25–26). Negative moral influences are not the only reason why al-Nābulusī confined himself to his house in Damascus for several years. At the same time, to interpret his actions as motivated merely by a desire for spiritual edification would be to overlook its complexity. The immediate cause seems to have been captured in the following remarks:

> I was severely affected by the wretched state of affairs that seriously affected our land, Damascus, as well as the dangerous pronouncements and severe calamities which had befallen her. These state of affairs determined that I cease meeting with people except a few who believed in what I had to say and shared the same convictions. I resolved not to leave my house except if necessary. This was due to the appearance of disbelief and its spread between them [the Muslims] without any compunction.

> I counted and relied on God in bearing harm, patience at misfortune, excessive hypocrisy, the appearance of schisms and felt much alienation from people when I did not find anyone who agreed on the clear truth, let alone someone helpful, due to the incredible amount of corruption of this age, sinfulness, widespread misguidance among laity and scholars alike.
>
> AL-NĀBULUSĪ 1995, 130

Abdul-Karim Rafeq highlights the disaffection al-Nābulusī had felt when he had been informed about the injustices of excessive taxation "inflicted on the peasants by the *sipahi*s, the feudal lords, which resulted in the emptying of the countryside" (Rafeq 2009, 10). This urbanisation led to prominent *ʿulamāʾ* from the four schools of Sunnī jurisprudence to issue verdicts censoring the sultanic orders and the feudal practices which had led the *sipahi*s to drive this poor class from their villages and their "homeland" (*waṭan*). They urged the peasants to take a stand against their oppressors who were brazenly contravening the Sharīʿa. Al-Nābulusī himself had issued a *fatwa* on this issue entitled: *Takhyīr al-ʿIbād fī Suknā al-Bilād* ("Giving People the Option to Live where they Choose"). He rebuked the *sipahi*s (Ottoman cavalrymen) for attempting to coerce the peasantry to return to ruralisation and till the lands so that tax revenues may be collected after having driven them out in the first instance (Rafeq 2009, 10–11). His unequivocal denunciation of those in power demonstrates how earnestly al-Nābulusī treated issues of social justice.[12]

Al-Nābulusī was not retreating as a monadic hermit who simply sought to indulge in esoteric practices for personal spiritual gain but, rather, or perhaps also, someone that was deeply concerned with the social injustices affecting his people. The withdrawal therefore was, in some regards, a protest and many of his writings during this period were the medium by which he raised his voice and deep dissatisfaction.[13] This supports Nir Shafir's observation that the widespread pietistic turn in the tenth/sixteenth and eleventh/

12 Social concerns are deemed to be emotions that are influenced by the welfare of others, emotions such as happiness or joy, "or outcomes that would lead to those feelings." These are also known as "fortunes-of-others" emotions (see Mesoudi and Jensen 2012, 419–433, 426–427). Being sensitive to the emotions and states of others motivate prosocial behaviours, which is behaviour intended to help other people (see Mesoudi and Jensen 2012, 426–427). For more on whether religions influence prosociality (see Preston, Salomon and Ritter 2014, 149–169).

13 He only elaborates on political oppression but there is a sense that other vices are being left unsaid. The following chapter brings some of these to surface based on records towards the end of al-Nābulusī's life but which are likely to have resembled some of the problems which poverty will likely have caused when he was remonstrating about the

seventeenth centuries Ottoman Empire as captured by its "morality literature," or the *naṣīḥat-nāma* (advice book) genre which mushroomed in the period, was not simply religious in the devotional sense but had political implications and, indeed, was sometimes motivated by overwhelmingly political events, as the above case shows.

## 4 Motives for Withdrawal: A Selection of *Aḥadīth* from the *Takmīl*

The *Takmīl* was compiled during al-Nābulusī's retreat and its first two chapters seek to justify his seclusion by reference to sixty-two *ḥadīth*s that are occasionally interspersed with brief social commentary.[14] In this way, al-Nābulusī revealed how he personally read the contemporary state of affairs to which the traditions were meant to apply.[15] The first chapter of his work pertains to

prevalence of vices in society, such as prostitution and mercenary-harlot alliances in defiance of public morality (see Rafeq 2009, 180–196).

14 This combination of *aḥadīth* and social commentaries marries elements of timelessness and contemporary social issues. The Qur'ānic and *ḥadīth* sources foreground the first half of the book, several digressions notwithstanding, while the latter half of the book refers to the corruption besetting society and with which those sources are in conversation. For more on the commentarial impulse to timeliness/timelessness (see Blecher 2018, 184–145). The disadvantage of this approach, rather than a more specific but not necessarily atomistic one, is that we do not attain a nuanced insight into exactly which traditions are used for which particular purpose, or how some are even relevant to the argument being made. Even if the current work is not hermeneutically sophisticated it manifests a thorough engagement with the tradition in the first half, before assessing the practices and views of other Muslim scholars which are used as auxiliaries. This opposes the accusation of intellectual decline by showing the vibrancy of al-Nābulusī's production on this theme. Even the longstanding military decline had some recovery in the eleventh/seventeenth century, albeit embedded in centuries of steady decline. To say that the military decline, or irregularities in the provincial governments' rule (such as the rise of "dynasty governors"), signifies intellectual decline is unfair, as it compares the modernisation of the thirteenth/nineteenth and fourteenth/twentieth centuries with the "allegedly static" tenth/sixteenth, eleventh/seventeenth and twelfth/eighteenth centuries (see Barbir 1980, 3–6). Furthermore, due to inflation and the rise of an expanding janissary army in Istanbul, the livelihoods of the military forces spread throughout the Ottoman provinces were threatened. This resulted in the need to strengthen the governors of those regions to maintain local order. The state also resettled thousands of janissaries away from Istanbul to keep them away from brewing trouble in the political heartland; which led to trouble elsewhere (see Barbir 1980, 16–17).

15 In al-Nābulusī we see the fleshing out of the *eschaton* "end" when using *ḥadīth* traditions. Eschatological discourse is either futuristic or realised. In futuristic eschatology, the *eschaton* foretold by the scripture is still to happen; eschatological events are still in

disassociating from the public in times of "tribulation" (*fitna*), the second is on shunning the *imāms* of "*fitna*" in the mosques. My focus will be on the first of these chapters as it has a broader application, applied as it is to the masses.

Al-Nābulusī's use of the *aḥadīth* to bolster his case for seclusion is somewhat selective. It is notable that the general thrust of *aḥadīth* in the major *ḥadīth* collections on "the ethics of sociality" (*ādāb al-ṣuḥba*) push in the direction of prioritising companionship (*ṣuḥba*) and brotherhood (*ukhuwwa*).[16] *ʿUzla* removes one from fulfilling the ethical imperatives promulgated in these *aḥadīth*, even though *ʿuzla* in itself is not considered an absolute virtue, in the same way that "compassion" or "generosity" are considered (both of which, ironically, require others).[17] Usually Sufis are thought to have other higher spiritual objectives which lead them to pursue isolation from society. This does not seem to be the case with al-Nābulusī. As we will see from a sample of some of the *aḥadīth* considered below, there are traditions which portend various

---

the future. Realised eschatology are those traditions which contain events which have been fulfilled; the *eschaton* is thus in the past. The Prophet Muḥammad's death inaugurated eschatological expectations relating to seclusion. None of the traditions recounted by al-Nābulusī refer to events which may occur in the Prophet's life. For credit for these terms and for a useful comparison with a Christian typology on eschatology see (DeRoo and Manoussakis 2009, 5–6). By bringing texts of futuristic tendencies, as well as antecedent application to the present, the case is made to make both the past and future predictions causally efficacious in the present.

16 This is because *suḥba* is a part of a spiritual foregrounding of moral philosophy, a *sine qua non* of attaining optimal spiritual maturity. Attaining the virtuous self is hardly ever a solitary exercise. It is both achieved in relation to interacting with others as well as through the input of others' ethical assistance especially spiritual masters. For instance, al-Muḥāsibī encouraged seeking venerable masters as moral guides (see al-Muḥāsibī quoted in Yazaki 2013, 37). Al-Nābulusī encourages people to keep the company of the friends of God but then states, in an essay completed four years prior to his retreat, that owing to people's negative opinions of others and most people's corrupt objectives such pious people are in a state of "necessary obscurity" (*khifā ḍarūrī*) (see al-Nābulusī 1998, 181–183).

17 The requirement for *ʿuzla* is much more subjectively determined and applies to a narrow range of circumstances. This is different from saying, in the Nietzchean conception, that references to absolute values are futile and that one must guide their actions or limit them by the "juridical sanctions of positive law" (see Rocci 1990, 219–225, 219). Murtaḍā al-Zabīdī's commentary *Itḥāf al-Sāda al-Muttaqīn* on al-Ghazālī's *Iḥyāʾ ʿUlūm al-Dīn, Kitāb Ādāb al-Ulfa wa-l-Ukhuwwa wa-l-Ṣuḥba wa-l-Muʿāshara* ("Book on the Etiquettes of Affection, Brotherhood, Companionship and Social Interaction") stretches to three hundred pages while his commentary on *ʿuzla* amounts to a mere one hundred pages, highlighting the importance placed on both topics but the predominance of the former.

ominous circumstances where Muslims have been told to withdraw from society on account of certain problems within that society.

Some *aḥadīth* refer to specific types of events, usually internecine conflict, while others address a generally foreboding time in the distant future, and may have application in a variety of situations. An example of a specific event during "the time of strife" (*zaman al-fitna*) when the Prophet's companions were at war is alluded to in the following tradition. In response to whether he should carry his sword, Abū Dharr al-Ghifārī (d. 32/652) was told by the Prophet that if the olive trees are sullied by blood (in reference to the trees in Medina) then: "stick to your houses" (*kūnū aḥlāsa buyūtikum*) (al-Nābulusī 1998, 7).[18]

Of those traditions which describe a general state of widespread corruption or anarchy several problems arise to which attention will now be drawn. The ethical precept in many such *aḥadīth* either recommends or strongly proposes one to withdraw from society given various states of tumultuous affairs. Both Sufyān al-Thawrī (d. 97/778) and al-Ghazālī were of the opinions that it was permissible to isolate oneself from society.[19] Referencing their opinions al-Nābulusī goes one step further by claiming it is "*wājib* and *farḍ*" (both terms implying varying degrees of obligation with it being intensified in the latter) to isolate oneself from society in his time. He does not provide specific "evidence" (*dalīl*) for this point, instead proclaiming:

> It is equivalent to Islam and faith (*īmān*) in our times. Whoever therefore ignores this and intermingles with people then his Islam and *īmān* are mere lip service without a reality in the heart, like the Islam of a hypocrite.
> AL-NĀBULUSĪ 1998, 22[20]

Another *ḥadīth* which al-Nābulusī refers to is the tradition narrated by Abū Burda (d. 103/721 or 104/722 or 723):

18 The *ḥadīth* is related by Abū Dāwūd 2009, 6:319: *Awwal Kitāb al-Fitan* ("Book of Tribulations"), *Bāb al-Nahy 'an al-Sa'y fī l-Fitna* ("Chapter on the Prohibition of Engaging in Vice"). *Ḥils* or *ḥalas* is a cloth used to prevent saddle-sore on the back of a riding beast. The metaphor aptly compares material which is pressing upon the animal and is firmly in place with the way a person should remain confined to his house. The cloth also prevents major friction which is painful to the animal, just as a person avoids civil strife by withdrawing from society.

19 There were others who held this belief too such as: Ibrāhīm b. Adham (d. 161/778), Dāwūd al-Ṭā'ī (d. 165/782), Fuḍayl b. 'Iyāḍ (d. 187/803), Yūsuf b. Asbāṭ (d. 110/810) and Bishr al-Ḥāfi (d. 227/841) (see al-Zabīdī 2012, 317).

20 For al-Nābulusī's understanding on Islam and *īmān* see (al-Nābulusī 2000, 95–128).

> There will be strife, hostile separation and grave disagreement. When that time arrives you must take your sword and break it. Then sit in your house, until a sinful hand comes to you or a preordained death.
>
> AL-NĀBULUSĪ 1998, 9[21]

Abū Burda confirms that the prophecy of the Prophet was realised when he says: "what the Prophet Muḥammad said, happened" (al-Nābulusī 1998, 9). Al-Nābulusī's reliance on this *ḥadīth* suggests that he favours withdrawal from society in times of strife, as well as adopting a passive acceptance of one's fate in such times. The act of isolation, itself, in such traditions is justified by those facing unpalatable circumstances, rather than stemming from a mystical or spiritual motive for those with a surfeit of numinous stamina. This externalist approach of al-Nābulusī impresses upon the reader that it is the situations highlighted in the traditions and their attendant precepts that are the cause of his motivation to withdraw.

## 5 Corruption, Deprivation of Benefit to Others and Obligations to Society

It is important to explore al-Nābulusī's views of "others" during his seclusion from mainstream society. A paradox occurs with his decision to seclude himself which involves the relationality between the individual and society. His ethical outlook, informed by his epistemology, required him to disengage from the corruption of society. However, some of the *aḥadīth* he relied upon suggest it is society rather than al-Nābulusī that may benefit most from his withdrawal. For instance, in one *ḥadīth* which he quotes, Abū Saʿīd al-Khuḍrī says the Prophet Muḥammad was asked: "Who is the best person?" Among the people mentioned is a believer in a valley (or a barren area) who fears his Lord and distances people from his evil (al-Nābulusī 1998, 10).[22] Muḥammad

---

21 The *ḥadīth* is related by Ibn Māja 2009, 5:109: *Kitāb Abwāb al-Fitan* ("Book of Tribulations"), *Bāb Idhā Iltaqā l-Muslimāni bi-Sayfayhimā* ("Chapter on When Two Muslims Confront One Another with Their Swords"); Ibn Ḥanbal 1999, 29:496.

22 The *ḥadīth* is related by al-Bukhārī 1422]2001[, 4:15: *Kitāb al-Jihād wa-l-Siyar* ("Book on Fighting for the Cause of Allāh"), *Bāb Afḍal al-Nās Muʾmin Mujāhid bi-Nafsih wa-Mālih fī Sabīl Allāh* ("Chapter on the Best Man is the Believer who Participates in the Fight with His Life and Property"); Muslim 1991, 3:1503: *Kitāb al-Imāra* ("Book on Government"), *Bāb Faḍl al-Jihād wa-l-Ribāṭ* ("Chapter on the Virtue of *Jihād* and Keeping Watch over the Frontier").

ʿAbd al-Raḥmān al-Mubārakpūrī (d. 1353/1934) explains its rationale thus: "So he does not wrangle with people nor argue with them" (al-Mubārakpūrī 2011, 296). The above tradition is quoted by al-Nābulusī, but another which he does not mention might reflect upon him more positively and would better explain his actions:

> I heard the Prophet – upon him blessings and peace – say, "People will see a time when the best property will be sheep. A person leads them to the summit where it rains, fleeing for the sake of his religion away from strifes."[23]

The former narration depicts the isolationist as sparing society his own harm, while the latter sees him fleeing from society's harm.

Although some of the *aḥadīth* which al-Nābulusī quotes seem to suggest that society may benefit from the seclusion of certain difficult individuals, al-Nābulusī's own view is that seclusion from a corrupt society benefits the individual who chooses such an isolated path. Irrespective of which attitude is adopted, arguably, the path of seclusion contains a paradox. On the one hand, if society is corrupt, surely an ethical individual – not least a scholar – has a duty to engage in and reform that society, a point captured in a number of letters which al-Nābulusī writes (al-Nābulusī 2010, 121). If, on the other hand, an individual is corrupt, while his withdrawal may benefit society, it is unlikely that a corrupt individual will seclude himself simply to benefit society. Nonetheless, it could also be argued that the semi-isolation of some of the spiritual elite might raise the spiritual aspirations of ordinary believers by representing an exemplary ethical standard and this may have partly motivated al-Nābulusī. Such a strategy may confer religious repute to those who practice seclusion (as it certainly did to al-Nābulusī) and help gain admiration which results in a following. This may, in turn, benefit society if the secluded individual is a virtuous person seen as worthy of emulation.

Withdrawing from society, while it faces moral upheaval rather than seeking to improve it from within, does have its antecedents in Islamic literature. Precisely such a line of argument is enlisted by ʿAbd al-Raḥmān Ibn al-Jawzī (d. 597/1200) in *Ṣayd al-Khāṭir* ("Capturing the Mind's Destructive Tendencies"): "that I benefit myself alone is better than I benefit others while harming myself" (Ibn al-Jawzī 2011, 140). This reasoning may well be based on the understanding that privileging spiritual self-care is one's primary obligation. Does

23 Al-Bukhārī 1422 [2001], 9:53: *Kitāb al-Fitan* ("Book of Tribulations"), *Bāb al-Taʿarrub fī l-Fitna* ("Chapter Staying with the Bedouins during Tribulations").

the pursuit of spiritual self-interest in the midst of such corruption then constitute [Sharīʿa-justified] "psychological egoism," a term used by Joel Feinberg. Psychological egoism being a theory which states that humans pursue their own self-interests. Al-Nābulusī's position, however, might be better described as "ethical egoism:" all people ought to pursue their own well-being; it is about what ought to be the case (Feinberg 2013, 167). This stance indicates, "saving" oneself – however an individual defines it so – is given precedence over contributing to the welfare of others and it seems that this is al-Nābulusī's outlook during the said period. In al-Nābulusī's own words the following were some of the intolerable moral and ethical problems he encountered that led him to focus inwardly:

> Know that the tribulations which demand seclusion from people in our age, have been enumerated by the Prophet, as narrated in the explicit traditions quoted earlier. These include corruption becoming rampant and widespread. It is now so pervasive and has burgeoned to the extent that people have declared its permissibility, they have been assisted in that by the wicked scholars who ridicule a person and then declare: "He is a public sinner and backbiting a public sinner is not considered unlawful." As for the laity they say: "We have only spoken the truth." It also includes: honouring materialistic people, to the extent that they pardon every transgression of theirs and call it "obedience;" out of coveting their wealth, while severely despising the destitute, whom they consider bereft, wretched. They say: "If God was pleased with them, he would have provided them with material provisions and enriched them." It also includes the dominance of evil people over the people of truth so that you will see the pious believer fearful religiously and personally from slipping in front of a hypocrite, a profligate and criminal who is undeterred what religion he belongs to (even after claiming Islam and of having faith). You will see this believer around such type of people suffer considerably, at the hands of those who excoriate him and attack him with despicable actions and words relating to his honour, his religion, his intellect, assisted by a coterie of wicked people. Various other examples exist that would prolong this work. These matters then and their likes, are corruptions like a "sliver of the dark night," [to those who do] not find anything wrong in them in the slightest and indulge in them without compunction. They do not recognise them as problematic and nor consider them consequential. Some conceited folk even consider this age superior to the past, praising their contemporaries out of sheer ignorance, blind hearts, an extinguished insight due to eating the unlawful: "And whoever God wants to

> try with strife, you will not avail him from God in the slightest" [Q 5:41]. How incomparable: that age of mutual love to this age of hypocrisy, tyranny and hostility?
>
> AL-NĀBULUSĪ 1998, 25–26

The Qurʾānic call to pay heed to one's own affairs (which appends his work dedicated to the theme of seclusion), as well as al-Nābulusī's interpretations in the previous quote, apparently gave him the justification to withdraw the benefit of his presence from others and to focus on preserving himself.

This leads us to the question of whether spiritual self-preservation amounts to tacit harm of others and how to determine benefit and harm for oneself and society. Indeed, al-Ghazālī, but not al-Nābulusī, suggests that one drawback of seclusion is that it prevents one from "inviting to virtue and curtailing evil" (*al-amr bi-l-maʿrūf wa-l-nahy ʿan al-munkar*). Echoing this, albeit politically, according to Abū Naṣr al-Farābī (d. 339/950), the virtuous political regime is one in which its inhabitants' souls are all as healthy as possible: "the one who cures souls is the statesman and he is also called the king" (Butterworth 2010, 42; al-Farābī 1971, 24).[24] However, al-Nābulusī forestalls such objections of social and political apathy by bringing a tradition of Anas b. Mālik (d. 93/712) where he asserts that someone asked the Prophet when should inviting to virtue and curtailing evil be ceased:

> He said: "If what manifested in previous communities (*umam*) manifest in you." "We said: O Messenger of God what was it that manifested in previous communities." He said: "Sovereignty among the young, depravity among senior folk and knowledge being the lot of those who are despicable (*wa-l-ʿilm fī rudhālatikum*)."
>
> AL-NĀBULUSĪ 1995, 33[25]

Here al-Nābulusī brings in Zayd b. Yaḥyā b. ʿUbayd al-Khuzāʿī (d. 463–464/1071) to explain the meaning of the latter phrase as: "if knowledge is borne by the

24 According to Nāṣir al-Dīn al-Ṭūsī (d. 672/1274), virtuous friendship is the crucial element that was missing in al-Farābī's utopian vision. "The best friendship is the love between good and virtuous men, who share a hunger for perfection and for the Divine" (Gianotti 2015, 82). It seems it was precisely this quality of friendship which al-Nābulusī searched for but could not find.

25 The *ḥadīth* is related by Ibn Māja 2009, 5:147: *Kitāb Abwāb al-Fitan* ("Book of Tribulations"), *Bāb Qawlihi: "Yā Ayyuhā l-Ladhīna Āmanū ʿAlaykum Anfusakum"* ("Chapter on the Words of Allāh: 'O You Who Believe! Take Care of Your Own Selves'").

profligate" (*idhā kāna al-ʿilmu fī l-fussāq*) and then elaborates who the "*fussāq*" (profligates) are in his opinion:

> The profligate are those who insist on backbiting in their gatherings, spreading gossip, envy, arrogance, self-conceit, consuming the unlawful, hypocrisy, ostentation, giving verdicts to curry favour with popular sentiments and in order to side with their objectives, and the use of subterfuge "in legal matters" (Sharīʿa), to make falsehood truth and truth falsehood, to terminate endowments and ownership, to meddle in Sharīʿa contracts for the sake of temporal gains and other such matters which would be too long to illustrate and which would be unsavoury to spread.
>
> AL-NĀBULUSĪ 1995, 33

It appears that there are more sinister affairs that are rife in society, and that al-Nābulusī does not deign to mention these matters because he finds them deeply abhorrent. His emphatic outbursts elsewhere are not similarly truncated which supports the idea that al-Nābulusī's arguments and condemnation for virtually excommunicating his entire society are not expressed in full in the *Takmīl*.

In order to further disambiguate the moral dimension which he mentions we must delve into another of his texts, the *Ghāyat al-Maṭlūb*. This work offers a more integrated insight into the struggles al-Nābulusī faced, and which led him to perceive his contemporaries so morally wanting that he could not bear to associate with them.[26] Although his opinion of people was derogatory, and possibly contemptuous, he did not go so far as to insinuate that they were "ruined" and perhaps he proves that by eventually abandoning his retreat. In the discussion on "gazing at beautiful faces" (*al-naẓar ilā wujūh al-ḥisān*), al-Nābulusī appeals to a *ḥadīth*, for his own defence, in which the Prophet Muḥammad is reported to have said: "If you hear a person say that people are ruined; assuredly, most ruined is he."[27] He appeals to the commentary of Yaḥyā al-Nawawī (d. 676/1277) to clarify two possible interpretations of this depending on whether the word "ruined" (*ahlak*) is in the nominative or accusative case. If in the former case, then it means that the person referring to them, is himself the most ruined among the people. While in the latter situation it

26 This text was also written during al-Nābulusī's seclusion and hence complements some of the critiques made about society contained in the *Takmīl*.

27 Muslim 1991, 4:2024: *Kitāb al-Birr wa-l-Ṣila wa-l-Ādāb* ("Book on Virtue, Joining of the Ties of Kinship and Enjoining Good Manners"), *Bāb al-Nahy ʿan Qawl Halaka al-Nās* ("Chapter on the Prohibition of Saying: 'The People are Doomed'").

means that he presumes them to be ruined, not that they are, in reality, ruined (al-Nābulusī 1995, 83). Were one to say that "people are ruined", the supercilious pronouncement belies a callous proclamation of omniscience which, unsurprisingly, al-Nābulusī does not use in the *Takmīl*, even though his opinions regarding fellow residents of Damascus seemingly betrayed such an attitude.

After relaying numerous incidents from the Prophet Muḥammad's times concerning the "dissolute conduct of some Muslims," including sexual liaisons and prostitution, al-Nābulusī says the "acts of ignorance" (*jāhiliyya*) during that period were greater than his own era's corruption and evil (al-Nābulusī 1995, 87). As further examples to highlight the impiety characteristic of that age – yet similarly present in his own time – he mentions theft, fraudulent activity, armed robbery, homosexuality, extra-marital sex, drinking alcohol, false accusations, hurling insults and having the worst suspicions about others (al-Nābulusī 1995, 88).[28] Al-Nābulusī further clarifies that one is not to think that iniquity, evil, abhorrence and licentiousness are an exclusive feature of his times and that the past, even the virtuous era, was somehow empty of such decadence.[29] The prominent wars between the companions are better forgotten and not spread, he says, as well as those that occurred after them. Evil is present in all times, and much in that way could be mined from the books of "*ḥadīth*, narrations and history" (al-Nābulusī 1995, 83). Still, licentiousness, false testimonies, and calumny were sparse in the first "three-favoured-centuries" (*khayr al-qurūn*) which represented greater virtue, it is later that these vices became widespread (al-Nābulusī 1995, 89). The predecessors would consider thinking ill of one another as being forbidden, spying as unlawful and it would only be hypocrites who would fall foul of such sins. Nowadays, he inveighs, "no one thinks such things to be forbidden; very few individuals are free from

28 *Ḥadīth* commentaries, even the non-conventional type, like al-Nābulusī's *Takmīl*, may function as "an exegetical history that connects the audiences' current social and historical context to the past" (see Blecher 2018, 177). Al-Nābulusī was not a historian, yet his overview of Damascene society portrays insights that are useful for analysing his moral thought. In this sense, his value might be likened to when al-Ṭabarī writes contemporary history as its author, rather than a compiler or editor; his self-authored section is recognised as "highly distinctive" and valuable (see Shoshan 2004, xxxiii). Al-Nābulusī's decision to seclude himself because of corruption appears to contradict his confession of the Prophet's era being mired more in vice than his own, unless, it may be argued that, certain vices of his age – and he does differentiate between the two – were more malignant and nefarious, thus compelling his drastic course of action. It may also be the case that he was more personally affected by the issues prevalent in his society, hence, the need to consider his emotional state. Perhaps he was overwhelmed as the target of hatred, which evoked such an extreme reaction from him.

29 This is said in reference to the first three generations of Muslims, beginning with the first who witnessed the Prophet Muḥammad in their lives and so forth.

them" (al-Nābulusī 1995, 91). His arguments continue to pivot almost entirely on the explicitly moral.

One understands the moral duty to speak boldly which al-Nābulusī feels (and duly responds to in writing) when he quotes a tradition on the authority of Abū Saʿīd al-Khudrī (d. 74/693) that the Prophet Muḥammad said in a sermon: "Let a man not be prevented, out of awe for the people, from speaking the truth if he knows it." Al-Khudrī then cried and said: "by Allāh we saw things and were 'timorously reticent' (*fa-hibnā*) (al-Nābulusī 1995, 91)."[30] In yet another instance he quotes the Prophet:

> Let none of you detest himself. The companions asked: "O Messenger of God, how are we able to detest ourselves?" He said: "He sees an affair pertaining to the rights God speaks of, and about which he should interject, but he refrains from doing so. God will say to him on Judgement Day: 'what prevented you from speaking about such and such?' He will say: 'fear of people.' God will respond: 'It was me from whom you should have been more afraid.'"
>
> AL-NĀBULUSĪ 1995, 17[31]

Silence, al-Nābulusī goes on to say, would be tantamount to a blemish in the character of the Prophet Muḥammad, contradicting God's epithet for him in the Qurʾān: "Your virtues are indeed magnificent" (Q 68:4; al-Nābulusī 1995, 17). By mentioning this, al-Nābulusī presents himself as someone following in the footsteps of the Prophet by making knowledge-driven interventions.

Indeed, many of the scholars al-Nābulusī includes as practitioners of isolation taught from the privacy of their homes and did not entirely deprive others of their knowledge, even if the number of their beneficiaries may have dwindled post-isolation. This is referred to by Gibril Haddad as "qualified asociality" and quite accurately sums up the manner in which most scholars mentioned in the *Takmīl* practiced seclusion (Haddad 2017, 91). Withholding knowledge, besides being a condemned practice, is evidence of miserliness.[32] Knowledge

---

30 The *ḥadīth* is related by al-Tirmidhī 1996, 4:58: *Kitāb Abwāb al-Fitan* ("Book of Tribulations"), *Bāb Mā Jāʾa Mā Akhbara al-Nabī Aṣḥābahu Mā Huwa Kāʾin ilā Yawm al-Qiyāma* ("Chapter on What the Prophet Informed His Companions Would Occur until the Day of Resurrection"); Ibn Māja 2009, 5:141: *Kitāb Abwāb al-Fitan* ("Book of Tribulations"), *Bāb al-Amr bi-l-Maʿrūf wa-l-Nahy ʿan al-Munkar* ("Chapter on Commanding the Right and Forbidding the Wrong").

31 The *ḥadīth* is related by Ibn Māja 2009, 5:142: *Kitāb Abwāb al-Fitan* ("Book of Tribulations"), *Bāb al-Amr bi-l-Maʿrūf wa-l-Nahy ʿan al-Munkar* ("Chapter on Commanding the Right and Forbidding the Wrong"); Ibn Ḥanbal 1999, 17:359.

32 Al-Nābulusī clearly laments the lack of enthusiasm among people who have not appreciated their scholars and have consequently not preserved their scholars' written or

is the foundation of love, a silent person who is knowledgeable cannot uplift others ethically. Through the generosity of his speech, however, he can bring deliverance and tranquillity to them (Khalifa 2010, 227). One might still incline to charging a recluse like al-Nābulusī with ingratitude as Abū ʿUthmān ʿAmr al-Jāḥiẓ (d. 254/868 or 255/869) states: "you cannot show gratitude to God; you cannot show it except through speech" (al-Jāḥiẓ 1906, 136; also quoted in Khan 2008, 54). Al-Jāḥiẓ's argument seeks to convince his reader of the inferiority of silence – a typical characteristic of seclusion – "were silence more preferable ... the superiority ...[of] human beings over other [creatures] would not be recognised" (Khan 2008, 155). If one were to accept the above premise as a charge against al-Nābulusī, ignoring his thirsty pen during his retreat would ironically mean this narrow interpretation would itself lend to an uncharitable constriction of generosity, the pen too has a tongue. Moreover, al-Nābulusī permits occasional access to himself which vindicates him from this charge.[33] Considering this, to reinforce the earlier point of al-Nābulusī's engagement, it is likely that he did not see himself as being taken to silence and he certainly did not forego all human contact, as a small flock of his close associates maintained visits. Therefore, contrary to a lone undertaking concerned solely with interior progress and spiritual unveilings, al-Nābulusī continued to seek engagement with and benefit society especially through his prodigious output.[34]

## 6 Attitudes to Seclusion: A Reflection of True Humility or False Humility?

Demonstrating humility to God is different from showing humility to fellow humans. Al-Nābulusī's departure from the view of earlier self-deprecatory scholars, who believed that one should ascribe corruption to themselves, ostensibly appears arrogant. The argument might be inferred from those

intellectual legacy. This clarifies his stance on knowledge-sharing as being a bountiful act from which others may benefit (see al-Nābulusī 1995, 132).

33 He does feel unvalued; gaining respect was seen as important for him as a public figure (see al-Nābulusī 1995, 130). Reference to respect as an important interpersonal commodity can be seen in many works such as the following example where ʿAbd al-Raḥmān Ibn al-Jawzī contrasts two people, one of whom has far greater knowledge but due to a particular obnoxious sin is disgraced by people and they no longer pay him respect. His counterpart with far less knowledge, fulfils the rights of God and is held in higher esteem in people's hearts (see Ibn al-Jawzī 2011, 277).

34 We know al-Nābulusī had great faith in books having the power to educate and transform people. As Bakri Aladdin has pointed out, it was the books themselves that were the real teachers of al-Nābulusī (see Aladdin 1985, 82–84).

earlier scholars, that in order to preserve one's spiritual integrity, assumption of exogenous corruption was woefully self-defeating, as it would lead to one's ego assuming one was better than others.[35] Rather, despite evident societal dissolution, one is required to reflexively contort their perception, and to regard themselves as being of a lesser moral standing than people in society, or at least to outwardly manifest this position. The empirical reality to undergird the Damascene *shaykh*'s dismay with his social circumstances is supported *prima facie* by his personal account, our limited accessibility to the effects on his personal state notwithstanding. Therefore, should al-Nābulusī have affected self-diminution if he was unable to genuinely view himself as being corrupt and society as virtuous, in contradistinction to the advice of others such as al-Ghazālī and Abū l-Qāsim al-Qushayrī (d. 465/1073) who thought it proper to view oneself as being the party guilty of moral deficiencies in such a scenario?[36] Al-Nābulusī was unwilling to do so and thus radically departs from what would seem a fundamental commitment to any serious spiritual-mystical sojourn in the lives of some earlier practitioners of this type of seclusion, perhaps even undermining its spiritual essence.

To reiterate, self-perception when considering isolation is explained in the following two ways: one leaves society because people are noxious or, conversely, that one regards themselves as objectionable and ethically-wanting. Al-Ghazalī and al-Qushayrī say one must view themselves as being corrupt and loathsome. This latter position, al-Qushayrī asserts, emerges from having crushed one's ego while adopting the former stance is to manifest superiority over creation. Whoever effaces his ego is humble; he who feels supercilious towards any individual is arrogant (al-Qushayrī 2013, 138). Al-Nābulusī adopts the opposite position. Among the *aḥadīth* which address this conundrum are two *prima facie* paradoxical traditions. The first suggests seclusion to stave off one's evil from people; the second that seclusion is meant to protect one from the evil of others. Nonetheless, sequestering oneself in the above *aḥadīth* is meant as a protective measure rather than to prevent corruption, either to oneself or others. Therefore, one who solely seeks spiritual edification through

35 This is a common trope in Sufi discussions on humility. In Sufi parlance, humility, is to see everything which comes to you as coming from God. Al-Shiblī is said to have asked Yūsuf b. Asbāṭ about the extreme limit of humility. He replied: "when you come out of your house, you consider everyone you see better than yourself" (Nurbaksh 1988, 81–82). Fuḍayl said: "Whoever sees himself as having worth has no share in humility," while Bayazid said humility was when a person "sees himself as possessing neither station nor state and sees no one among God's creatures worse than himself" (Nurbaksh 1988, 86).

36 Philosophers during the Enlightenment such as Spinoza (d. 1677), Friedrich Nietzsche (d. 1900) and David Hume (d. 1776) vehemently opposed this view, disparaging humility and disregarding it as a virtue; ostensibly they would laud al-Nābulusī's stance on this point (see McPherson 2016, 163, 212).

reclusion is not *ipso facto* directly acting on those *aḥadīth* which encourage isolation, based on al-Nābulusī's compilation. Al-Nābulusī does not seem to be acting primarily for the achievement of such esoteric rewards and nor therefore sees "humility" as an important issue to address within the *Takmīl*.

If the content of al-Nābulusī's literary output and others' high-esteem of him and his self-perception were to be taken at face value, then it seems he was justified in taking his stance: society was corrupt, he was not. This does not seem contrary to humility or objectionable on moral grounds albeit, the stance is highly controversial in light of the principles of Sufi thought discussed above. Given al-Nābulusī's extensive use of source-texts we must admit that his rationale for seclusion was to some degree motivated by the Prophet through his traditions. In addition, it is incontrovertible that his emotions and sentiments clearly influenced his undertaking. It is arguable that if al-Nābulusī was less morally incensed and sensitive he may not have been incentivised by the *aḥadīth* alone to forego contact with mainstream society, particularly if he had achieved a prominent teaching position. This seems realistic given that he gave up his seclusion in 1098/1687 and led an integrated public life buttressed by a swell in following that will ostensibly have helped subdue residual feelings of emotional detachment and pain (Shafir 2019, 613–614). The emotions and feelings evinced by al-Nābulusī give us a better idea of his attitude in a way that a list of *aḥadīth* or impersonal anecdotes of others who undertook this practice would never disclose. After all, "emotions are part and parcel of ethical deliberation" (Nussbaum 2009, 172).

As illustrated above, the foundation of al-Nābulusī's moral epistemology is seen through the lens of received tradition and is heavily supported by his personal interpretations and experiences. Neither the religious elite nor the common-folk are spared vitriolic diatribes, effectively dismissing them as wastrels. Together the *Takmīl* and *Ghāyat al-Maṭlūb* – both of which were written during the seven-year seclusion – functioned as justifications for al-Nābulusī's extreme measures and sought to persuade readers of his moral judgement about the unbearable inhabitants of his city. What makes this period of his life relevant to study is that solitary action produces reflexives, these are insights that are developed when alone through sustained, focussed, concerted effort, which lead to a "culturally skilful development of thought" (Cohen 2016, 153–155). The salience of this self-society relation almost *in absentia* through a written corpus expresses al-Nābulusī's reading of his milieu and his subsequent ascription of meaning to religious texts, which reflect the underlying spirit of those texts according to his view, and in application to his particular circumstances. Hans Gadamer would concur that the undertaking of the interpreter of a text is that he must relate it to his situation in order to understand it at all

(Gadamer 1989, 324). Historical interpretation expresses not merely the linguistic expression of texts, but what the texts betray by delving "behind them and the meaning they express to inquire into the reality they express involuntarily" (Gadamer 1989, 336). Texts need explication, so that they are understood not only in terms of what they say but also what they exemplify (Gadamer 1989, 336). What al-Nābulusī's arguments exemplify is that he was eminently capable of weaving the rich *aḥadīth* corpus to his context and skilfully apply it in a demonstrably favourable manner in congruence with his moral constitution.

## 7 Conclusion

The underlying rationale and the hermeneutic employed in al-Nābulusī's analysis of severing social ties with most others is generously expatiated in the *Takmīl*. Beyond quoting *aḥadīth* extensively in the latter work, the *Ghāyat al-Maṭlūb* further captures his arguments related to the prevailing social and moral injustices which undergird his case for seclusion (al-Nābulusī 1995, 130). Together these texts display considerable insight into his moral sentiments at the time of writing. The theoretical basis of al-Nābulusī's claim uses *aḥādīth* to support his actions, but it is clear they were not the only motivating force. Of course, al-Nābulusī may have felt compelled by the influence of religious texts to withdraw from society around 1090–1091/1679–1680, but arguably other forces were also at play, like unbearable societal corruption and his feelings of alienation (Nābulusī 2010, 97).[37] Even though he was palpably a Sufi, the mystical element appears dim in his considerations to "withdraw" or practice *ʿuzla* from society.

The *Takmīl* and *Ghāyat al-Maṭlūb* are personal attempts by al-Nābulusī to combine his judgement on society with his religious hermeneutics to justify the drastic measures he takes. Written prior to the conclusion of his retreat, the former does not account for the reasons why he subsequently gives it up. Yet, it does show that moral issues were the significant rationale for his social disengagement even as no coherent moral theology is exposited. Together with other works written during the seclusion, much about his self-perception and personal struggles is revealed, giving us a glimpse of this understudied perspective about him which, as the above analysis demonstrates, in this instance,

---

37 The context, which for brevity I do not delve into here, plays a crucial part in convincing al-Nābulusī to seek refuge from social interactions. It is worth noting: "People often overestimate the degree to which language itself determines meaning and underestimate the role that context plays in every act of interpretation" (see Camper 2018, 17).

was driven largely by his moral theology. We also better understand his independence in the conclusions he came to, based on his reading of the texts, history and his specific context, for example, in the discussion on humility. This shows Islam to be a discursive tradition that may diverge considerably on ethical issues which are not straightforward to navigate based upon a simple reading of primary texts. Indeed, the texts about seclusion provided the necessary rationale for both engagement with, and the abdication of, the lauded social responsibilities towards others so emphasised in Islam. The application of these texts may change based on the subjective judgement of an individual, not only due to the reading of such texts, or even external socio-political circumstances, but also subject to the vicissitudes of inner emotional rifts caused, to some extent, by society's reception of one's ideas and their personal admiration or dislike of a public figure. Useful as the *Takmīl* is, it would be a stretch to attribute a coherent ethics of seclusion to al-Nābulusī's writings on this topic, yet, that he was ethically motivated in his withdrawal from society is undeniable, and it was the *aḥādīth* that were ostensibly the mainstay of such an undertaking.

## Bibliography

Abū Dāwūd, Sulaymān b. al-Ashʿath. 2009. *Sunan Abī Dāwūd*, edited by Shuʿayb al-Arnāʾūṭ and Muḥammad Kāmil Qurrah Balalī. Damascus: Dār al-Risāla al-ʿĀlamiyya.

Aladdin, Bakri. 1985. "ʿAbd al-Ghanī al-Nābulusī (1143/1731): Oeuvre, vie et doctrine." PhD diss., Sorbonne University, Paris.

Ateş, Ahmed. 1968. "Ibn al-ʿArabī." In *Encyclopaedia of Islam, Second Edition*, vol. 3, 707–711. Leiden: Brill. DOI: 10.1163/1573-3912_islam_COM_0316.

al-Baghdādī, Abū ʿAlī l-Ḥasan b. Aḥmad b. ʿAbd Allāh. 1988. *Al-Risāla al-Mughniya fī l-Sukūt wa-Luzūm al-Buyūt*, edited by ʿAbd Allāh b. Yūsuf al-Judayʿ. Riyad: Dār al-ʿĀṣima.

Barbir, Karl. 1980. *Ottoman Rule in Damascus: 1708–1758*. Princeton, NJ: Princeton University Press.

Barbour, John D. 2004. *The Value of Solitude: The Ethics and Spirituality of Aloneness in Autobiography*. Charlottesville, VA: University of Virginia Press.

al-Bayhaqī, Aḥmad b. Ḥusayn. 2015. *Al-Zuhd al-Kabīr*, edited by Taqī l-Dīn al-Nadwī. Amman: Arwiqa.

Blecher, Joel. 2018. *Said the Prophet of God: Hadith Commentary across a Millenium*. Oakland, CA: University of California Press.

al-Bukhārī, Muḥammad b. Ismāʿīl. 1422 [2001]. *Al-Jāmiʿ al-Ṣaḥīḥ*, edited by Muḥammad Zuhayr b. Nāṣir al-Nāṣir, 9 vols. Beirut: Dār Ṭawq al-Najāt.

Butterworth, Charles. 2010. "Early Thought." In *A Companion to Muslim Ethics*, edited by Amyn B. Sajoo, 31–51. London: I.B. Tauris.

Camper, Martin. 2018. *Arguing over Texts: The Rhetoric of Interpretation*. Oxford: Oxford University Press.

Cohen, Ira J. 2016. *Solitary Action: Acting on our own in Everyday life*. Oxford: Oxford University Press.

Cuneo, Terence. 2014. "Moral Realism." In *The Bloomsbury Companion to Ethics*, edited by Christian Miller, 3–28. London: Bloomsbury.

Demiri, Lejla and Samuela Pagani. 2019. *Early Modern Trends in Islamic Theology*. Tübingen: Mohr Siebeck.

DeRoo, Neal and John P. Manoussakis. 2009. *Phenomenology and Eschatology: Not Yet in the Now*. Aldershot: Ashgate.

al-Farābī, Abū Naṣr. 1971. *Fuṣūl Muntazi'a*. Beirut: Dār al-Mashriq.

Feinberg, Joel. 2013. "Psychological Egoism." In *Ethical Theory: An Anthology*, edited by Russ Shafer-Landau, 2nd edition, 166–177. West Sussex: Blackwell Publishers.

Gadamer, Hans. 1989. *Truth and Method*, 2nd edition. London: Sheed and Ward.

Gianotti, Timothy J. 2015. "Toward a Muslim Theology of Interreligious Friendship." In *Friendship Across Religions: Theological Perspectives on Interreligious Friendship*, edited by Alon Goshen-Gottstein, 77–95. Lanham: Lexington Books.

Goldziher, Ignaz. 1888–1890. *Muhammedanische Studien*. Halle: Niemeyer.

Haddad, Gibril Fouad. 2017. "Quietism and End-time Reclusion in the Qur'ān and Ḥadīth: al-al-Nābulusī and His Book *Takmīl al-Nu'ūt*." *Islamic Sciences* 15(2): 91–124.

Ibn Abī l-Dunyā, Abū Bakr 'Abd Allāh b. Muḥammad b. 'Ubayd. 1997. *Al-'Uzla wa-l-Infirād*. Riyad: Dār al-Waṭan.

Ibn Bājja, Abū Bakr Muhammad b. Yahyā. 1978. *Tadbīr al-Mutawaḥḥid*, edited by Ma'n Ziyāda. Beirut: Dār al-Fikr.

Ibn al-Jawzī, 'Abd al-Raḥmān. 2011. *Ṣayd al-Khāṭir*. Mansoura: Dār al-Yaqīn.

Ibn Māja, Abū 'Abd Allāh. 2009. *Al-Sunan*, edited by Shu'ayb al-Arnā'ūṭ et al. Damascus: Dār al-Risāla al-'Ālamiyya.

Ibn Ḥanbal, Aḥmad. 1999. *Musnad al-Imām Aḥmad Ibn Ḥanbal*, edited by Shu'ayb al-Arnān'ūṭ et al. Beirut: Mu'assasat al-Risāla.

al-Jāḥiz, Abū 'Uthmān. 1906. "Tafḍīl al-Nuṭq 'Alā l-Ṣamt." In *Majmū'at al-Rasā'il: Ithna 'Ashara Risāla*, edited by Maḥmūd al-Sāsī al-Maghribī. Cairo: Matba'at al-Taqaddum.

Khalifa, Nouha. 2010. *Deliverance and Hardship in the Islamic Tradition: Theology and Spirituality in the Works of al-Tanūkhī*. London: I.B. Tauris.

Khan, Ruqayya Yasmine. 2008. *Self and Secrecy in Early Islam*. South Carolina: University of Carolina Press.

al-Khaṭṭābī, Abū Sulaymān Ḥamd b. Muḥammad. 1990. *Kitāb al-'Uzla*, edited by Abū 'Ubayda Mashhūr b. Ḥasan Āl Salmān. Damascus: Dār Ibn Kathīr.

Knysh, Alexander. 1999. *Islamic Mysticism: A Short History*. Brill: Leiden.

Landolt, H. 1977. "Khalwa." In *Encyclopaedia of Islam, Second Edition*, vol. 4, 990–991. DOI: 10.1163/1573-3912_islam_SIM_4178.

Leaman, Oliver. 1999. *Key Concepts in Eastern Philosophy*. London: Routledge.

Lee, Robert D. 2018. *Overcoming Tradition and Modernity: The Search for Islamic Authenticity*. London: Routledge.

McPherson, A.C. Kirstin. 2016. "The Secular Transformation of Pride and Humility in the Moral Philosophy of David Hume." PhD diss., Marquette University, Milwaukee, WI.

Mesoudi, Alex and Keith Jensen. 2012. "Culture and the Evolution of Human Sociality." In *The Oxford Handbook of Comparative Evolutionary Psychology*, edited by Jennifer Vonk and Todd K. Shackelford, 419–433. Oxford: Oxford University Press.

al-Mubārakpūrī, ʿAbd al-Raḥmān. 2011. *Tuḥfat al-Aḥwazī fī Sharḥ Jāmiʿ al-Tirmidhī*, 10 vols. Damascus: Dār al-Fayḥāʾ.

al-Muḥāsibī, al-Ḥārith. 1986. *Al-Waṣāyā*, edited by ʿAbd al-Qādir Aḥmad ʿAṭā. Beirut: Dār al-Kutub al-ʿIlmiyya.

Muslim b. al-Ḥajjāj. 1991. *Ṣaḥīḥ Muslim*, edited by Muḥammad Fuʾād ʿAbd al-Bāqī. Cairo: Dār Iḥyāʾ al-Kutub al-ʿArabiyya.

al-Nabhānī, Yūsuf. 1983. *Jāmiʿ Karāmāt al-Awliyāʾ*, 2 vols. Beirut: n.p.

al-Nābulusī, ʿAbd al-Ghanī. n.d. *Takmīl al-Nuʿūt fī Luzūm al-Buyūt*, MS Istanbul, Süleymaniye, Çelebi ʿAbd Allāh Effendi 385/40, fols. 356b–376a.

al-Nābulusī, ʿAbd al-Ghanī. 1995. *Ghāyat al-Maṭlūb fī Maḥabbat al-Maḥbūb*, edited by Samuela Pagani. Roma: Bardi.

al-Nābulusī, ʿAbd al-Ghanī. 1998. *Al-Muslimūn fī Zaman al-Fitan Kamā Akhbara al-Rasūl*, edited by Majdī b. Manṣūr Sayyid al-Shūra. Cairo: Maktabat al-Qāhira.

al-Nābulusī, ʿAbd al-Ghanī. 2010. *Wasāʾil al-Taḥqīq wa-Rasāʾil al-Tawfīq*, edited by Samer Akkach. Leiden: Brill.

al-Nābulusī, ʿAbd al-Ghanī. 2017. *The Virtues of Seclusion in Times of Confusion*, translated by Abdul Aziz Suraqah and foreword by Shadee Elmasry. Toronto: Ibriz Media.

Nurbaksh, Javed. 1988. *Sufism IV*, translated by William Chittick. London: Khaniqahi Nimatullahi Publisher.

Nussbaum, Martha. 2009. *Upheavals of Thought*. Cambridge: Cambridge University Press.

al-Qushayrī, Abū l-Qāsim ʿAbd al-Karīm b. Hawāzin. 2013. *Al-Risāla al-Qushayriyya*. Beirut: Dār al-Kutub al-ʿIlmiyya.

Picken, Gavin. 2010. *Spiritual Purification in Islam: The Life and Works of al-Ḥārith al-Muḥāsibī*. Abingdon: Routledge.

Preston, Jesse Lee, Erika Salomon and Ryan S. Ritter. 2014. "Religious Prosociality: Personal, Cognitive, and Social Factors." In *Religion, Personality, and Social Behaviour*, edited by Vassilis Saroglou, 149–169. New York: Psychology Press.

Radtke, Bernd and John O'Kane. 1996. *The Concept of Sainthood in Early Islamic Mysticism*. Surrey: Curzon Press.

Rafeq, Abdul-Karim. 2009. "Abd al-Ghani al-Nabulsi: Religious Tolerance and 'Arabness' in Ottoman Damascus." In *Transformed Landscapes: Essays on Palestine and the Middle East in Honor of Walid Khalidi*, edited by Camille Mansour and Leila Fawaz, 1–17. Cairo: The American University Press.

Ritter, Hellmut. 2003. *The Ocean of the Soul: Man, the World, and God in the Stories of Farīd Al-Dīn 'Aṭṭār*, translated by John O'Kane. Leiden: Brill.

Rocci, Giovanni. "Ethics in the Psyche's Individuating Development Towards the Self." In *The Moral Sense and its Foundational Significance: Self, Person, Historicity, Community: Phenomenological Praxeology and Psychiatry*, edited by Anna-Teresa Tymieniecka and Analecta Husserliana, 219–225. Dordrecht: Kluwer.

Rossi, Osvaldo. 1990. "Ethics and Subjectivity Today." In *The Moral Sense and Its Foundational Significance: Self, Person, Historicity, Community: Phenomenological Praxeology and Psychiatry*, edited by Anna-Teresa Tymieniecka and Analecta Husserliana, 107–110. Dordrecht: Kluwer.

Sainsbury, Mark R. 1996. "Concepts Without Boundaries." In *Vagueness: A Reader*, edited by Rosanna Keefe and Peter Smith, 186–205. Cambridge, MA: MIT Press.

al-Sariyy, Hannād. 1986. *Al-Zuhd*. Kuwait: Dār al-Khulafā'.

Shafir, Nir. 2019. "Moral Revolutions: The Politics of Piety in the Ottoman Empire Reimagined." *Comparative Studies in Society & History* 61(3): 595–623.

al-Shaybānī, al-Muʿāfā b. Ismāʿīl. 2011. *Uns al-Munqaṭiʿīn ilā ʿIbādat Rabb al-ʿĀlamīn*. Damascus: Dār Saʿd al-Dīn.

Shoshan, Boaz. 2004. *Poetics of Islamic Historiography: Deconstructing Tabari's History*. Leiden: Brill.

al-Sindī, Abū l-Ḥasan b. 'Abd al-Ḥādī. 2013. *Shurūḥ Sunan Ibn Māja*, 2 vols. Amman: Bayt al-Afkār al-Dawliyya.

Stocker, Michael. 1976. "The Schizophrenia of Modern Ethical Theories." *The Journal of Philosophy* 73(14): 453–466.

Suhrawardī, Shihāb al-Dīn 'Umar b. Muḥammad. 1891. *A Derwish Textbook from the 'Awārif al-Ma'ārif: Written in the Thirteenth Century*, translated by Wilberforce Clarke, London: The Octagon Press.

al-Tirmdhī, Abū 'Īsā. 1996. *Al-Jāmiʿ al-Kabīr*, edited by Bashshār 'Awwād Maʿrūf, Beirut: Dār al-Gharb al-Islāmī.

Von Schlegell Rosenow, Barbara. 1997. "Sufism in the Ottoman Arab World: Shaykh 'Abd al-Ghanī al-Nābulusī." PhD diss., University of California, Berkeley.

Yaldiz, Yunus. 2016. "The Afterlife in Mind: Piety and Renunciatory Practice in the 2nd/8th- and early 3rd/9th-Century Books of Renunciation (Kutub al-Zuhd)." PhD diss., Utrecht University.

Yazaki, Saeko. 2013. *Islamic Mysticism and Abu Talib Al-Makki: The Role of the Heart*. London: Routledge.

al-Zabīdī, Muḥammad b. al-Ḥusaynī. 2012. *Itḥāf al-Sāda al-Muttaqīn bi-Sharḥ Iḥyā' 'Ulūm al-Dīn*, 12 vols., 5th edition. Beirut: Dār al-Kutub al-'Ilmiyya.

CHAPTER 8

# The Ethical in the Transmission of Sunna

## *Rethinking the* ʿUlamāʾ-Quṣṣāṣ *Conflict*

*Safwan Amir*

## 1 Introduction

In a world of information-at-your-fingertips, the idea of transmitting knowledge from a pious individual to others, as seen in the Sunna's case, might seem regressive and antithetical. While contemporary knowledge practices are but numerous chains of signifiers producing a further number of contexts, the Islamic tradition has held on to a unique system that tries to maintain its link to the Prophet Muḥammad. What is the relevance of such hand-picking and fixation around establishing these links? How can a premodern method of knowledge transmission provide us with material to realise our dissonances in modern comprehension?

This chapter addresses early Islamic ethics and transmission through the premodern *ʿulamāʾ-quṣṣāṣ* dichotomy. I argue that the *qāṣṣ-ʿālim* (preacher-scholar) relationship was one of a methodological approach rather than conflict that triggered true and false traditions of knowledge. This can better be characterised as a large scale premodern *jadal* (argumentation) and *munāẓara* (debate) that took its gradual course within the Islamic tradition and was not specifically attuned to the operations of rupture or continuity as ascribed by contemporary historians. With the Prophetic tradition being a main site of contention for these two groups, I will first compare *ḥadīth* and *qiṣṣa* with an overarching idea of *sunan* in the background, then I look at that which is desired, in place of a telos, through the activities of the storyteller-preachers and *ḥadīth* scholars. The chapter moves on to elucidate the kind of selves (and *self-lessness*) the two groups cultivated and disciplined. This allows us to locate possible genealogies of the *isnād* and *matn* approach, shaped by the *muḥaddithūn*, and how the *ʿulamāʾ* came to privilege it. Finally, I will end with a suggestion on how to approach such dispersed categories in history without falling for continuity and rupture as the only way out.

Absence and presence are two interconnected themes that direct this chapter – be it mediums analysed or characters cast. Since storyteller-preachers

 | DOI:10.1163/9789004525931_010

are seen as marginal entities, and are extinct in later centuries, present scholarship has engaged sparsely with them. This chapter then draws attention to the exuberant life of the *qāṣṣ* and his indubitable role in the everyday ethics of Islam. The work is historical but does not entitle any specific period in the premodern, and rather seeks to contribute to anthropological debates around transmission and inculcation of ethics.

## 2 The Scholar Meets the Preacher: Tradition and Authenticity

This chapter begins with an intriguing account. Aḥmad Ibn Ḥanbal (d. 241/855), the revered Sunnī scholar, and his friend and *ḥadīth* transmitter Yaḥyā Ibn Maʿīn (d. 233/847) were in for a shock one day after the noon prayers. They heard a Baṣran *qāṣṣ* preaching:

> Aḥmad Ibn Ḥanbal and Yaḥyā Ibn Maʿīn once related to me, on the authority of ʿAbd al-Razzāq (d. 211/827), from Maʿmar (d. 153/770), from Qatāda (d. 117/735), from Anas (d. 93/712), that the Messenger of God is reported to have said: "He who says *lā ilāha illā Llāh* causes a bird to be created from every word, with the beak made of gold, and feathers of pearls …"
>
> JUYNBOLL 1983, 158–159

The *qāṣṣ* went on for an equivalent of twenty pages while the two scholars conferred among themselves if either had transmitted this *ḥadīth*. Testifying that neither had heard this narration till date, they signalled to the *qāṣṣ* after his session and enquired from whom he had learnt this *ḥadīth*. The *qāṣṣ* immediately replied,

> "Yaḥyā Ibn Maʿīn and Aḥmad Ibn Ḥanbal." Ibn Maʿīn said: "But I am Yaḥyā Ibn Maʿīn and this man here is Aḥmad Ibn Ḥanbal and we have never heard of this mentioned as a Prophetic tradition."
>
> JUYNBOLL 1983, 159

To this the *qāṣṣ* retorted "grinningly,"

> I have always heard Yaḥyā Ibn Maʿīn is stupid … As if there were in the whole world no other Yaḥyā's or Aḥmad's except you two! I have

> written down traditions from seventeen different people called Aḥmad Ibn Ḥanbal apart from this one here.
>
> JUYNBOLL 1983, 159[1]

This is a classic example of an academically studied encounter with a *qāṣṣ* (pl. *quṣṣāṣ*) in medieval Islamic literature.

The linear story of the storyteller, *qāṣṣ*, is not new to students of premodern Islam. It begins in the initial centuries, following the death of Prophet Muḥammad (d. 11/632), with the *qāṣṣ* or storyteller-*cum*-preacher seen as instrumental in spreading the tradition. Acting as a bricoleur, the *qāṣṣ* dons several religious odd-jobs that include, more frequently, narrating tales of an edifying nature, reciting Qurʾān (*qurrāʾ*), instructing, admonishing and exhorting (*wuʿʿāẓ*), as well as being transmitters of *sunan*, and, occasionally serving a s *qāḍī* (judge) and *khaṭīb* (Macdonald 1927; Goldziher 1971; Pellat 1976; ʿAthamina 1992; Armstrong 2017).

With a clientele that usually involved a large following of the masses, they were hastily concluded as "popular preachers" (Berkey 2001). Drawing ire of more well-trained *ʿulamāʾ* and *muḥaddithūn*,[2] the *qāṣṣ* were severely criticised and ridiculed for their exaggeration and lack of authenticity. The storytellers' tale, then, was bound to be a tragic one. The fall of the *qāṣṣ* was ensured by subsequent generations of *ʿulamāʾ* who saw to it that they put an end to the storyteller's lies (Halldén 2006; Firestone 2006). Few were roped in, and most were vilified. While the dominant position within academic scholarship has been to read this compelling story from the perspective of the *ʿulamāʾ* and *muḥaddithūn*, in descending linear time, few (Afsaruddin 2002) have been sympathetic to the *qāṣṣ* by showcasing their gradual loss in social standing to the *ʿulamāʾ*. However, what remains common in these two seemingly opposite standpoints is that the *qāṣṣ*'s hazy modes and vague means evolve into the *ʿālim*'s certain and coherent ones. The Baṣran *qāṣṣ* instance above highlights this very movement (and moment) of imprecision to a more concrete approach towards the Islamic tradition. By exhibiting and asserting what fabrications are, these discourses have also, inadvertently, enabled definitions of

1 Many modern academics cite this example showcasing premodern scholar's contempt for the preacher (see also Juynboll 1983, 158–159; Goldziher 1971, 151–152). The story was cited in Ibn ʿAsākir 1995, 65:27; al-Dhahabī 1985, 11:86; Ibn Ḥajar 2002, 1:315. Al-Dhahabī (d. 748/1348) said: "this is a weird story (*ḥikāya ʿajība*). Its narrator, [Ibrāhīm b. ʿAbd al-Wāḥid] al-Bakrī is not known to me. It might be forged by him." Ibn Ḥajar (d. 852/1449) also said: "I don't know him. He narrated unbelievable story (*ḥikāya munkara*). It might be forged by somebody else."

2 Primarily, my comparison is between the *muḥaddithūn* and *quṣṣaṣ*. I use the term *ʿulamāʾ* because in the end they privilege the *isnād* and *matn* form and method of the *ḥadīth* scholars.

the contours of truth within what came to be known as the Islamic tradition, and more importantly how one needs to go about labelling authenticity.[3]

The earlier example, however, can generate other possible readings besides typical insinuations. The Baṣran *qāṣṣ* appears to playfully engage the two scholars – challenging their certitude and critiquing their method. He is quick in his responses, uses the right amount of rhetoric, and leaves the scholars irresolute for a short period. We only get to learn bits of the preacher's content but can, undeniably, contend that the imaginative expanse being built-up was beautiful to the spectators' ears. The scholars are left dumbfounded and forced to leave without any comeback. It is also important to observe the interesting oral to written comparison the scholar makes when he equates the length of the preacher's utterance to a twenty-page entry (Goldziher 1971, 151). Apart from being a testimony to the fact that the *quṣṣāṣ* have left us with scant written evidence, we also catch glimpses of the rugged terrain in these mediums of transmission. It is accurate that influential premodern scholars have chastised storytellers.[4] Nevertheless, it goes unwarranted to state that this represented a major practice among scholars post third/ninth century. Nor does it justify the teleological premise that the *qāṣṣ* paved way for the *ʿulamāʾ*. What can be said, in the least, is that the *ʿālim* and *qāṣṣ* entered into contestations over practices now and then, but this did not define/limit their relationship.

## 3 *Ḥadīth* and *Qiṣṣa*: A Comparison of Sunna

Works of *ṭabaqāt* (Islamic biographical literature) help us understand the lives of scholars, as *ʿilm al-rijāl* (the study of *ḥadīth* transmitters/narrators) is an important criterion for discerning the validity of a *ḥadīth*. There are special biographical genres for *ḥadīth* transmitters (*ṭabaqāt al-muḥaddithīn*) and the same can be found for the *fuqahāʾ* (jurists), *quḍāt* (judges), Sufis, etc. However, there is a strong absence of *ṭabaqāt* works specifically revolving around the *quṣṣāṣ*. And yet, the *qāṣṣ* is mentioned across most *ṭabaqāt* and similar biographies in passing. While we have to leave the reasons for this particular omission for later sections, we can nevertheless begin by observing the material the scholars and storytellers undertook.

---

3 Before entertaining the idea that this work takes a Shahab Ahmed (2015) turn, I would like to maintain that my interests are exceedingly around how modern academia have engaged with such discourses, rather than showcase supposed internal contradictions within the tradition.

4 See, for example, Ibn al-Jawzī 1983; Ibn Taymiyya 1988; al-Suyūṭī 1974.

The origins of both the *ḥadīth* and *qiṣaṣ* lie in the *sunan*, and yet the Sunna itself was never a fixed category. The *sunan* (guidelines for exemplary conduct) were never the sole purview of Prophet Muḥammad, especially in the initial centuries after his death. This does not mean that the Prophet's mode of conduct was not ideal, or that the companions competed with the Prophet's Sunna, but that the earlier phase of Sunna in the Islamic tradition included conducts of the Prophet's companions as well (*athar*),[5] as there was no consensus on the use of terms like "*ḥadīth*" (Ansari 1972, 256). The companions, as well as people of particular cities (Medina, for instance), considered various aspects of Prophetic and non-prophetic modes of conduct as *sunan* out of their deep connection with the Prophet. Wael Hallaq locates the history of Sunna and distinguishes between "practice-based *sunan*" and literary *ḥadīth*, by elaborating on how the former was primarily transmitted by storytellers, while the latter found prominence after the proliferation of a class of mobile traditionalists by the end of the second/eighth century (Hallaq 2009, 39–43). Such practice-based Sunna has to be identified with the very living processes of early everyday Islam, and even though the proliferation of literary *ḥadīth* at the hands of these newly emergent traditionists gains primacy, the role of the *qāṣṣ* and his transmission of *sunan* does not reduce in any way. Though the literary and living can be said to coalesce and overlap in this era,[6] they do not have to eclipse each other. Let us focus on the two separately to understand the fine points with which they approached the Sunna.

*Ḥadīth* transmitters can be cited as some of the first to develop the *isnād* and *matn* (source and content) form. Thus, the entirety of any *ḥadīth* would include a set of proper names (*kunya*, nicknames, regional affiliations would also be included) to indicate the *sanad* that has been followed in capturing a particular Prophetic tradition. Such traditions are usually actions and sayings of the Prophet, as recounted by his companions, and these make up the *matn* (main content), the primary text within quotes. These narrations can also be followed by commentaries made by various scholars across time and space. Memory and religiosity (ethicality rather) are primary considerations that *ḥadīth* transmitters have to demonstrate for the validity of *ḥadīth*. While *uṣūl al-ḥadīth* has many ways of dealing with a *ḥadīth* and its transmitter, I am interested in these fundamental ones because it gives us a sense of the basic

5 Literally means "trace." They are modes of conduct as well and can include artefacts related to the Prophet and his Companions.

6 The best example is to think of how the Qur'ān was never considered as learnt but as embodied. See Rudolph Ware (2014) for "embodiment as epistemology." More on this in subsequent sections.

premises with which the scholar engages in such activities. Even within the domains of memory, the method was made further rigorous by the inclusion of only that Sunna that could be recollected verbatim. Contrarily, in a famous instance, while al-Ḥasan al-Baṣrī (d. 110/728) knew a Prophetic Sunna regarding a theological position, he was unable to give a "verbal transmission" attesting the same (Hallaq 1997, 14). Can the religiosity/ethicality of a noted *tābiʿī* (companion of the Companions) like al-Baṣrī be contested? Or does memory dictate the certainty of a *sunna*? How can such Sunna find life under such strenuous measures? One way is to go by the standards set by the *muḥaddithīn* themselves and consider the varying degrees of *ḍaʿīf* (weak), *maqbūl* (acceptable), *ḥasan* (good), and *ṣaḥīḥ* (authentic) *ḥadīth*. And yet, this approach is only attained after a long and arduous procedure of sieving that gave these Sunna their respective degrees. It is perhaps for this reason that Louis Massignon, the French scholar of Islam, said:

> If the *muḥaddithīn* had succeeded in imposing their method and eliminating all *ḥadīth* with apocryphal *isnād* from the "authentic" collections, believers would now have only dried meat to feed meditation: a few prescriptions concerned only with hygiene and civility, sandal cleaning, and the right wood for making toothpicks.
>
> MASSIGNON 1997, 85–86

What happens to the remaining *sunan*? Are they never to be actualised in the Islamic tradition?

The *quṣṣāṣ* place us in a unique predicament given that they are hardly studied in any relevant manner, especially regarding how they engaged ethically or their transmission of Sunna. The fact that focus has never been on the *qāṣṣ*, even at the minimal level of a storyteller, is indicative of an issue of obsession around *who wrote* over *who spoke*. Much of the *qiṣaṣ* that are available from early Islam are anonymous entries, repetitions, and a combination of various *ḥikāyāt* (stories). Lyall Armstrong writes:

> The term *qiṣṣa* (pl. *qiṣaṣ*) is more problematic; "story" does not adequately encompass the breadth of the term … [A] *qiṣṣa*, during the period of time in question, seems to indicate any general piece of instruction given by a *qāṣṣ* [preacher/storyteller] … The term incorporates number of different types of instruction, including actual stories, verses of poetry, legal rulings, *ḥadīth*, as well as martial statements given on the field of battle.
>
> ARMSTRONG 2017, 9

My concern is not with the written author or the original narrator, but with those who related and passed on the *qiṣṣa* generation after generation. These "storytellers" are never mentioned or given their due because western scholars have indulged in a larger historian's disdain for the storyteller in studies on the Islamic tradition. In doing so, they follow the legacy of historians like John Wansbrough (1977) and Patricia Crone (1987) who saw the storyteller with suspicion and as a source of inauthenticity in the tradition (Armstrong 2017, 81). This absence and dearth of sources then imply that we must look at other places for answers. Concentrating on the root *q-ṣ-ṣ*, we learn from Arabic lexicons (especially Ibn Manẓūr's (d. 711/1311) *Lisān al-ʿArab* ("The Tongue of the Arabs")), from the eighth/fourteenth century onwards, that the words "trace," "echo," and "footprint" are equally important when locating the multiple definitions of the term "*qāṣṣ*."[7] A shared quality of traces, footprints, and echoes is that they do not have an ever-active presence, and yet their absence is never fully realised. Derrida (d. 2004) puts it succinctly:

> Trace is not a presence but is rather the simulacrum of a presence that dislocates, displaces, and refers beyond itself. The trace has, properly speaking, no place, for effacement belongs to the very structure of the trace.
>
> DERRIDA 1973, 156

This peculiar potential of the term *qāṣṣ* needs to be read as a built-in mechanism that challenges standard mnemonic practices and mediums.

To illustrate the same, let us look at the narrative strategies employed by the *qāṣṣ* in their *qiṣaṣ*. Stories (*qiṣaṣ*) did not take the prominent *isnād* and *matn* form, but the storyteller (*qāṣṣ*) took the Prophet Muḥammad as their model (Abbott 1967, 14). The *quṣṣāṣ* played a major role in extending the Prophetic imagination in the initial centuries after his death. The form of the *qiṣṣa* would generally include narratives of and around the Prophet. The Prophet would appear in various ways – in dreams or in other spatio-temporalities (*al-isrāʾ wa-l-miʿrāj* being an example), or, simply, in the Ḥijāz. There would be an added local flavour to these stories – generally a story of how the ruler of the locale embraced Islam and how he felt intense love for the Prophet. They would also include the *ṣaḥāba* (Companions), *tābiʿūn* (Companions' companion), and other well-known Islamic figures. Tellings of *qiṣaṣ al-anbiyāʾ* included stories of other Prophets and these would usually lead to a story of the Prophet Muḥammad. Emphasis and inclination always tend to the Prophet

7 To cut, narrate, and shear are other meanings.

and this is the widespread rule of the *qiṣṣa*. Reception is of key importance here and the audience enters into the world of the storyteller (Berkey 2001, 43–52; Armstrong 2017, 161–163).

The *qāṣṣ* does not rely much on memory and improvises most of the time. These improvisations were often called *bidʿa* (innovations) and admonished by scholars. An interesting example is the reason for the ninth/fifteenth century scholar al-Suyūṭī (d. 911/1505) writing *Taḥdhīr al-Khawāṣṣ min Akadhīb al-Quṣṣāṣ* ("A Warning to the Retinue against the Lies of the Storytellers"). The grand *ʿālim* says that he had come across a *qāṣṣ* (preacher/storyteller) who was transmitting a Prophetic Sunna without verifying or attributing it to the "right sources." The preacher retorted to this blatant criticism by saying, "I will verify them with the people!" and the audience who were witness to al-Suyūṭī's admonishing turned against the *ʿālim* and threatened to stone him (Berkey 2003, 255–256). We have two interconnected points to reflect on: one, an organic relationship between the larger public (the masses) and the *qāṣṣ* as seen in this instance, and second, the concept of "verifying with the people." When the preacher says that he derives his verification from the people, he is not implying a popular idea of religion or subscribing to a status of the popular. The *qāṣṣ* observes the community he is attached to, interacts with people, is knowledgeable about their issues, spends time with them, is privy to their moral fibre, recognises the various classes, gives advice when sought, and prays for them.[8] It is for this reason that Ibn al-Jawzī (d. 597/1201) notes:

> The common people ... rarely meet a jurist, so they discuss things with [the preacher]. The preacher is like the trainer of animals, who educates them, reforms them and refines them.
>
> BERKEY 2001, 24

Coming back to the genre of the *qiṣṣa*, we learn from al-Khāzin (d. 741/1340) that a *ḥikāya* (story) is called a *qiṣṣa* because the "narrator releases the story bit by bit" (bin Tyeer 2016, 12; see also al-Khāzin 2004, 2:511). This releasing in piecemeal is deliberate and is based on the depth and breadth of knowledge the audience is accustomed to. The *qāṣṣ* is careful not to overdo the amount of preaching and storytelling, and is highly receptive to the moods and sentiments of the audience. In such instances, the *qāṣṣ* has to then "verify" with

---

8 Ideally, the *qāḍī*, should intimately know the society where he is placed or know ethically sound people from the society who have knowledge in these matters. It comes as no surprise that the *quḍāt* and *quṣṣāṣ* were one and the same for a brief time in Islamic history. It is highly possible that those whom the *qāḍī* sought for intimate social knowledge were the *qāṣṣ*.

the people as to what they want and how well they can be instructed and narrated appropriate tales worthy of that period. These could vary from specific Islamic months, impending war, water scarcity, famine, extensive *fitna*, severe debt, and social crises to numerous everyday personal issues. In all these cases, the *qāṣṣ* would narrate and mention the Prophet, instil hope, and bring about unity among people. In short, these were not mere *qiṣaṣ* but *aḥsan al-qaṣaṣ* (the best of stories) as the fifth/eleventh-century exegete and mystic al-Qushayrī (d. 465/1074) maintains – such *qiṣaṣ* would mention the beloved Prophet Muḥammad and his beloveds, usually contain imitable and inspiring "ideal behaviour," and are not "explicitly didactic (command/forbid)" as these could induce "feelings that insinuate shortcomings" (bin Tyeer 2016, 12; see also al-Qushayrī 2000, 2:166–167).

## 4 Medium beyond Absence and Presence

In one of his earlier works, Jacques Derrida rereads the origin myth of writing through Plato (d. 347 BCE). He shows how Western philosophy privileges speech over writing since it was believed that the latter was a mere representation of higher forms of truth and presence (Derrida 1981). Muslim societies privilege a "culturally specific logocentrism," in the Derridean sense, of the spoken word via recitation (both textually and from oral/rote memory) (Messick 1993, 25). The dichotomy between the written and spoken word can be seen right from the beginning of Islam, with various close associates and teacher-student ties diverging on this question (Afsaruddin 2002, 20). And yet, our previous discussion on the *quṣṣāṣ* and their trace-based characteristics, points to different modalities of absence/presence from the western one. Regarding a mark or trace, Derrida believes that absence is key to communication, and words can be grafted onto other contexts which results in endless chains of signifiers, divorced from its origins and a metaphysics of presence (Derrida 1982). It is crucial to locate Derrida's idea of absence/presence in more concrete terms. His commentary on communication and transmission of ideas *vis-à-vis* absence is an apt representation of the conditions with which modernity moves about. Rather than the mere breakdown of authority or specific sites of dissemination, absence involves the blurring of ethical contours that were in place.

I propose reading Derrida's transformation of a metaphysics of presence to an ontology of absence as an insightful reading of the very shift from premodern knowledge practices (like the ones seen in the Sunna) to a modern-day information explosion. While the written and oral came to be identified as modes that changed due to its explicit nature, the ethical has often gone unrecognised as the larger site for transformations. Derrida's re-reading of the origin myth of writing in Plato is crucially an attempt to showcase the ethical value at stake in the written and oral. The various Gods involved in this reading are not tropes to give an essential Greek flavour but attempts to provide metaphors to the deep shifts that are studied and witnessed by Derrida.

In this chapter, I invoke the Derridean trace only because there are no clear concepts of absence and presence in an immediately available language of Islam.[9] In a different spatio-temporal context, the *ḥadīth*, as chains of transmission that harbour on pious individuals throughout the premodern, allowed for some kind of presence.[10] This can be seen as late as al-Suyūṭī who wrote *Kitāb al-Farq Bayna al-Muṣannif wa-l-Sāriq* ("Book on the Difference Between the Compiler and the Thief") to expose another *ʿālim*'s "misdoings" (Abdel-Ghaffar 2018). The latter's crime was that he had not attributed a particular work to al-Suyūṭī. The work in question is not one that al-Suyūṭī composed himself, rather his labour was in organising, gathering, and ordering narrated accounts of the Prophet. This book is "a tissue of quotations" and al-Suyūṭī believed that proper attribution to the one who found them, gathered them from a variety of sources, and ensured their authenticity is essential to respect the effort put in to make the book's knowledge available (Abdel-Ghaffar 2018). The book is not al-Suyūṭī's words and yet the kind of attribution that he seeks is one of presence or harbouring around pious individuals who could authorise the content within. Al-Suyūṭī's concerns, almost like a premonition, also give us a sense of the world that was about to emerge (early modernity/colonialism) – a strong threat to both knowledge and ethics wherein it could be communicated in absence. Thus, we learn that the *ʿulamāʾ* were not necessarily attacking the *quṣṣāṣ* alone but were wary of an impending approach to knowledge and ethics, and it was the realm of practices that they sought to redress.

All the same, what did presence and absence mean to the *qāṣṣ* and his followers? It can be noted that various *qiṣaṣ* were translated into the written format at the hands of author-jurists and scholars who attended their sessions

9 Without doubt, *fanāʾ* might be one. However, the term has been so closely associated with the mystical that reimagining it, or working through its standardised meaning, might be difficult.

10 "Allowed" in the past tense, because *ḥadīth* and other Prophetic sayings are almost always used in the present, out of context, or contexts are given to them when people use them for various purposes, including rhetoric and polemics, in their lives. Modernity has made it possible to by-pass the pious individuals they usually were harboured around. "So and so" reports "such and such" is only important for the text and content that is iterable and graftable to new contexts.

in the sixth/twelfth century, and onwards. People and their *qāṣṣ*, nonetheless, do not seem interested in this transitional phase. If anything, it has probably only been of application for later day historians. To advance the question we have set for ourselves at the beginning of this section, it is pertinent to tap into multiple potentials of the trace within the *qāṣṣ*.

The legendary tale of Abū Ḥāmid al-Ghazālī (d. 505/1111) and the marauders give us a starting point to think of the diverging ways in which presence/absence plays in an Islamic setting. The story goes that a group of raiders stopped al-Ghazālī's caravan and robbed him of his most prised possession – numerous books he had written, collated, and held close to heart. A desperate al-Ghazālī tells the chief raider to take away his possessions except for his cherished books. To this the chief retorts that if al-Ghazālī requires the presence of these books then the scholar has not benefited from studying them (Macdonald 1899, 76). This leaves the great *ʿālim* in deep reflection and initiates his second phase of heightened truth-seeking. The thief is not coincidental here, just like nothing else is in the Islamic tradition. His statements are not mere statements but are quite similar to those of the *qāṣṣ*. They are effective and powerful. They hit exactly where they are supposed to and *Imām* al-Ghazālī undergoes a thorough transformation thereafter. I am not suggesting that the thief is a *qāṣṣ* in disguise. Rather, the potential of the verb "*qāṣṣ*" can only be found in such extreme or unusual instances. The thief is interesting because, in his act of thievery, he is also advising (*naṣīḥa*) al-Ghazālī. The advice is also not a direct statement issued to al-Ghazālī, which is quite similar to the edifying content of the *qiṣaṣ*. He is not commanded to enjoin right or forbid wrong (*al-amr bi-l-maʿrūf wa-l-nahy ʿan al-munkar*).[11] And yet, the nature of this transformation is an ethical one.

In an important essay on the category of *maʿrūf*, Kevin Reinhart comments that ethical content and reflection must be found outside the Qurʾān in relation to changing environments (Reinhart 2017). He also suggests that solutions to "socially fraught situations" (especially those that concern the micro doings of people) that require Muslims to enact *maʿrūf* cannot be directly found in the Qurʾān. Reinhart's premise is based on the closing of tradition in the early centuries of Islam and postulates that people in the present end up distorting the

11 While I agree that *maʿrūf* can include lots of possibilities beyond a fixed category of "good," my case is against those who try to read Islam's entire ethical content through a shallow rendition of *al-amr bi-l-maʿrūf wa-l-nahy ʿan al-munkar*.

Qur'ān, a debate that I will not enter into.[12] Reinhart, nevertheless, mentions in passing that such social situations demand "tact," and "creative openness," and these are "qualities" that the "*Sīra* emphatically attributes the Prophet himself" with (Reinhart 2017, 67). The essay works towards the scripture with an overt presence, privileging the written, and yet, it cannot do this without mentioning (even in passing) an aspect that he considers to be absent – the Prophet's unique life. What the scholarly analysis fails to do is take up this crucial aspect of the *sīra* when it comes to dealing with *maʿrūf*, ethics, and the Qur'ān itself. This could stem from modern scholarship that presumes law and ethics as confused in the Sharīʿa, or a predominant focus on the textual without bringing out their deeply embodied characteristics. The human body is disciplined to bring about necessary ends, with the ethical being an important one.

In his exceptionally brilliant ethnography, Rudolph Ware examines Qur'ān schools in Africa to show that the Qur'ān and knowledge that emanates from it is not learnt, but, rather, embodied.[13] The Prophet, simply, is the walking Qur'ān, while the *ḥadīth* cannot be treated as scripture but "are best understood as historical traces of normative practice that can also be known through chains of embodied transmission" (Ware 2014, 13). The medium then is not about written or oral, but about the very person who transmits the Prophetic Sunna.

If so, ethics and *maʿrūf* (and the diverse possibilities the term offers) need to be understood through the ways in which they are actualised through the body rather than consider them as a mental process of choices to be found in quotes or texts.[14]

But how do we understand this embodiment in the case of the *qāṣṣ*? How do we think of the *qāṣṣ* as a medium beyond absence and presence in the usual Western philosophical sense? al-Qushayrī cites Abū ʿAlī l-Thaqafī (d. 328/940) in his *Risāla* ("Epistle") to say:

---

12 For more on the closing of the gate tradition and *ijtihād*, see Hallaq 1984. For more on the modern construction of the Muslim subject *vis-à-vis* fundamentalism, see Mamdani 2004.

13 The idea of habitus is relevant here while thinking of knowledge, bodies, and their intimate connections. Habitus are those aspects of tradition that are effective, learnt, and acquired by the body through transmission which includes essentially *oral*, imitative, and repetitions among others (Mauss 1973; 2006). Ibn Khaldūn (d. 808/1406) theorised the concept of "*malaka*" which can be said to be a forerunner of the concept of habitus (Messick 1993, 261).

14 This is not to return to the debate between "lived" and "textual" Islam, but to look at the very nature of tradition as primarily embodied discourses (Asad 2015).

> If someone could absorb all the sciences … he would still be unable to attain the rank of the real men (*lā yablughu mablagha al-rijāl*) unless he engages … in exercises under the supervision of a master (*shaykh*), religious leader (*imām*) or a sincere preacher (*mu'addib nāṣiḥ*).
>
> AL-QUSHAYRĪ 2007, 63[15]

This move beyond the usual sciences in the attainment of higher degrees of being is characterised by exercising on the self with the help of a set of experts. That the sciences alone could not get one to a higher degree of piety or closeness with his Lord is stressed here. Thus, we come to realise an aspect of knowledge through the potential of the trace. It is to such experts and exercises that we need to turn to realise what and who the storyteller-preacher is. The *quṣṣāṣ* as a medium beyond the oral, written, presence, and absence point to their trajectory as ethical repositories.

## 5 Self and Self-Lessness

Let us focus on this bodily aspect of ethics in detail. As we have seen in the previous section, the one who moves beyond nominal knowledge and sciences makes use of assistance from particular experts to attain the "rank of real men." But, how does such assistance work out? One of the standard ways in which internalisation of ethics is understood is via what Foucault has given currency to – "technologies of the self." However, the subject does not transform themselves on their own in all scenarios. They avail "*the help of others*" to orient their "own bodies and souls, thoughts, conduct, and way of being" to attain particular states of living (Foucault 1988, 18; 1997, emphasis added). Within an Islamic context, especially picked up by the anthropology of Islam, such operations on the self (and soul) have been studied in detail to show how the body becomes a site for the cultivation of virtues and discouraging of vices as defined by the tradition (Asad 2003; Mahmood 2005; Hallaq 2013).

What interests me are these "others" who "help" people with their desired ethical practices and states of living. What kind of disciplining do they go through to ensure this service? There is literature available on how the *fuqahā'*, *'ulamā'*, and Sufis go through disciplinary training, and yet, as indicated earlier, given the kind of attitude historians have taken towards the *quṣṣāṣ*, the

15 Whether al-Ghazālī's thief was "*mu'addib*" is, nevertheless, contested. We do, however, know through this very *Risāla*, that thieving marauders can undergo events which set deep transformations in motion (al-Qushayrī 2007, 18, 390).

question of internalisation and pedagogic exercises can hardly be found even among those who studied the various facets of the storyteller-preacher. To reach this point of what went into training the *qāṣṣ*, we are forced to look for answers elsewhere again. We learn from multiple sources that preachers were generally associated with or mentioned alongside *zuhd* in premodern Islam (al-Qushayrī 2007, 37–38; Massignon 1997, 112–115; Berkey 2001, 50–53; Afsaruddin 2007, 142). The concept of *zuhd* is a complex one to explain predominantly due to the easy translation in "asceticism" that it receives. While numerous premodern scholars have defined and thought about this in detail, I will (due to my limitations) merely term it here as "moving away from the self." Controlling the self or *nafs* is a common trope in the Islamic tradition,[16] and it comes as no surprise that the *quṣṣāṣ* took it up as an important component of their work while preaching and narrating.[17]

Exploring the subtle details of preaching led me to locate a few significant roles that the storyteller-preacher engaged in. Healing in its multiple dimensions happened to be a role that the *quṣṣāṣ* took up, or had to pick up, given the intimate nature of their relationship with the society they were placed in or visiting, as mentioned earlier. A couple of verses composed, as late as the ninth/fifteenth century, in honour of a preacher is illuminating here:

> Our imam preached [*waʿaẓa*] to mankind – the eloquent man who poured out the sciences like an ocean filled to overflowing and healed hearts with his knowledge and his preaching for only the preaching of a righteous man [*ṣāliḥ*] can heal.
>
> BERKEY 2001, 39

"Healing hearts" can be said to have a spiritual angle to it.[18] However, the heart is also about the body – a body that is at once individual and social.[19] The

16 The *nafs* is again differentiated into many types and is beyond the scope of this chapter. *Imām* al-Ghazālī's works have influenced much scholarship to this day on this subject.

17 A good example is *Qiṣṣat Shakarwatī Farmāḍ* or "Tale of the Great Chera King" (Kugle and Margariti 2017, 362) where the *qāṣṣ* includes a separate prayer seeking features of *zuhd*, and pushes the audience to think and reflect beyond their selves.

18 Which is not to divide the spiritual from other aspects of life. Rather, my point is to extend this argument alone.

19 A famous *ṣaḥīḥ ḥadīth* goes like this: "You see the believers as regards their being merciful among themselves, showing love among themselves and being kind among themselves, resembling one body, so that, if any part of the body is not well then the whole body shares the sleeplessness (insomnia) and fever with it." Al-Bukhārī 1997, 8:36: *Kitāb al-Adab* ("Book of Good Manners"), *Bāb Raḥmat al-Nās wa-l-Bahāʾim* ("Chapter on Being Merciful to the People and Animals").

*qāṣṣ* with his intimate approach to people allows for not merely an advisory or counseling relationship, but one where he is in the centre of things. A deeply grounded kind of *ḥikma* (wisdom) arises from such intimacy. This is an organic relationship and needs to be addressed and read in that manner. By interacting and intervening in social issues that take the breadth and expanse of day to day problems, family complications, bodily ailments, mental issues, the *qāṣṣ* attempts solutions. *Ḥikma* now expands in prospect and we get to see multiple meanings of the concept in play. There is a sense of signifying "wisdom" which is also about holding things in equilibrium and harmony. The body (social and individual) needs to be healed to maintain its equilibrium. The *qāṣṣ* would initially diagnose a problem and try to come to a point that attempts to balance issues. This can be found in the case of a heated argument between two families where the *qāṣṣ* would play the role of a moderator and try to ease the tension by alluding to simple examples or sayings. This moderator role can be found among many learned men, but the *qāṣṣ* stands out for uniquely submitting themself to this particular role. Thus, the *zuhd* that they engage in can be seen to derive from moving away from their selves in the service of other-selves. I term this as technologies of self-lessness.

But, we are still not clear on the exact nature of this pedagogical training that the *qāṣṣ* enters into. How does one discipline the self to move away from the self? A point that goes hand-in-hand with this is the anonymous nature of the *qiṣaṣ* that the storyteller-preacher-*ḥakīm* (wiseman) entertains the society with. Why do they remain anonymous when we have seen scholars, like al-Suyūṭī, take strong positions on attributing and referencing people? Why have the *qāṣṣ* remained anonymous to the extent that there are no specific *ṭabaqāt* that discuss them as their primary topic? Humility is an overarching concept of *zuhd* and is perhaps the most common among all who have practiced self-lessness (al-Qushayrī 2007, 134–138). Thus, anonymity was part of the humility that the *zāhid-qāṣṣ* cultivated which led them to stay unnamed, care less for titles or labels, and, at times, forget their designations.

It is important to take this point in direct comparison with that of the *ʿālim*, not to privilege a dichotomy, but to understand the divergent ways in which selves can also be thought of.[20] One primary goal in a fast-changing world, that the scholars had rightly anticipated throughout – the idea of ensuring proper attribution, is also part of moving away from this world and still being

20 I do not want to engage with the self in terms of a telos because a set of ethical practices only lead to another or affirm/better the ongoing ones. Thus, to read the disciplining of selves as aimed only for the next world can limit the potential of thinking around cultivation of ethical selves.

remembered and prayed for. Al-Suyūṭī's purpose in writing *al-Farq* is also to ensure this very aspect of life and afterlife (Abdel-Ghaffar 2018). As part of cultivating humility and other virtues, the *qāṣṣ* went about preaching and narrating without naming themselves but would often name others. By attributing others – fictitiously and genuinely – they were not entering into the realm of what constitutes honesty/dishonesty, but were ensuring that one of the goals of the scholar lives on. It is this kind of service that needs to be thought of when we take up narratives like that of Ibn Ḥanbal and Yaḥyā Ibn Maʿīn which we saw in the beginning. Thus, the grin that appears on the Baṣran *qāṣṣ* needs to be rethought through what the Prophet taught: "*smile*, it's Sunna."[21]

## 6 Transmission and Development

Having learnt the divergent approaches to disciplining the self, we are now left with the question of transmission, itself. Once again, the lives of the *ʿulamāʾ* and *quṣṣāṣ* need to be read as intertwined if we are to unearth the ways in which transmission took place among the *qāṣṣ*. We are aware of the presence of scholars in various *qāṣṣ* sessions – *imām* al-Ghazālī being quintessential here (Berkey 2001, 53). Easy deductions allow us to say with some clarity that preachers attended other preaching sessions. This is seen through numerous renditions of the same story in several *qiṣaṣ* – few characters and a basic narrative stand while additions play out now and then. A storyteller follows another storyteller only to the extent where the fundamentals of the story are intact. The rest is left to what has been accused as innovation/imagination (*bidʿa*).

Let us focus on this imaginative aspect of such "accretions." While charges against the *quṣṣāṣ* are that of giving free rein to people's imaginations, the counter can also be claimed. By being highly performative and moving beyond ordinary conventions of *lisān* (linguistic abilities),[22] the world that the storyteller-preacher presents are minutely detailed. This richness in description can be compared to the Geertzian "thick description," for a lack of a better analogy.[23] The ethnographer utilises this method to describe the field in

21 Various instances of the Prophet smiling are commonplace in all major *ḥadīth* sources. "Your smiling in the face of your brother is charity (*ṣadaqa*), commanding good and forbidding evil is charity …" Al-Tirmidhī 2007, 4:62: *Kitāb Abwāb al-Birr wa-l-Ṣila* ("Book on Righteousness and Maintaining Good Relations With Relatives"), *Bāb Mā Jāʾa fī Ṣanāʾiʿ al-Maʿrūf* ("Chapter on What Has Been Related about Various Kinds of Good Deeds").

22 On a detailed engagement of the *qāṣṣ* with *lisān*, please refer to Armstrong (2017, 157–159).

23 Clifford Geertz (d. 2006) is an anthropologist of fame for developing the ethnographic method of "thick description" which is still used and taught in the discipline of

detail – taking in every aspect, big or small, a wink or a fight, while analysing the various subjective positions and meanings that can be generated – the same can be said of the storyteller. The "twenty-page" equivalency that the writer imputes to the Baṣran *qāṣṣ*' preaching in the initial example can be understood as a kind of thick description. We get to learn only the introductory bit and are left to imagine what may have followed. However, the storyteller's audience is enthralled by the kind of "thick description" they are privy to. In short, the *qāṣṣ* steers the imagination of the audience and limits their capacity to do so on their own. Perhaps a *ḥadīth*, in contrast, with its short and crisp layout might evoke an untethered imagination in the contemporary era.

As the *qāṣṣ* were ethical repositories, a point we have delved in detail in earlier sections, it can also be safe to add that the imaginative they encouraged via these "thick descriptions" was well within the boundaries of the ethical. In a way, if the *ʿulamāʾ* were attentive to scrupulousness in sources, the *quṣṣāṣ* can be said to have shown scrupulousness in the daily lives of the people around them. This is not to say that the *ʿulamāʾ* were not careful of their outward behaviour, but it can be said that their over emphasis on texts might have kept them aloof from the laity. The *qāṣṣ*, on the other hand, derived their sources from other ethically sound *qāṣṣ* (quite similar to the *muḥaddithūn*). The only difference happens to be their diverging approaches to presence and absence on a longer duration. The *qāṣṣ* are aware that the *qiṣaṣ* have been transmitted through a kind of presence that is almost-ever absent, while the *ʿulamāʾ* are wary of losing an ongoing presence within the tradition.

To further this argument, it is necessary to recognise the kind of transformation the *qāṣṣ* went about themselves. This will also partially answer questions on the public nature of their preaching and the idea of public religion. The evolution of the *quṣṣāṣ* is to be read along lines with the evolution of the guild system post the fourth/tenth century. The close association of the *qāṣṣ* with the guilds provide us some direction as to how transmission itself was undertaken. Association with a guild was the only credential to possessing knowledge and later being able to transmit it (Makdisi 1993, 377). However, associating with guilds would also mean opening up the category of the storyteller to include other vocations – that of the blacksmith or the barber or any occupation that would ensure humility while staying mobile.

---

anthropology (Geertz 1973). However, subsequent anthropologists have critiqued the method for being ahistorical and limiting the idea of "religion," see Asad (1993), especially chapter one. The analogy here is strictly to describe the lengths to which the storyteller goes into describing a narrative.

The *isnād* and *matn* approach has been the major site of methodology in most contemporary scholarship on Islam. But, once again, it should be noted that during the premodern period it was a matter only for those who were concerned about it. Or rather, to put the same idea in another way – fixating around absence and presence in terms of authority/authenticity was not the concern of all scholars. While many modern scholars are quick in pointing to "political" issues, especially that of the Kharijīs, as the reason for obsessing around authenticity (Juynboll 1983), we have already seen that the ethical can be equally important. However, we have hardly been able to think of the context in which the ethical has been placed by and for the scholar. Reception might give us a faint idea in this regard. Scholarly works were read, copied, transmitted, and memorised by a group that, though spread across time and space, were overtly beginning to identify themselves as one. Their interlocutors, and quite often concerns, were not the people or the larger masses directly. The *qāṣṣ*, on the other hand, was one among the people, their audience was the common mass, and the society they were placed in were their interlocutors. By this comparison, the aim has been to suggest that the idea of the ethical when it comes to scrupulousness need not be the same for the *ʿulamāʾ* and others. When we approach the *isnād* and *matn* method in this fashion, we need to admit that it was more a scholarly engagement among a few, rather than a methodology to approaching Islam as a whole, till at least the tenth/sixteenth century.

But the question remains how did we, in modern academia, come to privilege the *isnād* and *matn* approach as the only one? I believe the issue stems from how we have looked at the concept of *trust* itself. If anything, our entire argument till now shows that the dialectic between the *ʿulamāʾ* and *quṣṣāṣ* has been based on various ideas that take the breadth and length of methodology, approach, and sources but not overarchingly around trust. How people came to trust their peer in the premodern has nothing to do with how contemporary scholarship has come to trust and obsess around positivist facts and phenomena.

## 7 Conclusion

Rather than summarising what has been done in this chapter, I would like to conclude by suggesting that reading premodern Islam through the historical methods of both conflict/rupture and continuity need not be the only ways in which the past needs to be studied. While they do make for important analyses, one is left wondering whether our privileging of such binary methods can explain and expand the scope of matters that have deeper non-material underpinnings.[24] Rather than seeing the *qāṣṣ* and *ʿālim* (preacher-scholar) relation as one of conflict that spurred separate traditions of knowledge, I have tried to argue that the issue was one of a methodological approach to knowledge itself. This chapter should not be read as overemphasising the scholar versus preacher-storyteller theme to reimpose a binary, but to recognise how important the scholar is to any historical understanding of knowledge in the Islamic tradition. It is through a comparison with the scholar that the storyteller's method can be traced and closely read.

Further their diverging methods of transmission also converge at many junctures, and hence they need not be seen as drastically in opposition to one another. They were not in competition but were interested in maintaining and propagating their approach (and the subsequent chains of transmission) as the best/unique one for their varied reasons. This can better be characterised as a large scale premodern *jadal* (argumentation) and *munāẓara* (debate) that took a gradual course over time within the Islamic tradition and was not specifically attuned to the operations of rupture or continuity as ascribed by historians. Or, this can be thought in terms of how learned members of the society would balance practices that stretched between overt-piety and extreme laxity. *Ḥikma* (wisdom) would be sought in these cases to, then, induce a new set of dialectics in place. While the *ʿulamāʾ* did come to represent all walks of engagement with knowledge in the Islamic world, knowledge itself came to be defined by historians within the ambit of "religion."

The history of the *quṣṣāṣ* is a way to initiate discussion into preconceived notions of what knowledge meant, how they were authorised, and in what ways people responded to them. It also attempts to think of the ethical beyond literal scriptures and manifest in pious individuals who walked across the length and breadth of the premodern world, imitating the Prophet Muḥammad. While the chapter attempted to answer the question of what happened to all the *sunan* that did not go through the rigorous method of *isnād* and *matn*, we are left with another matter to end with: What happened to the *quṣṣāṣ* after the early period of transmission? Where did they disappear into with the coming of stronger authorities and established knowledge traditions?

To attempt a history of the storyteller beyond the initial centuries of the Islamic tradition will then require us to also move along with these preachers and enter into domains away from the "centre." The periphery, in a way,

24 The attempt is to include the non-material, or rather *immaterial*. This does not mean that the material is a separate domain or cannot be perceived through the non-material. Rather, privileging the material is contested.

being the site for conversion and future conversations, allows for a richer history of the storyteller-preacher. The preacher's connection with guilds and the way they moved about preaching the word of Islam will give us a better lead to the lives of these storytellers that is not limited to the activity of storytelling. This will also mean analysing not only the standard *ḥikāya* or *qiṣṣa*, but also the multiple forms that such genres would later merge with such as shadow puppetry, *kissa pattu*, *dastangoi*, and other storytelling forms in South and Southeast Asia. The storyteller, if anything, is yet to complete his tale.

## Acknowledgements

I would like to thank Dr. Mutaz al-Khatib, Dr. Ali Altaf Mian, Omar Abdel-Ghaffar, Shirin Saifuddeen and the anonymous reviewers for their valuable comments and suggestions.

## Bibliography

ʿAthamina, Khalil. 1992. "Al-Qasas: Its Emergence, Religious Origin and Its Socio-Political Impact on Early Muslim Society." *Studia Islamica* 76: 353–74.

Abbott, Nabia. 1967. *Studies in Arabic Literary Papyri II: Qurʾānic Commentary and Tradition*. Chicago: The University of Chicago Press.

Abdel-Ghaffar, Omar. 2018. "Medieval Islamic Work and Robbery: A Study of Al Suyuti's Fariq." *Borderlines*, November 5. www.borderlines-cssaame.org/posts/2018/11/5/medieval-islamic-work-and-robbery-a-study-of-suyutisfariq.

Afsaruddin, Asma. 2002. "The Excellences of the Qurʾān: Textual Sacrality and the Organization of Early Islamic Society." *Journal of the American Oriental Society* 122(1): 1–24.

Afsaruddin, Asma. 2007. *The First Muslims: History and Memory*. Oxford: Oneworld.

Ahmad, Shahab. 2015. *What Is Islam? The Importance of Being Islamic*. Princeton: Princeton University Press.

Ansari, Zafar Ishaq. 1972. "Islamic Juristic Terminology before Šāfiʿī: A Semantic Analysis with Special Reference to Kūfa." *Arabica* 19(3): 255–300.

Armstrong, Lyall R. 2017. *The Quṣṣāṣ of Early Islam*. Leiden: Brill.

Asad, Talal. 1993. *Genealogies of Religion: Discipline and Reason of Power in Christianity and Islam*. Baltimore: Johns Hopkins University Press.

Asad, Talal. 2003. *Formations of the Secular: Christianity, Islam, Modernity*. Stanford, CA: Stanford University Press.

Asad, Talal. 2015. "Thinking about Tradition, Religion, and Politics in Egypt Today." *Critical Inquiry* 42(1): 166–214. DOI: 10.1086/683002.

Berkey, Jonathan Porter. 2001. *Popular Preaching and Religious Authority in the Medieval Islamic Near East*. Seattle: University of Washington Press.

Berkey, Jonathan Porter. 2003. *The Formation of Islam: Religion and Society in the Near East, 600–1800*. Cambridge: Cambridge University Press.

bin Tyeer, Sarah R. 2016. *The Qur'an and the Aesthetics of Premodern Arabic Prose*. London: Palgrave Macmillan.

al-Bukhārī, Muhammad b. Ismāʿīl. 1997. *The Translation of the Meaning of Ṣaḥīḥ al-Bukhārī, Kitāb al-Adab*, translated by Muhammad Muhsin Khan. Riyad: Darussalam.

Crone, Patricia. 1987. *Meccan Trade and the Rise of Islam*. Princeton: Princeton University Press.

al-Dhahabī, Shams al-Dīn. 1985. *Siyar Aʿlām al-Nubalāʾ*, edited by Shuʿayb al-Arnāʾūṭ, 18 vols. Beirut: Muʾassasat al-Risāla.

Derrida, Jacques. 1973. *Speech and Phenomena: And Other Essays on Husserl's Theory of Signs*, translated by David B. Allison. Evanston: Northwestern University Press.

Derrida, Jacques. 1981. "Plato's Pharmacy." In *Dissemination*, translated by Barbara Johnson. Chicago: University of Chicago Press.

Derrida, Jacques. 1982. *Margins of Philosophy*, translated by Alan Bass. Chicago: University of Chicago Press.

Firestone, Reuven. 2006. "Tales of the Prophets." In *Medieval Islamic Civilization: An Encyclopedia*, edited by Josef W. Meri, vol. 1, 644–646. London: Routledge.

Foucault, Michel. 1988. "Technologies of the Self." In *Technologies of the Self: A Seminar with Michel Foucault*, by Huck Gutman, Patrick H. Hutton, Luther H. Martin and Rux S. Martin. Amherst: University of Massachusetts Press.

Foucault, Michel. 1997. "On the Genealogy of Ethics: An Overview of Work in Progress." In *Ethics: Subjectivity and Truth: Vol. 1, Essential Works of Foucault, 1954–1984*, edited by Paul Rabinow, 253–280. New York: New Press.

Geertz, Clifford. 1973. *The Interpretation of Cultures: Selected Essays*. New York: Basic Books.

Goldziher, Ignaz. 1971. *Muslim Studies*, edited by S.M. Stern and translated by Stern and C.R. Barber, vol. 2. Albany: State University of New York Press.

Hallaq, Wael. 1997. *A History of Islamic Legal Theories: An Introduction to Sunnī Uṣūl al-Fiqh*. Cambridge: Cambridge University Press.

Hallaq, Wael. 1984. "Was the Gate of Ijtihad Closed?" *International Journal of Middle East Studies* 16(1): 3–41.

Hallaq, Wael. 2009. *Sharīʿa: Theory, Practice, Transformations*. Cambridge: Cambridge University Press.

Hallaq, Wael. 2013. *The Impossible State: Islam, Politics, and Modernity's Moral Predicament*. New York: Columbia University Press.

Halldén, Philip. 2006. "Rhetoric." In *Medieval Islamic Civilization: An Encyclopedia*, edited by Josef W. Meri, vol. 1, 679–681. London: Routledge.

Ibn ʿAsākir, Abū l-Qāsim. 1995. *Tārīkh Dimashq*, edited by ʿUmar b. Gharāma al-ʿAmrawī, 80 vols. Beirut: Dār al-Fikr.

Ibn Ḥajar, Aḥmad b. ʿAlī. 2002. *Lisān al-Mīzān*, edited by ʿAbd al-Fattāḥ Abū Ghudda, 10 vols. Beirut: Dār al-Bashāʾir al-Islāmiyya.

Ibn al-Jawzī, ʿAbd al-Raḥmān b. ʿAlī. 1983. *Kitāb al-Quṣṣāṣ wa-l-Mudhakkirīn*, edited by Luṭfī l-Ṣabbāgh. Beirut: al-Maktaba al-Islāmiyya.

Ibn Manẓūr, Muḥammad b. Mukarram. 2005. *Lisān al-ʿArab*. Beirut: Dār Ṣādir.

Ibn Taymiyya, Taqī al-Dīn. 1988. *Aḥādīth al-Quṣṣāṣ*, edited by Luṭfī l-Ṣabbāgh. Beirut: al-Maktaba al-Islāmiyya.

Juynboll, G.H.A. 1983. *Muslim Tradition: Studies in Chronology, Provenance, and Authorship of Early Hadith*. Cambridge: Cambridge University Press.

al-Khāzin, ʿAlāʾ al-Dīn. 2004. *Lubāb al-Taʾwīl fī Maʿānī al-Tanzīl*, edited by ʿAbd al-Salām Muḥammad ʿAlī Shāhīn. Beirut: Dār al-Kutub al-ʿIlmiyya.

Kugle, Scott and Roxani Eleni Margariti. 2015. "Narrating Community: the Qiṣṣat Shakarwatī Farmāḍ and Accounts of Origin in Kerala and around the Indian Ocean." *Journal of the Economic and Social History of the Orient* 60(4): 337–380.

Macdonald, D.B. 1899. "The Life of al-Ghazzālī, with Especial Reference to His Religious Experiences and Opinions." *Journal of the American Oriental Society* 20: 71–132.

Macdonald, D.B. 1927. "Ḳiṣṣa." In *Encyclopaedia of Islam, First Edition (1913–1936)*. DOI: 10.1163/2214-871X_ei1_SIM_4241.

Mahmood, Saba. 2005. *Politics of Piety: The Islamic Revival and the Feminist Subject*. Princeton: Princeton University Press.

Makdisi, George. 1993. "*Ṭabaqāt*-Biography: Law and Orthodoxy in Classical Islam." *Islamic Studies* 32(4): 371–396.

Mamdani, Mahmood. 2004. *Good Muslim, Bad Muslim: America, the Cold War, and the Roots of Terror*. Kampala: Fountain Publishers.

Massignon, Louis. 1997. *Essay on the Origins of the Technical Language of Islamic Mysticism*. Notre Dame: University of Notre Dame Press.

Mauss, Marcel. 1973. "Techniques of the body." *Economy and Society* 2(1): 70–88.

Messick, Brinkley. 1993. *The Calligraphic State: Textual Domination and History in a Muslim Society*. Berkeley: University of California Press.

Pellat, Ch. 1976. "Ḳāṣṣ." In *Encyclopaedia of Islam, Second Edition*, vol. 4, 733–735. DOI: 10.1163/1573-3912_islam_SIM_4002.

al-Qushayrī, ʿAbd al-Karīm. 1989. *Al-Risāla al-Qushayriyya*, edited by Maḥmūd b. Sharīf. Cairo: Muʾassasat al-Shaʿb.

al-Qushayrī, ʿAbd al-Karīm. 2000. *Laṭāʾif al-Ishārāt*, edited by Ibrāhīm Basyūnī, 3 vols. Cairo: al-Hayʾa al-Miṣriyya al-ʿĀmma lil-Kitāb.

al-Qushayri, Abu ʾl-Qasim. 2007. *Al-Risala al-Qushayriyya fi ʿIlm al-Tasawwuf*, translated by Alexander D. Knysh. Reading, MA: Garnet Publishing.

Reinhart, A. Kevin. 2017. "What We Know about Maʿrūf." *Journal of Islamic Ethics* 1: 51–82.

al-Suyūṭī, ʿAbd al-Raḥmān b. Abī Bakr. 1974. *Taḥdhīr al-Khawāṣṣ min Akādhīb al-Quṣṣāṣ*, edited by Luṭfī al-Ṣabbāgh. Beirut: al-Maktaba al-Islāmiyya.

al-Tirmidhī, Mohammad b. ʿĪsā. 2007. *Jāmiʿ al-Tirmidhī*, translated by Abū Khalīl, vol 4. Riyad: Darussalam.

Wansbrough, John. 1977. *Quranic Studies: Sources and Methods of Scriptural Interpretation*. Amherst, NY: Prometheus Books.

Ware, Rudolph T. 2014. *The Walking Qurʾan: Islamic Education, Embodied Knowledge, and History in West Africa*. Chapel Hill: The University of North Carolina Press.

CHAPTER 9

# Abū Shuqqa's Approach to the *Ḥadīth*

***Towards an Egalitarian Islamic Gender Ethics***

*Faqihuddin Abdul Kodir*

## 1 Introduction

Over the past three decades, many feminist and progressive Muslims have criticised the *ḥadīth* and dismissed them from their projects on egalitarian gender ethics in Islam. Fatima Mernissi (d. 2015) argued that all *ḥadīth*s demeaning women are traditions of misogyny falsely attributed to the Prophet and accordingly are not authoritative sources of Islamic teachings (Mernissi 1991). Riffat Hassan (b. 1943) and Ali Asghar Engineer (d. 2013) also contended that the *ḥadīth* is a source of patriarchal Islam and are not authoritative enough to construct a notion of egalitarian Islam (Hassan 1991; Engineer 2001). On the other side, many contemporary religious scholars still utilise *ḥadīth* to perpetuate entrenched traditional interpretations of Islam that discriminate against women.

On the basis of traditional interpretation and some *ḥadīth*s, many religious scholars have reduced the ideal Muslim woman, in this contemporary age, as completely invisible from the public domain. They forbid women to drive cars, walk in the middle of the road, travel alone, work in public (especially in radio or television stations), or participate in political activities. They have also conceptualised that the ideal Muslim woman a domestic role of being an obedient wife whose religious duty is to serve and please her husband. This *ḥadīth*-based interpretation is observed in the works of ʿAbd al-ʿAzīz Ibn Bāz (d. 1999) and of Muḥammad b. Ṣāliḥ al-ʿUthaymīn (d. 2001) (Ibn Bāz 1988; 1994; and 1995; al-ʿUthaymīn 1989; and 1998), the most revered scholar for contemporary Wahhabī Muslims. This traditional interpretation is also visibly observed in the contemporary *ḥadīth* collections on gender issues by Muḥammad ʿAlī al-Hāshimī (d. 2015), Muḥammad Farīja, and Ṣādiq b. Muḥammad al-Hādī (al-Hāshimī 2013; Farīja 1996; al-Hādī 2009).

Other scholars seem uneasy with interpretations adopted about women by traditional religious scholars, but they also do not want to disregard the authority of *ḥadīth* in Islam. They generally accept the *ḥadīth* literature and

DOI:10.1163/9789004525931_011

prefer rather to circumvent the seemingly harsh element of literal meanings of *ḥadīth* texts. They attempt to find an ethical message from each *ḥadīth* to draw out a more women-friendly interpretation. This approach is noticeably observed in the works of many scholars, such as Ghāda al-Khurasānī, Muḥammad al-Ghazālī (d. 1996), Kaukab Siddique (b. 1943), Yūsuf al-Qaraḍāwī (d. 2022), Hiba Ra'ūf 'Izzat (b. 1965), and Mohja Kahf (b. 1967) (al-Khurasānī 1979; al-Ghazālī 1989; Siddique 1990; al-Qaraḍāwī 1991; 'Izzat 1995; Kahf 2000).

In line with this interpretative approach is the work of 'Abd al-Ḥalīm Muḥammad Abū Shuqqa (d. 1995) in his book, *Taḥrīr al-Mar'a fī 'Aṣr al-Risāla: Dirāsa 'an al-Mar'a Jāmi'a li-Nuṣūṣ al-Qur'ān wa-Ṣaḥīḥay al-Bukhārī wa-Muslim* ("The Liberation of Women at the Time of the Message: A Study on Women Composed of the Qur'ānic Texts, and the *Ṣaḥīḥ*s of al-Bukhārī and Muslim").[1] It is the first work that collects a large number of the *ḥadīth*s on women's issues. It brings many inspiring interpretative examples from the *ḥadīth* that have influenced some conservative Muslims to hold more women-friendly opinions (al-'Awwā, 2000, 13–14). It has also been used by some Muslim women activists to challenge male authority within Islamic spaces that often restrict women's mobility (Berglund 2011, 505–508). The book was even celebrated at a 2003 international conference held in Cairo on Islam and the liberation of women (al-Lajna al-Islāmiyya al-'Ālamiyya lil-Mar'a wa-l-Ṭifl 2004). It also inspired some female scholar-activists on gender justice to argue that some *ḥadīth*s can be the basis to claim necessary social recognition of Muslim women's roles in both the private and public spheres (Abū Bakr and Shukrī 2002). Indeed, Abū Shuqqa's work is transformative for gender justice discussions within Islamic interpretation at the start of the 21st century.

This chapter analyses the methodological approaches of Abū Shuqqa disclosed in the *Taḥrīr* to present some enabling interpretations of the *ḥadīth*, and establish a theological basis for an egalitarian gender relations ethics from within an Islamic perspective. I argue that the work of Abū Shuqqa can be regarded as a genre of "conflicting *ḥadīth*s" (*mukhtalif al-ḥadīth*) in the sciences of *ḥadīth* (*'ulūm al-ḥadīth*), since it prefers to circumvent seemingly harsh elements of the literal meanings of some *ḥadīth* and attempts to find an ethical message to present a more women-friendly interpretation. In his interpretation, Abū Shuqqa suggests promising approaches towards the *ḥadīth* to produce more favourable interpretations of egalitarian gender relations ethics by promoting an Islamic ethics of mutuality and reciprocity between women and

1 While this chapter cites the 2002 edition of Abū Shuqqa's work, his collection was first published in 1990.

men, both in domestic and public spheres. I argue that the *Taḥrīr* has paved the way for methodological approaches to the *ḥadīth* that establish the means for interpreting an Islamic egalitarian gender ethics.

## 2 Abū Shuqqa's Interpretation on Gender Relations

The main elements of Abū Shuqqa's interpretation of egalitarian gender relation can be identified in four themes: the humanity of women; a non-segregated society as an ideal Muslim community; the active agency of women in public activities; and mutuality and reciprocity in all matters related to spousal relationship, including sexual intimacy. He suggests that his work is a form of Islamic women's liberation that differentiates from and repairs conservative interpretations. In his perspective, liberation means to free women from the burden of oppressive and discriminatory interpretations, by promoting teachings of Islam towards the humanity of women (*insāniyya*) and the equality of gender relationships (*musāwāt*) (Abū Shuqqa 2002, 1:28–61).

Abū Shuqqa argued that, in Islam, women and men are human and should be principally treated equally in all matters of life. He emphasised six principles to avow the humanity of women. They are: the entitlement of women to human dignity; their ability to be responsible for their own labour; their right to freedom and independency; their potentiality for human perfection, just like men; their capability to play their roles in the public sphere; and their ability to have proper personalities as normal human beings.

To prove his argument, Abū Shuqqa refered to verses of the Qur'ān that assert the humanity of women. In fact, the term *musāwāt*, which means "no other than equality," is the first word he used to open his entire interpretation. He quoted Qur'ānic verse 4:1 to state that women and men are created from the same entity. Based on the verses 3:190–195, 4:124, 16:97, and 40:40, he also affirmed that Islam demonstrates the equal responsibility of women and men. The personality of women, and men as well, is respected and dignified in Islam on the grounds of many verses of the Qur'ān (see for example Q 24:11–12, 33:35, 48:5, 48:25, 57:12, 57:18 and 71:28). In dealing with the reward and punishment by God, these verses demonstrate equal treatment of women and men. Moreover, the verses 66:10–12 maintain the independency of women from their husbands in terms of their own responsibility towards God (Abū Shuqqa 2002, 1:69–110). Indeed, these verses, according to Abū Shuqqa, clearly reveal the idea of equality between men and women in Islam, allowing him to argue for equality in his interpretation of *ḥadīth*.

Abū Shuqqa established the humanity of women from the *ḥadīth* of Umm Salama (d. 62/681).[2] To my knowledge, there has been no attempt prior to the *Taḥrīr* that uses a *ḥadīth* to demonstrate the equal humanity of women in Islam. Abū Shuqqa reinterprets the *ḥadīth* of Umm Salama to affirm that a woman, in the Prophet's time, was declared as a member of humanity and, thus, as equal to men. This attempt has been acknowledged and appreciated by Omaima Abou Bakr during her opening discussion on Islamic feminism. On the grounds of Umm Salama's saying, alongside other *ḥadīth*s that detail female questions and demands, she argues that women in Islam are encouraged to engage in social matters, to obtain acknowledgement and praise by the society, and that their voices should be heard, and their problems solved in any stage of history (Abū Bakr and Shukrī 2002, 14–16).

Abū Shuqqa established the equality of men and women as the principle of Islam on the grounds of the saying of the Prophet, "women are the counterparts of men" (*al-nisāʾ shaqāʾiq al-rijāl*).[3] Based on this saying, he starts to establish the principle of gender equality, aiming intentionally to criticise the basic assumption about women prevalent in the traditional interpretation. This saying along with his discussion in the *Taḥrīr* becomes, borrowing the argument of Mohammed Fadel, "an explicit textual basis for a presumptive norm of gender equality" (Fadel 2012, 13). In his introduction of the main argument of the *Taḥrīr*, Abū Shuqqa quoted the phrase, "women are the counterparts of men," alluding to the equality of women and men (Abū Shuqqa 2002, 1:30). This phrase is also quoted to point out the importance of women's position in Islam, which has been neglected for centuries. It is included mainly as an epitome of the whole discussion of *ḥadīth*s on the characteristics and personality of women in Islam. This phrase is conflated with the statement of ʿUmar b. al-Khaṭṭāb (d. 23/644), who argued that Islam guaranteed the rights of women. It is repeated again as the opening remark of Abū Shuqqa's second volume on equal participation of women and men in public activities. When Abū Shuqqa reinterpreted the temptation of women, he also quoted this phrase to emphasise equal partnership between two sexes in avoiding unlawful sexual attraction, rather than focusing on the temptation of one sex only (Abū

2 Muslim 2000, 2:989: *Kitāb al-Faḍāʾil* ("Book of Virtues"), *Bāb Ithbāt Ḥawḍ Nabiyyinā wa-Ṣifātih* ("Chapter on the Cistern of Our Prophet and its Attributes").

3 Abū Dāwūd 2000, 1:39: *Kitāb al-Ṭahāra* ("Book of Purification"), *Bāb fī l-Rajul Yajidu al-Billa fī Manāmih* ("Chapter on a Man Who Sees Some Wetness on his Clothes after Sleeping"); al-Tirmidhī 2000, 1:34: *Abwāb al-Ṭahāra* ("Book of Purification"), *Bāb fī l-Rajul Yajidu Balalan wa-lā Yadhkuru Iḥtilāman* ("Chapter on A Man Who Awakens to Find Wetness, but Does Not Recall Having a Wet Dream").

Shuqqa 2002, 1:30, 69–79, 115, 295 and 302–303). Indeed, Abū Shuqqa's interpretation is one of gender equality in all situations, including perceived *fitna*.

The argument for equality (*musāwāt*) in the *Taḥrīr* appears in three forms: women as individuals, women as part of the family, and women as members of society. As individuals, women are described by Abū Shuqqa as equal to men in all essential rights and duties towards Allāh, the Absolute. They are created from the same essence (*nafs wāḥida*) as men, not from the crooked rib of men. To Abū Shuqqa, Allāh makes no distinction between women and men in the origin of creation. They are addressed by the revelation equally for faith and its teachings. They are also to be equally rewarded or punished for their deeds. In terms of moral responsibility, both women and men are equally accountable for their actions. In terms of legal status, women are allowed to have their own contracts, to run their own business, to possess their own property, and to vote based on their own political choices equally and independently from their husbands or any relatives (Abū Shuqqa 2002, 1:67–147 and 295).

As part of the family, women are equal to men in all principal rights and duties in the familial relationship. To begin family life, consent of both bride and groom is essential in Abū Shuqqa's interpretation. A woman, therefore, cannot be forced to enter into marriage without her agreement; indeed, she has the right to withdraw from a marriage to which she does not agree to. In daily familial life, both women and men are equally required to treat and to be treated with mutuality and reciprocity when it comes to taking care, respecting, and serving each other. Familial relationships in Abū Shuqqa's interpretation are based on the principle of respect, mutual understanding, and helping each other. This principle is emphasised in his discussion of the notions of male leadership (*qiwāma*) and guardianship (*wilāya*), and conjugal rights and duties among the spouses (Abū Shuqqa 2002, 1:47–48, 128–130, 173–175, 296–311, 3:15, 53, 216 and 5: 96–214).

In contrast to interpretations that enforce gender hierarchy, Abū Shuqqa conceptualised the *wilāya* of fathers over their daughters, or of brothers over their sisters, and the *qiwāma* of a husband over his wife as the right of *mushāwara*, or giving consultation in the interest of the daughters, the sisters, and the wife. It is, rather, a responsibility to guarantee protection, safety, maintenance, and the well-being of family members than a right to lead and command them. This right also should be exercised in a friendly manner and for the good purpose of the wife and other members of the family. Otherwise, a wrongly practiced right should be redressed so that it results in its initial purpose. Abū Shuqqa presented examples of *ḥadīth*s to show how guardians were required, when they arbitrarily misused their right of guardianship, to turn back to the purpose of the *ḥadīth* to result in what was best for the ward, women or wife. For example, Abū Shuqqa points to how the Prophet asked Maʿqil b. Yasār (d. 58/678) not to prevent his sister from marrying a man of her choice; how the Prophet enforced Khansāʾ bint Khidām's right to annul her forced marriage by her father; the way he let the aunt of Jābir b. ʿAbd Allāh (d. 76/697) work outside her home during the waiting period after divorce (*ʿidda*); to how the Prophet forbade men from preventing their wives from going to the mosque; and to how the Prophet rejected the desire of ʿAlī b. Abī Ṭālib (d. 40/661) to marry another woman without the consent of his wife Fāṭima bint Muḥammad (d. *c.*18/605) (Abū Shuqqa 2002, 1:296–299).

In this regard, the *qiwāma* of a husband over his wife along with her obedience (*ṭāʿa*) to him are discussed in Abū Shuqqa's interpretation as the right of both partners to – and their responsibility for – caring and protection. To ease these rights and responsibilities, the husband is charged with the responsibility of *qiwāma* and maintenance while the wife is entitled with the responsibility of rearing children and managing the house. This division is, however, subject to change and negotiation under the notions of "helping each other" (*taʿāwun*), and "giving and getting consultation" from each other (*mushāwara*), particularly when realities require the exchange. These notions of *taʿāwun* and *mushāwara* are very fundamental in Abū Shuqqa's interpretation of all aspects of the marital relationship, which is rooted in the norms of mutuality, reciprocity, and partnership. For instance, the wifely duty of obedience is interpreted as being part of helping the husband fulfil his duty to manage the matters of the whole family and to take care of them. When the *qiwāma* is practiced outside of this purpose, the wife has the right to disobey her husband and to rectify his *qiwāma* by giving him an alternative. This giving of an alternative is part of the notion of *mushāwara*. In turn, the husband embracing the opinion proposed by his wife is part of *mushāwara* and *taʿāwun* as well. During the absence of the husband, the wife's taking of *qiwāma* and *riʿāya* becomes necessary as a part of the requirement that spouses help each other (Abū Shuqqa 2002, 5:99–115).

To Abū Shuqqa, *nafaqa* (marital financial support) is primarily a duty of the husband, not the wife. However, since there is the principle of *taʿāwun*, to him, the wife is also encouraged to provide maintenance for the family depending on her capacity and capability. During the absence of the husband, for instance, or his lack of capacity to provide, it becomes a wifely duty to feed the family. We find in the *Taḥrīr* examples of women from the early Islamic period who worked for their family during the life of the Prophet, such as Jābir b. ʿAbd Allāh's aunt, Umm Mubashshir al-Anṣāriyya, and Zaynab (d. after 32/653), the wife of ʿAbd Allāh b. Masʿūd (d. 32/653). We can also mention Umm Shurayk (d. *c.*50/670), who was well known for her richness, generosity, and her strong work ethic (Abū Shuqqa 2002, 2:343–345, 359–364 and 5:109–115). Indeed, these women are examples of *taʿāwun* that present wives actively providing for their families.

Whereas the husband maintains the health of his family by working outside the house, the wife is obliged to rear children and manage the house at home. This responsibility of the wife appears and takes form in the *Taḥrīr* as her obedience to the husband within the spirit of helping him to fulfil his responsibility as the holder of *qiwāma*. However, the principle of *taʿāwun* here operates also to encourage the husband to do the rearing, caring, and managing of domestic matters while he has time at home, particularly if the wife is very exhausted, or busy with her profession outside of the home. Indeed, women should have access to the benefits of cultural activities outside of their homes. Doing the rearing, caring, and managing of domestic matters, in turn, may become the obligation of the husband when the wife is obliged to go out to work for the family, for society, or for the sake of developing her own personality. In ordinary circumstances, argues Abū Shuqqa, a believing Muslim should follow an example of the Prophet as he served his family while he was at home (Abū Shuqqa 2002, 2:364–366, 5:132–133).

On this basis, women are equal to men in all aspects of enjoying and participating in public activities that relate to building society. In Abū Shuqqa's interpretation, women not only have full freedom but should also be encouraged to develop their personalities by participating in and shaping a better society for the sake of all. To prove his claim, Abū Shuqqa draws from the images of virtuous women during the time of the first generations of Muslims. They are portrayed as individuals who actively took part in public life; who went to the mosque for prayers and took part in other social activities with men; who joined their colleagues in migration for faith; who sought knowledge and taught it to other people; who engaged with men in military expeditions; who worked and looked after the maintenance of the family; and who gave alms to the needy. Essentially, they participated in all aspects of religious, social, economic, and political spheres, bringing benefits to society. Since this equality is mandatory, Abū Shuqqa urges men and all members of society not to burden women alone with domestic responsibilities in which they are prevented from their participation in public life. Indeed, this public participation is beneficial to women's self-development, and women's participation is beneficial to society (Abū Shuqqa 2002, 2:15–72).

## 3 Abū Shuqqa's Methodological Approach to *Ḥadīth*

There are many sources in the *Taḥrīr* on which Abū Shuqqa based his interpretation to advocate for his notion of gender equality (*musāwāt*). The sources are verses of the Qur'ān, *ḥadīth* texts, *ḥadīth* commentaries of classical scholars, events from the past, history related to the subject, opinions of classical and contemporary scholars, as well as experts' analysis of the context of contemporary social changes. However, *ḥadīth* texts are the primary sources in the *Taḥrīr* while the other sources are complementary. As his concern is mostly interpretation, Abū Shuqqa did not discuss the issue of authenticity. He followed the judgments of *ḥadīth* texts as *ṣaḥīḥ* and *ḥasan* made by classical scholars such as al-Bukhārī (d. 256/870), Muslim (d. 261/875), Abū Dāwūd (d. 275/889), al-Tirmidhī (d. 279/892), and Ibn Ḥajar al-ʿAsqalānī (d. 852/1449), and even by contemporary scholars such as his teacher Nāṣir al-Dīn al-Albānī (d. 1999).

With regard to methodological approach, I suggest that there are five main approaches to the *ḥadīth*, through which Abū Shuqqa established his interpretation in the *Taḥrīr* for what he called gender equality (*musāwāt*). As the next sections will explore, he advocated for an inclusive definition of the *ḥadīth* which focused on examples of the female Companions of the Prophet, for pairing the *ḥadīth* with the Qur'ān on gender issues, for a reorganisation of themes in the *ḥadīth* (*tarājim al-abwāb*), for a hermeneutics of equality (*musāwāt*), and for a reinterpretation of problematic *ḥadīth*s (*ta'wīl mushkil al-ḥadīth*).

### 3.1 *Inclusive Definition of the* Ḥadīth

Abū Shuqqa used the terms Sunna and *ḥadīth* interchangeably, as one is identical to other. Both are about general principles and examples of the Prophet understood from detailed case law and teachings recorded in the *ḥadīth* literature. Following the definition of the term "*ḥadīth*" that includes sayings and deeds of the Companions of the Prophet (ʿItr 1985, 27–30; al-Bughā 1990, 9–10), Abū Shuqqa regarded the experiences of female Companions as part of the definition of "*ḥadīth*" of the Prophet. He also attributed prophetic guidance (*hady al-nabī*) to the deeds of ʿĀ'isha (d. 58/678), Umm Ḥarām (d. *c.*27–28/648–649), and Zaynab bint Jaḥsh (d. 20/641) (Abū Shuqqa 2002, 1:28–31).

The following texts are examples of how Abū Shuqqa focused on the experiences of female Companions, in addition to the actions and statements of the Prophet, and unlike the *Ṣaḥīḥ*s of al-Bukhārī and Muslim:

> Abū Saʿīd al-Khudrī [d. 74/693] reported that a woman came to Allāh's Messenger (may peace be upon him) and said: "Allāh's Messenger, men receive your instructions (*dhahaba al-rijāl bi-ḥadīthik*); kindly allocate at your convenience a day for us also, on which we would come to you and you would teach us what Allāh has taught you." He said: "You assemble on such and such a day." They assembled and Allāh's Messenger (may peace be upon him) came to them and taught them what Allāh had taught him

> and he then said: "There is no woman amongst you who sends her three children as her forerunners (to the Hereafter) but they would serve for her as a protection against Hell-Fire." A woman said: "What about two and two and two?" Thereupon Allāh's Messenger (may peace be upon him) said: "Even if they are two and two and two."[4]

This text above is found in the *Ṣaḥīḥ* of al-Bukhārī in a chapter titled *Ta'līm al-Nabī Ummatahū Min al-Rijāl wa-l-Nisā'* ("On the Teachings of the Prophet to His People, Men and Women"), and in the *Ṣaḥīḥ* of Muslim in a chapter titled *Faḍl Man Yamūt wa-lahu Walad fa-Yaḥtasibuh* ("The Merit of the One Who Dies while He has a Child, through Whom He Will Be Rewarded"). A similar text is placed by al-Bukhārī in a chapter titled *Hal Yuj'al lil-Nisā' Yawm 'alā Ḥida fī l-'Ilm* ("Should a Specific Day be Allocated to Women for Knowledge?"), and in another chapter titled *Faḍl Man Māt wa-lahu Walad fa-Ḥtasab* ("On the Merit of the One Who Died while Leaving a Child through Whom He Will be Rewarded") (al-Bukhārī 2000, 1:28, 235). However, In the *Taḥrīr* of Abū Shuqqa, the above text is placed in a chapter titled: *Namādhij min Quwwat Shakhṣiyyat al-Mar'a al-Muslima wa-Ḥusn Idrākihā li-Ḥuqūqihā wa-Wājibātihā* ("On Examples of Strong Characteristics of a Muslim Woman and Her Good Discernment on Her Rights and Obligations") in a sub-chapter about women who demanded the Prophet have more chances for his teaching (Abū Shuqqa 2002, 1:171). Thus, the chapters of Abū Shuqqa are focusing on the experiences of female Companions.

The following is the second example of female Companions presented by Abū Shuqqa.

> Narrated by Ibn 'Abbās [d. *c.*68/687]: 'Umar b. al-Khaṭṭāb said: "It so happened that I was thinking about some matter that my wife said: 'I wish you had done that and that.' I said to her: 'It does not concern you and you should not feel disturbed in a matter which I intend to do.' She said to me: 'How strange is it that you, o son of al-Khaṭṭāb, do not like anyone to retort to you, whereas your daughter retorts to Allāh's Messenger (peace be upon him) until he spends the day in vexation.'" 'Umar said: "I took hold of my cloak, then came out of my house, visited Ḥafṣa [d. 41/661] and said to her: 'O daughter, (I heard) that you retort upon Allāh's

---

4 al-Bukhārī 2000, 3:1477: *Kitāb al-I'tiṣām bi-l-Kitāb wa-l-Sunna* ("Book on Holding Fast to the Qur'ān and Sunna"), *Bāb Ta'līm al-Nabī Ummatahu min al-Rijāl wa-l-Nisā' mimmā 'Allamahu Allāh* ("Chapter on How the Prophet Taught His Followers, Men and Women, from What Allāh Taught Him").

> Messenger (peace be upon him) until he spends the day in vexation,' whereupon Ḥafṣa said: 'By Allāh, we do retort upon him.' I said: 'You should bear in mind, my daughter, that I warn you against the punishment of Allāh and the wrath of His Messenger (peace be upon him). You may not be misled by one whose beauty has fascinated her, and the love of Allāh's Messenger (may peace be upon him) for her.' I ('Umar) then visited Umm Salama because of my relationship with her and I talked to her. Umm Salama said to me: "Umar b. al-Khaṭṭāb, how strange is it that you meddle with every matter so much so that you are anxious to interfere between Allāh's Messenger (peace be upon him) and his wives?' And this perturbed me so much that I refrained from saying what I had to say, so I came out of her quarters."[5]

For the classical scholars of *ḥadīth*, such as al-Bukhārī and Muslim, the text above is only referenced as evidence that a man often loves one of his wives more than the rest, or that the husband may let his wives choose to leave him if they dislike to live with him. However, for Abū Shuqqa, the text is a lesson that women at the time of the Prophet were strong and knowledgeable (Abū Shuqqa 2002, 2:153).

Thus, Abū Shuqqa applies the term "*ḥadīth*" and "Sunna" inclusively, not only for the traditions of the Prophet, but also for sayings and deeds of the Companions of the Prophet. These experiences, according to Abū Shuqqa, represented the origin of prophetic guidance on gender relations. He named these experiences "practical and applied *ḥadīth*s" (*aḥādīth 'amaliyya taṭbīqiyya*) on the relationship between men and women in diverse aspects of life (Abū Shuqqa 2002, 1:28). Indeed, all of his work concentrated on including experiences of female Companions as religious authorities to which Islamic teachings on gender relations should refer.

### 3.2 *Pairing Qur'ān with the* Ḥadīth

For his interpretation on egalitarian gender relations (*musāwāt*), Abū Shuqqa paired the Qur'ān with the *ḥadīth* to dig up meanings of the latter which are suitable to principles of the former. This attempt is made on the grounds that there should be unity and coherence in telling the truth, since both are authoritative sources of it. Abū Shuqqa recognised the prevalent argument in Islamic legal theory (*uṣūl al-fiqh*) about the certainty of the Qur'ān and probability of

5 Muslim 2000, 1:617–618: *Kitāb al-Ṭalāq* ("Book of Divorce"), *Bāb fī l-Īlā'* ("Chapter on Keeping away from One's Wives").

the *ḥadīth*, but he did not polarise these two sources. Rather, he brought both together to figure out the truth about the equality between women and men.

The *Taḥrīr* is a collection of *ḥadīth*s on women's liberation, but it also presents verses of the Qur'ān related to the subject in question. He put the verses in the beginning of the collection to set up what he conceived as principles of Islamic teachings with regard to women. There are about thirty pages of the first volume where some verses of the Qur'ān are presented to support his argument about the equality of men and women when it comes to: the responsibility of women as human beings, the liberation of women from oppression, a recognition of their personality, their place in the family, their participation in public life, and celebrating stories of virtuous women in the Qur'ān. Indeed, there are 474 places in the *Taḥrīr* where Abū Shuqqa supported his interpretation with verses of the Qur'ān.

His main argument, that men and women are from the same essence, is established from verse 4:1 of the Qur'ān. The humanity of women, the nobility of their personality, and the independency of their responsibility of their own good and bad deeds, are also drawn from verses of the Qur'ān (3:190–195, 4:124, 16:97 and 40:40). He often starts his major topics with presentation of verses and follows by listing *ḥadīth*s on the subject in question. He establishes the major argument from the Qur'ān and put it in his title headings before he listed *ḥadīth* related to the subject. He then composed title headings inspired by Qur'ānic verses to categorise the *ḥadīth* he interpreted. His interpretation, then, of *ḥadīth* is coloured by his weight to principles deduced from Qur'ān; and evidenced in three major topics of the *Taḥrīr*, female participation in public, familial relationship, and sexual intimacy.

In some cases, Abū Shuqqa interprets the *ḥadīth* in light of the Qur'ān. The *ḥadīth*-text that states that people will not achieve their prosperity when led by a woman, for instance, is interpreted in favour of gender justice with the fact, which is recognised by verses 27:23–44 of the Qur'ān, that a woman (Bilqīs) ruled a kingdom successfully and that her people were happy and prosperous. In other cases, however, he interprets a verse from the Qur'ān using the teachings and practices of the Prophet. This is obvious in the verse of the right of men to slap their wives. The Qur'ān has dictated that wives who disobey (*nushūz*) their husbands are subject to being slapped after receiving advice if they still persist in disobeying (Q 4:34). In Abū Shuqqa's explanation, however, this right is explained under restricted conditions drawn from the teachings and practices of the Prophet, who did not condone wife-beating. Thus, whether the Qur'ān is interpreted through the *ḥadīth*, or vice versa, is defined by the question of what the meanings signify to the reader. There is no specific approach to textual interpretation that applies in all conditions and for all texts, other than the principle of reciprocity and equal humanity.

### 3.3 *Producing Themes Using Chapter Headings* (Tarājim al-Abwāb)

Before delving into discussing chapter headings, it is important to discuss the structure of Abū Shuqqa's collection. The titles of the six volumes of the *Taḥrīr* are (1) *Maʿālim Shakhṣiyyat al-Marʾa al-Muslima* ("Characteristics of Muslim Women"), (2) *Mushārakat al-Marʾa al-Muslima fī l-Ḥayāt al-Ijtimāʿiyya* ("Women's Participation in Public Social Life: Activities of Women During the Time of the Prophet"), (3) *Ḥiwārāt maʿ al-Muʿāriḍīn li-Mushārakat al-Marʾa fī l-Ḥayāt al-Ijtimāʿiyya* ("Extended Evidence of Women's Participation in Public Activities"), (4) *Libās al-Marʾa al-Muslima wa-Zīnatihā* ("Dressing and Adornment of Women"), (5) *Makānat al-Marʾa al-Muslima fī l-Usra* ("Marriage") and (6) *al-Thaqāfa al-Jinsiyya lil-Zawjayn* ("Sexual Education"). Each volume is divided into chapters and each chapter contains sub-chapters followed by texts of *ḥadīth*. The first volume contains eight chapters (*faṣl*); two are dedicated to the presentation of the verses of Qurʾān and six to the texts of *ḥadīth*. The third to eighth chapters of the first volume, that are designated for the texts of *ḥadīth*, are titled (3) *Baʿḍ Maʿālim Shakhṣiyyat al-Marʾa* ("Landmarks of Characteristics of Women"), (4) *Mawāqif Nisāʾiyya Karīma* ("Noble Feminine Stances"), (5) *Namādhij min Quwwat Shakhṣiyyat al-Marʾa al-Muslima wa-Ḥusn Idrākihā li-Ḥuqūqihā wa-Wājibātihā* ("Examples of Strong Characteristics of a Muslim Woman and Her Awareness of Her Rights and Her Responsibilities"), (6) *Shakhṣiyyāt Nisāʾiyya* ("Biographies of Virtuous Women"), (7) *Aḥādīth Ṣaḥīḥa ʿan Shakhṣiyyat al-Marʾa Asāʾa l-Baʿḍ Fahmuhā wa-Taṭbīquhā* ("Religiously Sound Texts of the *ḥadīth*s on Women, Understood and Applied Incorrectly by Some People"), and the last (8) *Taʿqībāt ʿalā Maʿālim Shakhṣiyyat al-Marʾa al-Muslima* ("Comments on Landmarks of Characteristics of Muslim Women").

Abū Shuqqa also came up with new themes using chapter headings to emphasise that women are visible, knowledgeable, have good characteristics, and that they should be active participants of domestic and public activities. The themes of familial relationships are also presented in much more favourable perspectives, as a partnership between women and men. All of these newly created themes are observed in the chapter headings of the *Taḥrīr*. Starting from the title of the book, Abū Shuqqa declares that women have been liberated since the time of the Prophet. His themes, as emphasised in his chapter headings are, then, composed to serve his notion of women's liberation, which is about the humanity of women and the rights of women to access public spheres.

The fifth chapter of the first volume, as an example, has 18 sub-chapters, each of which is followed by one or two texts from the two canonical collections, the *Ṣaḥīḥ* of al-Bukhārī, the *Ṣaḥīḥ* of Muslim, or both. The first ten sub-chapters that prove women's visibility, knowledge, and good characteristics are; *al-Nisāʾ Yuṭālibna al-Rasūl bi-Mazīd min Furaṣ al-Taʿlīm* ("Women Demand the Prophet More Opportunities for Education"); *Asmāʾ bint Shakl Tughālib al-Ḥayāʾ li-Tunfiquh fī l-Dīn* ("Asmāʾ bint Shakl (d. 73/692) Overcomes Her Shyness to Spend it on Religion"); *Sabīʿa bint al-Ḥārith Taʿrif Kayf Tataḥarrā li-Taṣil ilā l-Yaqīn* ("Sabīʿa bint al-Ḥārith Knows How to Search in Order to Come to Certainty of Knowledge"); *al-Marʾa al-Khathʿamiyya – wa-Hiya Shābba – Yushghiluhā Ḥukm al-Ḥajj ʿan Abīhā* ("A Woman of Khathʿamiyya – and She is Young – is Concerned with the Provision of Performing the Pilgrimage on behalf of Her Father"); *al-Marʾa Tatamassak bi-Ḥaqqihā fī Khtiyār al-Zawj* ("A Woman Upholds Her Right in Choosing a Husband"); *al-Marʾa Tatamassak bi-Ḥaqqihā fī Mufāraqat al-Zawj* ("A Woman Upholds Her Right in Repudiating Her Husband"); *ʿĀtika bint Zayd Zawj ʿUmar b. al-Khaṭṭāb Tatamassak bi-Ḥaqqihā fī Shuhūd al-Jamāʿa* ("ʿĀtika bint Zayd the Spouse of ʿUmar b. al-Khaṭṭāb Upholds her Right to Attend the Congregation"), *al-Marʾa Tumāris baʿḍ al-Ḥiraf li-Kasb al-Māl wa-Tataṣaddaq* ("A Woman Works to Earn Money and to give Alms"); *al-Nisāʾ Yulabbīn al-Daʿwa ilā Jtimāʿ ʿĀmm bi-l-Masjid* ("Women Come to a Public Meeting in the Mosque"); and *Umm Kulthūm bint ʿUqba Tufāriq Ahlahā Jamīʿan wa-Tuhājir Firāran bi-Dīnihā* ("Umm Kulthūm bint ʿUqba (d. 33/654) Leaves All of Her Family and Migrates for Her Religion") (Abū Shuqqa 2002, 1:169–176).

Another example of Abū Shuqqa's attention to upstanding Muslim women is the title of the fourth chapter in the first volume which is *Mawāqif Nisāʾiyya Karīma* ("Noble Feminine Stances"). Abū Shuqqa, here, explains facts concerning early Muslim women. This chapter implies his criticism against those who negatively pigeonhole women as religiously defective. Under this chapter of noble female characteristics, Abū Shuqqa lists sub-chapter headings, namely: *Badhl al-Nafs fī Sabīl Allāh* ("Sacrifysing Oneself for the Sake of God"), *al-Ṭumūḥ ilā l-Kamāl* ("Ambition towards Religious Perfection"), *al-Iqbāl ʿalā l-ʿIbāda* ("Action of Sincere Devotion"), *al-Ṣadaqa wa-l-Badhl* ("Gracious Giving"), *Birr al-Wālidayn* ("Obedience to One's Parents"), *Ḥusn al-Tawakkul ʿalā Llāh* ("Full Reliance on God"), *al-Ṣabr ʿalā l-Muṣība* ("Good Patience during Calamity"), *al-Istimsāk bi-l-ʿIffa* ("Holding on to Chastity"), *Surʿat al-Iʿtirāf bi-l-Dhanb* ("Quick Confession to Sins"), *al-Ḥirṣ ʿalā l-Taṭahhur bi-l-Rajm* ("Readiness to Redemption") (Abū Shuqqa 2002, 1:155–166).

The second volume is dedicated to exhibiting women's roles in public activities in the early period of Islam. Again, Abū Shuqqa here presents facts and stories that took place in Islamic history before he comes to a conclusion about the teachings of Islam in the subject matter. There are eight chapters and ninety-eight sub-chapters under the volume title *Mushārakat al-Mar'a al-Muslima fī l-Ḥayāt al-Ijtimā'iyya* ("Muslim Women's Participation in Public Social Life"). With the eight chapter headings titled: *Dawā'ī Mushārakat al-Mar'a al-Muslima* ("Positive Factors of Female Participation"), *Ādāb Ishtirāk al-Mar'a al-Muslima* ("Etiquette of Female Public Participation"), *Mushārakat al-Mar'a fī l-Ḥayāt al-Ijtimā'iyya fī 'Uhūd al-Anbiyā'* ("Female Participation in Public during the Ages of the Earlier Prophets"), *Liqā' Nisā' al-Nabī (Ṣ) al-Rijāl fī Majālāt al-Ḥayāt Qabl Farḍ al-Ḥijāb* ("The Prophet's (Ṣ) Wifes Meeting Men in Public Life before the Verse of the Veil"), *Tawāṣul Nisā' al-Nabī (Ṣ) ma' al-Mujtama' wa-Muḥādathatihinn al-Rijāl ba'd Farḍ al-Ḥijāb* ("The Wives of the Prophet Staying in Touch with Society and Talking to Men after the Obligation to Wear the Veil"), *Waqā'i' Mushārakat al-Mar'a al-Muslima fī l-Ḥayāt al-Ijitimā'iyya fī 'Aṣr al-Risāla* ("More Facts about Female Participation in Public Social Life during the Age of the Prophet"), *Mushārakat al-Mar'a al-Muslima fī l-'Amal al-Mihanī* ("Female Participation in Professional Labour"), *Mushārakat al-Mar'al al-Muslima fī l-Nashāṭ al-Ijtimā'ī* ("Female Participation in Female Participation in Social Activities") and *Mushārakat al-Mar'a al-Muslima fī l-Nashāṭ al-Siyāsī* ("Female Participation in Political Activities") (Abū Shuqqa 2002, 2:5–8).

In the rest of the volumes, there are many other chapter headings that indicate Abū Shuqqa's interpretation with regard to women's liberation. The abovementioned sub-chapters show women as the subjects of stories and as the active agents in the early period of Islam. Thus, Abū Shuqqa has approached the *ḥadīth* by inventing a new *tarjama* (translation) of the *ḥadīth*s in which women are visible to contemporary Muslims in the canonical collections. The Prophet, in Abū Shuqqa's perspective, was surrounded by powerful, honourable, and knowledgeable women in every part of his duty in delivering a revelatory message to the people at that time. In other words, women in the time of the Prophet are described by Abū Shuqqa as believing firmly in the faith, as caring to others, as being generous with their wealth for society, as active in social and public activities, as participating in very hard moments such as migration and war, as creative in their suggestions and demands for their own rights and the society, as independent of their marital rights, and as intelligent when it comes to the important knowledge of the time they lived. All of these descriptions of early women in Islam are apparent in Abū Shuqqa's chapter titles and sub-chapter headings.

Abū Shuqqa also categorises care, love, and sexual pleasure under a chapter titled *al-Ḥuqūq al-Mutamāthila lil-Zawjayn* ("Mutual Rights between the

Spouses") (Abū Shuqqa 2002, 5:6–9). There is a title heading in the *Taḥrīr*, *al-Ṭāʿa Masʾūliyyat al-Marʾa* ("Obedience is the Obligation of the Woman"), but it is followed by a discussion of mutual consultation in the sub-chapter *al-Taʿāwun bayn al-Zawjayn* ("Collaboration between the Spouses") to emphasise mutual obligation (Abū Shuqqa 2002, 5:103–109). This organisation reveals that "obedience" is for the sake of both, not only for the sake of one side. In other words, it connotes that the husband is also obliged to obey his wife in order to help her obligation of bringing goodness to the family. Rearing the children is discussed under *al-Masʾūliyya al-Ūlā lil-Marʾa* ("The First Obligation of the Woman") as well, but it is followed directly by *al-Taʿāwun bayn al-Zawjayn min Ajl Kamāl Adāʾ Masʾūliyyat al-Marʾa fī l-Ḥaḍāna* ("Collaboration between the Spouses to Accomplish the Obligation of Nurturing the Children") (Abū Shuqqa 2002, 5:116–126). Under this title, there are sub-titles that explain that rearing the children was also done by the Prophet and many men. The same is for the obligation of managing the house. The *Taḥrīr* classifies it under the obligation for the wife, but this is directly followed by *al-Taʿāwun bayn al-Zawjayn min Ajl Kamāl Adāʾ Masʾūliyyat Tadbīr Shuʾūn al-Bayt* ("Collaboration between the Spouses to Accomplish the Obligation of Managing the House") (Abū Shuqqa 2002, 5:126–130), which discloses that this obligation should be shared in the sense that the husband is also obliged to help his wife in accomplishment of managing the house. There are also sub-titles about the Prophet and male Companions managing their homes. This entire approach, which centres women in the very organisation of the text, when compared to classical works of *ḥadīth* on women's issues and contemporary ones as well, makes the *Taḥrīr* a very impressive and promising text for further attempts to read the *ḥadīth* literature through the lens of gender justice.

### 3.4 *Inclusive Hermeneutics on Gender*

Abū Shuqqa also came up with a method termed the hermeneutics of equality (*musāwāt*) to help dig up new meanings in the *ḥadīth*. Given that Arabic is a gender-specific language, in which expression of all things is classified either as male or female, Abū Shuqqa explains the rule of textual interpretation with regard to this matter. He suggested that the revelatory texts, the Qurʾān and *ḥadīth*, apply equally to both sexes, men and women, even though the language that is used is generally in male form. He acknowledged that there are limited texts delivered particularly to women, but the rule remains that both sexes are addressed intentionally, while the gender-particular texts are exceptional. To prove this argument, Abū Shuqqa quotes the sayings of Abū Bakr Ibn al-ʿArabī (d. 543/1148), Ibn Rushd (d. 595/1198), and Ibn al-Qayyim (751/1349) on the matter. Among classical scholars, however, the issue of whether the male form of sentence includes women is debatable since Arabic is originally a gendered-specific language (al-Ḥasanī 1992, 69–70).

According to Abū Shuqqa, every usage of masculine form in any sentence of the Qurʾān and *ḥadīth* is intended to include both male and female, equally, unless it includes a specific indication for its exclusive application to a male or female (Abū Shuqqa 2002, 1:70). Though Abū Shuqqa did not explain this rule, he exemplified it with many texts of the *ḥadīth*. There are at least twelve texts in the masculine form interpreted to include women as the subjects of meaning. These texts are about teachings that relate to building society, taking care of its members, giving advice and counsel, doing good deeds for the community, bringing peace to people, giving alms to the poor, and helping all the needy (Abū Shuqqa 2002, 2:394–396).

This perspective of understanding the Arabic language as gender inclusiveness, though the form is not so, leads to the belief in gender equality stated by Abū Shuqqa, in interpreting the Qurʾān and *ḥadīth*. This belief made him approach the *ḥadīth* in a way that treats women and men equally as subjects. Its meanings should not discriminate against women in particular. Even though he knew that the Arabic language is gender-specific, he attempted to propose an inclusive interpretation in which women are included in the statement of the masculine form and men are included in that of the feminine form as well. He was additionally aware that many texts are composed literally, not in favour of women, and they side-line and reduce the existence, role, and participation of women in public and private life. Moreover, he was cognisant of prevalent understandings of the available texts among people, the subject of his contention. He objected to an understanding that discriminated against and violated women's humanity. He also rejected any interpretation that maintained that women are bodily alluring and thus damaging to the "community," which positions them as sources of religious immorality.

Just after establishing his hermeneutics of inclusivity when it comes to the Arabic language, Abū Shuqqa goes directly to name the sub-chapter with the phrase "that man and woman are created from one origin." The example is stated in the *Taḥrīr* as an interpretation of the Qurʾān, which states that God created "you" (both sexes) from one soul or self, then, from it, God creates its pair, then from both, He created other men and women (Q 4:1). The "you" or *kum* in Arabic is composed in a male-gendered form. In the traditional interpretation, the verse means that the human being (*kum*, you) is created from Adam, then from his rib God created Eve, and then He created the rest of human beings, men and women (Ibn Kathīr 1999, 2:206). Abū Shuqqa was likely motivated by the traditional interpretation, which is argued by almost all classical exegesis, and moving to an interpretation that "man and woman are created from one origin" (Abū Shuqqa 2002, 1:70). Here, unlike traditional interpretation, Abū Shuqqa argued that the verse of creation does not exclusively address men, but is inclusive of both women and men, and that their creation, then, is the same from one origin.

He also inclusively interprets the verse of consultation (Q 42:38) which is composed in the plural masculine form, "and their affairs are consulted among them" (*wa-amruhum shūrā baynahum*), in favour of gender neutrality and, thus, applying equally to both men and women. In terms of specific familial life, in his interpretation, this verse prescribes a husband to consult his wife and a wife to consult her husband as well. It is odd to him that women are advised to consult men while men are not advised to do the reverse, for many women are wiser than men. Consultation is good conduct in Islam, and it is good for both man and woman to consult one another. He brings forth, then, many *ḥadīth*s to show how the Prophet also consulted his wife in matters of both religious and ordinary life (Abū Shuqqa 2002, 5:103–109).

He also reads many *ḥadīth*s with this hermeneutics of equality in mind. Among them is the following *ḥadīth*:

> Narrated by Anas (d. 93/712): The Prophet said, "None of *you* will have faith till *he* wishes for *his* (Muslim) *brother* what *he* likes for *himself*."[6]

This *ḥadīth* is composed in the Arabic masculine form which is then translated into "he," "his," "brother" and "himself" (*lā yu'minu aḥadukum ḥattā yuḥibba li-akhīhi mā yuḥību li-nafsih*). Abū Shuqqa included this *ḥadīth* in his discussion about the principles of affection among spouses in familial life. To him, this *ḥadīth* directs both husband and wife to love each other and to do her/his best for her/his spouse, since bringing affection to the family is the responsibility of both of them, together. In this regard, the verse of affection in the Qur'ān (30:21),[7] when interpreted from this inclusive linguistic perspective, is interpreted by Abū Shuqqa reciprocally in two directions, from husband to wife and vice versa (Abū Shuqqa 2002, 5:98, 144, and 163).

---

6 Al-Bukhārī 2000, 1:8: *Kitāb al-Īmān* ("Book of Faith"), *Bāb min al-Īmān an Yuḥibba li-Akhīhi mā Yuḥibbu li-Nafsih* ("Chapter on Desiring for One's Muslim Brother What One Desires for Himself is Part of Faith").

7 "And one of His signs is that He created for you spouses from among yourselves so that you may find comfort in them. And He has placed between you compassion and mercy. Surely in this are signs for people who reflect" (Q 30:21).

Another example is the *ḥadīth* of Abū Hurayra (d. 57/678, or slightly later) which is composed in clear gender- specific language, and addressing a husband about his wife. However, Abū Shuqqa reads this *ḥadīth* reciprocally address the wife about her husband (Abū Shuqqa 2002, 5:164).

> Abū Hurayra (Allāh be pleased with him) reported that Allāh's Messenger (may peace be upon him) said: A believing man should not hate a believing woman; if he dislikes one of her characteristics, he will be pleased with another.[8]

Having these hermeneutics of equality, then, he attempted to counter traditional hermeneutics that put the onus only on women as responsible for everything regarded to be religious deviation. He has called for a balance of this meaning by centring women in the stories of the *ḥadīth* text. For example, the following report on a saying of the Prophet operates with two indispensable features, by awakening consciousness of the discriminatory context of the text and moving to that of an egalitarian understanding of it as well.

> Narrated by Abū Mūsā (d. *c.*48/668): Allāh's Apostle said: "Many amongst men reached (the level of) perfection but none amongst the women reached this level except Āsiya, Pharaoh's wife, and Mary, the daughter of ʿImrān."[9]

This *ḥadīth* is recorded in the *Ṣaḥīḥ* of al-Bukhārī and the *Ṣaḥīḥ* of Muslim. Abū Shuqqa put it in conversation with other traditions about virtuous women, making a specific argument under the heading *al-Mar'a wa-Bulūgh al-Kamāl* ("Woman and Achieving Religious Perfection"). In its explanation, he begins to quote opinions of classical scholars such as Abū l-Ḥasan al-Ashʿarī (d. 324/925) and Ibn Ḥajar al-ʿAsqalānī claiming that women can be prophets and indeed there are many female prophets such as Eve, Sara, Āsiya, the mother of Moses, and Mary the mother of Jesus. Characteristics linked to prophecy, as quoted from Ibn Ḥajar, are indeed evidenced in many women of the world, but heard of little. The *ḥadīth* mentions three virtuous women, and female prophets. Having this report on female prophets and its interpretation in classical works,

8 Muslim 2000, 1:608: *Kitāb al-Raḍāʿ* ("Book of Suckling"), *Bāb al-Waṣiyya bi-l-Nisā'* ("Chapter on Advice With Regard to Women").

9 Al-Bukhārī 2000, 2:672: *Kitāb Aḥādīth al-Anbiyā'* ("Book of Traditions of the Prophets"), *Bāb Qawl Allāh Taʿālā wa-Ḍaraba Allāhu Mathalan lil-Ladhīna Āmanū* ("Chapter on Allāh Almighty's Statement: 'And Allāh Sets Forth as an Example to Those Who Believe'").

Abū Shuqqa made his argument by drawing from this *ḥadīth*, explained in the seven points below (Abū Shuqqa 2002, 1:312–315):

1. The nature of being elevated to religious perfection (*kamāl*) is initially embedded in both men and women. Abū Shuqqa has argued that women and men have equal potential to become elevated to the state of religious perfection.
2. This potential will be possible only by having a readiness for religious consciousness, and the ability to conduct religious activities that may elevate one to the state of being religiously perfect. Learning, teaching, and preparing supportive conditions for both women and men are necessary to reach this state. The more these conditions are accessible for her or him, the more possibilities are open for her or him to move towards perfection.
3. Taking the two notes above into consideration, Abū Shuqqa clarified that the little number of virtuous women stated in the report above is not because they are women, but because the society they lived in encouraged them to have other duties that were not considered part of "religious perfection," such as getting pregnant, giving birth, rearing children, and taking care of all familial matters. In such conditions, women are not prepared by society to become elevated to the state of religious perfection. Muslims should open equal spaces to women as they do to men for this elevation to perfection.
4. Abū Shuqqa has also questioned his readers; does the *ḥadīth* above indicate only the perfection that has been seen, known, and heard by people? Thus, could there be other perfection, particularly pertaining to women, that has not been seen, known, and heard by them? This question comes to mind from reading verses 66:11–12 of the Qur'ān.[10] Indeed, according to him, there are many honourable and perfect women who are not known yet.
5. Since public spaces, in which acts take place such as worship, teaching, and preaching, through which one may be elevated to perfection are already occupied by men, Abū Shuqqa proposed that "female spaces" should also be considered as grounds for this religious perfection. Activities related to taking care of the family are considered commonly

10 "And Allāh sets forth an example for the believers: the wife of Pharaoh, who prayed, 'My Lord! Build me a house in Paradise near You, deliver me from Pharaoh and his [evil] doing, and save me from the wrongdoing people.' [There is] also [the example of] Mary, the daughter of 'Imrān, who guarded her chastity, so We breathed into her [womb] through Our angel [Gabriel]. She testified to the words of her Lord and His Scriptures, and was one of the [sincerely] devout" (Q 66:11–12).

as mundane. Since these activities are very important, even from a religious perspective, they should be reconsidered as religious and spiritual and thus as a pathway towards perfection. Unfortunately, these activities are unseen, unknown, and unrecognised by society, and those who participate in these activities are also unseen, unknown, and unrecognised. The unknown, to him, does not mean unimportant. Indeed, he argued that there are many unknown soldiers who save society and who make its history. In his view, women are the unknown soldiers of society.

6. The *ḥadīth*, according to Abū Shuqqa, encourages women to be part of those who elevate to perfection. It does not state that women are not able to elevate. Natural hindrances such as menstruation may prevent women from certain types of worship, primarily prayer and fasting, but they may conduct many other good things that will take them to perfection. Abū Shuqqa has asked those who experience reproductive duties and dedicate themselves to familial responsibilities to be patient, aware of their important position, and faithful when educating people in their arms. This will elevate them to religious perfection.
7. Abū Shuqqa has also urged contemporary Muslims to do their best to support women in elevating to religious perfection and to make them visible in society.

If all *ḥadīth*s are approached with such hermeneutics, we will have many more interpretations of egalitarian gender relations from an Islamic perspective.

### 3.5 *Reinterpreting Problematic* Ḥadīths

In classical discussion of the sciences of *ḥadīth*, there is a branch that explains interpretative attempts made for *ḥadīth*s that literally contradict each other or contradict the principles of Islam derived from the Qurʾān and *ḥadīth*. These contradictory *ḥadīth*s are called *mukhtalif al-ḥadīth* and *mushkil al-ḥadīth*, which literally mean "conflicting *ḥadīth*s" and "problematic *ḥadīth*s," respectively. The classical scholars often defined conflicting or problematic *ḥadīth*s as accepted *ḥadīth*s despite apparently contradicting the principles of the Qurʾān or other authoritative texts, so a serious attempt to avoid a literal understanding of these *ḥadīth*s is necessary (al-Ghawrī 2010, 2:169). In the classical discussion, only very few reports concerning gender issues are deemed to be problematic *ḥadīth*s. In modern times, many *ḥadīth*s concerning gender issues and which appear to condone discrimination and marginalisation of women are subjects of reinterpretation; thereby, they are considered as conflicting and problematic *ḥadīth*s.

Abū Shuqqa also discussed the genre of problematic *ḥadīth*s, and in the *Taḥrīr*, there are many valid *ḥadīth*s regarded as conflicting and problematic.

Since women's participation in public spaces is Sunna, Abū Shuqqa reinterpreted many *ḥadīth*s that are traditionally understood literally to be contrary to the principle of Sunna, and, thus, problematic. The *ḥadīth*: "[the] *jihād* of women is pilgrimage,"[11] for instance, according to Abū Shuqqa, is not to ban women from the *jihād* of military expedition. The *ḥadīth* is to explain that women may make pilgrimage if they want to receive the rewards of *jihād*. This *ḥadīth* is rather to acknowledge the physical paucity of women to be as involved as men in war. Women are still, however, allowed to go on military expeditions. There are many *ḥadīth*s showing that the women of early Islam were involved in this activity, preparing food, nursing the wounded, and even bearing arms. Fifteen women, for instance, took part in the war of Khaybar (7/628). Umm Sulaym bore arms in the war of Ḥunayn (8/630). Umm ʿAmmāra (d. 13/634) bore arms and protected the Prophet in Uḥud (d. 3/625) when the Muslims were defeated and most of the men ran away to save themselves, leaving the Prophet unprotected (Abū Shuqqa 2002, 1:31, 177, 2:53–45, 221–222, 3:36–38). Thus, Abū Shuqqa interprets the above-mentioned *ḥadīth* of *jihād* in a different way: that this *ḥadīth* acknowledges the conditions of women in society but does not discriminate against them.

The *ḥadīth* "[the] prayer of a woman in her house is better than in the mosque" (Aḥmad b. Ḥanbal 1996, 45:37–38) does not contradict the right of women to pray in the mosque. This *ḥadīth* should be understood in its context, which is the busy woman with domestic duties. This *ḥadīth*, according to Abū Shuqqa, appreciates domestic activities and acknowledges the hardships that might exhaust a woman who works in her house, and also longs to pray at the mosque. This *ḥadīth*, he argued, does not require women to conduct prayer at the house, as many female Companions were active in praying at the mosque. When the Prophet heard a woman's baby cried during congregational prayer, he did not command her to pray at her house; he still welcomed her come to the mosque. Moreover, when the Prophet was reminded that ʿIshāʾ prayer was conducted late at night, and thus women and children would not be able to attend as they were sleeping, he performed it in the early evening. All of these *ḥadīth*s, according to Abū Shuqqa, reveal that women are not to be kept away from the mosque and that their houses are not better than the mosque. The main message addressed by the *ḥadīth* is that a woman's hardships should be acknowledged and her work should be appreciated. In this context, only when a women is exhausted from domestic work, or when a prayer is conducted very

11 Al-Bukhārī 2000, 2:558: *Kitāb al-Jihād wa-l-Siyar* ("Book on Fighting for the Cause of Allāh"), *Bāb Jihād al-Nisāʾ* ("Chapter on the *Jihād* of Women").

late at night and could jeopardise her safety, then, her prayer at home is better for her than in the mosque (Abū Shuqqa 2002, 3:27–31, 39 and 53).

Furthermore, Abū Shuqqa argued that *ḥadīths* on the prohibition of handshakes between men and women, and preventing men and women from being in seclusion with each other, are not meant to bar them from jointly participating in social activities. These *ḥadīths* are understood by Abū Shuqqa, alongside other teachings such as veiling women and lining them behind men in congregational prayers, as advice to men and women on how to meet each other, while also practicing self-dignity, honesty, and modesty. Abū Shuqqa also cites many *ḥadīths* in his text that show how on many occasions the Prophet was in a situation where he touched and was touched by a woman and was in seclusion with a woman as well. For example, Anas b. Malik related that "Any of the female slaves of Medina could take hold of the hand of Allāh's Messenger and take him wherever she wished."[12] This assures Muslims that for many good purposes, a man may touch a woman and he can be in seclusion with her as long as they maintain self-dignity and honesty, while avoiding illicit sexual intimacy. There are also many *ḥadīths* quoted by Abū Shuqqa regarding this point that support his suggestion. He puts them under the title *Nuṣūṣ Tufīd Jawāz al-Lams ʿind al-Ḥāja bidūn Shahwa* ("Texts of *Ḥadīth* Denoting the Permissibility of Touching (Woman and Man) If Need Be without Temptation") (Abū Shuqqa 2002, 2:91–93). Indeed, according to Abū Shuqqa, the *ḥadīths* do not ask men to stay away from women, or even prescribe separate societies for women and men.

There is also a famous *ḥadīth* recorded in the collection of al-Bukhārī where the Prophet says: "I haven't left behind any *fitna* (trial or affliction, etc.) that is more harmful to men than women" (*mā taraktū baʿdī fitnatan hiya aḍarr ʿalā al-rijāl min al-nisāʾ*).[13] This *ḥadīth* often becomes the grounds for conservatives to perpetuate the idea that women are dangerous sources of temptation, explicitly using the word *fitna*. From their perspective, in order to prevent men from destruction stirred by women, there should be abundant restrictions placed upon women. They should be veiled, segregated, confined at home, and their public activities should be significantly restricted. Abū Shuqqa suggested that conservative exaggerations of texts on the temptation of women are shaped mainly in the spirit of "oppression of women by men and arrogance of men over women" (*istiḍʿāf al-dhakar lil-unthā wa-stiʿlāʾ al-rijāl wa-stikbāruhum*

---

12 Al-Bukhārī 3:1240: *Kitāb al-Adab* ("Book of Manners"), *Bāb al-Kibr* ("Chapter on Pride and Arrogance").

13 Al-Bukhārī 2000, 3:1064, *Kitāb al-Nikāḥ* ("Book of Marriage"), *Bāb mā Yuttaqā min Shuʾm al-Marʾa* ("Chapter on What Evil Omen of a Lady is to be Warded Off").

*ʿalā l-nisāʾ*) (Abū Shuqqa 2002, 3:203). This is evidenced in the way conservatives selectively emphasise only the temptation of women while they deliberately omit other texts that focus on the temptation of family, wealth, and social status.

In Abū Shuqqa's description, the notion of *fitna*, or temptation, is a general term for the state of condition in which one may be allured from the right path to conduct a wrong deed. Abū Shuqqa criticised conservatives who exaggerate the notion of the temptation of women by inferring restrictions that confine the freedom of women, while they do not create any restrictions to keep away from the temptations of family and wealth (Abū Shuqqa 2002, 3:200–203). The only reason for this is, according to him, because restrictions on temptation when it comes to family and wealth might harm men's freedom and rights. Hence, conservatives prefer to control women and restrict their mobility, while they allow men to widely enjoy their freedom. This kind of conservative interpretation contradicts the principle of equality, partnership, and mutuality between men and women. It also contradicts the principle that women have equal humanity to men. Here, argued Abū Shuqqa, *fitna* should be understood inclusively as a general test of life, addressed to both women and men, that can take the forms of any kind of worldly desires that may turn them away from the truth. Women, family, and wealth are only examples of those forms.

Unlike the conservatives, arguing on the grounds of verses in the Qurʾān (specifically 12:23, 24, 31 and 33), Abū Shuqqa explained that both women and men are susceptible to sexual temptation, they both are reciprocally attractive to and attracted by each other. Abū Shuqqa recognised the potential temptation of both women and men, to each other. The *ḥadīth*s, according to him, advise people to establish relationships between the different sexes with self-dignity without labelling one sex as the only source of temptation. In other words, the notion of sexual temptation applies to men as they are attractive to women and to women as they are attractive to men. Being attractive to and attracted by is natural. Indeed, it is not the concern of the *ḥadīth*s on this issue. Rather, the *ḥadīth*s pertaining to this issue are about how to behave in relation to one another in a respectful manner and about not luring each other to illicit sexual intimacy. To burden women with the onus of all immoralities that happen in the society is an obvious injustice and not intended by the *ḥadīth*s. This way of giving a reciprocal meaning to the *ḥadīth*s when it comes to sexual desire is, to my knowledge, only observed in the *Taḥrīr* of Abū Shuqqa. Moreover, the consciousness that male biases may influence *ḥadīth*-based interpretations concerning the temptation of women is also only observed in the *Taḥrīr*.

In the discussion on the interplay between text and context, Abū Shuqqa also maintained that problematic *ḥadīth*s should be reinterpreted by focusing on their main message. For instance, the *ḥadīth* that says: "A woman should not travel unless accompanied by her husband or her relative,"[14] is to guarantee a woman's safety during her trip, not to restrict her from travel. According to Abū Shuqqa, the *ḥadīth* is not to ban women from travelling or any activity in public spheres. The task of providing safety is also not necessarily performed by her relative since there are many other means to guarantee safety. In fact, a woman is allowed to have any person, man or woman, whom she trusts to accompany her when she needs it for her travel (Abū Shuqqa 2002, 2:280–282). This is to say that the main message of the *ḥadīth* is not to require male accompaniment for a woman during her trip, but to provide for her safety. With this approach, the *ḥadīth* is not used as the basis for banning women from their basic rights to travel, study, and work. Rather, it encourages society to facilitate women's complete safety when traveling for study, work, or other purposes.

## 4 Conclusion

Abū Shuqqa's interpretive attempts, when it comes to the *ḥadīth* texts, are generally characterised by his acknowledgement of male biases within prevalent interpretations of the *ḥadīth*; hence, his seeking of strategies to centre women is inevitable, and can be observed in particular by the way he mainstreamed the notion of partnership, mutuality, and reciprocity. Compared to the traditional and conservative views, Abū Shuqqa's interpretation ensures that women's involvement in public activities is not only allowed in Islam, but is also recommended; thereby, society is encouraged to provide proper inclusion for women. Though he still envisages traditional divisions between gender roles as important and primary, they are neither universal nor immutable.

From the methodological approaches of Abū Shuqqa, analysed above, this study finds that there are possibilities for reinterpreting *ḥadīth* to encourage egalitarian gender ethics. Indeed, this study finds three favourable approaches of the *Taḥrīr* with regard to advocacy for gender equality. First is its inclusive concept of *ḥadīth* in which experiences of the female Companions are imparted as a constitutive element of the Prophetic guidance. Second is its reorganisation of the *ḥadīth* in themes that make female agency observable and recognisable. Third is its equality-based reading of the texts in which

14 Muslim 2000, 1:548: *Kitāb al-Ḥajj* ("Book of Pilgrimage"), *Bāb Safar al-Mar'a maʿ Maḥram* ("Chapter on A Woman Travelling With an Unmarriageable Kin or Her Husband").

women's perspectives are centered much more than the readings of the conservatives and the moderates. Its conception that Islamic sources have established three principles on human dignity, independency, and responsibility of both women and men is also favourable for the development of this ethics.

The above discussion was a hermeneutical analysis about the reinterpretation of the *ḥadīth* within the context of Muslims' contemporary struggle for equality between women and men. It was concerned with an interpretative attempt in which the *ḥadīth* is perceived positively, as a source of Islamic teachings for a meaningful life and just relations between women and men. I used the *Taḥrīr* of Abū Shuqqa to point out some of its enabling moments when it comes to reading Islamic sources, as practiced by advocates of gender equality within Islam. While Abū Shuqqa's interpretation of egalitarian gender relations is debatable, his methodological approach to the *ḥadīth* deserves ample appreciation, as his work suggests that reinterpretation of *ḥadīth* in the light of women's and men's equality can retrieve key aspects of the texts that have been neglected through tendentious assumptions prevalent among many Muslims. His interpretation of mutuality when it comes to the relationship between women and men in domestic and public spheres therefore deserves further study as we work towards egalitarian gender ethics in Islam.

## Bibliography

Abū Bakr, Umayma and Shirīn Shukrī. 2002. *Al-Mar'a wa-l-Jandar: Ilghā' al-Tamyīz al-Thaqāfī wa-l-Ijtimā'ī Bayn al-Jinsayn*. Damascus: Dār al-Fikr.

Abū Dāwūd, Sulaymān b. al-Ash'ath. 2000. *Sunan Abī Dāwūd*, 2 vols. Cairo: Jam'iyyat al-Maknaz al-Islāmī.

Abū Shuqqa, 'Abd al-Ḥalīm Muḥammad. 1974. "Khawāṭir ḥawla Azmat al-'Aql al-Muslim al-Mu'āṣir." *Al-Muslim al-Mu'āṣir* 0(al-'Adad al-Iftitāḥī): 12–28.

Abū Shuqqa, 'Abd al-Ḥalīm Muḥammad. 1975. "Khawāṭir ḥawla Azmat al-Khuluq al-Muslim al-Mu'āṣir." *Al-Muslim al-Mu'āṣir* 1–2: 41–74.

Abū Shuqqa, 'Abd al-Ḥalīm Muḥammad. 2001. *Naqd al-'Aql al-Muslim: al-Azma wa-l-Makhraj*. Kuwait: Dār al-Qalam lil-Nashr wa-l-Tawzī'.

Abū Shuqqa, 'Abd al-Ḥalīm Muḥammad. 2002. *Taḥrīr al-Mar'a fī 'Aṣr al-Risāla. Dirāsa 'an al-Mar'a Jāmi'a li-Nuṣūṣ al-Qur'ān wa-Ṣaḥīḥay al-Bukhārī wa-Muslim*, 6 vols. Kuwait: Dār al-Qalam.

Aḥmad b. Ḥanbal. 1996. *Musnad al-Imām Aḥmad b. Ḥanbal*, edited by Shu'ayb al-Arnā'ūṭ and 'Ādil Murshid. Beirut: Mu'assasat al-Risāla.

Ali, Syed Mohammed. 2004. *The Position of Women in Islam: A Progressive View*. Albany: State University of New York Press.

al-ʿAwwā, Muḥammad Salīm. 2000. *Al-Islāmiyyūn wa-l-Marʾa*. Mansoura: Dār al-Wafāʾ.

Balṭājī, Muḥammad. 2005. *Makānat al-Marʾa fī l-Qurʾān al-Karīm wa-l-Sunna al-Ṣaḥīḥa*. Cairo: Dār al-Salām.

Berglund, Jenny. 2011. "Global Question in the Classroom: The Formulation of Islamic Religious Education at Muslim Schools in Sweden." *Discourse: Studies in the Cultural Politics of Education* 32(4): 487–512.

al-Bughā, Muṣṭafā. 1990. *Buḥūth fī ʿUlūm al-Ḥadīth wa-Nuṣūṣih*. Damascus: Maṭbaʿat al-Ittiḥād.

al-Bukhārī, Muḥammad b. Ismāʿīl. 2000. *Ṣaḥīḥ al-Bukhārī*. Cairo: Jamʿiyyat al-Maknaz al-Islāmī.

Engineer, Ali Asghar. 2001. "Islam, Women, and Gender Justice." In *What Men Owe to Women*, edited by John C. Raines and Daniel C. Maguire. New York: State University of New York Press.

Fadel, Muhammad. 2012. "Muslim Reformists, Female Citizenship, and the Public Accommodation of Islam in Liberal Democracy." *Politics and Religion* 5: 2–35.

Farīja, Muḥammad. 1996. *Huqūq al-Marʾa al-Muslima fī l-Qurʾān wa-l-Sunna*. Beirut and Damascus: al-Maktab al-Islāmī.

Franzmann, Majella. 2000. *Women and Religion*. Oxford: Oxford University Press.

al-Ghawrī, Sayyid ʿAbd al-Mājid. 2010. *Maṣādir al-Ḥadīth wa-Marājiʿuh: Dirāsa wa-Taʿrīf*. Damascus and Beirut: Dār Ibn Kathīr.

al-Ghazālī, Muḥammad. 1989. *Al-Sunna al-Nabawiyya bayna Ahl al-Fiqh wa-Ahl al-Ḥadīth*. Cairo: Dār al-Shurūq.

al-Hādī, Ṣādiq b. Muḥammad. 2009. "Al-Marʾa fī l-Sunna al-Nabawiyya al-Muṭahhara." *Al-Alūka*, 7 May 2009: www.alukah.net/publications_competitions/0/6525/.

al-Ḥakīm, Razān ʿAbduh. 2008. *Ṣūrat al-Marʾa fī l-Ḥadīth al-Nabawī*. Damascus: Dār al-Fikr.

al-Ḥasanī, Muḥammad ʿIṣām ʿIrār. 1992. *Bahjat al-Wuṣūl bi-Sharḥ al-Lumaʿ fī ʿIlm al-Uṣūl li-Abī Isḥāq al-Shīrāzī*. Damascus: Dār al-ʿIlm lil-Ṭibāʿa.

Hassan, Riffat. 1991. "Muslim Women and Post-Patriarchal Islam." In *After Patriarchy: Feminist Transformation of the World Religions*, edited by Paula M. Cooey, William R. Eakin and Jay B. McDaniel. New York: Orbis Book.

al-Hāshimī, Muḥammad ʿAlī. 2013. *Shakhṣiyyat al-Marʾa al-Muslima ka-Mā Yaṣūghuhā l-Islām fī l-Kitāb wa-l-Sunna*. Cairo: Dār al-Salām.

al-Hibri, Azizah Y. 2000. "An Introduction to Muslim Women's Rights." In *Windows of Faith: Muslim Women Scholar-Activists in North America*, edited by Gisela Webb, 51–71. New York: Syracuse University Press.

Ibn Bāz, ʿAbd al-ʿAzīz. 1988. *Khaṭar Mushārakat al-Marʾa lil-Rajul fī Maydān ʿAmalih*. Cairo: Maktabat al-Sunna lil-Tawzīʿ.

Ibn Bāz, ʿAbd al-ʿAzīz. 1994. *Fatāwā l-Nisāʾ*. Medina and Cairo: Dār Ibn Rajab and Dār al-Ṭibāʿa.

Ibn Bāz, ʿAbd al-ʿAzīz. 1995. *Fatāwā l-ʿUlamāʾ lil-Nisāʾ*. Cairo: Maṭbaʿat al-Sunna.

Ibn Kathīr, Ismāʿīl. 1999. *Tafsīr al-Qurʾān al-ʿAẓim*. Riyad: Dār Ṭayba.

Ibn Māja. 2000. *Sunan Ibn Māja*. Cairo: Jamʿiyyat al-Maknaz al-Islāmī.

Ibn Qarnās. 2011. *Al-Ḥadīth wa-l-Qurʾān*. Baghdad: Manshūrāt al-Jamal.

ʿItr, Nūr al-Dīn. 1985. *Manhaj al-Naqd fī ʿUlūm al-Ḥadīth*. Damascus: Dār al-Fikr.

ʿIzzat, Hiba Raʾūf. 1995. *Al-Marʾa wa-l-ʿAmal al-Siyāsī: Ruʾya Islāmiyya*. Herndon, VA: al-Maʿhad al-ʿĀlamī lil-Fikr al-Islāmī.

Kahf, Mohja. 2000. "Braiding the Stories: Women's Eloquence in the Early Islamic Era." In *Windows of Faith: Muslim Women Scholar-Activists in North America*, edited by Gisela Webb, 147–71. New York, NY: Syracuse University Press.

al-Khurasānī, Ghāda. 1979. *Al-Islām wa-Taḥrīr al-Marʾa: Awwal Mawsūʿa ʿan al-Marʾa al-ʿArabiyya ʿabr al-ʿUṣūr*. Beirut: Dār al-Siyāsa.

al-Lajna al-Islāmiyya al-ʿĀlamiyya lil-Marʾa wa-l-Ṭifl. 2004. *Taḥrīr al-Marʾa fī l-Islām. Aʿmāl al-Muʾtamar al-Munʿaqad bi-l-Qāhira min 22–23 Fibrāyir 2003*. Cairo: Dār al-Qalam.

Mālik b. Anas. 2000. *Muwaṭṭaʾ Mālik*. Cairo: Jamʿiyyat al-Maknaz al-Islāmī.

Mernissi, Fatima. 1991. *The Veil and the Male Elite: A Feminist Interpretation of Women's Rights in Islam*. Reading, MA: Addison-Wesley.

Muslim b. al-Ḥajjāj. 2000. *Ṣaḥīḥ Muslim*, 2 vols. Cairo: Jamʿiyyat al-Maknaz al-Islāmī.

al-Qannūjī, Muḥammad Ṣiddīq Ḥasan Khān. 2008. *Ḥusn al-Uswa bi-Mā Thabata ʿan-Allāh wa-Rasūlih fī l-Niswa*, edited by Bashīr Muḥammad ʿUyūn. Damascus: Maktabat Dār al-Bayān.

al-Qaraḍāwī, Yūsuf. 1991. *Kayfa Nataʿāmal maʿ al-Sunna al-Nabawiyya: Maʿālim wa-Ḍawābiṭ*. Riyad: Maktabat al-Muʾayyad.

al-Sharqāwī, Aḥmad b. Muḥammad. 2009. *Ḥuqūq al-Marʾa fī l-Sunna*. Riyad: Dār al-Ṣamīʿī.

Siddique, Kaukab. 1990. *Liberation of Women Thru Islam*. Kingsville, MD: American Society for Education and Religion.

al-Tirmidhī, Muḥammad b. ʿĪsā. 2000. *Sunan al-Tirmidhī*, 2 vols. Cairo: Jamʿiyyat al-Maknaz al-Islāmī.

al-ʿUthaymīn, Muḥammad b. Ṣāliḥ. 1989. *Fatāwā wa-Rasāʾil lil-Nisāʾ*. Cairo: Maktabat al-Turāth al-Islāmī.

al-ʿUthaymīn, Muḥammad b. Ṣāliḥ. 1998. *Al-Fatāwā l-Nisāʾiyya*. Cairo: Maktabat al-ʿIlm.

CHAPTER 10

# Islamic Ethics and the *Ḥadīth* of Intention

*Ali Altaf Mian*

## 1 Introduction

The capacity of the doer to give purpose and meaning to the deed, or intentionality, is a major theoretical and practical concern of Islamic ethics. This chapter illuminates this concern by recourse to a study of the Prophetic report often called the *ḥadīth* of intention: "Actions are indeed [evaluated] according to intentions." I approach this report as an entry point into broader debates on human agency in Islamic ethics. To that end, this chapter pursues the following questions: What is the relationship between intention and action? Does the former cause the latter, or does action construct inner life? How do commonly shared motivations create community and how are such motivations cultivated? Where have Muslim jurists and Sufis converged and diverged in their approaches to intentionality? Are intentions performative (embedded in devotional practices and social transactions) or a matter of the heart (presupposing a self that stands behind bodily actions)?

I grapple with these questions in three conceptual frameworks, which is to say that I relate the *ḥadīth* of intention to (1) the dialectic of inside (*bāṭin*) and outside (*ẓāhir*), (2) communal formation, and (3) the distinction between the transcendental and empirical aspects of juridical-moral norms. My argument, simply put, is that studying the *ḥadīth* of intention in relation to these conceptual frameworks reveals the resourcefulness of *ḥadīth* discourse for thinking about ethical agency, since the commentarial literature on this report elaborates a complex view of intention as a psychosomatic orientation that conjoins the self to the Other, the individual to the community, and morality to legality.

At the outset, I find it apropos to mention my personal motivation for pursuing the question of intentionality and *ḥadīth* discourse. I suspect that this chapter is an attempt on my part to grapple with the challenges posed to intentionality by psychoanalysis, especially the writings of Sigmund Freud (d. 1939) and Jacques Lacan (d. 1981). I have especially struggled to come to terms with two challenges stemming from my study of their writings. First, they hold that the subject of consciousness is not fully self-transparent and one often acts without total knowledge of one's latent motivations. Second, they contend that it might be impossible to constantly orient oneself towards a transcendental signifier, that is, to constantly focus on God, when most of one's actions are embedded in social networks of recognition.

The commentarial literature on the *ḥadīth* of intention allows us to think creatively about both challenges posed by psychoanalysis. This is so because Muslim ethicists have elaborated nuanced views of interiority that approach inner life as a theatre of struggle between instinct and reason. They have also acknowledged the social nature of action as well as the communal, even political, import of intentionality. Thus, I read the Islamic ethical insistence on the necessity of introspection, the struggle to purify motivation, as an attempt to constantly destabilise the moral certitude practitioners of piety might enjoy about their actions. In other words, by linking intention to self-probing ethical reasoning, the Islamic ethical tradition posits moral action as a site of self-transcendence.

Now, a note on what follows. I commence with a brief discussion of the *ḥadīth* of intention that locates my inquiry in the turn to practice on the part of religious studies scholars. This section also illuminates how thinking about intention through the lens of religious practice involves attention to its historical scene of emergence, its meaning in concrete social contexts, and the "discursive formations" (or what I have called conceptual frameworks) in which it has been historically understood. To that end, the following sections consider the biography of the *ḥadīth* scholar who popularised this report in the middle of the second/eighth century (section 3); how this report has been linked to political action and communal formation (section 4); the textuality of its citation in its *locus classicus*, namely, al-Bukhārī's (d. 256/870) *Ṣaḥīḥ* ("Authentic") (section 5); the reception of this report, and intentionality more broadly, in classical-era Sufi writings (section 6); the necessity of approaching intention in Islamic ethics as simultaneously empirical and transcendental (section 7); finally, the conclusion considers the methodological salience of using *ḥadīth* texts to think about key concepts in the study of Islamic ethics.

## 2 Intention and the Turn to Practice

The three conceptual frameworks I mentioned above are alluded to in the "the *ḥadīth* of intention," which I cite below:

> Actions are indeed [evaluated] according to intentions, and in fact what belongs to a man is what he intends. So, whosoever migrates towards God and His Messenger, let it be known that his migration is for God and

> His Messenger. So, whosoever migrates to pursue the world or to marry a woman, let it be known that his migration is for what he migrates towards.
>
> AL-BUKHĀRĪ 2011, 1:180–181[1]

The report's ethical significance was clear to classical-era Muslim religious scholars. For instance, the famed jurist Muḥammad b. Idrīs al-Shāfiʿī (d. 204/820) allegedly said: "This *ḥadīth* contains seventy portals into 'religious understanding' (*fiqh*) … and encompasses one-third of 'religious knowledge' (*ʿilm*)."[2] This Prophetic report has thus been cited copiously and continuously in Muslim religious discourses to underscore the ethical principle that the doer's motive is an important source for determining the moral status of the deed. The *ḥadīth* fleshes out this principle by recourse to an example, what I call "ethnographic illustration," that is, an example considering how people might practice the principle at hand.

The *ḥadīth* of intention places motive at the heart of action, a move that has wide-ranging purchase in both legal and Sufi ideas about human agency (that is, the capacity to transform oneself and one's social world through action). Yet the Islamic ethical principle concerning intention (*niyya*) is not only about being conscious of one's motivations; it also involves truthfulness and sincerity: "intention signifies sincerity; it is a unitary act for the sake of God, the One without peers" (Ibn Ḥajar 1969, 1:12). This is what we might call the pietistic understanding of intention, which has often been elaborated in Sufi texts. At the same time, the idea that Sufi theologians are concerned solely with the transcendental aspects of intentionality is also problematic. As the foremost Sufi theologian and Muslim mystical author of the seventh/thirteenth century Ibn ʿArabī (d. 638/1240) writes: "While intention is unitary with respect to its essence, it changes with respect to its object, and so the consequence of an intention, too, depends on its object" (Ibn ʿArabī 1997, 1:256). *Niyya* thus concerns *how* one desires in the heart but also *what* one desires in the world. Muslim jurists, in turn, consider the moral status of devotional rituals, social transactions, and criminal behaviour. The key question here is: How does empirical action mirror inner motive? Jurists answer this question on a case-by-case basis, complicating our understanding of the inside-outside relationship.

---

1 This *ḥadīth*, which is the first report recorded by al-Bukhārī in his *Ṣaḥīḥ*, appears with slight modifications in six additional "books" of this collection. Here, I cite the opening version in *Kitāb Badʾ al-Waḥy* ("Book of the Beginning of Revelation"), *Bāb Badʾ al-Waḥy ʿalā Rasūl Allāh* ("Chapter on How the Divine Revelation Started to Be Revealed to Allāh's Messenger"). For an insightful analysis of this report, see de Francesco (2013).

2 The first saying is cited from al-Khaṭīb's (d. 463/1071) *al-Jāmiʿ* ("The Compendium") and the second from al-Bayhaqī (d. 458/1066) (al-Suyūṭī 1986, 42–43).

The broader ethical principle underlined by this *ḥadīth* thus becomes: because bodily action can reveal, conceal, and displace inner motive, we must approach *niyya* in contextual, concrete terms. This is another way of underscoring the centrality of practice and contingency in ethical theory. The fact that Sufis and jurists have accentuated different aspects of this ethical principle does not necessarily imply that we are talking about two different religious practices. Rather, we can take the Sufi insistence on the inside and the juristic emphasis on the outside as reflecting the two sides of religious practice: the transcendental and the empirical. I address the latter conceptual dichotomy below. Here, let me say more on the advantages of approaching intentionality through the lens of religious practice.

Several scholars of religion have argued for nuanced approaches to religious practice. In her influential ethnography of Egyptian Muslim women's participation in the so-called Islamic Revival of the 1990s, anthropologist Saba Mahmood underscores "the morphology of moral actions" (Mahmood 2005, 25, 119). She argues that when examined as micropolitical strategies, Muslim women's practices of piety can no longer be depoliticised as docile submission to authority, as is often done within secular liberal feminist frameworks. In her focus on practice as a site for understanding ethical life, historian of religion and social ethicist Anna Peterson posits practices of "morality as a living, collective, and active undertaking" (Peterson 2020, 6). The sociologist of religion Robert Wuthnow argues that intention cannot be ignored in any examination of religious practice, since practitioners use rituals to "articulate and enact their intentions" (Wuthnow 2020, 104). He further argues that we must attend to the macrostructures in which religious practices are situated and in which intentions are "reinforced, aligned, and favorably [or unfavorably] assessed" (Wuthnow 2020, 104). These macrostructures include "power dynamics, social interactions, and discursive formations" (Wuthnow 2020, 13). The turn to practice in religious studies, therefore, allows us to place intentionality in Islamic ethics in multiple historiographical, political, and conceptual frameworks. In what follows, I have especially attempted to situate the *ḥadīth* of intention in relation to its salient "discursive formations," namely, the dialogue of the inside and outside, political action and communal formation, and the transcendental and empirical aspects of juridical-moral norms.

## 3 The Popularisation of the *Ḥadīth* of Intention

To appreciate how this report underscores the dialogue between the inside and outside (as well as the implications of this dialogue for the practice of

Islamic ethics), it is important to first study its historical scene of emergence. It was the traditionist Yaḥyā b. Saʿīd al-Anṣārī (d. 143/760 or 144/761) who first brought this report into wide circulation in the middle of the eighth century. A student of the so-called "seven jurists of Medina," Yaḥyā b. Saʿīd was a famed scholar of Prophetic traditions and a master-jurist in his own right. His pre-eminent status as a man of piety – according to some observers he was an urbane ascetic – made him attractive to the administrators of law and order in the Islamic imperium. The Umayyads appointed him judge (*qāḍī*) of Medina around the year 743 (Judd 2014, 158). The ʿAbbāsids followed suit and appointed him *qāḍī* when they established rule in the Iraqi city of Hāshimiyya. The prosopographical literature remembers Yaḥyā for emphasising sincere intentions and pious actions. The Damascene historian and *ḥadīth* scholar Shams al-Dīn al-Dhahabī (d. 748/1348) informs us that "Yaḥyā is the [chief] narrator of the Prophetic report about actions and intentions, and it is from him that this *ḥadīth* became popular. It is said that around 200 people narrated this report from him" (al-Dhahabī 1996, 5:476–481).

Yaḥyā is therefore the "common link" between narrators of this report before his time period and the succeeding generations of narrators. The term, "common link," was coined by the Orientalist Joseph Schacht (d. 1969) to refer to the narrator who popularised a tradition: "the existence of a significant common link (N.N.) in all or most *isnāds* of a given tradition would be a strong indication in favour of its having originated in the time of N.N." (Schacht 1979, 172). The Dutch historian of *ḥadīth* G.H.A. Juynboll (d. 2010) brought a more nuanced view to this phenomenon and joined Schacht in using "the common link" to "establish the date and place of origin of individual *ḥadīths*" (Motzki 2004, xxxviii). Yet both Schacht and Juynboll associated the common link phenomenon with forged reports. Harald Motzki (d. 2019) challenged their view by insisting that the common link is not necessarily the forger of a tradition, but in many instances a narrator who might be "characterised as an early systematic collector who professionally passed his material on to students in a teaching circle" (Motzki 2004, xl). This view is more sympathetic to the approach of Muslim traditionists, since for them the common link phenomenon did not automatically imply forgery or invention; rather, it only signalled one of the many defects of transmission that must be considered in evaluating a report's authenticity and normative evidentiary status (Aghaei 2020, 114–115).

The point to underscore here is that it was Yaḥyā who popularised the *ḥadīth* of intention, as is brought out in Juynboll's "chain of narration" (*isnād*) for this report:

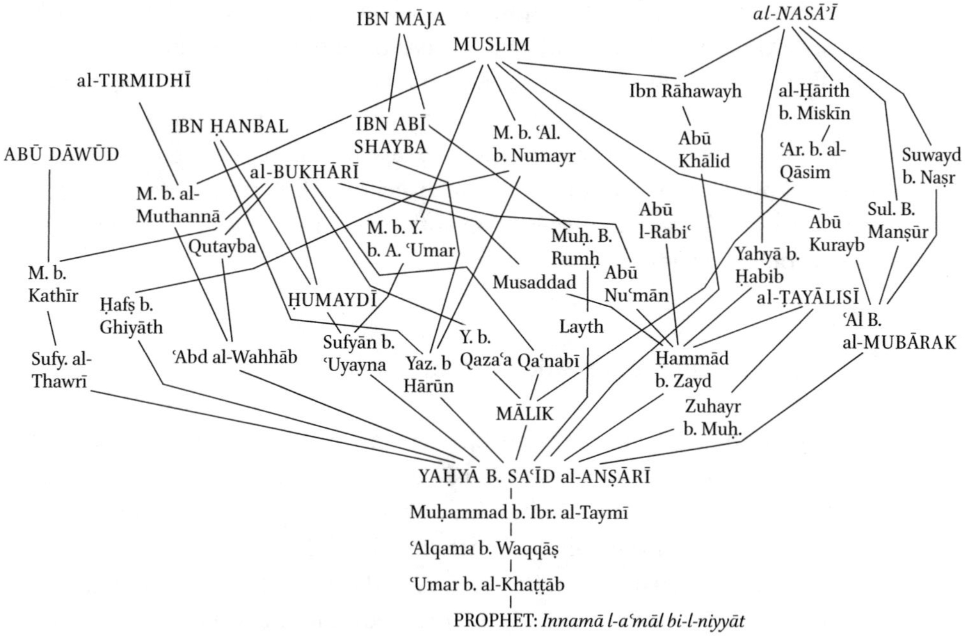


FIGURE 10.1 *Isnād* chart of the *ḥadīth* of intention (Juynboll 2007)

We can only speculate why Yaḥyā might have frequently engaged in the teaching of this *ḥadīth*, since "the early historical literature on *ḥadīth* and *rijāl* does not contain a single clue as to the reason why … Yaḥyā … may have brought the tradition into circulation" (Juynboll 2007, 677). At the same time, Juynboll does insinuate that Yaḥyā's "judicial activities may have dictated the need for such a *niyya* maxim" (Juynboll 2007, 677). This is a valid interpretation because intention is an important aspect to consider when judging human actions in juridical settings. Let me suggest two additional interpretations.

First, the time period in which Yaḥyā was a *qāḍī* coincided with the tumultuous decades that witnessed the transition from the Umayyads to the ʿAbbāsids. While recent scholarship has emphasised a continuity between the two empires instead of the "rupture" presumed by earlier scholars, the two decades of the 740s and the 750s nonetheless saw significant transition in power and patronage. The era was therefore ripe, one might argue, for proliferating a Prophetic teaching that used intention to emphasise loyalty to religion, including in acts of migration. In fact, Yaḥyā himself migrated from Medina to Iraq. This contextualisation allows us to appreciate how ethical ideas accrue value, and how moral practices become normative, in relation to particular social and political dynamics.

Second, the biographical literature on Yaḥyā portrays him to be incredibly learned in *ḥadīth* and jurisprudence and also exceptionally committed to devotional religion (al-Bukhārī 1941–1964, 4.2:275–276; al-Mizzī 1983, 31:346–359; al-Dhahabī 1996, 5:468–481; Juynboll 2007, 668). I would like to suggest that he might have popularised this *ḥadīth* for the sake of exhorting his co-religionists to monitor their motives and to cultivate sincerity. Thus, his profuse transmission of this *ḥadīth* might be seen as an antidote to the habituated, dry practice of devotional religion.

## 4 Community and Political Action

The attention to Yaḥyā b. Saʿīd enables us to identify the possible social and political contexts in which early Muslims might have cited this report. Yet it is important to underscore that this *ḥadīth*'s linking of intention to political action resonates generally with how intentionality figures in the broader *ḥadīth* discourse. This section first mentions those reports that maintain this link and then discusses the political implications of intention. To begin with, let me mention a report mentioned in Shīʿī sources:

> Actions are indeed according to intentions, and in fact what belongs to a man is what he intends. So, whosoever fights for the sake of what is with God the Loftiest, he will surely find his reward with God the Loftiest. And whosoever fights desiring something of this world, then there is nothing for him except what he intends.
>
> AL-MAJLISĪ 1983, 67:212[3]

3 Let me mention here a few Shīʿī reports in order to illustrate the fact that intentions are central in both Sunnī and Shīʿī *ḥadīth* canons. ʿAlī b. al-Ḥusayn (d. 95/713) is reported to have said: "No action is valid without intention." The Prophet Muḥammad is reported to have said: "The intention of a believer contains more goodness than his action, whereas the intention of the unbeliever contains more wickedness than his action, and every doer does according to his intention." Here, action only brings forth a part of the intention, which contains more goodness in case of a good action and more wickedness in case of an evil action. This view of intention coheres with Ibn ʿArabī's views discussed above, as soul and meaning are the standing reserves of potentiality from which bodies and words derive their actuality. Several reports attributed to Jaʿfar al-Ṣādiq (d. 148/765) are especially illuminating. For example: "The needy and believing servant of God prays, 'Oh Lord! Grant me so that I can do this or that act of goodness. So, because God the Most Sublime and Sanctified knows the truth of his intention, God grants him the same reward that he would have received had he performed that action, for God is All-Encompassing and Ever-Kind." In another narration, Jaʿfar al-Ṣādiq justifies the eternity of hellish punishment and paradisiacal pleasure based on the fact that

Consider also the tradition, "There is no migration after the Conquest of Mecca, but in terms of armed struggle and intention and if you are called to go forth, then go forth [in armed struggle]" (al-Bukhārī 2011, 6:7–8).

In his discussion of intention, the famed Muslim moral theologian Abū Ḥāmid al-Ghazālī (d. 505/1111) mentions the following reports that further link intention to political acts such as warfare and migration:

- Anas b. Mālik (d. 93/712) reports: "The Prophet said during the Tabūk campaign: 'There are many in Medina who, while still in the city, are joined with us in every valley we have crossed, every path we trod that vexed the unbelievers, every provision spent or hunger felt.' The Companions asked, 'How could it be, O Messenger of God, if they were not with us?' He replied: 'They were excusably detained and partook by way of good intention'" (al-Ghazālī 2010, 6:132; al-Ghazālī 2013, 6; al-Bukhārī 2011, 8:619–620).
- "He who fights with the intention only to have his share [of the booty] shall have only what he intends" (al-Ghazālī 2010, 6:133; al-Ghazālī 2013, 6).
- "Fighters fight according to intentions" (al-Ghazālī 2010, 6:134; al-Ghazālī 2013, 7).
- "When the two rows meet, the angels descend to record men their rank: so-and-so fought for the world (*dunyā*); so-and-so fought zealously (*ḥamiyya*); so-and-so fought for clan (*ʿaṣabiyya*). Therefore, say not that this person fell in the path of God, for only he who fights to make God's word supreme is on God's path" (al-Ghazālī 2010, 6:135; al-Ghazālī 2013, 7).

While scholars have questioned the authenticity of some of these reports, these reports do enable us a glimpse of how later authors such as al-Ghazālī underscored the political context in which intention mattered as a concept in early Islam. These reports suggest that communal belonging and political action were especially relevant to early Muslims' ethical thought and practice. Thus, Kevin Reinhart identifies "membership in/leadership of the community" as one of the two primary concerns of formative "Islamic theological ethics," the other being "predestination/moral responsibility" (Reinhart 2005, 250). He insightfully explains that these two issues were "inextricably bound together" and posed a major question for those who aspired to the "moral rigorism of early Islam:" Does "moral failure mean expulsion from the community?" (Reinhart 2005, 250).[4] The moral failure that was linked to political belonging included failures in both devotional rituals and pious intentions.

---

God has perfect, eternal knowledge of believers' and unbelievers' intentions. For all reports, see al-Māzandarānī 2008, 8:265–268.

4 Roy P. Mottahedeh briefly discusses the link between *niyya* and political loyalty with reference to vows in fourth/tenth century Būyid contexts (Mottahedeh 1980, 65–67).

How do intentions become political? The *ḥadīth* of intention uses the example of migration, namely, the migration of the early believers from Mecca to Medina. We know that according to the standard biographical tradition, the Prophet Muḥammad migrated to Medina after thirteen years of preaching in his hometown of Mecca. For a believer to migrate with Muḥammad implied leaving behind home and family ties. Migration was thus an act of fidelity, which demonstrated one's commitment to an ideological community (instead of a tribal community). However, what if a believer had migrated for a reason other than pleasing God and joining Muḥammad's community? What if one had migrated for the sake of a prospective marriage partner or to sell one's merchandise in a new market? Is this migration also an act of fidelity and does it also secure political belonging? The *ḥadīth* of intention questions this type of migration. *Ḥadīth* commentators state that this report is about a person who had allegedly migrated from Mecca to Medina for the sake of marrying a woman named Umm Qays (Ibn Ḥajar 1969, 1:10; al-Suyūṭī 1986, 37–38). Consequently, the man became known as "the migrant of Umm Qays" (*muhājir Umm Qays*). While the story is hard to verify, it does furnish us with the context needed to understand the practical, and in fact political, implications of intention. The strong connection we see between the *ḥadīth* of *niyya* and community-forming political actions, such as migration and warfare, suggests that the idea of pure intentions served to consolidate loyalty in believers' hearts, so that the onset of adversity and adversaries would not weaken believers' attachment to the faith community. The particular example of "the migrant of Umm Qays" gives an incredibly political charge to intention, signifying intentions as personal and political.

## 5 Al-Bukhārī's Creative Citation

The above explanations underscore the point that the *ḥadīth* of intention is deeply connected to the dialectic of inside and outside and that intentionality is at once a matter of private devotion and political belonging. I now turn to the *locus classicus* of this *ḥadīth*, namely al-Bukhārī's *Ṣaḥīḥ*, to examine some further aspects. This famed collection of Prophetic speech commences with this report, and it is significant that al-Bukhārī placed it at the beginning of a chapter concerning the lofty theme of divine revelation (*waḥy*), suggesting, albeit implicitly, that the Prophet's sincere search for truth was rewarded in the form of Qurʾānic revelation, for God gifts one according to one's intentions. Recall the Prophet's foundational migration, one that took him from commercial engagements to contemplative experiences on the Mount of Light. By taking up solitude in a cave outside Mecca, the Prophet Muḥammad intended to find transcendental meaning and message. Because what God gifts people corresponds to their intentions, the Prophet received divine revelation as the reward of his foundational quest/intention to find God. Here, at least two questions must be addressed. First: Why does al-Bukhārī include the *ḥadīth* of intention at the beginning of "The Book of Revelation?" Second: What is the significance of starting with "revelation?"[5] The *ḥadīth* commentator, Ibn Ḥajar al-ʿAsqalānī (d. 852/1449), addresses both questions.

Ibn Ḥajar speculates about al-Bukhārī's possible intent behind the textual decision to commence with this *ḥadīth*. Imagine, the commentator asks his readers, the following words on al-Bukhārī's lips: "I intended to collect the revealed Sunna transmitted from the Prophet Muḥammad – who is the best of all created beings – so that my [sincere] intention would ensure the goodness of my action [of compiling *ḥadīths*]" (Ibn Ḥajar 1969, 1:8; see also al-Qasṭallānī 1996, 1:67). Note how these words posit the Sunna a revealed text, hearkening back to al-Shāfiʿī's point that the Prophet's speech was "cast into his heart" by God.[6] This is also the reason that al-Bukhārī begins a collection of *ḥadīth* with "revelation," accentuating the revealed or scriptural nature of Prophetic speech. Thus, the reader is encouraged both to think of *ḥadīth* as revelation and to engage in an act of purifying his or her intention for engaging in the study of *ḥadīth*. In other words, the reader is indirectly being directed to contemplate this question: What motivates my engagement with divine revelation? In this way, al-Bukhārī's textual decision to commence his collection by coupling revelation and intention performs the communicative work that is usually reserved for exhortative prefaces.

Ibn Ḥajar mentions that some commentators have suggested that al-Bukhārī cites this report in lieu of an opening "sermon" or *khuṭba* ("exhortative preface" in this textual context). This is so because in some traditions it is reported that the Prophet's companion ʿUmar b. al-Khaṭṭāb (d. 23/644) recited this *ḥadīth* "on the pulpit," and in another narration, the *ḥadīth* begins with the Prophet saying, "O people! Actions are indeed according to intentions." These textual cues lend support to the idea that this *ḥadīth* is exhortative in substance, an ideal Prophetic aphorism befitting the sermon genre. We must also mention that by opening with this *ḥadīth*, al-Bukhārī might be merely following tradition, an

5 The *ḥadīth* scholar Muslim b. al-Ḥajjāj (d. 261/875) opens his collection with "Faith," while "Purification" opens the other four books of the six canonical books (*al-kutub al-sitta*) in Sunnī Islam.

6 In his *al-Risāla* ("Epistle"), al-Shāfiʿī (d. 204/820) remarked: "Both [the Qurʾān and the Sunna] came to him [Muḥammad] from God's grace, just as God intended, and just as other acts of grace came to him" (al-Shāfiʿī 2015, 48–49).

established custom of his righteous predecessors. In this regard, the following textual fragment from another Mamluk-era commentator, namely, Badr al-Dīn al-ʿAynī (d. 855/1451), sheds some light: "The predecessors [of the community] have preferred starting their discourse with the *ḥadīth* of intention for the sake of indicating their sincerity" (al-ʿAynī 1970, 1:13). Note that ʿAbd al-Raḥmān b. Mahdī (d. 198/814) is reported to have said, "he who wants to write a book, let him start with the tradition: works are to be judged by their intentions (*man arāda an yuṣannifa kitāban fa-l-yabdaʾ bi-ḥadīth al-aʿmāl bi-l-niyyāt*)" (Juynboll 2007, 676).[7] These explanations attest to al-Bukhārī's success in compiling a text that invites such rich observations on the part of commentators and readers. Let us now examine how other Muslim scholars approached the theme of intentionality.

## 6 Intention in Sufi Writings

The interplay between inside and outside as being a major feature of the Islamic ethical tradition's understanding of intentionality is especially brought out in Sufi writings.[8] In his *al-Riʿāya li-Ḥuqūq Allāh* ("Observing God's Due"), a text that was "composed in the form of counsels given to a disciple in response to questions on his part" (Smith 1935, 44), the mystical theologian al-Ḥārith al-Muḥāsibī (d. 243/857) defines *niyya* as "the resolution on the part of the believer to align his action to an idea from among ideas. Hence, when he determines that he will perform *this* particular action for *this* particular idea, then such a resolution is called *niyya*, be it for God's sake or for another's" (al-Muḥāsibī n.d., 246). Furthermore, al-Muḥāsibī says, "intention thus covers two meanings: the resolution to do a particular action and doing something while desiring a particular meaning [object of thought]" (al-Muḥāsibī n.d., 246). It is in this sense that I term *niyya* a psychosomatic orientation; it is an inner movement that is expressed by and embodied in physical action.

In his *Qūt al-Qulūb* ("Nourishment of the Hearts") Abū Ṭālib al-Makkī (d. 386/996) adopts a holistic approach to the centrality of *niyya* in everyday ethics: intention pervades not only the formal practices of piety but, also,

> eating, drinking, attire, sleeping, and marital relations, since these are all actions for which one shall be questioned [by God]. If one performs these actions for God's pleasure, then they increase his tally of good works.

7 Ibn Taymiyya (2004, 18:246) makes a similar point in his analysis of this *ḥadīth*.
8 This paragraph and the next two are also discussed in Mian 2022.

> However, if one undertakes these actions in pursuit of lust or for the sake of another's pleasure, then they end up amplifying the tally of evil deeds. This is [the meaning of the Prophet's words] for every man is what he intends.
>
> AL-MAKKĪ 2001, 3:1342

Al-Makkī additionally says that *niyya* is a gift of God and that a single action can contain multiple motivations. In this way, a single action becomes a source of plentiful merit. Such merit, however, is contingent on not only the doer's knowledge of and assent to the revealed norms but also the grace of God (al-Makkī 2001, 3:1343).

In al-Ghazālī's thinking we find a finessed account of *niyya*. He retains the link between action and what al-Muḥāsibī calls idea (that is, between *ʿamal* and *maʿnā*) and also al-Makkī's idea of "multiple intentions." However, instead of "idea" or "meaning" (*maʿnā*), al-Ghazālī opts for a more psychologically-laden word, namely, *gharaḍ* (aim or purpose). To that end, he cites the *ḥadīth* under study in this chapter in a refined discussion of intention as well as sincerity (*ikhlāṣ*) and truthfulness (*ṣidq*).[9] For al-Ghazālī intention becomes especially relevant for highlighting the dialogue between the inside and outside, since he defines *niyya* as an "intermediate attribute" (of the soul). He writes, "intention is the soul's springing forth, direction, and inclination towards what it perceives as its purpose [intended object], in this life or in the hereafter" (al-Ghazālī 2010, 6:155). "The springing forth of the soul" – *inbiʿāth al-nafs*, which one might even translate as the flow of the inner onto the outer – is a beautiful phrase that captures the dynamic way in which *niyya* mediates the inside and outside.

Ibn ʿArabī illuminates the relationship between the inside and outside through three analogies. Intention is like the body's soul; it is similar to the rainwater that nourishes the ground of action; finally, action and intention are akin to word and meaning (Ibn ʿArabī 1997, 1:256–259). These multiple analogies allow us to view intention as source, sustainer, and substance of action. Yet Ibn ʿArabī also encourages us to approach intentions as taking place in a liminal space that is the scene of both coherence and displacement, unity and difference. He further complexifies this view when he posits the relationship between water and intention as ontological and not merely analogical. He does so in his discussion of purification rituals, where he elaborates the

9 Al-Ghazālī approaches *niyya* under five subheadings: the virtues of good intention, its reality, how intention is superior to action, the relationship between action and intention, and the difference between intention and choice.

ingenious insight that the reason why some jurists do not require intention as a necessary condition for ritual ablution is because of the role water plays in this practice. Recall that according to Qurʾānic discourse, water is the source of all life (Q 21:30). In Ibn ʿArabī's imaginal schema, life/soul and intention are structurally identical (*niyya* for him is *rūḥ maʿnawī*). Thus, because water is life, its use in the practice of ablution already presupposes the presence of the soul (read: intention). Hence, there is no need to identify formal intention-making as a condition of ritual ablution, since the liquid substance one uses in this practice assumes the same relationship to flesh as intention does to action (Ibn ʿArabī 1997, 1:397).

## 7 Scholarship on Intentionality in Islamic Ethics

The deep resonance between the inside and outside insofar as the concept of intentionality in Islamic ethics is concerned has not always been appreciated by scholars. Paul Powers has studied the ritualistic and performative dimensions of *niyya* in Islamic law. He finds fault with those scholars who deploy *niyya* "to look for a 'deep' or spiritual component of ritual" (Powers 2006, 64). For Powers,

> *Niyya* is what one does with the mind while making certain ritualised bodily movements and verbal utterances … The legal texts do not indicate a capacity or mental mode such as "will" that is separate from, and which directs, the *niyya*. Rather, one simply intends, formulates *niyya*, and this is the inner self in a ritual mode. There is nothing "further inside" than *niyya*, no "self" standing back while the mind/body performs the acts of ritual.
>
> POWERS 2006, 203

While Powers rightly draws attention to the "physical, bodily, and praxis-oriented qualities so central to Islamic ritual law and practice," his limited sources reflect only a provisional and partial view of *niyya* in Islamic law and ethics (Powers 2006, 72). For Talal Asad, this position sees ritual prayer, for example, as "an external effect" even if "will and intent are viewed as a conjoined internal cause" (Asad 2018, 81).[10] On my reading, however, Powers effec-

10 Asad further states: "What worries me about this way of looking at the problem is that the most important point of the prayer (the subject learning to articulate her faith) is missed, and the traditional norm being learned is confused with the experience of the performed – that is, with what she thinks the prayer means. The recited words and body

tively partitions the inside and outside, leaving little room for understanding the meaning and function of ritual in the broader framework of Muslim piety.

I thus question Powers' hasty conclusion about "no self" in ritual worship. Unfortunately, he does not engage with works of moral philosophy and legal theory, which do presuppose a moral self and discuss the transcendental consequences of actions.[11] Pre-modern Muslim jurists in fact cited the *ḥadīth* of intention in both works of substantive law and in texts of legal theory. I provide two illustrations to make this point.

My first illustration comes from the Andalusian jurist and littérateur Ibn Ḥazm (d. 456/1064). He justifies his jurisprudential approach to the issue of buying and selling musical instruments by recourse to the *ḥadīth* of intention. On the one hand, the sale of musical instruments is forbidden, argues Ibn Ḥazm, when the buyer intends to use such instruments in sinful behaviour (*fisq*), such as listening to music in a way that arouses illicit sexual desire. On the other hand, the purchase of the same instruments is permissible for someone who seeks self-comfort and pleasure (*tarwīḥ al-nafs*), which in turn might strengthen one's willingness to perform the devotional rituals. "He seeks to enliven himself by means of music," explains Ibn Ḥazm, "and he is obedient and virtuous, and his action [of buying these instruments] is valid" (Ibn Ḥazm 2003, 7:567; cited in Kaddouri 2013, 234). It is noteworthy that Ibn Ḥazm makes repeated references to a self that intends and becomes either pious or impious due to the effects of intention. The invocation of this "self" thus problematises Powers' claim about the lack of a self behind ritual performance.

My second illustration comes from a text of legal theory. The Egyptian Ḥanafī jurist Ibn Nujaym (d. 970/1563) discusses *niyya* in a major text on legal rules and axioms. He invokes the *ḥadīth* of intention in his discussion of the juristic maxim, "there is no reward except with *niyya*." He explains that the *ḥadīth*

---

movements in prayer aim not at creating a belief (an intellectual doctrine) but an attitude of reverence and a desire (intention) to get closer to God. I stress that I refer here not to the private experience of every performer but to the point of the prayer as stipulated by the discursive tradition" (Asad 2018, 81).

11 Missing from Powers' account are several important treatments of *niyya* by pre-modern and modern Muslim jurists and theologians. A broader view of *niyya* reveals that a host of traditionists and jurists themselves recognise its spiritual dimensions. See, for example, the following works on *niyya*, which are all missing from Powers' book: Ibn Abī l-Dunyā (d. 281/894), *al-Ikhlāṣ wa-l-Niyya* ("Sincerity and Intention"); al-Suyūṭī (d. 911/1505), *Muntahā l-Āmāl* ("Ultimate Hopes"); al-Qārī (d. 1014/1606), *Taṭhīr al-Ṭawiyya* ("Smootheing the Folds"); al-Kūrānī (d. 1101–1690), *Iʿmāl al-Fikr* ("Activate the Thinking"); Ibn ʿAjība (d. 1224/1809), *Tashīl al-Madkhal* ("Simplifying the Introduction"); al-Ḥusaynī (d. 1332/1914), *Kitāb Nihāyat al-Iḥkām* ("Book on the Goal of Legislation"). In addition to these monographs, there are countless texts in various genres where Muslim authors from a range of disciplinary backgrounds comment on *niyya*.

of intention occasions "a verdict on or a moral assessment of actions" (*ḥukm al-aʿmāl*), which is of two types: transcendental and empirical. The first verdict or assessment "pertains to the afterlife and concerns the question of reward or punishment" (Ibn Nujaym 1999, 17). We can call this "the transcendental *ḥukm*," to borrow words from Ebrahim Moosa (1998). The second assessment – or, "the empirical *ḥukm*" – concerns "the validity or invalidity of actions in this world" (Ibn Nujaym 1999, 17). While a jurist often has to restrict himself to determine the empirical validity or invalidity of human actions, Ibn Nujaym acknowledges that intentions also have consequences in the afterlife and implicate a soul or self, a moral subject (al-Ḥamawī 2011, 1:63–67). The Ḥanafī jurist Aḥmad b. Muḥammad al-Ḥamawī (d. 1098/1687) further clarifies that the Ḥanafīs – as opposed to the Shāfiʿīs – lack consensus on the necessity of *niyya* as a prerequisite for the empirical validity of an action. Yet, the Ḥanafīs unanimously affirm the transcendental implications of *niyya*, that is, its significance for thinking about reward or punishment in the afterlife (al-Ḥamawī 2011, 1:63–67).[12] Thus, the transcendental *ḥukm*, which pertains to the afterlife and implicates a soul, forms a part of the legal discourse about *niyya* (Moosa 1998).

These two illustrations – the first from Ibn Ḥazm and the second from Ibn Nujaym – serve to demonstrate my point, namely, that jurists are cognisant of moral subjectivity and attend to both the empirical and transcendental aspects of norms. I thus remain wary of the claim, on the part of Powers, that Islamic substantive law does not presuppose a moral self. Below I consider how other scholars have studied intention to highlight some alternative perspectives on the subject matter in the study of Islamic ethics.

The legal historian Oussama Arabi has studied *niyya* in the context of modern legal reform by concentrating on the Egyptian jurist ʿAbd al-Razzāq al-Sanhūrī's (d. 1971) efforts to modernise Islamic law. The latter activated a subjectivist notion of intentions in legal practices by turning to the Ḥanbalī, and to a lesser extent Mālikī, treatment of intent or ulterior motive in contract law. The "pietist subjectivist bent of Ḥanbalī law" emphasises both the intent of the buyer and the seller (for example, with reference to an arms seller whose

12 See also Ibn Kamāl Pāshā's (d. 940/1534) discussion of this point in his treatise on the first "book" of al-Bukhārī's *Ṣaḥīḥ* (*Majmūʿ Rasāʾil al-ʿAllāma Ibn Kamāl Bāshā* ["Collection of Treatises of the Scholar Ibn Kamāl Pāshā"]). Already in the late third/ninth and early fourth/tenth centuries, the Egyptian Ḥanafī jurist Abū Jaʿfar al-Ṭaḥāwī (d. 321/933) argued that the report, "actions are indeed according to intentions," does not establish "the principle that the appropriate intention must accompany a speech act for the act to be deemed legally valid. He reinterprets the *ḥadīth* as confirming simply that Divine reward in the hereafter for a given action correlates with the agent's intention in performing the action" (Syed 2017, 160).

customer might use a purchased weapon to execute a mass shooting) (Arabi 1997, 220). This subjectivist bent appealed to al-Sanhūrī because of its resonance with "the modern French theory of the determining cause or motive" (Arabi 204). Al-Sanhūrī's reformist efforts illustrate that Islamic legal traditions can be read in multiple ways to support different ideas about ethics and moral responsibility.

The historical anthropologist Brinkley Messick directly approaches the question of subjectivity: is there a theory of the self that is implied in Islamic legal thought and practice? For Messick, the writings of Muslim theologians and jurists on intention elaborate "crucial components of the legal theory of the *sharʿī* subject" (Messick 2001, 153). Messick emphasises the usefulness of contextualising this ethical subject within "a history of the self and the individual" that is distinct from Eurocentric conceptualisations of subjectivity and individuality (Messick 2001, 151). The contours of the Muslim ethical self also become clear when this self is posited in relation to God. While a "separation of intentionality and expression" does not characterise the divine word, human language indicates a lack of equivalence between thought and expression (Messick 2001, 178). It seems to me that the crucial point here is to appreciate the vulnerability and uncertainty that infuses all human intentions and actions. Thus, a moral action, according to the Islamic ethical tradition, expresses the agency of a self, but its immediate and final meaning remains contingent on two factors that exceed the self, namely, public interpretation and divine judgment.

Arabi and Messick both highlight the need to situate the jurisprudence of intent in broader social, political, and intellectual contexts. Likewise, it is also important to acknowledge the complex intersectional realities in which contemporary Muslims observe norms that they take to be divinely sanctioned, that is, norms based in the Sharīʿa. Muslims' everyday practices are situated in networks of local and global histories (of nation-states, market economies, and ethical traditions) as well as vectors of embodied differences, such as race/ethnicity, class, gender, sexual orientation, and bodily capacity. As historian of Islam and Muslim feminist scholar Kecia Ali points out, "Our experiences differ dramatically based on our race and socio-economic status, our family configurations, our sexual orientations, our marital statuses, our geographic locations" (Ali 2016, 205). Thus, in our bid to identify the moral self, or ideas about interiority and subjectivity, we have to be cautious. The sources might reveal a reified self at work, but this generic "un-marked" self will not do for everyone. In other words, after recovering a moral self in classical Islamic law, there still remains the question: How do we bridge the gap between the legal tradition's idealised moral self, one who thrives in textual spaces, and ordinary

Muslim selves, those who survive in physical spaces? The key is to engage in critical and creative acts of translation, whether translating between textual representation or social reality, or interior states and physical actions.

The need to approach intentionality within the contingencies of social life was acknowledged by Muslim moral theologians such as al-Ghazālī. For Ebrahim Moosa, al-Ghazālī saw intention as the elixir that purifies knowledge and practice. A focus on inner motive, Moosa argues, has the capacity to humanise those moral acts that appear as improper or subversive (Moosa 2005, 131). Thus, our judgments about our own actions and others' actions should resist the convenient but crude binary of good and evil. Sometimes, evil intentions lurk behind good deeds and vice versa. It goes without saying that the interpretation of intention is not so easy, but the point here is that attention to intent and motive complexifies, and can thus humanise, a range of actions whose moral status we might not understand at first sight. In his insightful commentary on al-Ghazālī, Moosa also theorises the central dyad that concerns us in this chapter, namely, the relationship between the inside and outside. These two terms animate a paradox that consists of an "inwardness of faith that is incommensurate with its outwardness – an exterior of faith not identical with its interior" (Moosa 2005, 132). This incommensurability, however, sets the stage for approaching Islamic ethics as a project of self-transcendence.

## 8 Conclusion

This chapter has demonstrated the salience of *ḥadīth* texts as important sources for the study of Islamic ethics as well as the need to engage with ethical themes and questions on the part of researchers in *ḥadīth* studies. In the above analysis, I have situated "the *ḥadīth* of intention" in three discursive formations that illuminate its analytical purchase for the critical study of Islamic ethics. Intentionality in this ethical tradition is a psychosomatic orientation that presupposes the dialogue of self and society and relates to communal formation as well as the legal/moral divide of human actions (which I explored by looking at how intention is important for both the empirical and transcendental valences of juridical-moral norms). To a large extent, these three conceptual points of reference enabled me to grapple with the psychoanalytical challenges to the intentional subject. In the Islamic ethical tradition, the spiritual and material dimensions of intentionality are not easily separable. The actions we undertake with our limbs both extend and inform psychic life. The movements of the heart, too, seek bodily forms. Intention, therefore, is irreducible to inner experience or linguistic or bodily performatives. I have also suggested above that this view of intentionality resonates with scholarship on religious practices. Finally, I underscored the need to engage in critical and creative acts of translation when thinking about intention at the threshold of the inside and outside.

## Bibliography

Aghaei, Ali. 2020. "The Common Link and its Relation to Hadith Terminology." In *Modern Hadith Studies: Continuing Debates and New Approaches*, edited by Belal Abu-Alabbas, Michael Dann and Christopher Melchert, 97–128. Edinburgh: Edinburgh University Press.

Ali, Kecia. 2016. *Sexual Ethics and Islam: Feminist Reflections on Qur'an, Hadith, and Jurisprudence*. Oxford: Oneworld.

Arabi, Oussama. 1997. "Intention and Method in Sanhūrī's Fiqh: Cause as Ulterior Motive." *Islamic Law and Society* 4(2): 200–223.

Asad, Talal. 2018. *Secular Translations: Nation-State, Modern Self, and Calculative Reason*. New York: Columbia University Press.

al-ʿAynī, Badr al-Dīn. 1970. *ʿUmdat al-Qārī Sharḥ Ṣaḥīḥ al-Bukhārī*, edited by Idārat al-Ṭibāʿa al-Munīriyya et al., 25 vols. Beirut: Muḥammad Amīn Damaj.

al-Bukhārī, Muḥammad b. Ismāʿīl. 1941–1964. *Kitāb al-Tārīkh al-Kabīr*, 5 vols. Hyderabad: Dāʾirat al-Maʿārif al-ʿUthmāniyya.

al-Bukhārī, Muḥammad b. Ismāʿīl. 2011. *Al-Jāmiʿ al-Ṣaḥīḥ bi-Ḥāshiyat al-Muḥaddith Aḥmad ʿAlī al-Sahāranfūrī*, edited by Taqī l-Dīn al-Nadawī, 15 vols. Beirut: Dār al-Bashāʾir al-Islāmiyya.

de Francesco, Ignazio. 2013. "Il Lato Oscuro Delle Azioni: La Dottrina Della Niyya Nello Sviluppo Dell'Etica Islamica." *Islamochristiana* 39:45–69.

al-Dhahabī, Shams al-Dīn Muḥammad b. Aḥmad. 1996. *Siyar Aʿlām al-Nubalāʾ*, edited by Shuʿayb al-Arnāʾūṭ, 25 vols. Beirut: Muʾassasat al-Risāla.

Draz, Mohamed Abdallah. 1951. *La morale du Koran*. Paris: Presses Universitaires de France.

Drāz, Muḥammad ʿAbd Allāh. 1973. *Dustūr al-Akhlāq fī l-Qurʾān*, trans. into Arabic from French by ʿAbd al-Ṣabūr Shāhīn. Kuwait: Dār al-Buḥūth al-ʿIlmiyya.

al-Ghazālī, Abū Ḥāmid. 2010. *Iḥyāʾ ʿUlūm al-Dīn*, edited by ʿAlī Muḥammad Muṣṭafā et al., 6 vols. Damascus: Dār al-Fayḥāʾ.

al-Ghazālī, Abū Ḥāmid. 2013. *Al-Ghazālī on Intention, Sincerity, and Truthfulness*, translated by Anthony F. Shaker. Cambridge: Islamic Texts Society.

al-Ḥamawī, Aḥmad b. Muḥammad. 2011. *Ghamz ʿUyūn al-Baṣāʾir Sharḥ al-Ashbāh wa-l-Naẓāʾir*, edited by Naʿīm Ashraf Nūr Aḥmad, 2 vols. Karachi: Idārat al-Qurʾān wa-l-ʿUlūm al-Islāmiyya.

al-Ḥusaynī, Aḥmad Bey. 1903. *Kitāb Nihāyat al-Iḥkām fī Bayān Mā lil-Niyyati min al-Aḥkām*. Cairo: al-Maṭbaʿa al-Amīriyya.

Ibn Abī l-Dunyā. 1992. *Al-Ikhlāṣ wa-l-Niyya*, edited by Iyyād Khālid al-Ṭabbāʿ. Damascus: Dār al-Bashāʾir.

Ibn ʿAjība, Aḥmad b. Muḥammad. 2014. *Tashīl al-Madkhal li-Tanmiyat al-Aʿmāl bi-l-Niyya al-Ṣāliḥa ʿinda al-Iqbāl*, edited by ʿAbd al-Majīd Marzūqī. Essaouira: Maṭbaʿat Hiba.

Ibn al-ʿArabī, Muḥyī al-Dīn. 1997. *Al-Futūḥāt al-Makkiyya*, edited by Nawwāf al-Jarrāḥ, 9 vols. Beirut: Dār Ṣādir.

Ibn Ḥajar al-ʿAsqalānī, Aḥmad b. ʿAlī. 1969. *Fatḥ al-Bārī bi-Sharḥ Ṣaḥīḥ al-Imām Abī ʿAbd Allāh Muḥammad b. Ismāʿīl al-Bukhārī*, edited by ʿAbd al-ʿAzīz b. ʿAbd Allāh Ibn Bāz, 13 vols. Cairo: al-Maktaba al-Salafiyya.

Ibn Ḥazm, Abū Muḥammad ʿAlī b. Aḥmad b. Saʿīd. 2003. *Al-Muḥallā bi-l-Āthār*, edited by ʿAbd al-Ghaffār Sulaymān al-Bandārī, 12 vols. Beirut: Dār al-Kutub al-ʿIlmiyya.

Ibn Kamāl, Pāshā. 2018. *Majmūʿ Rasāʾil al-ʿAllāma Ibn Kamāl Bāshā*, edited by Muḥammad Khallūf al-ʿAbd Allāh et al., 8 vols. Istanbul: Dār al-Lubāb.

Ibn Nujaym, Zayn al-Dīn b. Ibrāhīm b. Muḥammad. 1999. *Al-Ashbāh wa-l-Naẓāʾir ʿalā Madhhab Abī Ḥanīfa al-Nuʿmān*, edited by Zakariyyā ʿUmayrāt. Beirut: Dār al-Kutub al-ʿIlmiyya.

Ibn Taymiyya, Taqī l-Dīn Aḥmad. 2004. *Majmūʿ Fatāwā Shaykh al-Islām Aḥmad Ibn Taymiyya*, edited by ʿAbd al-Raḥmān b. Muḥammad b. Qāsim and Muḥammad b. ʿAbd al-Raḥmān b. Muḥammad, 37 vols. Medina: Mujammaʿ al-Malik Fahd.

Juynboll, G.A.H. 2007. *Encyclopedia of Canonical Ḥadīth Online*. Leiden: Brill.

Judd, Steven C. 2014. *Religious Scholars and the Umayyads: Piety-Minded Supporters of the Marwānid Caliphate*. London: Routledge.

Kaddouri, Samir. 2013. "Ibn Ḥazm al-Qurṭubī (d. 456/1064)." In *Islamic Legal Thought: A Compendium of Muslim Jurists*, edited by Oussama Arabi, David S. Powers and Susan A. Spectorsky, 211–238. Leiden: Brill.

al-Kūrānī, Ibrāhīm b. Ḥasan. 2013. *Iʿmāl al-Fikr wa-l-Riwāyāt fī Sharḥ Ḥadīth Innamā l-Aʿmāl bi-l-Niyyāt*, edited by Aḥmad Rajab Abū Sālim. Beirut: Dār al-Kutub al-ʿIlmiyya.

Mahmood, Saba. 2005. *Politics of Piety: The Islamic Revival and the Feminist Subject*. Princeton: Princeton University Press.

al-Majlisī, Muḥammad Bāqir. 1983. *Biḥār al-Anwār al-Jāmiʿa li-Durar Akhbār al-Aʾimma al-Aṭhār*, 110 vols. Beirut: Dār Iḥyāʾ al-Turāth al-ʿArabī.

Makdisi, George. 1985. "Ethics in Islamic Traditionalist Doctrine." In *Ethics in Islam: Ninth Giorgio Levi Della Vida Conference, 1983, in Honor of Fazlur Rahman*, edited by Richard G. Hovannisian, 47–63. Malibu, CA: Undena Publications.

al-Makkī, Abū Ṭālib. *Qūt al-Qulūb*, edited by Maḥmūd Ibrāhīm Muḥammad al-Riḍwānī, 3 vols. Cairo: Maktabat Dār al-Turāth.

al-Māzandarānī, Muḥammad Ṣāliḥ. 2008. *Sharḥ Uṣūl al-Kāfī*, 12 vols. Beirut: Dār Ihyaʾ al-Turāth al-ʿArabī.

Messick, Brinkley. 2001. "Indexing the Self: Intent and Expression in Islamic Legal Acts." *Islamic Law and Society* 8(2):151–178.

Mian, Ali Altaf. 2022. "Agents of Grace: Ethical Agency between Ghazālī and the Anthropology of Islam." *American Journal of Islam and Society* 39(1–2): 6–40.

al-Mizzī, Jamāl al-Dīn Abū l-Ḥajjāj Yūsuf. 1983. *Tahdhīb al-Kamāl fī Asmā' al-Rijāl*, edited by Bashshār ʿAwwād Maʿrūf, 35 vols. Beirut: Mu'assasat al-Risāla.

Moosa, Ebrahim. 1998. "Allegory of the Rule (*Ḥukm*): Law as Simulacrum in Islam?" *History of Religions* 38(1):1–24.

Moosa, Ebrahim. 2005. *Ghazālī and the Poetics of Imagination*. Chapel Hill: The University of North Carolina Press.

Mottahedeh, Roy P. 1980. *Loyalty and Leadership in an Early Islamic Society*. Princeton: Princeton University Press.

Motzki, Harald. 2004. "Introduction." *Ḥadīth: Origins and Developments*, edited by Harald Motzki, xiii–liii. London: Routledge.

al-Muḥāsibī, al-Ḥārith. n.d. *Al-Riʿāya li-Ḥuqūq Allāh*. Beirut: Dār al-Kutub al-ʿIlmiyya.

Peterson, Anna L. 2020. *Works Righteousness: Material Practice in Ethical Theory*. Oxford: Oxford University Press.

Powers, Paul R. 2006. *Intent in Islamic Law: Motive and Meaning in Medieval Sunnī Fiqh*. Leiden: Brill.

al-Qārī, Mullā ʿAlī. 2018. *Taṭhīr al-Ṭawiyya bi-Taḥsīn al-Niyya*, edited by Māhir Adīb Ḥabbūsh. In *Majmūʿ Rasā'il al-ʿAllāma al-Mullā ʿAlī l-Qārī*, edited by Muḥammad Khallūf al-ʿAbd Allāh et al., 8 vols, 3:177–205. Istanbul: Dār al-Lubāb.

al-Qasṭallānī, Shihāb al-Dīn. 1996. *Irshād al-Sārī li-Sharḥ Ṣaḥīḥ al-Bukhārī*, edited by Muḥammad ʿAbd al-ʿAzīz al-Khālidī. Beirut: Dār al-Kutub al-ʿIlmiyya.

Reinhart, A. Kevin. 2005. "Origins of Islamic Ethics: Foundations and Constructions." In *The Blackwell Companion to Religious Ethics*, edited by William Schweiker, 244–253. Malden, MA: Blackwell.

Schacht, Joseph. 1979. *Origins of Muhammadan Jurisprudence*. Oxford: Clarendon Press.

al-Shāfiʿī, Muḥammad b. Idrīs. 2015. *The Epistle on Legal Theory: A Translation of al-Shāfiʿī's Risālah*, translated by Joseph E. Lowry. New York: New York University Press.

Smith, Margaret. 1935. *An Early Mystic of Baghdad: A Study of the Life and Teaching of Ḥārith b. Asad al-Muḥāsibī A.D. 781–A.D. 857*. London: The Sheldon Press.

Syed, Mairaj U. 2017. *Coercion and Responsibility in Islam: A Study in Ethics and Law*. Oxford: Oxford University Press.

al-Suyūṭī, Jalāl al-Dīn. 1986. *Muntahā l-Āmāl fī Sharḥ Ḥadīth Innamā l-Aʿmāl*, edited by Muṣṭafā ʿAbd al-Qādir ʿAṭā. Beirut: Dār al-Kutub al-ʿIlmiyya.

Wuthnow, Robert. 2020. *What Happens When We Practice Religion? Textures of Devotion in Everyday Life*. Princeton: Princeton University Press.

CHAPTER 11

# Consult Your Heart

## *The Self as a Source of Moral Judgment*

*Mutaz al-Khatib*

## 1 Introduction

The dichotomy of God versus human is central in Qurʾānic discourse and permeates most reflections in ontology, epistemology, and ethics. For example, God's roles as the Bestower of bounty (*al-Munʿim*) and the Speaker (*al-Mutakallim*) have been the focus of inquiries into the ethical obligations placed upon humans and the sources of knowledge in Islamic scholarship. The search for understanding this dilemma pushed Muslims to explore a methodology for understanding God's discourse and uncovering His will – either through the Qurʾān or through the Prophet Muḥammad's words and deeds.

The difference in methodology between jurists and Sufis around what is apparent (*ẓāhir*) and what is inward (*bāṭin*) formed a central axis in discussions within the fields of *tafsīr* (Qurʾānic exegesis), *ḥadīth* (Prophetic reports), *fiqh* (Islamic law), *uṣūl al-fiqh* (Islamic legal theory), and Sufism (Islamic mysticism). However, the search for the sources of ethical knowledge against the universality of the Lawgiver stimulates serious inquiry into the role of the individual in ethical judgment. The question of individual moral knowledge prompts us to explore interrelated issues such as: (1) the capacity to know an ethical judgment inwardly, which relates to the source of the judgment and its evidence; (2) the competence to understand the Lawgiver's intent addressed to individuals; (3) the ethical responsibility in applying general judgments and principles, or the *fatwā* (legal opinion) of the *muftī* (jurisconsult) to specific private realities (scrutiny and caution); and (4) individual moral responsibility and choice in the face of contradictions in *muftīs*' legal opinions – for example, in the case of different opinions on a particular case, how should the individual choose?[1]

1 Recently, few studies discussed the moral role of the individual in Islamic law. Mohammad Fadel discussed the ethical dilemma facing *muqallids* (imitators) as a result of the ethical pluralism generated by *uṣūl al-fiqh*'s individualist ethical paradigm, and he proposed that "the *muqallid* plays a central role in maintaining the integrity of Islamic law by monitoring

The issue of individual moral knowledge is not only limited to questions of ethical responsibility but also connected to the concept of "conscience" understood as

> The faculty within us that decides on the moral quality of our thoughts, words, and acts. It makes us conscious of the worth of our deeds and gives rise to a pleasurable feeling if they are good and to a painful one if they are evil.
>
> DESPLAND 2005, 3:1939

The concept of "conscience" in the Islamic tradition is a controversial issue for Western scholars. For instance, William Tisdall appealed to the Arabic language to prove that Islam lacks the ethical conception which is called "conscience" (*ḍamīr*) claiming that "[n]either in the Arabic itself nor in any other Muhammadan languages is there a word which properly expresses what we mean by conscience" (Tisdall 1910, 62). This approach led the *Encyclopedia of Religion* (Despland 2005, 3:1944) to conclude that: "The notion of conscience as internal organ is not found outside of Christianity. As commonly understood, it is peculiar to the West." This debate on the existence or non-existence of "conscience" in Islam began at the beginning of the twentieth century. Ignaz Goldziher's insight was critical when he noted: "The assumption that a word alone can be taken as a credible proof of the existence of a conception, has shown itself to be a prejudice" (Goldziher 1917, 16). Indeed, he quoted the two *ḥadīth*s under study here to prove that

> didactic sentences, principles mirroring ethical conceptions, should be tested by more than a word, a *terminus technicus*, such as those which are used in the consideration of the "question of conscience" in Islam.
>
> GOLDZIHER 1917, 16

In this vein, Bryan W. Van Norden coined the term "lexical fallacy" to argue that simply because a word for a concept does not exist in a particular tradition, it does not mean that the concept is not operative in it (Ban Norden 2003, 101–102). Rashīd Riḍā (d. 1354/1935) argued that the "*qalb*" (heart), in a specific context, refers to what is known in modern Arabic as "*ḍamīr*" (conscience).

---

would-be *mujtahids* to ensure that they conform to Islamic ethical ideals" (Fadel 2014, 106). Similarly, Baber Johansen suggested a differentiation between *forum internum* and *forum externum* inherent to Islamic Law which, "like most legal systems, obliges those that appeal to it to choose their own options and to take ethical decisions" (Johansen 1997, 20).

It means knowing from oneself through spiritual and emotional engagement (*al-wijdān al-ḥissī wa-l-maʿnawī*). He also quoted the first *ḥadīth* "consult your heart …" to prove this meaning (Riḍā 1367/1948, 9:419).[2]

The concomitant dichotomy of reason and revelation has also dominated modern discussions about Islamic ethics,[3] hindering further inquiry into conscience and its authority in the Islamic tradition. The present study unveils understudied spaces where Muslim jurists, legal theorists, Sufis, and ethicists have discussed the role of individual conscience in the development of moral judgments from different perspectives.

In order to flesh out these issues, this study shall investigate two central *ḥadīths*: "consult your heart and consult your self"[4] and "righteousness is good conduct, and sin is that which rankles in your chest and which you would hate for other people to look upon." These two *ḥadīths* have been chosen for their content and special status in the field of Islamic ethics. The two *ḥadīths* point to the innermost dimension in humans – that which takes place in the heart, stirs in the self, and occurs within thought – in order to distinguish between the righteous and the sinful. The special status of these two *ḥadīths* is attested by the fact that they were included by Imām al-Nawawī (d. 676/1277) in his collection of forty *ḥadīths*, wherein each is considered

> A core fundamental among the fundamentals of religion, described by scholars as [the core] upon which Islam is premised, or as being half of Islam, or one third of it, or something approximating that.
>
> AL-NAWAWĪ 2004, 14–15

The reception of the two *ḥadīths* will be explored within the disciplines of *ḥadīth* commentaries, *uṣūl al-fiqh*, *fiqh*, and Sufi literature. Looking at Muslim jurists' and theorists' engagement with these *ḥadīths*, I shall focus on al-Ghazālī's (d. 505/1111) understanding of *waraʿ* (abstinence), Ibn Taymiyya's (d. 728/1328) approach, and al-Shāṭibī's (d. 790/1388) interpretation of *ijtihād al-mukallaf* (exerting one's reasoning for personal judgment). My approach investigates the specific ethical question of the inward aspect (*bāṭin*) on three levels. First, it looks at meta-ethics, as it explores the theoretical and epistemological basis relating to the sources of judgment and the criteria for specifying

---

2 For more discussion about "*ḍamīr*" see Heck 2014, 292–324 and Leirvik 2006.

3 See for example: Makdisi 1983, 47–64; Frank 1983, 204–223; Hourani 1985, 57–66; Kelsay 1994, 101–126; Shihadeh 2016, 384–407; Al-Attar 2019, 98–111.

4 Lit. "seek *fatwā* from your heart and seek *fatwā* from yourself." The variant narrations of the two *ḥadīths* will be discussed below.

righteousness and sin. Second, I examine the scriptural ethics, represented by key *ḥadīth*s as the primary gateways for the study of ethics within the *ḥadīth* corpus.[5] And third, I turn to applied ethics, which focuses on specific cases and individual applications.[6]

## 2 References to the Inward Dimension (*Bāṭin*) in the *Ḥadīth* Corpus

The *ḥadīth*s associated with the issues of the role of the individual's inward dimension may be approached through scrutiny of the transmission and narrations, and/or interpretation, both direct and indirect. While the locus of direct interpretation can be accessed in the books of *ḥadīth* commentary, indirect interpretation may be gleaned from the titles of books and chapters in *ḥadīth* compendiums that employ the device of chapter and topic headings directly addressing this subject.

### 2.1 *The* Ḥadīths *of the Inward Dimension* (Bāṭin)

There are two central *ḥadīth*s that refer to the inward dimension of the human in the attainment of knowledge of righteousness (*birr*) and sinfulness (*ithm*): the *ḥadīth* of Wābiṣa b. Maʿbad (d. 89/708) and that of al-Nawwās b. Samʿān (d. 50/670). It was reported that Wābiṣa came to ask the Prophet about righteousness and sinfulness, so the Prophet said:

> O Wābiṣa! Consult your heart and consult your self (three times). Righteousness is that towards which the self feels tranquil, and sinfulness is that which rankles in the self, and wavers in the chest, even when people have offered you their opinion time and time again.[7]

---

5 Taha Abdurrahman (Ṭāhā ʿAbd al-Raḥmān, b. 1944) has mentioned that it has been customary for jurists not to pay heed to the ethical aspects of scriptural texts, as a result of their paramount interest in commandments, which he named the commandment-based (*iʾtimārī*) orientation. This orientation may be summarised as "seeking rulings simultaneously denuded from both the divine witness (*al-shāhid al-ilāhī*) and the inward ethical dimension (*al-bāṭin al-akhlāqī*)," whereas "divine command (*āmiriyya*) is the basis of the existence of the apparent legal decree, and divine witnessing (*al-shāhidiyya al-ilāhiyya*) is the basis of the existence of the inward ethical dimension of these rulings" (ʿAbd al-Raḥmān 2017, 1:205–206). However, I shall clarify in the course of this study the inaccuracy of this generalisation.

6 I have developed a specialised academic syllabus entitled "Scriptural Ethics: Ethics in the Qur'ān and the *Ḥadīth*" for graduate students specialising in the "Applied Islamic Ethics" MA program at the College of Islamic Studies, Hamad Bin Khalifa University, starting in fall 2019.

7 Narrated by Ibn Abī Shayba 1997, 2:259; Aḥmad 2001, 29: 533; al-Dārimī 2000, 3:1649: *Kitāb al-Buyūʿ* ("Book of Sales"), *Bāb Daʿ Mā Yarībuk ilā Mā lā Yarībuk* ("Chapter on Leaving That

As for al-Nawwās b. Samʿān, it was transmitted that he said:

> I asked the Messenger of God about righteousness and sinfulness, so he said: righteousness is good conduct (*ḥusn al-khuluq*), and sinfulness is that which rankles in your chest and which you would hate for other people to look upon.[8]

There is a slight difference in the narrations of the *ḥadīth* of Wābiṣa. Consultation is reported to be sought from both the heart and the self together in some narrations,[9] but in others, consultation is reported to be sought from

---

Which Stirs Doubt Within You in Favour of That Which Does Not"); al-Ḥārith 1992, 1:201: *Bāb fī l-Birr wa-l-Ithm* ("Chapter On Righteousness and Doubt"); Abū Yaʿlā 1984, 3:160; al-Ṭaḥāwī 1994, 5:386: *Bāb Bayān Mushkil Mā Ruwiya ʿan Rasūl Allāh fī l-Birr wa-l-Ithm Mā Humā?* ("Chapter Clarifying Problematic Narrations Attributed to the Messenger of God on Righteousness and Sinfulness: What Are They?"); and Abū Nuʿaym 1996, 2:24. Al-Nawawī (2004, 14–15) said: "a good (*ḥasan*) *ḥadīth*," and Ibn Rajab (1999, 2:95) said: "and this *ḥadīth* has been narrated from the Prophet – upon him be God's blessings and peace – via numerous routes, some of which are good."

8 Narrated by Ibn Abī Shayba 1989, 5:212: *Kitāb al-Adab* ("Book of Manners"), *Bāb Mā Dhukira fī Ḥusn al-Khuluq wa-Karāhiyyat al-Fuḥsh* ("Chapter on What Has Been Mentioned Regarding Good Conduct and the Abhorrence of Indecency"); Aḥmad 2001, 5:386; 29:180; al-Bukhārī 1989, 110–111: *Bāb Ḥusn al-Khuluq idhā Faqihū* ("Chapter "Good Conduct if [Only] They Understood"); Muslim 1991, 4:180: *Kitāb al-Birr wa-l-Ṣila wa-l-Ādāb* ("Book on Righteousness, Maintaining Relations, and Manners"), *Bāb Tafsīr al-Birr wa-l-Ithm* ("Chapter on Explaining Righteousness and Sinfulness"); al-Tirmidhī 1996, 4:196: *Kitāb Abwāb al-Zuhd* ("Book on the Doors of Temperance"), *Bāb Mā Jāʾa fī l-Birr wa-l-Ithm* ("Chapter on What Has Been Reported on Righteousness and Sin"); al-Kharāʾiṭī 1999, 35: *Bāb al-Ḥathth ʿalā l-Akhlāq al-Ṣāliḥa wa-l-Targhīb fīhā* ("Chapter on Encouragement and Promotion of Upright Conduct"); Ibn Ḥibbān 2012, 5:272: *Ikhbāruhu Ṣallā Llāh ʿalyahi wa-Sallam bi-l-Ajwiba ʿan Ashyāʾ Suʾila ʿanhā* ("Chapter on Reports of the Prophet's – upon Him be God's Blessings and Peace – Answers to Things About Which He Was Asked"), *Dhikr al-Ikhbār ʿammā Yajibu ʿalā al-Marʾ min al-Taʿāhud li-Sarāʾirihi wa-Tark al-Ighḍāʾ ʿan al-Muḥaqqarāt* ("Mention of Reports About What a Person is Obligated to do in Terms of Commitment to [Being Watchful of] his Secrets and Abstaining from Excusing Minor Sins"); al-Bayhaqī 2011, 21:30: *Kitāb Jimāʿ Abwāb Man Tajūzu Shahādatuhu wa-Man lā Tajūzu min al-Aḥrār al-Bālighīn al-ʿĀqilīn al-Muslimīn* ("Book on the Anthology of Chapters on Whose Testimony is Permissible and Whose is Not Among Free Muslims of Majority and Sound Mind"), *Bāb Bayān Makārim al-Akhlāq wa-Maʿālīhā allatī Man Kāna Mutakhalliqan bihā Kāna min Ahl al-Murūʾa Allatī Hiya Sharṭun fī Qabūl al-Shahāda ʿalā Ṭarīq al-Ikhtiṣār* ("Chapter on Clarifying the Noblest and Most Excellent of Manners, Which Render a Person as Among the People of Chivalry, Which is a Condition for the Acceptance of Testimony by Way of Abridgement"); and al-Bayhaqī 2003, 9:408: *Bāb fī Muʿālajat Kull Dhanb bi-l-Tawba minhu* ("Chapter On the Treatment of Each Sin by Repenting From It"), *Faṣlun fī Muḥaqqarāt al-Dhunūb* ("Section on Minor Sins").

9 As narrated by Aḥmad 2001, 29:533; Ibn Abī Shayba 1997, 2:259; Abū Yaʿlā 1984, 3:160; al-Ḥārith 1992, 1:201; and al-Dārimī 2000, 3:1649.

the self alone.[10] Whereas Wābiṣa's version enquires about the knowledge of righteousness and sinfulness, others seek the knowledge about the permissible (*ḥalāl*) and the prohibited (*ḥarām*), and some *ḥadīth*s even report mention of certitude (*yaqīn*) and doubt (*shakk*).[11] The sign of righteousness or certitude is occasionally expressed as "tranquility (*ṭumaʾnīna*) of the heart or the self," and on other occasions as "stillness (*sukūn*) of the heart or the self." Sinfulness is expressed on one occasion as "that which rankles in the self;" on another as "that which rankles in the heart and wavers in the chest" (Aḥmad 2001, 29:528), and on yet a third occasion as "that which rankles in the chest" (Abū Yaʿlā 1984, 3:162). Sufis have engaged in extended discussions on the self and the heart, but these *ḥadīth*s do not help in differentiating between the self and the heart, because they add in the term "chest." However, the central formulation in the *ḥadīth* of Wābiṣa is "Consult your heart. Consult your self" and the common denominator among all the narrations is turning towards the inner dimension of the human being. This is meant to distinguish between righteousness and sinfulness, between the permissible and the prohibited. The *ḥadīth* is connected to the dichotomy of the apparent (*ẓāhir*) and the inward (*bāṭin*), which manifested strongly thereafter, particularly in the writings of the Sufis, who speak of "the scholars of the apparent" (*ʿulamāʾ al-ẓāhir*) in opposition to "the scholars of the inward dimension" (*ʿulamāʾ al-bāṭin*), as we find, for instance, in Abū Ṭālib al-Makkī's (d. 386/998) work (al-Makkī 2001, 1:326, 423–424, 443).

The *ḥadīth* variant that mentioned certitude (*yaqīn*) and doubt (*shakk*) can be linked to the intensive discussions on knowledge (*ʿilm*), its definition and process as we find in philosophy, theology, and *ūṣūl al-fiqh*. The Muʿtazilīs considered *sukūn al-nafs* (lit., "tranquillity of the soul") a condition for knowledge. Thus, when conviction does not correspond to reality (*muṭābaqa lil-wāqiʿ*), it should be considered ignorance; which was criticised harshly by Sunnī *ūṣūl al-fiqh* (al-Bāqillānī 1998, 178–182; al-Shīrāzī 2003, 4; al-Kalwadhlānī 1985, 1:36). The Muʿtazilīs defined knowledge as "believing a thing to be as it is to one self's tranquility" (*iʿtiqād al-shayʾ ʿalā mā huwa bihi maʿa sukūn al-nafs ilayh*),[12] and a similar definition can be found in philosophy in relation to rhetorical argument. ʿAbd al-Jabbār (d. 415/1025) developed an epistemology of *sukūn al-nafs* as mental persuasion that corresponds to outward realities (*al-muṭābaqa fī l-khārij*), and he understood it as an additional attribute of scholarship (*ʿālim*) and not as an essential element of the definition of *ʿilm* itself. Hence,

---

10 As narrated by Aḥmad 2001, 29:528; and al-Ṭaḥāwī 1994, 53:386.

11 As narrated by al-Ṭabarānī 1984, 1:117; and al-Mukhallaṣ 2008, 2:265.

12 It seems that the Muʿtazilīs' definition of *ʿilm* has been developed and revised by some late Muʿtazilī scholars (see ʿAbd al-Jabbār n.d., 12:13; al-Baṣrī 1964, 1:10; al-Māzarī 2002, 97).

the subjective standard of inner conviction must be reinforced by an objective standard, and, thus, the tranquillity of the self belongs to rationality rather than psychology, because lay persons, *muqallid*s (people who follow others' opinions), psychologically can have the tranquillity of the self without its rational basis (ʿAbd al-Jabbār n.d., 12:16–33; al-Kindī 1950, 1:171; Butterworth 1977, 63; Rosenthal 2007, 47f, 63, 211; Wilmers 2018, 151–152, 156, 163; Elkaisy-Friemuth 2006, 58–60, 169; Goodman 2003, 148–149).[13] Note, however, that this understanding of *sukūn al-nafs* is outside the scope of this paper as it is related mainly to the rational process of attaining knowledge and not to the inward dimension and conscience.

Going back to the two mentioned *ḥadīth*s, I should note that they have provoked disagreement, as is clear from the words of Muḥammad b. Jarīr al-Ṭabarī (d. 310/923), who spoke of jurists being divided into two groups according to their stance:

> A group among the predecessors (*salaf*) advocated deeming them authentic (*ṣaḥīḥ*) and acting upon that which is indicated by their apparent meanings…, then there are reports attributing to others a position advocating attenuating them, deeming them weak (*ḍaʿīf*), and reinterpreting their meanings.[14]

As for the group, who ascribed a weak validity to these *ḥadīth*s, they did not only discourage people to act upon them, but also saw a contradiction between those *ḥadīth*s that restrict guidance (*hidāya*) to the Qurʾān and the Sunna and those that refer to consultation of the heart and the self. For, in their view, God is the Legislator (*al-Musharriʿ*) and He has clarified all matters of religion either directly or indirectly. Indeed, even the Prophet had been commanded in the Qurʾān to rule between people according to what God had shown him (Q 4:105), not according to his own opinion, nor by what his self had instructed. If this was the case with the Prophet himself, then it is all the more applicable

13 For more discussion on *sukūn al-nafs*, see al-ʿAskarī 1998, 81; Bouhafa 2019, 67; Johansen 2013, 127–144.

14 After relating a number of *ḥadīth*s, both *marfūʿ* (attributed to the Prophet) and *mawqūf* (attributed to a Prophetic companion (*ṣaḥābī*)), al-Shāṭibī summarised the words of al-Ṭabarī from his book *Tahdhīb al-Āthār* ("Refinement of the Traditions") (al-Shāṭibī 1992, 2:659). We do not know precisely which *ḥadīth*s have been deemed weak (*ḍaʿīf*), as some *ḥadīth*s to this effect have been verified in the two authentic books of *ḥadīth* (al-Bukhārī and Muslim) or in one of them. Also, the extant copy of *Tahdhīb al-Āthār* is incomplete and does not contain this discussion, nor could I find anyone else who has cited these words from al-Ṭabarī.

to others. Whosoever is ignorant of God's proclamations is obligated to ask the scholars who understand God's intention, not to ask his self. The scriptural evidence is the sole reference for knowing the permissible and the prohibited, the meaning of which is affirmed by a number of *ḥadīth*s and reports. It would seem that the choice for which this group has opted in order to resolve the supposed problem is to weigh between the *ḥadīth*s that gives preference to one over the other. This is done without attempting to interpret or harmonise them, or even claim abrogation – the available options for dealing with "contradictory *ḥadīth*s" (al-Khaṭīb 2011, 286–289; al-Shumunnī 2004, 157–161). It would have been possible to restrict consultation of the heart to cases in which scriptural texts are absent or in cases where divergence exists between scholars on a particular issue. However, this too was ruled out based on the aforementioned argument regarding the status of the scriptural text as the sole authority with proclamations encompassing all realities.

As for the other group who advocated classifying these *ḥadīth*s as authentic (*ṣaḥīḥ*) and acting upon their apparent meanings, al-Shāṭibī reported some disagreement but did not convey the arguments through al-Ṭabarī, although they are mentioned in the books of *uṣūl al-fiqh*. It appears that al-Ṭabarī opted for an intermediate position between the two groups, so he interpreted the *ḥadīth*s in a restricted manner,

> either because he considered the *ḥadīth*s to be authentic, or because he considered those among them that indicate their [apparent] meanings to be authentic.
>
> AL-SHĀṬIBĪ 1992, 2:663

However, the position advocating the attenuation of these *ḥadīth*s, deeming them weak (*ḍaʿīf*), did not continue after al-Ṭabarī. We find no clear trace of this position in the various sources of *ḥadīth*.[15] It would appear that numerous *ḥadīth*s that reported on this topic within the *ḥadīth* corpus precluded the endurance of the position advocating such *ḥadīth*s to be deemed forgeries. This is especially the case because these *ḥadīth*s buttress each other's reliability, due to the abundance of their sources and the trajectory of their chain

15 With the exception of that which appears, in a very limited fashion, in the criticism of the chain of transmission of the "consult your heart" *ḥadīth*, connected to the weakness of a particular transmitter, or one transmitter not hearing the narration from another transmitter. In all cases, this is a criticism directed at the chains of transmission, not to the *ḥadīth* in its origin, which is transmitted through numerous paths (see Ibn Rajab 1999, 2:94–95).

of transmission, as they were imparted from seven Companions (*ṣaḥāba*) and one among the Successors (*tābiʿūn*).

### 2.2 *Interpretations of the* Ḥadīth

With the decline of the position advocating the weak reliability of these *ḥadīth*s, the discussion turned to their interpretation and the search for their intended meaning. These *ḥadīth*s provoked a central dilemma connected to the sources of knowledge, namely the authority of the heart and the self. The interpretations of the scholars of *ḥadīth* reflect their positions *vis-à-vis* this issue. For if we examine the chapter headings under which these *ḥadīth*s have been included, we will find them revolving around ethical content, such as: righteousness and sinfulness; manners and good conduct; temperance, piety, and abstaining from ambiguous matters; in addition to some jurisprudential topics, such as the books of sales, testimony, judgments and rulings. The discussions of the *ḥadīth* commentators revolved around three central issues: (1) the boundaries of the authority of the heart and the self; (2) the concepts of righteousness and sinfulness; (3) How to reconcile and harmonise between the *ḥadīth* and others that might contradict it. We now turn to these issues in more detail.

#### 2.2.1 The Authority of the Heart

One group rejected the authority of the heart and the self, and on this basis, deemed these *ḥadīth*s to be weak. Another group took the opposite position and embraced the apparent meaning of these *ḥadīth*s. Al-Ṭabarī was opposed to taking these *ḥadīth*s in their general apparent meaning. He argued that the meaning of these *ḥadīth*s is restricted, "not as those have presumed, that it is a commandment directed to the ignorant (*juhhāl*) to act according to what their selves have arrived at and reject whatever they deem repulsive, without asking their scholars" (al-Shāṭibī 1992, 2:664). Thus, two central questions arise here: what are those things that one should refer to the heart? And is this applicable to all hearts?

Al-Ṭūfī (d. 716/1316) determined that

> the self (*nafs*) possesses an awareness, rooted in the *fiṭra* (innate disposition), of outcomes or results that are praiseworthy and those outcomes which are not. However, the appetite (*shahwa*) can overcome inner restrictions in such a way that it can obligate the person to act in a way that is self-harmful, such as the thief who is overcome by the appetite to steal, [despite] being afraid of the punishment that may befall him.
>
> AL-ṬŪFĪ 1998, 204

Ibn Rajab (d. 795/1393) affirmed the same meaning, maintaining the position that consultation of the heart is connected to those *ḥadīths* that speak of the innate disposition that God has built into people (*al-fiṭra al-latī faṭar al-nās ʿalayhā*).[16] However, something might arise that may corrupt this *fiṭra*, as a result of the actions of devils or parents. Thus, truth and falsehood are not ambiguous for the percipient believer – rather, he knows the truth from the light that surrounds it, so his heart accepts it; and he recoils from falsehood, so he condemns it and does not affirm it (Ibn Rajab 1999, 99–101).

However, because the *fiṭra* may become disturbed by external influence, the authority of the heart remains, on the one hand, imprecise and ill-suited for generalisation to all individuals and, on the other hand, also ill-suited for all issues about which one seeks consultation. The position advocating the authority of the heart in absolute terms would, thus, infringe upon the authority of the scriptural text and that of the scholars. It is possible here to distinguish between three interpretations.

The first interpretation followed the apparent meaning of the *ḥadīth*, while restricting its applicability to the person seeking an answer alone, namely Wābiṣa b. Maʿbad, for the specificity of the person's condition such as the tranquillity of his self in comparison to others, and being gifted with a light that distinguishes between truth and falsehood (al-Munāwī 1972, 1:495–496). However, the *ḥadīths* on this topic clearly demonstrate that Wābiṣa was not unique, as the question was reportedly raised by others. Because some *ḥadīths* are articulated in a general form, there is no rationale for such specification.

The second interpretation holds that the *ḥadīth* is not specific to the person seeking an answer. Rather, it is specific to a particular kind of heart. Thus, it is addressed to a person whose chest God has expanded with the light of certainty when he was given an opinion based on mere conjecture or inclination without *sharʿī* (legal) evidence (al-Munāwī 1972, 1:495). Al-Ḥakīm al-Tirmidhī (d. 320/932) predates others in advocating this meaning, as he specified that the heart an individual seeks consultation from should be the heart of "the truthful" (*muḥiqqūn*). By this, he means the people of truth possess a path towards God and their appetites have been controlled to the extent that their selves have become consorts of their hearts (al-Ḥakīm al-Tirmidhī 2010, 2:39–40). However, Ibn ʿIllān (d. 1057/1647) held that the intended meaning here is the self and the heart of a person among the people of *ijtihād*; for if this were not the case, then the person would be obligated to ask a *mujtahid* (Ibn ʿIllān 2004, 5:41). Thus, he reverts the entire issue to the actions and choices of the jurist, not to those of the *muqallid* (follower) of a *madhhab* (legal school), or the person seeking consultation.

---

16 On *fiṭra*, see Vasalou 2016; Holtzman 2015, 163–188.

The third interpretation attests that the *ḥadīth* is meant for all believing hearts, but that it is specific to ambiguous issues, or to the field of transactions (*buyūʿ*) in particular. Thus, whoever has said that seeking consultation of the heart is specific to ambiguous issues in general has interpreted the *ḥadīth* of Wābiṣa in light of the *ḥadīth* of al-Nuʿmān b. Bashīr, who narrated from the Prophet:

> That which is permissible is clear, and that which is prohibited is clear, and between these two are ambiguous matters that many people do not know.
>
> AL-BUKHĀRĪ 1895, 3:53; Muslim 1991, 3:1221

Al-Ṭabarī was among the first to advocate this position, as he dealt with the juristic applications of these *ḥadīth*s. Therefore, he "did not apply them in every domain of *fiqh*" (al-Shāṭibī 1992, 2:663). Thus, seeking consultation from the heart does not apply to the legislation of actions or instituting acts of worship, nor to leaving aside Sharīʿa rulings. The authority of the self and the heart, then, lies in issues that are licit (*mubāḥ*) or in cases where sinfulness has been cast in doubt. It covers the area of mundane choices (*muʿāmalāt*) in life where people find themselves hesitant about a decision.

Some of the jurists who have commented on the *ḥadīth*, such as al-Ṭūfī and Ibn Rajab followed al-Ṭabarī's construal. Ibn Rajab attempted to create a balance between the authority of the self, on the one hand, and the authority of the scriptural text and the *muftī*, on the other. Thus, he divided thoughts that occur in the self into those addressed by scriptural texts and those that are not. In the case of issues addressed by scriptural texts, the believer has no option but to obey God and his Prophet, and what occurs in the self is of no consequence. As for cases that have not been addressed by scriptural texts, authority belongs to the evidence, if it exists, or to the self of the tranquil believer, if no evidence exists (Ibn Rajab 1999, 2:103). This implies that Ibn Rajab remarkably narrowed the space in which one can refer to the heart, privileging the scriptural text, the actions of the predecessors (*salaf*), and the authority of the *muftī*.

### 2.2.2 The Concepts of Righteousness and Sinfulness

Wābiṣa and al-Nawwās had both inquired about righteousness and sinfulness but were provided different answers, which led to different interpretations by scholars. Righteousness, in the *ḥadīth* of Wābiṣa, is "that towards which the self feels tranquil (*mā iṭma'annat ilayhi al-nafs*)," whereas in the *ḥadīth* of al-Nawwās, it is "good conduct (*ḥusn al-khuluq*)." Al-Ṭaḥāwī (d. 321/933) strived to bring the two *ḥadīths* into harmony and suggested that since good conduct is occasioned by the tranquillity of the self, the two answers are in agreement (al-Ṭaḥāwī 1994, 5:387). However, Ibn Rajab considered the difference in the Prophet's explanation of righteousness to be due to a variance in the meaning of the term itself, as it carries two connotations. In the context of the treatment of the rest of creation, it means doing good (*iḥsān*), which includes doing good to one's parents (*birr al-wālidayn*). It also means performing all acts of obedience, both apparent and inward. Ibn Rajab considered the *ḥadīth* of al-Nawwās to encompass the second meaning, because "by good conduct, one might mean adopting the ethics of the Sharīʿa and the manner of God." However, he did not clarify which meaning is applicable to the *ḥadīth* of Wābiṣa (Ibn Rajab 1999, 2:97–99). As for al-Rāghib al-Iṣfahānī (d. 502/1108), the *ḥadīth* of Wābiṣa does not explain the concepts of righteousness and sinfulness, but somewhat clarifies their legal status (*ḥukm*) (al-Rāghib al-Iṣfahānī 2009, 64). This is because the meaning of righteousness is amplitude (*saʿa*), and the meaning of sinfulness is delay (*ibṭāʾ*), for "righteousness (*birr*) is amplitude in knowing truth (*ʿilm al-ḥaqq*) and doing good (*fiʿl al-khayr*)," and sinfulness (*ithm*) "is a name for actions that inhibit reward (*mubṭiʾa ʿan al-thawāb*)" (al-Rāghib al-Iṣfahānī 2007, 160; 2009, 114).

It seems, as such, that al-Rāghib wanted to suggest that the abundant commission of good actions bequeaths the self an expansion in the chest and tranquillity in the heart. As for al-Ṭūfī, he considered that if righteousness is opposed to sinfulness, then it pertains to what the Sharīʿa demands in terms of obligations or recommendations, sinfulness pertains to what the Sharīʿa prohibits; whereas if righteousness is opposed to ingratitude, then it means doing good (*iḥsān*). The *ḥadīth* of al-Nawwās includes two signs of sinful acts, namely, its effect on the self and its wavering within it, because of its sense of an ill outcome, and hating for others to look upon the thing. However, al-Ṭūfī gave preponderance to there being a single composite sign (al-Ṭūfī 1998, 204–205).

Al-Ṭūfī and Ibn Rajab attempted to translate righteousness and sinfulness into the juristic categories of human actions (*al-aḥkām al-fiqhiyya*). On the one hand, Al-Ṭūfī categorised the signs of righteousness and sinfulness into four possibilities: (1) *ithm* (sinfulness) or *ḥarām* is that which rankles in the self, with fears that other people will observe it, such as *zinā* and *ribā*; (2) *birr* (righteousness) is that which does not rankle in the self and there is no fear of the observation of others such as *ʿibāda*, eating and drinking; (3) *mushtabih* (ambiguous) is that which rankles in the self but with no fear of other people observing (4) or where one fears other people observing him but it does not rankle in the self. The last two (3 and 4) oscillate between sinfulness and righteousness and are encompassed by the category of abhorred acts from which one ought to distance oneself (*al-karāha al-tanzīhiyya*). Guarding against ambiguous acts is considered to be obligatory (*wājib*). Coming into contact with them is sinful, whereas guarding against them is a path to absolution for the religion (*dīn*) and honour (*ʿirḍ*). This is obligatory, for the path to what is obligatory is, in turn, also obligatory (al-Ṭūfī 1998, 210).

Ibn Rajab, on the other hand, considered sinfulness to be of two levels: the higher level is where both signs are established. The lower level is where the action is objectionable to the performer of the action. This is only applicable if the heart is among those that have been expanded by belief and the *muftī* offers his opinion merely on the basis of supposition (*ẓann*) or inclination toward whim (*mayl ilā hawā*) without *sharʿī* evidence where he grants the person the right to an individual review. However, Ibn Rajab did not clarify the legal status of referring to what is in the self in this case. Rather, he defined righteousness as that which is permissible (*ḥalāl*) and sinfulness as that which is prohibited (*ḥarām*). In so doing, he recognised the tranquil heart for which the chest expands (*mā sakana ilayhi al-qalb wa-insharaḥa ilayhi al-ṣadr*) is righteous and permissible, while its opposite is sinful and prohibited (Ibn Rajab 1999, 2:101).

Righteousness and sinfulness are ethical principles. Yet, commentators such as al-Ṭūfī and Ibn Rajab occupied themselves with the translation of the significations of righteousness and sinfulness into a juristic language within the system of the permissible and the prohibited (*manẓūmat al-ḥalāl wa-l-ḥarām*). Thus, the idea that righteousness implies amplitude, for example, pushes one to search for its constituent parts in an attempt to regulate and specify what is righteous and permissible, what is sinful and prohibited – and what is ambiguous. No acts of righteousness fall outside being either recommended (*mandūb*) or obligatory (*wājib*), as pointed out by al-Ṭūfī.

However, righteousness, in its qualification as an ethical principle, refers, in my opinion, to a broader conception than that as it encompasses two things: truthfulness (*ṣidq*) in action, i.e., achieving the intended aim of the action, and good conduct (*iḥsān*) in action, i.e., performing it in the most perfect way. This means that righteousness is a concept that refers to quality, not to quantity or the degree of obligation in action (obligatory and recommended). It thus aims to transcend the formalism of apparent judgments or mere performance apart from consideration for the intent or the anticipated value of actions. This meaning remains unexamined in the books of *ḥadīth* commentary. For righteousness is a concept that surpasses juristic language and transcends to the ethical sphere.

Al-Ḥakīm al-Tirmidhī held the position that ambiguity only occurs for the scholars of the apparent (*ʿulamāʾ al-ẓāhir*), because “they found no revelation in its regard, nor any tradition attributed to the Prophet, so it appears to them as ambiguous, sometimes as permissible and at other times as prohibited, and they corrupted the witness (*shāhid*) that is within their hearts and the proof (*ḥujja*) with which God provided them" (al-Ḥakīm al-Tirmidhī 2010, 2:42). But this does not occur for "the truthful ones" (*muḥiqqūn*) who find within their hearts the clarification of ambiguous matters. Whatever makes their hearts feel tranquil, they count among the permissible, and whatever makes their hearts waver and from which they recoil, they count among the prohibited. For in the view of "the truthful," no ambiguous matter falls outside what is either permissible or prohibited, and this is a level of reflection at variance with the aforementioned ambiguous matters with which the jurists occupied themselves. An ambiguous matter for the jurist does not fall outside the category of abhorred acts from which one ought to distance himself/herself (*al-karāha al-tanzīhiyya*), as made clear by al-Ṭūfī. However, al-Ḥakīm al-Tirmidhī counted that towards which the heart feels tranquil as permissible, and that for which the heart wavers as prohibited. I surmise that he had in mind a meaning specific to the jurists, which he clarified in another book when he spoke of abstaining from appetites and avoiding desires for the purpose of refining the self and training it so that the heart is not corrupted – not in the sense of prohibiting that which is permissible (al-Ḥakīm al-Tirmidhī 1993, 64). This meaning is connected to the principle of striving for perfection of action, which transcends the action of the people of the apparent (*ahl al-ẓāhir*).

These opinions have generally sought to present interpretations that preserve the authority of the scriptural text and that of its specialists and prevent the transformation of normative judgments into individual subjective judgments. This is particularly the case as the self is susceptible to contingencies, such as desires and appetites, which disrupt the objectivity of its judgments. Accordingly, there were three interpretations; the first interpretation understood "consulting the heart" as a reference specifically to the hearts of the people of truth who relinquished their appetites and submitted to psychological exercises that refined them and rendered their judgments as trustworthy. The second interpretation specified consulting the heart over ambiguous issues, where the line between permissible (*ḥalāl*) and prohibited (*ḥarām*) is blurred. This ambiguity occurs mainly in individual choices and in the absence of evidentiary arguments. Here individuals are addressed by the Sharīʿa because they are aware of the innermost aspects of their selves. The third interpretation understood consulting the heart as a reference to the heart of the independent jurist (*mujtahid*) or the critical *ḥadīth* scholar (*al-muḥaddith al-nāqid*) who has acquired cumulative evidentiary knowledge. In all these interpretations, scholars tried to minimise the subjective role of the individual in favour of the objective judgment of the scholars in general.

## 3 Consulting the Heart: Rational Proofs and the Sources of Knowledge

The previous discussion revolved around the text of the *ḥadīth* in two aspects: that of the *ḥadīth* being firmly established, and that of its signification and its relation to other scriptural texts. However, the authority of the inward dimension (*bāṭin*) is connected to discussions and branching issues that fall under the domains of *fiqh*, *uṣūl al-fiqh*, and Sufism. This is because the authority of the inward dimension relates to a central issue – namely, the sources of knowledge by which *sharʿī* knowledge is established and the arguments for the rulings (*aḥkām*) of actions, which are matters where the jurists differ from the Sufis. The *ḥadīths* of consulting the heart or referring to the stirrings of the heart (*ḥawāzz al-qulūb*) are connected to numerous issues; among them are inspiration (*ilhām*), juristic preference (*istiḥsān*), blocking the means of prohibited actions (*sadd al-dharāʾiʿ*), piety (*waraʿ*) and caution (*iḥtiyāṭ*).[17]

### 3.1 *Inspiration* (Ilhām) *and Rational Proofs*

The jurists based their knowledge on a master principle: theoretical speculation (*naẓar*) and evidentiary inference (*istidlāl*). In doing so, jurists held that in every ruling (*ḥukm*) there must be a fundamental principle (*aṣl*) upon which it is based. Thus, they did not deem it permissible for a legally obligated individual (*mukallaf*) to undertake an action if they do not know its *sharʿī* ruling. These rulings were specified according to an established methodology in *uṣūl al-fiqh*, which inquires into the evidence and proofs upon which *fiqh* is based. They applied this method to assess particular actions by attributing to them a specific ruling in the science of *fiqh*. However, inspiration (*ilhām*) is neither

17 *Istiḥsān* is defined by some *Ḥanafīs* as a nuanced and subtle evidence that the *mujtahid* is unable to express properly (*dalīl yanqadiḥu fī nafs al-mujtahid taqṣuru ʿanhu ʿibāratuh*), although he/she feels it in his/her heart. This definition, according to Shams al-Dīn al-Barmāwī (d. 831/1428), makes *istiḥsān* close to *ilhām* in the Ḥanafī view (al-Barmāwī 2015, 5:180), but *istiḥsān*, in contrast to Ibn Ḥazm's (d. 456/1064) view, is classified as a sort of evidence, not personal preference (*tashahhī*) (see al-Dabūsī 2009, 3:369, 404; al-Taftāzānī n.d., 2:163; Ibn Hazm n.d., 6:60). Furthermore, conceiving *ijtihād* as a *malaka* (faculty) that enables the *mujtahid* to do his job spontaneously, makes *istiḥsān* acceptable even beyond the Ḥanafī school (see al-Ṭūfī 1997, 3:192). As for *sadd al-dharāʾiʿ*, al-Shawkānī (1999, 2:196; see also al-Bājī 1995, 2:697–698) considered this *ḥadīth* as evidence that supports it; in the sense that the individual shall consult his heart in the case of doubt or uncertainty and leave out some permissible actions to avoid what is prohibited. These two concepts belong to the toolbox of the *mujtahid* per se. The other concepts belong to the space of individual moral judgment. Hence, the following headings will be dedicated to discussing them in detail.

theoretical speculation (*naẓar*), nor evidentiary inference (*istidlāl*), and, therefore, it has been a cause for controversy in *uṣūl al-fiqh* (Ibn ʿAqīl 1999, 1:18; Abū Yaʿlā 1990, 1:82). Can *fiqh* be based upon the inspiration of the heart? Is seeking the adjudication of the heart an action of the independent jurist (*mujtahid*) or the *madhhab*-follower (*muqallid*)? What is the authoritative reference if all proofs are absent? These questions fall directly under our discussion of the *ḥadīth*s under study.

The evidentiary inference has been employed with the "consult your heart" *ḥadīth* in order to prove the authority of inspiration.[18] This is an area of inquiry where the positions of the *uṣūlī*s (legal theorists) have differed and three positions are distinguishable.

The first position holds that inspiration is an absolute *sharʿī* proof and an inward revelation analogous to rational theoretical speculation and evidentiary inference. It would appear that the rejection of the authority of inspiration in the books of *uṣūl* is related to two issues: the jurists' conceptualisation of what may be deemed as adequate "proof" in their convention; and their response to those who pay no heed to rational theoretical speculation holding that "there is no proof except inspiration." So, they give precedence to it over rational theoretical speculation (al-Samarqandī 1984, 679; al-Māwardī 1994, 16:53; al-Dabūsī 2009, 3:369–391; al-Fanārī 2006, 2:445).

The second position holds that inspiration is not proof, neither with respect to the individual who is inspired (*mulham*), nor with respect to others, i.e., regardless of whether it is transitive or intransitive. The reason for this is the absence of divine basis and the distrust towards those who carry fallible meditations (al-Subkī 2003, 111; Ibn Amīr al-Ḥājj 1983, 3:296). Ruling out inspiration as a path to knowledge or as a proof among other proofs is due to the paths of knowledge and to the conceptualisation of the validity of proofs. The paths of *sharʿī* knowledge were restricted by al-Shāfiʿī (d. 204/820) to the scriptural text. He clarified elsewhere that resorting to *ijmāʿ* (consensus) and *qiyās* (analogy) is within the category of *ḍarūra* (exigency) (al-Shāfiʿī 1938, 39, 599). This means that the locus of *sharʿī* knowledge is either a revealed scriptural text, or, in absence of a direct scriptural text, rational theoretical speculation regarding a revealed scriptural text. However, the *uṣūlī*s who came after al-Shāfiʿī agreed upon the convention of *istidlāl* (evidentiary inference), which is to search for proofs outside the four sources (Qurʾān, *ḥadīth*, consensus, and analogy). *Istidlāl* is based upon rational theoretical speculation, thereby excluding

18 Those in support of the authority of inspiration have marshalled it as evidence in a number of sources, including: al-Dabūsī 2009, 3:372; al-Samarqandī 1984, 680; al-Barmāwī 2015, 5:182; al-Fanārī 2006, 2:445; al-Zarkashī 1994, 8:117; and al-Kūrānī 2008, 4:38.

inspiration (al-Dabūsī 2009, 3:375; al-Sarakhsī n.d., 2:185–186; al-Bukhārī n.d., 3:358).

The third position is that it is obligatory to act upon true inspiration, but only with respect to the individual who is inspired. It is impermissible to invite others to it. Al-Dabūsī and al-Samarqandī (d. 540/1145) attributed this position to the majority of scholars (al-Dabūsī 2009, 3:369; al-Samarqandī 1984, 679; Ibn Amīr al-Ḥājj 1983, 3:296; al-Zarkashī 1994, 8:114; Ibn al-Najjār 1993, 1:330–332; Ibn Rajab 1999, 2:104). However, those who hold this position consider inspiration to be conditional proof, not self-standing independent proof. Thus, it is not permissible to act upon it, except in the absence of all other proofs (al-Dabūsī 2009, 3:369; al-Samarqandī 1984, 679; Ibn al-Najjār 1993, 1:330–332).

According to the first position, inspiration is considered as a path to knowledge that is established in the heart without theoretical speculation or evidentiary inference. The testimony of the heart without proof holds precedence over the proof-based opinion of the *muftī*. This has been understood from the *ḥadīth* of Wābiṣa itself, meaning that the heart of the individual occupies a dynamic role in the ethical valuation of actions, owing to the fact that the inspiration of the heart is analogous to revelation. However, the problem with this position is the possibility that inspiration can stand independently from all other proofs, or in opposition to them (al-Dabūsī 2009, 3:388). Even if it is indeed an "inward proof" (*ḥujja bāṭina*), the characteristics of proofs sanctioned by the *uṣūlīs* in rulings do not apply. Proofs, according to them, are the rational proofs that depend on the one hand on scriptural texts and, on the other, on theoretical speculation and evidentiary inference. Further, among the necessary conditions of proof is that it should be expressed first, whereas in the case of inspiration, "the scope for expressing it narrows" (al-Ghazālī 1971, 177). A proof must be suitable for debate and be binding upon another (al-Dabūsī 2009, 3:377; 1:133–134), meaning that it is open to generalisation. Obligation and generalisation, however, are established upon the characteristic of what is apparent to everyone, which is not the same in the case of inspiration.

The majority of scholars did not deem inspiration to be entirely without merit, but they only resorted to it in cases of exigency where worthy proofs were absent. What is implied by this is that proofs vary in degree, so direct scriptural proofs are given precedence over indirect scriptural proofs. Thus, *qiyās* (analogy) and *ijmāʿ* (consensus) were considered to be an exigency in the absence of a scriptural text. If all apparent proofs are lacking, the individual who is inspired resorts to inspiration as an exigency. Such a ruling is established for the individual alone, so others should not be invited to it. Obviously, this avoids the arbitrariness of judgment and ensures stability while still allowing for some discretion in cases where no apparent evidence is available. This view remains consistent with the theory of the *uṣūlīs*.

### 3.2 *The Heart That Offers Opinion: al-Ghazālī, on Piety and Caution*

The *ḥadīth* of Wābiṣa, and others, are a fundamental principle within scholarship that addresses the subject of piety (*waraʿ*). The two *imāms* al-Juwaynī (d. 478/1085) and al-Ghazālī deemed it foundational within their chapters on this topic. Al-Ghazālī spoke of what he called "the heart that offers opinion (*al-qalb al-muftī*)," and he drew a parallel between the opinion (*fatwā*) of the heart and that of the *muftī* in terms of ethical responsibility and the jurist's connection to the actions of the heart. The individual "is taken with respect to his self – between himself and God – by the opinion of his heart" (al-Ghazālī 1982, 3:3; 2:113; see also al-Juwaynī 2007, 15:320). At the same time, the actions of the heart fall outside the authority of the jurist due to two reasons: the first is because the theoretical speculation of the jurist is specific only to the rulings of the actions of the limbs and that which becomes apparent from inward actions. In other words, the jurist is concerned only with what can be regulated and is general to all legally obligated individuals. This differs from "the piety of the God-conscious (*muttaqūn*) and the righteous (*ṣāliḥūn*)," who aspire to a station higher than that of the generality of the legally obligated. For that reason, the latter do not only stop at the boundary of the obligatory and the prohibited, rather, they abstain from everything in which there is ambiguity; and they also abstain from some things that are licit out of fear that they may lead to what is illicit. Then, if their station is elevated further, they abstain from many licit fortunes which distract them from the pleasure of proximity to God. The second reason is that the jurist "does not discuss the stirrings of the hearts and how to act upon them," because his theoretical speculation relates to the earthly world (*dunyā*) (al-Ghazālī 1982, 1:19, 2:113, 4:213). On this basis, the individual shoulders the majority of the heart's actions themselves since it is s/he who is acquainted with their own particulars. While this is a broad conception of piety that al-Ghazālī discussed at length, he did not grant the legally obligated individual complete authority to determine what is valid or invalid in piety in case he passes over into obsessiveness and affective overburdening. Some piety falls under the laws of *fiqh* in terms of regulation and codification, and that which cannot be regulated is deferred anew to the legally obligated pious individual (al-Ghazālī 1982, 2:112).

Importantly, consultation of the heart is not absolute. It is subject to restrictions and particulars at which one must stop for it not to disrupt the system of apparent rulings. This is because the purpose of scrutinising the conditions of the inward dimension is to arrive at a higher station of devotion in worship.

On this basis, al-Ghazālī stipulated that the intended meaning of consulting the heart is,

> that which the *muftī* has declared permissible. As for that which he has declared prohibited, it is obligatory to refrain.
>
> AL-GHAZĀLĪ 1982, 2:118

Here, it is possible for us to distinguish between two cases. The first is the case of conflict between the opinion of the *muftī* and the opinion of the heart, which is implied by the *ḥadīth* of Wābiṣa (al-Ghazālī 1982, 1:224), i.e., that the opinion of the heart is given precedence over that of the *muftī*, because the heart is the locus of accountability for blame and the acquisition of reward.

> So, if the heart of the *muftī* ruled in favour of deeming something obligatory and it was mistaken in so doing, he is rewarded for that. Indeed, whosoever presumed that he had performed ritual purification must pray, then if he prayed and then remembered that he had not performed the ablution, he receives a reward for his action. If he remembered and then left performing it, he is punished for it … and all that is by considering the heart to the exception of the limbs.
>
> AL-GHAZĀLĪ 2011, 5:153

Moreover, the heart might be harmed by accepting that in which there is a stirring. It is obligatory, therefore, to listen to it. Venturing upon any action with a stirring in the heart harms it and brings darkness upon it, irrespective of the reality of the ruling as determined by God or its formulation by the *muftī* (al-Ghazālī 1982, 2:113).

The second case is doubt and ambiguity, involving two competing beliefs, each with its own proper ground. Al-Ghazālī attempted to regulate the implications of ambiguous matters. He determined that in cases of doubt, the legally obligated individual shall consult his heart in the same way the Messenger of God commanded Wābiṣa to consult his heart. Al-Ghazālī thus calls upon the legally obligated individual to go beyond simply avoiding what is prohibited and to shun ambiguous matters. For a while the opinion of the *muftī* is grounded on probabilities, the opinion of the heart pertains to piety and needs to be shielded from ambiguous matters. Such a station is higher than the theoretical speculation of the jurist which stops at clear-cut boundaries. Although al-Ghazālī attempted to regulate the fundamental principles of ambiguous matters (*shubah*) by means of the logic of the jurist, the details and applications of these ambiguous matters cannot be regulated. On this basis, he delegated them to the heart, not to the *muftī* (al-Ghazālī 1982, 2:99, 103, 86, 118).

The heart's stirrings, in terms of their capacity as a standard in determining what is ethical, do not only depend on the heart as the locus of legal obligation. They also depend on the heart possessing "insights into discrete contextual indicants for which the scope of speech narrows" (al-Ghazālī 1982, 2:125). Thus, it is not possible to regulate them according to the laws of *fiqh*, but they may be realised by means of "the contextual indicants of conditions (*qarā'in al-aḥwāl*)" (al-Ghazālī 1982, 4:213).

Because the heart's stirrings differ according to individuals and realities, it is possible to posit a general fundamental principle for them. Namely, "that which he finds to be closer to his whim and to that which is implied by his nature, the opposite of it is more worthy" (al-Ghazālī 1982, 2:170). Because these issues and conditions are in the utmost of subtlety, "not every heart can be depended upon" (al-Ghazālī 1982, 2:118). For that reason, "[the Prophet] did not refer everyone to the consultation of the heart. Rather, he only said that to Wābiṣa because of what he had known of his condition" (al-Ghazālī 1982, 2:117). This does not mean that consultation is to be restricted to the hearts of specific individuals, but rather that the command revolves around specific characteristics that adorn hearts, which may be attained through cultivation, watchfulness, and avoiding ambiguous matters. For hearts are two extremes and a median: the two extremes are an obsessive heart that recoils from everything and a covetous indulgent heart that is at ease with everything, and these two hearts are to be given no consideration. Rather, consideration is owed to what al-Ghazālī on occasion called "the heart of the scholar who has attained success that is watchful of the subtleties of conditions," which on another occasion he called "the pure moderate heart (*al-qalb al-ṣāfī l-muʿtadil*)." Even though al-Ghazālī admits to the scarcity of this type of heart, he opens the door to whoever "does not trust his own heart" to "solicit the light from a heart bearing this description" in order that he may present his case to it (al-Ghazālī 1982, 113, 118).

## 3.3 *The Heart as Exhorter: Ibn Taymiyya and Giving Preponderance to the Heart*

Ibn Taymiyya reaffirmed the authority of the scriptural text, by holding the position that any belief or action needs to be grounded in *sharʿī* evidence (Ibn Taymiyya 2001, 2:101; 2005, 10:477; 1991a, 1:244; 2005, 18:65; 2005, 22:27; 1987, 5:134). According to him, the scriptural evidence reflects God's intent and what He loves and abhors. Hence, it behoves the legally obligated individual to examine the evidence without yielding to his or her whim. However, the Lawgiver's ruling may be absolute or specific. As clarified by the Lawgiver, absolute rulings are principles and generalities which encompass an infinite number of particularities (Ibn Taymiyya 2001, 2:102; 2005, 10:478). Specific rulings, on the other hand, are those technically termed "establishing the *ratio legis* (*taḥqīq al-manāṭ*)." If a specific scriptural text exists in which the ruling is clarified, this expresses God's intent more clearly. However, if God's intent is hidden due to the absence of evidence or its ambiguity, or because the proofs contradict one another, establishing what God loves and what God abhors becomes the locus of *ijtihād*.

It is here that Ibn Taymiyya cites three schools: the first is to give preponderance to one position by the mere choice and will of the legally obligated individual. This is the position of the theologians, jurists and some of the Sufis. However, he determined that,

> Giving preponderance to one position by mere will, without relying on any scholarly basis, whether hidden or apparent, is not a position that is held by any of the *imāms* of knowledge and temperance.
>
> IBN TAYMIYYA 2005, 10:269; 2001, 2:93

The second is to refer to pure *qadar* (divine decree), because of the absence of overriding authoritative reasons (*al-asbāb al-murajjiḥa*) from the perspective of the Sharīʿa, and to avoid the introduction of personal will and whim into the action. This is because the introduction of whim dithers between being prohibited, disapproved, or descending from the station of perfect obedience to God. Surrendering to *qadar* here is to give preponderance by means of something that cannot be attributed to the individual and in which he has no will. It is God's action with regard to the individual. This is, according to Ibn Taymiyya, the method of ʿAbd al-Qādir al-Jīlānī (d. 561/1166) and his like among the great *shaykhs*. The third is to give preponderance to one position based on an inward reason, such as taste (*dhawq*), inspiration (*ilhām*), or inclination of the heart (*mayl qalbī*). Here, Ibn Taymiyya added that if the heart that is abundant in God-consciousness (*al-qalb al-maʿmūr bi-l-taqwā*) gives preponderance to a position by its will, then it is a *sharʿī* overriding authority (*tarjīḥ sharʿī*) with respect to itself. Guiding indications may occur within the heart of the believer regarding things that cannot be expressed. This is because God has built within his servants an innate disposition (*fiṭra*) towards the truth, and has placed within the heart of each believer an exhorter (*wāʿiẓ*), just as he placed an exhorter for the believer within the Book and the apparent Sharīʿa. Within each of the two exhorters, there are commandments and prohibitions, accompanied by exhortations and admonitions. This implies that there is a correspondence between apparent commandments and inward commandments. And in the case of the heart that is abundant in God-consciousness, the commandments and prohibitions that occur within the believer's heart are identical to the commandments and prohibitions of the Qurʾān, so one is strengthened by the other. Thus, there is sinfulness and righteousness "roaming and wavering" (*taraddud wa-jawalān*) within the chests of creation. If the servant exerts their utmost in obeying God and guarding against God's wrath, God becomes his or her hearing and sight and comes to be within his or her heart and sense. Indeed, he or she mostly wills what God loves and detests that which He abhors. When a heart becomes abundant in God-consciousness, matters are disclosed and become open to it, unlike the darkened ruinous heart. The action of this heart (i.e., *al-qalb al-maʿmūr bi-l-taqwā*) here is stronger upon its bearer than the weak and illusory analogies, just as it is stronger than the many apparent meanings and claims of continuity (*istiṣḥāb*) that the jurists cite as proof (Ibn Taymiyya 2001, 2:98–99; 2005, 20:27–29, 44–46, 19:280–285, 10:268–273, 477; 1986, 8:70; 1991b, 1:7).

Resorting to the inward overriding authoritative factor (*al-murajjiḥ al-bāṭin*) here takes place after the exhaustion of all apparent evidentiary indicants. The believer in this case may either opt to give preponderance to this inward reason, or to give preponderance merely based on his or her will and choice. However, giving preponderance to something merely on the basis of personal choice is to be avoided because it can be unstable, oscillating between prohibition or disapproval, or descending from the station of perfect obedience to God. The servant may also be requested to contradict his or her whim.

### 3.4 *Everyone Is Their Own Jurist: al-Shāṭibī and Establishing the Ratio Legis*

Al-Shāṭibī argued that these *ḥadīth*s are connected to the legally obligated individual's *ijtihād* in establishing the *ratio legis* (*taḥqīq al-manāṭ*). When it comes to knowing its ruling, every action is in need of two exercises in theoretical speculation: the first is an exercise in theoretical speculation with respect to the scriptural evidence of the ruling (*dalīl al-ḥukm*). This is something in which the heart has no place. For deeming something detestable based on the extent to which the self feels at ease without any scriptural evidence is the methodology of the people of innovation (*bidʿa*), and opposed to the *ijmāʿ* of Muslims. The second is an exercise in theoretical speculation regarding the locus in which the ruling is revealed (*maḥall al-ḥukm*), as many of its applications are deferred to the legally obligated individuals without requiring them to meet the condition of fulfilling the status of *ijtihād* or of Sharīʿa knowledge.[19] If the layperson were to ask the *muftī* about actions that are not of the type performed in prayer – whether their commission by a person during the performance of prayer would render their prayer invalid – the *muftī* would answer: if the action is negligible, it is forgivable, but if it is excessive, it would invalidate the prayer. The layperson here is in no need of clarification from the *muftī* in specifying what is excessive and what is not, for such specific judgment goes back to each legally obligated individual self to decide. This means that judgments of validity and invalidity depend upon the self of the legally obligated individual, i.e., deferring to the heart is restrictive in nature, so it does not undermine the scriptural evidence of the Sharīʿa (al-Shāṭibī 1992, 2:666–667; 1997, 2:300, 5:16–17, 25). As for determining general rulings, engaging in theoretical speculation on scriptural evidence and establishing the *ratio legis* that require *ijtihād*, they are to be referred to the jurists. This is because the ruling authority of jurists rests on *sharʿī* knowledge, which is specific to their domain and distinguishes them from others. To refer to the jurist is to refer to the Sharīʿa, and the *muqallid* is in need of an exemplar to follow (al-Shāṭibī 1992, 2:858–862). This means that consultation of the heart does not nullify the authority of the jurist.

Al-Shāṭibī stresses the regularity of the Sharīʿa, the generality and consistency of its rulings, and its exemption from loopholes, and thus runs on a singular law encompassing all legally obligated individuals. This regularity, however, does not nullify the variances and differences between individuals, whether in terms of the difference in their conditions, or the variance in their cognitive abilities. On this basis, al-Shāṭibī determines that the purpose of *sharʿī* rulings relating to customs (such as transactions and adjudications), as well as many acts of worship, is the regulation of the avenues of benefits, so that people's affairs may become well-ordered. Regulation, to the extent that it is possible, is closer to abiding by God's intent. As for matters that cannot be regulated, they are deferred to the trust and private affairs of legally obligated individuals (*amānāt al-mukallafīn*), such as prayer, fasting, menstruation, ritual purity, and other such matters (al-Shāṭibī 1997, 2:526–527). Furthermore, absolute

19 After putting our *ḥadīth* in the context of doubtful cases where everyone is obliged to refer to his own conscience and abide by its response, Muhammad Abdulla Draz (Muḥammad ʿAbd Allāh Drāz, d. 1958) discussed the role that the individual conscience plays in the institution of moral duty based on two points: understanding a rule and applying it, where there is a whole gamut of options between the undetermined and the determined. A similar perception was discussed by al-Shāṭibī under "*ratio legis* (*taḥqīq al-manāṭ*)." Draz concluded that it is "the recourse to individual effort, to ensure that one's duty is in conformity with the objective reality, is a universal duty, incumbent upon the most ignorant man, as well as the most competent" (Draz 2008, 63–65).

commandments and absolute prohibitions (i.e., those for which the Lawgiver has not specified particular boundaries) are intended to be unregulated by the Lawgiver and are delegated to the theoretical speculation of the legally obligated individual to engage in *ijtihād*. This is because the commandments and prohibitions must have intelligible meanings that can be understood independently but are still left without regulation. The aim here is to accommodate individual differences and conditions and variances in the performance of duties, which fall outside the circle of well-regulated obligations in which all are equal (al-Shāṭibī 1997, 2:148). This includes commandments such as those in favour of justice, goodness, forgiveness, patience, and gratitude, and prohibitions against injustice, indecency, bad conduct, and transgression (al-Shāṭibī 1997, 3:235, 392–398, 401). This point opens the door for the individual creative effort,[20] which differentiates between people in their goodness, and for distinctions between ethics and *fiqh* where the ethical realm goes beyond what is licit.

As for the stirrings of the hearts, they cannot be regulated, and they encompass personal revelations (*mukāshafāt*) and miracles (*karāmāt*). These cannot validly be taken into consideration except on the condition that they do not contravene a *sharʿī* ruling nor a religious principle. Moreover, the domain of acting upon *mukāshafāt* and *karāmāt* is in matters that are licit, or desirable pursuits in which there is room for manoeuvre, such as warning, giving glad tidings, and the pursuit of benefits that one hopes may successfully be attained. All this is based upon the fundamental principle determined by al-Shāṭibī, namely that the Sharīʿa is general and not specific. Its fundamental basis cannot be contravened and its consistency cannot be broken (al-Shāṭibī 1997, 2:457, 466–468, 471–473).

Al-Ghazālī discussed exhaustively what cannot be regulated among the actions of legally obligated individuals under the topic of "piety (*waraʿ*)," and included a cryptic part to guide the pious scholar. Al-Shāṭibī, however, addressed the same point under what he called the theoretical speculation of legally obligated individuals (*naẓar al-mukallaf*), or under the *fiqh* of the self, which generally revolves around "establishing the *ratio legis*." The two approaches are complementary, as they refer to the individual's effort and role in the valuation of actions. Overlapping occurs between the approaches of al-Ghazālī and al-Shāṭibī in that issues of piety intersect with issues of establishing the *ratio legis*. If piety is taken to mean the avoidance of ambiguous matters, then establishing the *ratio legis* is a broader category, because it

20 It seems that Draz coined what he called "effort créateur" (creative effort) based on what al-Shāṭibī mentioned here. For more details see Draz 2008, 257 f.; al-Khatib 2017, 107–108.

addresses ambiguous matters and other issues. Al-Shāṭibī even made space for that which the Lawgiver deliberately left unregulated so that the legally obligated individual may move freely based on their *ijtihād* and according to their condition. Al-Ghazālī primarily occupied himself with the responsibility of the individual from a Sufi perspective, and therefore opened the door to the stirrings of the hearts in order that some licit things that may harm the self may be avoided. Al-Shāṭibī, on the other hand, occupied himself with the regulation of the fundamental principles of the Sharīʿa. He thus posited a cohesive theoretical framework for it, closing the door to the stirrings of the hearts except when they do not contravene *sharʿī* principles or rulings, such as *mushtabihāt* or licit actions, to exclude what some extremist Sufis did when they followed their inspiration and freed themselves from the juristic rulings.

## 4 The Sufi Discourse on Consciences

Ibn ʿAjība (d. 1224/1808) noted that "among the foundational principles of the people of *taṣawwuf* is to refer to God in all things" (Ibn ʿAjība 2002, 2:417). However, this absolute recourse to God cannot be achieved by sticking to the method of the jurists only and contenting oneself with the apparent actions. The Sufis, thus, expanded in two directions: first, in valuating human actions in such a way as to encompass actions of the heart, and that there are rights owed to God in the beliefs of the hearts and what they acquire. These are referred to as "the inward knowledge" (*ʿilm al-bāṭin*),[21] which pertain to what the Sufis call musings (*khaṭarāt*), which are, as al-Muḥāsibī (d. 243/857) says, "the causes for hearts to turn to every good or evil" (al-Muḥāsibī 2003:84–85). The second expansion came in the direction of the sources of knowledge of divine will, which governs people's actions. This will encompass "apparent commandments" (*awāmir ẓāhira*), expressed by scriptural texts, and "inward commandments" (*awāmir bāṭina*), embodied in inspiration (*ilhām*) and the consultation of the heart. Al-Qushayrī's (465/1073) definition of musings reflects this aforementioned expansion, as he defined musings as "a discourse that comes upon the consciences" (*khiṭāb yaridu ʿalā l-ḍamāʾir*) (al-Qushayrī 1989, 169). This is a definition that encompasses two meanings:

21 *ʿIlm al-bāṭin* refers to what al-Ḥārith al-Muḥāsibī called "inward worship" (*ʿibāda bāṭina*) which consists of the inward actions and virtues such as *waraʿ* (piety), *ikhlāṣ* (sincerity), and *niyya* (intention). In contrast, the apparent knowledge (*ʿilm al-ẓāhir*) consists of the knowledge of *ḥalāl* (permissible) and *ḥarām* (prohibited). This classification of knowledge emerged with al-Muḥāsibī, and then became popular in Sufi literature such as Abū Ṭālib al-Makkī's work (see al-Muḥāsibī 1975, 81–88; al-Makkī 2001, 1:363–380).

The first meaning is that the heart is a discrete power (*quwwa khafiyya*) or a divine spiritual subtlety (*laṭīfa rabbāniyya rūḥāniyya*). This is the discerning aspect of the human that is addressed, punished, admonished, and answerable. The *khaṭarāt*, which come upon this heart, vary based on their sources and types and are differentiated by means of signs and terminologies. Al-Muḥāsibī divided the musings of the hearts into three types: a forewarning from the Most Gracious (which may be direct, without an intermediary, or through the mediation of an angel), a command from the self, and a whispering from the devil. Al-Qushayrī clarifies that each of these types takes a convention specific to it, "so, if it is from an angel, it is inspiration (*ilhām*); if it is from the self, it is called presentiments (*hawājis*); if it is from the devil, it is the whispering (*waswās*); and if it is God who has placed it in the heart, it is a true musing (*khāṭir ḥaqq*)" (al-Muḥāsibī 1986, 297–299; al-Qushayrī 1989, 169–170). The Sufis were thus cognisant of the complexities of that which roams within the human and the different causes that prompt actions. This is a vision that is more layered and complex than that of the Greek philosophers regarding the three powers of the soul: the appetitive power, the irascible power, and the rational power.[22] This complexity can be explained based on the spiritual experience and the scriptural sources.

The second meaning is that the Sufis' inquiry into divine will (and what God loves and abhors) generated their interest in the varieties of discourse, both apparent and inward. With regard to the inward discourse, they considered all its forms regardless of the source because they believed that the inward revelation complements the apparent revelation. Inquiry into the inward revelation requires differentiating it from what may be confused with it, such as the whisperings of a devil or the whims of a self. The inward revelation takes two forms: inspiration from an angel and the true musing from God, each of which represents a source for the valuation of the individual's actions. On this basis, al-Suhrawardī (d. 632/1234) considered that "the esoteric sciences (*al-ʿulūm al-ladunniyya*) within the hearts of those devoted to God are a kind of communication" (al-Suhrawardī 2000, 2:37). However, this differs from the way of the jurists, who restricted themselves to knowing the discourse of revelation (scriptural texts) which represents the general and apparent divine will. In the absence of scriptural evidence, jurists had to negotiate how much leeway they were willing to give to the heart within the non-textual sources. By contrast,

22 This is the classic version of the Platonic tripartite soul, but some studies show that Plato (d. 347–348 BCE) was hesitant about the tripartite division or there is more than one tripartite relation in the *Republic* (see Plato 2003, 135 f; Finamore 2005, 35–52; Robinson 1995, 119–122; Fronterotta 2013, 168–178; Corrigan 2007, 99–113).

the Sufis did not have the same concern for they operated within the realm of the heart and had more space to elaborate and theorise. For jurists, it remained limited to psychology in relation to what is evident and what is apparent in terms of testimony, while for the Sufis it became completely grounded in the deep psychological domain of the heart, beyond the domain of what is apparent. While some *uṣūlī*s objected to the rejection of inspiration, for the lack of grounding of its source, the Sufis posited standards and signs that aid in differentiating between one musing and another.

From the sum total of their discussions, it is possible to say that the distinction between musings is based on two things. The first rests on the consideration of the musing in light of the apparent revelation. The second is premised on the special characteristics linked to taste and experience. The divine musing is in concord with a fundamental *sharʿī* principle, untouched by license or whim, and followed by a sense of calm and expansion (*burūda wa-inshirāḥ*). The musing of the self mostly invites following an appetite or a sense of pride, which is not in accord with a fundamental *sharʿī* principle. It also admits licenses and is followed by a sense of dryness and tightness (*yubs wa-inqibāḍ*). The angelic musing brings nothing but good, whereas the satanic musing mostly invites us towards sin, although it may also bring good, which is cause for ambiguity. The differentiating factor between the angelic and satanic muse is that the first is supported by evidentiary indicants and is accompanied by an expansion, contrary to the satanic, which turns one away from evidentiary indicants and is accompanied by restrictiveness. If a person is confused regarding the origin of their musing, it is up to them to stop and ascertain, either by looking into their heart or asking the scholars. Thus, according to Ibn ʿAjība, it is among the characteristics of the people of *taṣawwuf* "to consult the hearts regarding those matters that occur [to them]," i.e., if they did not find an apparent revelation in its regard (al-Muḥāsibī 2003, 89; al-Qushayrī 1989, 169–170; al-Jīlānī 1976, 26–27; Zarrūq n.d., 288–289; al-Ḥakīm al-Tirmidhī 2010, 2:42, 54; Ibn ʿAjība 2002, 3:14; 2:417).

The principle of referring to God in all things also affected the Sufis' way of gauging actions on the basis of the principle that all the servant's movements and moments of stillness ought to be through God. This is because referring to God absolutely demands following commandments that may be divided into two kinds: the first is to take from the earthly world (*dunyā*) sustenance (*qūt*) which is the self's right to avoid whims and desires (*ḥaẓẓ al-nafs*), and to perform obligations and become occupied with avoiding sins, both apparent and inward. This is the adherence to apparent commandments. The second is to follow the inward commandment, which comes from the exalted Truth. God commands His servants and prohibits them by means of true musing or by the inspiration of an angel. This inward commandment is linked to what is licit with no ruling in the Sharīʿa and is left to the servant's choice. However, here, the individual may relinquish choice and await the inward commandment regarding the issue at hand – and if he is then commanded, he complies. Indeed, al-Jīlānī and others "command the performance of that which is recommended and not obligatory, and proscribe that which is discouraged and not prohibited" (Ibn Taymiyya 2005, 10:265). Thus, there remains no scope for the five legal rulings[23] with respect to the specific individual. This is because the recommended (*mustaḥabb*) is subsumed into the obligatory (*wājib*), the discouraged (*makrūh*) is subsumed into the prohibited (*ḥarām*), and the licit (*mubāḥ*) does not exist, because it becomes appended either to commission or to omission. In fact, al-Jīlānī calls for the abandonment of those musings which, upon consideration in light of the Book and the Sunna, it becomes clear that they are of the self and its licit appetites (such as eating, drinking, sexual intercourse, and other such things).

Ibn Taymiyya highlighted the disputation among the jurists over the meaning adopted here by al-Jīlānī and others because the jurists affirm the five legal rulings. However, the work of the jurists applies to rulings in general (*ʿumūm*) and the work of the Sufis applies to the rulings of the elect (*khawāṣṣ*). Thus, al-Ḥakīm al-Tirmidhī differentiated between "refining the self," by barring it from some licit appetites and "prohibition," positing that by barring the self from its desires, the training of the self is achieved such that it is subdued and softened. Therefore, the renunciation of the heart is meant to purify the heart. For the sake of these meanings, *fiqh*[24] for the Sufis is the science of the path of the hereafter, as clarified by al-Muḥāsibī, al-Ghazālī, and others (al-Jīlānī 1976, 26–28; Ibn Taymiyya 2005, 10:296–299; al-Ḥakīm al-Tirmidhī 1993, 63–65). This provides room to both distinguish between *fiqh* and ethics and give more scope for the individual creative effort that is based on self-discipline.

## 5 Conclusion

This study has shown that the inward dimension, with its various interpretations and the scope of its authority, has occupied an important space in various disciplines of the Islamic moral tradition. However, taking the perspective of how the two *ḥadīth*s were interpreted offers a different outlook to what is often

23 The five legal rulings in *fiqh* are: obligatory (*farḍ*), recommended (*mustaḥabb, mandūb*), permissible/ licit (*mubāḥ*), discouraged/disapproved (*makrūh*), and prohibited (*ḥarām*).

24 Lit., "comprehension; understanding."

gleaned from Muʿtazilīs' and Ashʿarīs' discussions on the sources of moral value judgments (*taḥsīn* and *taqbīḥ*). Moral conscience is a third category, besides reason and revelation, used to assess the moral quality of our thoughts, words, and deeds. This chapter proves that the common assumption of the absence of individual decision making in Islamic ethics is an oversimplification.

The contemporary scholarship about Islamic ethics has reduced Islamic ethics to two meta-ethical theories: ethical rationalism and ethical voluntarism (divine command theory). This taxonomy has implicitly emphasised the common understanding among some Western scholars that the Islamic conscience is an external scriptural conscience. This study identifies the rich Islamic discussions on individual conscience and its authority in ethical judgments. The inward dimension of the soul is substantiated through the discussion of three concepts: (1) inspiration (*ilhām*) (2) the musings (*khawāṭir*) that come upon the individual conscience in general, and (3) the preponderation of the heart (*tarjīḥ al-qalb*) and its inclination towards a particular action or judgment.

Traditionally, there were two main positions *vis-à-vis* the two key *ḥadīth*s discussed here. The first is represented by *ḥadīth* commentators who reinforced the authority of the scriptural text and the scholars to prevent the transformation of juristic rulings into individual judgment based upon human whims. On this basis, the apparent or general meaning of the *ḥadīth* was rejected. Jurists, *uṣūlī*s and Sufis adopted the second stance and sought to negotiate the strength of the authority of the conscience. In fact, the majority of *uṣūlī*s considered that in the absence of rational proofs, inspiration plays the role of an inward proof with respect to the individual who receives inspiration to the exception of others. In so doing, the recourse to inward dimension is needed as a departure from the apparent sense-determinate towards the individual inward dimension that cannot be made apparent, generalised, or regulated. The Sufis, however, have a vision of divine command that is broader than that of the jurists. For them, the issue is no longer limited to the commands and prohibitions stated in the scriptural texts, nor to those dos and don'ts that can be gleaned from the apparent meanings of these texts, but also encompass the inward dimensions of individuals and the actions of hearts. In order for their position to be made feasible, Sufis needed to broaden the sources of knowledge of divine will. On this basis, they discussed "the inward revelation," represented in inspiration and consultation of the heart, because it is deemed a divine discourse, coming either directly from God or through the medium of an angel.

In the negotiations over the authority and space of individual conscience, some scholars such as al-Ghazālī, Ibn Taymiyya, and al-Shāṭibī pursued a middle route, through which they attempted to reconcile between the apparent and the inward in terms of the discussions about consultation of the heart and to give preponderance to it. Al-Ghazālī argued for "the heart as *muftī*," with the *ḥadīth* as a fundamental principle for piety (*wara*ʿ). This piety directs itself towards the actions and choices of individuals, an issue that does not occupy the jurist. The individual takes charge of the majority of the actions of the heart, as it is the individual who is acquainted with its particularities. The heart becomes the locus of legal and moral obligation and possesses "insights into discrete contextual indicants," which cannot be regulated by the laws of *fiqh*.

Ibn Taymiyya weighs between the action of the heart and some of the preponderations that the jurists adopt (such as weak analogy, the apparent meaning, and claims of continuity [*istiṣḥāb*]), and considers that the inclination of the heart in this instance is stronger with respect to the individual than the overriding authoritative claims of the jurists.

Al-Shāṭibī, while refusing the heart as a source of evidence or a source of issuing rulings, established a balance between the absolute and the individual, the regulated and unregulated, and the authority of the scriptural text and the jurist on the one hand, and the responsibility of the legally obligated individual on the other. Those issues that cannot be regulated are to be deferred to the trusts and private affairs of legally obligated individuals. Indeed, there are spaces which the Lawgiver intended to leave unregulated by delegating them to the theoretical speculation of legally obligated individuals so that they may engage in *ijtihād* according to their capacity, cognition, and condition. This is because affairs of the conscience come down to intelligible meanings in which individuals differ.

To conclude, subjective interiority was inherent in the Islamic tradition and not necessarily imported and introduced by modernity.[25] This goes against the widespread Weberian notion that the normative structure of Islamic law leaves no room for individual ethical decisions and moral resistance against legal authority and political power. According to Max Weber (d. 1920),

> a "sacred law" is unable to develop the concept and the institutions of a formally rational justice because the weight of material religious ethics will always force the judge to define justice in the light of material considerations inherent in the case which he has to try. It will, therefore, produce "Kadi-Justiz." The mixture of ethics and law is considered to be an efficient impediment against the formal rationalisation of law.
>
> JOHANSEN 1997, 2

25 Although Jakob Skovgaard-Petersen defended the opposite of this position (1997, 23–25, 384).

Mohammad Fadel (2014), Baber Johansen, and Talal Asad also proved that this assumption is untenable and the latter emphasised that,

> subjective interiority has always been recognised in the Islamic tradition … what modernity does bring in is a new *kind* of subjectivity, one that is appropriate to ethical autonomy and aesthetic self-invention – a concept of "the subject" that has a new grammar.
>
> ASAD 2003, 225

The classical discussions around the authority of the inward dimension and the boundaries of its investment in ethical knowledge fall within the core of *ḥadīth*-centric discussions around the idea of the ethical conscience and its role in specifying right and wrong, which in turn is worthy of attention in further studies.

## Acknowledgements

I would like to thank Mohammed El-Sayed Bushra for his valuable help in fixing the language of an early draft of this chapter. I also thank Samer Rashwani and Rajai Ray Jureidini for their editorial help in later versions, Feriel Bouhafa, and the anonymous reviewers for their valuable comments. A version of this chapter was previously published in the *Journal of Arabic and Islamic Studies*, edited by Bouhafa (see al-Khatib 2021).

## Bibliography

ʿAbd al-Jabbār, al-Qāḍī Abū l-Ḥasan. n.d. *Al-Mughnī fī Abwāb al-Tawḥīd wa-l-ʿAdl*, edited by Ibrāhīm Madkūr. Cairo: al-Dār al-Miṣriyya lil-Taʾlīf wa-l-Tarjama.

ʿAbd al-Rahmān, Ṭāhā. 2017. *Dīn al-Ḥayāʾ: Min al-Fiqh al-Iʾtimārī ilā l-Fiqh al-Iʾtimānī*. Beirut: al-Muʾassasa al-ʿArabiyya lil-Fikr wa-l-Ibdāʿ.

Abou El Fadl, Khaled, Ahmad Atif Ahmad and Said Fares Hassan, eds. 2019. *Routledge Handbook of Islamic Law*. London: Routledge.

Abū Nuʿaym, Aḥmad b. ʿAbd Allāh. 1996. *Ḥilyat al-Awliyāʾ wa-Ṭabaqāt al-Aṣfiyāʾ*. Beirut: Dār al-Fikr.

Abū Yaʿlā, Aḥmad b. ʿAlī. 1984. *Musnad Abī Yaʿlā al-Mawṣilī*, edited by Ḥusayn Salīm Asad. Damascus: Dār al-Maʾmūn lil-Turāth.

Abū Yaʿlā, Muḥammad b. al-Ḥusayn. 1990. *Al-ʿUdda fī Uṣūl al-Fiqh*, edited by Aḥmad al-Mubārakī. Riyad: n.p.

Adamson, Peter and Matteo Di Giovanni, eds. 2019. *Interpreting Averroes: Critical essays*. Cambridge: Cambridge University Press.

Aḥmad Ibn Ḥanbal. 2001. *Musnad al-Imām Aḥmad b. Ḥanbal*, edited by Shuʿayb al-Arnāʾūṭ, ʿĀdil Murshid and ʿĀmir Ghaḍbān. Beirut: Muʾassasat al-Risāla.

Asad, Talal. 2003. *Formations of the Secular: Christianity, Islam, Modernity*. Redwood City, CA: Stanford University Press.

al-ʿAskarī, Abū Hilāl. 1998. *Al-Furūq al-Lughawiyya*, edited by Muḥammad Ibrāhīm Salīm. Cairo: Dār al-ʿIlm wa-l-Thaqafa lil-Nashr wa-l-Tawzīʿ.

al-Attar, Mariam. 2019. "Divine Command Ethics in the Islamic Legal Tradition." In *Routledge Handbook of Islamic Law*, edited by Khaled Abou El Fadl, Ahmad Atif Ahmad and Said Fares Hassan, 98–111. London: Routledge.

al-Bājī, Abū l-Walīd. 1995. *Iḥkām al-Fuṣūl fī Aḥkām al-Uṣūl*, edited by ʿAbd al-Majīd Turkī. Beirut: Dār al-Gharb al-Islāmī.

al-Bāqillānī, Abū Bakr. 1998. *Al-Taqrīb wa-l-Irshād*, edited by ʿAbd al-Ḥamīd Abū Zunayd. Beirut: Muʾassasat al-Risāla.

al-Barmāwī, Shams al-Dīn. 2015. *Al-Fawāʾid al-Saniyya fī Sharḥ al-Alfiyya*, edited by ʿAbd Allāh Ramaḍān. Egypt: Maktabat al-Tawʿiya al-Islāmiyya.

al-Baṣrī, Abū l-Ḥusayn. 1964. *Al-Muʿtamad fī Uṣūl al-Fiqh*, edited by Muḥammad Ḥamīd Allāh, Muḥammad Bakr and Ḥasan Ḥanafī. Damascus: al-Maʿhad al-ʿIlmī al-Faransī lil-Dirāsāt al-ʿArabiyya.

al-Bayhaqī, Aḥmad b. al-Ḥusayn. 2003. *Al-Jāmiʿ li-Shuʿab al-Īmān*, edited by Mukhtār Aḥmad al-Nadwī. Riyad: Maktabat al-Rushd Nāshirūn.

al-Bayhaqī, Aḥmad b. al-Ḥusayn. 2011. *Kitāb al-Sunan al-Kabīr*, edited by ʿAbd Allāh b. ʿAbd al-Muḥsin al-Turkī and Markaz Hajar. n.p.

Bo, Mou, ed. 2003. *Comparative Approaches to Chinese Philosophy*. Burlington: Ashgate.

Bouhafa, Feriel. 2019. "Averroes Corrective Philosophy of Law." In *Interpreting Averroes: Critical essays*, edited by Peter Adamson and Matteo Di Giovanni, 64–80. Cambridge: Cambridge University Press.

al-Bukhārī, ʿAbd al-ʿAzīz. n.d. *Kashf al-Asrār: Sharḥ Uṣūl al-Bazdawī*. Beirut: Dār al-Kitāb al-ʿArabī.

al-Bukhārī, Muḥammad b. Ismāʿīl. 1312/1895. *Ṣaḥīḥ al-Bukhārī*. Cairo: al-Maṭbaʿa al-Amīriyya bi-Būlāq.

al-Bukhārī, Muḥammad b. Ismāʿīl. 1989. *Al-Adab al-Mufrad*, edited by Muḥammad Fuʾād ʿAbd al-Bāqī. Beirut: Dār al-Bashāʾir al-Islāmiyya.

Butterworth, Charles, trans. and ed. 1977. *Averroes' Three Short Commentaries on Aristotle's 'Topics,' 'Rhetoric,' and 'Poetics.'* Albany, NY: State University of New York.

Cook, Michael, Najam Haider, Intisar Rabb and Asma Sayeed, eds. 2013. *Law and Tradition in Classical Islamic Thought*. New York: Palgrave Macmillan.

Corrigan, Kevin. 2007. "The Organization of the Soul: Some Overlooked Aspects of Interpretation from Plato to Late Antiquity." In *Reading Ancient Texts*, edited by Suzanne Stern-Gillet and Kevin Corrigan, 99–114. Leiden: Brill.

al-Dabūsī, Abū Zayd. 2009. *Taqwīm Uṣūl al-Fiqh wa-Taḥdīd Adillat al-Shar'*, edited by 'Abd al-Raḥīm Ya'qūb. Riyad: Maktabat al-Rushd Nāshirūn.

al-Dārimī, 'Abd Allāh b. 'Abd al-Raḥmān. 2000. *Musnad al-Dārimī*, edited by Ḥusayn Salīm Asad. Riyad: Dār al-Mughnī lil-Nashr wa-l-Tawzī'.

Despland, Michel. 2005. "Conscience." In *Encyclopedia of Religion*, edited by Lindsay Jones, Mircea Eliade and Charles J. Adams, 2nd edition. Detroit: Macmillan Reference USA.

Draz, M.A. 2008. *The Moral World of the Quran*, translated by Danielle Robinson and Rebecca Masterton. London: I.B. Tauris.

Elkaisy-Friemuth, Maha. 2006. *God and Humans in Islamic Thought: 'Abd al-Jabbār, Ibn Sīnā and al-Ghazālī*. London: Routledge.

Fadel, Mohammad. 2014. "Istafti Qalbaka wa-in Aftāka al-Nāsu wa-Aftūka: The Ethical Obligation of the Muqallid between Autonomy and Trust." In *Islamic Law in Theory*, edited by A. Kevin Reinhart and Robert Gleave, 105–126. Leiden: Brill.

al-Fanārī, Muḥammad b. Ḥamza. 2006. *Fuṣūl al-Badā'i' fī Uṣūl al-Sharā'i'*, edited by Muḥammad Ḥasan Ismā'īl. Beirut: Dār al-Kutub al-'Ilmiyya.

Finamore, John F. 2005. "The Tripartite Soul in Plato's Republic and Phaedrus." In *History of Platonism: Plato Redivivus*, edited by John Finamore and Robert Berchman, 35–52. New Orleans: University Press of the South.

Finamore, John and Robert Berchman, eds. 2005. *History of Platonism: Plato Redivivus*. New Orleans: University Press of the South.

Frank, Richard M. 1983. "Moral Obligation in Classical Muslim Theology." *The Journal of Religious Ethics* 11(2): 204–223.

Fronterotta, Francesco. 2013. "Plato's Psychology in Republic IV and X: How Many Parts of the Soul?" In *Dialogues on Plato's Politeia (Republic): Selected papers from the nineth Symposium Platonicum*, edited by Noburu Notomi and Luc Brisson, 168–178. Lecce: University of Salento.

al-Ghazālī, Abū Ḥāmid. 1971. *Shifā' al-Ghalīl fī Bayān al-Shabah wa-l-Makhīl wa-Masālik al-Ta'līl*, edited by Aḥmad al-Kubaysī. Baghdad: Maṭba'at al-Irshād.

al-Ghazālī, Abū Ḥāmid. 1982. *Iḥyā' 'Ulūm al-Dīn*. Beirut: Dār al-Ma'rifa.

Goldziher, Ignaz. 1917. *Mohammad and Islam*, translated by Kate Chambers Seelye. New Haven: Yale University Press.

Goodman, Lenn. E. 2003. *Islamic Humanism*. Oxford: Oxford University Press.

al-Ḥakīm al-Tirmidhī, Abū 'Abd Allāh. 1993. *Adab al-Nafs*, edited by Aḥmad 'Abd al-Raḥīm al-Sāyiḥ. Cairo: al-Dār al-Miṣriyya al-Lubnāniyya.

al-Ḥakīm al-Tirmidhī, Abū 'Abd Allāh. 2010. *Nawādir al-Uṣūl*, edited by Maḥmūd Takla. Damascus: Dār al-Nawādir.

al-Ḥārith, b. Muḥammad. 1992. *Bughyat al-Ḥārith 'an Zawā'id Musnad al-Ḥārith*, selected by Nūr al-Dīn al-Haythamī, edited by Ḥusayn al-Bākirī. Medina: Markaz Khidmat al-Sunna wa-l-Sīra al-Nabawiyya.

Heck, Paul L. 2014. "Conscience across Cultures: The Case of Islam." *The Journal of Religion* 94: 292–324.

Holtzman, Livnat. 2015. "Human Choice, Divine Guidance and the *Fiṭra* Tradition: The Use of Hadith in Theological Treatises, Ibn Taymiyya and Ibn Qayyim al-Jawziyya." In *Ibn Taymiyya and His Times*, edited by Yossef Rapoport and Shahab Ahmed, 163–188. Oxford: Oxford University Press.

Hourani, George. 1985. Reason and Tradition in Islamic Ethics. Cambridge: Cambridge University Press.

Hovannisian, Richard, ed. 1983. *Ethics in Islam*. California: Undena Publications.

Ibn ʿAbd al-Barr, Abū ʿUmar. 1994. *Jāmiʿ Bayān al-ʿIlm wa-Faḍlih*, edited by Abū l-Ashbāl al-Zuhayrī. Riyad: Dār Ibn al-Jawzī.

Ibn Abī l-Dunyā, Abū Bakr. 1988. *Kitāb al-Waraʿ*, edited by Muḥammad b. Ḥamad al-Ḥamūd. Kuwait: al-Dār al-Salafiyya.

Ibn Abī Shayba, Abū Bakr. 1989. *Al-Kitāb al-Muṣannaf fī l-Aḥādīth wa-l-Āthār*, edited by Kamāl Yūsuf al-Ḥūt. Beirut: Dār al-Tāj.

Ibn Abī Shayba, Abū Bakr. 1997. *Musnad Ibn Abī Shayba*, edited by ʿĀdil al-Ghazzāwī and Aḥmad al-Mazīdī. Riyad: Dār al-Waṭan.

Ibn ʿAjība, Aḥmad. 2002. *Al-Baḥr al-Madīd fī Tafsīr al-Qurʾān al-Majīd*. Beirut: Dār al-Kutub al-ʿIlmiyya.

Ibn Amīr al-Ḥājj, Abū ʿAbd Allāh. 1983. *Al-Taqrīr wa-l-Taḥbīr*. Beirut: Dār al-Kutub al-ʿIlmiyya.

Ibn ʿAqīl, Abū l-Wafā. 1999. *Al-Wāḍiḥ fī Uṣūl al-Fiqh*, edited by ʿAbd Allāh b. ʿAbd al-Muḥsin al-Turkī. Beirut: Muʾassasat al-Risāla.

Ibn Ḥazm, Abū Muḥammad. n.d. *Al-Iḥkām fī Uṣūl al-Aḥkām*, edited by Aḥmad Shākir, introduced by Iḥsān ʿAbbās. Beirut: Dār al-Āfāq al-Jadīda.

Ibn Ḥibbān, Abū Ḥātim. 2012. *Al-Musnad al-Ṣaḥīḥ ʿalā l-Taqāsīm wa-l-Anwāʿ*, edited by Muḥammad ʿAlī Sūnmaz and Khāliṣāy Damīr. Doha: Wizārat al-Awqāf wa-l-Shuʾūn al-Islāmiyya.

Ibn ʿIllān, Muḥammad. 2004. *Dalīl al-Fāliḥīn li-Ṭuruq Riyāḍ al-Ṣāliḥīn*, edited by Khalīl Maʾmūn Shīḥā. Beirut: Dār al-Maʿrifa.

Ibn al-Najjār, Muḥammad b. Aḥmad. 1993. *Sharḥ al-Kawkab al-Munīr*, edited by Muḥammad al-Zuḥaylī and Nazīh Ḥammād. Riyad: Dār al-ʿUbaykān.

Ibn Rajab, Zayn al-Dīn. 1999. *Jāmiʿ al-ʿUlūm wa-l-Ḥikam fī Sharḥ Khamsīn Ḥadīthan min Jawāmiʿ al-Kalim*, edited by Shuʿayb al-Arnāʾūṭ and Ibrāhīm Bājis. Beirut: Muʾassasat al-Risāla.

Ibn Taymiyya, Taqiyy al-Dīn. 1986. *Minhāj al-Sunna fī Naqḍ Kalām al-Shīʿa al-Qadariyya*, edited by Muḥammad Rashād Sālim. Riyad: Muḥammad b. Suʿūd University.

Ibn Taymiyya, Taqiyy al-Dīn. 1987. *Al-Fatāwā al-Kubrā*, edited by Muḥammad Abd al-Qādir ʿAṭā and Muṣṭafā ʿAbd al-Qādir ʿAṭā. Beirut: Dār al-Kutub al-ʿIlmiyya.

Ibn Taymiyya, Taqiyy al-Dīn. 1991a. *Darʾ Taʿāruḍ al-ʿAql wa-l-Naql*, edited by Muḥammad Rashād Sālim. Riyad: Muḥammad b. Suʿūd University.

Ibn Taymiyya, Taqiyy al-Dīn. 1991b. *Al-Istiqāma*, edited by Muḥammad Rashād Sālim. Riyad: Muḥammad b. Suʿūd University.

Ibn Taymiyya, Taqiyy al-Dīn. 1999. *Al-Jawāb al-Ṣaḥīḥ li-man Baddala Dīn al-Masīḥ*, edited by ʿAlī b. Ḥasan b. Nāṣir, ʿAbd al-ʿAzīz b. Ibrāhīm al-ʿAskar and Ḥamdān b. Muḥammad al-Ḥamdān. Riyad: Dār al-ʿĀṣima.

Ibn Taymiyya, Taqiyy al-Dīn. 2001. *Jāmiʿ al-Rasāʾil*, edited by Muḥammad Rashād Sālim. Riyad: Dār al-ʿAṭāʾ.

Ibn Taymiyya, Taqiyy al-Dīn. 2005. *Majmūʿat al-Fatāwā*, edited by ʿĀmir al-Jazzār and Anwar al-Bāz. Mansoura: Dār al-Wafā.

al-Jīlānī, ʿAbd al-Qādir. 1976. *Futūḥ al-Ghayb*. Cairo: Maṭbaʿat Muṣṭafā l-Bābī l-Ḥalabī wa-Awlādih.

al-Jīlānī, ʿAbd al-Qādir. 1997. *Al-Ghunya li-Ṭālibī Ṭarīq al-Ḥaqq ʿAzza wa-Jall*, edited by Ṣalāḥ ʿUwayḍa. Beirut: Dār al-Kutub al-ʿIlmiyya.

Johansen, Baber. 1997. "Truth and Validity of the Qadi's Judgment. A Legal Debate among Muslim Sunnite Jurists from the 9th to the 13th Centuries." *Recht van de Islam* 14: 1–26.

Johansen, Baber. 2013. "Dissent and Uncertainty in the Process of Legal Norm Construction in Muslim Sunni Law." In *Law and Tradition in Classical Islamic Thought*, edited by Michael Cook, Najam Haider, Intisar Rabb and Asma Sayeed, 127–144. New York: Palgrave Macmillan.

al-Juwaynī, ʿAbd al-Malik. 2007. *Nihāyat al-Maṭlab fī Dirāyat al-Madhhab*, edited by ʿAbd al-ʿAẓīm al-Dīb. Riyad: Dār al-Minhāj.

al-Kalwadhānī, Abū l-Khaṭṭāb. 1985. *Al-Tamhīd fī Uṣūl al-Fiqh*, edited by Mufīd Abū ʿAmsha and Muḥammad b. ʿAlī b. Ibrāhīm. Riyad: Markaz al-Baḥth al-ʿIlmī wa-Iḥyāʾ al-Turāth – Umm al-Qurā University.

al-Kāsānī, ʿAlāʾ al-Dīn. 1986. *Badāʾiʿ al-Ṣanāʾiʿ fī Tartīb al-Sharāʾiʿ*. Beirut: Dār al-Kutub al-ʿIlmiyya.

Kelsay, John. 1994. "Divine Command Ethics in Early Islam: Al-Shāfiʿī and the Problem of Guidance." *The Journal of Religious Ethics* 22: 101–126.

al-Kharāʾiṭī, Muḥammad b. Jaʿfar. 1999. *Makārim al-Akhlāq wa-Maʿālīhā wa-Maḥmūd Ṭarāʾiqihā*, edited by Ayman ʿAbd al-Jābir al-Buḥayrī. Cairo: Dār al-Āfāq al-ʿArabiyya.

al-Khaṭīb, Mutazz. 2011. *Radd al-Ḥadīth min Jihat al-Matn: Dirāsa fī Manāhij al-Muḥaddithīn wa-l-Uṣūliyyīn*. Beirut: al-Shabaka al-ʿArabiyya lil-Nashr wa-l-Tarjama.

al-Khaṭīb, Mutazz. 2017. "Āyāt al-Akhlāq: Suʾāl al-Akhlāq ʿInda al-Mufassirīn." *Journal of Islamic Ethics* 1:83–121.

al-Khatib, Mutaz. 2021. "Consult Your Heart: The Self as a Source of Moral Judgement." *Journal of Arabic and Islamic Studies* 21: 229–257.

al-Kindī, Yaʿqūb. 1950. *Rasāʾil al-Kindī al-Falsafiyya*, edited by Muḥammad ʿAbd al-Hādī Abū Rīda. Cairo: Dār al-Fikr al-ʿArabī.

al-Kūrānī, Aḥmad b. Ismāʿīl. 2008. *Al-Durar al-Lawāmiʿ fī Sharḥ Jamʿ al-Jawāmiʿ*, edited by Saʿīd al-Majīdī. Medina: al-Jāmiʿa al-Islāmiyya.

Leirvik, Oddbjørn. 2006. *Human Conscience and Muslim-Christian Relations: Modern Egyptian Thinkers on al-Ḍamīr*. London: Routledge.

Makdisi, George. 1983. "Ethics in Islamic Traditionalist Doctrine." In *Ethics in Islam*, edited by Richard Hovannisian, 47–64. California: Undena Publications.

al-Makkī, Abū Ṭālib. 2001. *Qūt al-Qulūb fī Muʿāmalat al-Maḥbūb*, edited by Maḥmūd al-Raḍwānī. Cairo: Maktabat Dār al-Turāth.

al-Māwardī, Abū l-Ḥasan. 1994. *Al-Ḥāwī l-Kabīr*, edited by ʿAlī Muʿawwaḍ and ʿĀdil ʿAbd al-Mawjūd. Beirut: Dār al-Kutub al-ʿIlmiyya.

al-Māzarī, Abū ʿAbd Allāh. 2002. *Īḍāḥ al-Maḥṣūl min Burhān al-Uṣūl*, edited by ʿAmmār al-Ṭālibī. Beirut: Dār al-Gharb al-Islāmī.

al-Muḥāsibī, al-Ḥārith. 1975. *Kitāb al-ʿIlm*, edited by Muḥammad al-ʿĀbid Mazālī. Tunisia: al-Dār al-Tūnisiyya lil-Nashr.

al-Muḥāsibī, al-Ḥārith. 1986. *Al-Waṣāyā*, edited by ʿAbd al-Qādir ʿAṭā. Beirut: Dār al-Kutub al-ʿIlmiyya.

al-Muḥāsibī, al-Ḥārith. 2003. *Al-Riʿāya li-Ḥuqūq Allāh*, edited by ʿAbd al-Halīm Maḥmūd. Cairo: Dār al-Maʿārif.

al-Mukhallaṣ, Muḥammad. 2008. *Al-Mukhallaṣiyyāt*, edited by Nabīl Jarrār. Doha: Wizārat al-Shuʾūn al-Islāmiyya.

al-Munāwī, ʿAbd al-Raʾūf. 1972. *Fayḍ al-Qadīr: Sharḥ al-Jāmiʿ al-Ṣaghīr*. Beirut: Dār al-Maʿrifa lil-Ṭibāʿa wa-l-Nashr.

Muslim b. al-Ḥajjāj. 1991. *Ṣaḥīḥ Muslim*, edited by Muḥammad Fuʾād ʿAbd al-Bāqī. Cairo: Dār Iḥyāʾ al-Kutub al-ʿArabiyya.

al-Nawawī, Muḥyī al-Dīn. 2004. *Al-Arbaʿūn al-Nawawiyya*, edited by ʿAlī al-Rāziḥī. Sanaa: Dār al-Āthār.

Notomi, Noburu and Luc Brisson, eds. 2013. *Dialogues on Plato's Politeia (Republic): Selected Papers from the Nineth Symposium Platonicum*. Lecce: University of Salento.

Plato. 2003. *The Republic*, edited by G.R.F. Ferrari, and translated by Tom Griffith. Cambridge: Cambridge University Press.

al-Qushayrī, Abū al-Qāsim. 1989. *Al-Risāla al-Qushayriyya*, edited by ʿAbd al-Ḥalīm Maḥmūd and Muḥammad b. al-Sharīf. Cairo: Dār al-Shaʿb.

al-Rāghib al-Iṣfahānī, Abū al-Qāsim. 2007. *Al-Dharīʿa ilā Makārim al-Sharīʿa*, edited by Abū l-Yazīd al-ʿAjamī. Cairo: Dār al-Salām.

al-Rāghib al-Iṣfahānī, Abū al-Qāsim. 2009. *Mufradāt Alfāẓ al-Qurʾān*, edited by Ṣafwān ʿAdnān Dāwūdī. Damascus: al-Dār al-Shāmiyya.

Rappoport, Yossef and Shahab Ahmed, eds. 2015. *Ibn Taymiyya and His Times*. Oxford: Oxford University Press.

Reinhart, Kevin and Robert Gleave, eds. 2014. *Islamic Law in Theory*. Leiden: Brill.

Riḍā, Rashīd. 1367/1948. *Tafsīr al-Manār*. Cairo: Dār al-Manār.

Robinson, T.M. 1995. *Plato's Psychology*. Toronto: University of Toronto Press.

Rosenthal, Franz. 2007. *Knowledge Triumphant: The Concept of Knowledge in Medieval Islam*. Leiden: Brill.

al-Samarqandī, ʿAlāʾ al-Dīn. 1984. *Mīzān al-Uṣūl fī Natāʾij al-ʿUqūl*, edited by Muḥammad Zakī ʿAbd al-Barr. Doha: Maṭābiʿ al-Dawḥa al-Ḥadītha.

al-Sarakhsī, Shams al-Dīn. n.d. *Uṣūl al-Sarakhsī*, edited by Abū l-Wafāʾ al-Afghānī. Hyderabad: Lajnat Iḥyāʾ al-Maʿārif al-Nuʿmāniyya.

Schmidtke, Sabine, ed. 2016. *The Oxford Handbook of Islamic Theology*. Oxford: Oxford University Press.

al-Shāfiʿī, Muḥammad b. Idrīs. 1938. *Al-Risāla*, edited by Aḥmad Shākir. Egypt: Maṭbaʿat Muṣṭafā l-Bābī l-Ḥalabī wa-Awlādih.

al-Shāṭibī, Abū Isḥāq. 1997. *Al-Muwāfaqāt*, edited by Mashhūr Ḥasan Āl Salmān. Riyad: Dār ʿAffān.

al-Shāṭibī, Abū Isḥāq. 1992. *Al-Iʿtiṣām*, edited by Salīm al-Hilālī. Riyad: Dār ʿAffān.

al-Shawkānī, Muḥammad b. ʿAlī. 1999. *Irshād al-Fuḥūl ilā Taḥqīq al-Ḥaqq min ʿIlm al-Uṣūl*, edited by Aḥmad ʿIzzū ʿInāya. Beirut: Dār al-Kitāb al-ʿArabī.

Shihadeh, Ayman. 2016. "Theories of Ethical Value in *Kalam*: A New Interpretation." In *The Oxford Handbook of Islamic Theology*, edited by Sabine Schmidtke, 384–407. Oxford: Oxford University Press.

al-Shīrāzī, Abū Isḥāq. 2003. *Al-Lumaʿ fī Uṣūl al-Fiqh*. Beirut: Dār al-Kutub al-ʿIlmiyya.

al-Shumunnī, Aḥmad. 2004. *Al-ʿĀlī al-Rutba fī Sharḥ Naẓm al-Nukhba*, edited by Muʿtazz al-Khaṭīb. Beirut: Muʾassasat al-Risāla Nāshirūn.

Skovgaard-Petersen, Jakob. 1997. *Defining Islam for the Egyptian State: Muftis and Fatwas of the Dār al-Iftā*. Leiden: Brill.

Stern-Gillet, Suzanne, and Kevin Corrigan, eds. 2007. *Reading Ancient Texts. Volume II: Aristotle and Neoplatonism*. Leiden: Brill.

al-Subkī, Tāj al-Dīn. 2003. *Jamʿ al-Jawāmiʿ fī Uṣūl al-Fiqh*, edited by ʿAbd al-Munʿim Khalīl Ibrāhīm. Beirut: Dār al-Kutub al-ʿIlmiyya.

al-Suhrawardī, Shihāb al-Dīn. 2000. *ʿAwārif al-Maʿārif*, edited by ʿAbd al-Ḥalīm Mahmūd and Maḥmūd b. al-Sharīf. Cairo: Dār al-Maʿārif.

al-Ṭabarānī, Abū al-Qāsim. 1984. *Musnad al-Shāmiyyīn*, edited by Ḥamdī ʿAbd al-Majīd al-Salafī. Beirut: Muʾassasat al-Risāla.

al-Taftāzānī, Saʿd al-Dīn. n.d. *Sharḥ al-Talwīḥ ʿalā al-Tawḍīḥ li-Matn al-Tanqīḥ fī Uṣūl al-Fiqh*. Beirut: Dār al-Kutub al-ʿIlmiyya.

al-Ṭaḥāwī, Aḥmad b. Muḥammad. 1994. *Sharḥ Mushkil al-Āthār*, edited by Shuʿayb al-Arnāʾūṭ. Beirut: Muʾassasat al-Risāla.

al-Tirmidhī, Muḥammad b. ʿĪsā. 1996. *Al-Jāmiʿ al-Kabīr*, edited by Bashshār ʿAwwād Maʿrūf. Beirut: Dār al-Gharb al-Islāmī.

Tisdall, William St. Clair. 1910. *The Religion of the Crescent: Being the James Long Lectures on Muḥammadanism*. London: Society for Promoting Christian Knowledge.

al-Ṭūfī, Najm al-Dīn. 1997. *Sharḥ Mukhtaṣar al-Rawḍa*, edited by ʿAbd Allāh ʿAbd al-Muḥsin al-Turkī. Riyad: Wizārat al-Shuʾūn al-Islāmiyya wa-l-Awqāf.

al-Ṭūfī, Najm al-Dīn. 1998. *Al-Taʿyīn fī Sharḥ al-Arbaʿīn*, edited by Aḥmad Ḥājj Muḥammad ʿUthmān. Beirut: Muʾassasat al-Rayyān/Mecca: al-Maktaba al-Makkiyya.

Van Norden, Bryan W. 2003. "Virtue Ethics and Confucianism." In *Comparative Approaches to Chinese Philosophy*, edited by Mou Bo, 99–121. Burlington: Ashgate.

Vasalou, Sophia. 2016. *Ibn Taymiyya's Theological Ethics*. Oxford: Oxford University Press.

Wilmers, Damaris. 2018. *Beyond Schools: Muḥammad b. Ibrāhīm al-Wazīr's (d. 840/1436) Epistemology of Ambiguity*. Leiden: Brill.

al-Zarkashī, Badr al-Dīn. 1994. *Al-Baḥr al-Muḥīṭ fī Uṣūl al-Fiqh*. Damascus: Dār al-Kutubī.

Zarrūq, Aḥmad. n.d. *Qawāʿid al-Taṣawwuf wa-Shawāhid al-Taʿarruf*, edited by Nizār Ḥammādī. Sharjah: al-Markaz al-ʿArabī lil-Kitāb.

الفصل 12

# مصنفات المحدثين في الأخلاق: كشاف أوليّ

معتز الخطيب

## 1 مقدمة

بدت المكتبة الإسلامية الأخلاقية – في عمومها – محدودة جدًّا لدى محمد عبد الله دراز (ت. 1958) وغيره (دراز 1998، 4)؛ لأنهم حصروا أنفسهم في الأخلاق النظرية على طريقة الفلاسفة، في حين أننا لو اعتمدنا المفهوم الموسع للأخلاق الذي يشمل الفعل والفاعل، والظاهر والباطن، وينفتح على مقاربات ومناهج مختلفة (من حيث إن التفكير النظري ليس قاصرًا فقط على حقل الفلسفة)، ويشتبك مع حقول وتخصصات متعددة فإن المكتبة الأخلاقية ستتسع كثيرًا بلا شك، ولعل من أوسع فروعها مكتبة المحدثين التي شملت أبوابًا مختلفة في الأخلاق، ومع ذلك جرى تجاهلها من قبل عدد من الباحثين المعاصرين في حقل الأخلاق الإسلامية كما أوضحت في الفصل الأول من هذا الكتاب. ويُظهر هذا الأهمية القصوى لكتابة فهرست للكتب والمصادر الحديثية المتصلة بالأخلاق، فهي تشكل مادةً ثرية للأخلاق التحليلية (analytical ethics) بتعبير جورج حوراني (ت. 1984) الذي تجنب استعمال «الفلسفية» واستعاض عنها بـ«التحليلية» (Hourani 1985, 15–16).

ومن شأن هذا الفهرست أن يكون مرجعًا يوقفنا على ثراء المضامين الأخلاقية عند المحدثين أولًا، وأن يحرض الباحثين على دراسات مستقبلية في هذا الميدان الناشئ والخصب ثانيًا، حيث يمكن لهذه الدراسات أن تنهج نهجًا متعدد التخصصات يتوافق مع الطبيعة التي اكتسبها علم الأخلاق اليوم حيث إن أهم سماته أنه حقل متعدد التخصصات وعابر لها؛ من حيث إنه يتناول الأفعال الإنسانية وتقويم الفاعلين أنفسهم، ويشتبك مع ألوان النشاط الإنساني الشاسعة.بالإضافة إلى ذلك، من شأن فرع الأخلاق الحديثية أن يوسع آفاق البحث الحديثي الذي طالما انشغل بمسائل تقنية الطابع واستغرق – في العصر الحديث – في سؤال الموثوقية على حساب الكثير من الأسئلة المهمة وعلى حساب مضامين مدونات الحديث نفسها التي لم تكن محل اهتمام أو أولوية في الأكاديميا الغربية نفسها. أي أن الأخلاق الحديثية من شأنها أن تحدث تأثيرًا في حقل الحديث وحقل الأخلاق معًا.

قبل أن نستعرض فهرست المصنفات الحديثية في الأخلاق، سأتناول في هذه المقدمة التحليلية ثلاثة محاور رئيسة. في الأول منها سأوضح الأبعاد الأخلاقية لمدونة الحديث، وفي الثاني

منها سأقترح تصنيفًا للأخلاق الحديثية. أما الثالث فهو مخصص لبيان المعايير التي جرى – على أساسها – اختيار هذه الكتب واستبعاد غيرها من هذا الفهرست، ثم يأتي في المحور الرابع قائمة المصادر نفسها مرتبة تاريخيًّا.

## 2 المضمون الأخلاقي لمدونات الحديث

يمكن تصنيف محتوى مدونة الحديث – عمومًا – إلى ثلاثة أقسام: الأقوال والأفعال والصفات[1]، وهذه القسمة تتصل بالنقاشات الأخلاقية الحديثة التي تجري عادة وفق ثنائية الفعل (أو أخلاق الأفعال) والخُلق (أو أخلاق الفضيلة). وثنائية الأقوال والأفعال هي الغالبة على مصادر الحديث، ومن ثم سعى إلى جمعها واستيعابها كلٌّ من جلال الدين السيوطي (ت. 1505/911) وعلاء الدين المتقي الهندي (ت. 1568/975) (السيوطي 2005؛ والمتقي الهندي 1981). أما الصفات (ويُعبر عنها بلفظ الأخلاق إن تعلقت بالصفات غير الخَلْقية) فقد استوعبتها أنواع أخرى من المصنفات ككتب السيرة والشمائل النبوية التي تتضمن الصفات الجسدية والخُلقية معًا، كما تناولتها كتب مفردة حملت عناوين مثل «صفة النبي» أو «أخلاق النبي»، وصنف فيها محمد بن هارون (ت. 962/353) وأبو الشيخ الأصبهاني (ت. 979/369)، وأبو حيان الأصفهاني (ت. 1038/429)، وضياء الدين المقدسي (ت. 1245/643) وغيرهم.

وقد عملت هذه الأقسام الثلاثة (الأقوال والأفعال والصفات) على تثبيت مرجعية الحديث أو السنة التي صارت مصدرًا ثانيًا من مصادر التشريع بعد القرآن الكريم، كما ساهمت في رسم شخصية للنبي صلى الله عليه وسلم بوصفه مثلًا أعلى أو نموذجًا يُحتذى في هديه: قولًا وفعلًا وأخلاقًا (بمعنى الصفات الخُلقية)، ثم رتّبت له حقوقًا على المؤمنين تبدأ من أن حب النبي صلى الله عليه وسلم من الإيمان،[2] وتنتهي بالحقوق الواجبة على المسلم تجاه النبي، وقد جمعها القاضي عياض (ت. 1149/544) في كتاب سماه «الشفا بتعريف حقوق المصطفى» (2013).

1 انطوت كتب الحديث الرئيسة على فصل خاص (يُسمى كتابًا) بالفضائل أو المناقب، ويندرج تحته بعض ما يتعلق بصفات النبي وشمائله. وفي «أبواب البر والصلة» أدرج بعض المحدثين الأحاديث الخاصة بخلق النبي صلى الله عليه وسلم، كما فعل أبو عيسى الترمذي (ت. 892/279) في جامعه مثلًا، في حين أدرجه غيره من أصحاب كتب السنن تحت أبواب أخرى ككتاب الأدب مثلًا عند أبي داود (ت. 889/275) في سننه.

2 انظر مثلًا البخاري (1422هـ [2001]، 125/2)، كتاب الإيمان، باب حب الرسول صلى الله عليه وسلم من الإيمان.

وبالإضافة إلى المثل الأعلى والغايات، يستوعب المضمون الأخلاقي لمدونة الحديث نوعين من الأفعال: الأول: الأفعال الظاهرة (أو أفعال الجوارح) وقد استوعبتها المصنفات الحديثية الفقهية، ومن أبرزها كتب أحاديث الأحكام. والثاني: أفعال الباطن التي نشأت لها مصنفات مفردة وكَتَبَ في بعض موضوعاتها ابن أبي الدنيا (ت. 894/281) وأبو محمد الحسن بن إسماعيل الضرّاب (ت. 1002/392) وغيرهما، وأُدرجت أيضًا تحت أبواب مختلفة من كتب الحديث الرئيسة، وخاصة كتاب الرِّقاق من صحيح البخاري (ت. 870/256) ومن صحيح ابن حبان (ت. 965/354) بترتيب ابن بلبان (ت. 1339/739)، وكتاب البر والصلة والآداب من صحيح مسلم (ت. 875/261). ويستوعب المضمون الأخلاقي للحديث أيضًا نوعين من الأحاديث: الأول: الأحاديثَ المفردة التي تعالج قضايا جزئية أو حالات محددة (casuistry)، والثاني: الأحاديث الكلية التي تقدم مبادئ عامة، كالأحاديث التي اشتملت عليها «الأربعون النووية» لمحيي الدين النووي (ت. 1277/676) (النووي 2009).

وإن مشينا على المفهوم الموسّع للأخلاق، سنجد المضمون الأخلاقي موزعًا على العديد من الكتب - وفق التسمية الكلاسيكية للفصول - داخل مجاميع الحديث، ككتب الأحكام، والمظالم والغصب، والإكراه، والحيل، والقدَر، وغيرها من صحيح البخاري مثلًا. أما إذا مشينا على المفهوم المضيّق للأخلاق، فسنجد أحاديث الأخلاق في نوعين من المصادر: الأول: الكتب العديدة التي أُفردت إما لموضوع محدد كذم الرياء مثلًا، أو لبابٍ من أبواب الأخلاق كمكارم الأخلاق مثلًا، وسنأتي على تصنيف هذه الكتب لاحقًا. والثاني: مجاميع الحديث الرئيسة حيث نجد بعض أحاديث الأخلاق مصنفة ضمن أبواب محددة مثل كتاب الأدب من سنن أبي داود - مثلًا -، وهو كتاب ضخم اشتمل على أكثر من 500 حديث (أبو داود 2009، 7/153–545)، ومثل كتاب البر والإحسان وكتاب الرقائق من صحيح ابن حبان بترتيب ابن بلبان، وقد اشتملا على نحو 767 حديثًا (ابن حبان 1988، 1/506–3/310).

ومن مجموع عناوين الكتب التي انطوت عليها مجاميع الحديث الستة نخلص إلى أن ما يتصل منها بالأخلاق - بالمفهوم المضيق - يشمل الكتب الآتية: كتاب المناقب الذي ينطوي على بعض الفضائل، وكتب الأدب، والرِّقاق، والبر والصلة، والزهد. ومن اللافت أن أحاديث الأخلاق - بالمعنى المضيق - توزعت على كتب عدة في صحيح مسلم[3] هي: كتاب السلام، وكتاب ألفاظ من الأدب، وكتاب البر والصلة، وكتاب الآداب، وكتاب الفضائل، وكتاب التوبة، وكتاب الذكر والدعاء، وكتاب صفات المنافقين، وكتاب الزهد. ومن الواضح أنه تم التمييز هنا بين "الآداب"

---

3 بوّب مسلم بن الحجاج (ت. 875/261) كتابه ولكنه لم يترجم للأبواب، ثم جاء بعض العلماء بعده فوضع عناوين للأبواب بعضها جيد وبعضها ليس بجيد كما قال النووي (النووي 1929، 21/1).

وبين "الأدب" فجُعلا كتابين منفصلين، كما هو الحال – أيضًا – في سنن الترمذي (ت. 892/279) (الترمذي 1996).

## 3 تصنيف كتب الأخلاق الحديثية

سنتجاوز هنا ما سبق ذكره من الكتب الفرعية والأبواب التي اشتملت عليها مجاميع الحديث الرئيسة، كما سنتجاوز المفهوم الأخلاقي الموسع الذي يشمل أيضًا أجزاء من كتب أحاديث الأحكام التي غلب عليها المنظور الفقهي،[4] وسنركز فقط على الكتب المفردة في الأخلاق الحديثية التي هي محل اهتمامنا في هذا الفهرست، ويمكن أن نصنفها على ثمانية أقسام هي:

- كتب الأدب، وتشمل الأدب المفرد وأنواعًا أخرى من الآداب المتعلقة بالفروع المعرفية المختلفة، كآداب الراوي والسامع، والفقيه والمتفقه، والملي والمستملي وغيرها، بالإضافة إلى أدب النفوس، وآداب الوالدين، وآداب الصحبة، وآداب العشرة وقضاء الحوائج وغير ذلك من الكتب التي تسلك طرائق المحدثين في رواية الأحاديث المسندة، سواءً إلى النبي أم مَن دونه.
- كتب مكارم الأخلاق أو محاسن الأخلاق ومساوئها، وقد تحولت إلى لون من ألوان التصنيف المفرد، ويندرج ضمنها الحديث عن أخلاق النفس وطبائعها وفضائلها ورذائلها وصفات الفاضل والرذل، وكتب المحاسن والخصال، وكيفية تهذيب النفس ووعظها وترقيقها ومواساتها وبيان عللها إلى غير ذلك.
- كتب الترغيب والترهيب، وكتب فضائل الأعمال التي تنشغل بفضائل ومذام الأعمال، وتشتمل على جوانب تعبدية وأخرى أخلاقية.

4 وسَّع بعض المصنفين في أحاديث الأحكام مفهوم «الأحكام» لتشمل غير الفقهيات أيضًا، ومن هنا ضم عبد الحق الإشبيلي (ت. 1185/581) إلى «أحاديث الأحكام» بعض أبواب الأخلاق – بالمفهوم المضيق – وقال: إنه جمع في كتابه «لوازم الشرع وأحكامه وحلاله وحرامه، وضروبًا من الترغيب والترهيب وذِكر الثواب والعقاب»؛ لأن هذه الأحاديث "تُسعد العاملَ بها" (الإشبيلي 1993، 71/1). فهو قد وسع مفهوم «الأحكام» من جهة، وربطها بغاية تحصيل السعادة من جهة ثانية. وكذلك فعل ابن حجر العسقلاني (ت. 1449/852) فقد ضم – في كتابه – إلى الكتب الفقهية المعتادة كتابًا سماه «كتاب الجامع» على طريقة فقهاء المالكية، وأدرج ضمنه ستة أبواب هي: الأدب، والبر والصلة، والزهد والورع، والرهب من مساوئ الأخلاق، والترغيب في مكارم الأخلاق، والذكر والدعاء. وقد اشتملت هذه الأبواب على 131 حديثًا من مجموع 1582 حديثًا (ابن حجر العسقلاني 2003، 439–469).

- كتب شعب الإيمان التي تسعى إلى رصد شعب الإيمان الواردة في الحديث المشهور، وهي بضع وستون أو بضع وسبعون شعبة، ويتداخل في هذه الكتب الأبعاد الكلامية والفقهية والأخلاقية، كما يتداخل الاعتقادي والعملي.
- كتب المناقب والفضائل، وتتنوع هذه الكتب بحسب الأشخاص والأفعال والأزمنة وغيرها، أي أنها تذهب إلى مدى أبعد من مجال الأخلاق، ولكنها تشتمل على أبعاد أخلاقية تتصل بأخلاق الفضيلة.
- كتب الزهد والورع والرقائق التي أُفردت منذ زمن مبكر في القرن الثاني الهجري، وهي من أوائل الكتب التي ظهرت في التصنيف على الأبواب.
- كتب هدي النبي وأخلاقه وشمائله التي أُفردت بالتصنيف، وقد كانت جزءًا من السيرة النبوية، بالإضافة إلى سير الخلفاء الراشدين والصحابة والصالحين، وهي تقدم النموذج الأخلاقي الذي يجب أن يُحتذى، وتشكل كتب الطبقات كذلك مصدرًا ثريًّا لهذا وإن كان من العسير إدراجها ضمن كتب الأخلاق؛ لأنها ليست كذلك وإن انطوت على أبعاد أخلاقية.
- الكتب المخصصة لموضوع واحد من موضوعات الأخلاق، كذم الدنيا، وذم الرياء، واعتلال القلوب، والصبر على فقد الأولاد، والعزلة، والقناعة، والكذب، والنفاق، والصبر، والعدل، والزهد، والتوبة، والتواضع، والكبر، والرقة والبكاء، والرحمة، والفتوة، والعيال، والأمر بالمعروف والنهي عن المنكر، وغير ذلك، وقد ضرب ابن أبي الدنيا (ت. 281/894) مثلًا بارزًا في هذا الباب.

ويمكن أن نضيف -إلى ما سبق- بعض كتب الأربعينات؛ لأننا يمكن أن نميز فيها بين مسلكين: الأول: يقوم على معايير تقنية أو اصطلاحية أو لطائف إسنادية وهو كثير. أما الثاني فيتصل بالتصنيف على الأبواب والأخلاق والأحاديث الكلية، وقد أدرجت عددًا منها في هذا الفهرست. ومن أمثلة الأول الكثيرة جمع أربعين حديثًا عن أربعين شيخًا أو من أربعين بلدًا، وجمع أربعين حديثًا في المساواة، وهي أن يساوي الجامع في إسناده عدد رجال محدث آخر إلى النبي صلى الله عليه وسلم ولكن بإسناد غير إسناده، أو جمع أربعين حديثًا في الموافقة، وهي أن يوافق الجامع شيخ محدث آخر في الإسناد بإسناد عال يَقل عدد رجاله عن رجال الذي وافقه فيه، أو جمع أربعين حديثًا في الأبدال العوالي، والبدل أن يقع للجامع الحديثُ بإسناد عال عن غير شيخ محدث آخر، أو جمعُ أربعين حديثًا متباينة السماع، أو جمع أربعين حديثًا مسلسلة على صفة معينة، أو جمع أربعين حديثًا عشارية، إلى غير ذلك مما يتنوع ويكثر، وكلها اعتبارات لا مدخل لها هنا في حقل الحديث والأخلاق، ولذلك كان من الصعب أن ندرج نوع الأربعينات في القسمة الثمانية السابقة.

## 4 معايير اختيار الكتب وترتيبها

محور الاهتمام - في هذا الفهرست - الكتبُ ذات الصلة بالعلاقة بين الحديث والأخلاق. ويمكن تصنيف عموم الكتب - على هذا الشرط - إلى نوعين: الأول يضم المصادر الحديثية غير المطبوعة التي حدثتنا عنها كتب التراجم وفهارس المخطوطات، وهي تتوزع بين ما لا نعرف له أثرًا أو هو مفقود بالفعل، وبين ما لا يزال مخطوطًا،[5] ورغم أنني جمعت قائمة أولية بهذا النوع إلا أنني عدلتُ عن إدراجها في هذه الطبعة من كتابنا هذا على الأقل. أما النوع الثاني فيتناول المصادر المطبوعة فقط، وهو ما خصصت له هذا الفهرست. ولا يمكنني الادعاء بأن هذا الفهرست استقصى كل المصادر ذات الصلة، ولكن شرطي فيه أن أجمع ما أمكنني الاطلاعُ المباشر عليه، وقد بذلت جهدي في تخير الطبعة الأصلح للكتاب التي طُبعت على نسخ خطية إنْ وجدت أو أمكنني ذلك. وبالنظر إلى خصوصية علم الحديث، فإن الأهمية القصوى هنا للمصادر المبكرة، لما تنطوي عليه من قيمة معيارية؛ فهي تنتمي إلى المرحلة التأسيسية وتقل فيها الوسائط من جهة، وتشتمل على أحاديث وآثار مسندة، أي تتبع طريقة المحدثين في عصر الرواية. ومع ذلك استقصيت - ما أمكنَ - المصادر المتأخرة التي بلغت إلى حدود القرن العاشر الهجري تقريبًا، وإن كان ثمة أربعة مصادر تأخرت عن هذا التاريخ، آخرها مجموع حديثيٌّ صنفه الشيخ يوسف بن إسماعيل النبهاني (ت. 1350/1932). ويجب التورع عن بناء استنتاجات تخص حركة التأليف في الأخلاق الحديثية بالاستناد فقط إلى هذا الفهرست وذلك لسببين على الأقل: الأول أنني لا أستطيع الزعم بأنه شامل لكل ما طُبع في هذا المجال، والثاني أن ثمة كتبًا أخرى كثيرة لم تدرَج هنا وهي بين مفقود ومخطوط.

وبالنظر إلى مجموع مصادر هذا الفهرست، نستطيع أن نخلص إلى أنها تنطوي على ثلاث خصائص رئيسة:

5 على سبيل المثال، هناك الكثير من كتب الزهد التي هي بين مفقود ومخطوط، وقد ذكر عبد الرحمن الفريوائي في مقدمة تحقيقه لكتاب الزهد لوكيع بن الجراح (وكيع 1984، 1/144–153) قائمة مكونة من 62 كتابًا، وهناك - أيضًا - الكثير من الكتب في مكارم الأخلاق وأكثرها لا نعرفه، وقد ذكر محمد بن مصطفى في مقدمة تحقيقه لكتاب مكارم الأخلاق للطبراني (الطبراني 2013، 67–75) قائمة مكونة من 25 كتابًا في مكارم الأخلاق مع ذكر مصادرها وأماكن وجود ما هو موجود منها، وكان بشر فارس (ت. 1963) قد ذكر - قبل عقود - قائمة مكونة من 15 كتابًا (فارس 1939، 31–34). ومن الكتب التي تُذكر هنا أيضًا كتاب بعنوان «جوامع الكلم في المواعظ والحكم» للمتقي الهندي الحنفي (ت. 975/1568) جمع كمًّا كبيرًا من الحكم المختلفة من القرآن والأحاديث وكلام السلف وغيرهم، ويوجد منه نسخة خطية في المكتبة الوطنية بباريس، وهي متاحة على شبكة الإنترنت.

الخَصيصة الأولى: أنني أُدرج هنا – في الغالب – أعمال المحدثين أو من له اشتغال بالحديث مما له صلة بالأخلاق؛ فالكتب المُدرجة هنا تتخذ أشكالًا مختلفة فهي كتب رواية تجمع الأحاديث والآثار المُسندة التي يَذكر فيها مؤلفها أسانيده للأخبار، أو هي كتبٌ جمعت أحاديث وآثارًا في موضوعات أخلاقية وإن لم تعتنِ بذكر الأسانيد، ولكن مؤلفها عزا فيها الأخبار إلى مصادرها، أو هي كتبٌ بُنيت على الأحاديث والآثار وإن لم تكن كتب رواية خالصة. فعمدتنا هنا الجمع بين الحديث والأخلاق معًا، وبناء على هذا المعيار استبعدت من كتب المحدثين أنفسهم ما لا يشكل الحديث والآثار مكونًا رئيسًا فيها، وأدرجت بعض الكتب الأدبية التي كتبها محدثون؛ شكل الحديث مكونًا رئيسًا فيها تظهر فيه صنعتهم في الرواية والإسناد.

فبناء على معيار حضور الحديث والرواية في الكتاب أدرجت من مجموع كتب الحكيم الترمذي – مثلًا – كتابين حديثيين خالصين هما «نوادر الأصول» و«المنهيات»، وكتابًا آخر غلب عليه فيه الاستشهادُ بالحديث والأثر، ككتاب طبائع النفوس دون بقية كتبه، وأدرجت من كتب الحارث المحاسبي (ت. 857/243) كتابًا واحدًا هو «آداب النفوس». وأدرجت أيضًا كتاب «أخلاق حملة القرآن» لأبي بكر الآجري (ت. 970/360)؛ فقد قال في كتابه: "جميع ما ذكرته وما سأذكره إن شاء الله، بيانُه في كتاب الله تعالى وفي سنة رسوله صلى الله عليه وسلم، ومن قول صحابته رضي الله عنهم" (الآجري 2008، 37)، وقال: "واعلموا – رحمنا الله وإياكم – أني قد رويت فيما ذكرت أخبارًا تدل على ما كرهته لأهل القرآن فأنا أذكر ما حضرني ..." (الآجري 2008، 70)، وكذلك كتاب «العزلة» لأبي سليمان الخطابي (ت. 988/388) الذي ليس هو كتاب حديث خالصًا ولكن الحديث مكون رئيس فيه وصاحبه محدث.

ويمكن أن نرصد هنا شكلين لحضور الأحاديث والآثار في هذه الكتب: أولهما: مسلك السرد والرواية الذي يجري على الأبواب أو الذي يتمحور حول فكرة محددة، ويمكن أن نسميه الاحتجاج غير المباشر لنصرة فكرة أو الدعوة إليها، وهذا المسلك هو الغالب هنا في هذا الفهرست. وثانيهما: مسلك الحِجاج والاستدلال المباشر لفكرة معينة، ككتاب «تنبيه الغافلين» لابن النحاس (ت. 1411/814)؛ فقد مزج فيه مؤلفه بين طريقتين: طريقة الفقهاء وطريقة علماء التخلق وخاصة المتصوفة، وقد استدل – في كتابه – بكم كبير من الأحاديث والأخبار إلى جانب أقوال العلماء والفروع الفقهية التي أوردها، وحشد أيضًا الكثير من المناهي التي نقل فيها عن الحكيم الترمذي والكثير من مدونات الحديث.

وكونُ المؤلف محدثًا له وزنه هنا، وإن توسع في مصادره حتى شملت فنون الأخبار وأنواع الأشعار، ومن ثم أدرجتُ كتابي «عيون الأخبار» لابن قتيبة (ت. 889/276) و«روضة العقلاء» لابن حبان (ت. 965/354) في هذا الفهرست. فابن قتيبة محدث ومتكلم وأديب، وهو من المتقدمين أصحاب الإسناد، وكان من أوائل من كتب في علم مختلف الحديث، وابن حبان

محدث مشهور صاحب أحد دواوين الحديث الكبرى وإن كان الكتابان ليسا كتابي حديث خالصين. أما كتاب عيون الأخبار فقد احتوى على الكثير من الآيات القرآنية والأحاديث النبوية المسندة كما يتضح من فهارسه. وأما ابن حبان فقد جعل كتابه على خمسين بابًا، وقال: إن "بناء كل باب منها على سنة رسول الله صلى الله عليه وسلم" (ابن حبان 1949، 26). وفي المقابل، استبعدت كتبًا احتوت على أحاديث ولكن مؤلفيها أدباء؛ فهم وإن افتتحوا أبواب كتبهم بآيات وأحاديث إلا أن صنعتهم الأدب، ككتاب «غرر الخصائص الواضحة وغرر النقائص الفاضحة» مثلًا لأبي إسحاق الوطواط (ت. 718/1318)؛ فقد جمع أخبارًا في "المحامد والمذامّ المتخلقة بها نفوس الخواص والعوام" (الوطواط2008 ، 7)، ولكن كتابه أليق بحقل الأدب لا الحديث.

الخصيصة الثانية: أنني حاولت – قدرَ الطاقة – أن أراعي خصوصية حقل الأخلاق من خلال التركيز على الموضوعات الأخلاقية، بالإضافة إلى أولوية الصلة بين الحديث والأخلاق أو كيفية استثمار الحديث نفسه في المجال الأخلاقي. فكون الأخلاق حقلًا متعدد التخصصات لا يعني أن يذوب في حقل الحديث فيصبحا شيئًا واحدًا. ومن ثم ضربتُ صفحًا عن إدراج مدونات الحديث الكبرى من جوامع وصِحاح ومسانيد وسنن ومعاجم ومصنفات، ولم أُدرج – أيضًا – كتب السيرة النبوية؛ بالرغم من أنها تنطوي على أبعاد أخلاقية تتصل بأخلاق الفضيلة؛ فالسيرة – كالسنة – هي ما رُسِم ليُحتذى أو يُؤتسى به، ولكن لما غلب عليها المنحى التأريخي لم أدرجها هنا. ولم أدرج – أيضًا – كتب أحاديث الأحكام وهي كثيرة لغلبة المنظور الفقهي عليها، وكتب شروح الحديث، كشروح كتاب «الشهاب» لأبي عبد الله القضاعي (ت. 454/1062)، وشروح «رياض الصالحين» و«الأربعين النووية» وشروح كتب الشمائل وشروح أحاديث مفردة مثل حديث النية وغيره، وكتب الدعاء والكتب المفردة لفضائل أشخاص أو شخص معين، فإن ذلك مما يعسر استيعابه، والتوسع فيه من شأنه أن يجعل الأخلاق حقلًا سائلًا يتضمن كل مصادر الحديث والسيرة والتاريخ، فوجود أبعاد أخلاقية للموضوع غير كافٍ لإدراجه في هذه القائمة وإن كانت تلك الأبعاد مما يستحق أن يُدرس في حقل الأخلاق.

الخصيصة الثالثة: أنني لم أنشغل بالمصادر المعاصرة؛ لأن ذلك مما يَعسر ضبطه أو استيعابه، وذلك ككتاب «شعب الإيمان» لعبد السلام ياسين (ت. 2012)، وهو مجموع حديثي أعاد فيه ترتيب شعب الإيمان ترتيبًا يراعي "المراحل التي ينبغي أن يسلكها الفرد والجماعة تربيةً وتنظيمًا وجهادًا" (ياسين 2018، 8)، وكالأربعينات الحديثية التي جمعها بعض المعاصرين كتلك التي جمعها صالح السدلان (ت. 2017) في الخصال،[6] وغير ذلك.

6 جمع صالح بن غانم السدلان – مثلًا – مجموعة من الأربعينات في أحاديث الخصال، وقد أفرد لكل أربعين منها كتابًا مفردًا، بدأ بالأحاديث التي كل حديث منها خصلة واحدة، ثم كل حديث خصلتان، وهكذا حتى وصل إلى الأربعين التي كل حديث منها عشر خصال، وهي مطبوعة.

وفي الختام، لا بد من الإشارة إلى أنني رتبت المصادر ترتيباً تاريخيًّا، وسأذكر التاريخ الهجري لوفاة المؤلف مضافاً إليه التاريخ الميلادي، والله الموفق.

## مصادر المقدمة[7]


ابن حبان، أبو حاتم محمد. 1949. **روضة العقلاء ونزهة الفضلاء**، تحقيق وتصحيح محمد محيي الدين عبد الحميد ومحمد عبد الرزاق حمزة ومحمد حامد الفقي. القاهرة: دار الكتب العلمية.

ابن حبان، أبو حاتم محمد. 1988. **الإحسان في تقريب صحيح ابن حبان**، حققه وخرج أحاديثه وعلق عليه شعيب الأرناؤوط. بيروت: مؤسسة الرسالة.

ابن حجر العسقلاني، أبو الفضل أحمد بن علي. 2003. **بلوغ المرام من أدلة الأحكام**، تحقيق سمير بن أمين الزهري. الرياض: دار الفلق.

أبو داود، سليمان بن الأشعث. 2009. **سنن أبي داود**، حققه وضبط نصه وخرج أحاديثه وعلق عليه شعيب الأرناؤوط ومحمد كامل قره بللي. بيروت: دار الرسالة العالمية.

الإشبيلي، أبو محمد عبد الحق بن عبد الرحمن. 1993. **الأحكام الشرعية الصغرى**، تحقيق أم محمد بنت أحمد الهليس. القاهرة: مكتبة ابن تيمية، جدة: مكتبة العلم.

البخاري، أبو عبد الله محمد بن إسماعيل. 1422هـ [2001]. **الجامع المسند الصحيح المختصر من أمور رسول الله صلى الله عليه وسلم وسننه وأيامه**، تحقيق محمد زهير بن ناصر الناصر. بيروت: دار طوق النجاة.

الترمذي، أبو عيسى محمد بن سورة. 1996. **الجامع الكبير**، حققه وخرج أحاديثه وعلق عليه بشار عواد معروف. وبيروت: دار الغرب الإسلامي.

دراز، محمد عبد الله. 1998. **دستور الأخلاق في القرآن**، ترجمة عبد الصبور شاهين، بيروت: مؤسسة الرسالة.

السيوطي، جلال الدين عبد الرحمن. 2005. **جمع الجوامع المعروف بالجامع الكبير**، تحقيق مختار إبراهيم الهائج وعبد الحميد محمد ندا وحسن عيسى عبد الظاهر. القاهرة: الأزهر الشريف.

عياض بن موسى اليحصبي السبتي. 2013. **الشفا بتعريف حقوق المصطفى**، تحقيق عبده علي كوشك. دبي: حكومة دبي.

فارس، بشر. 1939. **مباحث عربية**. القاهرة: مطبعة المعارف ومكتبتها بمصر.

المتقي الهندي، علاء الدين علي بن حسام الدين. 1981. **كنز العمال في سنن الأقوال والأفعال**، ضبطه وفسر غريبه بكري حياني، صححه ووضع فهارسه ومفتاحه صفوة السقا. بيروت: مؤسسة الرسالة.

مسلم بن الحجاج. 1991. **صحيح مسلم**، وقف على طبعه وتحقيق نصوصه وتصحيحه وترقيمه محمد فؤاد عبد الباقي. القاهرة: دار إحياء الكتب العربية عيسى البابي الحلبي وشركاه.


7 اقتصرت - في هذه القائمة - على المصادر التي لم يرد ذكرها في فهرست المصنفات الحديثية في الأخلاق. أما المصادر الأخرى التي وقعت الإحالة إليها ولم يرد ذكرها في هذه القائمة فيمكن الرجوع إليها في الفهرست أدناه.

النووي، محيي الدين. 1929. **صحيح مسلم بشرح النووي**، القاهرة: المطبعة المصرية بالأزهر.
الوطواط، أبو إسحاق محمد بن إبراهيم الكتبي. 2008. **غرر الخصائص الواضحة وغرر النقائص الفاضحة**، ضبطه وصححه وعلق حواشيه إبراهيم شمس الدين. بيروت: دار الكتب العلمية.
ياسين، عبد السلام. 2018. **شعب الإيمان**، خرج أحاديثه عبد اللطيف أيت عمي، وراجعه وشرح غريبه عبد العلي المسؤول. بيروت: دار لبنان للطباعة والنشر.
Hourani, George F. 1985. *Reason and Tradition in Islamic Ethics*. Cambridge: Cambridge University Press.

## 6 فهرست المصنفات الحديثية في الأخلاق

### القرن الثاني/الثامن

ابن المبارك، عبد الله (ت. 181/797). **الزهد والرقائق**. تحقيق حبيب الرحمن الأعظمي. الهند: مجلس إحياء المعارف، بيروت: مؤسسة الرسالة، 1966م.[8]

ابن المبارك، عبد الله (ت. 181/797). **البر والصلة (مطبوع مع مسند عبد الله بن المبارك)**. تحقيق مصطفى عثمان محمد. بيروت: دار الكتب العلمية، 1991م.[9]

---

8 هذا الكتاب من رواية الحسين بن الحسن المروزي عن ابن المبارك، وقد زاد المروزي روايات أخرى كثيرة على ابن المبارك بلغت نحو 373 رواية، كما أن يحيى بن صاعد (ت. 318/930) الذي سمع الكتاب على المروزي سنة 245/859 زاد عليه روايات أخرى عن ابن المبارك أيضًا، وقد أُلحق بالكتاب ما رواه نُعيم بن حماد (ت. 228–229/844) في نسخته زائدًا على ما رواه المروزي عن ابن المبارك. ومع وجود روايات أخرى في الكتاب عن غير ابن المبارك فإن الكتاب اشتهر باسم ابن المبارك؛ لأن أكثر من ثلاثة أرباعه عن ابن المبارك.

9 هذه النسخة مطابقة لكتاب البر والصلة المنشور باسم الحسين بن الحسن المروزي، وكلاهما منشور عن النسخة الخطية المحفوظة في المكتبة الظاهرية بدمشق، وقد نبه محمد سعيد بخاري إلى أن كل من نسب هذه النسخة إلى ابن المبارك قد أخطأ، وأن مصدر الخطأ هو الشيخ محمد ناصر الدين الألباني (ت. 1999) حيث ذكر هذا المخطوط – في الفهرس الذي وضعه لكتب الظاهرية – ضمن مؤلفات ابن المبارك. فابن المبارك له كتاب باسم البر والصلة، وسمعه واستجاز روايته غيرُ واحد، ولكن النسخة المحفوظة في المكتبة الظاهرية بدمشق والتي نُشرت باسم ابن المبارك إنما هي من تأليف الحسين بن الحسن المروزي (ت. 246/860)، وقد روى المروزي في كتابه هذا عن ابن المبارك (151 رواية)، وروى عن غير ابن المبارك (200 رواية). انظر مقدمة تحقيق محمد سعيد بخاري لـ«كتاب البر والصلة عن ابن المبارك وغيره»، الرياض: دار الوطن، 1419هـ [1998]، 10.

ابن المبارك، عبد الله (ت. 797/181). **كتاب الأربعين حديثًا** (طُبع جزءٌ منه ضمن كتاب: **الإمام عبد الله بن المبارك المروزي المحدث الناقد**). تحقيق محمد سعيد بخاري. الرياض: مكتبة الرشد، 2003 (ص186–200).

الموصلي، أبو مسعود المعافى بن عمران (ت. 801/185). **الزهد**. تحقيق عامر حسن صبري. بيروت: دار البشائر الإسلامية، 1999.

وكيع بن الجراح، أبو سفيان (ت. 812/197). **الزهد**. تحقيق عبد الرحمن عبد الجبار الفريوائي. المدينة المنورة: مكتبة الدار، 1984.

### القرن الثالث/التاسع

أسد بن موسى، أبو سعيد (ت. 827/212). **الزهد**. تحقيق أبي إسحاق الحويني. مصر: مكتبة التوعية الإسلامية لإحياء التراث الإسلامي، 1993.

المدائني، أبو الحسن علي بن محمد (ت. نحو 839/224). **التعازي**. تحقيق إبراهيم صالح. بيروت: دار البشائر، 2003.

أبو عبيد، القاسم بن سلاّم (ت. 838/224). **الخطب والمواعظ والحض على أعمال البر وطلب الخير**.[10] تحقيق رمضان عبد التواب. القاهرة: مكتبة الثقافة الدينية، 1986.

ابن أبي شيبة، أبو بكر (ت. 850/235). **الأدب**. تحقيق محمد رضا القهوجي. بيروت: دار البشائر الإسلامية، 1999.

القرطبي، عبد الملك بن حَبِيب (ت. 853/238). **أدب النساء الموسوم بكتاب الغاية والنهاية**. تحقيق عبد المجيد تركي. بيروت: دار الغرب الإسلامي، 1992.

البُرْجُلاني، محمد بن الحسين (ت. 853/238). **كتاب الكرم والجود وسخاء النفوس**. تحقيق عامر حسن صبري. بيروت: دار ابن حزم، 1991.

ابن حبيب الأندلسي، أبو مروان عبد الملك (ت. 853/238). **كتاب الورع**. تحقيق نبيل أحمد بلهي. القاهرة، الإسكندرية: دار السلام للطباعة والنشر والتوزع والترجمة، 2020.

ابن حنبل، أبو عبد الله أحمد (ت. 855/241). **الزهد**. تحقيق محمد جلال شرف، بيروت: دار النهضة العربية، 1991.

ابن حنبل، أبو عبد الله أحمد (ت. 855/241). **كتاب الورع**. رواية أبي بكر المَرُّوذي (أحمد بن محمد بن الحجاج ت. 888/275)، ومعه **زوائد الورع**، رواية تلميذه أبي بكر الورّاق (أحمد بن محمد بن عبد الخالق ت. 701/309). تحقيق مصطفى بن محمد القباني. الرياض: مركز الملك فيصل (تحت الطبع).[11]

---

10 هكذا سماه أبو عبيد، وهكذا جاء في العنوان الداخلي للكتاب وفي التعريف به ص 73، ولكن اقتصر المحقق على الغلاف بالعنوان الآتي فقط: «المواعظ والخطب».

11 ذكر هذا الكتاب الحافظ ابن حجر العسقلاني فقال: "كتاب الورع للإمام أحمد رواية أبي بكر المروذي عنه." ابن حجر. 1998. **المعجم المفهرس أو تجريد أسانيد الكتب المشهورة والأجزاء المنثورة**. تحقيق

الطوسي، محمد بن أسلم (ت. 856/242). **كتاب الأربعين**. تحقيق مشعل بن باني الجبرين المطيري، بيروت: دار ابن حزم، 2000.

هَنَّاد بن السَّرِي (ت. 857/243). **كتاب الزهد**. تحقيق عبد الرحمن عبد الجبار الفريوائي. الكويت: دار الخلفاء للكتاب الإسلامي، 1985.

المحاسبي، الحارث بن أسد (ت. 857/243). **آداب النفوس**. تحقيق عبد القادر أحمد عطا. بيروت: دار الجيل، 1991.

المروَزي، الحسين بن الحسن (ت. 860/246). **كتاب البر والصلة عن ابن المبارك وغيره**. تحقيق محمد سعيد بخاري. الرياض: دار الوطن، 1419هـ [1998].

الأهوازي، أبو محمد الحسين بن سعيد (ت. بعد 868/254). **الزهد**. تحقيق وإخراج وتنظيم غلام رضا عرفانيان. قم: حسينيان، 1402 هـ [1982].

البخاري، محمد بن إسماعيل (ت. 870/256). **الأدب المفرد**. تحقيق محمد فؤاد عبد الباقي. القاهرة: المطبعة السلفية ومكتبتها، 1955.

أبو داود، سلمان بن الأشعث (ت. 888/275). **كتاب الزهد**. رواية ابن الأعرابي عنه. تحقيق ياسر بن إبراهيم بن محمد وغنيم بن عباس بن غنيم، قدم له وراجعه محمد عمرو بن عبد اللطيف. حلوان: دار المشكاة، 1993.

ابن قتيبة، أبو محمد عبد الله بن مسلم (ت. 889/276). **عيون الأخبار**. تحقيق منذر محمد سعيد أبو شعر. بيروت: المكتب الإسلامي، 2008.

أبو حاتم الرازي، محمد بن إدريس (ت. 890/277). **الزهد**. تحقيق: منذر سليم محمود الدومي. الرياض: دار أطلس للنشر والتوزيع، 2000.

الترمذي، أبو عيسى محمد بن عيسى (ت. 892/279). **الشمائل المحمدية**. اعتنى به محمد عوامة. الرياض: دار اليسر، دار المنهاج، 2015.

البرقي، أبو جعفر أحمد بن محمد (ت. 274-887/280-893). **المحاسن**. تحقيق السيد مهدي الرجائي. قم: المجمع العالمي لأهل البيت، 2011.

---

محمد شكور المياديني. بيروت: مؤسسة الرسالة، 1، 91. وقد طُبع الكتاب عدة طبعات ونُسب خطأ. منها طبعة دار الكتاب العربي في بيروت بتحقيق محمد السعيد بسيوني زغلول وقد جعله من تصنيف "أبي بكر أحمد بن محمد بن هارون المروَزِي المعروف بالخلال،" وجاء اسمه في طبعة دار ابن رجب (المنصورة، 2002) بتحقيق نشأت بن كمال المصري هكذا: "أحمد بن محمد المرُّوزيّ." أما طبعة دار الصميعي (الرياض، 1997) بتحقيق سمير بن أمين الزهيري فلم يُذكر اسم أحمد على غلافها، فجعل المحقق الكتاب من تأليف أبي بكر المروذي نفسه وبين أن نسبته لأحمد غير صواب، وأنه "عبارة عن مسائل سألها للإمام أحمد." انظر مقدمة الزهيري للكتاب ص 6، 10. وثمة طبعة أخرى بعنوان: «جزء من كتاب الورع لأبي بكر أحمد بن محمد بن الحجاج المرّوذيّ عن نسخة مسندة مرتبة تحوي زيادات كثيرة»، بتحقيق ودراسة محمد بن عبد الله السريع، طبعتها دار الحديث الكتانية سنة 2019.

ابن أبي الدنيا، أبو بكر عبد الله (ت. 894/281). **الزهد**. تحقيق ياسين محمد السواس. دمشق: دار ابن كثير، 1999.

ابن أبي الدنيا، أبو بكر عبد الله (ت. 894/281). **إصلاح المال**. تحقيق محمد عبد القادر عطا. بيروت: مؤسسة الكتب الثقافية، 1993.

ابن أبي الدنيا، أبو بكر عبد الله (ت. 894/281). **كتاب مكارم الأخلاق**. حققه وشرحه وقدم له جيمز أ. بلمي. فيسبادن: فرانز ستاينر، 1973.

ابن أبي الدنيا، أبو بكر عبد الله (ت. 894/281). **مكايد الشيطان**. (مطبوع ضمن: **رسائل ابن أبي الدنيا في الزهد والرقائق والورع**). جمعها وضبطها وخرج أحاديثها وعلق عليها أبو بكر بن عبد الله سعداوي. الشارقة: المنتدى الإسلامي، والمركز العربي للكتاب، 2000.

ابن أبي الدنيا، أبو بكر عبد الله (ت. 894/281). **اصطناع المعروف**. تحقيق محمد خير رمضان يوسف. بيروت: دار ابن حزم، 2002.

ابن أبي الدنيا، أبو بكر عبد الله (ت. 894/281). **العمر والشيب**. (مطبوع ضمن: **رسائل ابن أبي الدنيا في الزهد والرقائق والورع**). جمعها وضبطها وخرج أحاديثها وعلق عليها أبو بكر بن عبد الله سعداوي. الشارقة: المنتدى الإسلامي، والمركز العربي للكتاب، 2000.

ابن أبي الدنيا، أبو بكر عبد الله (ت. 894/281). **الأمر بالمعروف والنهي عن المنكر**. تحقيق صلاح بن عايض الشلاحي. الرياض: مكتبة الغرباء الأثرية، 1997.

ابن أبي الدنيا، أبو بكر عبد الله (ت. 894/281). **الأهوال**. تحقيق مجدي فتحي السيد. مصر: مكتبة آل ياسر، 1413هـ [1992].

ابن أبي الدنيا، أبو بكر عبد الله (ت. 894/281). **الأولياء**. تحقيق: محمد السعيد بن بسيوني زغلول. بيروت: مؤسسة الكتب الثقافية، 1992.

ابن أبي الدنيا، أبو بكر عبد الله (ت. 894/281). **مجابو الدعوة** (مطبوع ضمن: **رسائل ابن أبي الدنيا في الزهد والرقائق والورع**). جمعها وضبطها وخرج أحاديثها وعلق عليها أبو بكر بن عبد الله سعداوي. الشارقة: المنتدى الإسلامي، والمركز العربي للكتاب، 2000.

ابن أبي الدنيا، أبو بكر عبد الله (ت. 894/281). **الإخلاص والنية**. تحقيق إياد خالد الطباع. بيروت: دار البشائر، 1992.

ابن أبي الدنيا، أبو بكر عبد الله (ت. 894/281). **الإخوان**. تحقيق مصطفى عبد القادر عطا. بيروت: دار الكتب العلمية، 1988.

ابن أبي الدنيا، أبو بكر عبد الله (ت. 894/281). **الإشراف في منازل الأشراف**. تحقيق: نجم عبد الرحمن خلف. الرياض: مكتبة الرشد، 1990.

ابن أبي الدنيا، أبو بكر عبد الله (ت. 894/281). **كتاب الاعتبار وأعقاب السرور والأحزان.**[12] تحقيق نجم عبد الرحمن خلف. عمان: دار البشير، 1993.
ابن أبي الدنيا، أبو بكر عبد الله (ت. 894/281). **التواضع والخمول.** تحقيق لطفي محمد الصغير، إشراف نجم عبد الرحمن خلف. القاهرة: دار الاعتصام، 1986.
ابن أبي الدنيا، أبو بكر عبد الله (ت. 894/281). **كتاب التوبة.** تحقيق مجدي السيد إبراهيم. القاهرة: مكتبة القرآن، 1991.
ابن أبي الدنيا، أبو بكر عبد الله (ت. 894/281). **التوكل على الله.** تحقيق مصطفى عبد القادر عطا. بيروت: مؤسسة الكتب الثقافية، 1993.
ابن أبي الدنيا، أبو بكر عبد الله (ت. 894/281). **الجوع.** تحقيق: محمد خير رمضان يوسف. بيروت: دار ابن حزم، 1997.
ابن أبي الدنيا، أبو بكر عبد الله (ت. 894/281). **الحلم.** تحقيق محمد عبد القادر عطا. بيروت: مؤسسة الكتب الثقافية، 1993.
ابن أبي الدنيا، أبو بكر عبد الله (ت. 894/281). **الرضا عن الله بقضائه [والتسليم لأمره].**[13] تحقيق ضياء الحسن السلفي. مومباي: الدار السلفية، 1990.
ابن أبي الدنيا، أبو بكر عبد الله (ت. 894/281). **الرقة والبكاء.** تحقيق محمد خير رمضان يوسف. بيروت: دار ابن حزم، 1998.
ابن أبي الدنيا، أبو بكر عبد الله (ت. 894/281). **كتاب الشكر لله عز وجل.** حققه وعلق عليه ياسين محمد السواس وراجعه وخرج أحاديثه عبد القادر الأرناؤوط. دمشق: دار ابن كثير، 1987.
ابن أبي الدنيا، أبو بكر عبد الله (ت. 894/281). **الصبر والثواب عليه.** تحقيق محمد خير رمضان يوسف. بيروت: دار ابن حزم، 1997.
ابن أبي الدنيا، أبو بكر عبد الله (ت. 894/281). **كتاب الصمت وآداب اللسان.**[14] حققه وخرج أحاديث أبو إسحاق الحويني. بيروت: دار الكتاب العربي، 1990.

12 في الطبعة التي نشرها أبو بكر بن عبد الله السعداوي (الشارقة: المنتدى الإسلامي، والمركز العربي للكتاب 2000، 2، 97): «رسالة الاعتبار وإعقاب السرور الأحزان»، وهي هكذا في النسخة الخطية من المنتقى من الكتاب التي اعتمدها أيضًا خلف!

13 هكذا جاء عنوان الرسالة في النسخة الخطية التي اعتمدها المحقق، ولكنه أسقط من عنوان الكتاب ما بين المعقوفتين. ورغم أن النسخة الخطية التي اعتمدها أبو بكر بن عبد الله السعداوي (2000، 1، 34) جاءت بنفس العنوان، إلا أنه جعل عنوانها هكذا: «رسالة الرضا عن الله والصبر على قضائه» (2000، 1، 165)!

14 طبعها أبو بكر السعداوي (2000، 2، 613) بعنوان «الصمت وحفظ اللسان».

ابن أبي الدنيا، أبو بكر عبد الله (ت. 894/281). **العزلة والانفراد**. ضبط نصه وقدم له وعلق عليه وخرج أحاديثه أبو عبيدة مشهور بن حسن آل سلمان، الرياض: دار الوطن، 1997.

ابن أبي الدنيا، أبو بكر عبد الله (ت. 894/281). **العقل وفضله**. تحقيق محمد زاهد الكوثري، عُني بنشره السيد عزت العطار الحسيني، القاهرة: مكتب نشر الثقافة الإسلامية، 1946.

ابن أبي الدنيا، أبو بكر عبد الله (ت. 894/281). **العقوبات**. تحقيق محمد خير رمضان يوسف. بيروت: دار ابن حزم، 1996.

ابن أبي الدنيا، أبو بكر عبد الله (ت. 894/281). **الفرج بعد الشدة**. تحقيق ياسين محمد السواس وعبد القادر الأرناؤوط. دمشق: دار البشائر، 1992.

ابن أبي الدنيا، أبو بكر عبد الله (ت. 894/281). **القبور**. تحقيق طارق محمد سكلوع العمود. المدينة المنورة: مكتبة الغرباء الأثرية، 2000.

ابن أبي الدنيا، أبو بكر عبد الله (ت. 894/281). **القناعة والتعفف**. تحقيق مصطفى عبد القادر عطا. بيروت: مؤسسة الكتب الثقافية، 1993.

ابن أبي الدنيا، أبو بكر عبد الله (ت. 894/281). **كتاب المتمنين**. تحقيق محمد خير رمضان يوسف. بيروت: دار ابن حزم، 1997.

ابن أبي الدنيا، أبو بكر عبد الله (ت. 894/281). **كتاب المحتضرين**. تحقيق: محمد خير رمضان يوسف. بيروت: دار ابن حزم، 1997.

ابن أبي الدنيا، أبو بكر عبد الله (ت. 894/281). **المرض والكفارات**. تحقيق عبد الوكيل الندوي. مومباي: الدار السلفية، 1991.

ابن أبي الدنيا، أبو بكر عبد الله (ت. 894/281). **المنامات**. تحقيق مجدي السيد إبراهيم. القاهرة: مكتبة القرآن، 1989.

ابن أبي الدنيا، أبو بكر عبد الله (ت. 894/281). **كتاب العيال**. قدم له وحققه وعلق عليه نجم عبد الرحمن خلف. الدمام: دار ابن القيم، 1990.

ابن أبي الدنيا، أبو بكر عبد الله (ت. 894/281). **الهم والحزن**. تحقيق مجدي فتحي السيد. القاهرة: دار السلام، 1991.

ابن أبي الدنيا، أبو بكر عبد الله (ت. 894/281). **الهواتف**. تحقيق مجدي السيد إبراهيم. القاهرة: مكتبة القرآن، 2005.

ابن أبي الدنيا، أبو بكر عبد الله (ت. 894/281). **الوجل والتوثق بالعمل**. تحقيق مشهور حسن آل سلمان. الرياض: دار الوطن، 1997.

ابن أبي الدنيا، أبو بكر عبد الله (ت. 894/281). **كتاب الورع**. تحقيق وتعليق أبي عبد الله محمد بن حمد. الكويت، الدار السلفية، 1988.

ابن أبي الدنيا، أبو بكر عبد الله (ت. 894/281). **كتاب اليقين**. تحقيق ياسين محمد السواس. بيروت: دار البشائر الإسلامية، 2004.

ابن أبي الدنيا، أبو بكر عبد الله (ت. 894/281). **كتاب حسن الظن بالله**. حققه وعلق عليه وخرج أحاديثه مخلص محمد. الرياض: دار طيبة، 1988.

ابن أبي الدنيا، أبو بكر عبد الله (ت. 894/281). **كتاب ذم البغي**. تحقيق نجم عبد الرحمن خلف. الرياض: دار الراية للنشر والتوزيع، 1988.

ابن أبي الدنيا، أبو بكر عبد الله (ت. 894/281). **كتاب ذم الدنيا**. تحقيق محمد عبد القادر أحمد عطا. بيروت: مؤسسة الكتب الثقافية، 1993.

ابن أبي الدنيا، أبو بكر عبد الله (ت. 894/281). **ذم الغيبة والنميمة**. تحقيق بشير محمد عيون. دمشق: مكتبة دار البيان، الرياض: مكتبة المؤيد، 1992.

ابن أبي الدنيا، أبو بكر عبد الله (ت. 894/281). **كتاب ذم المسكر**. تحقيق ياسين محمد السواس. بيروت: دار البشائر الإسلامية، 1992.

ابن أبي الدنيا، أبو بكر عبد الله (ت. 894/281). **ذم الملاهي**. تحقيق عمرو عبد المنعم سليم. القاهرة: مكتبة ابن تيمية، 1416 هـ [1995].

ابن أبي الدنيا، أبو بكر عبد الله (ت. 894/281). **قِرَى الضيف**. تحقيق عبد الله بن حمد المنصور. الرياض: أضواء السلف، 1997.

ابن أبي الدنيا، أبو بكر عبد الله (ت. 894/281). **قِصَر الأمل**. تحقيق محمد خير رمضان يوسف. بيروت: دار ابن حزم، 1997.

ابن أبي الدنيا، أبو بكر عبد الله (ت. 894/281). **قضاء الحوائج**. تحقيق محمد خير رمضان يوسف. بيروت: دار ابن حزم، 2002.

ابن أبي الدنيا، أبو بكر عبد الله (ت. 894/281). **كلام الليالي والأيام لابن آدم**. تحقيق محمد خير رمضان يوسف. بيروت: دار ابن حزم، 1997.

ابن أبي الدنيا، أبو بكر عبد الله (ت. 894/281). **محاسبة النفس**[15] (منشور ضمن **موسوعة ابن أبي الدنيا**). تحقيق فاضل بن خلف الحمادة الرقي. الرياض: دار أطلس الخضراء، 2012.

ابن أبي الدنيا، أبو بكر عبد الله (ت. 894/281). **مداراة الناس**. تحقيق محمد خير رمضان يوسف. بيروت: دار ابن حزم، 1998.

ابن أبي الدنيا، أبو بكر عبد الله (ت. 894/281). **من عاش بعد الموت** (منشور ضمن **مجموعة رسائل ابن أبي الدنيا**). تحقيق محمد حسام بيضون. بيروت: مؤسسة الكتب الثقافية، 1993.

ابن أبي الدنيا، أبو بكر عبد الله (ت. 894/281). **ذم الكذب وأهله**. تحقيق محمد غسان نصوح عزقول. دمشق: دار السنابل، 1993.

15 في بعض النسخ المطبوعة زيادة في العنوان: «والإزراء عليها»، كما في نسخة دار الكتب العلمية، بيروت، 1986.

ولابن أبي الدنيا رسائل عديدة فُقدت أو لم تطبع.[16]

الحربي، أبو إسحاق إبراهيم (ت. 898/285). **إكرام الضيف**. تحقيق عبد الله عائض الغرازي، راجعه وقدم له مقبل بن هادي الوادعي. طنطا: مكتبة الصحابة، 1987.

ابن أبي عاصم، أبو بكر أحمد (ت. 900/287). **الزهد**. تحقيق عبد العلي عبد الحميد حامد. بومباي: الدار السلفية، 1987.

الحكيم الترمذي، أبو عبد الله محمد بن علي (ت. نحو 908/296).[17] **المنهيات وكل حديث جاء بالنهي**. تحقيق السيد إبراهيم الجميلي وأحمد عبد الرحيم السايح. القاهرة: مركز الكتاب للنشر، 2001.

الحكيم الترمذي، أبو عبد الله محمد بن علي (ت. نحو 908/296). **نوادر الأصول في معرفة أحاديث الرسول**. تحقيق توفيق محمود تكلة. دمشق: دار النوادر، 2010.

الحكيم الترمذي، أبو عبد الله محمد بن علي (ت. نحو 908/296). **طبائع النفوس وهو الكتاب المسمى بالأكياس والمغترين**. دراسة وتحقيق أحمد عبد الرحيم السايح والسيد الجميلي. القاهرة: المكتب الثقافي للنشر والتوزيع 1989.

الحكيم الترمذي، أبو عبد الله محمد بن علي (ت. نحو 908/296). **بيان الكسب (مطبوع مع آداب المريدين للحكيم الترمذي)**. تحقيق وتعليق وتقديم عبد الفتاح عبد الله بركة. القاهرة: مطبعة السعادة، 1976.

وللحكيم كتب أخرى ذات صلة بالأخلاق لم أرها مطبوعة.[18]

### القرن الرابع/العاشر

الفِرْيابِي، أبو بكر جعفر (ت. 913/301). **صفة النفاق وذمّ المنافقين**. تحقيق عبد الرقيب بن علي، إشراف ومراجعة مقبل بن هادي الوادعي. بيروت: دار ابن زيدون، 1990.

البَرْديجي، أبو بكر أحمد بن هارون (ت. 914/301). **جزء من روى عن النبي صلى الله عليه وسلم في الكبائر (منشور مع كتاب الكبائر للذهبي)**. قرأه وقدم له وعلق عليه وخرج أحاديثه مشهور بن حسن آل سلمان. عمّان: مكتبة الفرقان، 2003.

---

16 نشر صلاح الدين المنجد رسالة بعنوان «معجم مصنفات ابن أبي الدنيا» لمؤلف مجهول، واستدرك عليها عناوين أخرى من مصادر أخرى. انظر: المنجد، مجلة المجمع العلمي بدمشق، 1974، 47/579–594، ثم جاء محمد زياد التكلة فنشر الرسالة بعنوان «أسماء مصنفات أبي بكر عبد الله بن محمد بن عبيد بن أبي الدنيا على حروف المعجم»، وأوضح أنها للحافظ جمال الدين المزي، وأعقبها بما أسماه «معجم مصنفات ابن أبي الدنيا». نشر على موقع الألوكة على الإنترنت بتاريخ 2012: https://2u.pw/qN8yJ.

17 ثمة خلاف حول سنة وفاة الحكيم الترمذي، وقد رجح آرثر آربري وعلي حسن عبد القادر أنها في حدود 909/296. انظر: الحكيم الترمذي. 1947. كتاب الرياضة وأدب النفس. عُني بإخراجه أ. ج. آربري وعلي حسن عبد القادر. القاهرة: مطبعة مصطفى البابي الحلبي وأولاده، 11.

18 كالعقل والهوى، ومسألة في الإسلام والإيمان والإحسان. انظر قائمة الكتب وأماكن وجود نسخها الخطية في مقدمة آربري وعبد القادر، 1947، 14.

النسائي، أحمد بن شعيب (ت. 915/303). **عمل اليوم والليلة**. دراسة وتحقيق فاروق حمادة. بيروت: مؤسسة الرسالة، 1985.

النَّسَويّ، أبو العباس الحسن بن سفيان (ت. 916/303). **كتاب الأربعين**. تحقيق محمد بن ناصر العجمي. بيروت: دار البشائر الإسلامية، 1993.

الدوري، أبو محمد الهيثم بن خلف (ت. 919/307). **ذم اللواط**. تحقيق خالد علي محمد. الرياض: مكتبة الصفحات الذهبية، 1409هـ [1988].

ابن المَرْزُبان، أبو بكر محمد بن خلف (ت. 921/309). **المروءة وما جاء في ذلك عن النبي صلى الله عليه وسلم وعن الصحابة والتابعين**. تحقيق محمد خير رمضان يوسف. بيروت: دار ابن حزم، 1999.

الخلّال، أبو بكر أحمد بن محمد (ت. 923/311). **الأمر بالمعروف والنهي عن المنكر من مسائل الإمام المبجل أبي عبد الله أحمد بن حنبل**. تحقيق يحيى مراد. بيروت: دار الكتب العلمية، 2003.

الخلّال، أبو بكر أحمد بن محمد (ت. 923/311). **الحث على التجارة والصناعة والعمل والإنكار على من يدعي التوكل في ترك العمل والحجة عليهم في ذلك**. اعتنى به عبد الفتاح أبو غدة. حلب: مكتب المطبوعات الإسلامية، 1995.

البيهقي، إبراهيم بن محمد (ت. 932/320). **المحاسن والمساوئ**. تحقيق محمد أبو الفضل إبراهيم. القاهرة: دار المعارف، 1991.

الخرائطي، أبو بكر محمد بن جعفر (ت. 939/327). **مكارم الأخلاق ومعاليها ومحمود طرائقها ومرضيها**. تحقيق سعاد سليمان إدريس الخندقاوي، تقديم موسى شاهين لاشين، مراجعة وتقديم محمد رشاد خليفة. القاهرة: مطبعة المدني، 1991.

الخرائطي، أبو بكر محمد بن جعفر (ت. 939/327). **كتاب فضيلة الشكر لله على نعمته وما يجب من الشكر للمنعم عليه**. تحقيق محمد مطيع الحافظ، قدم له عبد الكريم اليافي. دمشق: دار الفكر، 1982.

الخرائطي، أبو بكر محمد بن جعفر (ت. 939/327). **مساوئ الأخلاق ومذمومها**. تحقيق مصطفى بن أبو النصر الشلبي. جدة: مكتبة السوادي للتوزيع، 1992.

الخرائطي. أبو بكر محمد بن جعفر (ت. 939/327). **اعتلال القلوب**. تحقيق حمدي الدمرداش. مكة المكرمة: مكتبة نزار مصطفى الباز، 2000.

الخرائطي، أبو بكر محمد (ت. 939/327). **هواتف الجنان**. تحقيق إبراهيم صالح. بيروت: دار البشائر، 2001.

الخرائطي، أبو بكر محمد بن جعفر (ت. 939/327). **المنتقى من كتاب مكارم الأخلاق ومعاليها ومحمود طرائقها**. انتقاء الحافظ أبي طاهر أحمد بن محمد السِّلَفي الأصبهاني، تحقيق محمد مطيع الحافظ، وغزوة بدير. دمشق: دار الفكر، 1986.

الدينَوَري، أبو بكر أحمد بن مروان (ت. 945/333). **المجالسة وجواهر العلم**. خرج أحاديثه وآثاره ووثق نصوصه وعلق عليه أبو عبيدة مشهور بن حسن آل سلمان. بيروت: دار ابن حزم، 1998.

ابن الأعرابي، أبو سعيد أحمد بن محمد (ت. 952/340). **الزهد وصفة الزاهدين**. تحقيق مجدي فتحي السيد. طنطا: دار الصحابة للتراث، 1988.

ابن المرزبان، محمد بن سهل (ت. نحو 952/340). **التهاني والتعازي**. تحقيق إبراهيم محمد البطشان. الرياض: نادي القصيم الأدبي، 2003.
الخُلْدي، جعفر بن محمد بن نُصير (ت. 348/959–960). **الفوائد والزهد والرقائق والمراثي**. تحقيق مجدي فتحي السيد. طنطا: دار الصحابة للتراث، 1989.
الأنصاري، محمد بن هارون (ت. 353/964). **صفة النبي صلى الله عليه وسلم وصفة أخلاقه وسيرته وأدبه وخفض جناحه**. حققه وشرحه أحمد البزرة. دار المأمون للتراث، 2003.
ابن حبان، أبو حاتم محمد (ت. 354/965). **روضة العقلاء**.[19] دراسة وتحقيق محمد عايش. عمان: دار أروقة، 2022.
الطبراني، أبو القاسم سليمان بن أحمد (ت. 360/970). **مكارم الأخلاق**. تحقيق أبي بسطام محمد بن مصطفى. بيروت: دار البشائر الإسلامية، 2013.[20]
الآجري، أبو بكر محمد بن الحسين (ت. 360/970). **أخلاق حملة القرآن**. تحقيق غانم قدوري الحمد. عمان: دار عمار، 2008.
الآجري، أبو بكر محمد بن الحسين (ت. 360/970). **كتاب الأربعين حديثًا**. حققه بدر بن عبد الله البدر. الرياض: أضواء السلف، 2000.
الآجري، أبو بكر محمد بن الحسين (ت. 360/970). **ذم اللواط**. دراسة وتحقيق مجدي السيد إبراهيم. القاهرة: مكتبة القرآن للطبع والنشر والتوزيع، 1990.
الآجري، أبو بكر محمد بن الحسين (ت. 360/970). **أدب النفوس**. علق عليه وخرج أحاديثه أبو عبيدة مشهور بن حسن آل سلمان. جدة: دار الخرّاز، بيروت: دار ابن حزم، 2001.

19 طُبع الكتاب طبعات عدة مع اختلاف جزئي في العنوان؛ ففي طبعة محمد عايش (عمان: دار أروقة، 2022) جاء العنوان على الغلاف هكذا: «روضة العقلاء»، وقد اعتمد المحقق على ست نسخ خطية إحداها تمثل الإبرازة الثانية للكتاب. وفي طبعة محمد بن عوض بن عبد الغني المصري (الجزائر العاصمة: دار الميراث النبوي، 2017) جاء العنوان هكذا: «روضة العقلاء وما يحتاج إليه الملوك والنبلاء»، وقد اعتمد المحقق على أربع نسخ خطية. أما طبعة طارق بن عبد الواحد بن علي (الرياض: دار ابن الجوزي، 2012) فقد جاء العنوان فيها هكذا: «روضة العقلاء ونزهة الفضلاء»، وهو العنوان الذي حملته الطبعة القديمة التي حققها محمد محيي الدين عبد الحميد ومحمد عبد الرزاق حمزة ومحمد حامد الفقي (القاهرة: دار الكتب العلمية، 1949)، وقد طُبعت هذه النسخة لاحقًا وأُسقط منها اسما الشيخين محمد محيي الدين عبد الحميد ومحمد عبد الرزاق حمزة!

20 طُبع الكتاب أكثر من طبعة، أبرزها طبعة بتحقيق فاروق حمادة (الدار البيضاء: دار الثقافة، 1988)، ولكن الطبعة المشار إليها في المتن قوبلت على ثمان نسخ خطية، وقد زعم المحقق أن النسخ المنشورة قبله ناقصة، ولكنه لم يوضح أي تفاصيل عن النقص الذي فيها، وهل يتمثل النقص في كلمات أو أحاديث؟ انظر ص 78 من مقدمة المحقق.

الآجري، أبو بكر محمد بن الحسين (ت. 970/360). كتاب الغرباء. تحقيق بدر البدر. الكويت: دار الخلفاء للكتاب الإسلامي، 1983.

الآجري، أبو بكر محمد بن الحسين (ت. 970/360). أخلاق العلماء. قام بمراجعة أصوله وتصحيحه والتعليق عليه إسماعيل محمد الأنصاري. وقابله مع عبد الله بن عبد اللطيف آل الشيخ على النسخة المصرية. الرياض: رئاسة إدارات البحوث العلمية والإفتاء والدعوة والإرشاد، 1978.

الآجري، أبو بكر محمد بن الحسين (ت. 970/360). تحريم النرد والشطرنج والملاهي. دراسة وتحقيق واستدراك محمد سعيد عمر إدريس. الرياض: رئاسة إدارة البحوث العلمية والإفتاء والدعوة والإرشاد، 1982.

الآجري، أبو بكر محمد بن الحسين (ت. 970/360). كتاب الشريعة. دراسة وتحقيق عبد الله بن عمر بن سليمان الدميجي. الرياض: دار الوطن، 1997.

ابن السني، أبو بكر أحمد (ت. 974/364). القناعة. تحقيق ودراسة عبد الله بن يوسف الجديع. الرياض: مكتبة الرشد للنشر والتوزيع، 1989.

ابن السني، أبو بكر أحمد (ت. 974/364). عمل اليوم والليلة. حققه وخرج أحاديثه عبد الرحمن البَرني. بيروت: دار الأرقم، 1998.

أبو الشيخ الأصبهاني، أبو محمد عبد الله بن محمد (ت. 979/369). كتاب أخلاق النبي صلى الله عليه وسلم وآدابه. حققه وكتب حواشيه أبو الفضل عبد الله محمد الصديق الغماري. مصر: مطابع الهلالي، 1959.

أبو الشيخ الأصبهاني، أبو محمد عبد الله بن محمد (ت. 979/369). التوبيخ والتنبيه. تحقيق وتعليق أبي الأشبال حسن بن أمين بن المندوه. القاهرة: مكتبة التوعية الإسلامية للطبع والنشر والتوزيع، 1408هـ [1987].

السمرقندي، أبو الليث نصر بن محمد (ت. 983/373). تنبيه الغافلين. حققه وعلق عليه يوسف علي بديوي. دمشق: دار ابن كثير، 2000.

الكلاباذي، أبو بكر محمد بن إبراهيم (ت. 990/380). بحر الفوائد المشهور بمعاني الأخبار. دراسة وتحقيق وجيه كمال الدين زكي. القاهرة: دار السلام للطباعة والنشر والتوزيع، 2008.

الصدوق (ابن بابويه)، أبو جعفر محمد بن علي (ت. 991/381). علل الشرائع. قدم له السيد محمد صادق بحر العلوم. النجف: منشورات المكتبة الحيدرية ومطبعتها في النجف، 1963.

الصدوق (ابن بابويه)، أبو جعفر محمد بن علي (ت. 991/381). الخصال. قدم له محمد مهدي السيد حسن الخرسان. النجف: المطبعة الحيدرية، 1971.

الصدوق، أبو جعفر ابن بابويه (ت. 991/381). مصادقة الإخوان. إشراف السيد علي الخراساني الكاظمي. الكاظمية: منشورات مكتبة الإمام صاحب الزمان العامة، 1982.

ابن شاهين، أبو حفص عمر بن أحمد (ت. 995/385). الترغيب في فضائل الأعمال وثواب ذلك. صالح أحمد مصلح الوعيل، إشراف أكرم ضياء العمري. الدمام-الرياض: دار ابن الجوزي، 1995.

ابن أبي زيد القيرواني، أبو محمد عبد الله (ت. 386/996). **كتاب الجامع في السنن والآداب والمغازي والتاريخ**. حققه وقدم له وعلق عليه محمد أبو الأجفان وعثمان بطيخ. بيروت: مؤسسة الرسالة، تونس: المكتبة العتيقة، 1983.

الخطابي، أبو سليمان حمد بن محمد (ت. 388/998). **العزلة**. حققه وعلق عليه ياسين محمد السواس. دمشق: دار ابن كثير، 1990.

السيلقي، أبو القاسم زيد بن عبد الله (ت. قبل 390/1000). **الأربعون حديثًا السيلقية**. تحقيق عبد الله بن حمود العزي. صنعاء: مؤسسة الإمام زيد بن علي الثقافية، 2002.

الضرّاب، أبو محمد الحسن بن إسماعيل (ت. 392/1002). **ذم الرياء في الأعمال والشهرة في اللباس والأحوال وكراهية الصفْق والزفْن عند سماع الذكر**. تحقيق محمد با كريم محمد با عبد الله. المدينة النبوية: دار البخاري للنشر والتوزيع، 1416 هـ [1995].

## القرن الخامس/الحادي عشر

الحَليمي، أبو عبد الله الحسين بن الحسن (ت. 403/1012). **كتاب المنهاج في شعب الإيمان**. تحقيق حلمي محمد فوده. بيروت: دار الفكر، 1979.

أبو عبد الرحمن السلمي، محمد بن الحسين (ت. 412/1021). **كتاب الأربعين في التصوف**. حيدرآباد: مطبعة مجلس دائرة المعارف العثمانية، 1981.

أبو عبد الرحمن السلمي، محمد بن الحسين (ت. 412/1021). **كتاب آداب الصحبة وحسن العشرة** (مطبوع ضمن **مجموعة آثار أبو عبد الرحمن السلمي** ج2). تحقيق نصر الله بورجوادي. طهران: مركز نشر دانشگاهى 1372 هـ ش [1993].

السلمي، محمد بن الحسين (ت. 412/1021). **الفتوة**. تحقيق إحسان ذنون الثامري ومحمد عبد الله القدحات. عمان: دار الرازي للطباعة والنشر والتوزيع، 2002.

الماليني، أبو سعد أحمد بن محمد (ت. 412/1022). **كتاب الأربعين في شيوخ الصوفية**. تقديم وتحقيق وتعليق عامر حسن صبري. بيروت: دار البشائر الإسلامية، 1997.

أبو نعيم الأصبهاني، أحمد بن عبد الله (ت. 430/1038). **صفة النفاق ونعت المنافقين من السنن المأثورة عن رسول الله صلى الله عليه وسلم**. تحقيق وتقديم عامر حسن صبري. بيروت: البشائر الإسلامية، 2001.

أبو نعيم الأصبهاني، أحمد بن عبد الله (ت. 430/1038). **فضيلة العادلين من الولاة ومن أنعم النظر في حال العمال والسّعاة**. ضبط نصه وعلق عليه مشهور بن حسن آل سلمان. الرياض: دار الوطن، 1997.

أبو نعيم الأصبهاني، أحمد بن عبد الله (ت. 430/1038). **كتاب الأربعين على مذهب المتحققين من الصوفية**. حققه وخرج أحاديثه بدر بن عبد الله البدر. بيروت: دار ابن حزم، 1993.

القضاعي، أبو عبد الله محمد بن سلامة (ت. 1062/454). **مسند الشهاب**.[21] تحقيق حمدي عبد المجيد السلفي. بيروت: مؤسسة الرسالة، 1985.

القضاعي. أبو عبد الله محمد بن سلامة (ت. 1062/454). **دستور معالم الحكم ومأثور مكارم الشيم من كلام أمير المؤمنين علي بن أبي طالب كرم الله وجهه**. تحقيق طاهرة قطب الدين. نيويورك: المكتبة العربية، 2013.

الجوهري، أبو محمد الحسن بن علي (ت. 1062/454). **مجلس في التواضع من أمالي أبي محمد الحسن بن علي بن محمد الجوهري**. تحقيق حسين آيت سعيد. بيروت: دار البشائر الإسلامية، 2007.

البيهقي، أبو بكر أحمد بن الحسين (ت. 1066/458). **الآداب**. اعتنى به وعلق عليه عبد الله السعيد المندوه. بيروت: مؤسسة الكتب الثقافية، 1988.

البيهقي، أبو بكر أحمد بن الحسين (ت. 1066/458). **شعب الإيمان**. تحقيق عبد العلي عبد الحميد حامد. الرياض: مكتبة الرشد للنشر والتوزيع، 2003.

البيهقي، أبو بكر أحمد بن الحسين (ت. 1066/458). **كتاب الزهد الكبير**. تحقيق تقي الدين الندوي، تقديم أبي الحسن الندوي ونخبة من العلماء. عمان: دار أروقة، 2015.

البيهقي، أبو بكر أحمد بن الحسين (ت. 1066/458). **الأربعون الصغرى المخرجة في أحوال عباد الله تعالى وأخلاقهم**.[22] حققه محمد نور بن محمد أمين المراغي. الدوحة: إدارة إحياء التراث الإسلامي، 1980.

الخطيب البغدادي، أبو بكر أحمد بن علي (ت. 1072/463). **الجامع لأخلاق الراوي وآداب السامع**. تحقيق محمود الطحان. الرياض: مكتبة المعارف، 1983.

الخطيب البغدادي، أبو بكر أحمد بن علي (ت. 1072/463). **كتاب الفقيه والمتفقه**. حققه أبو عبد الرحمن عادل بن يوسف العَزازي. الدمام: دار ابن الجوزي، 1996.

---

21 هذا الكتاب أسند فيه القضاعي أحاديث كتاب «شهاب الأخبار» له أيضًا، وقد سماه حاجي خليفة وإسماعيل البغدادي هكذا: «شهاب الأخبار في الحكم والأمثال والآداب من الأحاديث النبوية»، وجاء في بعض نسخه الخطية هكذا: «شهاب الأخبار في الحكم والأمثال والآداب من الأحاديث المشتهرة»، وفي بعضها الآخر هكذا: «شهاب الأخبار في الوصايا والآداب والمواعظ والأمثال». انظر: حاجي خليفة. 1941. **كشف الظنون عن أسامي الكتب والفنون**. بغداد: مكتبة المثنى، 2، 1067؛ إسماعيل البغدادي. 1951. **هدية العارفين أسماء المؤلفين وآثار المصنفين**. إسطنبول: طبع بعناية وكالة المعارف الجليلية في مطبعتها، 2، 71، وانظر خزانة المخطوطات على شبكة الإنترنت.

22 وقع اختلاف في تسمية كتاب البيهقي، وقد ناقش ذلك المحقق ص 50–51 ثم رجح التسمية التي اعتمدها، ثم جاء محمد السعيد بسيوني زغلول فتابعه عليها (بيروت: دار الكتب العلمية، 1987)، وطُبع الكتاب طبعة أخرى بعنوان «الأربعون الصغرى» فقط، مع تخريج مطول لأحاديثه فاق حجم الكتاب، صنعه أبو إسحاق الحويني الأثري (بيروت: دار الكتاب العربي، 1988).

الخطيب البغدادي، أبو بكر أحمد بن علي (ت. 1072/463). **المنتخب من كتاب الزهد والرقائق**. تحقيق عامر حسن صبري. بيروت: دار البشائر الإسلامية، 2000.
القشيري، أبو القاسم عبد الكريم بن هوازن (ت. 465/1072–1073). **كتاب الأربعين في تصحيح المعاملة**. تحقيق محمد السيد البرسيجي. عمان: دار الفتح: 2013.
ابن البناء، أبو علي الحسن بن أحمد (ت. 1078/471). **الرسالة المُغنية في السكوت ولزوم البيوت**. تحقيق عبد الله بن يوسف الجديع. الرياض: دار العاصمة، 1409هـ [1989].
الأصبهاني، أبو عبد الله القاسم بن الفضل الثقفي (ت. 1096/489). **كتاب الأربعين المسمى: (الأربعون حديثًا فيما ينتهي إليه المتقون ويستعمله الموفقون وينتبه به الغافلون ويلازمه العاقلون)**، مطبوع مع كتاب الأربعين للطوسي (ت. 658/242). تحقيق مشعل بن باني الجبرين المطيري. بيروت: دار ابن حزم، 2000.
الحلواني، الحسين بن محمد بن الحسن (ت. القرن الخامس/الحادي عشر). **نزهة الناظر وتنبيه الخاطر**. تحقيق ونشر مدرسة الإمام المهدي عليه السلام. قم: مطبعة مهر، 1408هـ [1988].

## القرن السادس/الثاني عشر

الديلمي، أبو شجاع شيرُوْيِه بن شهردار (ت. 1115/509). **الفردوس بمأثور الخطاب**.[23] تحقيق السعيد بن بسيوني زغلول. بيروت: دار الكتب العلمية، 1986.
أُبَيّ النَّرْسيّ، أبو الغنائم محمد بن علي (ت. 510/1116–1117). **ثواب قضاء حوائج الإخوان وما جاء في إغاثة اللهفان**. تحقيق وتخريج عامر حسن صبري. بيروت: دار البشائر الإسلامية، 1993.
البغوي، أبو محمد الحسين بن مسعود (ت. 1122/516). **الأنوار في شمائل النبي المختار**. تحقيق إبراهيم اليعقوبي، قدم له محمد اليعقوبي. دمشق: دار المكتبي، 1995.
أبو القاسم الأصبهاني، إسماعيل بن محمد (ت. 1141/535). **كتاب الترغيب والترهيب**. تحقيق أيمن بن صالح بن شعبان. القاهرة: دار الحديث، 1993.

23 جاء عنوان الكتاب في الطبعة التي نشرها وقدم لها وحققها وخرج أحاديثها فواز أحمد الزمرلي ومحمد المعتصم البغدادي (بيروت: دار الكتاب العربي، 1987) هكذا: «كتاب فردوس الأخبار بمأثور الخطاب المخرّج على كتاب الشهاب»، وهذا العنوان لا يرد في صور المخطوطات التي أرفقها المحققان بالنسخة، بل إن الديلمي نفسه يقول في المقدمة: إنه سماه «الفردوس بمأثور الخطاب». وجاء عنوانه في بعض النسخ الخطية المحفوظة في مكتبة فيض الله بتركيا هكذا: «كتاب الفردوس بمأثور الخطاب مرتبًا على كتاب الشهاب». وقد وقع الخلط أيضًا بين كتاب الفردوس ومسند الفردوس الذي صنفه ابنه أبو منصور شهردار بن شيرويه (ت. 1163/558) وأسند فيه أحاديث كتاب أبيه: الفردوس، ولمسند الفردوس نسخة خطية متاحة على شبكة الإنترنت.

عياض، أبو الفضل عياض بن موسى اليحصبي (ت. 1149/544). **الشفا بتعريف حقوق المصطفى صلى الله عليه وسلم**. حقق نصوصه وخرج أحاديثه وعلق عليه عبده علي كوشك. دبي: دائرة دبي الدولية للقرآن الكريم، 2013.

الطبرسي، أبو علي الفضل بن الحسن (ت. 1153/548). **الآداب الدينية للخزانة المعينية**. تحقيق وترجمة أحمد عابدي. قم: انتشارات زائر، 1380 هـ ش [2001].

الآمدي التميمي، عبد الواحد بن محمد (ت. 1155/550). **تصنيف غرر الحكم ودرر الكلم**. تحقيق مصطفى درايتي. قم: مكتب الإعلام الإسلامي، 1407هـ [1986].

أبو الفتوح الطائي، محمد بن محمد (ت. 1160/555). **كتاب الأربعين في إرشاد السائرين إلى منازل المتقين أو الأربعين الطائية**. تحقيق عبد الستار أبو غدة. بيروت: دار البشائر الإسلامية، 1999.

السمعاني، أبو سعد عبد الكريم بن محمد (ت. 1166/562). **كتاب أدب الإملاء والاستملاء**. تحقيق ماكس فايسفايلر. بيروت: دار الكتب العلمية، 1981.

ابن عساكر، أبو القاسم علي بن الحسن (ت. 1176/571). **مدح التواضع وذم الكبر**. تحقيق محمد عبد الرحمن النابلسي. دمشق: دار السنابل للطباعة والتوزيع والنشر، 1993.

ابن عساكر، أبو القاسم علي بن الحسن (ت. 1176/571). **التوبة (ضمن مجموع رسائل)**. تحقيق مشعل بن باني الجبرين المطيري. بيروت: دار ابن حزم، 2001.

ابن عساكر، أبو القاسم علي بن الحسن (ت. 1176/571). **ذم الملاهي**. تحقيق العربي الدائز الفرياطي. دمشق: دار البشائر الإسلامية، 2003.

ابن عساكر، أبو القاسم علي بن الحسن (ت. 1176/571). **ذم ذي الوجهين واللسانين (ضمن مجموع رسائل)**. تحقيق مشعل بن باني الجبرين المطيري. بيروت: دار ابن حزم، 2001.

ابن عساكر، أبو القاسم علي بن الحسن (ت. 1176/571). **ذم قرناء السوء (ضمن: مجلسان من مجالس الحافظ ابن عساكر في مسجد دمشق)**. تحقيق محمد مطيع الحافظ. دمشق: دار الفكر، 1979.

ابن عساكر، أبو القاسم علي بن الحسن (ت. 1176/571). **ذم من لا يعمل بعلمه (ضمن: مجلسان من مجالس الحافظ ابن عساكر في مسجد دمشق)**. تحقيق محمد مطيع الحافظ. دمشق: دار الفكر، 1979.

ابن عساكر، أبو القاسم علي بن الحسن (ت. 1176/571). **فضيلة ذكر الله عز وجل**. صححه وخرج أحاديثه أحمد البزرة. دمشق: دار المأمون للتراث، 1994.

ابن عساكر، أبو القاسم علي بن الحسن (ت. 1176/571). **تعزية المسلم عن أخيه**. دراسة وتحقيق وتعليق مجدي فتحي السيد. جدة – الشرقية: مكتبة الصحابة، 1991.

ابن عساكر، أبو القاسم علي بن الحسن (ت. 1176/571). **الأربعون في الحث على الجهاد**. تحقيق عبد الله بن يوسف. الكويت: دار الخلفاء للكتاب الإسلامي، 1984.

أبو الفتح الجويني، عمر بن علي (ت. 1181/577). **المنتخب من كتاب الأربعين في شعب الدين لأبي القاسم علي بن الحسن بن محمد الصفّار (ت. 1128/522)**. حققه وعلق عليه مرهف حسين أسد بإشراف حسين سليم أسد، إسطنبول: دار السمان، 2020.

ابن الجوزي، أبو الفرج عبد الرحمن بن علي (ت. 1201/597). **المُقلق**. حققه وعلق عليه مجدي فتحي السيد. طنطا: دار الصحابة للتراث 1991.
ابن الجوزي، أبو الفرج عبد الرحمن بن علي (ت. 1201/597). **منهاج القاصدين ومفيد الصادقين**. تحقيق كامل محمد الخراط. دمشق: دار التوفيق للطباعة والنشر والتوزيع، 2010.
ابن الجوزي، أبو الفرج عبد الرحمن بن علي (ت. 1201/597). **كتاب البر والصلة**. تحقيق عادل عبد الموجود وعلي معوض. بيروت: مؤسسة الكتب الثقافية، 1993.
المقدسي، عبد الغني بن عبد الواحد (ت. 1203/600). **كتاب الأمر بالمعروف والنهي عن المنكر**. تحقيق سمير بن أمين الزهيري. مصر: دار السلف، 1995.
الطبرسي، أبو نصر الحسن بن الفضل (ت. القرن السادس/الثاني عشر). **مكارم الأخلاق**. تحقيق علاء آل جعفر. قم: مؤسسة النشر الإسلامي التابعة لجماعة المدرسين بقم المقدسة، 1425هـ [2004].

## القرن السابع/الثالث عشر

ورّام بن أبي فراس المالكي (ت. 1208/605). **تنبيه الخواطر ونزهة النواظر**. تحقيق وتعليق باسم محمد مال الله الأسدي. كربلاء المقدسة: العتبة الحسينية المقدسة، 2013.
الطبرسي، أبو الفضل علي بن الحسن (ت. أوائل القرن السابع/الثالث عشر). **مشكاة الأنوار في غرر الأخبار**. تحقيق مهدي هوشمند. قم: دار الحديث، 1418هـ [1997].
القصري، أبو محمد عبد الجليل (ت. 608/1211–1212). **شعب الإيمان**. تحقيق سيد كسروي حسن. بيروت: دار الكتب العلمية، 1995.
المقدسي، شرف الدين علي بن المُفَضَّل (ت. 1214/611). **كتاب الأربعين في فضل الدعاء والداعين** (مطبوع مع **كتاب الأربعين على مذهب المتحققين من الصوفية** لأبي نعيم الأصبهاني). تحقيق بدر بن عبد الله البدر. بيروت: دار ابن حزم، 1993.
أبو الفرج المقرئ، عفيف الدين محمد بن عبد الرحمن (ت. 1221/618). **كتاب الأربعين في الجهاد والمجاهدين**. تحقيق بدر بن عبد الله البدر. بيروت: دار ابن حزم، 1995.
ابن قدامة المقدسي، موفق الدين عبد الله بن أحمد (ت. 1223/620). **الرقة والبكاء**. تحقيق محمد خير رمضان يوسف. دمشق: دار القلم، بيروت: الدار الشامية، 1994.[24]

24 نسب عبد الرحمن الفريوائي في مقدمة تحقيقه لكتاب الزهد لوكيع بن الجراح (المدينة المنورة: مكتبة الدار، 1984، 1، 153) كتاب **الرقة والبكاء** لعبد الغني بن عبد الواحد المقدسي الجماعيلي (ت. 1203/600) وأن منه نسخة مصورة في مكتبة الجامعة الإسلامية مجموع 132، الرقم العام 1487، فلا أدري إن كان هو نفسه أم أن لعبد الغني كتابًا آخر بالعنوان نفسه.

التبريزي، أبو الخير بَدَل بن أبي المُعَمَّر (ت. 1238/636). **النصيحة للراعي والرعية.** حققه أبو الزهراء عبيد الله الأثري. طنطا: دار الصحابة للتراث، 1991.

ابن زُهرة الحلبي، محيي الدين محمد بن عبد الله الحسيني (ت. 1241/639). **الأربعون حديثًا في حقوق الإخوان.** تحقيق نبيل رضا علوان. قم: مطبعة مهر، 1405هـ [1985].

المقدسي، ضياء الدين محمد بن عبد الواحد (ت. 1245/643). **صفة النبي صلى الله عليه وسلم وجميل أخلاقه وأدبه وبِشْره وحسن سيرته في أمته، وأجزاء حديثية أخرى.** حققه وخرج أحاديثه فواز أحمد زمرلي. بيروت: دار ابن حزم، 2004.

المقدسي، ضياء الدين محمد بن عبد الواحد (ت. 1245/643). **كتاب فضائل الأعمال.** دراسة وتحقيق غسان عيسى محمد هرماس. بيروت: مؤسسة الرسالة، 1987.

المنذري، عبد العظيم بن عبد القوي (ت. 1258/656). **الترغيب والترهيب.** حكم على أحاديثه وآثاره وعلق عليه محمد ناصر الدين الألباني. اعتنى به أبو عبيدة مشهور بن حسن آل سلمان. الرياض: مكتبة المعارف للنشر والتوزيع، 1424هـ [2003].

المنذري، زكي الدين عبد العظيم بن عبد القوي (ت. 1258/656). **أربعون حديثًا في اصطناع المعروف.** علق عليه وقدم له محمد بن تاويت الطنجي. الرباط: وزارة الأوقاف والشؤون الإسلامية، 1985.

المنذري، عبد العظيم بن عبد القوي (ت. 1258/656). **كفاية المتعبد وتحفة المتزهد.** تحقيق وتعليق علي حسن علي عبد الحميد. عمان: المكتبة الإسلامية، 1410هـ [1990].

ابن عبد السلام، عز الدين عبد العزيز (ت. 1262/660). **شجرة المعارف والأحوال وصالح الأقوال والأعمال.** تحقيق إياد خالد الطباع. دمشق: دار الفكر، 2006.

القونوي، صدر الدين محمد بن إسحاق (ت. 1275/673). **شرح الأربعين حديثًا.** حققه وعلق عليه حسن كامل ييلماز. قم: انتشارات بيدار، 1372 هـ ش [1993].

النووي، أبو زكريا محيي الدين (ت 1277/676). **رياض الصالحين من كلام رسول الله صلى الله عليه وسلم سيد العارفين.** تحقيق اللجنة العلمية بمركز دار المنهاج، جدة: دار المنهاج، 2015.

النووي، أبو زكريا محيي الدين (ت. 1277/676). **الأربعون النووية.** عُني به قصي محمد نورس الحلاق وأنور بن أبي بكر الشيخي. جدة: دار المنهاج للنشر والتوزيع 2009.

النووي، أبو زكريا محيي الدين (ت. 1277/676). **الأذكار من كلام سيد الأبرار.** عني به صلاح الحمصي وعبد اللطيف عبد اللطيف ومحمد شعبان. جدة: دار المنهاج للنشر والتوزيع، 2005.

ابن قدامة المقدسي، أحمد بن عبد الرحمن (ت. 1283/682). **مختصر منهاج القاصدين.** علق عليه شعيب الأرناؤوط وعبد القادر الأرناؤوط. دمشق – بيروت: مكتبة دار البيان، ومؤسسة علوم القرآن، 1978.

السَّبزَواري، محمد بن محمد (ت. القرن السابع/الثالث عشر). **جامع الأخبار أو معارج اليقين في أصول الدين.** تحقيق علاء آل جعفر. بيروت: مؤسسة آل البيت لإحياء التراث، 1993.

## القرن الثامن/الرابع عشر

ابن تيمية، تقي الدين أحمد بن عبد الحليم (ت. 1328/728). **الكلم الطيب.**[25] تحقيق محمد ناصر الدين الألباني. الرياض: مكتبة المعارف للنشر والتوزيع، 2001.

الذهبي، شمس الدين محمد بن أحمد (ت. 1347/748). **الأربعين في صفات رب العالمين.** قدم له وحقق نصوصه وخرج أحاديثه وعلق عليه عبد القادر بن محمد عطا صوفي، المدينة المنورة: مكتبة العلوم والحكم، 1413هـ [1993].

الذهبي، شمس الدين محمد بن أحمد (ت. 1347/748). **الكبائر.** قرأه وقدم له وعلق عليه وخرج أحاديثه مشهور بن حسن آل سلمان. عمان: مكتبة الفرقان، 2003.

العلائي، صلاح الدين خليل بن كيكلدي (ت. 1359/761). **جزء فيه أربعون حديثًا منتقاة من كتاب الآداب للبيهقي.** تحقيق محمد مطيع الحافظ. دمشق: دار البيروتي، 2006.

العلائي، صلاح الدين خليل بن كيكلدي (ت. 1359/761). **الأمالي الأربعين في أعمال المتقين.** دراسة وتحقيق محمد إسحاق محمد آل إبراهيم. الرياض، د.ن. 2021.

اليافعي، عبد الله بن أسعد (ت. 1367/768). **الترغيب والترهيب.** تحقيق محمد فارس. بيروت: دار الكتب العلمية، 1996.

الديلمي، أبو محمد الحسن بن أبي الحسن (ت. نحو 1370/771). **إرشاد القلوب المُنجي مَن عمل به من أليم العذاب.** تحقيق هاشم الميلاني. طهران: دار الأسوة للطباعة والنشر، 1424هـ [2003].

الديلمي. أبو محمد الحسن بن أبي الحسن (ت. نحو 1370/771). **أعلام الدين في صفات المؤمنين.** بيروت: مؤسسة آل البيت لإحياء التراث، 2015.

ابن كثير، أبو الفداء إسماعيل (ت. 1373/774). **شعب الإيمان.** تحقيق وليد بن محمد بن عبد الله العلي. بيروت: دار البشائر الإسلامية، 2005.

السُّرَّمَرِّي، جمال الدين يوسف بن محمد (ت. 1374/776). **خصائص سيد العالمين وما له من المناقب العجائب على جميع الأنبياء عليهم السلام.** تحقيق خالد بن منصور المطلق. د.ن، 2015.

الحُبيشي الوصابي، محمد بن عبد الرحمن (ت. 1380/782). **النورين في إصلاح الدارين.** جدة: دار المنهاج للنشر والتوزيع، 2018.

الحُبيشي الوصابي، محمد بن عبد الرحمن (ت. 1380/782). **البركة في فضل السعي والحركة.** القاهرة: مكتبة الخانجي، 1934.

المَنبجي، أبو عبد الله محمد بن محمد (ت. 1383/785). **تسلية أهل المصائب.** القاهرة: مكتبة الخانجي-مطبعة السعادة، 1929.

ابن رجب الحنبلي، زين الدين عبد الرحمن (ت. 1393/795). **جامع العلوم والحكم في شرح خمسين حديثا من جوامع الكلم.** تحقيق شعيب الأرناؤوط وإبراهيم باجس. بيروت: مؤسسة الرسالة، 1999.

25 في نسخة خطية بين يدي نسخها نصر بن محمد بن نصر بن رضوان الجعبري الشافعي بتاريخ 1312/712- جاء فيها العنوان هكذا: «كتاب فيه جوامع الكلم الطيب».

ابن رجب الحنبلي، زين الدين عبد الرحمن (ت. 1393/795). **كشف الكربة في وصف أهل الغربة**. بيروت: دار المقتبس، 2014.

ابن رجب الحنبلي، زين الدين عبد الرحمن (ت. 1393/795). **ذم قسوة القلب**. بيروت: دار المقتبس، 2014.

ابن رجب الحنبلي، زين الدين عبد الرحمن (ت. 1393/795). **شرح حديث "ما ذئبان جائعان"**. تحقيق وتعليق أبي القاسم عبد العظيم. الرياض: دار القبس، 2013.

العاقولي، محمد بن محمد بن عبد الله (ت. 1394/797). **الرصف لما روي عن النبي صلى الله عليه وسلم من الفعل والوصف**. بيروت: مؤسسة الرسالة، 1994.

## القرن التاسع/الخامس عشر

ابن النحاس، أبو زكريا أحمد بن إبراهيم (ت. 1411/814). **تنبيه الغافلين عن أعمال الجاهلين وتحذير السالكين من أفعال الهالكين**. حققه وعلق عليه عماد الدين بعاس سعيد. بيروت: دار الكتب العلمية، 1987.[26]

ابن الوزير، محمد بن إبراهيم (ت. 1436/840). **العزلة**. تحقيق ودراسة قسم التحقيق بدار الصحابة. طنطا: دار الصحابة للتراث، 1999.

ابن ناصر الدين الدمشقي، محمد بن عبد الله (ت. 1438/842). **برد الأكباد عند فقد الأولاد**. تحقيق عبد القادر أحمد عبد القادر. عمان: دار النفائس، 1993.[27]

ابن ناصر الدين الدمشقي، محمد بن عبد الله (ت. 1438/842). **سلوة الكئيب بوفاة الحبيب صلى الله عليه وسلم**. تحقيق صالح يوسف معتوق وهاشم صالح مناع. دبي: دار البحوث للدراسات الإسلامية، د.ت.

ابن حجر العسقلاني، أحمد بن علي (ت. 1449/852). **مختصر الترغيب والترهيب**. حققه وأتم اختصاره سائد بكداش. بيروت: دار السلام، 2021.

---

26 سمى الحافظ السخاوي (ت. 1497/902) هذا الكتاب باسم: «تنْبِيه الغافلين في معرفة الكبائر والصغائر والمناهي والمنكرات والبدع». انظر: السخاوي. د.ت. **الضوء اللامع لأهل القرن التاسع**. بيروت: دار الجيل، 1، 203.

27 طُبع أيضًا بتحقيق مشهور بن حسن آل سلمان (الرياض: دار ابن عفان، 2010). وهناك طبعة قديمة له (القاهرة: مطبعة السعادة، 1332هـ [1914])، ولكن باسم جلال الدين السيوطي! وقد عزا كتاب «برد الأكباد» لابن ناصر، الشيخ محمد بن يوسف الصالحي تلميذ السيوطي في مقدمة كتابه «الفضل المبين» المذكور في هذا الفهرست، وذكر الصالحي في مقدمته بعض الكتب المصنفة في الموضوع، ثم قال: إن كتاب السخاوي "أجمعها وأكثرها فائدة،" ولذلك رأى اختصاره مع الزيادة عليه وإعادة ترتيبه في كتابه «الفضل المبين».

ابن حجر العسقلاني، أحمد بن علي (ت. 1449/852). **الغرائب الملتقطة من مسند الفردوس المسمى زهر الفردوس**. تحقيق جماعة. دبي: جمعية دار البر، 2018.

ابن حجر العسقلاني، أحمد بن علي (ت. 1449/852). **معرفة الخصال المكفرة للذنوب المقدَّمة والمؤخَّرة**. تحقيق وتعليق جاسم الفهيد الدوسري. بيروت: دار البشائر الإسلامية، 2005.

ابن حجر العسقلاني، أحمد بن علي (ت. 1449/852). **الأربعون في ردع المجرم عن سب المسلم**. تحقيق مجدي السيد إبراهيم. القاهرة: مكتبة القرآن، 1989.

الخيضري، محمد بن محمد (ت. 1487/892). **كتاب اللفظ المكرم بخصائص النبي صلى الله عليه وسلم**. تحقيق محمد الأمين بن محمد الجكني الشنقيطي. المدينة المنورة: د.ن.، 1996.

## القرن العاشر/السادس عشر

السخاوي، شمس الدين محمد بن عبد الرحمن (ت. 1497/902). **ارتياح الأكباد بأرباح فَقد الأولاد**. حققه وعلق عليه إياد القيسي وأمجد العبد اللات. بيروت: مؤسسة الرسالة ناشرون، 2018.

السيوطي، جلال الدين عبد الرحمن (ت. 1505/911). **الشمائل الشريفة وشرحها للمناوي** (مُنتَزَع من الجامع الصغير وشرحه فيض القدير). إعداد حسن بن عبيد باحبيشي. جدة: دار العلم للطباعة والنشر، 1991.

السيوطي، جلال الدين عبد الرحمن (ت. 1505/911). **حُسْنُ السَّمْت في الصَّمْت**. حققه وخرج أحاديثه وعلق عليه نجم عبد الرحمن خلف. بيروت: دار المأمون للتراث، 1985.

السيوطي، جلال الدين عبد الرحمن (ت. 1505/911). **ذم المكس**. تحقيق مجدي فتحي السيد. طنطا: دار الصحابة للتراث، 1991.

السيوطي، جلال الدين عبد الرحمن (ت. 1505/911). **ما رواه الأساطين في عدم المجيء إلى السلاطين**. تحقيق مجدي فتحي السيد. طنطا: دار الصحابة للتراث، 1991.

السيوطي، جلال الدين عبد الرحمن (ت. 1505/911). **ذم القضاء وتقلد الأحكام**. تحقيق مجدي فتحي السيد. طنطا: دار الصحابة للتراث، 1991.

السيوطي، جلال الدين عبد الرحمن (ت. 1505/911). **منتهى الآمال في شرح حديث إنما الأعمال**. تحقيق وتعليق أبي عبد الرحمن محمد عطية. بيروت: دار ابن حزم، 1998.

السيوطي، جلال الدين عبد الرحمن (ت. 1505/911). **الأربعون حديثًا في قواعد من الأحكام الشرعية وفضائل الأعمال والزهد**. حققه وخرج أحاديثه وعلق عليه باحث بن أحمد الخزرجي الأنصاري. جدة: دار المنارة للنشر والتوزيع، 1997.

السيوطي، جلال الدين عبد الرحمن (ت. 1505/911). **فضل الجلد عند فقد الولد**. تحقيق عبد القادر أحمد عبد القادر. الكويت: مكتبة السندس، 1989.

السيوطي. جلال الدين عبد الرحمن (ت. 1505/911). **أنموذج اللبيب في خصائص الحبيب**. قابل أصوله الخطية واعتنى به عباس أحمد صقر الحسيني. الدار البيضاء: مطبعة النجاح، 1995.

السيوطي، جلال الدين عبد الرحمن (ت. 911/1505). **الخصائص الكبرى أو كفاية الطالب اللبيب في خصائص الحبيب**. تحقيق محمد خليل هراس. القاهرة: دار الكتب الحديثة، 1967.
السيوطي. جلال الدين عبد الرحمن (ت. 911/1505). **الأرج في الفرَج**. وقف على طبعه أحمد عبيد. دمشق: المكتبة العربية، 1350هـ [1931].
السيوطي، جلال الدين عبد الرحمن (ت. 911/1505). **تمهيد الفرش في الخصال الموجبة لظل العرش**. ويليه مختصره: **بزوغ الهلال في الخصال الموجبة للظلال**. تحقيق أبي عبيدة مشهور بن حسن آل سلمان. المدينة المنورة: مركز سطور للبحث العلمي، دار الإمام مسلم، 2019.
القسطلاني، أحمد بن محمد (ت. 923/1517). **منتقى تحفة الحبيب للحبيب بما زاد على الترغيب والترهيب** (مطبوع مع الترغيب والترهيب لليافعي). تحقيق محمد فارس. بيروت: دار الكتب العلمية، 1996.
الشامي الصالحي، محمد بن يوسف (ت. 942/1536). **الفضل المبين في الصبر عند فقد البنات والبنين**. تحقيق خلود محمد الحسبان. عمان: دار أمواج، 2013.
ابن طولون، شمس الدين محمد بن علي (ت. 953/1546). **كتاب الأربعين في فضل الرحمة والراحمين**. تحقيق محمد خير رمضان يوسف. بيروت: دار ابن حزم، 1995.
ابن حجر الهيتمي، شهاب الدين أحمد بن محمد (ت. 973/1566). **أربعون حديثًا في العدل**. تحقيق ودراسة سمير كتاني. بغداد - بيروت: منشورات الجمل، 2012.
العاملي، حسين بن عبد الصمد (ت. 984/1576). **أربعون حديثًا [في مكارم الأخلاق]**.[28] أخرجه حسين علي محفوظ. طهران: مطبعة الحيدري، 1957.
الغزي، أبو البركات بدر الدين محمد (ت. 984/1577). **آداب العشرة وذكر الصحبة والأخوة**. عني بتحقيقه عمر موسى باشا. دمشق: مطبوعات مجمع اللغة العربية، 1968.

## القرن الحادي عشر/السابع عشر

المناوي، زين الدين عبد الرؤوف (ت. 1029-1032/1620-1623). **الدر المنضود في ذم البخل ومدح الجود**. حققه وعلق عليه وخرج أحاديثه أبو الفضل الحويني الأثري. طنطا: دار الصحابة للتراث، 1990.
الغزي، نجم الدين محمد بن محمد (ت. 1061/1651). **حسن التنبه لما ورد في التشبه**. دمشق: دار النوادر، 2011.

## القرن الثاني عشر/الثامن عشر

السفاريني، شمس الدين محمد الحنبلي (ت. 1188/1774). **تناضل العمال لشرح فضائل الأعمال**. تحقيق محمد عصام الشطي. الدوحة: وزارة الأوقاف والشؤون الإسلامية، 2017.

28 تمت إضافة ما بين المعقوفتين إلى عنوان الكتاب في طبعة لاحقة نشرتها دار الأضواء في بيروت سنة 1998.

## القرن الرابع عشر/التاسع عشر

النبهاني، يوسف بن إسماعيل (ت. 1932/1350). **الأربعين أربعين من أحاديث سيد المرسلين.**[29] القاهرة: مطبعة مصطفى البابي الحلبي وأولاده بمصر، 1952.

---

29 جاء العنوان على الغلاف هكذا «مجموع الأربعين أربعين ...»، ولكن المؤلف يقول في مقدمة كتابه ص 3 إنه سماه «الأربعين أربعين ...».

# فهرس


آداب السلوك 89
الآداب الشرعية 89
آداب النفوس 312
آدم 97
الابتداع في الدين 65
ابن أبي الدنيا راجع أيضا
Ibn Abī l-Dunyā 87–113، 308، 310
الأخلاق الأثرية 89–91
حدود أخلاقياته 109–113
رسائله في الأخلاق والرقائق 88
العقل وفضله 87
العقل في الأخلاق 91–97
عن التقوى الشخصية 91
مكارم الأخلاق 87
ابن أبي زيد القيرواني 60، 65–67
ابن أبي داود، عبد الله 63–64
ابن الأثير الجزري، ضياء الدين 55
ابن الأعرابي، أحمد بن محمد 62، 99
ابن بلبان 308
ابن تغري بردي 88
ابن تيمية راجع أيضا
Ibn Taymiyya 57، 109
ابن جبير، سعيد 106
ابن جريج، عبد الملك 95
ابن الجوزي راجع أيضا Ibn al-Jawzī, ʿAlī b.
ʿAbd al-Raḥmān 62، 64، 98، 104
ابن حبان راجع أيضا
Ibn Ḥibbān 92، 98، 101، 104، 109،
308، 312–313
ابن حجر العسقلاني راجع أيضا Ibn Ḥajar
al-ʿAsqalānī 48، 52–53، 56–57، 64،
66، 68، 78، 309
ابن حنبل، أحمد راجع أيضا
Ibn Ḥanbal 60، 62، 78، 92، 102
ابن دقيق العيد 52
ابن ذكوان، عبد الله 52
ابن راهويه، إسحاق 60، 62
ابن رجب الحنبلي 51–55، 57–58، 60–62،
64، 70–72، 78
ابن سُراقة العامرى 61
ابن سيرين، محمد 93
ابن شهاب الزهري، محمد 54
ابن الصلاح راجع أيضا Ibn al-Ṣalāḥ 48،
50–51، 57–58، 60، 68–72
ابن عباس راجع أيضا Ibn ʿAbbās 69، 92
ابن العربي راجع أيضا Ibn al-ʿArabī,
Muḥyī l-Dīn 53، 78
ابن عمر 68
ابن عيينة 67
ابن قتيبة راجع أيضا Ibn Qutayba 111، 312
ابن المقفع 111
ابن الملقن 60–61، 64، 66، 70
ابن منظور 99
ابن مهدي 78
ابن النحاس 312
أبو إسحاق الوطواط 313
أبو بكر الآجري 312
أبو بكر الخفاف 60–62
أبو بكر الصديق راجع أيضا
Abū Bakr 106–107
أبو بكر القفال الشاشي الكبير 71
أبو داود (السِّجِستاني) راجع أيضا
Abū Dāwūd 49، 60، 62–65، 67، 70،
72، 78، 307–308

أبو الزناد 52
أبو عبيد القاسم بن سلام 60–61، 66
أبو هريرة راجع أيضا Abū Hurayra 63، 102
أحاديث الأحكام 49، 308–309، 313
الأحاديث الكلية 48–49
أصل من الأصول في موضوع معين 77
تأريخ 60–72
عند الأئمة المتقدمين 60–68
عند المتأخرين 68–72
تحديد 57–59
تعبر عن الشريعة بكليتها 76–77
تقدير العدد 66
ثنائية الأمر والنهي 77
صلة بين القواعد الفقهية والأحاديث الكلية 68
ثلث العلم أو ربعه 57
جزء من جوامع الكلم 56
متجاوزة للأبواب 78–79
نصف العلم أو نصف الشريعة أو نصف أدلة الشرع 77
وجه الكلي في 76–79
وحقل الأخلاق 74–76
وسؤال الأخلاق 72–79
أحاديث، بعض المواضع
أركان الإسلام 58، 61–63، 65، 72
إكرام الجار 75
إكرام الضيف 75
الابتداع في الدين 72
الإخلاص 75
الإخلاص لله 73
الأخوة 75
« الأعمال بالنيات » 61–63
الأمة 54
تحليل الحلال وتحريم الحرام 73
التقوى 75
جبريل 52
« الحلال بين » 66
الحلال والحرام 72
الرضاع 57، 71
الزهد 72–73
سببية الأعمال للجزاء 73
الصدقة 70، 75
الطهارة 59
الطُّهور 70
الظلم 70
عصمة دم المسلم 61، 72، 74
القدر 53
قواعد الدين 52
مسكر 54، 58، 71
مناسك 59
منافق 71
النصيحة 72
الورع 73
اليوم الآخر 52
أخبار الصالحين 88
الإخلاص 75، 77–78، 112
الأخلاق الأثرية 89–91، 109، 114
أخلاق الأفعال 307
الأخلاق التحليلية 306
أخلاق الفضيلة 75، 307
أخلاق الفعل 74
أخلاق النبي 307
الأخلاق باعتبارها صونا لإنسانية الإنسان 109

أخلاق حملة القرآن 312
الأخلاقيات العربية الدنيوية 101
أخلاقيات المكارم 87
أخلاقيات فضيلة 113
الأخوة 75
أداء الأمانة 108
الأربعون النووية 308
الأربعين النووية 56–57
أرسطو 113
أركان الإسلام 58
أركون، محمد 112
استفت قلبك 76
الإسماعيلية 110
إسناد 97، 101، 310
الأصبهاني، أبو نُعيم 71
الأصفهاني، أبو حيان 307
أصول الأحاديث 57، 65
أصول الإسلام 65
أصول السنن 57، 65
أفعال الباطن 308
أفعال الجوارح 308
الأفعال الظاهرة 308
الأفلاطونية المحدثة 110
الأقسام والخصال 60
أكثم بن صيفي 95
إكرام الجار 75
إكرام الضيف 75، 108– 109
إكرام الغير من ذوي القربى 108
الأمة 54
أمر الآخرة 65
الأنصاري، محمد بن هارون 307
الأنطاكي، عبد الله بن خَبيق 94
الاهتداء بالعقل 109
الإيجاز وجوامع الكلم 71
أيوب بن القِرِيّة 95

البخاري، محمد بن إسماعيل راجع أيضا al-Bukhārī, Abū ʿAbd Allāh Ismāʿīl b. Muḥammad 48، 50، 3–54، 57–59، 66، 71، 96، 99، 102، 109، 307–308
بدر الدين العيني 52–53
بدعة 52
بستان العارفين 51
البطرني المقري، أبو العباس 70
البويطي 67، 78
بيلمي، جيمس 90، 112
البيهقي، أبو بكر 67، 79
التجيبي، القاسم بن يوسف 64، 66، 70
التذمم للجار 108
التذمم للصاحب 108
الترمذي، الحكيم 78، 97، 104، 312
تصنيف السنن 49
تصنيف على الأبواب أو الموضوعات 48–49
تصنيف على المسند 48–49
التصنيف في الحديث 48–49
تصنيف كتب الأخلاق الحديثية 309–310
كتب الأدب 309
كتب الترغيب والترهيب 309
كتب الزهد والورع والرقائق 310
كتب شعب الإيمان 310
كتب فضائل الأعمال 309
كتب مكارم الأخلاق 309
كتب المناقب والفضائل 310
كتب هدي النبي وأخلاقه وشمائله 310

تفسير ﴿أُوْلِي ٱلْأَيْدِي وَٱلْأَبْصَٰرِ﴾ 92
التقوى 75، 99، 111
تهذيب الأسماء واللغات 51

ثنائية العقل والهوى في الفكر الأخلاقي في
الإسلام 94–95
ثنائية الفعل 307

الجابري، محمد عابد 89
الجاحظ 55
جامع العلوم والحكم في شرح خمسين حديثًا من
جوامع الكلم 52
جبريل 52، 69
جزاء للصالحات 100–101
الجهد المبدع 76
جوامع الكلم 50–56، 72
الأحاديث الكلية كجزء من 56
الإيجاز في اللفظ 56
تحديد 54–56
القرآن كجزء من 55
كصفة لكلام النبي 55
وبدائع الحكم 71
الجود وإعطاء السائل 108

الحافظ أبو عمرو عثمان بن عبد الرحمن، راجع
ابن الصلاح
الحاوي 59
« الحِجر » والعقل 93
حديث جبريل 75–76،78
حديث السيدة عائشة 109
حديث المكارم العشر 103–105
حديث النية 48، 66–68، 78

الحسن البصري راجع أيضا al-Ḥasan
al-Baṣrī 89، 93، 97
الحلم 111
الحُميدي، الحافظ أبو عبد الله 55، 59
حوراني، جورج 111، 306
الحياء 105، 113

خالد بن الوليد 108
الخطابي، أبو سليمان 52، 55–56، 312
الخطيب البغدادي 49
الخُلُق 307
الخليل بن أحمد 93

دار السلام في مدار الإسلام 70
الدارَقُطْني، أبو الحسن 60، 64، 67، 78
الدارِمي، عثمان بن سعيد 60، 64
الداني، أبو عمرو 64
دراز، محمد عبد الله 76، 306
دو بوفون 112
ديكارت 93
الديلمي، شيرويه بن شهردار 71

الذهبي، شمس الدين 72، 88، 109

الرازي، أبو بكر محمد بن زكرياء 95، 98–99،
104
الراغب الأصفهاني 87، 98–99، 111
الذريعة إلى مكارم الشريعة 87
رسالة « العقل وفضله » 91–92، 98
رسالة « المكارم » 103
تفصيل القول في 105–108
الحياء 105–106
رسالة « فضل العقل » 91

رسالة « مكارم الأخلاق » 91، 96، 98–107
أحد أعمدة الدين 103
مقدمة 98–103
الرقائق 90
« روضة العقلاء ونزهة الفضلاء » 111

الزبير بن العوام 108
الزهد 90، 111
زيد بن أسلم 100

السدلان، صالح 313
سعداوي، عبد الله 88
السعدي، عبد الرحمن بن ناصر 56
سعيد بن العاص 113
سعيد بن المسيَّب 93، 106
السكر 54
سليمان بن عبد الملك 94
سنن أبي داود 308
سنن الترمذي 309
سير الخلفاء الراشدين والصحابة والصالحين 310
السيرة النبوية 310
السيوطي، جلال الدين راجع أيضا ,al-Suyūṭī
Jalāl al-Dīn 307

الشافعي، محمد بن إدريس 59، 60، 61، 67، 78
شرعية العقل في الأخلاق 91–92
شعر الأعرابية 107
شكل الحديث 312
الشهاب في الحكم والآداب 71

صالح الشامي 56، 73
صحيح ابن حبان 308
صحيح البخاري 66، 109، 308
صحيح مسلم 50، 109، 308
الصدق 107
صدق البأس 107–108
صدقة 70
صفة النبي 307
صلاح الرجل الصالح 96

الضحاك بن مُزاحم 93، 96
الضرّاب، أبو محمد الحسن بن إسماعيل 308

طاعة الله 100
طلحة بن عبيد 108
الطهارة 59
الطوفي، نجم الدين 51، 57، 60–61، 70، 76

عائشة 62، 91، 103–105، 107، 114
العاقل مرادفًا للمؤمن الكامل 95
العامري، أبو الحسن 111
عبد الجبار 100
عبد الرحمن بن مهدي 48، 60–62، 71، 78
عبد الله بن أحمد 62
عبد الله بن عمر 103
عبيد الله بن سعد بن إبراهيم القرشي 93
عتر، نور الدين 56
عثمان بن عفان 59، 61
العدل والعقل 93
العِرباض بن سارية 69
العقل
كآلة التمييز 97
كالفاروق الذي يُعرض عليه دين
المرء 96
وفضله 88
وملكات الإنسان 94

العقل الفطري والعقل المكتسب 93
« العقل عن الله » 96
علي بن أبي طالب 94، 107
علي بن المديني 48، 60–61، 78
عليّ بن عبيدة 94
علي القاري، ملا 51
عمران الزّنّاتي 68
عمر بن الخطاب 61، 92، 107، 112
عمر بن المظفر 70
عمر بن عبد العزيز 106
عيون الأخبار 312

الغماري، عبد الله بن الصديق 72
غولدتسيهر 110

الفاكِهاني، تاج الدين 68
فخري، ماجد 89
الفراء، يحيى بن زياد 99
الفِردوس بمأثور الخطاب 71
فضائل الأعمال 111
فضائل الخصال 111
فضل العقل 90
فهرست المصنفات الحديثية في الأخلاق 306–335

القاضي عياض 78، 307
قَتادة بن دِعامة السَّدوسي 95
القطان، يحيى بن سعيد 48
القُضاعي، أبو عبد الله 71، 313
القوتلي، حسين 110

كتاب الأذكار 50
كتاب البر 308
كتاب تنبيه الغافلين 312
كتاب التوحيد والتوكل 88
كتاب الرِّقاق 308
كتاب روضة العقلاء 312
كتاب الزهد 308
كتاب السنن لأبي داود 65
كتاب الشفا بتعريف حقوق المصطفى 307
كتاب طبائع النفوس 312
كتاب العزلة 312
كتاب « العقل وفهم القرآن » 110
كتاب العقل ومكارم الأخلاق 88
كتاب عيون الأخبار 312–313
كتاب غرر الخصائص الواضحة وغرر النقائص الفاضحة 313
كتاب « مائية العقل ومعناه » 93
كتاب المذمومات 88
كتاب مستفاد الرحلة والاغتراب 70
كتاب « مكارم الأخلاق » 104
كتاب المناقب 308
كتاب اليقين 90
هيكله 105
الكتب الستة 114
كلي الباب 58
الكِناني، حمزة بن محمد 60، 64، 66، 78
الكندي، أبو يوسف 95، 99

لبراند، ليونارد 90
اللغة الأخلاقية 75–76
لقمان الحكيم 95

مائية العقل 93
ما بعد الأخلاق 75–76
مالك بن أنس 67

مالك بن دينار 99
الماوردي 59، 94، 98
المتقي الهندي، علاء الدين 307
مجاهد بن جبر 92
المحاسبي، الحارث 93، 96، 110، 312
محمد بن أبي إسماعيل 97
محمد بن بكر بن داسة 63
محمد بن علي بن المديني 61
محمد بن كعب 107
محمد زاهد الكوثري 91
مدار الإسلام 65
مدار الحديث 65
مدار السنن 65
مدار الفقه 65
المدارس الأخلاقية في الفكر الإسلامي 90
مدونات الحديث
المضمون الأخلاقي 307–308
المروءة 109، 111–113
والعقل 92
المزي، الحافظ جمال الدين 88
مسلك الحِجاج 312
مسلك السرد والرواية في أبواب المصنفات
الحديثية 312
مصادر التقويم الأخلاقي 75–76
معاذ بن جبل 69
معاوية بن أبي سفيان 93
معاوية بن قرة 106
مفهوم « الكرم » 99–100
مفهوم « المكارم » 99، 101–103
قيمة الحِلم 102–103
مفهوم « مكارم الأخلاق » 112

المقدسي، ضياء الدين 307
المقدسي، نصر بن إبراهيم 63
مكارم الأخلاق 87–88، 90–91
المكارم والكرم 98–103، 111
الموروث العربي 98، 111–113
المكافأة بالصنائع 108
المُكتفين بالمدونة الأخلاقية الإسلامية 111
منصور بن المعتمر 97
المنهيات 312

النبراوي، عبد الله 56
النبهاني، يوسف بن إسماعيل 311
النزعة النقلية في الأخلاق 90
نَصْرَوَيه، ورد بن محمد 95
النعمان بن بشير 62–63
نقد الإسناد 110
نوادر الأصول 312
النووي، يحيى بن شرف 48–52، 55–60، 63،
65، 68–73، 308
النية 72
النيسابوري، الحاكم 62

الهروي، أبو عبيد 55
هوميروس 112
وصل البلاغات الأربعة في الموطأ 72
الوضوء 59
وكيع بن الجراح 96
وهب بن منبه 95، 107

ياسين، عبد السلام 313
يحيى بن أبي كثير 100

# Index


ʿAbbāsids 252–253
ʿAbd al-Awwal b. ʿĪsā 130
ʿAbd al-Jabbār 273
ʿAbd al-Qādir al-Jīlānī 3, 5, 147–148, 150–151, 155–156, 158–166, 177, 288, 294–295
  on *taḥbīb* 158–165
ʿAbd al-Raḥmān b. Mahdī 258
ʿAbd al-Wahhāb b. al-Ḥāfiẓ 130
ʿAbduh, Muḥammad 136
absence (Derridean concept) 206–208
Abū ʿAbd Allāh Muḥammad b. ʿUmar b. Rashīd 21
Abū ʿAlī l-Thaqafī 209
Abū ʿAwāna 148
Abū Bakr. *See also* أبو بكر الصديق 155
Abū Burda 182–183
Abū Dāwūd 2, 4, 13, 40
Abū Dharr al-Ghifārī 182
Abū Ḥanīfa 156
Abū Ḥudhayfa b. al-Yamān 174
Abū Hurayra. *See also* أبو هريرة 238
Abū Mūsā 238
Abū Saʿīd al-Khuḍrī 183, 228
Abū l-Shaykh, ʿAbd Allāh 2
Abū Shuqqa, ʿAbd al-Ḥalīm Muḥammad 5–6, 221–245
Abū ʿUbayda Maʿmar b. al-Muthannā 37
*Adab al-Imlāʾ wa-l-Istimlāʾ* 10
*Adab al-Kātib* ("Manners of the Scribe") 41
*al-Adab al-Mufrad* 9
*Adab al-Nufūs* 10
*Adab al-Ṣuḥba* 10
*adab* (pl. *ādāb* manner, ettiquette) 2, 4, 16, 23
  *ādāb al-sulūk* (etiquette of spiritual wayfaring) 9
  *al-ādāb al-sharʿiyya* 9
  conceptual shift in Islam 35–38
  definition and ethical dimension 30
  historical conceptualisation 32–33
  in *ḥadīth* collections 38–43
  pre-Islamic use 32
*adīb* (educator [in etiquette] or educated) 32, 36
*afʿāl al-bāṭin* (inner actions) 14
*aḥādīth al-aḥkām* (traditions on *fiqhī* rulings) 16
*al-aḥādīth al-mushtahira* (viral *ḥadīth*) 149
al-ʿAjlūnī 149, 156
al-Ājurrī, Abū Bakr 10
*akhlāq* (ethics) in Islam
  *al-akhlāq al-athariyya* (narration-based ethics) 14–15
  based on *ḥadīth* 1–2, 4, 19–22
    applied studies 25
    comparative studies 25
    history and development 23–24
    nature of 24–25
    primary sources 6
    Sunna as a source 25
    terminology and concepts 23
  conception of 14–15
  conscience (the heart/self) as a source 269–271, 282–292
    Sufi discourse on 292–295
  gender 221–222
    Abū Shuqqa on 223–242
  intention 248–251, 260–264
    in Sufi writings 258–260
  of seclusion (*ʿuzla*) 170–173, 181–192
  Sufi 147
  the inward (*bāṭin*) dimension 271–281
  virtue 120–124
al-Albānī, Nāṣir al-Dīn 136, 138, 228
ʿAlī b. Abī Ṭālib 155, 226
Ali, Kecia 263
ʿAlī l-Qārī 155
ambiguous matters (*shubah*) 286
Anas b. Mālik 148–149, 186, 242, 255
annihilation and subsistence (*al-fanāʾ wa-l-baqāʾ*) 128
al-Anṣārī, Yaḥyā b. Saʿīd 252
anti-Arab sentiment (*shuʿūbiyya*) 41
*anwāʿ ʿulūm al-ḥadīth* (types of *ḥadīth* sciences) 19
*al-ʿAql al-Akhlāqī al-ʿArabī* 1, 8
Arabi, Oussama 262
ʿArafāt 133
*al-Arbaʿūn al-Nawawiyya* 18
Arkoun, Mohammed 21

Armstrong, Lyall 203
al-Arnāʾūṭ, Shuʿayb 138
al-Arnāʾūṭ, ʿAbd al-Qādir 138
Asad, Talal 260, 298
al-Aṣbahānī, Abū l-Shaykh b. Ḥayyān 17, 22, 149
al-Aṣfahānī, Abū Ḥayyān 17
asceticism (*zuhd*) 2, 9, 18–19, 40, 129, 132, 134, 147, 150–151, 158, 161, 165–166, 170, 173–174, 177, 211–212
and marriage 150–152
al-Ashʿarī, Abū l-Ḥasan 238
*āthār* 133–134, 141
al-Attar, Mariam 13
authenticity of traditions 199–201
*ʿAwārif al-Maʿārif* ("The Esoteric Insights of the Gnostics") 176
ʿĀʾisha 34, 126, 150, 228

Badr al-Dīn al-ʿAynī 258
Baghdad 126
banquets (in *adab* literature) 32–33, 35–37
*baqāʾ* 148, 150, 155, 158, 160, 164
al-Barrāk, ʿAbd al-Raḥmān Nāṣir 152
*bāṭin*. *See* inner
al-Bayhaqī, Aḥmad b. Ḥusayn 22, 33, 148, 176
Beaumont, Daniel 43
begging 131
Bilqīs 231
*birr* (righteous virtue) 33–34
Bishr al-Ḥāfī 151
al-Bīṭār, Muḥammad Bahjat 137
blocking the means of prohibited actions (*sadd al-dharāʾiʿ*) 282
bodily aspect of ethics 210
Brockelmann, Carl 127
brotherhood (*ukhuwwa*) 181
al-Bukhārī, Abū ʿAbd Allāh Muḥammad b. Ismāʿīl. *See also* البخاري، محمد بن إسماعيل 6, 9–10, 12–14, 17–18, 20, 22, 35, 39–40, 42, 123–124, 130, 133, 147, 157, 183, 222, 228–230, 233, 237–238, 241–242, 249–250, 254–258, 262, 272, 274, 278, 284
and the *ḥadīth* of intention 256–258
Burrell, David 135

Carra de Vaux, Bernard 8
casuistries in *ḥadīth* 18
caution (*iḥtiyāṭ*) 282
certitude (*yaqīn*) 273
classification of books on *ḥadīth*-based ethics 21–22
common link between *ḥadīth* narrators 252
companionship (*ṣuḥba*) 181
Companions of the Prophet (*ṣaḥāba*) 202–203, 276
conflicting *ḥadīth*s (*mukhtalif al-ḥadīth*) 222
conscience in Islam 269–270
authority of the heart 276–278
Sufi discourse on 292–295
consultation between genders 237
Crone, Patricia 204

al-Dabūsī 284
Damascus 138
al-Dārānī, Abū Sulaymān 131
al-Ḍarrāb, Abū Muḥammad al-Ḥasan b. Ismāʿīl 18
Demiri, Lejla 178
Derrida, Jacques 204, 206
al-Dhahabī, Shams al-Dīn 252
*Dhamm al-Dunyā* ("Condemnation of the Worldly") 153
*Dhamm al-Hawā* ("Disparagement of Passion") 139
*dhikr* (the recollection of God) 174
al-Dihlawī, ʿAbd al-Ḥaqq 155
al-Dihlawī, Walī Allah 20
al-Dīnawarī, Abū Bakr 9
Donaldson, Dwight M. 10
doubt (*shakk*) 273
Drāz, Muḥammad ʿAbd Allāh 8, 21
Dahmān, Muḥammad Aḥmad 137, 141
*duʿāʾ* (supplication in prayer) 37

earliest generations (*al-salaf al-ṣāliḥ*) 120
earthly world (*dunyā*) 147, 285, 294
egoism 185
El Calamawy, Sahair 43
*Encyclopaedia of Islam* 11
Engineer, Ali Asghar 221
equality (*musāwāt*) of gender relationships 223–228, 230, 235

esoteric sciences (*al-ʿulūm al-ladunniyya*) 293
establishing the *ratio legis* (*taḥqīq al-manāṭ*) 288–292
*Ethical Theories in Islam* 1
ethics 30, 39–41, 268–271, 291
ettiquette. *See* adab (pl. *ādāb* manner, ettiquette)
evidence of the ruling (*dalīl al-ḥukm*) 289
evidentiary inference (*istidlāl*) 282–283

Fadel, Mohammad 224, 298
Fakhry, Majid 1, 11
family life 147
*fanāʾ* (annihilation) 128, 148, 150, 155, 158, 160, 162–166, 207
al-Farābī, Abū Naṣr 186
Farīja, Muḥammad 221
*al-Fatḥ al-Rabbānī* ("The Sublime Revelation") 147
Fāṭima bint Muḥammad 226
Feinberg, Joel 185
female prophets 238–239
"female spaces" 239
*fiṭra* (innate disposition) 276–277, 288
Foucault, Michel 210
fragrance. *See* perfume
Freud, Sigmund 248
*Fuṣūṣ al-Ḥikam* ("Bezels of Wisdom") 156
*Futūḥ al-Ghayb* ("Revelations of the Unseen") 147

Gabriel 155, 239
Gadamer, Hans 171
gazing 187
Geertz, Clifford 213–214
gender ethics 5–6
gender relations
- and the Arabic language 235–236
- hermeneutics on 235–240
- in *ḥadīth* 228–230
- in the Qurʾān 230–231

*Gharīb al-Ḥadīth* ("Strange Traditions") 37
*Ghāyat al-Maṭlūb fī Maḥabbat al-Maḥbūb* ("The Peak of the Goal in Loving the Beloved") 171, 173, 187
al-Ghazālī, Abū Ḥāmid 3, 5, 24, 120, 122–142, 149, 151, 153, 171, 173, 177, 181, 186, 191, 208, 210–211, 213, 222, 255, 259, 264, 270, 284–287, 291, 295–296
- on the study of *ḥadīth* 123–124

al-Ghazālī, Muḥammad 222
al-Ghazzī 152
*al-Ghunya li-Ṭālibī Ṭarīq al-Ḥaqq* ("Richness for the Seeker of the Truth") 161
Gibb, Hamilton 11
giving and getting consultation from each other (*mushāwara*) 226–227
Goldziher, Ignaz 269

Haddad, Gibril Fouad 178, 189
al-Hādī, Ṣādiq b. Muḥammad 221
*ḥadīth* 6, 35
- and the Arabic language 35, 41
- as a corpus on ethics 15–19
- as examples of wisdom 42
- as intermediary divine communication 35
- as *khabar* (narrative) 43
- categories of *ḥadīth* content 17
- classifying and compiling 20–21
- criticism 120–123, 138–140
- etymology and relation to *adab* 31
- forged (*mawḍūʿ*) 120–121, 125, 127
- inaccessibility to non-Arabs 13
- inclusive definition of 228
- in contemporary scholarship on ethics 8–15
- *maqṭūʿ* 16
- *marfūʿ* 15–16
- *mawqūf* 15–16
- of intention 248–264
  - *isnād* and popularisation 251–254
- on the inward dimension (*bāṭin*) 271–275
- pairing the Qurʾān with 230–231
- position after Qurʾānic verses 42
- reinterpretation of problematic *ḥadīth* (*taʾwīl mushkil al-ḥadīth*) 240–244
- rejection (*iʿtibār*) of 21
- reorganisation of themes (*tarājim al-abwāb*) 232–235
- scope 15–16
- texts (*mutūn*, sing. *matn*) 16
- transmitter of (*musnad*, pl. *masānīd*) 16
- verbal transmission of 202–203

*ḥadīth* (*cont.*)
weak (*ḍaʿīf*) 120–121, 125
works on
*adab* 22, 38–43
*al-targhīb wa-l-tarhīb* (persuasion and intimidation) 22
*manāqib* (merits) and excellences (*faḍāʾil*) 22
noble virtues (*makārim al-akhlāq*) 22
Prophetic guidance (*hady al-nabī*) 22
*shuʿab al-īmān* (branches of faith) 22
*ḥadīth al-taḥbīb* 5, 147, 154–156
in al-Jīlānī's works 158–165
theosophical perspective 156–158
*ḥadīth* collections 39–40
Abū Dāwūd 13, 18, 39–42, 228
al-Bukhārī 12, 14, 18, 20, 39–42, 123–124, 130, 137, 228–229, 249
Ibn Ḥibbān 18
Ibn Māja 39
Muslim 12–14, 18–19, 39–42, 123–124, 130, 137, 228–229
al-Tirmidhī 39–42, 130, 228
*ḥadīth* of *taḥbīb* 148
*Ḥajj* 133
Ḥājjī Khalīfa 127
al-Ḥalīmī 22
Hallaq, Wael 202
al-Ḥamawī, Aḥmad b. Muḥammad 262
al-Ḥasan al-Baṣrī. *See also* الحسن البصري 203
al-Hāshimī, Muḥammad ʿAlī 221
Hāshimiyya 252
Hassan, Riffat 221
*hawā* (desire) 161
Ḥawwā, Saʿīd 138–140
heart (*qalb*) 6
helping each other (*taʿāwun*) 226–227
*hijra* (migration from Mecca to Medina) 256
*ḥikma* (wisdom) 212
historical science of ethics (*ʿilm al-akhlāq al-tārīkhī*) 19
Hourani, George 11, 21

Ibn ʿAbd al-Salām, ʿIzz al-Dīn 18, 21
Ibn Abī l-Dunyā. *See also* ابن أبي الدنيا 3, 5, 18, 21–22, 24, 40, 134, 174
Ibn Abī ʿĀṣim 149, 151
Ibn Diḥya al-Kalbī, Abū l-Khaṭṭāb 18
Ibn al-Ḥasan, Muḥammad 23
Ibn al-Jawzī, ʿAbd al-Raḥmān b. ʿAlī. *See also* ابن الجوزي 5, 120–121, 124–141, 184, 190, 201, 205
on Sufism in the *Iḥyāʾ* 128–129
Ibn al-Mubārak, ʿAbd Allāh 20, 22, 174
Ibn al-Munayyir 20
Ibn al-Muqaffaʿ 23
Ibn al-Qayyim 139, 236
Ibn al-Ṣalāḥ. *See also* ابن الصلاح 4, 19, 21
Ibn al-Sikkīt 36
Ibn al-ʿArabī, Abū Bakr 235
Ibn al-ʿArabī, Muḥyī al-Dīn. *See also* ابن العربي 147, 151–152, 154, 156–157, 176, 250, 254, 259–260
Ibn Bāz, ʿAbd al-ʿAzīz 221
Ibn Fūrak 149
Ibn Ḥajar al-ʿAsqalānī. *See also* ابن حجر العسقلاني 20–21, 148–149, 200, 228, 238, 250, 256–257
on al-Bukhārī 257
Ibn Ḥanbal. *See also* ابن حنبل، أحمد 22, 130–131, 133, 149–150, 183, 189, 199–200, 213
Ibn Hārūn, Muḥammad 17
Ibn Ḥazm 261–262, 282
Ibn Ḥibbān. *See also* ابن حبان 2, 18, 272
Ibn Kathīr, Abū l-Fidāʾ Ismāʿīl b. ʿUmar 139
Ibn Manẓūr, Abū al-Faḍl Jamāl al-Dīn Muḥammad 37, 204
Ibn Masʿūd, ʿAbd Allāh 35–36, 131, 133, 226
Ibn Maʿīn, Yaḥyā 199, 213
Ibn al-Mulaqqin, Sirāj al-Dīn 18
Ibn Nujaym 261–262
Ibn Qayyim al-Jawziyya 149
Ibn Qudāma 5, 121, 125, 127–129, 131–132, 135, 137–141
Ibn Qutayba. *See also* ابن قتيبة 41–42
Ibn Rajab al-Ḥanbalī 121–122, 152, 272, 275, 277–280, 284
Ibn Rushd 236
Ibn Shihāb al-Zuhrī 33
Ibn Taymiyya. *See also* ابن تيمية 162, 201, 258, 270, 287–289, 295–297
Ibn ʿAbbās. *See also* ابن عباس 133
Ibn ʿAjība 292, 294

Ibn ʿIllān 277
Ibrāhīm b. Adham 131
*Iḥyāʾ ʿUlūm al-Dīn* ("Revival of the Religious Sciences") 24, 120–140, 149, 151, 177, 181
criticism
modern 135–140
premodern 124–129
modern epitomes of 136–140
*ijmāʿ* (consensus) 283–284, 289
*ijtihād* 152, 209, 270, 277, 282, 288–292, 297
*ʿilm al-rijāl* (the study of *ḥadīth* transmitters/narrators) 201
inclination of the heart (*mayl qalbī*) 288
inner (*bāṭin*) 6, 14–15, 18, 248, 268, 270–271, 273, 282, 289, 292
in *ḥadīth* compendia 271–281
innovation (*bidʿa*) 205, 213, 289
inspiration (*ilhām*) 282
intentionality in Islamic ethics 260–264
modern legal reform and 262–263
ritualistic and performative dimensions 260–262
subjectivity 263
intention (*niyya*) 248–249
and action 250–251
and political action 254–256
in Sufi writings 258–260
of religious practice 251
inward knowledge (*ʿilm al-bāṭin*) 292
al-ʿIrāqī, al-Ḥāfiẓ Zayn al-Dīn ʿAbd al-Raḥīm 139
al-ʿIrqsūsī, Naʿīm 138
Islamic legal theory (*uṣūl al-fiqh*) 1
*isnād* 43, 141, 198, 200, 202–204, 215–216, 252
*al-ʿUzla wa-l-Infirād* ("Seclusion and Isolation") 174
*istiṣḥāb* (continuity) 289, 297
*Itḥāf al-Sāda al-Muttaqīn* ("The Benefactions of the Cultivated-Faithful") 177
ʿIzzat, Hiba Raʾūf 222
*Iʿlām al-Aḥyāʾ bi-Aghlāṭ al-Iḥyāʾ* ("Informing the Living about the Mistakes in the Revival") 126

Jābir b. ʿAbd Allāh 226
al-Jābirī, Muḥammad ʿĀbid 1, 8
*jadal* (argumentation) 198
al-Jāḥiẓ, Abū ʿUthmān ʿAmr b. Baḥr 41, 190
*Jāmiʿ al-Tirmidhī* ("The Compilation of al-Tirmidhī") 154
*al-Jāmiʿ li-Aḥkām al-Qurʾān* ("Compilation of the Rulings of the Qurʾān") 36
*al-Jāmiʿ li-Akhlāq al-Rāwī wa-Ādāb al-Sāmiʿ* 10
*Jamʿ al-Jawāmiʿ* 16
*al-jarḥ wa-l-taʿdīl* (impugning and approving) 136
*jihād* 241
Job, Prophet 131
Johansen, Baber 298
al-Junayd, Abū l-Qāsim 124, 163, 166
juristic categories of human actions (*al-aḥkām al-fiqhiyya*) 279–281
juristic preference (*istiḥsān*) 282
al-Juwaynī 123, 285
Juynboll, G.H.A. 252

Kahf, Mohja 222
al-Kalābādhī, Abū Bakr 21, 149, 153–154
*al-Kāmil fī l-Lugha wa-l-Adab* ("The Comprehensive Work on Language and Manners") 42
*Kanz al-ʿUmmāl fī Sunan al-Aqwāl wa-l-Afʿāl* 16
*al-Kasb wa-l-Maʿāsh* ("Earning and Livelihood") 129, 140
al-Kāshānī, Maḥmūd b. ʿAlī 172
*Kashf al-Khafāʾ* ("Uncovering the Hidden") 149
*Kashf al-Ẓunūn* ("Removal of Uncertainties") 127
*al-Kashshāf* ("The Revealer") 149
Khalidi, Tarif 31, 39
al-Khalīl b. Aḥmad al-Farāhīdī 32
*khalwa* (seclusion) 172
as an innovation of Sufis 172
attitudes towards 190–193
benefits of 183–189
historiography of 173–178
in time of strife and corruption 182–183
motives for 180–183
al-Kāndihlawī, Muḥammad Zakariyyā 20
Khansāʾ bint Khidām 226
al-Kharāʾiṭī 22
Khārijīs 215
al-Kharrāṭ, Kāmil Muḥammad 138

al-Khaṭīb al-Baghdādī, Abū Bakr 10
al-Khaṭṭābī, Abū Sulaymān Ḥamd b. Muḥammad 173, 174–175
al-Khāzin 205
al-Khudrī 189
al-Khurasānī, Ghāda 222
al-Khuzāʿī 186
al-Kindī, Abū Yūsuf 23
*Kitāb al-Adab* ("Book of Manners") 40
*Kitāb al-Alfāẓ* ("The Book of Words") 36
*Kitāb al-Amr bi-l-Maʿrūf wa-l-Nahy ʿan al-Munkar* ("Book of Commanding the Right and Forbidding the Wrong") 129
*Kitāb al-Birr wa-l-Ṣila wa-l-Ādāb* ("Book on Virtue, Maintaining the Ties of Kinship and Manners") 40
*Kitāb al-Farq Bayna al-Muṣannif wa-l-Sāriq* ("Book on the Difference Between the Compiler and the Thief") 207
*Kitāb al-Khalwa wa-l-Tanaqqul fī l-ʿIbāda wa-Darajāt al-ʿĀbidīn* ("The Book of Seclusion and Movement in Worship, and the Levels of Worshippers") 176
*Kitāb al-Qabas* ("The Book of Allusion") 154
*Kitāb al-Samāʿ wa-l-Wajd* ("Book on Audition and Ecstasy") 129
*Kitāb al-Tawakkul* ("Book on Providence") 134
*Kitāb al-Tawḥīd wa-l-Tawakkul* ("Divine Unity and Reliance") 134
*Kitāb al-ʿUzla* ("The Book of Seclusion") 174
*Kitāb ʿIshrat al-Nisāʾ* ("Kind Treatment of Women") 149
knowledge seeker (*ṭālib al-ḥadīth*) 19
knowledge, sources of 282–291
knowledge, withholding of 189–190

Lacan, Jacques 248
Landolt, Hermann 178
legal categories in Sharīʿa 13
*Lisān al-ʿArab* ("The Tongue of the Arabs") 37, 204
livelihood and work, ethics of 129–131
Lucas, Scott C. 13
Luqmān the Wise 131

Mahmood, Saba 251
*Makārim al-Akhlāq* ("The Noblest Moral Character") 40
al-Makkī, Abū Ṭālib 120, 126, 129, 136, 151, 258, 273, 292
*al-Maktab al-Islāmī* 138
male guardianship (*wilāya*) 225
male leadership (*qiwāma*) 225
Mālik b. Anas 42
*al-Manār* ("The Lighthouse") 136
manner. *See adab*
*al-Maqāṣid al-Ḥasana* ("The Good Purposes") 149
*Maqāyīs al-Lugha* ("Analogical Templates of Language") 36
al-Maqdisī, Ḍiyāʾ al-Dīn 17
March, Andrew 10
marriage 147–148, 151–153, 157, 161–162, 166, 225–226, 256
al-Marwazī, Muḥammad b. Naṣr 148
Massignon, Louis 203
material world (*dunyā*) 152–153
*matn* 16, 43, 198, 200, 202, 204, 215–216
*al-Mawāhib al-Ladunniyya* ("The Divine Providences") 150
*al-mawrūth al-ʿarabī* (Arab heritage) 10
*Mawʿiẓat al-Muʾminīn min Iḥyāʾ ʿUlūm al-Dīn* ("Exhortation of the Believers from the Iḥyāʾ") 136
Maʿqil b. Yasār 226
*maʿrifa* (gnosis) 157
*maʿrūf* (known or prescribed) 208–210
Medina 253
Mernissi, Fatima 221
Messick, Brinkley 263
*Minhāj al-Qāṣidīn wa-Mufīd al-Ṣādiqīn* ("The Way of the Strivers and the Benefit of the Truthful") 121, 124–129, 139
*Minhāj al-ʿĀbidīn* ("The Curriculum of Worshippers") 177
*Minhāj al-ʿĀrifīn* ("The Curriculum of the Gnostics") 177
miracles (*karāmāt*) 160, 291
*Misbāḥ al-Hidāya* ("Lantern of Guidance") 172
*Mishkāt al-Maṣābīḥ* ("The Niche of Lamps") 155
Miskawayh, Abū ʿAlī 23
misogyny 221
Moosa, Ebrahim 262, 264
moral exhortation (*mawāʿiẓ*) 16
Motzki, Harald 252

Mount Ḥirāʾ 172
al-Mubārakpūrī, Muḥammad ʿAbd al-Raḥmān 183
al-Mubarrid 42
*muḥaddithūn* (Traditionists) 9–11, 14–16, 20, 22–23, 203
Muḥammad, Prophet 147, 200, 204, 226, 256–257, 268, 271
  as role model/example in *ḥadīth* 17, 32–35
  retreats in solitude 172
al-Muḥāsibī, al-Ḥārith 24, 175–176, 258–259, 292–295
*al-Mujālasa wa-Jawāhir al-ʿIlm* 9
*mukhālaṭa* (social interaction) 170
*Mukhtaṣar Minhāj al-Qāṣidīn* ("Summary of the Way of the Strivers") 121, 124–129, 139
  modern editions 137–140
al-Munāwī, ʿAbd al-Raʾūf 158
*munāẓara* (debate) 198
*al-Muntaẓam fī Taʾrīkh al-Mulūk wa-l-Umam* ("Compilation on the History of Kings and Nations") 126
Murtaḍā al-Zabīdī 140, 177
*Muṣannaf* of ʿAbd al-Razzāq al-Ṣanʿānī 24
musings (*khaṭarāt*) 292–293
Muslim Brotherhood 138
*Musnad Aḥmad* 137
*Mustakhraj* ("The Extracted") 148
*muṣṭalaḥ al-ḥadīth* (*ḥadīth* classification) 136
al-Muttaqī l-Hindī, ʿAlāʾ al-Dīn 16
*al-Muwaṭṭaʾ* ("The Well-Trodden Path") 42, 154
*muʾaddib* (educator in *adab*) 32–35
*al-Muʿjam al-Awsaṭ* ("The Middle Sized *Muʿjam*") 149
Muʿtazila 1, 273

al-Nabhānī, Yūsuf 173
al-Nābulusī, ʿAbd al-Ghanī 3, 5, 170–173, 176–194
*nafaqa* (marital financial support) 226
names of God
  Bestower of bounty (*al-Munʿim*) 268
  Lawgiver/Legislator (*al-Musharriʿ*) 268, 274, 288, 291–292, 297
  Most Gracious 293
  Speaker (*al-Mutakallim*) 268
al-Nasāʾī 20, 42, 148, 150
al-Nawawī 4, 18–20, 40–41, 270
al-Nawwās b. Samʿān 271–272, 278–279
al-Naysābūrī, al-Ḥākim 21, 33, 148
*Nuzhat al-Majālis wa-Muntakhab al-Nafāʾis* ("Unwinding Councils and Precious Selections") 155
al-Nuʿmān b. Bashīr 278

opinion of the heart 285–287
outer actions (*afʿāl al-jawāriḥ or al-ẓāhir*) 18
outer (*ẓāhir*) 6, 18, 248, 268, 273, 280–281, 292
overriding authoritative reasons (*al-asbāb al-murajjiḥa*) 288–289

Pagani, Samuela 178
patriarchal Islam 221
people of the apparent (*ahl al-ẓāhir*) 281
perfume 5, 147, 149–150, 152, 154–156, 158–159
Peterson, Anna 251
piety (*waraʿ*) 40–41, 44, 210, 216, 249, 251–252, 258, 261, 276, 282, 285–286, 291–292, 297
Plato 206
poverty (*faqr*) 129
Powers, Paul 260
predecessors (*salaf*) 278
presence (Derridean concept) 206–208
printing 135
prophetic guidance (*hady al-nabī*) 228
purification of Sunna 127, 135

*qadar* (fate) 165, 288
*qaḍāʾ* (divine decree) 165
al-Qāḍī ʿIyāḍ 17, 150–151
al-Qalqashandī 41
al-Qaraḍāwī, Yūsuf 140, 222
al-Qāsimī, Jamāl al-Dīn 136–137
*qāṣṣ* (preacher) 198–209, 211–216
al-Qasṭallānī 150, 156
*Qawāʿid al-ʿAqāʾid* ("The Foundations of Religious Convictions") 129
*Qawāʿid al-Taḥdīth* ("The Foundations of Narrating Prophetic Traditions") 136

al-Qazwīnī, Aḥmad b. Fāris 36
*qiṣṣa* (story)
 aspect of thick description 213–215
 narrative strategies of 204–206
 versus *ḥadīth* 201–206
 writing and orality 206–210
*qiwāma* 226–227
*qiyās* (analogy) 283–284
Qurʾān
 verses on rulings (*āyāt al-aḥkām*) 17
*Qurrat al-ʿayn* (coolness of the eyes) 159
al-Qurṭubī, Muḥammad b. Aḥmad 36–37
al-Qushayrī, Abū l-Qāsim 191, 206, 209–212, 292–294
*Qūt al-Qulūb* ("The Nourishment of the Hearts") 120, 124, 126, 129, 136, 151, 258

Rabīʿ b. Khuthaym 174
Rafeq, Abdul-Karim 179
al-Rāfiʿī, Muṣṭafā Ṣādiq 19
al-Rāghib al-Iṣfahānī 279
rational proofs 282
Raymond, Andre 178
al-Rāzī, Abū Bakr 23
reason and revelation dichotomy 270–271
Reinhart, Kevin 208, 255
reliance on God (*tawakkul*) 129, 132
religious perfection (*kamāl*) 239
remembrance of death (*dhikr al-mawt*) 134
revelations (*mukāshafāt*) 291
Riḍā, Rashīd 124, 136, 269
righteousness (*birr*) 271–273, 278–281
*al-rijāl* (transmitters) 19
*Risāla fī l-ʿUlūm* ("Epistle on the Classification of Knowledge") 42
*Riyāḍ al-Ṣāliḥīn* ("Gardens of the Righteous") 40
*al-Riʿāya li-Ḥuqūq Allāh* ("Observing God's Due") 258
*Rubʿ al-ʿĀdāt* ("Quarter of Habits") 129
*rūḥ* (spirit) 157

*ṣabr* (patience) 165
al-Ṣaffūrī 155–156
*ṣaḥāba* (Companions) 204
Sainsbury, Mark 173
al-Sakhāwī 149
*ṣalāt* (prayer) 148
al-Ṣāliḥiyya 126
al-Samarqandī 283–284
*ṣamt* (silence) 174
al-Samʿānī, Abū Saʿd 10, 33, 174
*sanad* (chain of transmission) 174
al-Ṣanʿānī, ʿAbd al-Razzāq 24
al-Sanhūrī, ʿAbd al-Razzāq 262, 263
al-Sarī al-Saqaṭī 124
*Ṣayd al-Khāṭir* ("Capturing the Mind's Destructive Tendencies") 184
Schacht, Joseph 252
scholars of the apparent (*ʿulamāʾ al-ẓāhir*) 273, 280
seclusion (*ʿuzla*) 3, 5, 151, 170, 174, 176–177, 181, 193
sexuality in Islam 235
Sezgin, Fuat 174
Shafir, Nir 179
al-Shāfiʿī, Muḥammad b. Idrīs 17, 23, 42, 156, 250, 257, 283
*shamāʾil* (qualities and attributes of the Prophet) 17, 150, 154–156
al-Shāmī, Ṣāliḥ 139–140
Sharīʿati, ʿAlī 172
al-Shāṭibī 270, 274–276, 278, 289–291, 296
al-Shaʿrānī 158
*al-Shifāʾ bi-Taʿrīf Ḥuqūq al-Muṣṭafā* 17
*al-Shifāʾ* ("The Healing") 150
Shuʿayb b. Ḥarb 174
Siddique, Kaukab 222
al-Sindī 155
sinfulness (*ithm*) 271–272, 278–281
*sīra* (prophetic biography) 17
speculative theology 125
Sperl, Stefan 30, 38–39
stirrings of the heart (*ḥawāzz al-qulūb*) 282
al-Subkī, Tāj al-Dīn 140
Successors (*tābiʿūn*) 276
Sufi orders
 Khalwatiyya 177
 Kubrāwiyya 177
 Naqshabandiyya 172
 Qādiriyya 177
 Shādhiliyya 177
Sufyān al-Thawrī 182
*suḥba* (companionship) 170
al-Suhrawardī, Shihāb al-Dīn 176
*sukūn al-nafs* (tranquillity of the soul) 273–275
al-Sulamī, Abū ʿAbd al-Raḥmān 10

*al-Sunan al-Kubrā* ("The Great Sunnas"). *See also ḥadīth* collections 148
*Sunan al-Nasāʾī* ("The Traditions of al-Nasāʾī") 154
*sunan* (exemplary behaviour) 16
Sunna 17–18, 42–43
sustenance (*qūt*) 294
al-Suyūṭī, Jalal al-Din. *See also* السيوطي، جلال الدين 16, 19, 21, 37–38, 41, 154–155, 201, 205, 207, 212–213, 250, 256, 261

*ṭabaqāt* (Islamic biographical literature) 201–202
al-Ṭabarānī 22, 137, 149
al-Ṭabarī, Muḥammad b. Jarīr 274–276
*tābiʿūn* (Companions' companion) 204
Tabūk campaign 255
*tahdhīb al-nafs* (disciplining the self) 14
*Taḥdhīr al-Khawāṣṣ min Akadhīb al-Quṣṣāṣ* ("A Warning to the Retinue against the Lies of the Storytellers") 205
*Taḥrīr al-Marʾa fī ʿAṣr al-Risāla* ("The Liberation of Women at the Time of the Message) 222
*Takhyīr al-ʿIbād fī Suknā l-Bilād* ("Giving People the Option to Live where they Choose") 179
*Takmīl al-Nuʿūt fī Luzūm al-Buyūt* ("Perfecting Praiseworthy Qualities by Imposing Home-Seclusion") 171
*Talbīs Iblīs* ("The Deception of the Devil") 128
al-Tanūkhī, Abū ʿAlī 41
taste (*dhawq*) 288
*tawakkul* 129, 132, 134–135, 141
*tawḥīd* 132
*tawḥīd as tawakkul* 132–135
al-Tawḥīdī, Abū Ḥayyān 42
*al-Tawshīḥ ʿalā l-Jāmiʿ al-Ṣaḥīḥ* ("The Strophic Work on the Authentic Collection") 37
al-Ṭayālisī, Abū Dāwūd 133
*Taʿẓīm Qadr al-Ṣalāt* ("The Aggrandizement of the Status of Prayer") 148
Thābit 38
The Moral World of the Qurʾān 8
theoretical speculation (*naẓar*) 282–283
al-Tirmidhī 19, 22
al-Tirmidhī, al-Ḥakīm 21–22, 176, 277, 295
Tisdall, William 269
"tribulation" (*fitna*) 181
al-Ṭūfī 276, 278

*ʿubūdiyya* (worship) 153
*ukhuwwa* 171, 181
*ʿulamāʾ-quṣṣāṣ* dichotomy 198
*ʿulūm al-sharīʿa* (Islamic sciences) 1
ʿUmar b. al-Khaṭṭāb 131, 155, 224, 229–230, 233, 257
Umayyads 252–253
Umm Ḥarām 228
Umm Mubashshir al-Anṣāriyya 226
Umm Qays 256
Umm Shurayk 226
unity (*tawḥīd*) 165
unsound *ḥadīth* (*ḥadīth al-ḍuʿafāʾ*) 21
*uṣūl al-ḥadīth* (sciences of *ḥadīth*) 19
al-ʿUthaymīn, Muḥammad b. Ṣāliḥ 221
ʿUthmān 155
*ʿuzla*. *See* seclusion
*al-ʿUzla wa-l-Infirād* ("Seclusion and Isolation") 174

Van Norden, Bryan W. 269
virtuous acts (*faḍāʾil al-aʿmāl*) 120, 141

Wābiṣa b. Maʿbad 271–273, 277
*waḥdat al-wujūd* 156
Walzer, Richard 11
Wansbrough, John 204
Ware, Rudolph 209
*al-Waṣāyā* ("The Commandments") 175
*Wasāʾil al-Taḥqīq wa-Rasāʾil al-Tawfīq* ("The Means of Truth-Seeking and the Letters of Providential Guidance") 173
*al-Waʿẓ al-Maṭlūb min Qūt al-Qulūb* ("The Required Exhortation from The Nourishment of the Hearts") 136
Weber, Max 297
wisdom (*ḥikma*) 42
women 5–6, 147, 153, 157–159
  and *jihād* 241
  as *fitna* 242–243
  humanity (*insāniyya*) of women 223–224
  liberation 234–235
  meeting and touching men 242
  Muslim ideal of 221–222

women (*cont.*)
praying in mosque 241
religiosity of 233
roles in public activities in early Islam 234
sexuality in Islam 235
travelling 244
working outside the house 227
*wujūd* (existence) 163
Wuthnow, Robert 251

*ẓāhir*. *See* outer
al-Zamakhsharī 149
Zayd b. Thābit 131
Zaynab bint Jaḥsh 149, 226, 228
Zuhayr al-Shāwīsh 138
*al-Zuhd al-Kabīr* ("The Major Epistle on Asceticism") 176
*zuhd*. *See* asceticism
*al-Zuhd wa-l-Raqāʾiq* 174